P9-DTS-006

Behavioral Assessment:
A PRACTICAL HANDBOOK

Behavioral Assessment:
A PRACTICAL HANDBOOK

EDITED BY

MICHEL HERSEN

Department of Psychiatry, Western Psychiatric Institute and Clinic, University of Pittsburgh School of Medicine, Pittsburgh, Pennsylvania

ALAN S. BELLACK

Department of Psychology, University of Pittsburgh, Pittsburgh, Pennsylvania

PERGAMON PRESS

OXFORD · NEW YORK · TORONTO · SYDNEY
PARIS · FRANKFURT

U. K.	Pergamon Press Ltd., Headington Hill Hall, Oxford OX3 0BW, England
U. S. A.	Pergamon Press Inc., Maxwell House, Fairview Park, Elmsford, New York 10523, U.S.A.
CANADA	Pergamon of Canada Ltd., P.O. Box 9600, Don Mills M3C 2T9, Ontario, Canada
AUSTRALIA	Pergamon Press (Aust.) Pty. Ltd., 19a Boundary Street, Rushcutters Bay, N.S.W. 2011, Australia
FRANCE	Pergamon Press SARL, 24 rue des Ecoles, 75240 Paris, Cedex 05, France
WEST GERMANY	Pergamon Press GmbH, 6242 Kronberg-Taunus, Pferdstrasse 1, Frankfurt-am-Main, West Germany

---

First edition 1976

Library of Congress Cataloging in Publication Data

Main entry under title:

Behavioral assessment.

(Pergamon general psychology series; 65)
1. Behavioral therapy. 2. Mental illness—Diagnosis.
I. Hersen, Michel. II. Bellack, Alan S.
RC489.B4D4354 1976 616.8'914 76-7376
ISBN 0-08-020532-1
ISBN 0-08-020531-3 pbk.

Printed in Great Britain by A. Wheaton & Co., Exeter

TO LYNN AND JONATHAN

AND

BARBARA AND JONATHAN

Contents

Preface

One of the hallmarks of behavior modification is its emphasis on empiricism, experimentation, and precision. This emphasis had led to an integral relationship between treatment and assessment. In contrast to most traditional clinical approaches in which assessment is functionally independent of treatment, behavior modification strategy requires careful assessment before, during, and after treatment. Given the specificity of behavioral treatment, selection of an intervention strategy is impossible without measurement and assessment. And contrary to the thinking of some of the critics of behavior modification, measurement has meant evaluation of all three response modalities—the motoric, the physiological, and the cognitive. Indeed, there is no question that behavior modifiers are very much interested in what their clients and patients think and feel as well as how they behave overtly. This point has been underscored in and by many of the chapters that comprise this volume.

The volume, itself, is in response to what we perceived as a growing need in the field after discussion with many colleagues and students. Although behavioral assessment is being conducted and practiced in the clinic and laboratory as well as being written about in various singular publications, there is no one place where the student, clinician, or researcher can turn to when particular assessment problems are encountered. In many cases, the most current assessment techniques and data are available only in a few laboratories. Therefore, our initial intention was to prepare a "how-to-do-it" manual. However, our eminent contributors pleasantly surprised us by being much more thorough and comprehensive in their presentations. Thus, as the reader goes through the various chapters, it will be clear that there are many unresolved issues and that there are some unique differences in the behavioral assessments conducted for clinical purposes, during the course of single case experimental evaluations, and group comparison designs.

Although we have attempted to be comprehensive in our topical headings, we do not think this is the "last word" and recognize possible omissions. However, we do hope that material in this volume may stimulate further thinking in the field and lead to refinement of assessment strategies.

The material is organized into three major sections. The first part deals with broad issues and involves an overview of assessment in general and behavioral assessment in particular. The second part deals with the initial stages of behavioral assessment. Finally, the bulk of the volume, Part Three, deals with evaluation for treatment planning. Here the intricate relationships between assessments and treatments are highlighted for a variety of disorders.

Many individuals have contributed to this volume. *First*, we would like to express our gratitude to our contributors who agreed to concretize their thinking in writing. *Second*, we would like to thank our colleagues in psychology, psychiatry, and social work who have encouraged us to pursue our academic endeavors. *Third*, we would like to acknowledge the cooperation and encouragement we have received from Robert Miranda, Senior Vice-President of Pergamon Press. *Finally*, but hardly least of all, we would like to express our appreciation to Mary Newell, Kaylee Shank, John Watts, and Martin Williams for their technical assistance.

Pittsburgh, Pennsylvania

Michel Hersen
Alan S. Bellack

About the Editors

Michel Hersen (Ph.D., State University of New York at Buffalo) is Professor of Clinical Psychiatry and Director of the Resocialization Treatment Center in the Department of Psychiatry, Western Psychiatric Institute and Clinic, University of Pittsburgh School of Medicine. In addition, Dr. Hersen is Director of the Clinical Psychology Internship Training Program in the Department of Psychiatry, University of Pittsburgh School of Medicine. He also holds an appointment as Professor in the Psychology Department at the University of Pittsburgh. Dr. Hersen is Editor-in-Chief of *Progress in Behavior Modification*, Editor-in-Chief of *Behavior Modification*, Associate Editor of *Addictive Behaviors*, and is on the editorial boards of *Behavior Therapy* and *Behavior Therapy and Experimental Psychiatry*. He is consultant to the Veterans Administration Medical Research Service Merit Review Board in Behavioral Sciences and is editorial consultant for numerous journals.

Dr. Hersen has published over 90 papers, chapters and books in the fields of clinical psychology and psychiatry including *Single-Case Experimental Designs: Strategies for Studying Behavior Change* (with David H. Barlow). Dr. Hersen's professional interests are in the area of behavior modification and social skills training.

Alan S. Bellack (Ph.D., Pennsylvania State University) is Assistant Professor in the Department of Psychology at the University of Pittsburgh. He also holds an appointment as Assistant Professor of Clinical Psychiatry in the Department of Psychiatry of the University of Pittsburgh School of Medicine. Dr. Bellack is Associate Editor of *Behavior Modification* and has been an editorial consultant for several journals and publishing companies. He has published numerous journal articles and chapters in the areas of behavioral assessment, self-control, and social skills training.

PART ONE

Overview

CHAPTER 1

*Historical Perspectives in Behavioral Assessment**

MICHEL HERSEN

Department of Psychiatry
Western Psychiatric Institute and Clinic
University of Pittsburgh School of Medicine
Pittsburgh, Pennsylvania

Introduction

In this chapter the historical developments leading to the recent surge of interest in behavioral assessment (e.g., Bellack & Hersen, in press; Cautela, 1968, 1973; Goldfried & Pomeranz, 1968; Kanfer & Saslow, 1969; Hersen, 1973; Hersen & Barlow, 1976; Hersen & Bellack, in press) will be briefly reviewed. The assessment techniques used in behavioral practice and research are to be considered in light of: (1) the unreliability of psychiatric diagnosis and the invalidity of the current nosological scheme, (2) traditional psychological assessment (i.e., the use of projective techniques and/or diagnostic devices tapping presumed "traits"), (3) the relationship of traditional diagnosis to treatment planning and implementation, (4) the emergence of behavior modification as an accepted therapeutic methodology, and (5) parallel developments in diagnostic practice (i.e., the problem-oriented record) first applied in internal medicine (Weed, 1964) and more recently in psychiatry (e.g., Hayes-Roth, Longabaugh & Ryback, 1972) and in the clinical practice of behavior modification (Katz & Woolley, 1975). A number of schemes proposed for conducting comprehensive behavioral assessment will be examined. The importance of evaluating *all* three response systems (motoric, physiological, and cognitive), whenever possible, will be underscored. Different strategies carried out when engaged in consulting room practice, outcome research, and single case experimental research will be contrasted. Finally, an attempt will be made to prognosticate future directions and trends that are likely to emerge in the area of behavioral assessment.

As the historical developments in this field unfold, it will become apparent that behavioral assessment has had its greatest impetus and initial support from clinical psychologists intent on taking psychodiagnosis out of the realm of "art" and moving it into the realm of *science*. Although some of these earlier attempts to observe, measure, and classify behavior may in future years strike the reader as "primitive" or even "comical," undoubtedly others will be hailed as milestones in the field.

With the emergence of behavioral assessment and modification, the role of the clinical psychologist has undergone considerable change. The changing dimensions of that role will also become apparent throughout this examination of the historical developments in assessment. An important distinction will be highlighted between the assessor of behavior who functions merely as a consultant who may or may not have had any impact on actual treatment (i.e., the traditional assessor) and the assessor (i.e., the behavioral assessor) whose evaluation has a *direct* relationship to developing viable treatment programs. This relationship is not at all surprising in light of the fact that assessment and treatment in behavioral practice are typically carried out by the same individual or team of individuals.

Psychiatric Diagnosis and Issues of Reliability and Validity

In a review of research studies concerned with various aspects of psychiatric diagnosis, Frank (1969) regrettably concluded that, ". . . the review of this research leaves one with the uncomfortable feeling that the results of all the studies that have utilized psychiatric diagnosis as a dependent or independent variable are of questionable validity. The data reviewed herein suggest that an entirely new system of classification is needed, one which can encompass the many variables that define psychological functioning and behavior in the human, including the viewing of these functions from a developmental frame of reference" (p. 167). In a more recent and still more comprehensive review of the area, Frank (1975) came to a similar conclusion for the second time. During the course of examining the ethical and legal issues of behavior modification, Begelman (1975), somewhat sardonically, referred to the DSM I and DSM II classification systems as "twice told tales." Apparently, the American Psychiatric Association, itself, is dissatisfied with the current nomenclature, and is currently at work developing DSM III. However, advanced word has it that many of the problematic features inherent in DSM I and DSM II are being retained in DSM III![1] Writing in the *Archives of General Psychiatry*, two psychiatrists, Hine & Williams (1975), recently pointed out the difficulties in teaching medical students about psychiatric diagnosis when using the current categorical model. Underscored in their critique are the problems of applying

[1]Kupfer, D. J. Personal communication, July 25, 1975.

diagnostic labels to "real patients" and the current nosological system's limited relevance to general medical practice. The solution proposed involves ". . . presenting psychiatry in the framework of a multidimensional schema that uses familiar terms but treats them as dimensions with severe, moderate, and mild degrees of impairment rather than as categories of mutually exclusive psychiatric diseases" (Hine & Williams, 1975, p. 525).

Reliability

While the present nosological system can be readily criticized on a number of conceptual and empirical bases (e.g., confounding etiology and symptomatology; specific signs and symptoms not being able to differentiate among diagnostic groupings), perhaps the most frequently leveled criticism at the system is that it does not allow for reliable psychiatric diagnoses. The concern involving reliability when making diagnostic assessments has been articulated for four decades in the literature (see Ash, 1949; Blashfield, 1973; Cohen, Harbin & Wright, 1975; Doering, 1934; Nathan, Andberg, Behan & Patch, 1969; Sandifer, Pettus & Quade, 1964). While occasional criticisms and reanalyses of data obtained in studies assessing reliability do appear (e.g., Ley, 1972), the overwhelming evidence suggests that when assessments of patients are made by independent clinicians, the resulting inter-rater agreements are of low magnitude (Frank, 1969).

For example, Ash (1949) conducted a study (using a conference interview method) in which 52 male outpatients were evaluated by at least two psychiatrists. In 35 of the cases three psychiatrists made the evaluations. For *specific* diagnostic categories, inter-rater agreement was found in only 20% of the cases when there were three psychiatrists. Agreement was somewhat higher (31.4 to 43.5%) when data were examined for pairs of psychiatrists. When *major* diagnostic categories were examined, inter-rater agreements reached 45.7%, and 57.9 to 67.4% when data were once again examined for pairs of psychiatrists. In a more recent study, Sandifer, Pettus & Quade (1964) examined inter-rater agreement for 14 senior medical diagnosticians (11 of whom were psychiatrists) who were asked to evaluate (when sitting in a group) 91 first admissions to a psychiatric hospital. The probability of a second opinion coinciding with the first averaged to about 57%. Although there was considerable variability in inter-rater reliability across diagnostic categories, under- or over-use of categories as well as diagnostic "expectancy" were not significant variables contributing to disagreement. In a still more recent study, Nathan, Andberg, Behan & Patch (1969) asked 32 health professionals attending a case conference at the Psychiatry Service of the Boston City Hospital to fill out the Boston City Hospital-Behavior Check List after presentation of a 36-year-old male patient.

The patient was a chronic alcoholic who evidenced both organic and "psychiatric" symptomatology. "When the 32 health professionals were divided into four separate groups on the basis of experience with psychiatric patients and psychiatric diagnosis, it was found that the most experienced group gave more 'organic' diagnoses than the less experienced ones . . . experienced observers saw certain symptoms of 'organicity', . . . while the less experienced clinicians saw symptoms of perceptual disorder, often considered of significance for the diagnosis of schizophrenia and severe depression which more experienced observers did not see" (Nathan, Andberg, Behan & Patch, 1969, p. 15).

Finally, Cohen, Harbin & Wright (1975) present convincing data showing that the psychiatrist's psychosocial biases will affect the diagnostic label he places on his patient at the time of discharge. Of 267 adult inpatients admitted to a university hospital psychiatry service, it was found that in 33 cases (12%) the original admission diagnosis of psychosis was changed to neurosis or character disorder upon discharge. Interviews held with the 18 psychiatric residents who made these changes indicated that different psychiatric labels were applied at discharge to protect their patients from adverse environmental reactions rather than due to any changes observed in the patients' psychopathology. Noble though the gesture may be, if this phenomenon repeats across psychiatric settings, Frank's (1969) caution with respect to using psychiatric diagnosis as either an independent or dependent variable is doubly well taken.

Validity

One method for assessing the validity of a diagnostic system would involve a comparison across diagnostic categories of standard diagnostic symptoms and signs (e.g., Nathan, Zare, Simpson & Andberg, 1969). Similar discriminatory validity might be evaluated more indirectly. For example, are specific stressors leading to psychiatric hospitalization associated with specific diagnostic categories? And, in complementary fashion, are treatment expectations of specific diagnostic groupings significantly different across diagnoses? The first of the two experimental questions was examined by Eisler & Polak (1971) in a carefully designed investigation. Frequency of occurrence of specific life stressors (e.g., divorce, death in the family, economic loss, etc.) was tabulated for 172 patients (categorized as schizophrenics, depressives, personality disorders, and transient situational personality disorders) admitted as inpatients to a large state hospital facility. The resulting data analyses indicated that there were no differences among diagnostic groups with respect to number of stressors experienced or in terms of the relationship of particular stressors and diagnostic groups. When phrased in the positive, it appears that each of the diagnostic groups experienced an equal number and type of stressors prior to seeking and obtaining admission.

The second experimental question posed above was assessed in a subsequent investigation by Eisler, Hersen, Miller & Wooten (1973). In this study the treatment expectations (e.g., personal behavior change, interpersonal change, job and school, psychiatric symptom, physical symptom, etc.) of 103 newly admitted male patients to a Veterans Administration Hospital were examined in relation to their psychiatric diagnoses (labeled neurotic, psychotic, character disorder, alcoholic, and transient personality disorder). With few exceptions, there appeared to be a minimal relationship between psychiatric diagnosis and the patients' stated treatment expectation. Both of the studies reported failed to provide validation for some of the more general aspects of the classification system currently in use in most psychiatric facilities.

A more direct test of the symptom-sign notion as related to psychiatric diagnosis had earlier been carried out by Peter Nathan and his colleagues (Nathan, 1969; Nathan, Gould, Zare & Roth, 1969; Nathan, Robertson & Andberg, 1969; Nathan, Simpson & Andberg, 1969; Nathan, Zare, Simpson & Andberg, 1969) in an extended series of studies at the Boston City Hospital. The strategy followed in these studies involved evaluation of 924 patients seen between 1966 and 1968. Each of these patients received a diagnosis by a psychiatric resident and was rated on the Boston City Hospital-Behavior Check List (a 100-item questionnaire eliciting signs and symptoms of psychopathology). The validity of signs and symptoms pathognomonic of particular disorders (e.g., depressed mood in depression) were evaluated across the following major diagnostic categories and their sub-divisions: psychosis, psychoneurosis, personality disorder, acute brain disorder, chronic brain disorder. Although some of the symptoms and signs differentiated among the major categories, there was considerable overlap. Moreover, for the sub-categories, overlap was greater, and consequently the differentiating value of particular signs was markedly decreased. In commenting on their series of investigations, Nathan, Gould, Zare & Roth (1969) note that, ". . . study of the diagnostic process revealed only limited differential diagnostic validity for many of the most common signs and symptoms of psychopathology. These findings were partially explained as a function of the decidedly skewed distribution of diagnoses in the sample of psychiatric patients studied, i.e., 27% of the patients in this population were schizophrenic, of whom almost half were paranoid schizophrenic. This meant that many symptoms 'predicted' paranoid schizophrenia, because the greatest *number* of patients with these symptoms were often given this diagnosis, even though the highest *percentage* of patients showing the same symptoms were almost always drawn from a different, usually much less frequently conferred diagnostic category" (p. 370). Again, these studies highlight the problems associated with the use of a categorical model of classification. In addition, it seems clear that the low reliability of the psychiatrists' appraisals must have contributed to the difficulties in differentiating among the categories when the sign-symptom approach was employed.

Traditional Psychological Diagnosis

Quite frequently in the past (and even now at this time), clinical psychologists working in psychiatric settings have contributed substantially to the diagnostic process by conducting evaluations using indirect measurement devices such as projective tests and objective personality inventories containing disguised properties (e.g., Minnesota Multiphasic Personality Inventory, California Personality Inventory). Using such measurement techniques, the clinical psychologist was cast in a role analogous to an x-ray technician whenever a psychiatrist required confirmation of his differential diagnosis based on historical and interview data. Whether the psychologist's report had any impact on the ensuing treatment process seemed immaterial. His role was that of assessor.

From an historical framework, it is interesting that clinical psychology, as a visible profession in the mental health field, emerged at the end of World War II and began to blossom thereafter. However, because of the restrictive policies of the "psychiatric establishment" of the times, psychologists often were not permitted to engage in psychotherapeutic practice and were relegated to assessing "behavior" of patients. Given such contingencies, some clinical psychologists were able to develop lucrative practices (within and outside of institutions) in which they were adept at "peddling their wares" (i.e., providing the "psychiatric establishment" with the only commodity it then was willing to purchase—assessment along psychodynamic lines).

Not only did many clinical psychologists become quite proficient at describing patients in psychoanalytic jargon using a maximum of inference and a minimum of data, but they were highly valued for this reason by their psychiatric confrères. In the late 1940s and early 1950s, some clinical psychologists were able to penetrate the defenses erected by the "psychiatric establishment," and began developing their role as that of treatment agent. These clinicians frequently modeled themselves after their more successful psychiatric colleagues both in terms of style and theoretical orientation (e.g., the "lay analysts"). However, such clinicians lost their unique position in the psychiatric world by so emulating the psychiatrist with whom they previously had engaged, at times, in acrimonious debate. It will be recalled that the *unique* function (in which few challenged his expertise) of the clinical psychologist had been his role in providing support for diagnostic decisions reached by practicing psychiatrists.

Other psychologists (clinical), consistent with their training in scientific methodology, remained empirical in orientation and conducted research studies of academic import but of remote relevance to pressing clinical issues. Although the role of the clinical psychologist has changed considerably since the early 1950s, the advent and eventual (or partial) acceptance of behavior modification again permitted the clinical psychologist to resume a *unique* role (occasionally that of the "token" behavior modifier) within most psychiatric facilities. This time, however, a close relationship was obtained between his training in empiricism and his application of more scientifically based assessment and treatment techniques. The impact of behavior modification on the role of the clinical psychologist in psychiatric settings will be discussed in greater detail in a subsequent section.

Indirect Measurement

Even today the question is frequently posed: "What is wrong in using an indirect means of measurement (e.g., projectives) when evaluating psychiatric patients? After all, responses to projectives constitute data albeit indirect. A lengthy disquisition on this topic is well beyond the scope of this chapter, and the reader is referred to Mischel (1968) for a most comprehensive analysis of the issues. However, some of the problems associated with indirect assessment warrant brief mention here. *First*, the validity (construct, concurrent, or predictive) of indirect measurement techniques has generally not been adequately established (see Goldfried & Kent, 1972; Hersen & Barlow, 1976, Chapter 4; Mischel, 1968, 1971, 1972). Indeed, when the validities of direct and indirect personality tests are comparatively evaluated (e.g., Holmes & Tyler, 1968; Scott & Johnson, 1972), the results are usually in favor of the *direct* approach. Along these lines, Cronbach (1956) earlier had argued that, "Assessors have been foolhardy to venture predictions of behavior in unanalyzed situations, using tests whose construct interpretations are dubious and personality theory which has more gaps than solid matter" (pp. 173–174). *Second*, it is clear that the assessor in the projective test situation is not simply an impartial evaluator, but through his covert and overt manipulations is able to affect the testee's responses. In the last several years numerous *experimental* and *clinical* (conducted retrospectively) studies have documented the various types of examiner bias influencing the projective test situation (e.g., Hersen, 1970; Hersen & Greaves, 1971; Masling & Harris, 1969). *Third*, and perhaps most important, there is an unclear relationship between assessment (i.e., diagnosis) and treatment when using indirect measurement techniques. Thus, as has been implied elsewhere (Hersen & Bellack, in press), with the absence of a direct relationship between diagnosis and treatment, the assessment process represents little more than a meaningless "academic" exercise rather than a useful clinical function. Differences between the relationship of diagnosis and treatment in traditional and behavioral assessment will be underscored in the next section.

Relationship of Diagnosis and Treatment

The most succinct statement illustrating the differences between traditional and behavioral approaches to assessment appeared in an excellent paper by

Goldfried & Kent (1972). They note there that, "Whereas traditional tests of personality involve the assessment of hypothesized personality constructs which, in turn, are used to predict overt behavior, the behavioral approach entails more of a direct sampling of the criterion behaviors themselves. In addition to requiring fewer inferences than traditional tests, behavioral assessment procedures are seen as being based on assumptions more amenable to direct empirical test and more consistent with empirical evidence" (p. 409). The relationship of overt behavior (e.g., responses to TAT stories or Rorschach inkblots) in traditional assessment has been labeled the "indirect-sign paradigm" by Mischel (1972). In essence, it is assumed here that an individual's underlying depositions have the capacity for manifesting themselves in a variety of situations (e.g., responses to projective materials), but such overt behaviors are always representative of the underlying dynamics. On the other hand, the behaviorist views the behavior within the context of a given stimulus situation, and is interested in its direct manifestation, be it motoric, verbal, or physiological. Thus, traditional assessment favors a "trait" description whereas behavioral assessment is more supportive of a "state" description.

Hersen & Barlow (1976, Chapter 4) commenting on the direct approach to measurement, point out that, ". . . it is hardly surprising proponents of direct measurement favor the observation of individuals in their natural surrounding whenever possible. When such naturalistic observations are not feasible, analogue situations approximating naturalistic conditions may be developed to study the behavior in question (e.g., the use of a behavioral avoidance test to study the degree of fear of snakes). When neither of the two methods is available or possible, subjects' self-reports are used as criterial. However, it should be underscored that *self-reports are also used as criteria* and, at times, may be operating under the control of different sets of contingencies than those governing motoric responses . . ." In addition, the evaluation of physiological measurements (e.g., heart rate, muscle tension, blood pressure, skin conductance, respiration) is becoming increasingly common in behavioral assessment paradigms.

Largely as a function of the major philosophical-theroretical-empirical differences between traditional and behavioral approaches to assessment, there then exists an even greater difference in the relationship between diagnosis and treatment for the two strategies. Whereas in the behavioral approach the behaviors evaluated during the course of assessment are the very ones subjected to modification procedures in treatment, the same does not hold true in the case of the traditional approach. Obviously when dealing with presumed unconscious dynamics and their putative behavioral manifestations, the major target for modification (in the psychodynamic treatment sense) is not the overt behavior (i.e., the signs and symptoms), but the underlying conflict that produces such symptoms and signs. This being the case, to be consistent with psychodynamic theory, a direct approach linking assessment and treatment would be untenable. Parenthetically, and as has been noted elsewhere (e.g., Hersen & Bellack, in press), it is remarkable that psychiatry is one of the few medical specialties where the one-to-one relationship between diagnosis and treatment frequently does not hold. Of course, this is most prevalent when the relationship of psychodiagnosis and psychotherapy is examined. A closer relationship, however, does exist between traditional psychiatric diagnosis (when reliability is obtained) and pharmacological treatments (see Detre & Jarecki, 1971; Woodruff, Goodwin & Guze, 1974, for excellent discussions).

Emergence of Behavior Modification

Hersen, Eisler & Miller (1975) have documented, in their review of historical developments in behavior modification, that although sporadic reports of behavioral treatment efforts followed Watson & Rayner's (1920) applied work in the conditioning of fear in a child, the greatest impetus to behavioral treatment can be traced to publication of Wolpe's (1958) *Psychotherapy by Reciprocal Inhibition*. Despite intense criticism at the hands of his antagonists, after publication of this landmark in the field, Wolpe began to acquire a coterie of admirers and followers (most of whom were clinical psychologists), Totally independent of Wolpe's influence, followers of the Skinnerian model, (e.g., Ayllon & Michael, 1959) were also beginning to apply principles of experimental psychology to applied settings (i.e., the use of operant conditioning techniques in the state hospital). These singular applications of operant methodology eventually led to ward-wide management and treatment for large chronic psychiatric populations (Ayllon & Azrin, 1968). However, whether clinical applications followed a classical or operant conditioning paradigm, the empirical influence of laboratory psychology was keenly felt. Thus, it is not at all surprising that data oriented clinical psychologists were extremely enthusiastic about the application of empirically-based techniques to human problems. For the first time, such clinical psychologists were able to combine their training in scientific psychology with that of clinical application.

Although major contributions to behavior modification have and still do appear from individuals who are not clinical psychologists by professional affiliation (e.g., Agras, 1972; Brady, 1966; Liberman, 1970; Marks, 1969; Stuart, 1971; Wolpe, 1958, 1969), and in spite of the fact that there is an increased number of non-psychologists engaged in the application of behavioral techniques (see Brady, 1973), the preponderance of papers published in behavior modification today are still authored by clinical psychologists. Moreover, the greatest number of clinical practitioners of behavioral modification at this time are also clinical psychologists (see Davison & Neale, 1974).

With the advent of behavior modification and its continuing proliferation (see Hersen, 1973) and acceptance by the psychiatric world (see Task Force Report 5, 1973), a new role emerged for the clinical psychologist. Not only because of his inclination and interest, but because of his training in scientific psychology, the clinical psychologist, of all the mental health professionals, seemed best equipped to pinpoint and measure specific behaviors and ascertain the contingencies supporting targeted behaviors. Further, his expertise in the theory and clinical application of classical and operant conditioning techniques now enabled him not only to exercise his authority as an assessor in the psychiatric setting (as had been the case when the clinical psychologist functioned in the role of expert in psychodiagnosis by using psychological tests), but now as an important dispenser of treatment strategies. (This is also largely a function of the fact that assessment and modification of targeted responses in the behavioral paradigm are inextricably tied together.) Once again, the clinical psychologist had resumed his *unique* role within the psychiatric setting in addition to developing a *primary* role within many educational and rehabilitation settings (included are administrative roles previously not accorded to clinical psychologists in all of the aforementioned settings).

The Process of Behavioral Assessment

Although earlier theoretical expositions of behavioral assessment and modification (e.g., Eysenck, 1960) may have contributed to the notion that the diagnostic and treatment procedures followed in this orientation were both simple and "cut-and-dried," more recent examples of behavioral applications (Blanchard & Hersen, 1976; Hersen, Turner, Edelstein & Pinkston, 1975; Lazarus, 1973) clearly indicate that multiple assessment channels and multi-treatment applications (conducted sequentially and/or in concert) are more frequently the case. Lazarus (1973) has conceptualized such an approach under the rubric of "multimodal behavior therapy." Given the complexity of the typical clinical situation (rare in the case to be found where a uni-phobia can be treated in isolation), it naturally follows that a careful assessment of a particular patient is equally complicated, thus requiring the examination of many sources of data.

Cautela (1968) has shrewdly recognized that, "The mistaken notion of assessment in Behavior Therapy has led some traditionally trained clinical psychologists, as well as some experimental psychologists, to assume that specific training in behavioral assessment is not a requisite for the practice of Behavior Therapy" (p. 175). To the contrary, Cautela goes on to show how behavioral assessment plays its role during the various stages of treatment. In his scheme the treatment process is divided into three distinct stages. In the *first* stage the behavioral clinician identifies those behaviors that are maladaptive. In addition to using interview techniques designed to determine antecedent conditions maintaining maladaptive responses, several questionnaires including the Life History Questionnaire (Wolpe & Lazarus, 1966), the Fear Survey Schedule (Wolpe & Lang, 1964), and the Reinforcement Survey Schedule (Cautela & Kastenbaum, 1967) are employed to elicit relevant information. The *second* stage involves the choice of the appropriate treatment strategy (or strategies) and its application.[2] Cautela further sub-divides stage two into three phases during which time assessment and treatment are intertwined. Specifically, Phase 1 involves a determination of treatment procedures, Phase 2 an evaluation of on-going treatment procedures, and Phase 3 a decision regarding when to terminate the treatment (or treatments). Finally, the *third* stage consists of a careful follow-up of evaluation of the outcome of treatment. Throughout assessment and treatment, Cautela emphasizes the importance of being attuned to a variety of manifestations of the patient's behavior. Included are cognitions, dreams and imagery, overt motoric behavior, and physiological responsivity. In addition, confirmation of certain data by significant others in the patient's immediate environment is considered to be extremely important, particularly during follow-ups.

Somewhat more elaborate schemes for assessing behavior have been proposed by Kanfer & Saslow (1969) and Lazarus (1973). Kanfer & Saslow (1969) carefully outline the procedures required for a *seven* part analysis of any given behavioral problem. *First* is an initial evaluation of the problem situation. A determination is made as to whether a particular behavior represents an excess, a deficit, or an asset. Issues of frequency, intensity, duration, and stimulus conditions for its elicitation are all considered. *Second* is the clarification of the problem situation. "The questions raised here are derived from the assumption that maladjusted behavior requires continued support" (p. 432). *Third* is the motivational analysis. Here, essentially, a determination is made with respect to the most potent reinforcers (e.g., achievement of recognition, sexual satisfaction) for the patient and the main stimuli that prove to be aversive. *Fourth* involves a developmental analysis of the individual. Included in this assessment are concerns over biological, sociological, and behavioral changes. *Fifth* is an analysis of self-control. Among the questions posed are: "To what extent can the patient's self-controlling behavior be used in a treatment program? Is constant supervision or drug administration necessary to supplement self-control?" (p. 435). *Sixth* consists of an analysis of pertinent social

[2]Contrary to the practice of traditional psychotherapy, where there is a tendency to apply a rather uniform therapy irrespective of the presenting problem(s), the choice of treatment in behavior modification is determined on the basis of the findings derived from the behavioral analysis. If a maladaptive behavior is anxiety-based, the application of an anxiety management technique (e.g., systematic desensitization or implosion) might be warranted. On the other hand, if the maladaptive behavior is supported through environmental contingencies (e.g., parental reinforcement of a child's acting-out behaviors), then a more operantly-oriented treatment strategy such as differential reinforcement would be considered more appropriate.

relationships, and *seventh* comprises assessment of the patient's social-cultural-physical environment.

Kanfer & Saslow (1969) do point out, however, that their approach to assessment is not at all meant to supplant the existing psychiatric diagnostic scheme, with respect to statistical or administrative bases, in spite of its current limitations. Rather, this seven part analysis *is* designed ". . . to replace other diagnostic formulations purporting to serve as a basis for making decisions about specific therapeutic interventions" (p. 437).

Lazarus' (1973) scheme for assessment has humorously been categorized using the acronym of BASIC ID, with B = behavior, A = affect, I = imagery, C = cognition, I = interpersonal relationships, and D = the need for pharmacological intervention (drugs) in many patients. Lazarus contends that if sufficient attention (both diagnosis and treatment) is not accorded to each of the seven categories, then the diagnostic process will remain incomplete, therefore resulting in only partial treatment and partial success. Of course, it should be clear that all patients will not require remediation in all the seven categories, or for that matter with regard to equal intensity of treatment. However, as a function of the behavior analysis, if deficits or surplusses are identified in some or possibly all of the categories, then the treatment modality for each will be in direct relationship to the assessment procedure. That is, the same targets identified during assessment will then undergo modification during treatment.

Additional behavioral assessment schemes have (e.g., Cautela, 1973) and undoubtedly will make their appearance in the future. Presumably such schemes will represent further refinements in terms of both measurement and categorization. However, it would appear that the basic concerns with precision of measurement, comprehensiveness of the channels examined, and the close (i.e., isomorphic) relationship between diagnosis and treatment will prevail.

Parallel Developments: The Problem Oriented Record

A parallel but essentially independent development leading to improved assessments of patients in psychiatric settings is the introduction of the problem oriented system of record keeping (i.e., the problem oriented record). First introduced and applied on medical wards (Weed, 1964, 1968, 1969) to sharpen both diagnostic and record-keeping operations, the problem oriented record (POR) is enjoying a current surge of popularity in a variety of inpatient psychiatric settings (Hayes-Roth, Longabaugh, & Ryback, 1972; Katz & Woolley, 1975; Klonoff & Cox, 1975; McLean & Miles, 1974; Scales & Johnson, 1975). Although users of the POR in psychiatry do not uniformly eschew the application of traditional psychiatric labels to their patients, they generally are sufficiently concerned with the inherent difficulties in pinpointing target behaviors during traditional diagnosis and the poor concordance between traditional diagnosis and treatment (be it psychotherapeutic or pharmacological) so as to recognize the importance of preparing *problem lists*.

According to Hayes-Roth, Longabaugh, & Ryback (1972), the POR, when used in psychiatry, can be divided into four sections: (1) the data base, (2) the problem list, (3) the treatment plans, and (4) the use of follow-up data. Although all four sections of the POR have their counterparts in the behavioral analysis, the clearest analogy with behavioral assessment involves the problem list (i.e., the targeted behaviors selected for treatment) and the treatment plans (i.e., the relationship of the assessment and subsequent modification procedures directed at targets).

Despite the fact that the POR represents, for psychiatry, a vast improvement over the type of record-keeping and diagnostic practice previously followed, the level of precision in describing problem behaviors and the treatments to be used remedially *does not* yet approach the kind of precision reached in the carefully conducted behavioral analysis. On the other hand, mutually beneficial influences of behavioral assessment and the POR are beginning to emerge (e.g., Atkinson, 1973; Katz, 1973; Katz & Woolley, 1975). Focusing on the limitations of the POR, Katz & Woolley (1975) argue convincingly that, "Problem-oriented records should not be construed as a panacea for solving complex psychiatric problems. Nor do they guarantee high standards of quality in assessing (behaviorally or otherwise) and treating the patient. On the other hand, they do provide a potentially useful means of reorganizing existing patient records so that relevant clinical information is collected, displayed, and more easily dealt with in a logical way" (p. 123). Such steps in the right direction, small though they may presently seem, can only be applauded at this time. If the current mutual interest in behavioral assessment and problem oriented record-keeping were to persist, then a highly sophisticated approach to diagnosis in psychiatric settings might evolve.

Issues in Behavioral Assessment

Probably the first question to be asked when doing a behavioral assessment is: "What are the appropriate data that need to be obtained when conducting such an evaluation?" Although evaluation circumstances will, at times, severely limit the number of response channels (motoric, self-report, and physiological)[3] and the complexities of responses observed and recorded, the answer to this question should always be: "Assess as many of the systems concurrently that a given evaluation situation will permit." In this connection, Hersen (1973) and Lang (1968) have suggested that rather than expecting one response system to change as a result of changes obtained in another, modification procedures

[3]In some disorders (e.g., the sexual dysfunctions; when pharmacological treatments are being administered) biochemical assays should be added to the list.

should be applied directly to each of the response systems. However, the luxury of such precision will often be determined by whether assessment and modification are being conducted in clinical or research paradigms. (Differences between behavioral assessment in the clinical and research situations are to be discussed in a later section.)

The Three Response Systems

The naive behaviorist and other professionals of differing theoretical persuasion often wrongly assume that a behavioral assessment involves little more than an evaluation of the patient's overt (i.e., motoric) behavior in either a naturalistic setting or in some contrived laboratory analogue situation. However, this assumption is totally erroneous as it does not reflect current practices in the field (e.g., Begelman & Hersen, 1973; Bellack & Hersen, in press; Hersen, 1971, 1973; Hersen & Bellack, in press; Lang, 1968; Wolpe & Lazarus, 1966). Indeed, behaviorists are very much interested in what their patients say they have done or would do in a particular situation in addition to what they actually *will do* in the same situation when put to the test. In spite of the problems of reliability and validity (e.g., the low correlations obtained between self-reports and motoric performance) associated with the use of self-reports, such data cannot and should not be discarded. Hersen (1973) had previously argued that, "Verbilizations of discomfort from distressed patients cannot be discounted either for clinical, ethical, or moral reasons" (p. 255).

When examining the large verbal-motor discrepancies of schizophrenics in a fear arousing situation, Begelman & Hersen (1973) concluded, ". . . that the verbal performance is a criterion of a different psychological variable. It is a criterion of a *S*'s belief that he has a fearful attitude. Whether or not he does will be clarified for him as well as others in light of how he behaves motorically" (p. 179). In a more recent discussion of the issues, Bellack & Hersen (in press) speculate that a factor possibly contributing to low correlations between self-report and motoric assessments is the manner in which items are presented in the typical self-report inventory. Considering the fact that in most of these inventories items eliciting self-reports frequently involve, at best, an incomplete or partial description of what the subject may be asked to do (or has done) in the actual behavioral test, such absence of concordance between the two response systems is less surprising. However, studies supporting Bellack & Hersen's (in press) contention have yet to appear and need to be conducted.

Similarly, correlations between physiological responses and those obtained via motoric and self-report indices are not consistently of high magnitude (Bellack & Hersen, in press; Hersen & Bellack, in press; Lang, 1968; Leitenberg, Agras, Butz, & Wincze, 1971). However, in most studies only one measure (e.g., heart rate) is usually obtained. When such assessment procedures are evaluated in light of genetically determined response preferences in physiological reactivity (Lacey, 1950, 1956, 1962; Lacey & Van Lehn, 1952), these low correlations are better understood. In a carefully done behavioral assessment (again when conditions permit) a multi-channel physiological evaluation is, of course, to be preferred.

Behavioral Assessment in the Clinic and in Research Paradigms

Four elements are needed to conduct the ideal behavioral assessment: time, money, equipment, and personnel. This will become apparent as the reader peruses through the many chapters presented in this volume. It will also be apparent that some of the procedures recommended herein will obviously be limited by the specific settings in which they are applied. The most striking differences will appear for those conducting behavioral assessments in consulting room practice and those performing their behavioral assessments in research settings where naturalistic observation, personnel required to assess behavior *in vivo*, and equipment are all readily available. The analogy is to the ship's doctor attempting to make a differential diagnosis with the limited facilities available to him and the physician attempting to make the same differential diagnosis working within a university hospital in a large metropolitan city where all the latest diagnostic procedures and methodologies for carrying them out are present. Thus, it should be underscored that behavioral assessment is not the same (or is it currently possible) across all settings in which it occurs.

The question to be raised is then: "How does the clinician working in a consulting room practice conduct a reasonably adequate behavioral assessment when given the restrictions of his office?" Unfortunately, the answer to this question is not at all simple. However, several possibilities present themselves. *First*, if the problem is so complex that assessment is not feasible within an office practice, the ethical and moral responsibility of such a practitioner is to refer his patient to a facility that is capable of providing the type of complicated assessment procedures that are required. Being that treatment strategies are based on the behavioral assessment and that periodic re-evaluations are needed throughout the course of treatment, a return for treatment to the independent practitioner following initial evaluation, in this hypothetical case, is not recommended. *Second*, if the assessment problem is less complex and requires less equipment and fewer observational recordings, it is possible to conduct an adequate assessment within the context of the office practice. Although still the exception, there are some practitioners who use videotape recordings and have access to physiological monitoring devices within their practices. *Third*, if naturalistic observations are not feasible (either through videotape recording or standardized observations by significant others), the astute clinician might evaluate behaviors in simulated situations (role played) and might also rely on retrospective reports from interested individuals in the patient's environment who fill out standard rating scales and questionnaires. *Fourth*, at times the clinical practitioner will be compelled to rely on self-reports and his own "clinical" observations of behavior. Of all the alternatives, this is the least desirable and the lowest priority for recommendation.

Not only are there major differences in behavioral assessment between clinical and research settings, but within the research setting different experimental paradigms allow for varying degrees of diagnostic flexibility. Consider, for example, the differential flexibility permitted by the single case experimental design and the pre-post outcome study in which large groups of subjects are compared (see Hersen & Barlow, 1976). Certainly in the former (the single case approach), the nature of the research strategy followed permits the kind of flexibility where, at times, different assessment procedures as well as different modification techniques may be introduced during the course of the study. On the other hand, when conducting group comparison research, the nature of the typical pre-post design forces a strict adherence to assessment and modification procedures outlined in the research protocol irrespective of the vicissitudes found in the resulting data.

Future Trends

The area of behavioral assessment is new, and despite its relative brevity historically, a vast array of assessment techniques encompassing many parameters of behavior have been developed by clinicians and researchers working in behavior modification. Numerous developments and innovations have taken place since the earlier concerns with behavioral assessment were first articulated (Cautela, 1968; Goldfried & Pomeranz, 1968; Kanfer & Saslow, 1969). Although further developments stemming from existing behavioral techniques and their refinements undoubtedly will have their effects in the assessment area, the influence from the increasing empiricism found in academic psychiatry should also prove important.

Three current trends in the psychiatric scene (two of them emanating from biological psychiatry) are likely to influence the course of behavioral assessment (and vice versa). The *first*, already mentioned, involves the convergence of behavioral assessment and the application of problem oriented record keeping, particularly in psychiatric inpatient settings. (Of course, there is absolutely no reason why the problem oriented approach should not be equally applicable to outpatient settings.) The *second* concerns the issue of drugs and behavior analysis (see Hersen, Turner, Edelstein & Pinkston, 1975; Liberman & Davis, 1975; Liberman, Davis, Moon & Moore, 1973; Pacoe, Himmelhoch, Hersen & Guyett, 1975; Turner, Hersen & Alford, 1974). Liberman & Davis

(1975) forsee the marriage of behavioral and pharmacological approaches along four dimensions: "... (1) drugs as facilitators or adjuncts to behavior therapy; (2) behavioral and environmental strategies for prompting and reinforcing the appropriate and prescribed use of antipsychotic drugs; (3) single-case experimental designs using direct and continuous observations of behavior to assess the effects of psychotropic drugs; (4) drugs as agents of punishment, reinforcement and extinction of clinically important behaviors" (p. 325). Cutting across the four dimensions is the fact that behavioral assessment procedures would be performed in each case.

Finally, the *third* trend involves the use of nightly EEG recordings coupled with telemetric measurements of activity levels and biochemical evaluations in order to improve the diagnostic process across the major psychiatric dimensions (e.g., Foster & Kupfer, 1973, 1975). The use of objective data such as indicated in the aforementioned are entirely consistent with the spirit of behavioral assessment. In years to come the standardized use of automated measurement devices in behavioral assessment paradigms should be commonplace.

References

Atkinson, C. Data collection and program evaluation using the problem-oriented medical record. Paper presented at the meeting of the Association for Advancement of Behavior Therapy, Miami. December 1973.

Agras, W. S. (Ed.), *Behavior modification: Principles and clinical applications.* Boston: Little, Brown, 1972.

Ash, P. The reliability of psychiatric diagnoses. *Journal of Abnormal and Social Psychology*, 1949, **44**, 272–276.

Ayllon, T., & Azrin, N. H. *The token economy: A motivational system for therapy and rehabilitation.* New York: Appleton, 1968.

Ayllon, T., & Michael, J. The psychiatric nurse as a behavioral engineer. *Journal of the Experimental Analysis of Behavior*, 1959, **2**, 323–334.

Begelman, D. A. Ethical and legal issues in behavior modification. In M. Hersen, R. M. Eisler, & P. M. Miller (Eds.), *Progress in behavior modification: Volume I.* New York: Academic Press, 1975.

Begelman, D. A., & Hersen, M. An experimental analysis of the verbal-motor discrepancy in schizophrenia. *Journal of Clinical Psychology*, 1973, **29**, 175–179.

Bellack, A. S., & Hersen, M. Use of self-report inventories in behavioral assessment. In J. D. Cone, & R. P. Hawkins (Eds.), *Behavioral assessment: New directions in clinical psychology.* New York: Brunner/Mazel, in press.

Blanchard, E. B., & Hersen, M. Behavioral treatment of hysterical neurosis: Symptom substitution and symptom return reconsidered. *Psychiatry*, 1976, **39**, 118–129.

Blashfield, R. An evaluation of the DSM-II classification of schizophrenía as a nomenclature. *Journal of Abnormal Psychology*, 1973, **82**, 382–389.

Brady, J. P. Brevital-relaxation treatment of frigidity. *Behaviour Research and Therapy*, 1966, **4**, 71–77.

Brady, J. P. The place of behavior therapy in medical student and psychiatric resident training: Two surveys and some recommendations. *Journal of Nervous and Mental Disease*, 1973, **157**, 21–26.

Cautela, J. R. Behavior therapy and the need for behavioral assessment. *Psychotherapy: Theory, Research and Practice*, 1968, **5**, 175–179.

Cautela, J. R. A behavioral coding system. Presidential address to the seventh annual meeting of the Association for Advancement of Behavior Therapy, Miami, December 1973.

Cautela, J. R., & Kastenbaum, R. A. A reinforcement survey schedule for use in therapy, training, and research. *Psychological Reports*, 1967, **20**, 1115–1130.

Cohen, E. S., Harbin, H. T., & Wright, M. J. Some considerations in the formulation of psychiatric diagnoses. *Journal of Nervous and Mental Disease*, 1975, **160**, 422–427.

Cronbach, L. J. Assessment of individual differences. *Annual Review of Psychology*, 1956, **7**, 173–196.

Davison, G. C., & Neale, J. M. *Abnormal psychology: An experimental clinical approach.* New York: John Wiley & Sons, Inc., 1974.

Detre, T. P., & Jarecki, H. G. *Modern psychiatric treatment.* Philadelphia: J. B. Lippincott, 1971.

Doering, C. R. Reliability of observation of psychiatric and related characteristics. *American Journal of Orthopsychiatry*, 1934, **4**, 249–257.

Eisler, R. M., Hersen, M., Miller, P. M., & Wooten, L. S. Treatment expectations of psychiatric inpatients and their relationships to psychiatric diagnosis. *Journal of Clinical Psychology*, 1973, **29**, 251–253.

Eisler, R. M. & Polak, P. R. Social stress and psychiatric disorder. *Journal of Nervous and Mental Disease*, 1971, **153**, 227–233.

Eysenck, H. J. (Ed.), *Behavior therapy and the neuroses.* Oxford: Pergamon Press, 1960.

Foster, F. G., & Kupfer, D. J. Psychomotor activity and serum creatine phosphokinase activity. *Archives of General Psychiatry*, 1973, **29**, 752–758.

Foster, F. G., & Kupfer, D. J. Psychomotor activity as a correlate of depression and sleep in acutely disturbed psychiatric inpatients. *American Journal of Psychiatry*, 1974, **132**, 928–931.

Frank, G. Psychiatric diagnosis: A review of research. *Journal of General Psychology*, 1969, **81**, 157–176.

Frank, G. *Psychiatric diagnosis: A review of research.* Oxford: Pergamon Press, 1975.

Goldfried, M. R., & Kent, R. N. Traditional versus behavioral personality assessment: A comparison of methodological and theoretical assumptions. *Psychological Bulletin*, 1972, **77**, 409–420.

Goldfried, M. R., & Pomeranz, D. M. Role of assessment in behavior modification. *Psychological Reports*, 1968, **23**, 75–87.

Hayes-Roth, F., Longabaugh, R., & Ryback, R. The problem-oriented medical record and psychiatry. *British Journal of Psychiatry*, 1972, **121**, 27–34.

Hersen, M. Sexual aspects of Rorschach administration. *Journal of Projective Techniques and Personality Assessment*, 1970, **34**, 104–105.

Hersen, M. Fear scale norms for an in-patient population. *Journal of Clinical Psychology*, 1971, **27**, 375–378.

Hersen, M. Self-assessment of fear. *Behavior Therapy*, 1973, **4**, 241–257.

Hersen, M., & Barlow, D. H. *Single case experimental designs: Strategies for studying behavior change.* New York: Pergamon Press, 1976.

Hersen, M., & Bellack, A. S. Assessment of social skills. In A. R. Ciminero, K. S. Calhoun, & H. E. Adams (Eds.), *Handbook for behavioral assessment.* New York: John Wiley & Sons, in press.

Hersen, M., Eisler, R. M., & Miller, P. M. Historical perspectives in behavior modification: Introductory comments. In M. Hersen, R. M. Eisler, & P. M. Miller (Eds.), *Progress in behavior modification: Volume I.* New York: Academic Press, 1975.

Hersen, M., & Greaves, S. T. Rorschach productivity as related to verbal reinforcement. *Journal of Personality Assessment*, 1971, **35**, 436–441.

Hersen, M., Turner, S. M., Edelstein, B. A., & Pinkston, S. G. Effects of phenothiazines and social skills training in a withdrawn schizophrenic. *Journal of Clinical Psychology*, 1975, **31**, 588–594.

Hines, F. R., & Williams, R. B. Dimensional diagnosis and the medical student's grasp of psychiatry. *Archives of General Psychiatry*, 1975, **32**, 525–528.

Holmes, D. S., & Tyler, J. D. Direct versus projective measurement of achievement motivation. *Journal of Consulting and Clinical Psychology*, 1968, **32**, 712–717.

Kanfer, F., & Saslow, G. Behavioral diagnosis. In C. M. Franks (Ed.), *Behavior therapy: Appraisal and status*, New York: McGraw-Hill, 1969.

Katz, R. C. Further advantages of the problem-oriented record. Paper presented at the Association for Advancement of Behavior Therapy, Miami, December 1973.

Katz, R. C., & Woolley, F. R. Improving patients records through problem orientation. *Behavior Therapy*, 1975, **6**, 119–124.

Klonoff, H., & Cox, B. A problem-oriented system approach to analysis of treatment outcome. *American Journal of Psychiatry*, 1975, **132**, 836–841.

Lacey, J. I. Individual differences in somatic response patterns. *Journal of Comparative and Physiological Psychology*, 1950, **113**, 338–350.

Lacey, J. I. The evaluation of autonomic responses: Toward a generalization. *Annals of the New York Academy of Sciences*, 1956, **67**, 123–164.

Lacey, J. I. Psychophysiological approaches to the evaluation of psychotherapeutic process and outcome. In F. Rubinstein, & M. B. Parloff (Eds.), *Research in psychotherapy*. Washington, D. C.: American Psychological Association, 1962.

Lacey, J. I., & Van Lehn, R. Differential emphasis in somatic response to stress. *Psychosomatic Medicine*, 1952, **4**, 71–81.

Lang, P. J. Fear reduction and fear behavior: Problems in treating a construct. In J. M. Shlien (Ed.), *Research in psychotherapy: Volume III*. Washington, D. C.: American Psychological Association, 1968.

Lazarus, A. A. Multimodal behavior therapy: Treating the "basic id". *Journal of Nervous and Mental Disease*, 1973, **156**, 404–411.

Leitenberg, H., Agras, S., Butz, R., & Wincze, J. Relationship between heart rate and behavioral change during the treatment of phobias. *Journal of Abnormal Psychology*, 1971, **78**, 59–68.

Ley, P. The reliability of psychiatric diagnosis: Some new thoughts. *British Journal of Psychiatry*, 1972, **121**, 41–43.

Liberman, R. A behavioral approach to group dynamics: I. Reinforcement and prompting of cohesiveness in group therapy. *Behavior Therapy*, 1970, **1**, 141–175.

Liberman, R. P., & Davis, J. Drugs and behavior analysis. In M. Hersen, R. M. Eisler, & P. M. Miller (Eds.), *Progress in behavior modification: Volume I*. New York: Academic Press, 1975.

Liberman, R. P., Davis, J., Moon, W., & Moore, J. Research design for analyzing drug-environment behavior interactions. *Journal of Nervous and Mental Disease*, 1973, **156**, 432–439.

Marks, I. M. *Fears and phobias*. London: Heinemann Medical, 1969.

Masling, J., & Harris, S. Sexual aspects of TAT administration. *Journal of Consulting and Clinical Psychology*, 1969, **33**, 166–169.

McLean, P. D., & Miles, J. E. Evaluation and the problem-oriented record in psychiatry. *Archives of General Psychiatry*, 1974, **31**, 622–625.

Mischel, W. *Personality and assessment*. New York: Wiley, 1968.

Mischel, W. *Introduction to personality*. New York: Holt, Rinehart & Winston, 1971.

Mischel, W. Direct versus indirect personality assessment: Evidence and implications. *Journal of Consulting and Clinical Psychology*, 1972, **38**, 319–324.

Nathan, P. E. A systems analytic model of diagnosis: V. The diagnostic validity of disordered consciousness. *Journal of Clinical Psychology*, 1969, **25**, 243–246.

Nathan, P. E., Andberg, M., Behan, P. O., & Patch, V. D. Thirty-two observers and on patient—a study of diagnostic reliability. *Journal of Clinical Psychology*, 1969, **25**, 9–15.

Nathan, P. E., Gould, C. F., Zare, N. C., & Roth, M. A systems analysis of diagnosis: VI. Improved diagnostic validity from median data. *Journal of Clinical Psychology*, 1969, **25**, 370–375.

Nathan, P. E., Robertson, P., & Andberg, M. M. A systems analytic model of diagnosis: IV. The diagnostic validity of abnormal affective behavior. *Journal of Clinical Psychology* 1969, **25**, 235–242.

Nathan, P. E., Simpson, H. F., & Andberg, M. M. A systems analytic model of diagnosis: II. The diagnostic validity of abnormal perceptual behavior. *Journal of Clinical Psychology*, 1969, **25**, 115–119.

Nathan, P. E., Zare, N. C., Simpson, H. F., & Andberg, M. M. A systems analytic model of diagnosis: I. The diagnostic validity of abnormal psychomotor behavior. *Journal of Clinical Psychology*, 1969, **25**, 3–9.

Pacoe, L. V., Himmelhoch, J. M., Hersen, M., & Guyett, I. Pharmacologic and behavioral approaches to the treatment of unipolar (non-psychotic) depression: A needed integration. Unpublished manuscript, 1975.

Sandifer, M. G., Jr., Pettus, C., & Quade, D. A study of psychiatric diagnosis. *Journal of Nervous and Mental Disease*, 1964, **139**, 350–356.

Scales, E. J., & Johnson, M. S. A psychiatric POMR for use by a multidisciplinary team. *Hospital and Community Psychiatry*, 1975, **26**, 371–373.

Scott, W. A., & Johnson, R. C. Comparative validities of direct and indirect personality tests. *Journal of Consulting and Clinical Psychology*, 1972, **38**, 301–318.

Stuart, R. B. Behavioral contracting within the families of delinquents. *Journal of Behavior Therapy and Experimental Psychiatry*, 1971, **2**, 1–11.

Task Force Report 5. *Behavior therapy in psychiatry*. Washington, D. C.: American Psychiatric Association, 1973.

Turner, S. M., Hersen, M., & Alford, H. Effects of massed practice and meprobamate on spasmodic torticollis: An experimental analysis. *Behaviour Research and Therapy*, 1974, **12**, 259–260.

Watson, J. B., & Rayner, R. Conditioned emotional reactions. *Journal of Experimental Psychology*, 1920, **3**, 1–14.

Weed, L. L. Medical records, patient care, and medical education. *Irish Journal of Medical Science*, 1964, **6**. 271–282.

Weed, L. L. Medical records that guide and teach. *New England Journal of Medicine*, 1968, **278**, 593–600.

Weed, L. *Medical records, medical education, and patient care*. Cleveland: Case Western Reserve University Press, 1969.

Wolpe, J. *Psychotherapy by reciprocal inhibition*. Stanford: Stanford University Press, 1958.

Wolpe, J. *The practice of behavior therapy*. New York: Pergamon Press, 1969.

Wolpe, J., & Lang, P. J. A fear survey schedule for use in behavior therapy. *Behaviour Research and Therapy*, 1964, **2**, 27–30.

Wolpe, J., & Lazarus, A. A. *Behavior therapy techniques*. New York: Pergamon Press, 1966.

Woodruff, R. A., Goodwin, D. W., & Guze, S. B. *Psychiatric diagnosis*. New York: Oxford University Press, 1974.

CHAPTER 2

Behavioral Classification

D. A. BEGELMAN

Division of the Social Sciences
Kirkland College

Introduction

Basic to any scientific enterprise is the act of classification. It constitutes the initial effort undertaken by investigators whose subsequent work gives shape to increasingly complex and sophisticated forms of scientific activity. Nowhere has the discrepancy between the necessity for rational taxonomic schema and the perceived drawbacks of those in use been as noteworthy as it is in the study of human abnormal behavior. The pressing need for clinical theory to address itself to the problem of human suffering both on the pure and applied levels has remained strong. Even so, diagnostic systems on which the clinician has relied in ordering his subject matter have been considered deficient for the purposes for which they were developed. This chapter will examine issues in the area of behavioral classification which the present author believes still require comment or clarification. Without exception, they pertain to fundamental concepts of the field. For this reason, more painstaking attention to the details of discussions as they relate to basic aspects of the area might have a salutary effect for any position the clinician ultimately adopts.

Historical Themes of Classification

Zigler & Phillips (1961a, 1961b) contend that classification systems in clinical work should be viewed as tools of discovery in contrast to spurs for polemical debate. Nonetheless, the observed frequency of such debates attests to the judged inadequacy of systems already in use, while Zigler & Phillips' call for moderation perhaps reflects the more conservative view they espouse about the utility of diagnostic systems. Traditionally relied on systems, especially psychiatry's *Diagnostic and Statistical Manual of Mental Disorders* (DSM-I and DSM-II) have been faulted from a number of standpoints: (1) over-reliance on the so-called "medical model" of human abnormal behavior (Adams, 1964;

Albee, 1968; Begelman, 1971; Szasz, 1960; Ullmann & Krasner, 1969); (2) facilitating the stigmatization of clients, especially the institutionalized (Goffman, 1973; Millon & Millon, 1974; Rosenthal & Jacobsen, 1968; Sarbin & Mancuso, 1970; Scheff, 1973; Stuart, 1970); (3) incorporating debatable theoretical notions (Cautela & Upper, 1973; Panzetta, 1974); (4) possessing low reliability and validity (Kreitman, 1961; Sandifer, Pettus & Quade, 1964; Schmidt & Fonda, 1956; Seeman, 1953; Stoller & Geertsma, 1963; Zubin, 1966); (5) having little value as regards prognosis, treatment implications, or predicting future behavior in general (Dershowitz, 1974); (6) dehumanizing the client-therapist relationship (Laing, 1967); (7) failing to achieve consistency of categorical groupings (Cautela & Upper, 1973); (8) the introduction of negative biases stemming from arbitrary decision-rules, as when a client with "mixed symptomatology" is diagnosed on the basis of the behavioral pattern deemed most "severe" (Millon, 1969; Panzetta, 1974); and (9) favoring a presumption of homogeneity among individuals labeled in the same way (King, 1954; Wittenborn, 1951, 1952; Zigler & Phillips, 1961a, 1961b).

Increasingly, professional complaints over the drawbacks of standard nosologies and nomenclature generally coincide with a period of self-appraisal within the social sciences (Zigler & Phillips, 1961a, 1961b). Criticisms of "diagnosis" and "labeling" in scientific circles—in addition to their intrinsic methodological justification—have mirrored the adverse social and philosophical reaction to them which was rife in the 1960s. Consequently, mounting disenchantment with this aspect of the clinical role has probably reflected the impact of broader cultural issues. Indeed, the popularity among sociologists of the perspective called "labeling theory" (Becker, 1963; Erikson, 1964; Goffman, 1961; Kitsuse, 1964; Lemert, 1967; Scheff, 1966) is well in keeping with this intellectual trend, in spite of recent evidence of its limitations (Angrist, Lefton, Dinitz & Pasamanick, 1968; Freeman & Simmons, 1963; Gove, 1970; Sampson, Messinger & Towne, 1964; Yarrow, Schwartz, Murphy & Deasy, 1955). The creation of deviance, according to labeling theory, is an outcome of the societal reaction to it, rather than due to its inherent features. The emphasis is quite consistent with a skeptical attitude towards the diagnostic practices of psychiatry and psychology. Indeed, labeling theorists in sociology might tend to regard scientific attempts to validate nosological systems as misconceived, if deviant behavior is basically their creation, rather than pre-existing reality they are devised to describe. The validity of labeling theory appears to hinge on a clarification of precisely what sense of the term "creation" (as in labeling individual A an "X," creates "X-ness") figures importantly in the theoretical formulation. There is a sense of "create" for which it is obvious no diagnostic act ever "created" anything, and another sense in which diagnostic creation is inevitable. It behooves the labeling theorist to show how deployment of the latter meaning of "create" in a sociological formulation is non-trivial.

As Millon & Millon (1974) have indicated, efforts to resolve the problem of the current limitations of classification schema comprise three broad strategies: (1) recommendations to abandon them completely (Laing, 1967; Sarbin & Mancuso, 1970); (2) to revise them drastically (Cautela, 1968; Hayes-Roth, Longabaugh & Ryback, 1972; Kanfer & Saslow, 1965; Millon, 1969); and (3) attempts merely to refine them further (Lorr, 1966; Overall & Gorham, 1962, 1963; Spitzer, Endicott, Cohen & Fleiss, 1972; Zigler & Phillips, 1961a, 1961b). It is difficult to envision how a commitment to a vigorous program of research into the behavior disorders is possible without a corresponding (even if implicit) assumption about the necessity, hence legitimacy, of behavioral classification. Obviously, a research orientation to problem behaviors presupposes the possibility of making requisite taxonomic distinctions (Eysenck, 1952). By the same token, it need not follow that recommendations to abandon classification schema suggest a negative attitude towards research. On the contrary, an important distinction is seldom drawn between two altogether different motives behind the rejection of diagnostic or coding practices: (1) that they *inherently* do violence to, or distort, that which they purport to characterize (Menninger, 1955; Noyes, 1953; Rogers, 1951; Rotter, 1954); and (2) that the sociological disadvantages of their adoption outweigh the gains attendant on their use in scientific inquiry (Laing, 1967; Szasz, 1957). The former view has been associated with investigators favoring the so-called "idiographic" approach to problem behaviors (Beck, 1953; Eysenck, 1954; Falk, 1956). On this view, the uniqueness of the individual client referred for treatment is all but obliterated by classificatory procedures under which he is identified with others in a group who differ from him in essential ways. By contrast, the second point of view is the considered outcome of a social cost-analysis. The acknowledged utility of classification is made subordinate to the necessity of avoiding stigmatization, institutionalization, or other untoward consequences of labeling. The motive behind the first recommendation is, whatever its final merit, *scientific*; whereas the motive behind the second is *moral*.

The confusion between empirical issues and those in the value-sphere is rife in debates over the validity of classification systems. For example, in calling current nosological practices in psychiatry a "Tower of Babel," Szasz (1957) has pointed out that diagnostic categories as presently used are "unserviceable" and "meaningless" when applied in contexts differing from those in which they originated. Accordingly, the category *psychosis* "justifies forcible retention" when applied in a state hospital system, "refers only to certain mental mechanisms" in the private practice situation, and "pertains to the ascription of criminal responsibility, hence punishment," in legal contexts, such as court hearings. However, a case for the *conceptual* weakness of nosological labels cannot be made on these grounds. At best, Szasz has shown that the practical consequences to the client of applying diagnostic labels shift depending on context, not that their use involves diverse meanings. Indeed, it is possible that variations in contextual consequentiality may occur using labels of acknowledged precision (e.g., "epilepsy"). Szasz appears to have confused the semantic meaning of a diagnostic term with the pragmatic implications of applying it (Begelman, 1971). It may transpire that the term "psychosis" is indeed used in distinguishable or confused ways, as regards its meaning. However, this is no more indicated by the facts Szasz cites than is the semantic meaninglessness of "epilepsy" assured when appreciably different social reactions to it on the part of mothers, recruitment sergeants, or employers are observed in consequence of its application! Szasz's concern here is not with the meaning of a label, since semantic precision alone cannot ensure that the social consequences of applying a diagnostic term serve to augment the client's interest. More likely, his concern is with legal or ethical implications of the practice of psychiatric labeling, in the context of its tendency to jeopardize an individual's freedom or self-interest. Szasz's critique of psychiatric diagnosis parallels the growing tendency of negativism toward the labeling process itself, rather than the societal reaction to those made the willing or unwilling recipients of the process. As a consequence, mental health professionals—in accordance with the *caveats* urged by the general semanticists (Chase, 1938; Hayakawa, 1954; Korzybski, 1933)—have developed a noticeable sensitivity to admissible or inadmissible ways to speak. Approaches to treatment issues, the legality or morality of much of traditional mental health practice, the plight of the institutionalized person, and other weighty questions receive strikingly varied answers, while there is a much wider consensus over linguistic proprieties. For instance, while there remains a latitude of opinion concerning the boundaries of our collective admissible approach to hospitalized "psychotic" individuals, it is obvious that calling them "mentally ill patients" is otiose, the preferred substitute being "clients with behavioral problems." In a previous publication (Begelman, 1971), the present author pointed out how difficult it is to justify magnifying the importance of such terminological revision when progress in other spheres cannot keep pace with it. The world is not magically transformed by giving everything a new name, when all else remains the same (e.g., nothing is changed by exchanging "moron" for "retarded person" or "underachiever," while continuing to deal with the individual in question as if he or she were a moron).

The Problem of Definition

The definition and classification of a subject matter are two closely interwoven activities in the early stages of theorizing. Acknowledgement of this fact is clearly in evidence in textbooks on abnormal psychology (Davison & Neale, 1974; Millon & Millon, 1974; Nathan & Harris, 1975; Rosen, Fox & Gregory, 1972; Suinn, 1970; Ullman & Krasner, 1969; Zax & Cowen, 1972), in which one of the first chapters is typically devoted to "defining" abnormal or maladaptive behavior. Defining a concept may be a hazardous task, especially when one considers the haste with which it is so frequently dispatched. Moreover, it is not obvious that "definitions" are in every case the same species of thing. Indeed, the business of "defining" is a complex and multifaceted affair; it can encompass logically distinct undertakings, each of which runs the occasional risk of becoming confused with another. Specifically, there are at least eleven distinguishable activities which in the clinical literature have all been identified as defining. To wit:

1. Categorizing
2. Stipulating
3. Substituting
4. Abstracting
5. Distributing
6. Operationalizing
7. Verifying
8. Mapping
9. Theorizing
10. Judging
11. Pointing

(1) We frequently "define" a particular response-class, act, or behavioral pattern when we *categorize* it as a member of a larger class. For example, delusions have been defined as a symptom of mental illness (or an expression of problems in living, or an abnormal or maladaptive behavioral pattern). In so defining them, we classify delusions as a sub-group in a broader membership of problem behaviors, including such phenomena as hallucinations. Analogous definitions through categorization in law would be the classification of burglary as a felony or in biology, the classification of a platypus as a mammal. Categorization is not an arbitrary act. In biology, designation of a platypus as a mammal rather than a reptile is hardly a matter of convention (Cain, 1954).

Categorization is frequently confused with causal explanation. Skinner's (1974) assault on mentalism and Szasz's (1961) attack on the so-called mental illness myth may be examples of such confusions. Thus, among the various types of explanation given for behavior, "He is jealous," and "He is mentally ill" are sometimes supplied. Skinner insists that the former is a mentalistic explanation of overt behavior in that it posits an internal mental state in contrast to the contingencies of reinforcement to account for overt behavior, whereas Szasz has complained that the latter explanation reifies a presumed internal disease process to account for observations which are more properly dealt with by means of psychosocial, ethical, and legal concepts. Both men agree that "jealousy" and "mental illness" cannot be deployed as explanatory concepts since they are, in the last analysis, merely descriptions of the behavior to be explained. A similar argument is sometimes sustained against "retardation" as an explanatory concept. Accordingly, it is argued that it is circular to assume that "John is retarded" can ever function as a substantive explanation of John's behavior. If "retardation" is a term describing a person's intellectual behaviors, "John behaves as he does because he is retarded," communicates no more than "John behaves in a retarded manner because he is retarded," which is circular. In commenting on what they take to be the fallacy of transforming descriptive labels into explanations, Millon & Millon (1974) attribute the resulting "circular reasoning" to adherence to the medical model. They further conclude that it is the transparency of this fallacy that has led clinical theorists to argue prematurely for the wholesale rejection of diagnostic labels.

Unfortunately, the foregoing critique is weakened by the failure to systematically distinguish among logically different types of explanation. In accounting for behavior, attributions of such things as mental illness, jealousy, or retardation are intended as explanations, although not causal ones. Specifically, they are meant only to evaluate overt behavior, as such evaluation relates to the proper categorization of patterns under scrutiny. In other words, "He behaves that way because of jealousy" is intended to inform as to the classification of a response-pattern, not as to the independent variables of which it is a function (Begelman, 1966). If explanations incorporating emotion terms like "jealousy" were causal in scope, jealousy would be construed as an internal independent variable, the occurrence of which can at best only be inferred. If so, how is it then possible for us to reject the suggestion that jealousy may be experienced as a result of striking our thumb with a hammer as a *logical absurdity* in contrast to an empirical improbability? Furthermore, how is it possible to reconcile Skinner's account of such explanations with the fact that emotions such as jealousy are frequently not "inferred" at all? They can be established with certainty (Austin, 1961). With respect to the mental illness concept, the presumed "circularity" of explanations employing it also happen to characterize those explanations involving its preferred alternatives. Thus, "problems in living" is vulnerable to criticism on similar grounds, since "Jones behaves as he does because of problems in living" translates as "Jones has problems in living because he has problems in living." Obviously, impatience with the expression "mental illness" has in this case prompted many to argue for its deletion from the psychological vocabulary prematurely; the argument based on circularity has the embarrassing consequence of backfiring (Begelman, 1966).

(2) *Stipulatory* definitions involve a speech convention. As regards the clinical concept of delusions, we establish that the term "delusion" will henceforth be used as the name (label, tag, word) for a given pattern of behavior. In this manner, we have defined the term "delusion." Stipulatory definitions contrast with (3) *substitutive* definitions specifying the alternative terms of expressions in a language that may be substituted for, or regarded as synonymous

with, the clinical term in question. With respect to delusions, the term "paranoid" would undoubtedly be of service in fashioning a substitutive definition, although it is not exactly a synonymous expression. In defining the term "delusion" for a foreign person, substitutive definitions may consist in locating a term in his language which is synonymous with "delusion" in English. A substitutive definition is accordingly the current cash-value of an expression on an exclusively verbal exchange.

(4) *Abstract* definitions are verbal formulae specifying the criteria for a behavioral concept, whereas (5) *distributive* definitions are conjunctive in scope. They specify all possible instances of a behavioral concept that would be classified as such, whether or not those instances are occurring. The glossaries of textbooks on abnormal psychology usually attempt to supply abstract definitions of behavioral disorders, based upon the distributive definitions of concepts it is presumed are already operating. An accurate grasp of the actual distributive definition of a concept is therefore a pre-condition for a well-formulated abstract definition.

(6) The *operational* definition of a concept is most frequently identified as the measure or barometer of an entity, structure, concept, or process, especially in research. A misconceived relationship between operational definitions and concepts they purport to measure forebodes problems in the area of construct validity. In behavioral research, the most persistent difficulties of operational defining pertain to inconsistencies among several measures of the same concept. For example, the observed low correlations among the verbal, physiological, and behavioral indices of "fear" (Lang, 1968; Smith, Diener & Beaman, 1974) are noteworthy.

Defining a behavioral pattern as "delusional" is sometimes identified as an operation or procedure undertaken in determining that some pattern is an illustration of the concept. Here, the defining act is most closely aligned in meaning with the notion of (7) *verification*: the getting of the goods on someone. When we make use of an abstract definition of, say, "delusions" in order to determine the incidence or prevalence of this behavioral pattern, we supply a definitional (8) *mapping* of the concept. In mapping a concept, we therefore review those behaviors to which the abstract definition currently applies. Such definitions would understandably change over time, in accordance with the appearance or disappearance of those patterns they cover.

(9) *Theoretical* definitions exhibit the influence of particular theories, formulations, or paradigms (Kuhn, 1962) in obvious ways. Examples would be Freud's "definition" of delusional thinking as "repressed homosexuality" (Freud, 1959) or the one favored by several applied behavior analysts (Ayllon & Michael, 1959) as the verbal behavior of clients discriminated as "delusional" by a diagnostic community. Needless to say, theoretical definitions can be seen as false, without the necessity of abandoning a paradigm. In line with this,

Freud's definition of paranoia appears to have been an unwarranted extrapolation from the Schreber case (Schreber, 1955), whereas the mistake of viewing verbal responses as the only criteria of delusions casts considerable doubt on the aforementioned behavioristic definition of the disorder.

(10) *Judgmental* definitions are the outcome of decision-processes most closely resembling verdicts. They constitute *rulings*, rather than *discoveries*, as to whether a particular sample of behavior qualifies as the type which counts as, for example, delusional thinking. Judgmental definitions are made in contexts wherein persons may be responding in ways that dramatize a degree of *vagueness* (Waismann, 1963) in diagnostic concepts. On some occasions, in order to define an observed pattern as one to which a given concept applies, a quasi-legal ruling must be undertaken. More often than not, such rulings will affect which topographical features of behavioral patterns we come to regard as criteria for applying various concepts. Is a blue lemon a lemon? What indeed are we to say concerning the fearfulness of a subject, when there is a lack of correlation among the measures of fear obtained from him? Lastly, there is (11) the *ostensive* definition, for persons of action, and few words. The problem of supplying definitions can become a badly muddled one: the more so when we fail to distinguish which of the foregoing eleven is functioning when we purport to define something.

Interrelationships among the foregoing definitional acts can be manifold. They may overlap, as when, for example, supplying a theoretical definition simultaneously constitutes a fresh categorization or operational definition. Under the Freudian theoretical definition, delusional thinking is categorized as "verbal behavior" according to one behavioral approach to the problem. Understandably, the latter categorization yields an operational definition of "delusion" for the purposes of applied behavioral analysis: verbal operants of a given kind. Freud's reclassification of hysterics as "sick" in contrast to "malingerer" has been construed by some writers (Begelman, 1966; Margolis, 1966) as springing from an original theoretical definition of hysteria. Conversely, others have insisted the reclassification is without theoretical justification, and represents merely a move calculated to enhance the lot of a hitherto despised social group—malingerers (Szasz, 1961). Space does not permit a detailed discussion of the myriad problems generated by interrelationships among all eleven definitional acts. However, the interface between *abstract* definitions on the one hand, and the *judgmental*, *distributive*, and *ostensive* kind on the other will be singled out for special comment.

Abstract and Judgmental Definitions

In keeping with the aforementioned recent criticisms of diagnostic labeling, one line of argument has been that these classificatory practices are futile exercises in subjectivity, as evidenced by the less than satisfactory results from reliability studies. It would perhaps be more accurate to point out that reliability is high for broader behavioral classifications than it is for sub-classifications (e.g., of "schizophrenia") (Buss, 1966; Quay, 1963; Schmidt & Fonda, 1956). However, even this statement requires qualification, since, as Ullmann & Krasner (1969) have indicated, precisely how great inter-rater reliabilities must be in order to approximate requisite levels cannot be divorced from interpretations unique to particular decisions.

Any finding of reliability levels lower than those deemed acceptable for particular purposes is of little comfort to diagnosticians who place great importance on this aspect of their clinical work. It has been pointed out that such findings directly reflect differences in meaning which diagnosticians attach to given nosological labels. That is, it is frequently assumed that the only plausible interpretation of the lack of agreement among diagnosticians attaching different labels to a client are inconsistencies in interpretation of their semantic content. This need not be true. The difference may relate to disparities in *judgment* as to whether a particular pattern is sufficiently illustrative of that which takes a given diagnostic label. Here, the familiar phenomenon of ambiguity introduced by the lack of correspondence between the clinical data and textbook "syndromes" compels the diagnostician to rule on whether a suitable enough match exists between clinical behavior under scrutiny and a given diagnostic term. The lack of agreement among diagnoses may thus reflect factors intrinsic to all diagnostic activities, not merely those conducted by mental health professionals. Oddly, disagreements among pathologists as to the malignant nature of a biopsy is rarely construed as evidence of substantial disagreement over what "carcinoma" means. Nor is the consistent diasgreement between defense and prosecution attorneys in court proceedings viewed as decisive evidence of different meanings attaching to the legal concepts of "innocent" and "guilty" (Begelman, 1966).

The assumption of disparities in meaning of diagnostic labels is a further interest in connection with the famous controversy between Kraepelin (1896) and Bleuler (1950). The irony here is that the controversy has many of the earmarks of a purely semantic quibble, although it is invariably referenced as a confrontation in theoretical outlook over schizophrenia on the part of the two psychiatrists (Davison & Neale, 1974; Zigler & Phillips, 1961a, 1961b). Specifically, in taking issue with Kraepelin that schizophrenia inevitably involves a deteriorative course, Bleuler is credited with a discovery which Kraepelin had overlooked: schizophrenia is not irreversible. Nevertheless, such a view prejudges a crucial issue concerning the equivalence of the concepts *dementia praecox* and *schizophrenia*. If irreversibility were among the criteria of Kraepelin's abstract definition of dementia praecox, there are no Bleulerian "discoveries" of exceptions to Kraepelin's view. Rather, Bleuler simply developed a newer concept, which was not conceptually wedded to the notion of irreversibility. Whether the controversy actually involved a case of the failure to observe reversible schizophrenia or the creation of a wider concept would depend upon the importance Kraepelinians attached to irreversibility as a criterion of the syndrome. Kraepelin's abiding interest in underlying disease processes suggests that it held more importance for him than most modern texts would have us believe.

Abstract and Distributive Definitions

There is a neglected aspect of the relationship between *abstract* and *distributive* definitions. The relationship is typically interpreted as being governed by a model which may only frequently, rather than invariably apply. To take an unrelated example, we may cite the concept of a fever. Its *abstract* definition is: "a body temperature in excess of 98.6°F," whereas its *distributive* definition is all possible body temperature in excess of 98.6°F. As regards "fever," *abstract* and *distributive* definitions of the concept have a singular relationship. The criterion of the concept represented in the abstract definition is common to all distributions of "fever." There is a widespread assumption that the same isomorphism holds with respect to other concepts—that every instance of a concept has a particular feature in common with every other instance. Indeed, this isomorphism is believed to be the only conceivable basis on which concept-formation itself is possible. Thus, it is held that, for example, beliefs A, B, C, D, E can all be identified as "delusional" only if there is some property or properties that A, B, C, D, E share in common, in virtue of which they are so defined. This "common ingredient" picture of concepts has been influential and compelling. If two instances of a concept were observed to share no common feature, many theorists would suspect something amiss with the original application of the concept (or the concept itself), in contrast to suspecting some drawback in their view of concepts.

Wittgenstein (1953) is credited with formulating a plausible alternative to the ingredient picture of concepts, called the "family resemblance" analysis. According to Wittgenstein, many concepts are built up on the basis of commonalities shared by some of their instances, but not all. The difference between the ingredient picture and the family resemblance notion may be illustrated as follows:

Common Ingredient Picture

A	B	C	D	E
abcd	*abce*	*abef*	*abfg*	*abgh*

Family Resemblance Analysis

A	B	C	D	E
abcd	*abce*	*abde*	*acde*	*bcde*

(Upper-case letters A–E represent instances of a concept, lower-case letters, the empirical features of each instance. Under the CI model, features *ab* are common to all instances, whereas under the FR model, there is no given feature common to all instances.) Taxonomic and evolutionary biologists will recognize the similarity between the structure of Wittgenstein's FR model and the notion of a *Rassenkreis* (Rensch, 1959) in speciation. A *Rassenkreis* (mosaics of races) is a polymorphic species of several geographically distributed races of animals that may not hybridize consistently.

In an impressive attempt to expose the "mythic" roots of the mental illness concept, Sarbin (1964, 1968) has argued for the elimination of several of its constituent bulwarks, like *anxiety*, *schizophrenia*, and *hallucination*, the criteria for which he finds equivocal (Sarbin, 1968, p. 318). Nevertheless, an uncomfortable degree of "equivocality" is precisely what one should expect to observe if a CI model is assumed to operate for the clinical concepts of Sarbin dissects. Under an FR model, the investigator should anticipate no necessarily shared commonalities, nor should he rule out in advance a considerable overlap among instances and non-instances of a concept. In spite of this, one method Sarbin resorts to in dismantling the mental illness myth is to invite experimental subjects to discriminate between a written "schizophrenic" communication and a poem by Dylan Thomas (Sarbin, 1968). He concludes that the failure of subjects to properly distinguish the two productions out of context as confirming the unnecessary reification of the concept of "hallucination." Sarbin's conclusion is vitiated for two important reasons. *First*, contextual embedding of behavior is scarcely a minor element in ascertaining whether a clinical concept holds. We would obviously have something quite different to say about a person shadow-boxing in Stillman's Gymnasium in contrast to engaging in the same behavior at the wake of his 5-year-old daughter. *Second*, Sarbin's methodology is ultimately self-defeating in relation to his professed broader program. If the failure to discriminate between a Dylan Thomas poem and an hallucinatory production casts doubt on the deployment of a time-honored clinical concept, why is this conclusion so asymmetrical? Might not an equally sceptical conclusion be drawn concerning the reality of Welsh poetry? Cannot the data be used to argue with equal force that schizophrenics are actually Welsh poets, or that Dylan Thomas was "hallucinating," or both, or neither (in the sense that both enjoy parity status on some higher level of synthesis)?

Abstract and Ostensive Definitions

Efforts to mark the proper relationship between abstract and ostensively defined concepts are among the most problematic in clinical theory. Put differently, this is the problem of making the right connections between extra-linguistic events (i.e., those "pointed to") and abstract characterizations of them. Basically, the most significant problems arising here are of two distinct types: ingredient picture sequelae and sequelae of value-sphere quandries.

Over-reliance on the ingredient picture discussed above may have the effect of prompting the clinical theorist to attempt assays at formulating abstract criteria that have a tenuous relationship to clinical events they are meant to characterize. For example, while there may be a degree of consistency among clinicians about the ostensive definition of, for example, delusional thinking, it is questionable whether abstract criteria many investigators claim define this clinical phenomenon actually do. Sarason (1972) and others contend that certain ostensively defined clinical occurrences can be abstractly defined as "fixed, false beliefs which are maintained even in the face of clear evidence to the contrary." The problem is that this abstract definition is not congruent with the clinical occurrences usually designated as "delusional." If we restrict attention to delusions which involve an intelligible truth-claim (e.g., *Neighbors are trying to poison me*, or *Martians are controlling my mind*, or *My wife is unfaithful*), it appears the falsity of the belief cannot be a criterion for delusional thinking. Delusions can incorporate *true* beliefs, as when the allegation they contain is true independently of the specific grounds for which it is held. Alternatively, it is possible to make an allegation of infidelity falsely and vehemently, and yet not engage in delusional thinking, as when a scenario without foundation in fact is elaborately planned and staged by wife and friend for a wager. Orson Welles' "War of the Worlds" created numerous non-delusional convictions about an invasion from Mars. When certain current beliefs about Martian invasions are diagnosed as "delusional," they are hardly deemed so on the basis of a diagnostician's intimate knowledge of the progress of plans for space conquest by extra-terrestrial aliens. Yet there is a presupposition behind the conviction that the delusion in question must contain a *false* belief. Furthermore, there is a huge class of delusional beliefs that do not appear to qualify as "false," because they cannot qualify as being either true or false. These are the beliefs which are incoherent or unintelligible as regards a truth-claim, such as, "*My soul has left my body*," "*I am growing my father's hair*," "*Our minds have been exchanged*." It would be odd in the extreme to characterize such beliefs as "false," unless they are understood to be symbolic or metaphoric transformations of cognitions which can be decoded as those that are either true or false. However, such transformations themselves presuppose a rather speculative body of translation-rules peculiar to versions of psychodynamic theory, and devised—as best as one can determine—for the express purpose of disallowing anyone from speaking utter nonsense with conviction.

In the case of psychological concepts intrinsically *normative*, in contrast to *descriptive* in scope, the problem of drawing connections between abstract criteria and ostensively defined behaviors becomes knotty indeed. For example' Maslow's (1968) notion of self-actualization involves a "metamotivational" repertoire of behaviors including increased "autonomy," "creativeness," and "superior perception of reality" (Maslow, 1968, p. 26). On an abstract level, there ordinarily would be little disagreement as to the value of such characteristics. In so far as this is true, "self-actualization" may be non-controversially conceived as encompassing them. (Maslow purported to "discover" such patterns to characterize the behavior of self-actualizers, although such a claim courts the fallacy of *petitio principii.* On what basis are so-called "self-actualizers" selected for study in the first place? Because they are, *inter alia,* "autonomous," "creative," and possessed of "superior perceptions of reality"?) The problem surfaces in determining what is to count as, for example, "autonomy," and is highlighted by the discrepancy between the consensus obtained over the formal requirements of abstract definitions and the lack of consensus over those behaviors to which they are perceived to apply. Thus, observers who agree on the value of "autonomy" might disagree strenuously as to which patterns are likely to illustrate it. Obviously, an implicit value-scheme will influence the extent to which virtues like "autonomy" describe given behaviors. In a related way, clinical concepts many assume are distinguishable because of the topographic features of behaviors to which they apply dramatize the same problem. For example, the notions of *assertivity* and *aggressivity* are widely supposed to be so distinguished. We thus may come under the grip of a certain picture of their relationship: assertivity is a sort of low magnitude aggressivity (i.e., we are brought, as it were, over into the realm of the latter by "juicing up" the former, hence overstepping permissible limits of socially sanctioned behaviors). However, it might be more correct to view the substantive distinction between assertivity and aggressivity as relating to positive and negative value judgments. That is, a response may be correctly labeled "assertive" because it is judged to be a proper or desirable one in the circumstances in which it is emitted. On the other hand, "aggressive" responses are those uncalled for or undesirable in some sense, not simply those differing topographically from the assertive kind. The tendency in clinical theory to foster explanations of differences among key concepts on the basis of the descriptive features of the behaviors to which they apply is a misconceived program. Commentators in the womens' movement have long ago recognized that to describe a female as "aggressive" need not imply she behaves any differently from men universally characterized as "assertive." On the contrary, the discrimination conventionally made here is between behaviors that resemble each other topographically. The discrimination itself is a historical consequence of an ingrained value-scheme dictating the boundaries of permissible female conduct. It follows that denying a particular woman to be "aggressive" is not to deny that she challenges men on matters important to her own identity, but to question whether this is rightfully identified as "aggression," and therefore something with a negative connotation. The example of "aggressivity" is interesting in another respect. The perceived justification of newer female sex-roles has been accompanied by either: (1) an acceptance of the charge that certain women are "aggressive," but are ideologically justified in so responding in order to combat oppression, or (2) a denial that the behavior in question can be classified as "aggressive" in contrast to "assertive," explicitly because it is ideologically demanded.

The application of a bewildering range of clinical concepts like "aggression" presuppose an elaborate body of background assumptions in the value, political, and ideological spheres. On the personal side, the present author's critique of traditional approaches to the treatment of the so-called "problem" of homosexuality (Begelman, 1975b) was faulted by one medical psychoanalyst as "hostile." Yet, the latter's response as well as those of his medical colleagues to proposals for socialized medicine or accountability for malpractice are seen by them as "righteous indignation" in contrast to some meaner emotion. In the sixties, youngsters who rebelled against conventional values were frequently perceived as "disturbed," consequently diagnosable. In the seventies, California physicians who endanger public health through a work-stoppage are not "socipaths" incapable of those guilt feelings requisite for inhibiting antisocial conduct; they are only devoted campaigners against the depredations of the legal system! In his play *Man and Superman*, Bernard Shaw had Don Juan castigate the Devil for the latter's celebration of virtues which were unreal because they could be turned inside out like a glove, depending upon the moral stance initially taken: beauty, purity, respectability, patriotism, bravery, and so forth (Shaw, 1952). As regards the much discussed concepts of behavioral normality and disorder, the same point applies with a vengeance.

The Definition of Abnormal Behavior

Clinicians have for many years now been led quite naturally to pose the question "What is a problem behavior?" with that kind of innocence born of the conviction that the answer is just around the corner, and not the anguished product of inquiries forever plagued by false starts (Benedict, 1934; Foley, 1935; Hacker, 1945; Marzolf, 1947; Shoben, 1957; Skaggs, 1933; Wegrocki, 1939). Essentially, traditional abstract definitions of behavioral disorder have been based on the assumption that a correct formulation of abnormal behavior could be supplied as an abstraction of empirical qualities common to all instances of maladaptive behavior. An alternative model has a lower visibility, although much can be said in its favor. According to it, the very notion of a problem behavior itself is conceptually linked to issues in the realm of law, ethics, and value, and admits of a family resemblance analysis. A recent, although most probably inadequate formulation of abnormality has received few formal adherents with the exception of the phenomonologists (Laing, 1967; Rogers, 1951). It is the view that problem-behaviors are self-defined. As usually referenced, this definition of behavior disorder is ambiguous. It is not altogether clear whether client "self-definition" is, according to this formulation: (1) necessary for the purpose of providing a reasonable basis for initiating therapy, (2) along with such elements as "informed consent" necessary in developing a proper legal or ethical basis for initiating treatment, or (3) supplying a criterion of a behavioral problem. For example, Bandura (1969) is sympathetic to the view that only the client should define his or her own problem behaviors, although it is unclear as to whether his emphasis on "client decision-making in the value-realm" is intended as a guide to the proper approach to treatment or as a definition of the concept of problem behavior itself. If the latter, the viewpoint is counter-intuitive.

If the actual existence of a behavior disorder logically required the element of self-definition, it would be inconsistent to speak of a behavior disorder in advance of assuming such self-definition has occurred. According to this view, clients such as non-verbal retardates or autistic persons cannot be classified as problem behavers. In addition, the view entails the absurd consequence that an individual cannot have a behavioral problem of which he is unaware. This one entailment is of great importance, since it compels us to acknowledge that we cannot honor a first-person phenomenological criterion of the concept of behavior disorder, and simultaneously insist that clients are sometimes unaware of their problems. (A, possible qualification to this would be a definition of "behavioral problem" that requires first-person criteria, but not "self-definition" as it entails awareness. For example, a person may self-define a particular behavioral pattern as "abnormal" were he to emit it—without realizing, alas, he has been emitting it all along.) Either the existence of problem behaviors is conceptually linked to an individual's tendency to define them as such, *or* he can fail to recognize them, but not both. This manner of having one's cake while eating it is a sometime reflection of the attempt to push in opposite directions at once. Because of philosophical upheavals in current views about normality and abnormality, there is a trend towards rejecting institutional definitions in favor of personalistic ones. At the same time, there is an understandable reluctance to abandon the view that persons experience problems of which they are unaware, even conceding the damage perpetuated historically by reliance on social or institutional definitions of abnormality.

It is safe to say that problem-behaviors are patterns of disturbance in people's lives that are undesirable only because such a characterization is vacuous and empty. The relationship among the expressions "behaviors which qualify for treatment," "problem behaviors," "disturbances," "undesirable patterns," and so forth, are among substitutive definitions, as discussed above. Thus, the sentence, "problem behaviors are undesirable patterns of responding" is uninformative; the notion of an undesirable pattern is already contained in the idea of a problem behavior. The individual who utters such a sentence is not an individual in receipt of important clinical information; he is merely one who has learned how to speak properly. As we use the expression "problem behavior," it can never apply to a desirable pattern without incurring the charge of self-inconsistency or language-abuse. If a pattern is a desirable one, it is logically debarred from being a problem-behavior; if the latter, it is logically guaranteed to be undesirable. Identifying concretely those events described by terms such as "problem-behavior" or "undesirable" is precisely the quandry of determining the correct relationship between abstractly and ostensively defined concepts, as discussed previously.

Abstract definitions of behavior disorder formulated in the past share a common failing. They seek to supply a *picture* of the concept at the very highest level of generality, as if the expression "abnormal behavior" were somehow a *name* for a group of inductively arrived at characteristics. (In a related way, the child who asks his mother to draw a picture of the keys that fit the front and back doors cannot quite grasp why it is that difficult for her to draw a similar picture of a "master key," where the latter is not merely the name of the key which will in fact open both the front and back doors of his house.) To call something a behavioral problem is not to *depict* it in the abstract, but to *judge* it concretely (Begelman, 1975a), typically in terms of a tacit system of values. When we say that a stuttering pattern is of a given frequency-rate, or when we describe the slope of an extinction curve for head-banging, we exhibit something about behavior altogether different from what is exhibited in calling them "problems." The so-called "objective" approach in behavior modification aimed at recasting abstract definitions of essentially normative concepts as psychological or descriptive ones is a hopeless enterprise. The term "problem behavior" is not a name for a set of as yet unformulated empirical properties; it expresses an evaluation of behavior. If "behavioral problem" were shorthand for the functional properties of a pattern solely, it is inconceivable how an orientation like, for example, homosexuality, should cease to be judged a "disturbance" in the way it traditionally has been (Tripp, 1975). Obviously, this sexual pattern has remained the same; our value-appraisal of it has undergone considerable change, relative to the past.

Hasty efforts to flesh out the concept of behavior disorder—to supply an abstract definition of it which matches its distributed instances—has, in the absence of a value-scheme, thrust the investigator back onto other substitutive equivalents, such as "dysfunctional patterns," "maladaptive behavior," "psychopathology," and the like. Nevertheless, a frequently encountered definition has been: a behavior disorder can be defined as a pattern of conduct which disturbs someone. Controversies over such definitions seem for the most part confined to whether the disorder is one because it upsets the individual displaying it, upsets others (hence the emphasis on the social unacceptability of a pattern), or both. Regardless of the focus involved, all such definitions will be found to be wanting because they are predicated on the root assumption of a behavior disturbance being a *psychological*, not a *moral* concept.

A pattern of responding is not classified as a behavior disorder simply because the person displaying it is distressed. The reason is eminently clear. Being upset, anxious, troubled, or distressed is neither a necessary nor sufficient condition for being "disturbed." A person can be severely disturbed without being distressed; those who experience manic episodes are a case in point. Similarly, there are numerous states of subjective distress and agitation it would be absurd or foolhardy to classify as behavioral disturbances. For example, it is the rule, not the exception, for political and religious leaders to experience intense discomfort in promulgating revolutionary or unpopular ideas, while the significance of their contributions is rarely judged by the presence of such negative states. Interestingly, it is the prior negative evaluation of their ideas on moral, religious, or philosophical grounds that will in turn largely determine whether the psychological distress in question is to be classified as maladaptive (Brotz, 1961). When such leaders proclaim ideas perceived as morally objectionable, the analysis of their psychological states by the community becomes a fascinating exercise in moral preachment, disguised as scientific pronouncement. In the case of Martin Luther, whether the personal anguish of the Reformation leader was regarded as moral fortitude or neurosis depended largely on whether one espoused a Catholic or Reformation viewpoint. The issue here is not whether the strength of a Catholic or Protestant moral bias colored observation in the sense of obscuring the truth. On the contrary, it involves the more fundamental question of whether we can supply an intelligible criterion of what truth is in the absence of a value-judgment about Luther. If it makes no sense to ask whether a historical personage like Martin Luther was "disturbed" independently of a tacit moral assessment, it is also impossible to determine whether he had a disorder merely on the basis of the descriptive aspects of his behavior.

The mistake of identifying problem behaviors as an aspect of a value-neutral enterprise is prompted in part by the failure to distinguish two quite different propositions: (1) behavioral criteria exist for defining disturbances, and (2) disturbances can be behaviorally defined. Specifically, the fact that Luther's psychological states admit of a behavioral analysis in no way implies that there exist purely behavioral criteria for determining their status as problem behaviors. The former amounts to no more than supplying a theoretical definition of a pattern: the latter, to the acknowledgement of a rule permitting the application of an essentially normative concept to that pattern.

If an acceptable substitutive definition of problem behavior is "undesirable pattern," attempts to flesh out the concept of undesirability along behavioral lines are likewise foredoomed. The customary move made here is to recast *undesirable* as *undesired*, a definitional substitute quite on the same naturalistic wave-length as the substitution of *disturbed* for *disturbance*. In spite of this, the judgment that a pattern is an undesirable one is normative, and does not reduce to a summary of individual or social attitudes or opinions prevailing about that pattern. A valid challenge to consensus as a criterion of desirability is requesting justification for the adoption of this or that social doctrine, a most mysterious move indeed if what is undesirable is defined by the social response to it. Whatever the merits of Mowrer's (1961) theory that behavior disorder is an indirect outgrowth of the violation of reference-group norms, it is a mistake to identify such violation as moral transgression, "sinning," or misbehavior. The latter concepts, in being normative, are properly applied as an outgrowth of tacit moral arguments as easily turned against reference-group norms themselves as they can be against the sinner. Because of this, demonstrating empirical relationships between the violation of reference-group mores and behavioral disturbance is not thereby to reveal the relationship between sinning and the latter, unless the equivalence of the concepts "social rule violation" and "sinning" is presupposed. The fact that their mutual identification in given cases must be established only as a consequence of a moral argument indicates no such presupposition exists. Furthermore, since ostensively defining "behavioral disturbance" must involve a value-judgment, Mowrer's attempt to operationally define "sinning" and "behavior disorder" in terms of measures that lend themselves easily to empirical inquiry is implausible.

The Behavioral Approach and the Medical Model

Recommendations for behavioral approaches to classification (Cautela & Upper, 1973; Goldfried & Pomeranz, 1968; Kanfer & Saslow, 1965, 1969; Mischel, 1968; Nathan & Harris, 1975) have arisen not only because of perceived weaknesses in psychiatric coding systems but also because of the debatable metapsychological assumptions their continued use involves. In a significant sense, the expression "behavioral classificatory approach" is redundant. It is impossible to conceive how any classification system can escape reliance on observable behaviors both in the initial stages of its creation and in later phases of its refinement. The criteria for ordering clinical phenomena, and making those taxonomic distinctions felt to be important, are ultimately behavioral in scope. Indeed, in a previous publication (Begelman, 1973) the present author pointed out that criticisms of the behavioral approach based upon the charge that it overlooks significant classes of underlying processes are self-defeating. A behavioral emphasis is an emphasis on the very criteria theoreticians of contrasting persuasions rely on in positing those processes behavior modifiers are charged with ignoring. Thus, the immediate reason for suspecting the existence of a so-called "psychic conflict" concerns the anomalies in the behavior of the individual to whom it is attributed. Furthermore, it is scarcely realized that the rather complete reliance on behavioral criteria in clinical work is not warranted on purely methodological grounds alone, or because of limitations as regards access to or knowledge of, internal physical events. On the contrary, and as Hebb (1968) has indicated, intimate knowledge of events on the neuroanatomical level has meaning only to the extent the latter are correlated with events in the behavioral category. Indeed, the very notion of a neuroanatomical defect itself is linked to its discovery in the nervous system of, say, psychotic, as opposed to normal persons.

Despite the fact that the behavioral orientation has in recent years been identified with an unequivocal rejection of the medical model, the latter has been perceived as being associated with a number of logically independent assumptions or policies (Begelman, 1971). An incomplete list would include the following partialities:

1. Behavior disorder is caused by organic dysfunction.
2. The treatment of the behavior disorders should be confined to physicians.
3. Patients with behavior disorders should not be held responsible for their condition.
4. Patients with behavior disorders should be treated as if "sick."
5. Expressions such as "mental illness," "patient," "psychopathology," and so forth, are legitimate.
6. The concepts of "insanity" and "responsibility" in court proceedings are psychiatric in meaning.
7. Mental patients benefit from hospitalization, since they are dangerous to themselves and others.
8. Disorder reflects underlying processes on the basis of which it is possible to predict behavior cross-situationally.
9. Mental illness is like any other illness.
10. Specific and effective treatment programs are associated with entities diagnosed according to DSM-II.
11. Standard nosology is a reliable system of diagnostic labeling.
12. Pathology resides within the individual, rather than in the external environment or social structures influencing his behavior.
13. Diagnosis and treatment are value-neutral.
14. Behavior disorders are marked by a natural course of a disease process on the basis of which prognosis is legitimate.
15. Biomedical modalities are the proper avenues of approach to behavior disorder.

Because the foregoing fifteen assumptions have at one time or another been identified with the medical model, there has been a corresponding tendency to view their interrelationships as mutual entailments. For example, assumption (4) and (15) are regarded as closely intertwined, although the present author has argued elsewhere (Begelman, 1971) that if "sick" is interpreted as "caused by an organic disease or impairment," it is a *non sequitur* to conclude that the proper approach to treatment must be in the biomedical category. In fact, there are no unambiguous dictates as to the proper kind of treatment persons deemed "sick" should receive. Investigators partial to behavioral or biogenic theories of disorder are mandated only to explain why a given treatment procedure proves effective, in terms of concepts germane to their orientation. In spite of this, many maintain that there is an *a priori* relationship between the known etiology of a behavior disorder and the category of treatment suitable for it. Thus, if a behavior disorder has been learned, it is held that some form of behavior modification is the appropriate treatment approach to it, whereas if the etiology is held to be organic, a biomedical approach is called for. Not only are such assumptions demonstrably false ones, they appear to be maintained by a vicious circularity of reasoning. In line with this, if the criterion of a learning-process basis for a behavior disorder is nothing other than the responsiveness of the problem to behavior modification, then the possibility of adapting the latter to the treatment of organically-based conditions is precluded on logical grounds alone. Likewise, if the criterion of an organically-based disorder is its responsiveness to some biomedical technique, the possibility of adopting the latter (e.g., drugs) for the treatment of predominantly learned behaviors is ruled out for identical reasons. However, the criteria of etiology in current use are themselves muddled, as has already been indicated by Rimland (1964, 1969) and Davison (1969). The problem of the relationship between etiology and recommended treatment approach is further compounded by a category-mistake (Ryle, 1949). It is the error of supposing that learning-process explanations and biogenic explanations of deviant behavior belong to a logical type precluding their both holding true for the same behavior. In effect, most clinical theorists in the past have assumed that learning-theory and organic defect explanations are mutually inconsistent in casually explaining deviancy. Albee (1966), for example, endorses the prevailing view of psychopathologists that functionally psychotic disorders "are more social than biological in causation" (Albee, 1966). Mariner (1967) imagines that if "schizophrenia" were discovered to be based on a biochemical deficiency, its treatment should rightfully "pass out of the realm of the mental health professional and into the realm of organic medicine" (Mariner, 1967, p. 279). Szasz (1963) believes that if neurological defects are discovered which explain disorders of cognition and behavior, this "implies that people's troubles cannot be caused by conflicting needs, opinions, social aspirations, values, and so forth" (Szasz, 1963, p. 12). Ullmann & Krasner (1969) imply that if "schizophrenia" is largely the outcome of the treatment of persons so labelled, then this tends to preclude its causation by "something in the patient" (Ullmann & Krasner, 1969, p. 397). Lastly, Wolpe (1956, 1958, 1970), in citing the reasons why neurotic responses must be classified as learned, takes this to be a decisive basis upon which to rule out their being sequelae of cortical lesions.

The foregoing category-mistake can perhaps be revealed for what it is along the following lines. Biogenic explanations of behavior disorder (Kety, 1959a, 1959b; Meehl, 1962; Pauling, 1968; Rimland, 1969) are a subset of biogenic or physiological explanations with a respected place in psychological theorizing (Hebb, 1949; Pavlov, 1917). If physiological-psychological explanations of human behavior constitute accounts of it that have a different theoretical focus than does behavior-theory, they cannot as physiological accounts *per se* conflict with or supplant explanations on the behavioral level. In the same way, chemical accounts of intracellular processes do not as chemistry compete with accounts of the same processes in physics. However, if there is no inconsistency on the general theoretical level in developing separate behavioral and neurophysiological explanations of normal functioning, the same holds true as regards accounts of disordered behavior. The explanation of the latter involves supplying a causal account of patterns negatively valued for social and historical reasons. Thus, it makes as little sense to rule out serotonin (Wooley & Shaw, 1954) or tarazein (Heath, 1959) theories of "schizophrenia" because the latter is a learned pattern of responding, as it does to rule out a hypothesis about potassium levels in synaptic transmission because a group of delinquents have achieved cooperation through timely reinforcements delivered by their supervisor.

It is in light of the foregoing analysis that the present author regards the proposed diagnostic system of Nathan & Harris (1975) as based upon a spurious distinction. Nathan and Harris favor a dichotomous approach to behavior disorder, involving a dual classification system for organic and behavioral disorders. In their opinion, this would correspond to disorders diagnosable from etiological factors such as biochemical, metabolic, or toxic conditions, and those involving no such factors. Undoubtedly, there are numerous behavior disorders independent of such etiologies. On the other hand, identifying them would appear to be by dint of fiat, since this would involve proving the null hypothesis. Furthermore, Nathan and Harris indicate that diagnosing such conditions as organic brain syndromes and perhaps the functional psychoses from etiologic factors "makes sense" because "they are physical diseases" (Nathan & Harris, 1975, p. 141). The point of view presented thus far in this section regards the status of "being a physical disease" to possess no obvious implications for exclusion from that category of disorder the authors contend is diagnosable as "exercises in treatment design" or escape-avoidance conditions (Nathan & Harris, 1975, p. 141). Alternatively, determination of the appropriateness of a behavioral approach has little implication for the contribution of biogenesis to the acquisition of the disorder in question. It is interesting to note that some behaviorists (Ferster, 1961) have implied that the success of behavior modification argues exclusively for a learning-process acquisition in the case of childhood autism. Cases of behaviorally-induced improvement in retarded children whose disorder is based upon demonstrable organic impairment are alone sufficient to expose the invalidity of such arguments.

Another relationship deserving of comment is the one thought to obtain between assumptions (1) and (8). Specifically, attacks on the medical model as it involves partiality towards the theory of the biogenic causation of behavior disorder is frequently confused with its drawbacks as a model favoring the cross-situational consistency of behavior as specified by trait-theory (Alker, 1972; Bandura & Walters, 1963; Bem, 1972; Bowers, 1972, 1973; Mischel, 1968, 1969, 1971). However, hypotheses concerning organic impairment as a critical internal variable need not entail assumptions about the greater consistency of behavior across contexts, relative to the degree expected under situationism. Thus, it is possible that behavioral anomalies on the basis of which organic defect is suspected are nonetheless patterns that fluctuate appreciably, depending on situational context. Indeed, if the evidence for situationism is how much of the total variance is due to situational variables, it is conceivable that it be quite high in relation to a particular pattern independently revealed to have an organic basis. Typically, however, the assault on any theory of biogenic or biochemical dysfunction becomes confused with assaults on mentalism (Skinner, 1953), on trait-theory (Mischel, 1968, 1969, 1971), on cognitive explanations (Bowers, 1973), and on explanations of behavior referring to covert variables (Kanfer, 1970). Because of this, behavioristic antipathy to the medical model as the latter relates to assumption (1) above has a spurious validity, conferred as a result of the accumulated wisdom of arguments addressed to quite independent issues. Even at that, many of the behavioristic criticisms of, say, mentalism, are ill-suited for their avowed purpose, whatever the fate of a particular paradigm. Thus, behaviorists have attempted to expose the theoretical weakness of mentalistic explanations by indicating that mental states or traits get invoked as independent variables, although their own antecedents are largely ignored. Surely, this is not a valid criticism of mentalism. If the logical adequacy of any explanation were in question because it specified causal events which in turn go unexplained, all formulations are unsatisfactory unless they resolve the problem of infinite regress. In line with this, how can the contingencies of reinforcement maintaining a response-class constitute their explanation, until such contingencies themselves are causally accounted for, and so on *ad infinitum* (Keat, 1972)? The frequency with which such behavioristic arguments are mustered to deal with competing theories or doctrines lends credence to the Shavian lament that we tend to believe the world is progressing because it is always moving (Shaw, 1952).

References

Adams, H. B. "Mental Illness" or interpersonal behavior? *American Psychologist*, 1964, **19**, 191–197.

Albee, G. W. Needed: A conceptual breakthrough. Unpublished manuscript, 1966.

Albee, G. W. Conceptual models and manpower requirements in psychology. *American Psychologist*, 1968, **23**, 317–320.
Alker, H. A. Is personality situationally specific or intrapsychically consistent? *Journal of Personality*, 1972, **40**, 1–16.
Angrist, S., Lefton, M., Dinitz, S., & Pasamanick, B. *Women after treatment*. New York: Appleton-Century-Crofts, 1968.
Austin, J. L. Other minds. In J. O. Urmson, & G. J. Warnock (Eds.), *Philosophical papers*. Oxford: Clarendon, 1961.
Ayllon, T., & Michael, J. The psychiatric nurse as a behavioral engineer. *Journal of the Experimental Analysis of Behavior*, 1959, **42**, 3–21.
Bandura, A. *Principles of behavior modification*. New York: Holt, Rinehart & Winston, 1969.
Bandura, A., & Walters, R. W. *Social learning and personality development*. New York: Holt, Rinehart & Winston, 1963.
Beck, S. The science of personality: Nomothetic or idiographic? *Psychological Review*, 1953, **60**, 353–359.
Becker, H. *Outsiders: Studies in the sociology of deviance*. New York: The Free Press, 1963.
Begelman, D. A. Two criticisms of the mental illness concept. *Journal of Nervous and Mental Disease*, 1966, **141**, 598–604.
Begelman, D. A. Misnaming, metaphors, the medical model, and some muddles. *Psychiatry*, 1971, **34**, 38–58.
Begelman, D. A. Ethical issues in behavioral control. *Journal of Nervous and Mental Disease*, 1973, **156**, 412–419.
Begelman, D. A. Ethical and legal issues of behavior modification. In M. Hersen, R. M. Eisler, & P. M. Miller (Eds.), *Progress in behavior modification*. Vol. 1. New York: Academic Press, 1975a.
Begelman, D. A. Homosexuality and the ethics of behavioral intervention. Paper presented at the ninth annual meeting of AABT, San Francisco, Dec. 13, 1975b.
Bem, D. J. Constructing cross-situational consistencies in behavior: Some thoughts on Alker's critique of Mischel. *Journal of Personality*, 1972, **40**, 17–26.
Benedict, R. Anthropology and the abnormal. *Journal of General Psychology*. 1934, **10**, 59–82.
Bleuer, E. *Dementia praecox or the group of schizophrenias*. New York: International University Press, 1950.
Bowers, K. Situationism in psychology: On making reality disappear. *Research Reports in Psychology*, University of Waterloo, 1972, **37**.
Bowers, K. S. Situationism in psychology: An analysis and a critique. *Psychological Review*, 1973, **80**, 307–336.
Brotz, H. Functionalism and dynamic analysis. *European Journal of Sociology*, 1961, **2**, 170–179.
Buss, A. H. *Psychopathology*. New York: John Wiley, 1966.
Cain, A. J. *Animal species and their evolution*. London: Hutchinson Press, 1954.
Cautela, J. R. Behavior therapy and the need for behavioral assessment. *Psychotherapy: Theory, Research and Practice*, 1968, **5**, 175–179.
Cautela, J. R., & Upper, D. A behavioral coding system. Presidential address presented (by Dr Cautela) at the seventh Annual Convention, AABT, Miami Beach, Dec., 1973.
Chase, Stuart. *The tyranny of words*. New York: Harcourt, Brace, 1938.
Davison, G. C. Some problems of logic and conceptualization in behavior therapy research and theory. Paper presented at the 75th annual convention of the American Psychological Association, Washington, D. C., 1967.
Davison, G. C., & Neale, J. M. *Abnormal psychology: An experimental clinical approach*. New York: John Wiley, 1974.
Dershowitz, A. M. Dangerousness as a criterion for confinement. *Bulletin of the American Academy of Psychiatry and the Law*. 1974, **2**, 172–179.
Erikson, K. Notes on the sociology of deviance. In H. Becker (Ed.), *The other side*. New York: The Free Press, 1964.
Eysenck, H. The logical basis of factor analysis. *American Psychologist*, 1953, **8**, 105–113.
Eysenck, H. The science of personality: Nomothetic. *Psychological Review*, 1954, **61**, 339–341.

Eysenck, H. *The scientific study of personality*. London: Routledge and Kegan Paul, 1952.

Falk, J. Issues distinguishing idiographic from nomothetic approaches to personality theory. *Psychological Review*, 1956, **63**, 53–62.

Ferster, C. B. Positive reinforcement and behavioral deficits in autistic children. *Child Development*, 1961, **32**, 437–456.

Foley, J. P. The criterion of abnormality. *Journal of Abnormal and Social Psychology*, 1935, **30**, 279–290.

Freeman, H., & Simmons, O. Feelings of stigma among relatives of former mental patients. *Social Problems*, 1961, **8**, 32–321.

Freud, S. Psycho-analytic notes upon an autobiographical account of a case of paranoia (Dementia Paranoides). In *Collected papers. Vol. III*. New York: Basic Books, 1959.

Goffman, E. *Asylums*. New York: Doubleday, 1961.

Goffman, E. The inmate world. In T. Millon (Ed.), *Theories of psychopathology and personality*. Philadelphia: W. B. Saunders, 1973.

Goldfried, M. R., & Pomeranz, D. M. Role of assessment in behavior modification. *Psychological Reports*, 1968, **23**, 75–87.

Gove, W. R. Societal reaction as an explanation of mental illness: an evaluation. *American Sociological Review*, 1970, **35**, 873–884.

Hacker, F. H. The concept of normality and its practical significance. *American Journal of Orthopsychiatry*, 1945, **15**, 47–54.

Hayakawa, S. I. *Language, meaning and maturity*. New York: Harper, 1954.

Hayes-Roth, F. Longabaugh, R., & Ryback, R. The problem-oriented medical record and psychiatry. *British Journal of Psychiatry*, 1972, **121**, 27–34.

Heath, R. G. Physiological and biochemical studies in schizophrenia with particular emphasis on mid-brain relationships. *International Review of Neurobiology*, 1959, **1**, 299–331.

Hebb, D. O. *Organization of behavior*. John Wiley, 1949.

Hebb, D. O. *A textbook of psychology*. Philadelphia: W. B. Saunders, 1968.

Kanfer, F., & Saslow, G. Behavioral diagnosis, *Archives of General Psychiatry*, 1965, **12**, 529–538.

Kanfer, F. H. Self-regulation: Research, issues and speculations. In C. Neuringer, & J. L. Michael (Eds.), *Behavior modification in clinical psychology*. New York: Appleton-Century-Crofts, 1970.

Keat, R. A critical examination of B. F. Skinner's objections to mentalism. *Behaviorism*, 1972, **1**, 53–70.

Kety, S. Biochemical theories of schizophrenia. Part I. *Science*, 1959a, **129**, 1528–1532.

Kety, S. Biochemical theories of schizophrenia. Part II. *Science*, 1959b, **129**, 1590–1596.

King, G. Research with neuropsychiatric samples. *Journal of Psychology*, 1951, **58**, 147–154.

Kitsuse, J. Societal reaction to deviant behavior: Problems of Theory and Method. In Becker (Ed.), *The other side*. New York: The Free Press, 1964.

Korzybski, Alfred. *Science and sanity: An introduction to non-aristotelian systems and general semantics*. Lancaster, Pa.: Science Press, 1933.

Kraepelin, E. *Dementia praecox and paraphrenia*. (1st ed.), Edinburgh: Livingstone, 1896.

Kreitman, N. The reliability of psychiatric diagnosis. *British Journal of Psychiatry*, 1961, **107**, 876–886.

Kuhn, T. S. *The structure of scientific revolutions*. Chicago: University of Chicago Press, 1962.

Laing, R. D. *The politics of experience*. New York: Pantheon, 1967.

Lang, P. J. Fear reduction and fear behavior: Problems in treating a construct. In J. M. Schlien (Ed.), *Research in psychotherapy, Vol. III*. Washington, D. C. A.P.A., 1968.

Lemert, E. *Human deviance, social problems and social control*. Englewood cliffs, New Jersey: Prentice Hall, 1967.

Lorr, M. (Ed.), *Explorations in typing psychotics*. New York: Pergamon Press, 1966.

Margolis, J. *Psychotherapy and morality: A study of two concepts*. New York: Random House, 1966.

Mariner, A. S. A critical look at professional education in the mental health field. *American Psychologist*, 1967, **22**, 271–281.

Marzolf, S. S. The disease concept in psychology. *Psychological Review*, 1947, **54**, 211–221.

Maslow, A. H. *Toward a psychology of being*. New York: D. Van Nostrand Company, 1968.

Meehl, P. Schizotaxia, Schizotypy, Schizophrenia. *American Psychologist*, 1962, **17** 827–838.
Menninger, K. The practice of psychiatry. *Digest of Neurology and Psychiatry*, 1955, **23**, 101.
Millon, T. *Modern psychopathology*. Philadelphia: W. B. Saunders, 1969.
Millon, T., & Millon, R. *Abnormal behavior and personality*. Philadelphia: W. B. Saunders, 1974.
Mischel, W. *Introduction to personality*. New York: Holt, Rinehart and Winston, 1971.
Mischel, W. *Personality and assessment*. New York: Wiley, 1968.
Mischel, W. Continuity and change in personality. *American Psychologist*, 1969, **24**, 1012–1018.
Mowrer, O. H. *The Crisis in psychiatry and religion*. New York: Van Nostrand, 1961.
Nathan, P. E., & Harris, S. L. *Psychopathology and society*. New York: McGraw-Hill, 1975.
Noyes, A. *Modern clinical psychiatry*. Philadelphia: W. B. Saunders, 1953.
Overall, J. E., & Gorham, D. R. The brief psychiatric rating scale. *Psychological Review*, 1962, **10**, 799–812.
Overall, J. E., & Gorham, D. R. A pattern probability model for the classification of psychiatric patients. *Behavioral Science*, 1963, **8**, 108–116.
Panzetta, A. F. Towards a scientific psychiatric nosology. *Archives of General Psychiatry*, 1974, **30**, 154–161.
Pauling, L. Orthomolecular psychiatry. *Science*, 1968, **160**, 265–271.
Pavlov, I. P. *Conditioned reflexes*. London: Oxford University Press, 1927.
Quay, H. C. (Ed.), *Research in psychopathology*. Princeton, New Jersey: Van Nostrand, 1963.
Rensch, B. *Evolution above the species level*. New York: John Wiley, 1959.
Rimland, B. *Infantile autism*. New York: Appleton-Century-Crofts, 1964.
Rimland, B. Psychogenesis vs. biogenesis: The issue and the evidence. In S. C. Plog, & R. B. Edgerton (Eds.), *Changing perspectives in mental illness*. New York: Holt, Rinehart and Winston, 1969.
Rogers, C. R. *Client-centered therapy: Its current practice, implications and theory*. New York: Houghton, Mifflin Company, 1951.
Rosen, E., Fox, R. E., & Gregory, I. *Abnormal psychology*. Philadelphia: W. B. Saunders, 1972.
Rosenthal, R., & Jacobsen, L. *Pygmalion in the classroom: Teacher expectations and pupils' intellectual development*. New York: Holt, Rinchart & Winston, 1968.
Rotter, J. *Social learning and clinical psychology*. New York: Prentice Hall, 1954.
Ryle, G. *The concept of mind*. London: Macmillan, 1949.
Sandifer, M. G., Pettus, C., & Quade, D. A study of psychiatric diagnosis. *Journal of Nervous and Mental Disease*, 1964, **139**, 350–356.
Sarbin, T. R. Anxiety: Reification of a metaphor. *Archives of General Psychiatry*, 1964, **10**, 630–638.
Sarbin, T. R. The concept of hallucination. *Journal of Personality*, 1967, **35**, 359–380.
Sarbin, T. R., & Mancuso, J. C. Failure of a moral enterprise: Attitudes of the public toward mental illness. *Journal of Consulting and Clinical Psychology*, 1970, **35**, 159–173.
Sarason, I. G. *Abnormal psychology: The problem of maladaptive behavior*. New York: Appleton-Century-Crofts, 1972.
Scheff, T. J. *Being mentally ill*. Chicago: Aldine, 1966.
Scheff, T. J. The role of the mentally ill and the dynamics of mental disorder. In T. Millon (Ed.), *Theories of psychopathology and personality*. Philadelphia: W. B. Saunders, 1973.
Schmidt, H. O., & Fonda, C. P. The reliability of psychiatric diagnosis: A new look. *Journal of Abnormal and Social Psychology*, 1956, **52**, 262–267.
Schreber, D. P. *Memoirs of my nervous illness*. London: Dawson and Sons, 1955.
Seeman, W. P. Psychiatric diagnosis: An investigation of interperson-reliability after didactic instruction. *Journal of Nervous and Mental Disease*, 1953, **118**, 541–544.
Shaw, G. B. *Man and superman*. Baltimore, Md.: Penguin Books, 1952.
Shoben, E. J. Toward a concept of the normal personality. *American Psychologist*, 1957, **12**, 183–189.
Skaggs, E. B. The meaning of the term "abnormality" in psychology. *Journal of Abnormal and Social Psychology*. 1933, **23**, 113–118.
Skinner, B. F. *Science and human behavior*. New York: Macmillan, 1953.

Skinner, B. F. *About behaviorism*. New York: Alfred Knopf, 1974.

Smith, R. E., Diener, E. O., & Beaman, A. L. Demand characteristics and the behavioral avoidance measure of fear in behavior therapy analogue research. *Behavior Therapy*, 1974, **5**, 172–182.

Spitzer, R. L., Endicott, J., Cohen, J., & Fleiss, J. L. Constraints on the validity of computer diagnosis. *Archives of General Psychiatry*, 1974, **31**, 197–203.

Stoller, R. J., & Geertsma, R. H. The consistency of psychiatrists' clinical judgments. *Journal of Nervous and Mental Disease*, 1963, **137**, 58–66.

Stuart, R. B. *Trick or treatment: How and when psychotherapy fails*. Champaign, Ill.: Research Press, 1970.

Suinn, R. M. *Fundamentals of behavior pathology*. New York: John Wiley, 1970.

Szasz, T. S. The problem of psychiatric nosology: A contribution to a situational analysis of psychiatric operations. *American Journal of Psychiatry*, 1957, **114**, 405–413.

Szasz , T. S. The myth of mental illness. *American Psychologist*, 1960, **15**, 113–118.

Szasz, T. S. The uses of naming and the origin of the myth of mental illness. *American Psychologist*, 1961, **16**, 59–65.

Szasz, T. S. *Law, liberty and psychiatry: An inquiry into the social uses of mental health practices*. New York: Macmillan, 1963.

Tripp, C. A. *The homosexual matrix*. New York: McGraw-Hill, 1975.

Ullmann, L. P., & Krasner, L. *A psychological approach to abnormal behavior*. Englewood Cliffs, New Jersey: Prentice-Hall, 1969.

Waismann, F. Verifiability. In A. G. N. Flew (Ed.), *Logic and Language*. 1st Ser. Oxford: Blackwell, 1963.

Wittenborn, J. Symptom patterns in a group of mental hospital patients. *Journal of Consulting Psychology*, 1951, **15**, 290–302.

Wittenborn, J. The behavioral symptoms for certain organic psychoses. *Journal of Consulting Psychology*, 1952, **16**, 104–106.

Wolpe, J. Learning versus lesions as the basis of neurotic behavior. *American Journal of Psychiatry*, 1956, **112**, 923–927.

Wolpe, J. *Psychotherapy by reciprocal inhibition*. Stanford, California: Stanford University Press, 1958.

Wolpe, J. The discontinuity of neurosis and schizophrenia. *Behavior Research and Therapy*, 1970, **8**, 179–187.

Yarrow, M., Schwartz, C., Murphy, H., & Deasy, L. The psychological meaning of mental illness in the family. *The Journal of Social Issues*, 1955, **11**, 12–24.

Wegrocki, H. J. A critique of cultural and statistical concepts of abnormality. *Journal of Abnormal and Social Psychology*, 1939, **34**, 166–178.

Wittgenstein, L. *Philosophical investigations*. London: Macmillan, 1953.

Wooley, D. W., & Shaw, E. A biochemical and pharmacological suggestion about certain mental disorders. *Proceedings of the National Academy of Sciences*, 1954, **40**, 228–231.

Zax, M., & Cowen, E. L. *Abnormal psychology: Changing conceptions*. New York: Holt, Rinehart & Winston, 1972.

Zigler, E., & Phillips, L. Psychiatric diagnosis and symptomatology. *Journal of Abnormal and Social Psychology*, 1961a, **63**, 69–75.

Zigler, E., & Phillips, L. Psychiatric diagnosis: A critique. *Journal of Abnormal and Social Psychology*, 1961b, **63**, 607–618.

Zubin, J. A cross-cultural approach to psychopathology and its implications for diagnostic classification. In L. D. Eron (Ed.), *The classification of behavior disorders*. Chicago: Aldine, 1966.

PART TWO

Initial Stages of Assessment

CHAPTER 3

Behavioral Interviewing: The Initial Stages of Assessment

KENNETH P. MORGANSTERN

Psychology Clinic
University of Oregon
Eugene, Oregon

Introduction

In a recent report on the behavioral treatment of sexual dysfunctions (Lobitz, LoPiccolo, Lobitz & Brockway, 1974), an exhaustive, detailed analysis of the treatment process was presented. The authors' stated purpose was to provide practitioners with specific, step-by-step procedures for treatment, because they felt that readers had interpreted the existing literature as too general or assumed the techniques to be invariant. Similarly, reports on assessment often fail to supply specific guidelines and techniques to enable the therapist to accurately and completely define the problem so that effective treatment procedures may be instituted. Students are often encouraged to read Kanfer & Saslow (1969), for example, to understand what the requirements of multifaceted assessment are; yet the manner in which the necessary information is obtained is often unclear. While the process of assessment may be relatively straightforward once the specific target behaviors are *known*, inexperienced therapists may be uncertain how to determine what the problem *is*. Training in behavior therapy generally emphasizes the importance of observation, objective measurement, and experimental analyses of behavior. However, the interview itself, during which the therapist elicits information that leads to the specification and delineation of the behaviors to be assessed, is often ignored. The purpose of this chapter is to provide a framework for clinicians during the initial stages of assessment and to elaborate upon a number of issues and procedures in behavioral interviewing.

This chapter is divided into two sections. The first part discusses several

The author acknowledges Anthony Biglan, Edward Lichtenstein, Elizabeth Steinbock, and Helen Tevlin for their critical reading of an earlier draft of this manuscript.

important issues in behavioral interviewing. These involve: goals of assessment (including a review of the major multifaceted assessment strategies), ethical considerations, and the role of relationship variables. The second section focuses primarily on a few selected methods and procedures employed in the behavioral interview, with a number of clinical illustrations presented. While assessment often requires information from a variety of sources (including the client's family, employers, friends, co-workers, etc.), the major emphasis in this chapter is on the information provided by the client.

One of the major goals of the present paper is to provide some practical suggestions for the new or inexperienced behavior therapist. It is essential to note, however, that while the methods of behavioral *treatment* enjoy considerable empirical support, research on the effects of interview procedures are noticeably absent. The techniques and guidelines that are presented in this chapter, therefore, need to be considered cautiously. While the suggestion for future research in this area is, perhaps, obvious, it is nevertheless important that *every* component of the entire therapeutic process be empirically validated.

Behavioral Interviewing: Issues

Goals of Assessment

From the first contact between therapist and client, behavioral interviewing must be intimately tied to the ultimate goals of assessment. The anwer to the question, often asked by students, "What do I need to know about the client?" should be: "*Everything* that is relevant to the development of effective, efficient, and durable treatment interventions." And from an ethical (and economical) consideration, one could add, "And no more." Ideally, then, every question asked by the therapist (or for that matter, anything that occurs during the therapy situation) should have a purpose, the purpose being to gain a thorough functional analysis of the problematic behavior. This analysis establishes the precise covariations between changes in stimulus conditions and changes in selected behaviors (Mischel, 1971); that is, it defines the "ABC's (*a*ntecedents, *b*ehavior, and *c*onsequences) of behavior control" (O'Leary & Wilson, 1975, p. 25). Such an analysis is an important challenge to criticisms that behavioral approaches are superficial and narrow. It reduces the possibility that treatments will be ineffective or that new maladaptive responses will appear after the removal of a particular problem. While it is important to avoid the tautology that behavior therapy "successes" are the result of "thorough" analyses while "failures" are the product of inadequate ones (Kazdin, 1973), most behaviorists would agree with Lazarus' (1973) statement that "faulty problem identification (inadequate assessment) is probably the greatest impediment to successful therapy" (p. 407).

A complete functional analysis of problematic behavior often goes beyond first appearances in therapy (Mahoney, Kazdin & Lesswing, 1974). The "bridge phobia" described by Lazarus (1971a) is a well-known example. In this case, the client, originally complained of a fear of crossing bridges. Further exploration, however, revealed considerable anxiety and uncertainty in regard to work, competence, obligations, and achievements. In particular, the client was acutely sensitive to his mother's prejorative statements that "he would never amount to anything." What was actually being avoided, therefore, was a new work situation, and in turn, the potential criticisms of himself and his mother. Desensitization was, in fact, successfully employed, but it was primarily directed at the real or imaginal critical statements of the client's mother. Such cases are commonplace in the clinic: the obese individual who avoids work or heterosexual encounters by being overweight (Mahoney *et al.*, 1974) or the anxious client who receives social reinforcement for certain fears. In some instances, a complete assessment may reveal that a specific technique is inappropriate because of certain idiosyncracies of the client (Morganstern, 1974), or indicate that treatment is impossible without substantial changes in the client's environment.

A final caution is important. In their desire to be thorough, behaviorists need not, and should not, move toward the other extreme and attempt to assess everything in the background and present situation of their clients. Often, much of the information gathered by traditional therapists is unnecessary. Peterson (1968), for example, estimated that three-fourths of the material usually covered in interviews could probably be eliminated "with no loss whatever to the patient (since) only rarely do the conventional data have anything to do with treatment" (p. 119). Not only is such practice inefficient, it also raises an ethical question regarding the legitimacy of inquiry into diverse aspects of a client's life, however interesting they may be to the therapist or the client himself, when such content is irrelevant to treatment.

Multifaceted Assessment Strategies

It is clear that a thorough assessment is essential to ensure maximal treatment efficacy. Although many of the early reports of behaviorists were criticized for inadequate assessment (Goldfried & Pomeranz, 1968), a number of broad-spectrum, multifaceted assessment guidelines have been proposed in recent years. This section briefly reviews a few of the major strategies that have been proposed. Peterson (1968), one of the most outspoken critics of traditional assessment procedures in the late 1960s, described an overview of the entire interview strategy that included a scanning operation, extended inquiry, periodic reappraisal, and, ideally, a final phase that involved a follow-up study. He suggested that the content of the interview focus on two broad sets of variables: (a) the definition, severity, and generality of the problem (including the client's own view of his behavior), and (b) the determinants of the target behavior (e.g., the conditions which intensify or alleviate the problem, perceived antecedents, consequences, and the client's own suggested changes).

Goldfried & Pomeranz (1968) outlined four major classes of variables in any assessment process: (a) the antecedent stimulus variables, (b) organismic variables (psychological and physiological), (c) the overt maladaptive behavior itself, and (d) the consequent changes in the environment. The authors noted further that the target behavior selected in many behavioral reports were often oversimplified, and suggested the inclusion of cognitions, mediation responses, and cues, as well as directly observable behavior.

In probably the most extensive assessment scheme, Kanfer & Saslow (1969) described an approach that incorporated variables from both the client's current situation and his past history. They emphasized, however, that the selected focus on the past is only to determine the individual learning history, so that treatment strategies may be constructed to fit the unique environmental and behavioral characteristics of the client. That is, historical information is relevant only to the extent that it facilitates the description of current problematic behaviors and future therapeutic interventions. In order to accomplish this task, Kanfer and Saslow suggested examination of each of the following areas: (1) analysis of the problem situation (including behavioral excesses, deficits, and assets), (2) clarification of the problem situation that maintains the targeted behaviors, (3) a motivational analysis, (4) a developmental analysis (including biological, sociological, and behavioral changes), (5) a self-control analysis, (6) analysis of social relationships and (7) analysis of the social-cultural-physical environment. A noteworthy contribution of Kanfer & Saslow's outline is the inclusion of an assessment of the client's strengths, assets, skills, and talents.

Wolpe (1969) provided an assessment guideline that comprises four main areas of the client's life: (a) familial experiences while he was growing up, including information about influential "significant others" (friends, parents, siblings, etc.) and an exploration of the individual's religious background when relevant, (b) school experiences and employment history, (c) sexual history and the present status of sexual behavior, and (d) current social relationships.

Stuart (1970) outlined an assessment system that begins with the precise specification of problematic behaviors, followed by the identification of four classes of antecedent stimuli (instructional, discriminative, potentiating, and facilitating) and four classes of consequent events (positive reinforcement, punishment, extinction, and negative reinforcement). In addition, Stuart suggested that assessment strategies describe acceptable behaviors as fully as maladaptive responses, because more powerful techniques are available for increasing desired behaviors than for decreasing undesirable ones.

Lazarus (1971b), noting the "relapse" of many of his clients, proposed a multimodal behavior therapy approach. Assessment explores the modalities deemed essential by Lazarus (1973), the first letters of each forming the acronym *BASIC ID: B*ehavior, *A*ffect (e.g., joy, anxiety, anger), *S*ensation (e.g., muscle tension), *I*magery (positive or negative), *C*ognition (e.g., insights, ideas, philosophies), *I*nterpersonal relationships, and *D*rugs (the need, if any, for medication). While it would seem that Lazarus' assessment strategy is not significantly different than that of Kanfer and Saslow in terms of problem specification, many of his treatment strategies might be considered beyond the realm of behavior therapy (Franks & Wilson, 1974). An innovation that deserves consideration is the suggestion by Lazarus to assess anticipated areas of stress (perhaps through imaginal rehearsal) that the client is likely to experience at some future point.

Finally, Mischel (1973), whose classic work on assessment (Mischel, 1968) challenged every major assumption of traditional trait approaches to personality, is consistent with most behaviorists in his emphasis on the importance of specific environmental events in behavior control. He has proposed, however, a second class of variables ("person variables") that involve a number of cognitive social learning factors. Such person variables are thought to develop from each individual's unique social learning history, and influence or mediate the way in which environmental conditions affect his behavior. The specific person variables that Mischel suggested include: (a) cognitive and behavioral construction competencies, (b) encoding strategies and personal constructs, (c) behavior-outcome and stimulus-outcome expectancies, (d) subjective stimulus values, and (e) self-regulatory systems and plans.

In sum, a variety of broad, multifaceted assessment strategies have been proposed within recent years. Although some of the approaches suggest additional areas of attention that warrant exploration, all of them share the common emphasis on the specification of the "ABC's" of behavior control. It is important to note, however, that such comprehensive outlines as suggested by Lazarus or Kanfer and Saslow, while applicable in some cases, may be unnecessary for the majority of individuals. The identification, for example, of a client's strengths or the description of his learning history is often irrelevant for treatment planning. Multifaceted behavioral assessment, therefore, must always be guided by the principle of parsimony (Stuart, 1970).

Ethical Issues

Behavior therapy, characterized by empirically validated procedures for *client-stated objectives*, has considerably tempered Halleck's (1971) observation that therapists are never politically or ethically neutral. Nevertheless, several critical ethical considerations, particularly during the initial stages of assessment, remain. Important questions central to those issues involve: the determination of the client's goals, the degree of therapist-influence on the selection of those objectives, and the decision to "accept" the goals of the client and intervene, or refuse treatment accordingly. An additional ethical issue, regarding the client's right to minimal intrusion, has previously been discussed. In general, the arguments presented here assume the individual to be an adult volunteer in a non-institutionalized setting; however, many of the remarks may be equally applicable to clients not sharing these criteria. Questions concerning institutionalized individuals, while important, are beyond the scope of the present chapter (cf. Wexler, 1973).

It has been emphasized that behavior therapy "is a system of principles and not a system of ethics" (Bandura, 1969, p. 87). In addition, the focus of treatment is the client's, not the therapist's, goals. However, it is the rare individual that refers himself to therapy with his problems and future objectives clearly crystallized. Far more often, the client's needs and wants become clearer as he talks to the practitioner (Halleck, 1971), and thus the goals, desires, and values of the therapist are an inescapable reality in influencing both the interview process and the end-product of assessment. Recently, behaviorists have been called to task in relation to the target behaviors selected for institutionalized clients (Wexler, 1973) and school children (Winett & Winkler, 1972). The same issues are relevant to adult out-patients. The case of homosexuality provides an excellent example of the implicit (and often explicit) value judgements of therapists that influence the determination of the client's goals. Despite the fact that homosexuality is no longer included in the Diagnostic and Statistical Manual (DSM) II, most therapists, including behaviorists, "regard homosexual behavior and attitudes to be undesirable, sometimes pathological, and at any rate in need of change towards a heterosexual orientation" (Davison, 1974, p. 4). It is difficult to imagine such biases not entering into the assessment process in some, perhaps subtle, ways. Consider, for example, the decision made by Fensterheim (1972) to treat a homosexual who emphatically stated that he did not desire to change his sexual orientation:

> I do agree to confine the treatment to the specific target symptoms as best as I can. However, I also state that I will present for their consideration a plan for the treatment of homosexuality. All I ask is that I be permitted a brief time to present a possible treatment plan and that the client listen to it (pp. 25–26).

Although Fensterheim goes on to emphasize that there is no attempt to "sell" the treatment to the client, there is an implicit assumption in the therapeutic suggestion that the individual *should*, in fact, change. While the decision to accept the client's objective for treatment is a highly commendable one, it should be clear that additional suggestions on the part of the therapist may constitute very powerful influences on the client.

Ethical issues become even more complicated when it is the *client's* initially stated goals that require re-evaluation. It is unlikely that many practitioners would immediately accept a client's request to eliminate masturbation and proceed to treat the "problem." The therapist would almost certainly offer information to the individual in an attempt to re-educate him. Or desensitization might be instituted to reduce the anxiety associated with the target behavior. When the problem is homosexuality, therapists are far more likely to consider the behavior as problematic and to intervene accordingly. The very existence of a variety of techniques to change sexual orientation not only encourages their use, but may also condone the current societal prejudice concerning such behavior (Davison, 1974). While the resolution of such ethical problems may be exceedingly difficult, behaviorists need to be aware of the implications of "accepting" the client's goals when to do so explicitly reinforces the social *status quo* and may, in fact, impede social change. Winett & Winkler (1972) emphasize this point in their criticism of target behaviors that have often been selected for disruptive school children. In a similar fashion, Davison (1974) has suggested critical examination of the target behaviors involved in *any* anxiety-reduction procedure:

> Should we reduce anxiety, or should we perhaps address ourselves to the problematic educational system which can contribute to the kind of test anxiety we desensitize? ... Why do we engage in assertion training for people who are taken advantage of by an unfeeling society rather than attempt to persuade the offenders that their sometimes unkind actions cause others grief? (p. 3).

It would seem apparent, then, that behaviorists cannot separate themselves entirely from the important ethical and societal implications that are involved in any assessment and treatment intervention.

A related ethical question involves the therapist's refusal to treat a specific problem of the client. Such situations include instances where it would be ethically irresponsible to attack a certain target behavior, when the client insists on a technique that the practitioner has evidence to believe is ineffective, or when a specific "problem" may be beyond the realm of psychotherapy. The ethical choice to refuse treatment is often obvious in certain stereotypic examples (e.g. the anxious murderer seeking desensitization to feel better about killing, or the housewife who similarly desires desensitization so that she is no longer anxious anticipating her husband's beatings). More often, however, the implications are considerably more subtle, as in the case of homosexuality mentioned above. Even in situations where there is no ethical question about the client's objectives, a thorough assessment may reveal that the person is unwilling to change the contingencies that control the target behavior. It is the *responsible* practitioner who, after careful assessment, concludes that he cannot effectively treat the individual *unless* certain environmental conditions are considered, whether that means including the spouse in treatment, or involves the extensive rearrangement of contingencies. Kanfer (1975) has remarked that behavior therapy need not adopt a "Statue of Liberty" ("Give me your tired, your poor . . .") philosophy. That is, behaviorists need to accept their limitations and realize they cannot treat everybody, whether due to the fact that effective procedures may not exist for a specific problem (for example, the quest for the discovery of the "meaning of life"), or the individual's environment, which the client does not want altered, counterindicates treatment efficacy for a given target behavior.

Clients often come to therapy with a variety of expectations about what treatment will be like. Many of them request specific techniques such as hypnosis, bioenergetics, psychoanalysis, yoga, dream interpretation, and a host of other treatments. While it is probably sound clinical practice to incorporate those procedures which the client feels will be most helpful (since expectancy of therapeutic gain undoubtedly accounts for some portion of the outcome variance; cf. Lick & Bootzin, in press) the ethically responsible therapist must assess and communicate to the client the likelihood of success with any of these procedures. In many cases, the practitioner will refuse to adopt a particular method, either because he is unfamiliar with the technique or because there is no evidence that such a procedure is effective (especially when other, empirically tested, treatments are available). Of course, the behaviorist will often redefine certain problems within a social-learning framework, suggesting techniques that he feels are the most appropriate. However, even in situations in which the client is in complete agreement with the therapist with respect to both the assessment of the problem and the intervention planned, it is still the responsibility of the therapist to communicate to the individual the probabilities of success with a given technique (Biglan, 1975), the "emotional cost" of such a procedure (Morganstern, 1973), and the availability of alternative treatments.

In sum, behaviorists need to examine and be acutely aware of several ethical considerations and value judgments that are continually made. Whereas the principles of behavior modification may be relatively free of such biases, the interview and assessment process is not. In the final analysis, behavior therapy has little to apologize for, particularly when compared to the history of other therapeutic enterprises. The emphasis given to situational factors, functional analyses, and measurement of process and outcome, encourages accountability on the part of practitioners adopting a behavioral framework (Davison, 1974).

Interviewer-Client Relationship Variables

It is often assumed that behaviorists are cold, mechanistic, uncaring laboratory technicians with little regard for the "therapeutic relationship." On numerous occasions, students and clients have indicated surprise that the behaviorists they have seen or heard (or have been treated by) have been concerned, understanding, warm, and "human." Such surprise is not limited to laymen. Klein, Dittmann, Parloff & Gill (1969) noted that the behavior therapy they observed for five days was characterized by "experienced clinicians" who were seen as confident and skillful, and made "very effective use of the patient-therapist relationship to establish a context in which the specific behavioral techniques can be utilized most effectively" (p. 265). Apparently the stereotype of the "misanthropic behaviorist" is popular enough to compel some authors to caution the "would-be practitioner who chooses to be a behavior therapist because he finds it difficult to put clients at ease, through using a more traditional approach ... to rethink his professional goals" (Rimm & Masters, 1975, p. 35). Lazarus (1971a) has suggested, "If a person does not possess genuine compassion for the plight of his patients and have a strong desire to diminish their suffering, it would be a boon to psychotherapy if he would enter some other field of endeavor" (p. 56). While such statements may appear to be obvious (and perhaps even surprising that they have to be made), they raise a number of important questions that need to be considered. For example, *do* we want to communicate to professionals and trainees that behavioral techniques, well-validated and seemingly simple, may be instituted *without* regard to "therapist" or "relationship" variables? Or, *do* such variables relate to the completeness and accuracy of information obtained during interview and assessment, and, more importantly, to treatment outcome? Which variables are important and how do we know? Finally, *are* we then forced into the awkward position of advocating a variety of suggestions to students with precious little support for them?

There is considerable agreement that a variety of therapist behaviors relate to the openness, accuracy, and content of interviews (cf. Goldstein, 1975; Kanfer, 1968; Krasner, 1962; Marsden, 1971; Matarazzo, 1965; Salzinger, 1959; Truax & Carkhuff, 1967). Within the behavioral literature, Peterson (1968) has remarked that:

> The nature of the transaction . . . between interviewer and client . . . are of utmost importance in determining the amount and quality of information gained (and) a sense of (the interviewer's) interest on the part of the client probably has much to do with the extent and the accuracy of the information he provides (p. 123).

Rimm & Masters (1974) noted that an atmosphere of warmth and acceptance will facilitate the goal of assessment (i.e. to obtain considerable information from the client). Further, these authors point out that, "no therapy can succeed if the client perceives his therapist as cold and indifferent and, therefore, drops out of treatment" (p. 35). While one cannot question the logic that therapy cannot proceed without the client, it is unclear whether it is the therapist characteristics of "coldness" and "indifference" that drive the client away. Similarly, there is no substantial evidence that therapist variables affect the accuracy and completeness of assessment information to the degree that treatment outcome is impaired. Moreover, it is uncertain what combination of behaviors the clinician should have in his repertoire, since no practitioner could possibly possess the several dozen laudatory characteristics of the "ideal therapist" that have variously been proposed (Krasner, 1963). It could be argued that there is a huge literature to attest to the fact that such variables as empathy, warmth, and genuineness do relate to interview content (by increasing, for example, self-exploration and self-disclosure, Truax & Carkhuff, 1967), and in turn, to treatment outcome. The reliability of such measures, however, and the validity of the outcome variables in these studies are questionable. Even the goals of therapy are often vague and subjective, frequently reflecting the values and objectives of the therapist rather than the client. For this reason, such research may be irrelevant to an empirically oriented behavioral approach. This is not to suggest that such variables as empathy, warmth, genuineness, openness, honesty, etc. are *unimportant* in behavioral interviewing. On the contrary, it is strongly felt by the author that under some circumstances certain relationship variables will facilitate assessment and enhance treatment outcome. The point, however, is that very little is known about the effects of particular therapist characteristics on assessment information, continuance in therapy, compliance, and outcome measures *in behavior therapy*. Along these lines, it is interesting to note Bandura's (1969) challenge to the distinction made between "specific" and nonspecific" influences in therapy:

> It is difficult to conceive of nonspecific influences in social interchanges. Each expression by one person elicits some type of response from the other participant, which inevitably creates a specific reinforcement contingency that has a specific effect on the immediately preceding behavior (p. 77).

While it is beyond the scope of this chapter to discuss the relationship of therapist variables and treatment outcome, it should be noted that behaviorists have long acknowledged that social reinforcement processes assume a role of major importance in the modification and maintenance of behavior (Bandura, 1969). A few studies have investigated the effect of certain therapist characteristics on treatment outcome in behavior modification (Bergin, 1969; Harris & Lichtenstein, 1971; Morris & Suckerman, 1974a, 1974b). It is important to remember, however, that *no* technique can be expected to be effective across all clients under all circumstances. Even Truax (Truax & Mitchell, 1971), who concluded that, "the personality of the therapist is more important than his techniques" (p. 341), cautioned that high levels of warmth or accurate empathy could be totally inappropriate with certain clients.

In sum, it is awkward to reiterate the caution that cold, indifferent, and uncaring interviewers probably inhibit the assessment (and treatment) process, in the absence of clear evidence to support these notions. Effective behavioral outcome depends on thorough and accurate assessment, continuance in therapy, compliance with therapeutic intervention, as well as the treatment methods themselves. How client-therapist relationship variables affect each of these is, as yet, an unanswered, but empirical question.

Behavioral Interviewing: Methods and Procedures

While it is evident that a number of behavioral procedures need more detailed and explicit description to facilitate their use by practitioners (Lobitz *et al.*, 1974), behaviorists have, in general, been quite responsive in disseminating the necessary information and guidelines for *treatment.* Many journal articles contain complete procedures for specific interventions or authors furnish them upon request. Simplified texts of the "How-to" variety have been available for a number of years. Further, several manuals are available for relaxation, complete desensitization, obesity, alcoholism, smoking, self-control and many other areas; and there are movies, tapes, and records providing therapists with adequate descriptions of methods. In contrast, practical guidelines for behavioral *assessment* have only recently appeared. A few sources do provide examples of behavioral interviews, particularly the initial session (Fensterheim, 1972; Lazarus, 1971a; Peterson, 1968; Rimm & Masters, 1974; Wolpe, 1969, 1970). In addition, the reader is also referred to several traditional works, such as Menninger (1952), Sullivan's (1954) classic text, and more recently, Gorden (1969), which all provide valuable information that may be adapted by the behavioral clinician.

As previously discussed, the goal of assessment is an accurate functional analysis of the problematic behaviors, the environmental contingencies of those behaviors, the resources available to the individual, and any other information that is necessary in providing effective treatment. With this objective as the focal point of interviewing, the remainder of this section outlines a number of possible procedures, questions, and problems encountered in this process. While obvious, perhaps, it is important to note that there are many avenues to obtain the same end-product. Thus, one should view the following "techniques" and issues as only a few of the many conceivable strategies that may be employed. In addition, it should not be inferred that all of these procedures are always applicable or that any particular sequence must be rigidly followed. Finally, as emphasized before, how each of these methods relates to the essential variables of assessment, commitment, and treatment efficacy is a question of future empirical research.

The Initial Interview

The first session is often of critical importance. Several decisions need to be made, not the least of which concerns whether or not the client (and the therapist) wishes to continue. Both the client and the therapist will be (*should* be) asking the questions; Does the therapist understand what the problem is? What can I expect to gain from therapy? What are the probabilities that such outcomes will be reached? Are there alternative procedures that are as effective, more efficient, less risky, etc.? In addition, the client will no doubt be concerned about the therapeutic relationship (i.e., Does the therapist care about me? Will treatment be a pleasant or aversive process and, even, Does the therapist like me?).

Students awaiting their first contact with clients ask numerous questions about getting the interview started. They are often concerned about introductions, seating arrangements, whether they should remain silent until the client has spoken or if it is better for them to make some opening statements, and if so, what should they say. While anything but the most nondirective approach will shape and bias the interview to some degree, there are a number of advantages in having the therapist make some sort of introductory remarks. Such an opening statement is likely to reduce some of the client's initial anxiety about what to say and what he should expect. In almost every case, something is already known about the client. Often he has already been through one or more intake evaluations, has been referred with some accompanying statement, or, has communicated something about the nature of his problem on the telephone in setting up an appointment. Some introduction, therefore, briefly summarizing what is already known, is usually desirable. For example:

Therapist: Mr. Martin, whom you spoke to last week, has told me that you are presently having some difficulties in your relationship with your husband. From what I understand, you say that you are depressed much of the time and that you are also considering a separation. Apart from that, I really don't know much about you. What I would like for us to do today is to understand more fully what the problem is and what has brought you here. Can you tell me how *you* see the problem?

As brief and as simple as the above example seems, it provides the client with a framework from which to start and with some expectations about the purpose of the interview. The later is not as obvious as it sounds, considering many of the myths and practices of psychotherapy. Individuals, for example, often expect to be tested, answer long questionnaires, engage in free association, or dozens of other preliminaries. Another reason for this brief summary statement, is simply to communicate to the client that you have read the case material that is available, spoken to the referral source, or simply remember the telephone conversation. It may be frustrating for the client to have to repeat the story he has already told the therapist or others, and, at times, it may be evidence of a lack of care, consideration, and preparation on the part of the interviewer.

With such a minimal stimulus as this opening statement, a great many clients will begin to relate, often in very specific detail, the reasons they seek treatment. Within limits, it is useful to simply listen at this time, allowing the client to "tell his story." The decision to seek professional counseling is rarely an immediate, spur-of-the-moment step. He has most likely considered his problems over and over, with facts, thoughts, and feelings weighed and ordered. Just as it is often unsettling to have prepared at length for an important exam and *not* be tested when one arrives, so it is probably quite frustrating for the client to have carefully thought out his present difficulties and then not have a chance to share them. This is not to imply that the therapist adopt a nondirective attitude, following the client wherever, and for as long as, he leads. Certainly carefully considered questions are essential to both direct and clarify what is being said. Just listening to a client present his "autobiography" session after session is unnecessary, inefficient, and ineffectual.

Listening, then, would seem to be an essential skill of the interviewer. Interrupting with questions or premature "clarifications" of misconceptions may inhibit the client from relating certain information. It is possible for the therapist to distort what the client is saying since the therapist may actually prompt and shape inaccurate or partially accurate verbal statements by the client to coincide with the interviewer's initial perception of the problem. Annon (1974) provides some excellent examples of how this may occur in the assessment of sexual problems. For example, a client's statements, "I've been a homosexual for 10 years" or "I suffer from premature ejaculation" might immediately elicit reassuring comments or detailed inquiry on the part of the therapist, when the problems may lie elsewhere. In a similar fashion, middle-class interviewers may react inappropriately to such emotionally charged words as rape, abortion, suicide, etc., when in reality, the client experiences no "problem" in these areas. Listening, then, focuses on the problems of the client, not the preconceptions of the therapist.

During these first stages of behavioral assessment (and to a lesser extent throughout the course of therapy), a case can be made for the *selective* use of empathic statements, such as reflection and paraphrasing. One does not have to accept Rogers' deterministic notion of "self-actualization" nor believe in the need or utility of "unconditional positive regard" to effectively make use of reflective procedures. A number of behavior therapists have explicitly suggested such techniques (e.g., Lazarus, 1971a; Peterson, 1968), and the general use of reflective statements is apparent in most observations of behavioral assessments. The therapist, when reflecting, communicate to the client that he has heard and understood the message. Expanding upon Rogers' use of the word, one does not have to limit the reflections to feelings, since the content of such messages may be as or more important than the affect. Needless to say, the behavioral clinician cannot effectively intervene until he understands fully and accurately what the problem is. Training in reflection and paraphrasing, therefore, forces the therapist to listen and focus on what the client is saying. These techniques (in combination with direct questioning, probes, and provisional restatements, Peterson, 1968) may facilitate assessment in a number of ways. First, the experiences of being heard and understood may be extremely positive for many individuals, reinforcing them to continue and go into further detail. While good questions serve this purpose to some degree, reflective statements may, at times, communicate this message better. In addition, the therapist who is perceived as understanding may be a potent source of social reinforcement for the client. Finally, reflective remarks and restatements are often necessary to validate for the *interviewer* what is being said. In the following sample, a number of these techniques are illustrated:

Therapist: You say that you are very jealous a lot of the time and this upsets you a great deal.

Client: Well, I know it's stupid for me to feel that way, but I am hurt when I even *think* of Mike with another woman.

Therapist: You don't want to feel jealous but you do.

Client: I know that's not the way a "liberated" woman should be.

Therapist: What is your idea of how a liberated woman should feel?

Client: I don't know. In many ways I feel I have changed so much in the last year. I really don't believe you have the right to own another person—and yet, when it happens to me, I really feel hurt. I'm such a hypocrite!

Therapist: You're unhappy because you are not responding the way you really would like to?

Client: I'm sure not the person I want to be.

Therapist: So there's really "double jeopardy." When Mike is with someone else it really hurts you. And, then when you feel jealous, you get down on yourself for being that way.

Client: Yes. I guess I lose both ways.

In the above example, the reflective statements communicated to the client that she was being understood and helped her specify what she was experiencing. The final synthesis tied in the several feelings she was expressing, with the validation at the end that the therapist was, indeed, accurate. Quite often, however, the process is not as straightforward. In the example below, the reflections and questions are, at first, somewhat off the track. The therapist eventually narrows in on what the client is saying:

Client: Whenever my boss asks to see me, I almost start shaking, wondering what I've done wrong.
Therapist: The anticipation of criticism really makes you anxious?
Client: Well, it's not really that. I'm scared of what might happen.
Therapist: What might happen?
Client: I don't know what will happen; that's it.
Therapist: So it's the suspense that makes you feel uncomfortable.
Client: No, not the suspense—I keep saying to myself that if he starts chewing me out I'm just going to let him have it.
Therapist: How would you let him have it?
Client: Well, what I *think* I'm going to do is argue right back at him—or even quit right there.
Therapist: And what *do* you do?
Client: Nothing!
Therapist: Nothing?
Client: I never do anything. I just stand there while he's talking and never say a word.
Therapist: So what really makes you shake, as you say, is feeling a great deal of anger and not being able to express it?
Client: Yeah. And the one I'm really mad at is myself for being such a patsy all the time.
Therapist: What do you think would happen if you really did argue back with your boss?
Client: He probably would respect me a lot more than someone who's too scared to defend himself.
Therapist: What you're saying is that you're really afraid to challenge your boss' criticism. But when you think about it, you become angry at yourself for not being assertive.
Client: Yes.

It should be evident that reflective comments are not novel techniques. In most conversations, there is a continual exchange of information with feedback that the information has been received. The intention here is not to suggest that reflection be the sole, or even major, assessment procedure on the part of the therapist. Often it is useful to keep assessment flowing smoothly, to validate what the therapist is concluding, or simply to acknowledge that the client is being understood. However, it must be repeatedly emphasized that the goals of assessment are quite clear, underscoring the need for specific questions and direct behavioral measures. Thus, the extensive use of nondirective procedures may be, at best, inappropriate for behavioral interviewing (Suinn, 1974). At worst, it can be "an extremely hostile act to refuse to answer a direct and reasonable request or to withhold information from patients . . ." (Marquis, 1972, p. 44). Finally, by suggesting the selective use of reflective methods during the initial stages of the interview does not imply that such procedures are advocated as treatment techniques. Reflection of empathy, warmth, or genuineness is probably insufficient for the client presenting problems of anxiety, stuttering, sexual dysfunction, or the vast majority of other target behaviors for which the individual desires change. Noteworthy, in this regard, is Haley's (1969) inclusion of "Be reflective" in his satirical article outlining "The Five B's Which Guarantee Dynamic Failure."

Specification of the Problem

Quite often the client can specify in exacting detail the nature of his problems and, with the help of the therapist, provide the necessary data concerning both antecedent and consequent conditions. Many times, however, the client is unable to explain what is wrong. It is in these cases that the inexperienced therapist may encounter much difficulty. There are several ways to facilitate the narrowing process. Since the decision to seek professional services is related to some events that have recently occurred in the client's life, questions centering around the reasons that brought the client to treatment can be extremely useful. Often there have been recent changes such as a new job, marriage, divorce, moving, or other situations that may have radically shifted. In addition, the client may have recently had a number of unfortunate experiences such as being fired, rejected at a party, impotence, etc. Finally, in many cases the "problem" may have been defined by someone else. That is, the recommendation to go for treatment may have come from the client's spouse, parents, or friends, and information regarding the reasons for such referrals may be quite helpful. Such an analysis of the "labeling" process may, thus, provide very valuable information, although questions concerning "who is the client" and "to whom is the problem disturbing" must be considered.

Once the problem area has been broadly defined, a thorough behavioral analysis is derived. That is, a careful description of the behavior itself, as well as the antecedent and consequent variables is elicited. Even in situations in which the client reports that he is depressed *all* of the time, or *always* anxious, or a failure at *everything*, careful questions may delimit the problem considerably. A person who reports that he is depressed all of the time, almost certainly can think of circumstances in which he is more depressed than in others. Detailing certain activities, certain places, and certain people also serve to specify the problem more clearly. The client may also be able to relate experiences in the past, or imagine future situations in which the "depression" may be better or worse. Similarly, the individual who reports a global, undifferentiated fear, say of automobiles, will almost certainly be able to define situations in which the fear will be attenuated somewhat because of the time of day, type of automobile, number of people in the car, distance driven, etc.

In many cases, the interview material may be supplemented with observation in the natural setting or behavioral measurement (e.g., psycho-physiological measures) during the interview process. Tracking the frequency of certain behaviors may help the client more narrowly define the problem behavior and the circumstances surrounding it even when he has been previously unable to specify those variables. Behavior therapists, therefore, often ask their clients to carry around a diary in which frequency, duration, time, and other circumstances surrounding the target behaviors are carefully recorded. As O'Leary & Wilson (1975) have noted, most clients present themselves as "trait theorists" with descriptions such as "uptight," "lazy," "passive-aggressive," etc. A focused functional analysis with behavioral referents of the problem (using both the client's self-report during the interview and the tracked behavior) is probably one of the most essential activities of behavioral assessment. It is quite likely that the behavioral monitoring *itself* may be a "therapeutic" process, communicating to the client that he does not suffer from a deep-seated disease or some enduring underlying personality trait. Rather, the emphasis is on discrete behaviors, emitted at specific times, with certain frequencies, and intensities, and once these behaviors are changed, there is no longer a "problem."

A behavioral analysis also minimizes the possibility that certain self-reported feelings will be misinterpreted. Literally hundreds of commonly used words may imply very different things for different people. It is, therefore, a mistake for the therapist to assume that he knows what the client is talking about without any operational referents. It is quite illuminating, for example, to ask a class of students to define in one sentence what they mean by the words "anxiety" or "depression" or "assertive." Even in a group of professional counselors there is often a diverse array of meanings attached to these "feelings" or "states." In sum, it is sound advice for trainees to "be ignorant" when it comes to understanding what a client means by such words as uptight, heavy, angry, together, spaced out, freaky, dependent, passive, etc. The following examples illustrate, first, the acceptance without further exploration of several poorly defined terms used by the client; and second a more careful analysis of these self-reported feelings:

Client: When I'm in such "heavy" situations, I just get real "uptight."

Therapist: What makes you uptight?

Client: Well, the whole thing. Everybody kind of hanging out and running around. I can't seem to get it together with anybody, so I guess I freak out.

Therapist: And then what happens?

Client: I usually go home and go to sleep. But I'm usually pretty bummed out.

Therapist: Are you saying that you don't fit in with these people and that's what makes you feel bummed out?

Client: Well, I don't know. These are my friends, I guess—but it never seems to work out.

In this example, the therapist may have no idea what his client is talking about. And if he does, there is certainly no way of knowing whether he is accurate or not in his inferences. While it may, at first glance, appear that the therapist who does not understand such terminology is hopelessly naive, such "naivete" is probably essential in order to understand exactly what the client is saying:

Client: When I'm in such "heavy" situations, I just get real "uptight." You know, I just can't make it, so I kind of drop out.

Therapist: I think I have some idea of what you are saying, but everyone has slightly different interpretations. So I wonder if you can help me get a better understanding of what you mean. For example, when you say that you're uptight in these situations, what does that mean for you?

Client: Well, uptight, you know. Tense.

Therapist: You mean your muscles get tense?

Client: My neck gets very sore—and I get a headache lots of times.

Therapist: Anything else happen that you notice?

Client: Well, either because of my neck or my headache, I start sweating a lot.

Therapist: So when you say you're uptight you are really experiencing it physically. What kinds of things are you saying to yourself when this happens?

Client: I'm thinking, Man you really are paranoid. You just can't relax in any situation, You really are a loser. And then I want to get out of there fast...

In this example, the interviewer has tried to clarify the word "uptight." Although we all have some idea of what this means, there is much variation in the usage of the term depending on the individual. The client in this case was able to point to some very definite physiological changes that accompanied this feeling. In addition, there were a number of self-verbalizations (which would have required further elaborations and behavioral reference) as well as resultant avoidance behaviors. The therapist would have then proceeded in getting a good behavioral analysis of what the "heavy" situations were in the client's life and to what he was referring when he said he "couldn't make it." Although such questions may initially seem to the client evidence of a *lack* of therapist understanding (and hence provide some reason for early reflective statements), it is quickly communicated to the client that this inquiry is essential for *maximal* understanding of the problem. Care must be taken, however, to elicit the necessary information without insulting or punishing the client for using his own words.

The need for specific, operational terminology is especially well-illustrated in the area of sexual assessment, particularly since discussion of this material may be associated with a great deal of discomfort and embarrassment for the client and even the therapist. Annon (1974) has discussed the merits of using technical descriptions versus the street language that is commonly used, and indicates that a compromise between the two is sometimes the best strategy. Whatever the language, an exact understanding on the part of both the therapist and the client is important. Thus, the expressions "doing it" or "down there" may be so vague as to provide very little information to the interviewer. Even the use of precisely defined terms must be validated to insure that both individuals understand what is being communicated. Annon (1974) noted that some clients did not know what the word circumcized meant, or where exactly the clitoris was located; intervention in these cases might be doomed to fail unless such questions are clarified. In dealing with very sensitive topics, therapists as well as clients may be shaped into vague explanations and descriptions, depending on their own comfort with such terminology. The direct, straight-forward discussion and questioning on the part of the interviewer communicates to the client that it is quite acceptable to explore such areas. The therapist who models vague and euphemistic language may reinforce the client's belief that such topics should not be discussed and that it is better *not* to openly deal with these problems.

Redefinition of Problems

In a sense, the assessment demand for a functional analysis, with clear, operationalized behavioral referents, is a reinterpretation of the client's problems into a social-learning framework. An important question that arises is whether the same ethical objections that are raised about such redefinitions in insight-oriented therapies (Bandura, 1969) cannot also be raised concerning behavioral assessment. It is important to note, however, that behavior therapy differs from the more traditional approaches in two very important ways, *First*, behavioral approaches, unlike insight-oriented treatments, do not redefine the client's *goals* in terms of unmeasureable hypothetical constructs. *Second*, behavioral assessment is directed towards the selection of empirically supported treatment interventions.

Within a behavioral assessment it is useful, and ethically responsible for the interviewer to *explicitly* redefine the client's statements within a behavioral framework. Even from the very beginning, it is essential that the clinician not reinforce the client's self-explanations, be they psychodynamic notions, trait theories, or existential analyses. This is not to suggest that the behaviorist attempt to attack or antagonize his client by demanding well thought out operational definitions for everything the client says. The interviewer can, however, continually point out different ways of conceptualizing the problem. In sum, the therapist is both modeling and shaping a behavioral language and, at times, directly restating what the client has said in social-learning terms. This "reinterpretation" process communicates to the client that he is not "crazy," "paranoid," or "lacking in self-control." Rather, the client will hopefully begin to see his problems as specific behaviors emitted under specific circumstances, with well-defined psychological principles explaining its development and maintenance. The example below illustrates a few ways in which a client's statements are either questioned or "reinterpreted":

Client: I know I must be pretty "neurotic" to act like I do in all these situations.

Therapist: Can you tell me what you mean by "neurotic"?

Client: Somebody who is terrified by boys and starts crying every time one of them even puts his arm around her must be pretty crazy. Isn't that neurotic?

Therapist: Practically everything that we do is based, in large part, on experiences that we have had. Apparently, at some time you learned to be anxious when you were around boys, or at least when there was some sort of physical contact. That fear is now making you unhappy because there is no real danger in those situations and you would like to change how you react. I don't see that as either crazy or neurotic.

Client: But most girls don't act that way. Why is that?

Therapist: More than likely, most girls have not had the same learning experiences as you, but if they had, undoubtedly they would feel much the same way as you.

Client: But if I know this, why don't things change? I keep saying to myself that it is okay if my boyfriend touches me, that nothing bad is going to happen. But when he goes near me I cry like I always do.

Therapist: What happens when you cry?

Client: I feel terrible. I feel like a little girl.

Therapist: What does your boyfriend do?

Client: He is very nice. He is very understanding and we usually go someplace I like afterwards.

Therapist: So even though it is really painful for you, in a sense you get "rewarded" for reacting so intensely.

The therapist in this case refused to accept the client's self-labels of "crazy" and "neurotic." In addition, in very simple terms, the interviewer pointed out how the intense reactions might be reinforced. Finally, the brief explanation of the client's problems in terms of learning theory should be noted. Although the interviewer's attitudes and orientation are implicitly communicated to the client via the types of questions that are asked, the explanations that he offers, and the areas that are explored, an *explicit* "behavioral rap" at some time early in assessment is also desirable. Very often this is presented in the form of a summary and as a means of setting the stage for behavior therapy (Wolpe, 1969). Not only is an explanation provided for the development and maintenance of the problematic behavior, the rationale for certain treatment interventions is also outlined. But a behavioral framework does more than prepare the client for treatment. It very much affects the relationship between the client and therapist (Marquis, 1973) and may, as mentioned previously, be therapeutic in its own right. If the client's learning history, is to a great extent, the determining factor for his present difficulties, it is senseless for the therapist (and the client himself) to attach blame to the problems. Thus most behaviorists readily agree that, "if the therapist had had the same experiences as the client and vice versa, each would be sitting on the other side of the desk" (Marquis, 1973, p. 48). It should be emphasized, however, that the presentation of a social-learning model may be quite unexpected by the client. It is useful, therefore, to continually assess the reactions that the client may have to any analysis reinterpretation, or focal point that the interviewer offers. Lazarus (1971a), in fact, has suggested that every comment made by the therapist be followed with the question, "What do you think about (or, how do you feel about) what I have just said"? (p. 61). Although it is unnecessary to follow each statement with such a question, it is important to gauge whether or not the client understands what is being communicated to him. Just as important is the issue of whether the client *agrees with* or accepts the interviewer's explanation. From the standpoint of both treatment efficacy and ethical considerations, it is appropriate for therapy to proceed if an individual is insistent that a behavioral assessment (and the treatment that follows) are neither what he wants nor expects.

Therapists must also be sensitive to the fact that most clients have a variety of preconceptions about psychotherapy and a number of expectations about what treatment will entail. As Gottman and Leiblum (1974) have noted, clients upon entering the practitioner's office for the first time, may be thinking that only crazy, weak, or inadequate individuals come for therapy. They may be extremely concerned about what other people (neighbors, spouses, employers, friends, parents, etc.) may be saying. Additionally, clients will want to know whether they can afford therapy, how much it will be, and for how long it will last. They may also be wondering what will happen to them in therapy and what it will be like (Gottman & Leiblum, 1974). Needless to say, the behavior therapist should make every effort to both gauge and clarify the misconceptions and expectancies of the client. Finally, the therapist should be able to respond to the variety of criticisms and "ethical challenges" that have been directed towards behavior modification. Thus, the behaviorist must be comfortable in dealing with the issues of freedom, control, superficiality, etc. that are commonly questioned (cf. Bandura, 1969; Mahoney *et al.*, 1974, for good summaries of these arguments).

Toward a Broad Assessment

While the possession of certain professional credentials does not give an interviewer license to explore *anything* he wants in a client's life, the need for a thorough analysis is obvious. Not only must the therapist assess, in great detail, the specific presenting problems, he must also gain an understanding of how these problems have generalized and affect other areas in the client's life. In addition, a complete assessment forestalls the introduction of treatment strategies that are inappropriate or are likely to fail. Thus, modifying a child's behavior in therapy without intervening in the home environment and changing the important controlling variables may be pointless. Likewise, assessing a client's agressive behaviors and providing techniques to reduce or eliminate them without also assessing whether or not the client has other behaviors in his repertoire which can be equally reinforced is at best a sloppy and inefficient method of treatment.

A good functional analysis of the problematic behavior not only allows the interviewer to get a very specific understanding of the client's presenting difficulties, but also lends itself to a logical continuation into more broadly defined areas. A motivational analysis, for example, or explorations into the client's social relationships and his social-cultural-physical environment may all be important in defining not only the problem itself (and all the controlling variables), but also in assessing both the resources available to the client and what limitations must be considered in treatment (Kanfer & Saslow, 1969). A variety of multifaceted assessment outlines have already been reviewed, and the reader is referred to those sources for more detailed guidelines. It should be noted that a behavioral assessment rarely includes a complete life history of the client, since the past is considered relevant *only to the extent* that it affects the present. Some demographic data, of course, are essential to evaluate much of what the client reports. For example, career indecision may be viewed quite differently by both the therapist and the client, depending on whether the individual is 19 or 29. Similarly, lack of employment may be related to an entirely different set of circumstances for the uneducated, unskilled client, than for the person with a college degree.

In general, then, background information must have some relevance to either the client's present behavior, or the treatment intervention being planned, to warrant much time in exploration or to ethically justify the clinician's interest.

Closing the Interview

A sufficient amount of time at the end of the initial interview should be allowed for the therapist to provide the client with an overview of the process of behavioral assessment and therapy so that the client may know what to expect from future sessions. Such an overview includes: a summary of the information that has already been obtained, an explanation of additional data that is needed, and a reasonable estimate of the likelihood of successful intervention. A good summary communicates to the client that he has been understood and provides him with a behavioral framework to view his problems. Although the therapist has offered such "redefinitions" throughout the interview, it is desirable to reiterate many of these statements at the end of the session, integrating all of the material that has been covered. Caution must be taken to insure that this explanation is neither condescending nor too technical for the client to comprehend.

Quite often, additional information is necessary before any treatment interventions can be planned, and the client should know what areas need further delineation and what he can do to facilitate the process. Sometimes he may be asked to track certain behaviors, seek out information from others, or simply spend some time thinking about problems that he has had difficulty clarifying.

Even though assessment may be incomplete at this stage, clients should be provided with information concerning possible intervention strategies, length of treatment, and the financial and emotional costs of therapy. Most importantly, it should be clearly communicated to the client that he has a choice in every decision that is made.

At times the therapist may conclude, after the initial interview, that behavior therapy is appropriate for a particular individual. The client may present problems and goals for which there is no available treatment, he may not accept a behavioral explanation or treatment plan for his difficulties, or the objectives may be unacceptable to the *therapist* because of certain ethical or practical reasons. In such instances, the clinician may decide that appropriate referral is in the client's best interests.

Finally, when the joint decision is made to continue therapy, the client should be offered as much encouragement as is reasonably possible. As obvious as this may appear, trainees often either neglect to communicate any hope to the individual, or take the other extreme and make unrealistic promises that are doomed to fail. Unlike most traditional approaches, behavior therapy has considerable empirical support for a variety of treatments. Both therapist and client have a legitimate basis for optimism.

Summary

In contrast to the extensive literature on behavioral treatment procedures, and more recently assessment strategies, guidelines for interviewing techniques have been relatively neglected. This chapter has elaborated upon a number of issues and procedures in behavioral interviewing in order to provide a framework for clinicians during the initial stages of assessment.

Four major issues, interrelated to some degree, were discussed. *First*, the goals of assessment were specified, since every activity within the interview process is ultimately tied to such objectives. The basic task for the clinician is to obtain as complete a behavioral analysis as possible in order to develop effective, efficient, and durable treatment interventions. At the same time, there is an avoidance of gathering material that is unnecessary for such a task and which may overstep the ethical boundaries of legitimate inquiry when a wide range of the client's life history is explored.

Second, several multifaceted assessment strategies were reviewed. Although some suggested a number of new and different areas in which information might be useful, all of them emphasized that the major focus of assessment is on the antecedents, behavior, and consequences of targeted problems.

Third, two major ethical considerations were discussed: the degree of therapist influence on the determination of the client's objectives and the decisions to accept the client's goals and intervene, or to refuse treatment when it violates certain ethical responsibilities.

The *fourth* issue concerned the interviewer-client relationship in behavioral interviewing. It was concluded that cold, indifferent, and uncaring therapists probably inhibit the assessment process, although the absence of any empirical support for this conclusion was noted and the need for extensive research in the area underscored.

The second section of this chapter outlined a number of procedures and techniques available to the clinician during the early stages of assessment. Methods were proposed for conducting the initial interview, specification of target behaviors, redefinition of the problem, and, finally, closing the interview.

References

Annon, J. S. *The behavioral treatment of sexual problems* (Vol. 1: *Brief therapy*). Honolulu: Kapiolani Health Services, 1974.

Bandura, A. *Principles of behavior modification*. New York: Holt, Rinehart & Winston, 1969.

Bergin, A. E. A technique for improving desensitization via warmth, empathy, and emotional reexperiencing of hierarchy events. In R. D. Rubin, C. M. Franks, & A. A. Lazarus (Eds.), *Proceedings of the association for advancement of behavior therapy*. New York: Academic Press, 1969.

Biglan, A. Personal communication, July 1975.

Davison, G. C. *Homosexuality: The ethical challenge*. Presidential address presented at the meeting of the Association for Advancement of Behavior Therapy, Chicago, November 1974.

Fensterheim, H. The initial interview. In A. A. Lazarus (Ed.), *Clinical behavior therapy.* New York: Brunner/Mazel, 1972.

Franks, C. M., & Wilson, G. T. (Eds.), *Annual review of behavior therapy: Theory and practice* (*Vol. 2*). New York: Brunner/Mazel, 1974.

Goldfried, M., & Pomeranz, D. M. Role of assessment in behavior modification. *Psychological Reports*, 1968, **23**, 75–87.

Goldstein, A. P. Relationship-enhancement methods. In F. H. Kanfer & A. P. Goldstein (Eds.), *Helping people change.* New York: Pergamon Press, 1975.

Gorden, R. L. *Interviewing: Strategy, techniques, and tactics.* Homewood, Ill.: Dorsey Press, 1969.

Gottman, J. M., & Leiblum, S. R. *How to do psychotherapy and how to evaluate it: A manual for beginners.* New York: Holt, Rinehart & Winston, 1974.

Haley, J. The art of being a failure as a therapist. *American Journal of Orthopsychiatry*, 1969, **39**, 691–695.

Halleck, S. L. *The politics of therapy.* New York: Science House, 1971.

Harris, D. E., & Lichtenstein, E. The contribution of nonspecific social variables to a successful behavioral treatment of smoking. Paper presented at the meeting of the Western Psychological Association, San Francisco, April 1971.

Kanfer, F. H. Verbal conditioning: A review of its current status. In T. R. Dixon, & D. L. Horton (Eds.), *Verbal behavior and general behavior theory.* Englewood Cliffs, N.J.: Prentice-Hall, 1968.

Kanfer, F. H. Personal communication, June 1974.

Kanfer, F. H., & Saslow, G. Behavioral diagnosis. In C. M. Franks (Ed.), *Behavior therapy: Appraisal and status.* New York: McGraw-Hill, 1969.

Kazdin, A. E. The failure of some patients to respond to token programs. *Journal of Behavior Therapy and Experimental Psychiatry*, 1973, **4**, 7–14.

Klein, M. H., Dittmann, A. T., Parloff, M. B., & Gill, M. M. Behavior therapy: Observations and reflections. *Journal of Consulting and Clinical Psychology*, 1969, **33**, 259–266.

Krasner, L. The psychotherapist as a social reinforcement machine. In H. H. Strupp, & L. Luborsky (Eds.), *Research in psychotherapy* (Vol. 2). Washington, D. C.: American Psychological Association, 1962.

Krasner, L. The therapist as a social reinforcer: Man or machine. Paper presented at the meeting of the American Psychological Association, Philadelphia, September 1963.

Lazarus, A. A. *Behavior therapy and beyond.* New York: McGraw-Hill, 1971a.

Lazarus, A. A. Notes of behavior therapy, the problem of relapse and some tentative solutions. *Psychotherapy*, 1971b, **8**, 192–196.

Lazarus, A. A. Multimodal behavior therapy: Treating the "Basic Id". *Journal of Nervous and Mental Disease*, 1973, **156**, 404–411.

Lick, J., & Bootzin, R. Expectancy factors in the treatment of fear: Methodological and theoretical issues. *Psychological Bulletin*, in press.

Lobitz, W. C., LoPiccolo, J., Lobitz, G. K., & Brockway, J. A closer look at "simplistic" behavior therapy for sexual dysfunction: Two case studies. In H. J. Eysenck (Ed.), *Case studies in behavior therapy.* London: Routledge & Keegan Paul. 1974.

Mahoney, M. J., Kazdin, A. E., & Lesswing, N. J. Behavior modification: Delusion or deliverance. In C. M. Franks, & G. T. Wilson (Eds.), *Annual review of behavior therapy: Theory and practice* (Vol. 2). New York: Brunner/Mazel, 1974.

Marquis, J. N. An expedient model for behavior therapy. In A. A. Lazarus (Ed.), *Clinical behavior therapy.* New York: Brunner/Mazel, 1972.

Marsden, G. Content analysis studies of psychotherapy: 1954 through 1968. In A. E. Bergin, & S. L. Garfield (Eds.), *Handbook of psychotherapy and behavior change: An empirical analysis.* New York: Wiley, 1971.

Matarazzo, J. D. The interview. In B. B. Wolman (Ed.), *Handbook of clinical psychology.* New York: McGraw-Hill, 1965.

Menninger, K. A. *A manual for psychiatric case study.* New York: Grune & Stratton, 1952.

Mischel, W. *Personality and assessment.* New York: Wiley, 1968.

Mischel, W. *Introduction to personality.* New York: Holt, Rinehart & Winston, 1971.

Mischel, W. Toward a cognitive social learning reconceptualization of personality. *Psychological Review*, 1973, **80**, 252–283.

Morganstern, K. P. Implosive therapy and flooding procedures: A critical review. *Psychological Bulletin*, 1973, **79**, 318–334.

Morganstern, K. P. Cigarette smoke as a noxious stimulus in self-managed aversion therapy for compulsive eating: Technique and case illustration. *Behavior Therapy*, 1974, **5**, 255–260.

Morris, R. J., & Suckerman, K. R. The importance of the therapeutic relationship in systematic desensitization. *Journal of Consulting and Clinical Psychology*, 1974a, **42**, 148.

Morris, R. J., & Suckerman, K. R. Therapist warmth as a factor in automated systematic desensitization. *Journal of Consulting and Clinical Psychology*, 1974b, **42**, 244–250.

O'Leary, K. D., & Wilson, G. T. *Behavior therapy: Application and outcome*. Englewood Cliffs, N.J.: Prentice-Hall, 1975.

Peterson, D. R. *The clinical study of social behavior*. New York: Appleton-Century-Crofts, 1968.

Rimm, D. C., & Masters, J. C. *Behavior therapy: Techniques and empirical findings*. New York: Academic Press, 1974.

Salzinger, K. Experimental manipulation of verbal behavior: A review. *Journal of General Psychology*, 1959, **61**, 65–94.

Stuart, R. B. *Trick or treatment: How and when psychotherapy fails*. Champaign, Ill.: Research Press, 1970.

Suinn, R. M. Training undergraduate students as community behavior modification consultants. *Journal of Counseling Psychology*, 1974, **21**, 71–77.

Sullivan, H. S. *The psychiatric interview*. New York: Norton, 1954.

Truax, C. B., & Carkhuff, R. R. *Toward effective counseling and psychotherapy: Training and practice*. Chicago: Aldine, 1967.

Truax, C. B., & Mitchell, K. M. Research on certain therapist interpersonal skills in relation to process and outcome. In A. E. Bergin, & S. L. Garfield (Eds.), *Handbook of psychotherapy and behavior change: An empirical analysis*. New York: Wiley, 1971.

Wexler, D. B. Token and taboo: Behavior modification, token economies, and the law. In C. M. Franks, & G. T. Wilson (Eds.), *Annual review of behavior therapy: Theory and practice* (Vol. 2). New York: Brunner/Mazel, 1974. (Reprinted from *California Law Review*, 1973, **61**.)

Winnett, R. A., & Winkler, R. C. Current behavior modification in the classroom: Be still, be quiet, be docile. *Journal of Applied Behavior Analysis*, 1972, **5**, 499–504.

Wolpe, J. *The practice of behavior therapy*. New York: Pergamon Press, 1969.

Wolpe, J. Transcript of initial interview in a case of depression. *Journal of Behavior Therapy and Experimental Psychiatry*, 1974, **1**, 71–78.

CHAPTER 4

The Behavioral Inventory Battery: The Use of Self-Report Measures in Behavioral Analysis and Therapy

JOSEPH R. CAUTELA
Boston College
and
DENNIS UPPER
V. A. Hospital, Brockton, Mass.

Introduction

Behavioral analysis, which is central to the process of treating behavioral disorders, usually occurs in three stages. In the *first* stage, the maladaptive behaviors which will be the focus of therapy (together with their antecedents and consequences) are identified. In the *second* stage, the therapist develops and applies treatment strategies. This stage generally involves three phases: (1) deciding upon specific treatment procedures; (2) evaluating the on-going therapy process; and (3) deciding when to terminate treatment. In the *third* stage, an evaluation of treatment outcome is undertaken.

In contrast to the psychodynamic orientation, which focuses on the characteristics a person "has" (i.e., his "motives," "needs," "drives," "defenses," "traits," or other similar inferred traits), the behavioral approach to assessment places greater emphasis on what a person "does" in various situations (Mischel, 1968). The basic unit for consideration therefore becomes the individual's response to specific aspects of his environment. Human behavior is seen as being determined not only by the individual's previous social learning history, but also by the current environmental antecedents and/or consequences of the behavior in question.

Behavioral analysis is aimed at neither personality description nor the assignment of patients to particular personality types. Instead, it is designed to accomplish the following purposes: (1) identification of behaviors to be modified and their maintaining stimuli; (2) assessment of functional relationships among response classes and among discriminative and reinforcing stimuli;

(3) determination of available social resources, personal assets, and skills for use in therapeutic program, as well as of personal and environmental limitations and obstacles which might be encountered; and (4) determination of the availability of specific therapeutic techniques which are most consonant with the personal and environmental factors in the client's life situation (Kanfer & Phillips, 1970).

A variety of structured assessment instruments have proven useful to behaviorally oriented clinicians in their formulation of treatment strategies and evaluation of treatment effectiveness. The present chapter will focus on the use in behavioral analysis and therapy of assessment instruments which rely on the client's *self-report*. In addition to describing the most widely used behavioral self-report inventories, the chapter will introduce the Behavioral Inventory Battery (BIB), a standardized behavioral analysis procedure which the authors have found to have great clinical utility.

The Use of Self-Report Assessment Measures in Clinical Psychology

In the history of clinical psychology, there have been three general approaches to personality assessment: observation, personality projection, and self-description. Self-description, which shall be of primary interest here, has been described by George Kelly (1958, p. 332) as the method in which "the subject is asked to guess what the examiner is thinking," as contrasted with projective techniques, in which "the examiner tries to guess what the subject is thinking."

The prototype of the self-report assessment instrument is Woodworth's Personal Data Sheet, which was developed during World War I as a rough screening device for identifying seriously neurotic men who would be unfit for military service. Woodworth's inventory consisted of a number of questions dealing with common neurotic symptoms, which the individual answered about himself. It essentially was an attempt to standardize a psychiatric interview and to adapt the procedure for mass testing. A total score was obtained in terms of the number of symptoms reported. The Woodworth Personal Data Sheet served as a model for most subsequent emotional adjustment inventories, some of which attempted to subdivide emotional adjustment into more specific forms such as home, school, or vocational adjustment. Other tests concentrated more intensively upon a narrower area of behavior, or were concerned with more distinctly social responses, such as ascendance-submission in personal contacts. A later development was the construction of tests for quantifying the expression of interests and attitudes; these tests also were based essentially upon questionnaire techniques (Anastasi, 1961). Traditional self-descriptive inventories such as the Minnesota Multiphasic

Personality Inventory, the Edwards Personal Preference Schedule, the Guilford-Zimmerman Temperament Survey, the Strong Vocational Interest Blank, and the Cattell 16 PF Test have provided stepping stones toward the use of self-report measures by behaviorally oriented clinicians.

The Accuracy of Self-Report Data

In the early years of behaviorism, self-reports and the reports of others were held in poor repute among behaviorists, especially those reports used as indicators of behaviors that could be measured directly or of hypothetical mental states not amenable to measurement. While it is still true that most behaviour therapists would prefer direct measurement of a response to reports by the client or someone else about the behavior in question, behavioral researchers and therapists in recent years have found that checklists and schedules may be employed selectively to produce valuable data for research and therapy purposes.

Thomas (1974) points out that the critics of self-report measures often overlook two important factors. The *first* is that the client's self-reports are behaviors in themselves, and, in some cases, they are the primary responses of interest (e.g., when the client's inability to monitor his own behavior accurately is a major factor contributing to his problem). When self-reports are verbal behaviors that are themselves the main focus of interest, the question of their validity as indicators of other phenomena is not central.

A *second* factor often overlooked is that self-reports have not been shown to be any more unreliable or invalid than other types of measurement, with the possible exception of well-calibrated electro-mechanical devices. Walsh (1967), in his review of the literature concerning the validity of *interview data*, reported that 13 of the 27 studies reviewed demonstrated high validity, whereas nine reports indicated low validity and five yielded ambiguous results. Of seven studies investigating the validity of *questionnaire data*, three gave an impression of high validity and four indicated low validity. Finally, of five studies concerned with the validity of *personal data blank information*, three reports suggested high validity and two indicated that validity was low.

Walsh himself conducted two studies (1967, 1968) which investigated the accuracy of the interview, questionnaire, and personal data blank for collecting verifiable data; in both studies, he found that subjects gave quite accurate responses to most of the informational items and that no one method elicited more accurate self-reporting than another. Studies of college students' self-reported fears have shown that such self-descriptions are relatively reliable (Geer, 1965), have some predictive power with respect to behavioral measures (Geer, 1965; Lanyon & Manosevitz, 1966), and correlate moderately well with instruments which purport to measure conceptually related dispositions (Geer, 1965; Grossberg & Wilson, 1965).

Hilgard's research (1969) has illustrated that self-reports also may be used as indicators or summaries of more than one event. Using pain-state reports of subjects which were compared with different physiological indicators and pain-inducing stimuli, Hilgard found that pain reported verbally on a simple numerical scale yielded orderly and valid results. The reported pain bore a systematic relationship to the pain stimuli, and the lawfulness of the relationship was supported by the fit of the power function which has been found to hold for other perceptual modalities (Stevens, 1966). In regard to the reports in relationship to the physiological indicators, Hilgard said: "I wish to assert flatly that there is no physiological measure of pain which is either as discriminating of fine differences in stimulus conditions, as reliable upon repetition, or as lawfully related to change conditions, as the subject's verbal report" (p. 107).

Behavioral Analysis

As was previously stated, in the behavioral therapy model the process of behavioral analysis involves operationally defining the behaviors to be changed, identifying antecedents and consequences, and in determining behavioral parameters such as frequency, duration, and quality. In deciding which behaviors he will attempt to modify, the clinician must weigh a number of factors. For example, the modifiability of a particular behavior will depend in part on the stimuli which currently are maintaining that behavior. The choice of target responses is affected by the degree to which their modification would result in beneficial or detrimental consequences, not only for the patient but also for other persons close to him. The modification of some target behaviors offers the possibility of indirect beneficial changes in other responses that are functionally related to the problematic behavior; for example, the elimination of bed-wetting can result in improved parent-child relationships (the latter of which may be a target for its own sake). The practical resources (social, physical, temporal, and economic) which can be brought to bear on various potential target behaviors are likely to differ from client to client and from time to time, and factors such as the availability of a cooperative spouse, employer, teacher, or of funds for intensive treatment can alter the therapeutic goal. Even the setting in which the therapist and patient interact will make some treatment techniques—and hence some behavioral targets—more practical than others (Kanfer & Phillips, 1970).

Behaviorally-oriented clinicians utilize information from a number of sources in doing a behavioral analysis: interviews with the client or with significant others, direct observation of the client in different situations, and traditional psychological testing (although to a somewhat lesser degree than do non-behavioral clinicians). In addition, a variety of self-report assessment instruments have been developed and have proven useful to behavior therapists in their formulation of treatment strategies and evaluation of treatment effectiveness. Among these are (1) *life history questionnaires*, such as Cautela's Behavioral Analysis History Questionnaire (1970a) and Wolpe's Life History Questionnaire (c.f. Wolpe, 1969), (2) *problem checklists*, such as the Behavioral Self-Rating Checklist (c.f. Cautela & Upper, 1975), and (3) *survey schedules*, such as the Reinforcement Survey Schedule (Cautela & Kastenbaum, 1967), Homme's Reinforcement Menu (Homme, Csanyi, Gonzales & Rechs, 1969), and the Fear Survey Schedule (Wolpe & Lang, 1964).

In the case of individual behavior therapy, these structured assessment instruments generally are administered by having the client fill them out between therapy sessions, which does not necessitate taking time during treatment sessions for their administration. Since many of the behavioral treatment techniques require that the client do "homework" (i.e. practice specific procedures) between sessions, this structured type of assessment instrument helps to establish the expectation that therapy is going to consist of more than what goes on in the therapist's office, and provides a behavioral sample which indicates the client's probable degree of cooperation with treatment. If, for example, the client fails to return the completed instruments at the assigned time or hurriedly fills them out just before entering the therapist's office, it may be necessary for the therapist to stress strongly the importance of the work to be done by the client between sessions, particularly if therapy is not going to be needlessly prolonged.

After having administered the behavioral assessment instruments, the therapist generally goes over each of them in detail with the client, asking him to elaborate upon his responses, to give specific examples of situations in which the problematic behaviors in question occurred, and to indicate any relationships he sees between his problematic behaviors and environmental factors, or among his various problems. An important by-product of this detailed analysis of the client's behavior is that the client receives useful feedback which makes it possible to begin changing his behavior immediately. Often the mere process of counting the number of times a maladaptive behavior occurs can result in a more determined effort on the client's part to change the frequency of that behavior. The behavioral assessment process also provides the therapist with an opportunity to give the client new labels for his own behavior: for example, the client who says to himself, "I need to cut down on my drinking (i.e., to reduce the frequency of my drinking behavior) and to control my urges to drink alcoholic beverages" probably will show greater optimism about treatment success and more cooperation in treatment than will the client who says, "I'm a hopeless alcoholic!"

The Behavioral Inventory Battery

As a result of our experience in doing behavioral analysis and therapy in a wide variety of treatment cases, we have developed the Behavioral Inventory Battery (BIB), a standardized assessment strategy adaptable to a broad range of treatment settings and client populations. The self-report inventories comprising the BIB are structured into three levels: (1) the *primary* scales are the most general and the widest in scope, and they provide the type of information which is useful in planning treatment for virtually every client; (2) the *secondary* scales are somewhat more specific, and they yield information relevant to the use of the most commonly employed intervention techniques—relaxation, thought-stopping, assertive training, and covert techniques; and (3) the *tertiary* scales are relatively specific, and they are designed to provide the therapist with detailed information about the parameters of the client's problematic behaviors (see Table 4.1). The primary scales are the Behavioral Analysis History Questionnaire (Cautela, 1970c), the Behavioral Self-Rating Checklist (c.f. Cautela & Upper, 1975), the Fear Survey Schedule (Wolpe & Lang, 1964), and the Reinforcement Survey Schedule (Cautela & Kastenbaum, 1967). The secondary scales are the Thought-Stopping Survey Schedule (Cautela, 1972), the Assertive Behavior Survey Schedule (Cautela, 1973b), the Cues for Tension and Anxiety Survey Schedule (Cautela, 1973a), and the Imagery Survey Schedule (Cautela & Tondo, 1971; Tondo & Cautela, 1974). The tertiary scales are survey schedules and questionnaires related to the client's alcohol and drug intake, eating habits, sexual behavior, social performance, smoking, and weight.

TABLE 4.1
Behavioral Scales Used in Behavioral Analysis

Primary Scales	Secondary Scales	Tertiary Scales
Behavioral Analysis History Questionnaire (BAHQ)	Assertive Behavior Survey Schedule (ABSS)	Alcohol Questionnaire Drug Questionnaire
Behavioral Self-Rating Checklist (BSRC)	Thought-Stopping Survey Schedule (TSSS)	Eating Habits Questionnaire Sexual Behavior Questionnaire
Reinforcement Survey Schedule (RSS)	Cues for Tension and Anxiety Survey Schedule (CTASS)	Smoking Questionnaire Social Performance Survey Schedule
Fear Survey Schedule (FSS)	Imagery Survey Schedule (ISS)	Weight Questionnaire Etc.

Rationale Presented to the Client

During his first interview with the client, the therapist generally asks the client to describe his problematic behaviors in as much detail as possible. Then the therapist explains the rationale of the behavioral model and describes some of the possible treatment procedures that will be used. After the therapeutic contract has been agreed upon, the therapist may introduce the process of behavioral analysis in the following way:

> Behavior therapists generally believe that all behavior is determined, or at least influenced, by environmental circumstances. When we use the word "environment," we include covert processes such as thoughts, images, and feelings, as well as what is going on in the world around us. Rather than diagnosing a particular problem or person in the traditional way, we do a behavioral analysis on the particular problematic behaviors. The purpose of this behavioral analysis is to determine the frequency and intensity of the behavior to be changed and to identify the antecedents (i.e., what sets off the behavior) and the consequences (i.e., the results the behavior produces) of the behavior. Once we have identified these antecedents and consequences, we can set up a program to modify the behavior.
>
> We identify the antecedents and consequences by interviewing you, observing your behavior, and talking with significant others in your life. We also have developed a set of standardized inventories and questionnaires to help in our behavioral analysis and treatment. I'm going to give you several of these forms to fill out. Try to put down the first answer that occurs to you, and don't concern yourself if some of the questions seem ambiguous or if you feel that more elaboration is needed. I'll be going over each of these forms with you during our next session, so that we can note the answers which are most relevant to your problems. If a question seems ambiguous or difficult to answer, note it on the form so that we can discuss it next time. There are a number of forms, and I hope you'll try to fill them out as soon as possible. Ideally, I'd like to have you bring the completed forms to our next session.

The Primary Scales

The client then is given the four primary scales. The *Behavioral Analysis History Questionnaire* (BAHQ), when filled out by the client, provides the therapist with demographic and background data such as current marital and vocational status; family, religious, sexual, health, and educational histories; and specific information concerning the problems for which the client comes to therapy (see Table 4.2). This questionnaire usually takes the client about one hour to complete. At the second or third therapy session, depending upon the seriousness of the client's problematic behaviors, the therapist reviews each of the sections of the questionnaire with the client. The purposes of this inquiry are to clear up any ambiguous answers and to obtain any additional information which might be needed for treatment-planning purposes. During the inquiry (for the other assessment instruments as well as the BAHQ), the therapist makes notes about the client's responses, both on the assessment form and on the client's folder, for easy later reference.

TABLE 4.2

Behavioral Analysis History Questionnaire
(BAHQ)

This questionnaire is used to supply us with information from your past history and present situation that will help us to change your undesirable behavior. Your answers will be strictly confidential and will not be revealed to anyone without your full consent.

Date..........

I. Vital Statistics

Name.......... *Age*..........

Address.......... *Date of Birth*..........

....

Telephone Number (Home).......... (Work)..........

Sex Male.......... Female..........

Height..........ft..........in. *Weight*..........lbs.

Race White.......... Black.......... Oriental..........

Other..........

Color of eyes Blue.......... Brown.......... Green.......... Black..........

Glasses Yes.......... No..........

Complexion Dark.......... Medium-dark.......... Medium..........

Fair.......... Very fair..........

Distinguishing features ....

....

II. Referral and Previous Treatment

Who referred you?..........

What present complaints (maladaptive behaviors) do you have that make you feel you need help?..........

....

TABLE 4.2—continued

How often do these occur? Times per week .... Times per month ....

What do you think is presently causing these behaviors? ....

....

Have you sought treatment before? Yes .... No ....

If so, please list in chronological order the therapists and dates seen.

Name of therapist	*Dates seen*
....	....
....	....
....	....
....	....

Have you ever been hospitalized for a mental illness? Yes .... No ....

If so, list hospital(s) and dates.

Hospital(s)	*Dates*
....	....
....	....
....	....
....	....
....	....

III. Fears and Negative Thoughts

List below some of the fears that you have:

....

....

....

....

....

If you ever have any thoughts as listed below, check the frequency of their occurrences.

	hardly ever	*occasionally*	*frequently*
Life is hopeless	....	....	....
I am lonely	....	....	....
The future is hopeless	....	....	....
Nobody cares about me	....	....	....
I feel like killing myself	....	....	....
I am a failure	....	....	....
I am intellectually inferior to other people	....	....	....
People usually don't like me	....	....	....
I am going to faint	....	....	....
I am going to have a panic attack	....	....	....

Other negative thoughts you may have: ....

....

TABLE 4.2—continued

IV. Marital Status

Married............ Single............ Divorced............ Separated............ Widowed............

If married, wife's/husband's age and occupation: Age............

Occupation............

If any children, list their names and ages:

Name	*Age*
....	....
....	....
....	....
....	....
....	....

If divorced, or separated, for what reason?............

....

....

....

....

List the people who currently live in your household, and their relationship to you.

Name	*Relationship* (e.g., mother-in-law, daughter, roommate, etc.)
....	....
....	....
....	....
....	....
....	....
....	....
....	....

V. Family

Mother

Name............ *Age*............ *Occupation*............

Religion............ *Height*............ft............in. *Weight*............lbs.

How did she punish you?............

How did she reward you?............

What did she punish?............

What did she reward?............

How would others describe your mother?............

....

TABLE 4.2—continued

How would you describe your mother? ....

....

What activities did you do with your mother when you were a child? ....

....

How did you get along with your mother? ....

....

Father

Name .... *Age* .... *Occupation* ....

Religion .... *Height* ....ft. ....in. *Weight* ....lbs.

How did he punish you? ....

What did he punish? ....

What did he reward? ....

How would others describe your father? ....

....

How would you describe your father? ....

....

What activities did you do with your father when you were a child? ....

....

How did you get along with your father? ....

....

Brothers and Sisters

Name	Age	How did/do you get along with him/her?
....	......	....
....	......	....
....	......	....
....	......	....
....	......	....
....	......	....

Do (did) your mother or father favor any one? Yes .... No ....

If so, who and why? ....

....

How do (did) your mother and father get along? ....

....

VI. Education

	Name of School	*Location*	*Dates*	*How were your grades?*
Grammar	....	....	....	....
Secondary	....	....	....	....
College	....	....	....	....

TABLE 4.2—continued

Post-Graduate School(s)..............................

....

How well did you adjust to school situations?

poorly.......... fairly.......... well.......... excellently..........

List any significant events relating to school that you think had a bearing on your present problem.

....

....

....

Childhood hobbies and interests?..............................

....

Present hobbies and interests..............................

....

VII. Job

List the jobs you have held and their dates. Then note which aspects of each job were the most pleasurable for you (e.g., working with people, type of work, etc.) and which aspects gave you the most anxiety or trouble.

Dates	*Job Titles*	*Salaries*	*Liked*	*Disliked*
....	....	....	....	....
....	....	....	....	....
....	....	....	....	....
....	....	....	....	....

How often did you miss work?

(a) As a general estimate for all your jobs..............................

(b) For the jobs you enjoyed..............................

(c) For the jobs you disliked..............................

How did you get along with your fellow employees?

not at all.......... fairly well.......... very well..........

What bothers you most about your fellow employees?..............................

....

How did you get along with your supervisors?..............................

....

What bothers you most about your supervisors?..............................

....

What training or education have you had relevant to occupational skills? (List on-the-job training as well as course work.)

....

....

....

TABLE 4.2—continued

What job, if any, are you presently holding?..........

....

Does it satisfy you: intellectually.......... emotionally.......... physically..........

What ambitions do you have at the present time?..........

....

VIII. Sexual

When and how did you first learn about sex?..........

....

Was sex ever discussed at home? not at all.......... occasionally.......... a fair amount of the time.......... frequently..........

What was the attitude of your parents concerning sex?

it was considered shameful to discuss.......... not exactly shameful, but not discussed much.......... a natural function to be discussed without embarrassment..........

Describe your first sexual experience..........

....

If you masturbate, when did you first start?..........

When did you have your first sexual intercourse?..........

Have you ever had any homosexual experience?..........

What is your sexual activity at the present time?

	Times per week	*Times per month*
(a) Masturbation	....	....
What do you imagine when you masturbate?		
(b) Light petting (kissing and hugging)	....	....
(c) Heavy petting (touching sexual organs)	....	....
(d) Homosexual contacts	....	....
(e) Intercourse	....	....

For female clients

When did you have your first period?..........

Are your periods regular at the present time? Yes.......... No..........

How comfortable are your periods? very comfortable.......... uncomfortable.......... fairly comfortable.......... comfortable..........

Do you often feel depressed just before your period?..........

Do you use birth control devices or pills? Yes.......... No..........

If so, what types..........

....

TABLE 4.2—continued

Male and female clients

How well do you and your wife/husband get along. (Rate your relationship on a scale from 1 to 5:

1. very poor 2. poor 3. fair 4. good 5. excellent

How often do you and your wife/husband have intercourse?

per week.................................. per month..................................

How often do you and your wife/husband go out socially?

per week.................................. per month..................................

Who is the dominant member of your relationship?

you.................................. your wife/husband..................................

List some of the behaviors of your husband/wife that you find disagreeable.

....

....

....

List some of the behaviors of your husband/wife that you find agreeable.

....

....

....

IX. Health History

List any childhood diseases you've had:

....

....

List any operations you've had..

....

Have you had any significant illnesses in the past?..

....

List your present physical ailments (e.g., high blood pressure, diabetes, heart trouble etc.)

....

....

....

When was the last time you had a complete physical examination?

....

Results? ....

Name and address of your physician:

Name.. Address..

....

TABLE 4.2—continued

Do you have any trouble falling asleep? Yes........ No........

How long does it take you to fall asleep once you've gone to bed?........

Do you wake up during the night?........

If you wake up, can you get back to sleep easily?........

....

How is your appetite? poor........ average........ good........ very good........

What drugs are you presently taking and why?........

....

X. Religion

In what religion were you raised? Protestant........ Catholic........ Jewish........ Other........

Do you presently engage in any religious activity? Yes........ No........

If so, please describe........

XI. Behavioral

List any faults you think you have........

....

....

....

List your good points........

....

....

....

Please add anything you feel that could help us understand your problem.

....

....

....

....

....

A second primary scale, the *Behavioral Self-Rating Checklist* (BSRC), asks the client to indicate which of 73 adaptive behaviors he needs to learn in order to function more effectively or to be more comfortable (e.g., "I need to learn to feel less anxious when my work is being supervised"). The items deal with covert and overt behaviors and, unlike the Fear Survey Schedule, involve maladaptive *approach* behaviors as well as maladaptive avoidance. An advantage of using a comprehensive checklist of this type is that it requires the client to assess the adaptiveness of his functioning in a wide variety of behavioral areas, which may result in his identifying some problems on the checklist which he might not have brought up in general discussion with the therapist (and which might be related to the primary problems he presents). During the inquiry for the BSRC, each checked item is discussed briefly with the client, and a joint decision is made about whether to try to modify the problematic behavior under discussion. The behaviors to be modified then are ranked according to their priority for treatment, with those behaviors representing the greatest potential degree of interference with the client's life being given the highest priority (e.g., frequent thoughts about suicide or homicide would require immediate intervention).

The *Reinforcement Survey Schedule* (RSS), a third primary scale, is composed of 54 major items, which ask the client to rate the reinforcement value of a variety of stimuli and experiences which may be used as reinforcers in overt and covert conditioning programs. In the first three sections of the RSS, the client uses a five-point rating scale to indicate how enjoyable or satisfying he finds each stimulus—not at all, a little, a fair amount, much, or very much; in the fourth section, he is asked to list the things he does or thinks about relatively frequently. A number of research studies have indicated that both the reliability (Keehn, Bloomfield & Hug, 1970; Kleinknecht, McCormick & Thorndike, 1971) and the validity (Cautela, Steffan & Wish, 1970; Mermis, 1971; Steffan, 1971) of the RSS are sufficiently high to warrant its use as a clinical and research instrument. Cautela and Wisocki (1971) have outlined a number of ways in which the RSS can be used to aid the implementation of treatment in institutional and individual therapy settings. For example, in institutions the schedule may be used as follows: (1) responses can be used to choose the back-up reinforcers for a token economy or contingency contracting program; (2) idiosyncratic reinforcers for each patient can be employed in shaping responses not currently present in clients' repertoires; (3) changes in clients' responses on the schedule can be used as a measure of treatment success with certain types of behavioral problems, particularly depression, which has been shown to be related to decreased availability of significant reinforcers (Cautela & Wisocki, 1971); and (4) the RSS can be administered to treatment personnel in order to match therapists and clients on the basis of mutual reinforcers (and thus to increase the probability of rapport developing).

In individual therapy, the RSS is extremely useful in planning therapy involving covert reinforcement, a covert conditioning technique designed to increase response probability by having clients imagine themselves performing the behavior to be increased, followed by an imagined reinforcer. After the client has filled out the RSS, he is asked to imagine each of the items he has classified as bringing "much" or "very much" pleasure and to rate each of these items in terms of the clarity of his imagery. The items which are ranked highest in terms of both clarity of imagery and reinforcement value are employed in the covert reinforcement program.

The final primary scale, the *Fear Survey Schedule* (FSS), consists of 72 items which are related to maladaptive avoidance behavior, such as "fear of open wounds" or "fear of dead people." Clients are asked to rate each item according to the degree to which they experience that particular fear, once again on a five-point scale ranging from "not at all" to "very much." The present version of the FSS, perhaps the most widely used self-report schedule in behavior therapy, was earlier developed by Wolpe and Lang (1964). This version of the FSS was directly suggested and partially derived from a Fear Survey Schedule (FSS-I), which was developed to assess change in phobic behavior and generalized anxiety in experimental studies of desensitization (Lang & Lazovik, 1963). A second experimental form (FSS-II) has been constructed from the responses of a college population, and a factor analysis, as well as a study of the schedule's relationship to several personality scales, has been carried out by Geer (1965).

Items answered "much" or "very much" indicate possible behaviors to be modified by means of systematic desensitization and/or covert positive reinforcement. The FSS also can prove useful in identifying items for use in therapy involving covert sensitization or covert negative reinforcement. In covert sensitization (Cautela, 1966, 1967), the client is instructed to imagine that he is performing the behavior to be modified (in this case, reduced in frequency) and then to imagine an aversive stimulus, such as having an open wound. Theoretically, repeated pairings of this type should result in decreased behavioral frequency, a result which has been observed in a number of experimental investigations of covert sensitization (Ashem & Donner, 1968; Barlow, Leitenberg & Agras, 1969: Cautela, 1970b). In covert negative reinforcement (Cautela, 1970a), the client is asked to begin by imagining that he is exposed to an aversive stimulus and then to switch to a scene in which he performs an adaptive behavior (i.e., a behavior to be increased in frequency) upon the termination of the noxious scene. Experimental results (e.g., Ascher & Cautela, 1972) indicate that this procedure can be used effectively to increase adaptive behaviors.

In order to provide therapists with a relatively concise summary of information gathered from the four primary scales (i.e., the client's problems, fears, reinforcers, and significant biographical information, the Behavioral Inventory Battery Summary Sheet (see Table 4.3) has been devised. Biographical items that the therapist wants to pay special attention to during the inquiry are noted in the BAHQ summary section. Behaviors that the client has indicated he needs to learn are listed in the BSRC summary section, and items from the FSS and RSS which have been checked "much" and "very much" are listed

TABLE 4.3

BIB Summary Sheet

Name ....

Date ....

BAHQ Items for inquiry:	*BSRC* Behaviors to be changed:
....	....
....	....
....	....
....	....
....	....
....	....
....	....
....	....
....	....
....	....

RSS		*FSS*	
Much	*Very much*	*Much*	*Very much*
....	....	....	....
....	....	....	....
....	....	....	....
....	....	....	....
....	....	....	....
....	....	....	....
....	....	....	....
....	....	....	....
....	....	....	....
....	....	....	....
....	....	....	....
....	....	....	....

in the appropriate places. The **BIB** Summary Sheet provides a handy reference for behaviors to be changed, as well as items for use in overt or covert reinforcement or covert sensitization. It can be stapled to the inside of the cover of the client's folder for quick reference.

The Secondary Scales

As was mentioned above, the four secondary scales are somewhat more specifically focused than the primary scales and are intended to yield information relevant to the use of relaxation, thought-stopping, assertive training, and covert techniques. The *Cues for Tension and Anxiety Survey Schedule* (CTASS) consists of a list of sensations or behaviors which may accompany being tense or anxious (see Table 4.4). Items 1-10 involve autonomic responses, items 11-16 deal with voluntary motor responses, and items 17-21 involve behaviors associated with a panic attack. The client also is asked to specify what he commonly does to attempt to alleviate feelings of anxiety or tension (e.g., lying down until the feelings pass), information which can prove quite useful to the therapist in his attempts to teach the client how to use relaxation most effectively. When a client is taught how to relax, he is told to pay special attention to those parts of the body which are most affected when he is tense

TABLE 4.4

Cues for Tension and Anxiety Survey Schedule (*CTASS*)

Name ....

Date ....

Individuals have different ways that indicate to them that they are tense or anxious. Check below the ways that apply to you:

1. You feel tense in:
   (a) your forehead (   )
   (b) back of your neck (   )
   (c) chest (   )
   (d) shoulders (   )
   (e) stomach (   )
   (f) face (   )
   (g) other parts (   ). Specify where: ....
2. You sweat (   )
3. Your heart beats fast (   )
4. You can feel your heart pounding (   )
5. You can hear your heart pounding (   )
6. Your face feels flushed or warm (   )
7. Your skin feels cool and damp (   )
8. You tremble or shake in your:
   (a) hands (   )
   (b) legs (   )
   (c) other ....

TABLE 4.4—continued

9. Your stomach feels like you are just stopping in an elevator ( )
10. Your stomach feels nauseous ( )
11. You feel yourself holding onto something tightly (like a steering wheel or arm of a chair) ( )
12. You scratch a certain part of your body ( ). Specify where...
13. When your legs are crossed, you move the top one up and down ( )
14. You bite your nails ( )
15. Your grind your teeth ( )
16. You have trouble with your speech ( )
17. You feel like you are going to choke ( )
18. You feel faint ( )
19. You feel dizzy ( )
20. You find yourself breathing quickly or heavily ( )

When you feel tense or anxious, what ways do you commonly use to get rid of the feeling?

....

....

....

....

....

....

....

or anxious, and the therapist in fact may spend more time in teaching the client how to relax those exact parts. The client is also told to pay special attention to those physiological or behavioral cues which generally indicate that he is becoming tense (and which may have been identified by means of the CTASS). Some clients find it quite difficult, at first, to monitor their own sensations or behavior, and it is often helpful if these clients are instructed to pay special attention to how they feel and act in tension producing situations, so that they can become more aware of the relevant cues. The information gathered from the CTASS is useful not only in treatment implementation but in treatment evaluation as well; after the client has had sufficient time to learn relaxation as a self-control procedure, therapist and client can go over the CTASS items once again in order to determine those behavioral areas in which the intervention has achieved its goals (i.e., anxiety and tension control) and those in which further training and practice are needed.

Another of the secondary scales, the *Assertive Behavior Survey Schedule* (ABSS), is designed to elicit information which will aid the therapist in planning a therapy program involving assertive training. The schedule requires the client to indicate how he would respond in a variety of situations in which assertiveness on his part would be appropriate, as well as to speculate on what the interpersonal consequences of asserting himself will be (see Table 4.5). This information is used to determine the kinds of situations in which the client has greatest difficulty in displaying appropriately assertive behavior, which in turn will be those chosen for behavioral rehearsal (either overt or covert) during the course of treatment. Data concerning the client's perceptions about the interpersonal consequences of his behavior are especially significant in those instances when it appears that assertive behavior fails to occur because the client is fearful or anxious about the other person's response. Relaxation, thought-stopping, and covert reinforcement can be used quite effectively in such cases to increase assertive behavior. The ABSS items also can be used as the "take-off" points for discussions in assertion training groups.

TABLE 4.5

Assertive Behavior Survey Schedule (ABSS)

Name ....

Date ....

I. What would you do in the following situations? Indicate by circling number 1, 2, or 3.

A. In a restaurant, you have ordered your favorite meal. When it comes, it is not cooked to your liking.

1. You tell the waitress that it is not cooked to your taste or liking and have her take it back and cooked to your taste or liking.
2. You complain that it is not cooked to your taste or liking, but you say you will eat it anyway.
3. You say nothing.

B. You have been waiting in line to buy a ticket. Someone gets in front of you.

1. You say it is your turn, and get in front of him.
2. You say it is your turn, but you let the person go before you.
3. You say nothing.

C. In a supermarket, you are waiting in line at the checkout counter. Someone gets in front of you.

1. You say, "I'm sorry, but I was here first," and you take your turn.
2. You say, "I'm sorry, but I was here first," but you let the person go ahead of you.
3. You say nothing.

D. In a drugstore, the clerk has been waiting on someone for about five minutes. He finishes, and it is now your turn, but he starts to wait on someone else.

1. You speak up to him and say it is your turn, and take your turn.
2. You speak up to him and say it is your turn, but also say that you will let the other person go ahead of you.
3. You say nothing.

TABLE 4.5—continued

E. In a department store, the clerk talks on the phone for at least ten minutes while you are waiting.
   1. You say, "Will you please wait on me now? I've been here for ten minutes."
   2. You say, "Hurry it up, I've been waiting ten minutes."
   3. You say nothing.

F. At the dry cleaners, you notice that your shirt (or other clothing) is not properly cleaned.
   1. You say that your clothes are not properly cleaned and that they will have to do them over again.
   2. You say that your clothes are not properly cleaned but that you'll take them anyway.
   3. You say nothing.

Score..............................

II. What do you think will happen if you assert yourself in situations in which you are afraid to do so (i.e., speak up when an injustice is done to you by any of the following)?

A. mother
B. father
C. son or daughter
D. best friend
E. employer or immediate supervisor
F. clerk in a store
G. a waiter or waitress in a restaurant
H. boy friend
I. girl friend
J. wife
K. husband

III. In instances where you are afraid to speak up when an injustice is done to you, check which of the following consequences do you anticipate and are afraid of:

A. being yelled at ( )
B. being assaulted physically ( )
C. being given a dirty look ( )
D. having the person refuse to talk to you ( )
E. fearing the person will reject you in other ways ( )

IV. With certain important people in your life, you feel you give more than you receive and in these situations you usually:

A. Tell the other person you think the situation is unequal and you expect more from them.
B. Tend to avoid the person or give him less.
C. Do nothing.

The Thought-Stopping Survey Schedule (TSSS) is particularly useful in the implementation of treatment programs involving the technique of thought-stopping. The TSSS (see Table 4.6) consists of 51 items which involve thoughts, images, or feelings which can cause anxiety, depression, or other maladaptive behaviors (e.g., "People think I'm peculiar"). The client is asked to indicate how often he has each of these thoughts, using a five-point scale from "not at all" to "very much." He also is asked to list any other thoughts he has which occur more than 10 or 20 times a day, as well as any additional thoughts

TABLE 4.6

Thought-Stopping Survey Schedule (TSSS)

Name ....

Date ....

Check the appropriate box that indicates how often you have a particular thought.

	Not at all	A little	A fair amount	Much	Very much
1. I feel lonely					
2. Life is hopeless					
3. I feel stupid					
4. I don't look attractive					
5. People don't like me					
6. I'd like to have a drink (alcohol)					
7. I'd like to have something to eat					
8. I'd like to have a smoke					
9. I feel depressed					
10. I am going to make a mistake					
11. I am a failure					
12. I would like to expose myself					
13. The future looks hopeless					
14. I feel guilty about something I have done					
15. I am going crazy					
16. I am going to panic					
17. I want to kill myself					
18. I would like to have a homosexual experience					

TABLE 4.6—continued

	Not at all	A little	A fair amount	Much	Very much
19. The world is a mess					
20. What's wrong with me?					
21. I am afraid I'm going to die					
22. I am afraid of being left alone in life					
23. I will never find someone to love me					
24. I would like to hurt someone					
25. People will find out I am a phony					
26. I feel something terrible is going to happen to me					
27. I am going to lose my job					
28. I don't have enough money					
29. I am frigid (females) I am impotent (males)					
30. People think I am peculiar					
31. People think I am stupid					
32. I can't concentrate					
33. I need to take pills to calm down					
34. People will notice I am nervous					
35. Something is wrong with my sex life					
36. I don't want to go to work.					
37. Someone I care for might die					
38. I am too fat I am too thin					
39. I am not worthwhile					
40. I am afraid I will hurt someone					
41. People will think I am homosexual					
42. I wonder whether I am a homosexual					
43. I am a weak person					
44. No one seems to understand me					
45. The doctor can't find out what's wrong with me but I know I am sick					
46. If I have sex with someone, I want to be able to satisfy him/her					
47. I always going to be nervous					

TABLE 4.6—continued

	Not at all	A little	A fair amount	Much	Very much
48. Someone is going to hurt me or kill me					
49. I am growing old					
50. I wish I wasn't so short I wish I wasn't so tall					
51. I think about homosexual experiences					

List the thoughts not mentioned above that you have more than ten times a day:

....

....

....

....

....

....

....

....

....

....

List thoughts not mentioned above that you have more than twenty times a day:

....

....

....

....

....

....

....

....

....

List any other thoughts that bother you or make you feel anxious:

....

....

....

....

....

....

....

....

....

which bother him or make him feel especially anxious. Following inquiry about his responses on the TSSS, the client is instructed to monitor the occurrence of these thoughts and is taught to shout "STOP!" to himself every time one of the maladaptive thoughts occurs. The client also is told that, if he applies this procedure consistently, the problematic thoughts will occur less and less frequently, until they go away completely. The TSSS is particularly useful in clinical practice not only because it introduces the client to the process of monitoring his own maladaptive thoughts, but also because it provides a pre-treatment baseline against which his progress in mastering the thought-stopping technique can be measured.

The final secondary scale is the Imagery Survey Schedule (ISS), which requires that ratings be made of the ease, clarity, and pleasantness-unpleasantness of "images" elicited by single words within six separate sensory modalities: auditory, gustatory, kinesthetic, olfactory, tactile, and visual (see Table 4.7). The utility of formally assessing these parameters of the client's imagery is indicated by a number of experimental studies which have found a positive correlation between the vividness of imagery in the scenes presented to the client and the resulting behavioral changes (Tondo & Cautela, 1974; Wisocki, 1974). Since the use of imagery plays an important part in the implementation of a variety of behavior therapy techniques, including systematic desensitization and the covert conditioning procedures, a pre-treatment evaluation of the client's imagery can aid the therapist by identifying those clients who may need some pre-training in the use of imagery before hierarchy items or covert conditioning scenes are presented. Generally, this pre-training would involve practicing neutral scenes until they can be imagined easily and relatively vividly.

The Tertiary Scales

The tertiary scales listed in Table 4.1 are a variety of questionnaires and survey schedules, each of which is designed to elicit information relevant to the treatment of a particular clinical problem. If a therapist finds that he is treating a number of clients with the same general complaint (e.g., high alcoholic intake, frequent thoughts about suicide), he may find it useful to employ a structured assessment instrument which focuses on the problematic behavior of interest, rather than having to question each of these clients individually about behavioral parameters. Not only is clinical time saved, but the consistent use of this type of instrument can provide the clinician with a standardized data base which he can use in making broad-range treatment decisions. For example, if the clients' responses on the Eating Habits Questionnaire indicate that most clients tend to engage in maladaptive eating when they

TABLE 4.7

Two Sections of the Imagery Survey Schedule (ISS)

Section 1—Visual Imagery

Directions: This part of the questionnaire is concerned with visual imagery. For each work, read the word and then close your eyes and try to imagine that you are actually looking at something (anything) which the word may suggest to you. If you are able to obtain an image, or visual sensation, concentrate on it for a few seconds and then rate it. If the word does not produce an image within 15 seconds, indicate this by placing a checkmark in the appropriate column and go on to the next word. After you have followed the above procedure for all the words on this page, go on to the next section.

Words	Any image?		Ease			Vividness			Unpleasantness				Pleasantness				
	Yes	No	L	M	H	L	M	H	Very much	Much	Some	Not much	None	Not much	Some	Much	Very much
Attractive																	
Brown																	
Ugly																	
Glaring																	
Scenery																	

Section 2—Auditory Imagery

Words	Any image?		Ease			Vividness			Unpleasantness				Pleasantness				
	Yes	No	L	M	H	L	M	H	Very much	Much	Some	Not much	None	Not much	Some	Much	Very much
Crash																	
Laugh																	
Sound																	
Scream																	
Music																	

are feeling anxious, the therapist may decide to introduce relaxation training very early in treatment with his clients who overeat.

While structured questionnaires and survey schedules have been developed by Cautela for each of the areas listed in Table 4.1, these scales are being used on a limited basis clinically at present and have yet to be published or tested for validity and reliability. Rather than publishing them here, the present authors simply would like to indicate the potential clinical utility of developing and employing standardized questionnaires of this type, as well as to offer copies of our prototypes of these scales to those clinicians interested in testing their validity and reliability.

Problems in Administering the Scales

There are a number of problems which may arise during the administration of the Behavioral Inventory Battery. For example, some clients keep forgetting to bring in some or all of the scales which they were supposed to complete, or they claim that they have been too busy to complete them. In such cases, the therapist may tell them that time and money are being wasted until the forms have been completed, since data from the forms comprise an important part of the behavioral analysis. It also may be helpful if the therapist suggests that the delinquent client mail in each scale as it is completed.

Clients may feel that some items on the forms involve an unnecessary invasion of privacy—that is, they do not see the relevance of providing sexual information when the presenting complaint is a plane phobia. The therapist may respond by explaining that it might be a mistake to make *a priori* judgments about which information is relevant to the particular problem and which is not. For example, information about behaviors which are apparently irrelevant to the presenting problems may aid in the identification of behavioral antecedents or consequences.

A number of clients express concern about whether the information they give will be held in the strictest confidentiality; this has been especially true since the recent disclosures of alleged governmental tampering with the confidential files of psychiatrists and psychologists. Here it is helpful if the therapist has taken sufficient precautions to insure the confidentiality of his files that he can assure the client that the information he gives will be kept in strictest confidence (even to the point of preventing the therapist's secretary from seeing the files). Also, clients may be told that if there is some particular information which they are concerned will get into the wrong hands, they do not have to supply it in writing, and it does not have to be recorded in their files. The topic can be discussed verbally and not be noted by the therapist. In addition, the therapist can tell his clients that they may examine their case files at any time upon request and that the records contain no more than what has been discussed during the therapy session. Clients also may be informed that case records will be destroyed six months after the termination of treatment, unless otherwise requested; implicit here is the assumption that, if there is a relapse or if new problems occur after treatment has been completed, a new behavioral analysis probably will be necessary anyway.

Behavioral Analysis and the Issue of Diagnosis

Clients often express concern that their problematic behaviors will be seen by the therapist and by significant others in their lives as symptoms of a psychiatric illness, and they may express concern about being given a psychiatric diagnosis (e.g., "manicdepressive psychosis"). In general, most behavior therapists find diagnostic labels derived from standard psychiatric nomenclature to be of little value. Aside from the stigmatizing and dehumanizing aspects of such a labeling process (see Laing, 1967), criticisms have been leveled at the traditional system of psychiatric classification of purely practical grounds (Arthur, 1969; Ferster, 1966; Phillips & Draguns, 1971). Among these are: (a) that diagnostic categories are not based on any one consistent classificatory principle, but mix together data on age, behavior, severity, etiology, etc.; (b) that they are not based upon meaningful and discernible behaviors; and (c) that they do not address the question of what type of intervention is needed in order to help the person whose behavior disorder is being classified.

In order to meet the need for a standardized system of classifying behavioral disorders based upon clearly defined behaviors and related to therapeutic intervention procedures, the present authors (Cautela & Upper, 1973) have devised the Behavioral Coding System (B.C.S.). The B.C.S. includes 283 specific behaviors, divided into 21 major behavioral categories (e.g., fears, sex, imagery, vocational adjustment, emotional behavior). It is both a viable alternative to current psychiatric classification systems and a useful adjunct to the problem-oriented record-keeping procedures that have recently come into vogue. In individual therapy, the therapist and client can discuss the behavioral assessment material and can agree upon the appropriate behavioral diagnosis. The problematic behaviors can be listed in the order in which they will be treated during the course of therapy. Since behavioral diagnosis is directly related to specific client behaviors, the stigmatizing aspects of psychiatric labeling are absent.

Conclusion

One of the primary difficulties in constructing a battery such as the Behavioral Inventory Battery lies in choosing, from among a fairly extensive list of available instruments, those self-report inventories which will provide the greatest amount of relevant information in the most efficient way. The present authors have chosen these particular instruments for inclusion in the BIB because we have employed them relatively extensively in clinical practice and have found them to be quite useful to the process of behavioral analysis. Other clinicians and researchers, however, may find it just as effective to employ other inventories in their particular behavioral assessment batteries. Among the other instruments which might be considered are the following:

Life history questionnaires

Wolpe's Life History Questionnaire (cf. Wolpe, 1969)

Problem Checklists

The Mooney Problem Checklist (Mooney & Gordon, 1950)
The Willoughby Personality Schedule (Willoughby, 1934)

Reinforcement Schedules

Homme's Reinforcement Menu (Homme *et al.*, 1969)

Anxiety questionnaires

The Manifest Anxiety Scale (Taylor, 1953)
The Generalized Anxiety Scale (Gordon & Sarason, 1955)
The Assimilation Scale (McReynolds & Acker, 1966)
The IPAT Anxiety Scale (Cattell & Scheier, 1961)
The Saslow Screening Test (Saslow et al., 1951)

Assertiveness schedules

The Rathus Assertiveness Schedule (Rathus, 1973)
The Bernreuter Self-Sufficiency Inventory (cf. Wolpe, 1969)

The wide variety of self-report assessment instruments currently in use is a measure of the creativity which has marked the growth of the field of behavior therapy, but it also raises the question of whether the point of diminishing return is being approached. That is, if each clinician devises his own questionnaires and rating scales, will the process of behavioral analysis eventually become so idiosyncratic that communication among professionals and clinical research will suffer?

There are a number of advantages for developing a standardized assessment battery similar to the BIB. Assessment information can be communicated more efficiently from therapist to therapist and from setting to setting if similar behavioral analysis procedures are used. Repeated use of the same instruments across a variety of clinical cases should result in the clinician's becoming more skillful in their administration and interpretation. As was mentioned above, it permits the accumulation of a data base upon which broad-range clinical decisions can be made and fruitful research hypotheses developed. The widespread acceptance and use of a standardized battery also would have advantages in the areas of clinical research and training. More research effort could be directed toward investigating parameters of existing scales (e.g., reliability, validity, extended uses). Training in behavioral assessment could become somewhat more standardized, thus facilitating training with professional and paraprofessional treatment personnel.

In the last analysis, each clinician and clinical researcher must decide which avenue of behavioral assessment is most effective and efficient given his particular focus of interest. This decision is based on such factors as treatment setting, types of clients treated, available patient and treatment setting resources, time available, and types of intervention procedures being used. The use of self-report instruments in behavioral analysis, particularly when organized into a standardized battery, appears to offer sufficient advantages to warrant investigation of their usefulness in a wide variety of treatment situations.

References

Anastasi, Anne. *Psychological testing.* (2nd ed.) New York: Macmillan, 1961.

Arthur, A. Z. Diagnostic testing and the new alternatives. *Psychological Bulletin*, 1969, **72**, 183–192.

Ascher, L. M., & Cautela, J. R. Covert negative reinforcement: An experimental test. *Journal of Behavior and Experimental Psychiatry*, 1972, **1**, 1–5.

Ashem, B., & Donner, L. Covert sensitization with alcoholics: A controlled replication. *Behavior Research and Therapy*, 1968, **6**, 7–12.

Barlow, D. H., Leitenberg, H., & Agras, W. S. Experimental control of sexual deviation through manipulation of the noxious scene in covert sensitization. *Journal of Abnormal Psychology*, 1969, **6**, 596–601.

Cattell, R. B., & Scheier, I. H. *Handbook for the IPAT anxiety scale questionnaire.* Champaign, Ill.: Institute of Personality and Ability Testing, 1963.

Cautela, J. R. Treatment of compulsive behavior by covert sensitization. *Psychological Record*, 1966, **16**, 13–41.

Cautela, J. R. Covert sensitization. *Psychological Reports*, 1967, **20**, 459–468.

Cautela, J. R. Covert negative reinforcement. *Journal of Behavior Therapy and Experimental Psychiatry*, 1970a, **1**, 273–278.

Cautela, J. R. The use of covert sensitization in the treatment of alcoholism. *Psychotherapy: Theory, Research and Practice*, 1970b, **7**, 86–90.

Cautela, J. R. The Behavioral Analysis History Questionnaire. Unpublished questionnaire, Boston College, 1970c.

Cautela, J. R. The Thought-Stopping Survey Schedule. Unpublished survey schedule, Boston College, 1972.

Cautela, J. R. The Cues for Tension and Anxiety Survey Schedule. Unpublished survey schedule, Boston College, 1973a.

Cautela, J. R. The Assertive Behavior Survey Schedule. Unpublished survey schedule, Boston College, 1973b.

Cautela, J. R., Kastenbaum, R. A reinforcement survey schedule for use in therapy, training, and research. *Psychological Reports*, 1967, **20**, 1115–1130.

Cautela, J. R., Steffen, J. J., & Wish, P. Covert reinforcement: An experimental test. Paper presented at the 78th Annual Convention, American Psychological Association, Miami Beach, Florida, September 1970.

Cautela, J. R., & Tondo, T. R. The Imagery Survey Schedule. Unpublished survey schedule, Boston College, 1971.

Cautela, J. R., & Upper, D. A Behavioral Coding System. Presidential address presented (by J. R. Cautela) at the Association for Advancement of Behavior Therapy, Miami, Florida, December 1973.

Cautela, J. R., & Upper, D. The process of individual behavior therapy. In M. Hersen, R. M. Eisler, & P. M. Miller (Eds.), *Progress in behavior modification*. Vol. I. New York: Academic Press, 1975.

Cautela, J. R., & Wisocki, P. A. The use of the reinforcement survey schedule in behavior modification. In R. Rubin (Ed.), *Advances in behavior therapy*. New York: Academic Press, 1971.

Ferster, C. B. Classification of behavioral pathology. In L. Krasner, & L. P. Ullmann (Eds.), *Research in behavior modification*. New York: Holt, Rinehart & Winston, 1966.

Geer, J. H. The development of a scale to measure fear. *Behaviour Research and Therapy*, 1965, **3**, 45–53.

Gordon, E. M., & Sarason, S. B. The relationship between "Test Anxiety" and "Other Anxieties". *Journal of Personality*, 1955, **23**, 317–323.

Grossberg, J. M., & Wilson, H. K. A correlational comparison of the Wolpe-Lang Fear Survey Schedule and Taylor Manifest Anxiety Scale. *Behavior Research and Therapy*, 1965, **3**, 125–128.

Hilgard, E. R. Pain as a puzzle for psychology and physiology. *American Psychologist*, 1961, **24**, 103–114.

Homme, L. E., Csanyi, A. P., Gonzales, M. A., & Rechs, J. R. *How to use contingency contracting in the classroom*. Champaign, Ill.: Research Press, 1969.

Kanfer, F. H., & Phillips, J. S. *Learning foundations of behavior therapy*. New York: Wiley, 1970.

Keehn, J. D., Bloomfield, F. F., & Hug, M. A. Use of the Reinforcement Survey Schedule with alcoholics. *Quarterly Journal of Studies on Alcohol*, 1970, **31**, 602–615.

Kelley, G. A. Theory and techniques of assessment. *Annual Review of Psychology*. (Vol. 9) Palo Alto: Annual reviews, 1958.

Kleinknecht, R. A., McCormick, C. E., & Thorndike, R. M. Stability of stated reinforcers as measured by the Reinforcement Survey Schedule. Paper presented at the Annual Convention of the Association for Advancement of Behavior Therapy, Washington, D. C., September 1971.

Laing, R. D. *The politics of experience*. New York: Ballantine Books, 1967.

Lang, P. J., & Lazovik, A. D. Experimental desensitization of a phobia. *Journal of Abnormal and Social Psychology*, 1963, **66**, 519–525.

Lanyon, R. I., & Manosevitz, M. Validity of self-reported fear. *Behaviour Research and Therapy*, 1966, **4**, 259–263.

McReynolds, P., & Acker, M. On the assessment of anxiety: II. By a self-report inventory. *Psychological Reports*, 1966, **19**, 231–237.

Mermis, B. J. Self-report of reinforcers and looking time. Unpublished doctoral dissertation, University of Tennessee, 1971.

Mischel, W. *Personality and assessment*. New York: Wiley, 1968.

Mooney, R. L., & Gordon, L. V. *Manual: The Money problem check lists*. New York: Psychological Corporation, 1950.

Phillips, L., & Draguns, J. G. Classification of the behavior disorders. *Annual Review of Psychology*, 1971, **22**, 447–482.

Rathus, S. A. A thirty-item schedule for assessing assertive behavior. *Behavior Therapy*, 1973, **4**, 398–406.

Saslow, F., Counts, R. M., & Dubois, P. H. Evaluation of a new psychiatric screening test. *Psychosomatic Medicine*, 1951, XIII, 242–253.

Steffan, J. Covert reinforcement with hospitalized patients. Paper presented at the Annual Convention of the Association for Advancement of Behavior Therapy, Washington, D. C., September 1971.

Stevens, S. S. Matching functions between loudness and ten other continua. *Perception and Psychophysics*, 1966, **1**, 5–8.

Taylor, J. A. A personality scale of manifest anxiety. *Journal of Abnormal and Social Psychology*, 1953, **48**, 285–290.

Thomas, E. J. (Ed.). *Behavior modification procedure: A sourcebook*. Chicago: Aldine, 1974.

Tondo, T. R., & Cautela, J. R. Assessment of imagery in covert reinforcement. *Psychological Reports*, 1974, **34**, 1271–1280.

Walsh, W. B. Validity of self-report. *Journal of Counseling Psychology*, 1967, **14**, 18–23.

Walsh, W. B. Validity of self-report: Another look. *Journal of Counseling Psychology*, 1968, **15**, 180–186.

Willoughby, R. R. Norms for the Clark-Thurston Inventory. *Journal of Social Psychology*, 1934, **5**, 91–97.

Wisocki, P. A. A covert reinforcement program for the treatment of test anxiety. *Behavior Therapy*, 1973, **4**, 264–266.

Wolpe, J. *The practice of behavior therapy*. New York: Pergamon Press, 1969.

Wolpe, J., & Lang, P. J. A fear survey schedule for use in behavior therapy. *Behaviour Research and Therapy*, 1964, **2**, 27–30.

CHAPTER 5

Assessment for Self-Control Programs

ALAN S. BELLACK AND JEFFREY S. SCHWARTZ

University of Pittsburgh

Introduction

In an attempt to develop techniques applicable to naturally occurring behaviors of noninstitutionalized adult patients, behavior modifiers have increasingly turned to what Kanfer & Phillips (1966) have called "instigation therapies." Characteristically referred to as self-control (SC) strategies, these procedures involve the recruitment of the patient as the central force in his own treatment. The therapist serves primarily to instruct the patient in behavior theory and SC techniques, and to provide only as much external reinforcement as necessary to initiate and maintain the program. To this point, there has been sufficient clinical-empirical verification of the general SC approach that little question remains as to its clinical utility.

As with other new approaches, the major clinical research emphasis has been on validation of techniques and programs. A large number of techniques have been successfully applied to a wide variety of clinical problems. In contrast, there has been a dearth of material relative to the differential application or utility of the procedures. In reading the literature, one is left with the impression that SC is applicable for almost all non-psychotic patients and that once the clinician decides to use SC, success is guaranteed. As most workers in the area can attest, this picture is far from the truth. Self-control is not universally applicable and where it is, not all self-control procedures are equally effective. The clinician cannot simply *decide* to use an SC program, but must make a careful pre-treatment assessment in order to determine whether or not SC is the treatment of choice and, if so, how to apply it. It is considerably easier to generate faulty programs than effective ones. Familiarity with available techniques is not sufficient; programs must be *tailored* to individual patients.

Unfortunately, few guidelines are currently available to help the clinician conduct such an assessment. He is forced to rely on his general theoretical-clinical sophistication. The purpose of this paper is to provide a schema that can guide the assessment process. Much of what follows is based on our experience and research, and does not yet have strong empirical support. The emphasis will be on the questions that should be asked and issues that should be considered at various points in the assessment process. We will describe specific techniques that may be applicable wherever possible. The material will be divided into two sections, which represent the two major assessment considerations: (1) Is the target behavior amenable to an SC manipulation? (2) If so, what particular strategy, *if any*, is applicable for the individual patient?

Assessment of Target Behaviors

Initially, SC strategies were viewed as most applicable to behaviors which involved a conflict or disparity between immediate and long-term consequences. This category would include appetitive behaviors (e.g., eating, drinking, smoking) which have immediate positive consequences but delayed negative consequences, and such behaviors as studying which may be immediately aversive but ultimately positively reinforcing. Within the past few years, however, the SC approach has undergone a dramatic expansion in terms of the kinds of procedures utilized and the range of clinical disturbances seen as amenable to such interventions. Goldfried (1971) and Suinn & Richardson (1971) reconceptualized systematic desensitization as an SC procedure and suggested the use of muscle relaxation in vivo as a self-administered anxiety control technique. Meichenbaum (Meichenbaum, 1976; Meichenbaum & Cameron, 1974) has trained patients to emit controlling self-verbalizations, and D'Zurilla & Goldfried (1971) have described training in problem solving. Self-control strategies have also been applied to such problems as obsessions, self-mutilative behaviors, low self-esteem, depression, and hallucinations. As stated previously, however, the neophyte to the area has no road map to suggest why or when many of these techniques are to be applied.

In this section we will present some suggestions for the conceptualization and treatment of a variety of clinical problems in the context of SC. The focus will be behavioral dysfunctions which seem most consistent with an SC analysis, and for which SC techniques have been developed and elaborated. For each disorder we will present an SC conceptualization of etiology and maintenance, and an attempt will be made to present a suggested or typically employed treatment approach which reflects the various parameters of the problem. These proposed treatment programs are intended only as guidelines and not as the *sine qua non* for treatment of each dysfunction. (We hope to provide a demonstration of the SC approach, not an exhaustive survey).

Obesity

The behavior problem which has received the most attention in terms of the development of SC techniques has been weight control. Obesity is a major health problem in this country, affecting a large proportion of our population. As is the case with other appetitive problems, the reinforcement contingencies associated with eating do not promote restraint. Overeating has immediate positive consequences whereas the negative results (e.g., weight gain, impaired health) are generally much delayed. Similarly, dieting is aversive and the positive reinforcement for dietary restraint is often painfully delayed.

A second factor which contributes to the development and maintenance of obesity involves the relationship between eating and its situational determinants. Stimuli which are habitually associated with eating can become discriminative stimuli which will serve to initiate eating behaviors. For example, if an individual habitually eats while watching television, studying, or reading, these activities can gain a degree of control over the initiation of eating behavior. A wide variety of activities, situations, and emotional states can and do become associated with overeating. Some individuals, for example, tend to overeat primarily in social situations, others in the evening while studying or watching television, and for some people a variety of emotional states (e.g., anxiety, anger, depression, boredom) become discriminative stimuli for eating. A substantial body of research (see Schachter, 1971, for a review) suggests that the obese individual tends to be "stimulus bound." His eating behavior is thought to be controlled by external cues such as the availability of food, the sight, smell and taste of food, and the time of day, etc. In contrast, the eating behavior of individuals of normal weight occurs primarily in response to physiological hunger cues (i.e., gastric motility). Related to this issue of inappropriate stimulus control of eating is the lack of planning or intention involved in the time and amount of eating. Most obese individuals (are presumed to) eat in an automatic and impulsive manner and are often quite unaware of their actual consumption. Most overweight individuals substantially underestimate their actual caloric intake. At the beginning of treatment patients often maintain that they eat no more than friends or relatives who are slim. This often leads them to the mistaken conclusion that their problem is metabolic.

A number of SC strategies have been developed for the treatment of obesity. They all contain elements for the amelioration of the parameters of overeating outlined above: unfavorable reinforcement contingencies; external, situational control of eating; and inaccurate perception of consumption. Despite the generality of these factors, the particular patterns and problems of the obese patient are idiosyncratic. An individual analysis is therefore required. Self-monitoring (SM) is an invaluable tool for helping the patient and therapist arrive at a more accurate assessment of the patient's maladaptive eating patterns. The monitoring procedure involves the ongoing observation and recording of all eating behavior. The patient is generally instructed to keep a written record of all instances of eating as to time, place, form, amount, and caloric content of food consumed. Some therapists also ask the patient to record his emotional state at the time. Given the high frequency and relative invisibility (to the therapist) of eating, SM is the only way for the therapist to determine the patient's eating behavior, except in the rare instances in which an outside agent can be enlisted. The SM records should be carefully reviewed on an ongoing basis with a number of assessment questions in mind: Does the person tend to eat certain specific high calorie foods to excess? Does he generally eat excessively large portions? Does he tend to overeat at particular times of the day? Does he overeat in particular places or situations? Does he overeat with particular people? Are certain emotional states consistently associated with indulgence? Is his diet nutritionally sound? Does he get sufficient exercise? The therapist should be aware that SM has potentially reactive effects, and the records might therefore not accurately reflect pre-treatment eating behavior (Kazdin, 1974; Lipinski & Nelson, 1974). However, the reactive effects of SM appear to be shortlived and a return to baseline can be expected after a few weeks (Bellack, Glanz & Simon, 1976; Stuart, 1971).

The excessive control of eating by external determinants can be ameliorated through the use of stimulus control procedures (Bellack, Rozensky & Schwartz, 1974; Ferster, Nurnberger & Levitt, 1962; Schwartz & Bellack, 1975; Stuart, 1967,1971). Stimulus control procedures seek to make eating a "pure" behavior by dissociating it from other activities and situations. The patient is instructed to develop a routine schedule of eating, to eat in only one place (i.e., kitchen or dining room), and not to engage in other activities while eating. The availability of food (which is a powerful determinant of eating behavior for the obese) is modified by instruction to avoid bringing high calorie prepared foods into the house, to take small portions, to take only one portion at a time, to serve food from the kitchen, and to avoid placing serving platters on the table. The tendency to eat impulsively as a function of the mere presence of food is controlled by suggesting that the individual wait a fixed period after experiencing the urge to eat before actually eating, that he engage in an alternative pleasurable activity when confronted with the desire to snack, and that he set the table with a complete place setting *every* time he eats. Each stimulus control guideline will not necessarily be applicable or appropriate for each patient: only those that are relevant should be applied.

A third group of strategies have been employed to modify the balance of reinforcers associated with eating. Self-reinforcement (SR) techniques are used to provide more immediate positive reinforcement for dietary restraint and punishment for indulgence. The value of self-consequation seems particularly clear in the treatment of obesity. Eating is a behavior which occurs almost exclusively outside the therapist's presence. If appropriate remedial contingencies are to be applied, the patient himself is in an optimal position for systematic observation and reinforcement of the target behavior.

A typical procedure incorporates three stages. The individual is first instructed to monitor his behavior. The SM records serve as a basis for self-evaluation (SE), which involves comparing actual performance with some previously established performance criterion (e.g., comparing caloric consumption with a daily calorie intake goal). Some form of self-consequation is then provided contingent upon this evaluation. At this time, there is no general consensus on the optimal form of SE or SR. Self-evaluation for example, can be employed for each instance of eating. Bellack (1976) instructed clients to give themselves a written grade, (A, B, C, D, or F) for each instance of eating. Schartz & Bellack (1975) required subjects to evaluate themselves at the end of each day on the basis of their caloric intake and adherence to stimulus control guidelines. Similarly, a wide variety of reinforcers have been utilized including money (Jeffrey, 1974; Mahoney, 1974; Mahoney, Moura & Wade, 1973), cognitive imagery (Bellack *et al.*, 1976; Hall, 1972; Harris & Bruner, 1971; Harris & Hallbauer, 1973), and pleasurable high probability behaviors (Schwartz & Bellack, 1975). There is little empirical basis at this point for choosing from among these various SE and SR procedures. The decision should be made on an individual basis in terms of which technique seems most appropriate for a given patient. Further discussion of this issue will be provided below in the section concerned with assessment of the individual.

The most comprehensive program for weight reduction and weight control should include all of the techniques which have been discussed: SM, SE, SR, and stimulus control training. The initial phase of treatment is generally devoted to providing the patient with a veridical orientation to the behavioral theory of obesity and weight reduction and a one or two week period of SM. Assessment of current eating habits, as revealed by the SM records, then serves as a basis for the gradual introduction of appropriate stimulus control guidelines and SR techniques. We have also found it helpful to determine a daily calorie intake goal. This goal should be consistent with the requirements for gradual weight loss (1-2 pound/week) and should not place too severe a restriction on intake.

Most research reported in this area has involved brief treatment and follow-up periods (6-10 weeks each). The results for long term follow-up have not been very encouraging (Hall & Hall, 1974; Hall, Hall, Hanson & Borden, 1974), but this is not surprising in the light of the short treatment period generally employed. Although statistically significant weight losses can be achieved utilizing such brief treatment, it is likely that for clinically obese individuals, a much longer treatment period (perhaps 6-12 months) would be more efficacious.

Cigarette Smoking

Smoking is an appetitive problem which has much in common with obesity, but has received far less attention in terms of the development of SC interventions. As with overeating, the reinforcement contingencies associated with smoking do not promote restraint. For smokers, cigarette consumption is immediately reinforcing whereas its aversive consequences (e.g., increased risk of cancer and heart disease) are quite delayed. Similarly, resisting the urge to smoke is immediately aversive. The issue of situational control also applies to cigarette smoking. This behavior is generally associated with a wide range of social, environmental, and emotional stimuli. Naturalistic observation of smoking behavior reveals that it is generally related to a diverse variety of external determinants, including such activities as: drinking of coffee and alcohol, completion of a meal, reading, studying, watching television, engaging in social interactions, talking on the telephone, driving, etc. Emotional states (e.g., anxiety, depression, elation, relief) can also serve as discriminative stimuli which elicit smoking behavior. It has been suggested that smoking acquires secondary reinforcing properties through its association with other pleasurable activities (Nolan, 1968).

It can be seen that the factors maintaining smoking are in many ways parallel to those which promote overeating (i.e., unfavorable reinforcement contingencies, stimulus control). It is not surprising that an SC intervention for this behavior has much in common with a weight reduction program. Self-monitoring is employed to acquaint the patient and therapist with the former's pattern of smoking. Smokers are generally aware of the number of cigarettes they smoke on an average day, but SM can help to elucidate the situational determinants of smoking. An SM record for this behavior should probably include such parameters as time, place, situation, and emotional state. Patients can also be instructed to monitor each instance of resisting the urge to smoke (this can later be used as a basis for positive SR).

Stimulus control training should be aimed at restricting the number and range of situations associated with smoking in a manner analogous to that presented for overeating. For example, the patient can be instructed to gradually eliminate such patterns as smoking while drinking coffee, tea or alcohol; smoking while watching television or reading; smoking after meals, etc. Nolan (1968) reports an interesting example of such a procedure. The subject (his wife) was allowed to smoke only while sitting in a "smoking chair" and could not engage in other activities while smoking. Her rate of cigarette consumption dropped from 30/day to 12/day within 9 days. Cigarette consumption dropped to zero when the "smoking chair" was moved to the basement. The purpose of stimulus control training is to make smoking a "pure" act: independent of other activities. Smokers frequently report that smoking loses its appeal and, in fact, becomes boring when it is disassociated from other activities.

The unfavorable reinforcement contingencies associated with smoking should be modified by the introduction of remedial SR contingencies. As in the case of obesity, reinforcers should be selected on an individual basis after a thorough assessment of the patient's preferences and life style (see section on individual assessment). Any of a variety of possible positive reinforcers may be considered (e.g., money, cognitive imagery, pleasurable activities, etc.). Ober (1968) has reported that self-administered aversive contingencies were effective in reducing cigarette consumption. Subjects carried a portable shock device and self-administered a shock contingent on experiencing the desire for a cigarette. Homme (1965) has suggested an SR technique for smoking which seeks to modify attitudes about smoking. Pleasurable high probability behaviors (HPB's) are used as response contingent positive reinforcers to strengthen anti-smoking coverants (thoughts). The patient is instructed to compile a list of the long-term aversive consequences associated with smoking and to think of one of them just prior to engaging in a pleasurable HPB (e.g., drinking coffee).

A comprehensive treatment package for the reduction of cigarette smoking should include all the elements described: SM, stimulus control, and SR. After the initial assessment phase, stimulus control and SR should be gradually introduced. Initial (base rate) consumption level will be established via the client's SM records. At this point, the therapist might institute a daily consumption goal which begins just below the base rate level and is gradually reduced (e.g., at the rate of one cigarette every 3 days). Smoking at or below the goal level each day can be used as the criteria for SR. As stated earlier, resisting the urge to smoke can also be monitored and reinforced. As in the case with weight reduction, this sort of program seems ideally suited for group administration and (after the initial assessment and orientation phase) can probably be implemented with a minimum of the therapist's time. Relapse is a significant problem with this behavior (Hunt & Matarazzo, 1973). Treatment should probably be maintained, even at limited intensity for at least six months. Fading of therapist contact paired with periodic follow-up booster sessions are equally desirable.

Deficits in Work and Study Behaviors

A frequently encountered problem of either clinical or sub-clinical severity is so-called "underachievement" (i.e., functionally low levels or quality of performance in school or at work that are unrelated to intellectual ability or skill). Individuals reporting this difficulty frequently note that they simply lack the "will power" necessary to apply themselves to their work and that they are easily distracted. The problem may persist despite repeated failures and a variety of external pressures (e.g., spouse, parents, boss). This type of problem can also be conceptualized in terms of a behavioral SC perspective. The issue of the balance of reinforcers associated with this behavior is once again crucial. For most individuals, sitting down at a desk and spending hours studying or writing is quite aversive, and the payoffs are unfortunately quite delayed. While engaging in positively reinforcing behaviors (HBP's) is an obvious alternative that is frequently a problem, many individuals will engage in other behaviors that are mildly aversive in lieu of performing the highly aversive target behaviors.

The situational antecedents of study or work behaviors also seem crucial to an adequate understanding of this problem. Most individuals who report such problems are attempting to work under conditions which virtually eliminate the possibility of sustained concentration (e.g., studying while listening to the radio or watching television). Many such patients report that they work in an easy chair or while lying in bed, or if they do use a desk, it is situated in front of a window. Studying or working is often associated with such distracting activities as eating, drinking, or conversing with another individual in the room (Goldiamond, 1965).

Once again, treatment should be initiated with an assessment phase utilizing SM as a primary assessment device. The student should be instructed to record all instances of study behavior including time, place, work accomplished, situation, and which, if any, activities were engaged in simultaneously. In addition to its function for assessment, there is evidence that SM can have a reactive effect for the amelioration of study deficits. Johnson & White (1971) report that a group of college students instructed to simply monitor study time achieved significantly higher grade point averages than a nonmonitoring control group.

Stimulus control procedures are introduced to make work or studying independent of other (distracting) activities. The student, for example, should only study while sitting at a desk or table, in a quiet room free from distractions. This location should become a discriminative stimulus for studying. Therefore, it is important that he not engage in other activities at this desk (e.g., letter writing, eating, listening to music) even at times not reserved for studying. The student should be instructed that if he finds himself unable to work (e.g., if he is daydreaming) he should immediately get up from the desk and go to some other part of the house. Self-reinforcement procedures should be introduced to modify the balance of reinforcers associated with work behaviors. The range of possible reinforcers and the issue of individual assessment discussed in relation to obesity and smoking also pertains here.

Specific Symptom Disturbances

Reinforcement theory provides a relatively clear and plausible framework for conceptualizing the problems which have thus far been discussed. Overeating and smoking can clearly be maintained by the immediate positive consequences associated with these behaviors. Similarly, work and study deficits are promoted by reinforcement of incompatible behaviors. The practicing clinician, however, is confronted with an array of clinical problems for which an equally plausible reinforcement explanation does not present itself. We are referring here to a group of behavioral excesses which continue to persist despite the fact that they provide no obvious reinforcement to the patient, and in fact are generally experienced as quite aversive. These include such overt and covert behavioral excesses as compulsions, tics, various forms of self-multilation (e.g., scratching, hair pulling, eyebrow plucking, nail biting), and obsessions. The stubborn persistence of such problems often seems quite mystifying to the therapist and patient alike. Some behavioral theorists have suggested that such behaviors are reinforced by anxiety reduction (i.e., the individual often experiences acute discomfort if prevented from engaging in the behavior). However, as Bandura (1969) suggests, there are likely a variety of ways in which these behaviors can be developed and maintained.

Despite the lack of a definitive conceptualization framework, a number of clinicians have reported the successful application of SC strategies to the reduction or elimination of such behavioral excesses. The techniques which have been used (SM and SR) seek to: (1) increase the patient's awareness of the occurrence of the behavior; (2) provide the patient and therapist with a clearer understanding of the situational content in which the behavior is most likely to occur; and (3) increase response cost of engaging in the target behavior.

As is generally the case with SC interventions, the first phase should be a baseline-assessment period during which the patient is instructed to SM all occurrences of the target behavior. If the behavior occurs relatively infrequently, the individual can keep a complete written record of each occurrence as to time, place, situation, etc. If the target behavior occurs at high frequency such a recording procedure may be impossible. In that case the individual may be instructed to keep an hourly or daily cumulative total, or, if the frequency is high enough, to take time samples. A small pocket golf counter (generally available in sporting goods shops) is quite convenient for this purpose.

Aside from providing a baseline and a method for assessing the effects of an intervention, the SM records may facilitate a functional analysis of the target behavior. One frequent pattern involves occurrence of the behavior in response to stressful situations. The patient, for example, may seldomly or never engage in the behavior while alone, but may while at work or in social situations or while talking before a group. In most cases, however, a clear-cut relationship between a particular anxiety arousing situation and occurrence of the target behavior will not be apparent. The use of some form of self-conequation can, therefore, provide an alternative treatment approach. Before discussing SR techniques in this context, two issues related to the use of SM should be mentioned. *First*, there is reason to believe that SM may have particularly beneficial reactive effects in the treatment of these behavioral excesses. Such behaviors generally occur in a very automatic manner. Patients typically report that they are not aware of experiencing the intent to engage in the behavior, and are only aware after the entire behavioral chain has run off to completion. It is likely that SM will allow the individual to become more cognizant of the occurrence of the behavior and, therefore, be better able to control it.

Second, when used with behaviors (such as these) which occur at high frequency, SM can become a very repetitive and tedious chore. In this sense SM can function to increase the response cost of engaging in the target behavior and, therefore, decrease the probability of its occurrence. Similarly, SM of an undesirable behavior may serve as a discriminative stimulus for covert SE (negative) and SR. It is difficult, however, to draw any general conclusions as to the reactive effects of SM. Thomas and Abrams (1971) report that simple SM with therapist approval for low rates dramatically reduced the occurrence of vocal tics in a young male patient. Bayer (1972), however, reports that simple SM was not helpful in reducing the frequency of hair pulling. The reactivity of SM can only be determined on an individual, case by case basis. In the event that SM alone is effective, the therapist should be careful to continue assessment for a rather extended period as the reactive effects of SM may be only transient (Bellack *et al.*, 1976).

In most cases, the therapist will choose to employ some form of response contingent self-consequation. Self-reinforcement is well suited to these types of problems because the patient is in the best position to systematically observe such behavior. A variety of SR techniques have been reported as valuable in the reduction of behavioral excesses. One can employ negative (aversive) SR contingent on occurrence of the behavior or positive SR for low rates of occurrence or for engaging in behaviors antagonistic to the target response. Mahoney (1971) reported using aversive techniques with a 22-year-old, male patient who was troubled by persistent obsessions. After a baseline period (during which simple SM was not therapeutically beneficial) the patient was instructed to wear a heavy rubber band on his wrist, and snap it contingent on experiencing the obsessions. This procedure effectively extinguished the obsession according to the patient's report. This is an attractively simple technique, and certainly merits further clinical utilization and evaluation.

In terms of the use of positive SR, any of the techniques previously discussed may be used. The choice of a reinforcer must be based largely on individualized assessment. For illustrative purposes we will mention one report by Watson, Tharp & Krisberg (1972) which describes an innovative SC program designed by the patient. The patient was a student who was taking a course in SC techniques. She sufferred from neurodermatitis, a skin condition which was exacerbated by compulsive scratching. A program was designed in which she earned points for engaging in incompatible responses whenever she experienced an urge to scratch. Points could be used to purchase a powerful reinforcer (her daily bath). By the twentieth day of the program scratching had ceased and the rash had virtually disappeared. At 6, 12, and 18 month follow-ups, she reported only two brief recurrences, which were eliminated by reinstituting the program. This provides an excellent example of the manner in which patients can acquire the skill to serve as their own behavioral engineers, and even deal with relapses.

Depression and Low Self-esteem

Depression and self-depreciation are problems which occur with great frequency in virtually any clinical population. Marston (1965) and Bandura (1969) present essentially similar conceptualizations of these phenomena based upon SC theory. According to this view, SE and SR are learned behaviors, and as a function of divergent learning histories, marked individual differences can be expected in their typology. According to Marston and Bandura, individuals plagued by self-depreciation and depression tend to have excessively high standards for SE and consequently administer low rates of SR. Other behavioral theories of depression (Lewinsohn, 1975) also emphasize reinforcement problems (self or external) which are consistent with a self-control orientation.

A variety of SC techniques have been applied for enhancing self-esteem and the amelioration of depression. As one would expect, SM has been an integral component of such programs. Self-monitoring is generally employed to assess and record the frequency of covert SE's. The patient is instructed to tally (using a golf counter) or otherwise record instances of positive and/or negative thoughts about himself. Self-monitoring is also used to record the incidence of overt behaviors. MacPhillamy & Lewinsohn (1972) report that depressed psychiatric patients engage in significantly fewer pleasant activities than either nondepressed psychiatric patients or normal controls. Other investigators (Lewinsohn & Graf, 1973; Lewinsohn & Libet, 1972) report a significant correlation between mood state and the number and range of pleasant activities in which an individual engages. It would seem logical, therefore, that the therapist in treating a depressed patient would want to monitor and increase his participation in both pleasant and functional activities.

The most frequently reported SR technique, for promoting both positive covert SE and SR, as well as instrumental activity level, has involved utilization of the Premack Principle. Homme (1965), in his presentation of the coverant control paradigm (discussed earlier in relation to cigarette smoking), suggested that pleasurable HPB's might be used as response contingent positive reinforcers to increase the incidence of positive self-thoughts. Successful applications of this procedure for the treatment of depression have been reported by Hannum, Thoresen & Hubbard (1974), Mahoney (1971), and Todd (1972). In the Mahoney (1971) report, a 22-year-old patient with low self-esteem was instructed to write a number of positive self-statements on index cards, and to read one of them prior to smoking a cigarette (the HPB). The patient reported a subjective improvement in mood state and a number of beneficial behavioral changes. At a four month follow-up he had been able to leave his parent's home and had applied to college.

One example of a comprehensive SC program for depression is presented by Jackson (1972). This treatment followed Kanfer's three stage model of self-regulation, incorporating the techniques of SM, SE, and SR. The patient was a 22-year-old, married female who reportedly had been depressed for a number of years. At the time therapy was initiated the patient was depressed to the point of virtual immobility and was unable to complete even the simplest household chores. She was instructed to monitor her household activities, set performance goals, evaluate her performance, and reinforce herself for desirable behavior change. Self-praise and pleasurable HPB's were used as rewards. Jackson reported a significant reduction in the patient's self-rating of depression after only three weeks of treatment. Additional support for the efficacy of this approach to depression is provided by Fuchs (1975). In a controlled group study, depressed clients receiving a similar form of SC training (i.e., SM, SE, and SR) registered significantly greater gains than a matched control group which received non-directive, supportive psychotherapy. This appears to be a promising area of application for SC procedures. Initial enthusiasm should be tempered, however, pending further research. Durability of results is still uncertain, as is the number (or type) of depressed individuals for whom this approach is effective. Nevertheless, any success with depressed patients is notable.

We have focused in some detail on the SC conceptualization and treatment for a number of clinical problems. These disorders were selected as they were well represented in the literature. This is not meant to imply that these are the only problems for which SC interventions should be considered. Potential applications for a variety of additional clinical problems have been suggested by theorists and clinicians in the area including: marital discord (Goldiamond, 1965), dependency and deficits in problem solving (D'Zurilla & Goldfried, 1971), hallucinations (Bucher & Fabricatore, 1970), alcoholism (Sobell & Sobell, 1973), social anxiety (Rehm & Marston, 1968), and kleptomania (Epstein & Peterson, 1973). It would seem appropriate at this point to offer some general conclusions with regard to the types of problems that are or are not appropriate for SC. Our clinical experience and familiarity with the literature, however, make us reluctant to exclude virtually any target behavior or population from consideration. At this point the range of possible applications for SC interventions seems virtually limitless. Treatment programs for the disorders discussed have been clearly specified. Other populations have received little or no attention (e.g., psychotics, children, retardates, sociopaths, drug addicts). This is not to say, however, that the latter are not amenable to SC interventions. The SC approach is relatively new and largely unexplored. It is likely that in the near future, innovative researchers and clinicians wlil refine the existing strategies and discover a variety of additional applications.

Assessment of the Individual for Self-control

The discussion thus far has pertained to the applicability of SC strategies for the particular behavior problems manifested by the patient (i.e., can the target behavior be modified by SC procedures?). If the answer to that question is affirmative, a second question arises: Is SC the treatment of choice for this particular individual? The first question is comparatively easy to answer. The behavioral literature has described and evaluated a number of SC procedures for the modification of a wide variety of behaviors. Following identification of the target behavior, reference to this literature can provide a good indication of the treatment of choice. (Subsequent chapters will, however, demonstrate the complexity of identifying target behaviors.) In contrast, there is no existing resource for answering the second question. The existence of individual differences in the utilization of SC procedures (and their assessment) has been given scant attention in the literature. Because of the exigencies of empirical investigations, most studies employing group treatment have recruited subjects on the basis of target behavior criteria and assigned subjects to groups at random. Similarly, clinical reports have emphasized target behaviors and treatment techniques to the virtual exclusion of treatment planning considerations. The general assumption that patients come to treatment with similar skills or stylistic patterns, and that they are therefore equally susceptible to treatment manipulations, has been referred to by Kiesler (1966) as the "Patient Uniformity Myth." His admonition that treatment be matched to patient characteristics is highly relevant to SC based treatment procedures. In conducting SC programs one is struck by the high degree of variability among patients. Some individuals follow programs faithfully, while others simply do not employ the procedures regularly or contingently, regardless of the simplicity of the demands. The procedures are effective for most patients who employ them as directed, but some require other forms of intervention (e.g., therapist management).

The most probable explanation for these phenomena is that there are individual differences in ability and/or inclination to effectively utilize SC techniques. The major theoretical conceptualizations of SC all emphasize that SC behaviors are learned (Bandura, 1969; Kanfer, 1971; Thoresen & Mahoney, 1974). This contention is supported by numerous analogue studies. Bandura and his colleagues (Bandura, Grusec & Menlove, 1967; Bandura & Kupers, 1964; Bandura & Whalen, 1966) have demonstrated the importance of modeling in the development of SC. Model characteristics, the model-subject relationship, and model behavior have all been shown to affect SE and the administration of SR. Kanfer and his colleagues (Dorsey, Kanfer & Duerfeldt, 1971; Kanfer & Duerfeldt, 1968; Marston & Kanfer, 1963) have shown that the SC responses of adults are similarly affected by prior experience. Given the idiosyncratic nature of learning histories, it would not be surprising to find substantial individual differences in SC behavior.

Bellack (1975) and Bellack & Tillman (1974) have provided examples of the nature of such differences. Subjects in both studies were presented with a verbal recognition memory test. Thirty nonsense syllables were presented (on slides) one at a time, for one second each. After a brief rest period, 30 sets of three nonsense syllables were presented one at a time for five seconds each. One syllable on each slide had appeared on the original list; the subjects' task was to identify that syllable. Recognition accuracy for college populations is about 50–60%. Subjects in the Bellack & Tillman (1974) study were instructed to evaluate each response (SE) and administer self-reward (SR+) if they thought they were correct. SR+ consisted of a button press that illuminated a small orange lamp. No veridical feedback about accuracy was provided, placing the responsibility for SE and SR entirely on the "subjective" standard of the subjects. The number of reinforcements administered ranged from 0–20 (maximum possible was one per trial for a total of 30). More important than the range of SR's administered is the finding that the relationship between SR and number of correct responses was not significant. The ratio of SR's to correct responses ranged from 0–135.7. Since there were no cues available, these results do not reflect differential perception of stimulus factors. Rather, they reflect major differences in SE and SR behavior. The Bellack (1975) study involved the same memory task with several additions to the SE and SR procedure. Subjects were instructed to quantify their SE by assigning it a score from 0–10. Some subjects were also given the option of applying self-punishment (SP) after poor guesses. Self-punishment consisted of a button press that sounded a shrill tone and advanced a counter labeled "Incorrect" (a "Correct" counter was included for SR+). Once again the range of SR+ responses was extensive (5–30) and unrelated to recognition accuracy. The range of SP responses was similarly broad (2–23) and unrelated to accuracy. Self-punishment was to follow responses which the subject was confident were incorrect. It is interesting that any SP was administered given that the chance of being correct was one in three even on a blind guess. The mean SE scores ranged from 2.7 to 8.9 (again unrelated to accuracy). The mean SE after which an SR+ was administered ranged from 5.0 to 10.0, and the mean SE after which an SP was administered ranged from 1.0 to 5.5. As a final note, both studies compared the performance of Internal and External Locus of Control subjects. Externals gave themselves significantly lower SE's and were more dependent upon external input for their evaluation than Internals. These results provide strong support for the contention that substantial differences exist in SC skills and/or styles. Self-evaluative criteria and criteria for administration of SR (SR+ and SP) vary between individuals. The nature of information required to allow for SE also apparently varies.

As described above, SC treatment programs consist primarily of sets of instructions. The patient is expected to implement the procedures at his own initiative, with minimal guidance or control by the therapist. However, the existence of individual differences in SC repertoires suggests that not all patients will have equal success in applying the techniques. Schwartz & Bellack (1975), for example, found considerable variability in the extent to which subjects in a weight control program followed SE and SR instructions. Degree of application was significantly (positively) correlated with weight loss.

The need for careful evaluation of individual resources in this area is critical if treatment is to be successful. It should be recognized that the question is not simply whether the individual is capable of using SC. Kanfer (1975) has emphasized that SC programs can involve training in the use of SC and shaping of responses. Furthermore, SC and external control are not discrete, mutually exclusive elements, but exist on a continuum. The relative balance of self- and external control or consequation in a program can be tailored to meet individual needs and preferences. Assessment is needed to determine the extent of training and the relative degree of external control necessary for maximal results.

Motivation and Commitment

The question of whether or not SC is the treatment of choice can be divided into two secondary questions: (1) Can the patient apply the specified procedures? (2) Are the procedures effective when they are applied? The former question is based on the observation that some individuals do not follow program directions on a regular or contingent basis. Problems we have encountered include incomplete monitoring records, failure to administer SR, and monitoring or reinforcing on a delayed basis (e.g., before therapy sessions rather than when the targeted behavior occurs). This question subsumes a number of factors including motivation, commitment, and skill or ability. Inappropriate application probably represents the most frequent reason for failure of SC programs. In addition, it is likely that when procedures are ineffective, the patient ceases to apply them as directed. While resolution of the second question is important, the latter factor makes it exceedingly difficult to answer the second question independently of the first.

A widely considered factor in assessing the likelihood that instructions will be followed is "motivation." This term is loosely defined and typically refers to the patient's inclination to change (e.g., lose weight, quit smoking). Numerous self-report devices have been developed to assess the strength or breadth of the desire to change. The ability of these devices to predict success in treatment has been uniformly disappointing (see Bellack *et al.*, 1974, for an example). This result is not entirely surprising. All patients *voluntarily* coming for treatment can be presumed to desire change. This desire is not sufficient to generate change, and it is not predictive when considered in isolation. Factors that are more relevant in predicting (determining) change include: level of current distress, amount of distress or difficulty accompanying therapeutic procedures, expectations about the possibility of change, and the value of change (in terms of reduced distress and/or other reinforcement). If, for example, the distress associated with being overweight is less than the distress associated with a six month diet, or if the patient does not believe that weight loss will be reinforced (or reinforcing), a diet will not be followed regardless of the current level of distress. Alternatively, regardless of how strong the desire to lose weight, an individual will not diet if the diet is more aversive than his current weight. An alternative to the motivation construct which subsumes several of these factors is subjective expected utility (S.E.U.) (Mausner, 1973). S.E.U. relates current desire to change with the expected utility of change. Mausner (1973) has developed a self-report inventory to assess the S.E.U. of cigarette smoking and of non-smoking. Each item consists of three parts: a value statement relative to continuing to smoke (e.g., How much do you care about getting bronchitis ?), the expectation that the outcome would occur if smoking continued, and the expectation that the outcome would occur if smoking were not continued. The S.E.U. for smoking is determined by multiplying each value score by the associated expectancy for changing behavior and for continuing current behavior. The second product is subtracted from the first, and an overall total tabulated. The higher the score, the greater the value (S.E.U.) of behavior change. Note that the S.E.U. is a joint function of the value of possible outcomes *and* expectation that the outcomes will be achieved. If, for example, you do not believe *you* will get cancer, you will not value nonsmoking. Mausner (1973) reported that individuals able to quit smoking have higher S.E.U.'s for not smoking than those unable to quit, but the groups do not differ on S.E.U. for smoking (both before and after treatment). That is, both quitters and non-quitters value smoking, but only quitters see some positive result for not smoking. Assessment of S.E.U. accounts for more information and appears to be a more promising approach than assessment of motivation *per se*.

Another variation of the motivation construct is *psychological commitment*. Marston & Feldman (1972) described SC as a two component process consisting of a cognitive set (commitment) and specific self-controlling behaviors. The cognitive set includes such factors as attitudes, values, motivation, and expectancy. Commitment is viewed as a necessary factor if self-control responses are to be made. Marston and Feldman emphasized the importance of assessing commitment prior to treatment. However, their conceptualization does not provide specific behavioral referents that would allow for adequate assessment. Commitment and the factors underlying it (such as attitudes and motivation) are constructs which place primary emphasis for evaluation on self-report and retrospective inference. While the construct has face validity, it cannot be pragmatically useful unless concrete, assessable referents (i.e., an operational definition) are described.

Kanfer & Karoly (1972) also referred to commitment as a critical factor in SC. They conceive of commitment as a set of vocalized or cognized intention statements. These statements are defined as verbal operants, which include performance criteria and provisions for self- or externally-generated consequation for meeting (or failing to meet) the criteria. The commitment is essentially a contract in which the individual agrees to perform a certain response (or reach a goal). The terms of the contract include reinforcement for complying with the terms and/or penalties for failure to comply. Commitment is not simply a set of cognitions, it is a function of reinforcement that may include associated cognitions. Whether or not a patient becomes and remains committed is a function of the resolution of all sources of reinforcement currently experienced and expected in regard to the target behavior. Relevant reinforcers include SR and social reward or censure for fulfilling or failing to fulfill the contract, aversiveness of requisite responses, and value of expected rewards for reaching goals. The construct thus defined offers several advantages to those discussed previously. Rather than placing emphasis on a non-operational cognitive process, the contracting approach focuses on parameters that can be objectively evaluated (e.g., performance criteria and reinforcement). These two factors can be assessed *prior* to treatment and used for planning.

This concept is also useful for modifying faulty programs. Rather than explaining away failure by post hoc inference of a lack of motivation or commitment (which offers little guidance for modification), the therapist can re-evaluate performance criteria in terms of the patient's skills and the level of reinforcement provided. The factors that commonly contribute to program failure include the following:

1. *The specific intention statements:* Are goals and criteria realistic? Does the patient have an expectation that goals can be reached? Does the patient agree with the goals and their relationship to his referral complaint?
2. *The components of the program:* Does the patient have a clear understanding of what the component responses are and how to apply them? Does the patient agree that performing the component responses is necessary? Can the patient perform the requisite responses?

3. *The consequation involved in the program:* Are the consequences that prompted referral still applied (e.g., physical aversiveness of current state, spouse pressure for change, self-criticism, etc.)? What is the relative aversiveness of the treatment target and the treatment program (e.g., being overweight vs dietary restraint)? What is the value of reinforcement applied (or anticipated) for performing component responses and for failing to perform component responses (e.g. specific instance of eating in a weight reduction program)? What is the value of reinforcement contingent upon reaching goals?

The two fundamental parameters of commitment should become apparent from reading this list. *First*, as stated previously, commitment to a program is a function of the balance of the reinforcement expected and experienced in relation to the program. The greater the reinforcement value of following a program relative to not following it, the greater the commitment. *Second*, commitment is constantly changing as a function of shifts in reinforcement value. For someone attempting to lose weight, food is a much more potent reinforcer, and commitment to dieting is much less immediately before eating than after eating or while engaged in an activity incompatible with eating. The reduction in spouse pressure after a treatment program begins may reduce the patient's inclination to change. Pre-treatment assessment, therefore, will not necessarily continue to reflect the level of commitment after treatment has begun. Assessment must be an ongoing process in which the clinician is sensitive to variations in the sources and magnitude of reinforcements.

Assessment for Specific Program Components

Our discussion to this point has focused on general considerations. The therapist should attend to these issues during the initial stages of the therapeutic interaction in order to form a general picture of the applicability of SC procedures. However, prior to formally constructing and initiating a specific treatment plan, a more detailed assessment must be conducted. As with any behavioral treatment, the first step is a definition and functional analysis of the target behavior. The strategies and procedures for such an analysis are no different for SC programs than for other approaches. In addition to that analysis, SC programming requires evaluation of a number of other factors that are more or less specific to SC. The subsequent sections of this paper will focus on assessment questions and strategies relevant to specific components of SC programs.

Stimulus control. Procedures included under the rubric of stimulus control include a variety of self-generated environmental modifications. One form of manipulation involves response prevention. Examples are placing cigarettes in a locked box with a timer, not purchasing cigarettes or high caloric food items, not walking on the street where a favorite bar is located. These techniques are designed to prevent the occurrence of the target behavior when ability to control or abstain is low (i.e., the relative reinforcement value of indulging is high) by altering the environment at a time when ability to control is high (i.e., the relative reinforcement value of indulging is low). As discussed above, commitment and the ability to self-control vary over time, and this approach takes advantage of the variation. This form of behavioral control is sometimes differentiated from SC as it does not involve a conflict situation and no control is necessary once the initial response is made. The term SC is reserved for situations in which the controlling response (e.g., abstinence, SR) is made when the response to be controlled (e.g., smoking, eating) is of high valence. A second form of stimulus control involves restriction of the form or circumstances in which the target behaviors occur. Examples include limitations on the location in which the behavior can occur (e.g., smoking only in one chair, eating only in the dining room), the times at which it can occur (smoking or eating at fixed intervals), and the form in which it can occur (e.g., smoke without inhaling, set a complete place setting for any instance of eating). Rather than preventing the target response from occurring, these techniques are designed to modify their reinforcement value and bring them under the control of a narrower range of stimuli. This approach is considered to be SC, as the controlling response actually occurs when the response to be controlled is focal. Stimulus control (of one form or the other) is common to almost all SC programs. Several factors must be considered in applying either form of manipulation.

Preliminary evaluation of the target behavior should determine whether or not the use of stimulus control procedures is desirable or necessary. They are characteristically appropriate when: (a) the intermediary or overall goals are increase or reduction in frequency of a response; (b) when the target behavior is under the control of inappropriate discriminative stimuli; and (c) when appropriate discriminative stimuli do not control the behavior.

The use of stimulus control in the first situation could involve shaping, fading, or stimulus narrowing. This is characteristic of treatment for cigarette smoking, in which the range of stimuli under which smoking is permitted is gradually decreased. An example of the second situation is overweight. Schacter (1971) has hypothesized that the eating behavior of overweight individuals is highly controlled by environmental stimuli such as the sight of food and time of day. Weight reduction programs, therefore, emphasize reduction of situations in which eating occurs. The third situation often exists with insomniacs. They eat, read, watch television, and ruminate in bed; getting into bed is, therefore, not a stimulus for sleep.

Once it is determined that stimulus control is appropriate, a specific set of control techniques must be selected. There are usually numerous techniques that have some applicability, and the inclination is to present a set to the patient. This practice is rarely appropriate. During early stages of a program the patient will not be effective in following a large set of instructions. If presented with such a set, he will probably follow all only partially or select the easiest (and therefore the least important). The therapist must determine which procedures he wants followed and the most desirable number and sequences of procedures to be applied. There is a considerable amount of variability in the ease with which the techniques can be applied. Dieters characteristically report little difficulty in setting an eating schedule and taking one helping at a time, but experience considerable difficulty eating in only one place and engaging in no other activities while eating. They also follow the procedures to varying degrees. Difficulty level is a function of the individual's skills, the tediousness and complexity of the requirements, salience of cues (e.g., whether the patient is reminded to follow the procedure), and reinforcement.

The most effective approach for evaluating the patient's ability to follow any directive is an *in vivo* practice period. Focal situations or techniques should be ranked in order of importance to the program. For example, eating on schedule is probably more important for an impulsive eater than eating slowly or taking one helping at a time. The patient's subjective evaluation of difficulty should then be determined. The program should then be applied (for a few days or a week) sequentially, one element at a time, under observations (e.g., self- or spouse-monitoring). Patient report and monitoring data should both be used to evaluate performance, make necessary modifications, and determine when the next component can be added. The sequence of application should be based on importance to the program and likelihood of success. Periodic re-assessment should continue throughout treatment to guard against the gradual erosion of response adequacy.

Self-monitoring. Self-monitoring should be included in all SC programs. Self-modification of any form requires awareness of the environment and one's own behavior. Most individuals are able to account for their experiences on a general level (e.g., Did you smoke today? Did you study in the evening?). However, they are not sufficiently in touch with specific ongoing events to plan and implement behavior change strategies (e.g., How *many* cigarettes? How many puffs? What were the situations?). Self-monitoring provides an excellent vehicle for securing such information prior to treatment and maintaining the patient's awareness of his behavior during treatment. The latter consequence of SM is critical if procedures are to be followed immediately and contingently.

Despite the seeming simplicity of the SM procedure (e.g., keep a record of your eating behavior), this is one of the most problematic components of SC treatment. Two major difficulties are frequently encountered. First, a great number of patients do not regularly provide records of the desired form, based on ongoing monitoring. The most blatant violations are repeated failures to bring records to treatment sessions (typically explained by "I did them but forgot to bring them."). Other problems include production of narratives rather than specific records, and presentation of partial or incomplete data (often compiled retrospectively). The second major problem is validity of monitoring. Kazdin (1974) and Lipinski & Nelson (1974) have demonstrated that SM records are not highly accurate. It seems likely that this conclusion is more valid for some behaviors (e.g., high frequency, subtle, or covert behaviors such as tics, thoughts) than others (e.g., low frequency instrusive behaviors like time spent studying). Nevertheless, these findings suggest that caution be used in interpreting SM data.

A number of factors contribute to the relative difficulty involved in securing regular and valid records. SM is frequently tedious and difficult, requiring regular interruptions in the natural sequence of activity and thought. It is also potentially embarassing if the recording process is visible in interpersonal situations. Both of these problems are increased when recording must be descriptive rather than a simple tally or frequency count. Self-monitoring may also become aversive by forcing the patient to be aware of undesirable behavior or breach of contract. Individuals also differ in the extent to which they are characteristically aware of their own behavior and, therefore, the ease with which they can follow SM instructions. It is somewhat of a paradox that one must covertly SM in order to determine when a target behavior or situation occurs for which overt SM is required. Some individuals fail to monitor (overtly) because they do not monitor (covertly).

This specification of problems inherent in the use of SM suggests that SM must be a *target of assessment* as well as a technique for assessment. Whenever possible, the accuracy of monitoring records should be cross-validated. Third parties (e.g., spouse, room-mate) can sometimes be enlisted to make independent observations. In rare instances, such as inpatient settings, observations can be made by an agent of the therapist. When the target behavior occurs during treatment sessions (e.g., speech disfluencies, tics), the patient can be instructed to SM during sessions and the therapist can make independent observations. These procedures all presume that the target behavior is overt and can be observed by others. When the target behavior is covert or occurs out of the view of others (e.g., sexual behavior), a different approach is obviously necessary. A gross indication of general self-observational behavior can be garnered by comparing the patient's initial retrospective reports with objective data or initial SM records (the reactivity of SM should be kept in mind here) (e.g., Lipinski & Nelson, 1974). Another approach is to identify a non-clinical target behavior that can be self-monitored and observed by the therapist or others. If task factors are similar (e.g., rate and intrusiveness of behavior), accuracy of such neutral monitoring can be presumed to have some correspondence to the probable accuracy of the clinical monitoring.

In all cases, the purpose of the assessment is to compare monitored records with some external source of data about the behavior. This comparison can provide some indication of the patient's ability and inclination to follow instructions in general as well as to SM effectively. If it appears that the SM instructions are not being followed adequately, it is unwise to advance to the next stage of the program. *First*, treatment cannot be planned effectively without valid data. *Second*, SM provides an excellent behavioral test for the prediction of instruction-following. If monitoring instructions are not followed, it is likely that subsequent instructions will not be implemented properly. As with other program components, training, shaping, simplification of instructions and requirements, and some form of consequation (e.g., interpersonal censure and approval) are all possible procedures for remediation.

Self-evaluation. The second stage of the SC sequence is self-evaluation (SE). It involves comparing performance with some criterion in order to determine the adequacy of the response. The criteria for evaluation may be internally generated or established by some external agent. The nature of the evaluation can range from simple determination that a desired or undesired behavior occurred to a multiple appraisal of a variety of response components (e.g., evaluating a meal on the basis of calories, eating form, and daily and weekly goals). The process of SE presumes that some data (loosely defined) have been provided. In SC programs, the source of data will ordinarily be SM. As with SM, there are two major difficulties encountered with SE. The first involves the occurrence of SE: Will the patient evaluate regularly at appropriate times? This question is not as critical as the corollary question about the occurrence of SM. The major difficulties associated with monitoring (e.g., tediousness, complexity, embarrassment) are not manifest with SE. If the patient monitors as directed, it is highly probable that he will also SE.

The second and more critical question pertains to the nature of the evaluation. As was discussed earlier, there are substantial individual differences in self-evaluative behavior (Bellack, 1975) (A more detailed discussion of one particular evaluative difficulty will be presented in Chapter 9 on Depression). Patients will not all respond similarly to an instruction for SE, or evaluate similarly given the same objective quality of performance. The therapist must be aware of the criteria the patient uses and his ability to compare behavior with those criteria. A related issue is the patient's ability to adopt therapist generated criteria if treatment so requires. In assessing SM behavior, a major concern is the failure to monitor and/or to monitor accurately. Assessment of SE must consider the patient's evaluative *style* (e.g., characteristic performance expectancies) and *goals* (e.g., what does he consider to be acceptable behavior) as well as his deficits. A set of performance criteria might be entirely reasonable and appropriate for the patient and yet, as a function of inadequate communication (assessment), conflict with the therapist's expectations for treatment.

Difficulties with the SE component of treatment most often center around two facets: (1) the pool of information upon which evaluative criteria are based; and (2) the stringency of the criteria. The establishment of realistic performance criteria requires some objective information about the parameters of the target behavior. Relevant data include norms, individual capabilities, medical restrictions, and environmental-physical factors. For example, the patient attempting to lose weight should be aware of the caloric values of foods, the relationship between caloric intake, energy expenditure, and weight loss, nutrition, and numerous medical (health) considerations. An individual with a sexual disorder should be aware of the conformation and range of non-pathological functioning, physiology of the sexual response, and factors affecting development and performance of the sexual response. Most treatment programs provide a considerable amount of this type of material during the initial stages of treatment. However, presentation of such objective "trivia" to an anxious patient seeking an explanation and "cure" for his problem is not necessarily sufficient. The degree to which such information is mastered by the patient should be a target of assessment, *before* and *after* the information is provided.

Possession of relevant information is necessary but not sufficient to guarantee appropriate SE. In some instances, it is possible to select criteria that are entirely objectified and not subject to interpretation. Number of cigarettes allowed per day is an example. Once a contract is established between the therapist and patient, the SE is fixed. In most situations, however, the criteria that the patient establishes are essentially subjective (e.g., adequacy of an interpersonal response or a diet meal). They may or may not be based on an accurate, realistic appraisal of the information provided. Factors affecting selection of evaluation criteria include personal style, expectancies, fear, and social pressure. They can be so stringent that no response is seen as adequate (e.g., as in depression) or so lenient that no responses are considered inadequate. Bellack (1975) has pointed out that for some individuals (external locus of control) evaluative criteria are highly dependent upon external input; criteria employed by individuals under that constraint are apt to be highly variable and the evaluations would lack conviction. Whenever possible, criteria should be made entirely objective: occurrence—nonoccurrence of responses, rate and frequency of responses, and detailed definition of acceptable variations are typical forms of objectification.

When such an approach is not possible, quantification of subjective evaluations is desirable for both assessment and implementation. Likert scaling is useful in this regard. For example, we have required weight reduction patients to rate each meal they eat on a five point scale (1 = terrible diet meal, 5 = excellent meal) and record the ratings on their SM records. The ratings are based on an overall evaluation of caloric value of the meal, time and form of eating, daily caloric goals, and eating habit guidelines. Ratings could be made on each specific component or on the entire day's eating if desired. While the numerical values are still subjective, they offer a degree of objectification to an otherwise invisible (e.g., cognitive) and entirely subjective process. As such, they provide the therapist with a concrete representation which can be related to the objective parameters of the target response. Consistently high or low evaluations as well as specific errors can be identified, and training can be provided as needed. This procedure can be conducted in a role-playing format prior to the initiation of treatment. In that context, the therapist describes a series of potential situations in which the target behavior might occur, paired with a number of possible target responses varying in quality. The patient role plays or imagines the scenario and makes a numerical evaluation of the response. The evaluations can be appraised in a manner analogous to the retrospective examination of monitoring records. Both information deficits and inappropriate criteria can be identified in this manner.

The procedures described above are useful for examining relatively specific self-evaluative responses in restricted contexts. This degree of specificity is characteristically desirable for individual treatment planning. There are circumstances (e.g., group treatment, preliminary screening, troubleshooting faulty programs) in which more general assessment is appropriate. One approach for assessing general self-evaluative style was described by Bellack (1975). The procedure involves a verbal recognition memory test on which minimal performance feedback is available (see previous sections of this chapter for a more extensive description). Quantitative SE's are secured after each response and an overall SE score is calculated. This score can provide a general indication of stringency of evaluative criteria. While adequate norms are not yet available, scores of 1, 2, and 3 (low SE) and 9 and 10 (high SE) appear to be extreme. A critical aspect of this technique is that performance feedback is minimized so that SE is based on subjective criteria. Other tasks maintaining this aspect may be substituted for the memory task. The next section of this chapter will describe some clinically relevant empirical results using a related assessment procedure.

A final note should be added about Rotter's (1966) Locus of Control Scale. Bellack (1975) and Bellack & Tillman (1974) both found that individuals with external locus of control were highly reliant upon external input for SE. In the absence of such input, they were hesitant and conservative with their evaluations. These results suggest that externals would have difficulty in self-evaluating in vivo, under stressful conditions. Caution is therefore advised in emphasizing subjective evaluative criteria with externals (a conservative cutoff score on the IE scale is 15). This hypothesis and the clinical use of the IE scale in this regard should be explored further.

Self-reinforcement. The final stage in the SC sequence is SR. As Kanfer (1970) has conceptualized the SC process, the individual first monitors performance then compares it to some criterion, and based on that evaluation either self-rewards, self-punishes, or refrains from reinforcement. The SR processes are presumed to function analogously (and equivalently) to external reinforcement in maintaining or modifying behavior. SR can take any of a number of forms including concrete items (e.g., money, clothing), activities, covert products (e.g., imagery), and symbols (e.g., grades, points). The major assessment issues relative to SR pertain to whether or not the procedures will be applied as directed and whether or not the reinforcement will have the desired effect (e.g., have reinforcing properties).

To this point, we have described the assessment process as if it consisted of a series of discrete and potentially sequential steps. In fact, many questions can be answered simultaneously or make other questions superfluous. This is especially true with regard to whether or not the patient will follow SR instructions. Several of the factors relevant to this question will have been considered in evaluation of previous issues. These include commitment, stylistic preference, regularity and accuracy of SM, and appropriateness of SE. If the patient expresses reluctance to follow an SC program, has negative expectancies about such a program, is not experiencing distress, or does not adequately complete preliminary SM homework assignments, any questions about SE and SR are moot. Conversely, if the preliminary assessment indicates that SC is appropriate and that the patient can use stimulus control, SM and SE, the liklihood of SR being applied appropriately is high. At that point a more detailed assessment relative to factors specific to SR is required.

One such factor is the degree to which the patient characteristically applies SR. As discussed above, there is considerable variability in the tendency to administer self-reward and self-punishment (Bellack, 1975; Bellack & Tillman 1974). This variability suggests that not all individuals will respond equally well to programs requiring the administration of SR. Assessment of characteristic SR behavior or style, therefore, has potential utility for predicting response to SC treatment. Bellack & Rozensky (1976) administered the previously described recognition memory task to volunteers for a weight reduction program. They instructed subjects to administer SR for their responses, and classified subjects as high or low self-reinforcers based on a *median split* of SR scores (number administered per 30 trials). The median score was 21. High SR subjects lost more weight (although the difference did not reach statistical significance) than low SR subjects in an SC program. The reverse was true for an external control program (therapist controlled financial contingencies for weight loss). In fact, high SR subjects *lost no weight* during the course of the external control program.

The SC program in that study did not include explicit instructions for the use of SR. In a subsequent study Bellack *et al.* (1976) compared high and low self-reinforcers in a weight reduction program that involved the use of covert imagery as a reinforcer. A time estimation test consisting of 20 trials and intervals averaging 10 seconds was administered prior to treatment. Subjects were instructed to evaluate their estimates and reinforce themselves by writing a letter grade on a record sheet after each trial. It was presumed that grades were secondary reinforcers for most individuals. An SR score was calculated for each subject by converting the grades to numerical scores (A = 4, B = 3, etc.) and calculating the average score per trial. Subjects were again classified as high or low self-reinforcers by a median split. The median score was 3.0 (equivalent to a B). High SR subjects lost almost twice as much weight during treatment as low SR subjects. They continued to lose weight during the follow-up period while low SR subjects began regaining the small amount of weight they had lost. The differences between high and low reinforcers is especially noteworthy given that the groups were classified on the basis of a simple median split. Even greater differences might have been found if more extreme groups were compared.

The results of these two studies provide strong support for this approach to pre-treatment assessment. At this point, however, these techniques are more useful for general, pragmatic evaluation of SC behaviors than for resolution of specific SR questions. There is still some question about exactly what the tasks are actually measuring. Possible factors include self-evaluative style, tendency to administer SR, ability to use SR, or simply cooperation with the therapist's instructions (e.g., administer SR). The specific relationship between the test responses and treatment behavior is also uncertain at this point. Do high SR individuals follow instructions for SR more effectively? Is SR a greater source of reinforcement for them than it is for lows? Further examination of the procedures relative to these questions, collection of normative data, and experimental clinical application are all warranted.

We have been considering the question of whether or not SR procedures will be applied appropriately. A related question is whether or not the use of explicit SR techniques is necessary or desirable. Bellack & Rozensky (1976), Bellack *et al.* (1974), Romanczyk (1974), and Romanczyk *et al.* (1974) have all demonstrated that behavior change programs emphasizing SM rather than SR can be effective. While there also are some contradictory data (e.g., Bellack, 1976), it does appear that for some individuals SM instructions are sufficient to stimulate behavior change. These findings (and parallel results from analogue studies) suggests that SM is reactive, but do not exclude the possibility that covert, unsystematic SE and SR occur subsequent to SM. It is somewhat implausable that a clinical patient observing some change in his target behavior (e.g., studying for an increased period, not smoking in response to an urge) would not evaluate this behavior and administer positive or aversive self-statements and thoughts. It is also probably impossible to resolve this issue as the processes are covert and fleeting. Therefore, the assessment issue is not whether or not SR is appropriate, but whether or not it is necessary to impose explicit SR procedures. If there is an indication that behavior change is possible without the use of explicit procedures, they should not be applied. *First*, therapeutic strategy suggests that the least complicated yet effective intervention should be employed. Adding complicated procedures where they are not required is more likely to have negative than positive effects. *Second*, our experience indicates that many individuals find explicit SR procedures to be tedious, childish, and "gimmicky." A considerable amount of treatment time and false starts are often necessary to modify that attitude. It is, therefore, clinically appropriate to leave it unchallenged when behavior can be changed in other ways (e.g., SM and inexplicit SR).

All of the issues addressed thus far have been considered in terms of self-reinforcement as a unitary process. In actual practice, a more segmental analysis is appropriate. Self-reward and self-punishment behaviors have been found to be relatively independent (Bellack & Simon, 1976; Kanfer & Duerfeldt, 1968). Therefore, a patient capable of applying self-reward effectively will not necessarily use self-punishment adequately and vice versa. Logan (1973) argues that the use of self-punishment requires a considerably greater amount of external consequation than does self-reward. A similar breakdown is necessary in regard to the various forms of SR. As a function of preference, experience, or environment (e.g., resources available), patients will vary in their response to covert, concrete, activity, and symbolic reinforcers. While one individual will react to self-praise, another will find such self-statements irrelevant and respond to financial contingencies. It is also possible that a particular patient will respond to covert self-punishment but require concrete reward or vice versa. Furthermore, the magnitude of reinforcement necessary and the optimal timing and frequency of reinforcement (e.g., delay between response and reinforcement, need for intermediary reinforcers or tokens) will vary between and within individuals.

Formalized or objective techniques for conducting this detailed assessment have not yet been developed. The clinician must rely on a number of general procedures. The most effective approach is interviewing combined with imaginal role playing. The list of options can frequently be reduced significantly by ascertaining patient preferences, expectancies, prior experiences, and environmental resources. For example, financial contingencies are usually not feasible for the indigent patient and are not effective for the wealthy unless the amounts are substantial. An individual with a long history of self-criticism for his undesirable behavior will probably have satiated to this form of self-punishment. It is usually easier to rule out inappropriate procedures than identify appropriate ones on a purely conversational basis. A helpful adjunct involves describing a situation to the patient in which a positive or negative instance of the target behavior occurs. The patient imagines the situation as if it were really occurring and then imagines that SR of the form in question is administered. Reaction to that imagined trial can then be discussed. This procedure provides a more life like test of the reinforcer than discussion in the abstract. The Reinforcement Survey Schedule (Cautela & Kastenbaum, 1967) is also a useful addition to interviewing. This self-report inventory can be used to identify high valence activities (and objects) that can serve as Premack reinforcers or longer term goals for financial or token reinforcement systems.

It was suggested above that in vivo practice was a viable approach for evaluation of SM and SE. That procedure is not as applicable for SR. Techniques that are blatantly inappropriate or problematic will be identified by the patient quickly. However, the effects of SR are not readily discernable by introspection. It ordinarily requires a trial of several weeks under controlled conditions (e.g., the single subject experimental design; Hersen & Barlow, 1976) in order to clearly evaluate the effects of SR. Such ongoing assessment is *always advisable*, but it does not substitute for careful pre-treatment assessment and program planning.

Summary and Conclusions

While SC treatment procedures can be highly effective, they are far from universally applicable. Careful pre-treatment assessment is necessary to prevent misapplication of the procedures as well as to plan effective application. We have conceptualized the assessment process as a series of questions which should be answered in essentially sequential fashion. In most cases, a negative answer to a question will make subsequent questions irrelevant by ruling out the use of SC. The two major questions are: (1) Is the target behavior amenable to an SC strategy? and (2) Is SC applicable for the individual patient? The second question was subdivided into a series of component questions including: (1) Can the patient apply the procedures? (2) Are the procedures applied effectively?

Relatively few explicit techniques or empirical data are available with which to conduct the assessment process. Much of what we presented involved clinical interpretation of interview or role played material based on general principles. It should be obvious that thus far, insufficient attention has been paid to assessment issues. The material presented above is, therefore, aimed at researchers in the self-control area as well as practicing clinicians. It is our hope that it will be a stimulus to empirical evaluation of current techniques as well as to the development of new instruments and schemata.

In closing we would like to raise two issues that we have not discussed previously. The *first*, concerns the minimal criteria for effective use of SC in terms of age, psychopathology, and intellectual ability. There are several reports in the literature which indicate that children can be trained to use SC. Conversely, there are scant references to application with psychotics and the mentally retarded. Our view is that a functional analysis of the target behavior and behavioral resources is always appropriate. The use of SC should, therefore, not be excluded on the basis of gross categorization. Further research is necessary with these clinical populations. The second issue pertains to the use of SC when both high SC and high external control programs are feasible. The SC literature has implied that SC is the treatment of choice whenever it can be applied. However, we have not yet determined this empirically. It is our opinion that programs integrating both EC and SC elements are likely to be the most effective. Research is necessary to identify the best methods (e.g., sequence, emphasis) of combining elements and of determining the most effective combination in the individual case.

References

Bandura, A. *Principles of behavior modification*. New York: Holt, Rinehart & Winston, 1969.

Bandura, A., Grusec, J. E., & Menlove, F. L. Vicarious extinction of avoidance behavior. *Journal of Personality and Social Psychology*, 1967, **5**, 16–23.

Bandura, A., & Kupers, C. J. Transmission of patterns of self-reinforcement through modeling. *Journal of Abnormal and Social Psychology*, 1964, **69**, 1–9.

Bandura, A., & Whalen, C. K. The influence of antecedent reinforcement and divergent modeling cues on patterns of self-reward. *Journal of Personality and Social Psychology*, 1966, **3**, 373–382.

Bayer, C. A. Self-monitoring and mild aversion treatment of trichotillmania. *Journal of Behavior Therapy and Experimental Psychiatry*, 1972, **3**, 139–141.

Bellack, A. S. A comparison of self-monitoring and self-reinforcement in weight reduction. *Behavior Therapy*, 1976, **7**, 68–75.

Bellack, A. S. Self-evaluation, self-reinforcement and locus of control. *Journal of Research in Personality*, 1975, **9**, 158–167.

Bellack, A. S., Glanz, L., & Simon, R. Covert imagery and individual differences in self-reinforcement style in the treatment of obesity. *Journal of Consulting and Clinical Psychology*, 1976, in press.

Bellack, A. S., & Rozensky, R. H. Individual differences in self-reinforcement style and performance in self- and therapist-controlled weight reduction programs. *Behaviour Research and Therapy*, 1976, in press.

Bellack, A. S., Rozensky, R. H., & Schwartz, J. S. A comparison of two forms of self-monitoring in a behavioral weight reduction program. *Behavior Therapy*, 1974, **5**, 523–530.

Bellack, A. S., & Simon, R. Positive and negative self-reinforcement behavior under different instructional constraints. *Journal of General Psychology*, 1976, in press.

Bellack, A. S., & Tillman, W. The effects of task and experimenter feedback on the self-reinforcement behavior of internals and externals. *Journal of Consulting and Clinical Psychology*, 1974, **42**, 330–336.

Bucher, B., & Fabricatore, J. Use of patient-administered shock to suppress hallucinations. *Behavior Therapy*, 1970, **1**, 382–385.

Cautela, J. R., & Kastenbaum, R. A reinforcement survey schedule, for use in therapy, training and research. *Psychological Reports*, 1967, **20**, 1115–1130.

Dorsey, T. E., Kanfer, F. H., & Duerfeldt, P. H. Task difficulty and noncontingent reinforcement schedules as factors in self-reinforcement. *Journal of General Psychology*, 1971, **84**, 323–334.

D'Zurilla, T. J., & Goldfried, M. R. Problem solving and behavior modification. *Journal of Abnormal Psychology*, 1971, **78**, 107–126.

Epstein, L. H., & Peterson, G. The control of undesired behavior by self-imposed contingencies. *Behavior Therapy*, 1973, **4**, 91–95.

Ferster, C. B., Nurnberger, J. I., & Levitt, E. B. The control of eating. *Journal of Mathematics*, 1962, **1**, 87–109.

Fuchs, C. Z. The reduction of depression through the modification of self-control behaviors: An instigation group therapy. Unpublished doctoral dissertation, University of Pittsburgh, 1975.

Goldfried, M. R. Systematic desensitization as training in self-control. *Journal of Consulting and Clinical Psychology*, 1971, **37**, 228–234.

Goldiamond, I. Self-control procedures in personal behavior problems. *Psychological Reports*, 1965, **17**, 851–868.

Hall, S. M. Self-control and therapist control in the behavioral treatment of overweight women. *Behaviour Research and Therapy*, 1972, **10**, 59–68.

Hall, S. M., & Hall, R. G. Outcome and methodological considerations in behavioral treatment of obesity. *Behavior Therapy*, 1974, **5**, 352–364.

Hall, S. M., Hall, R. G., Hanson, R. W., & Borden, B. L. Permanence of two self-managed treatments of overweight in university and community populations. *Journal of Consulting and Clinical Psychology*, 1974, **42**, 781–786.

Hannum, J. W., Thoresen, C. E., & Hubbard, D. R., Jr. A behavioral study of self-esteem with elementary teachers. In M. J. Mahoney, & C. E. Thoresen (Eds.), *Self-Control: Power to the person*. Monterey, California: Brooks Cole, 1974.

Harris, M. B., & Bruner, C. G. A comparison of self-control and a contract procedure for weight control. *Behaviour Research and Therapy*, 1971, **9**, 347–354.

Harris, M. B., & Hallbauer, E. S. Self-directed weight control through eating and exercise. *Behaviour Research and Therapy*, 1973, **11**, 523–529.

Hersen, M., & Barlow, D. H. *Single-case experimental designs: Strategies for studying behavior change*. New York: Pergamon Press, 1976.

Homme, L. E. Control of coverants: The operants of the mind. *Psychological Record*, 1965, **15**, 501–511.

Hunt, W., & Matarazzo, J. D. Three years later: Recent developments in the experimental modification of smoking behavior. *Journal of Abnormal Psychology*, 1973, **81**, 107–114.

Jackson, B. Treatment of depression by self-reinforcement. *Behavior Therapy*, 1972, **3**, 298–307.

Jeffrey, D. A comparison of the effects of external control and self-control on the modification and maintenance of weight. *Journal of Abnormal Psychology*, 1974, **83**, 404–410.

Johnson, S. M., & White, G. Self-observation as an agent of behavioral change. *Behavior Therapy*, 1971, **2**, 488–497.

Kanfer, F. Maintenance of behavior by self-generated stimuli and reinforcement. In A. Jacobs, & L. Sachs (Eds.), *The psychology of private events: Perspectives on covert response systems*. New York: Academic Press, 1971.

Kanfer, F. H. Self-management methods. In F. H. Kanfer, & A. P. Goldstein (Eds.), *Helping people change*. New York: Pergamon Press, 1975.

Kanfer, F. H., & Duerfeldt, P. H. Comparison of self-reward and self-criticism as a function of types of prior external reinforcement. *Journal of Personality and Social Psychology*, 1968, **8**, 261–268.

Kanfer, F. H., & Karoly, P. Self-control: A behavioristic excursion into the lion's den. *Behavior Therapy*, 1972, **3**, 398–416.

Kanfer, F. H., & Phillips, J. S. Behavior therapy: A panacea for all ills or a passing fancy? *Archives of General Psychiatry*, 1966, **15**, 114–128.

Kazdin, A. E. Reactive self-monitoring: The effects of response desirability, goal setting and feedback. *Journal of Consulting and Clinical Psychology*, 1974, **42**, 704–716.

Kiesler, D. J. Some myths of psychotherapy research and the search for a paradigm. *Psychological Bulletin*, 1966, **65**, 110–136.

Lewinsohn, P. M. The behavioral study and treatment of depression. In M. Hersen, R. M. Eisler, & P. M. Miller (Eds.), *Progress in behavior modification: Volume I*. New York: Academic Press, 1975.

Lewinsohn, P. M., & Graf, M. Pleasant activities and depression. *Journal of Consulting and Clinical Psychology*, 1973, **41**, 261–268.

Lewinsohn, P. M., & Libet, J. Pleasant events, activity schedules, and depression. *Journal of Abnormal Psychology*, 1972, **79**, 291–295.

Lipinski, D., & Nelson, R. The reactivity and unreliability of self-recording. *Journal of Consulting and Clinical Psychology*, 1974, **42**, 118–123.

Logan, F. Self-control as habit, drive, and incentive. *Journal of Abnormal Psychology*, 1973, **81**, 127–136.

MacPhillamy, D. J., & Lewinsohn, P. M. Measurement of reinforcing events: Proceedings, *80th Annual Convention, American Psychological Association*, 1972, **7**, 399–400.

Mahoney, M. J. The self-management of covert behavior: A case study. *Behavior Therapy*, 1971, **2**, 575–578.

Mahoney, M. J. Self-reward and self-monitoring techniques for weight control. *Behavior Therapy*, 1974, **5**, 48–57.

Mahoney, M. J., Moura, N., & Wade, T. Relative efficacy of self-reward, self-punishment, and self-monitoring techniques for weight loss. *Journal of Consulting and Clinical Psychology*, 1973, **40**, 404–407.

Marston, A. R. Self-reinforcement: The relevance of a concept in analogue research to psychotherapy. *Psychotherapy: Theory, Research and Practice*, 1965, **2**, 1–5.

Marston, A., & Feldman, S. Toward the use of self-control in behavior modification. *Journal of Consulting and Clinical Psychology*, 1972, **39**, 429–433.

Marston, A. R., & Kanfer, F. H. Human reinforcement: Experimenter and subject controlled. *Journal of Experimental Psychology*, 1963, **66**, 91–94.

Mausner, B. An ecological view of cigarette smoking. *Journal of Abnormal Psychology*, 1973, **81**, 115–126.

Meichenbaum, D. A cognitive-behavior modification approach to assessment. In M. Hersen, & A. S. Bellack (Eds.), *Behavioral assessment: A practical handbook*. New York: Pergamon Press, 1976.

Meichenbaum, D., & Cameron, R. The Clinical potential of modifying what clients say to themselves. In M. J. Mahoney, & C. E. Thoresen (Eds.), *Self-control: Power to the person*. Monterey: Brooks Cole, 1974.

Nolan, J. D. Self-control procedures in the modification of smoking behavior. *Journal of Consulting and Clinical Psychology*, 1968, **32**, 92–93.

Ober, D. C. Modification of smoking behavior. *Journal of Consulting and Clinical Psychology*, 1968, **32**, 543–549.

Rehm, L. P., & Marston, A. R. Reduction of social anxiety through modification of self-reinforcement: An instigation therapy technique. *Journal of Consulting and Clinical Psychology*, 1968, **32**, 565–574.

Romanczyk, R. G. Self-monitoring in the treatment of obesity: Parameters of reactivity. *Behavior Therapy*, 1974, **5**, 531–540.

Romanczyk, R. G., Tracey, D. A., Wilson, G. T., & Thorpe, G. L. Behavioral techniques in the treatment of obesity: A comparative analysis. *Behaviour Research and Therapy*, 1973, **11**, 629–640.

Rotter, J. B. Generalized expectancies for internal vs. external control of reinforcement. *Psychological Monographs: General and Applied*, 1966, **80** (Whole No. 609).

Schachter, S. Some extraordinary facts about obese humans and rats. *American Psychologist*, 1971, **26**, 129–144.

Schwartz, J. S., & Bellack, A. S. Self-reinforcement and contracting in a behavioral weight reduction program. Unpublished manuscript, 1975.

Sobell, M., & Sobell, L. Individualized behavior therapy for alcoholics. *Behavior Therapy*, 1973, **4**, 49–72.

Stuart, R. B. Behavioral control of overeating. *Behaviour Research and Therapy*, 1967, **5**, 357–365.

Stuart, R. B. A three-dimensional program for the treatment of obesity. *Behaviour Research and Therapy*, 1971, **9**, 177–186.

Suinn, R. M., & Richardson, J. Anxiety management training: A non-specific behavior therapy program for anxiety control. *Behavior Therapy*, 1971, **2**, 498–510.

Thomas, E. J., & Abrams, K. S. Self-monitoring and reciprocal inhibition in the modification of multiple tics of Gilles de la Tourette's syndrome. *Journal of Behavior Therapy and Experimental Psychiatry*, 1971, **2**, 159–170.

Thoresen, C. E., & Mahoney, M. J. *Behavioral self-control*. New York: Holt, Rinehart & Winston, 1974.

Todd, F. J. Coverant control of self-evaluative responses in the treatment of depression: A new use for an old principle. *Behavior Therapy*, 1972, **3**, 91–94.

Watson, D. L., Tharp, R. G., & Krisberg, J. Case study in self-modification: Suppression of inflammatory scratching while awake and asleep. *Journal of Behavior Therapy and Experimental Psychiatry*, 1972, **3**, 213–215.

CHAPTER 6

A Cognitive-Behavior Modification Approach to Assessment

DONALD MEICHENBAUM

University of Waterloo
Waterloo, Ontario

Introduction

A major premise underlying the present chapter is that our client's cognitions, namely, what he says and/or fails to say to himself, as well as the images he emits, play a critical role in his presenting problem(s). That is, the client's appraisals, attributions, expectations, self-evaluations (which are all descriptive terms for the internal dialogues in which our client engages) are the appropriate and necessary concern for the diagnostician-therapist. The present chapter will describe in some detail how to assess the role our client's cognitions play in his maladaptive behavior and emotional upset. But before describing the specific assessment procedures, it is first necessary to present a framework of the conceptual alternatives available to the clinician as he sits in his chair listening to his client.

Exactly how the clinician assesses his client's thinking processes, the kinds of questions he asks, the tests he employs, and the homework assignments he gives, are influenced by the clinician's conceptualization of his client's cognitions. What the clinician says to himself about his client's thinking processes influences the assessment and therapy process. Permit me to share with you the internal dialogue of four clinicians, who have quite different orientations. We will see how their self-statements, images, and meaning-systems influence their assessment approach. We will briefly examine, in turn, the internal dialogues or conceptualization systems of a psychoanalyst, semantic therapist, behavior therapist, and finally, a "cognitive-behavior" therapist. We can then turn our attention to the internal dialogues of our clients.

The Clinician's Internal Dialogue

The Psychoanalyst

The clinician who is psychoanalytically oriented views the client's cognitions (i.e., thoughts and images) in terms of their defensive aspects. The client's cognitions are seen as manifest signs of underlying conflicts, many of which the client is unaware of. Illustrative of this approach is the work of D. Shapiro (1965), who has noted "neurotic" styles. This orientation leads to the use of projective techniques to assess the client's characteristic response style and the "unconscious" determinants and "latent meaning" underlying the manifest content.

Semantic Therapist

An alternative conceptualization is that of semantic therapists such as Albert Ellis and Aaron Beck. They view the client's cognitions as instances of faulty belief-systems and irrational thinking styles. Ellis (1961) emphasizes the so-called underlying premises that contribute to our client's faulty thinking, emotional disturbance, and maladaptive behavior. He encourages the clinician to note the themes, the irrational premises, that underlie the patient's self-statements, images, and cognitions. Supposedly, the client's preoccupation with what others think of him and the mistaken belief that an individual's self-worth is determined by others, contribute to his emotional disturbance. The assessment may include the administration of various tests of irrational beliefs and fear of negative evaluation, and rational analyses of the client's thinking processes, especially following specific behavioral homework assignments.

Aaron Beck (1970) assesses the stylistic qualities of his clients' cognitions: the distortions in their thought patterns. These distortions include (1) arbitrary inference—the drawing of a conclusion when evidence is lacking or is actually contrary to the conclusion; (2) magnification—exaggeration of the meaning of an event; (3) cognitive deficiency—disregard for an important aspect of a life situation; (4) overgeneralization—taking a single incident such as a failure as a sign of total personal incompetence, and in this way generating a fallacious rule; (5) other distortions, such as dichotomous reasoning, catastrophizing, etc. Such cognitive distortions result in the client's selectively attending to and inaccurately anticipating consequences, and making logical errors. The semantic therapist sees the task of assessment to be the pinpointing of such stylistic qualities. This is usually done by having the client describe in an interview the thoughts and images that precede, accompany, and follow the maladaptive behavior and affective disturbance. Braff & Beck (1974) have reported that the thoughts and images of depressed patients usually involve an assessment of worthlessness, whereas those of anxious patients involve personal danger. The interview procedures to solicit such thoughts will be described below. For now, it is important to appreciate that the semantic therapist views his client's cognitions as instances of irrational thinking styles.

The Behavior Therapist

The behavior therapist takes a somewhat different approach, viewing the cognitions that precede, accompany, and follow the client's maladaptive behaviors as "behaviors" themselves, similar in nature to other, nonverbal behaviors. In this tradition, a continuity assumption is made between overt and covert events; covert events are considered to be subject to the same "laws of learning" and social learning principles, such as reinforcement and contingency manipulations, as are overt behaviors. Homme (1965) has even offered the term "coverant" (i.e., covert-operant) to describe thinking processes. Thus, in assessing his client's cognitions the behavior therapist determines their positive and negative reinforcing value, and their stimulus and response properties. Quite often, cognitions become the target of therapy and/or are employed as tools in the therapy regimen, as in the case of covert sensitization, anxiety-relief-conditioning, and thought stoppage. Parenthetically, it should be noted that a number of recent studies have seriously questioned the continuity assumption and the validity of viewing and treating our client's cognitions in the same manner as overt behaviors (see Mahoney, 1974; Meichenbaum 1974a, 1975a, for a review of this literature).

The behavior therapist may also view his client's cognitions as instances of automatic thoughts that are part of the response chain. He is concerned with the nature and content of the cognitions occurring between the stimulus and response. Is the client given over to the immediate impression of the task or situation with little or no mediating processes intervening? Are the target behaviors habitual in nature (i.e., not premeditated), with little or no evidence of cognitive strategies intervening? The answers to these and related questions will indicate the degree to which the client's behavior is under his own verbal control, and the client's potential for developing self-control. According to this conception, the task of assessment and therapy is to have the client become aware of the role such thoughts (or their absence) play in the behavioral sequence. An attempt is made to return the client's maladaptive behavior(s) to a "deautomatized" condition, in which the habitual, maladaptive behaviors are then preceded by cognitive activity occurring within the client's awareness. Such "forced mediation" increases the separation between stimuli and responses, and thereby provides an additional opportunity for interrupting the maladaptive behavioral sequence.

Thus, the behavior therapist can view his client's cognitions as behaviors *per se*, and/or as part of a response chain. However, more often than not, the behavior therapy orientation leads him to view the cognitions as of secondary importance in the assessment process. The general strategy is to have the client produce incompatible behaviors, which lead to reinforcements, and in turn, it is assumed, the cognitions will follow suit. The focus is on the client's behavioral repertoire and the events antecedent and consequent to the target behavior(s). Little or no attention is directed at the client's internal dialogue.

The Cognitive-Behavior Therapist

The limitation of a strict behavior therapy approach in understanding the nature of a deficit was recently indicated in a study by Schwartz & Gottman (1974). Their research illustrates the cognitive-behavioral assessment approach. Schwartz and Gottman conducted a task analysis of the target behavior of unassertiveness. In a comparison of low-assertive and high-assertive male college students, they found that the low-assertive subjects did not differ from their more outgoing counterparts in knowledge of appropriate assertive responses, nor in the emission of such assertive responses under "safe" laboratory conditions (a "hypothetical" behavioral role-playing situation of having a friend ask how he should handle assertive situations). However, in a role-playing situation that simulated "real life," in which the subject was to imagine himself being confronted with an unreasonable request, the low-assertive subjects manifested a deficient repertoire. Therefore, the knowledge of the appropriate interpersonal behavior was in the low-assertive subjects' repertoire, but the subjects failed to emit such behavior when it was called for. Schwartz and Gottman found that it was the subjects' internal dialogues (i.e. the nature of their cognitions, negative self-statements, and images) that contributed to inferior performances. They determined this by having all subjects fill out a 34-item questionnaire entitled the Assertive Self-statement Test (ASST), following the role-playing situation. The ASST included 17 positive self-statements that would make it easier to refuse the request, and 17 negative self-statements that would make it harder to refuse. For example, positive self-statements included: "I was thinking that it doesn't matter what the person thinks of me;" "I was thinking that I was perfectly free to say no"; "I was thinking that the request is an unreasonable one." In contrast, the negative self-statements included: "I was worried about what the other person would think about me if I refused;" "I was thinking that the other person might be hurt or insulted if I refused." The subjects were asked to indicate on a scale from 1 to 5 (1 = hardly ever and 5 = very often) how frequently these self-statements characterized their thoughts during the preceding assertive situations.

The high-assertive subjects had significantly more positive than negative self-statements, whereas the low-assertive subjects did not differ in their positive and negative self-statements. For the high-assertive subjects there was a marked discrepancy between positive and negative self-statements, and usually little doubt in their minds about the appropriateness of their actions. In contrast, the low-assertive subjects could be characterized by an "internal dialogue of conflict" in which positive and negative self-statements compete against one another, interfering with interpersonal behavior. Thus, the cognitive-behavioral assessment approach focused on the nature of both the client's behavioral repertoire—his competencies—as well as the accompanying cognitive processes (e.g., knowledge, self-statements, images). How the cognitive and behavioral processes interact became the focus of assessment.

The clinical significance of such a cognitive-behavioral assessment approach was indicated in treatment studies by Glass (1974) and Shmurak (1974), who found that cognitive restructuring therapy, in the form of alteration of self-statements, was most effective in reducing nonassertiveness. Gottman, Gonso and Rasmussen (1974) have successfully applied a similar training program to socially withdrawn school children, whose internal dialogue also leads to inadequate interpersonal behaviors. These studies and others reviewed by Meichenbaum (1975a, 1975b) indicate that there is an interdependence between the client's cognitions and his overt behavior.

In the same way that psychologists have been seduced into arguing the either-or position of heredity versus environment, traits *versus* situationism, we have been seduced into arguing behavioral versus cognitive change. A similar artificial separation has evolved between cognitive versus affective assessment and therapy approaches. Instead, one may view that each cognition has an affective component and similarly, each affect, a cognitive component. As Bergin (1970) has suggested, "There may be highly specific interventions which have a behavioral or cognitive focus, but these are always embedded in a multidimensional context or have multiple consequences" (p.208). Our clients present problems that require assessment and change in motoric, affective, and cognitive domains. To focus on only behavior, *or* cognition, *or* affect would appear to be misguided and shortsighted. Thus, a hyphenated assessment and therapy approach, which examines each of these components, is proposed.

Murray & Jacobson (1971) have indicated that there appears to be some reluctance to see cognitive assessment and change as of central importance in psychotherapy. However, this reluctance may be based on several misconceptions. For many psychotherapists (e.g., Berenson & Carkhuff, 1967), cognitive change may imply an emphasis on purely intellectual insight. Cognitive assessment and therapy as described in this chapter refers to cognitive changes that are closely tied to emotional, motivational, and behavioral processes. For the cognitive-behavior therapist, the client's cognitions are viewed as one part of a complex repertoire of skills. The client's cognitions reflect his problem-solving ability and coping skills. A careful analysis of the client's cognitions reveals his skill in producing task-relevant strategies and the likelihood of his producing task-irrelevant cognitions, which interfere with the behavioral repertoire (i.e. the negative self-statements and images which are anxiety-engendering and often become self-fulfilling prophecies).

Thus, there is a shift of emphasis from the behavior therapist to the cognitive-behavior therapist. A shift from a focus on discrete, situation-specific responses and problem-specific procedures, to a general, coping-skills model. Whereas, for the behavior therapist the client's cognitions are of secondary importance or are viewed as behaviors *per se*, for the cognitive-behavior therapist the client's thoughts and images are of primary importance and are seen as cognitive skills that the client can use in preparing for and/or in confronting stressors.

In *summary*, a fulcrum that influences how we will conduct assessment and therapy is what we, as clinicians, say to ourselves about our client's thoughts and images. For, the way we view our client's internal dialogue will influence the questions we ask, the tests we administer, the nature of the homework assignments we give, and the way we conduct therapy.

How do you view your client's thoughts and images? Are they seen as defense mechanisms and reflections of unconscious processes, or reflections of irrational belief systems, and faulty thinking styles, or as instances of behavior *per se*, or automatic thoughts and part of the response chain, or as instances of problem-solving ability and coping skills? There are still other ways to view your client's cognitions including such factors as reflections or self-concept and interpersonal strategies.

In other words, as clinicians, we are trying to fabricate a meaning system, an understanding, a conceptualization to explain the internal dialogue of our patients. The marketplace is filled with a host of alternative conceptualizations, different paradigms, to make sense of our client's self-statements and images. Each of these conceptualizations has an accompanying set of assessment procedures, with specific tests, interview formats, homework assignments, and therapy regimes.

Assessment of the Client's Internal Dialogue

The Client's Conceptual Framework

In the same way that clinicians have a need to impose an explanatory system on client's behavior, clients have a similar need. Part of the reason they have come to see a clinician is to make sense of what is happening to them: how can they explain their behavior? What is likely to happen to them? A client comes to see the therapist with a "language" system, which includes a description of his presenting problem(s). The client's description often includes a sense that he is "losing control," that he feels helpless and hopeless. The clinician, with skill, enables the client come to view his problem from a different perspective, to fabricate a new meaning or explanation for the etiology and maintenance of the client's maladaptive behavior. Whereas prior to therapy the client may view his problem (e.g. an obsession, or compulsion, or phobia, etc) as a sign that he is "losing his wits," becoming depressed, anxious, etc., as a result of the clinical interview, the tests, the homework assignments, the therapy rationale, and therapy itself, the client will come to view his problem differently. The client may view his obsession as a communication problem, or as a manifestation of deep-seated conflict involving guilt, or as a behavioral repertoire maintained because of the secondary gains (reinforcers) that accrue. Many other conceptualizations could be offered. Indeed, the client may provide enough data to support each of these conceptualizations. Most clients do! The exact conceptualization adopted will vary with the therapist's orientation, the client's expectancies, and the goals of therapy. In fact, it is suggested that our clients have a sufficient life experience to provide data to support the conceptualizations of a host of therapists. If the therapist has a psychoanalytic orientation he can elicit from clients' life experiences that support his conceptualization. The same applies for a semantic, behavior, and cognitive-behavior therapist. The human life condition provides sufficient experience, and behavior is sufficiently multidetermined to maintain the employment of a host of therapists of different persuasions.

Thus, a major function of any assessment procedure is not only to analyze the nature of the client's deficit, but also to evolve with the client a common conceptualization or way to view his problem(s). For, once a particular conceptualization evolves between a client and therapist, then a host of therapeutic interventions and assignments are eagerly engaged in by the client (see Meichenbaum 1974b, 1975a, 1975b, for a fuller discussion).

Commission and Omission of Cognitions

As mentioned before, the cognitive-behavior therapist conducts a kind of "ethological" analysis of the client's thinking processes. The therapist attempts to discern the style and incidence of the client's internal dialogue and its relationship to the client's behavior. Two underlying questions influence the assessment procedure. First, what is the content of the client's cognitions that interfere with adaptive behavior? Second, what is the client failing to say to himself, which if present, would lead to adequate performance and adaptive behavior?

The Clinical Interview. In order to answer these questions the cognitive-behavior therapist uses a host of assessment procedures. Perhaps the most useful tool available is the clinical interview. The initial assessment session begins with an exploration of the extent and duration of the client's presenting problem. The therapist performs a situational analysis of the client's behavior. Table 1, taken from Donald Peterson's fine book, *The clinical study of social behavior* (1968), describes such an interview. In addition to the questions

TABLE 6.1
*Clinical Interview**

A. Definition of problem behavior
   1. Nature of the problem as defined by client
      "As I understand it, you came here because . . ." (discuss reasons for contact as stated by referral agency or other source of information) "I would like you to tell me more about this. What is the problem as you see it?" (Probe as needed to determine client's view of his own problem behavior, i.e., what he is doing, or failing to do, which he or somebody else defines as a problem.)
   2. Severity of the problem
      (a) "How serious a problem is this as far as you are concerned?" (Probe to determine perceived severity of problem.)
      (b) "How often do you . . . ?" (exhibit problem behavior if a disorder of commission, or have occasion to exhibit desired behavior if a problem of omission. The goal is to obtain information regarding frequency of response.)
   3. Generality of the problem
      (a) Duration "How long has this been going on?"
      (b) Extent "Where does the problem usually come up?" (Probe to determine situations in which problem behavior occurs, e.g., "Do you feel that way at work? How about at home?")

B. Determinants of problem behavior
   1. Conditions which intensify problem behavior "Now I want to you think about the times when . . . (the problem) is worst. What sort of things are going on then?"
   2. Conditions which alleviate problem behavior "What about the times when . . . (the problem) gets better? What sorts of things are going on then?"
   3. Perceived origins—"What do you think is causing . . . (the problem)?"
   4. Specific antecedents
      "Think back to the last time . . . (the problem occurred). What was going on at that time?"
      As needed:
      (a) Social influences "Were any other people around? Who? What were they doing?"
      (b) Personal influences "What were you thinking about at the time? How did you feel?"
   5. Specific consequences
      "What happened after . . . (the problem behavior occurred)?"
      As needed:
      (a) Social consequences "What did . . . (significant others identified above) do?"
      (b) Personal consequences "How did that make you feel?"
   6. Suggested changes
      "You have thought a lot about . . . (the problem). What do you think might be done to . . . (improve the situation)?"
   7. Suggested leads for further inquiry
      "What else do you think I should find out about to help you with this problem?"

*From Donald R. Peterson, *The Clinical Study of Social Behavior*, 1968, pp. 121–122. By permission of Prentice-Hall, Inc., Englewood Cliffs, N.J.

included in the Peterson interview, the cognitive-behavior therapist is interested in having the client share the feelings and thoughts he has preceding, accompanying, and following the presenting problem. For example, the client can be asked to close his eyes and imagine a recent situation when the anxiety, depression, anger, pain, or whatever the client's symptoms were particularly severe. The client is encouraged to imagine the scene, to "run a movie through this head" of a recent incident involving his problem(s). The client reports the sequence of thoughts, images, and behaviors. What are the thoughts that the client has when he first notices the problem (e.g., becoming depressed)? What are the thoughts as the client tries to cope with the depression? The client can be asked if he recognizes a common theme or link that runs through these thoughts.

By having the client close his eyes and use imagery, he is more likely to attend to aspects and details of the situation which may be overlooked and deemphasized in a direct interview. The set given to the client is to attend to the "nitty-gritty," the particular thoughts, images, fantasies, and feelings that he may have experienced in a given situation.

Following the description of the incident and after the imagery or "movie" reporting is over, the therapist can ask the client if he has similar thoughts and feelings in other situations. A number of options are available to the therapist. He can ask the client if he had such thoughts and feelings as a child, and thus conduct a developmental history. The client can consider the question, "How long have I been saying or thinking these things about myself?" The therapist can also focus on the "here and now" and wonder if the client had similar thoughts, images, and feelings during the assessment in the presence of the clinician. Moreover, the therapist can suggest that the client conduct a homework assignment of listening to himself with a "third ear," noting whether he experiences similar thoughts, images, and feelings over the course of the week. Such questions, homework assignments, etc., are all raised in the context of the therapist's curiosity, puzzlement as to the effect that such thoughts have on the client's behavior.

However, recall that part of what is going on in the assessment is not only an appraisal of the client's internal dialogue, but also an alteration of how the client views his problem. As a result of the assessment the client will come to entertain the notion that part of his problem results from what he says to himself. Implicit in this assessment is the notion that the client can control his thoughts and that he is not a victim of such thoughts, and feelings nor helpless in controlling what he says to himself. The therapist can wonder aloud, why does the client *choose* to have such thoughts and feelings? etc. That is, by the language and tenor of the interview and assessment, the client is given the impression that something can be done to exercise self-control. As a result of the assessment, the client comes to see how he is an active contributor to his presenting problem.

It should be emphasized that clients are not actively going around talking aloud to themselves prior to the assessment. But rather, as Goldfried, Decenteceo & Weinberg (1974) have indicated, because of the habitual nature of one's expectations or beliefs, it is likely that such thinking processes and images become automatic and seemingly involuntary, like most overlearned acts. The client's faulty cognitions—negative and anxiety-engendering self-statements and images—become habitual, and in many ways similar to the automatized thought that accompanies the proficiency of a motor skill such as driving a car. However, the clinician can make the client aware of such thinking processes and increase the likelihood that the awareness will be the trigger to produce incompatible thoughts and behaviors. In time, the client will try to convince the therapist that his negative self-statements and images are key aspects to his problem. This awareness provides the preparation for the therapist to present the therapy rationale and lay the groundwork for the therapeutic interventions.

By the act of assessment, we are changing what our client says to himself about his problem(s), and behavior(s). This is part and parcel of the assessment procedure. Instead of decrying this event we should recognize it and capitalize upon it. A similar process also occurs if we use a standardized battery of psychometric tests (e.g. Wechsler tests, Rorschach, TAT, MMPI) or reports of dreams, family interview, etc. It is interesting to contemplate how the client views his problem(s), his behavior(s) following such assessment procedures.

A variety of different techniques can be used in the assessment of cognitions, including the use of the imagery procedures, behavioral assessments, videotaping, projective devices (e.g. TAT-type pictures), group assessment, as well as homework assignments. Each of these topics will be discussed in turn.

Imagery. As described above, the imagery assessment procedure requires the client to close his eyes and "run a movie" of some critical incident in order to elicit the accompanying cognitions. This technique is illustrated by Novaco (1974), who had clients with anger problems close their eyes and relive a recent angry situation. During the course of the imagery, the clients were able to report their anger-eliciting and anger-fomenting self-statements and images. The provocation-related self-statements included, "Who the hell does he think he is; he can't do that to me;" "He wants to play it that way; okay, I'll show him;" "He thinks I'm a pushover; I'll get even;" etc. Such self-statements in combination with emotional arousal were defined as the anger-reaction. Under the influence of imagery the clients were able to relive their anger, reexperience their feelings and thoughts. Indeed, Sarbin (1972) viewed such imagery as muted role-taking, and one may supplement the present imagery assessment procedure with a behavioral role-playing assessment.

Such an assessment will reflect the client's interpersonal capabilities and reveal the degree to which the client's problem(s) is a reflection (to use a simplified model) of a "can't" problem versus a "won't" problem. Is the desirable response in the client's repertoire, and is the nature of his internal dialogue interfering with its emission? Or has the client failed, due to inadequate knowledge, information, modelling, and reinforcement history to acquire the appropriate behavioral and cognitive skills?

Novaco (1974) nicely demonstrated that after having clients become aware of the cognitive and emotional components of their anger, he could treat them by means of self-instructional training and relaxation procedures. Novaco's study illustrates how the assessment leads into the therapy regimen (see Meichenbaum & Turk, 1975, for other illustrations of how therapy naturally follows from assessment).

Meichenbaum, Gilmore, & Fedoravicius (1971), Meichenbaum (1972) and Meichenbaum, & Cameron (1973) used the imagery procedure for the assessment of interpersonal and evaluative anxiety and phobias. For example, a highly test-anxious client reported a set of behavioral rituals when taking a test that included knowing exactly which seat she would sit in, arriving in class early, remaining isolated from the other students in order to avoid hearing what other students were talking about, etc. Following the description of such behaviors the clinician can wonder aloud, using his own puzzlement, about the purpose of such patterns of behavior. A plausible answer the client will entertain is that these behaviors help control negative self-statements and the catastrophizing ideas that engender anxiety. A similar behavioral pattern was evident with individuals with interpersonal anxiety and unassertiveness. Recall Schwartz and Gottman's (1974) result (reported earlier) that an "internal dialogue of conflict" characterized the low-assertive subjects.

Another aspect of the internal dialogue became evident in our work with phobias. The fear or thought of having a phobic attack and losing control, with the accompanying social embarrassment, etc., was almost as terrifying as the phobic object or situation itself. The clients believed that a massive, *single-phase* phobic attack would overwhelm them. One result of the assessment procedure is a change in the way the client views such phobic attacks. By means of the clinician's thorough analytic probing the client will come to see that the phobic attack consists of several stages, including preparing for a stressor, confronting the stressor, possibly feeling overwhelmed by the phobic situation, and finally, having coped adequately, and reinforcing oneself for having done so. Whether the therapist is questioning the client in order to establish a hierarchy for desensitization or in order to appreciate the role the client's cognitions play in the phobic response, a consequence of such an assessment is a change in how the client views his presenting problem(s).

Moreover, what the client says to himself in trying to cope with the fear is also quite revealing. The client's criterion for having coped may be unrealistic and too demanding. The coping techniques may be in the client's repertoire, but the client's faulty appraisal, and self-defeating attributions may negate his handling of stressors. Assessing the client's cognitions will thus prove a useful tool in formulating plans for treatment.

An interesting variant of the imagery assessment procedure has been offered by Feather & Rhoads (1972). During the interview the clinician asks the client what is the worst thing that could happen if he were confronted by the phobic situation. The assessor presses for the "worst" fantasy. For example, a speech-anxious client might offer the fantasy of getting so angry with the audience and himself that he loses control and hurts someone. Feather & Rhoads solicit a detailed description of the fantasy (e.g., how he would hurt them, etc.). The client is taught the distinction between reality and fantasy, and examine the role that such fantasies play in the sequence of the maladaptive behavior. Feather & Rhoads go even further, and desensitize their client to his fantasy, teaching him to control the fantasy. They suggest that quite often the client is phobic to his own ideation and that much of the client's behavior is a learned avoidance of experiencing such thoughts.

In short, our clients emit cognitions (i.e., self-statements and images), and it is suggested that the interview questions and imagery procedures described will prove helpful in assessing them. Note that the client's faulty cognitions may take a pictorial form instead of or in addition to the verbal form. For example, Beck (1970) reports a woman with a fear of walking alone found that her spells of anxiety followed images of her having a heart attack, and being left helpless; a college student discovered that her anxiety at leaving the dormitory was triggered by visual fantasies of being attacked.

The focus on the imagery assessment so far has been on the negative aspects, namely, the images and self-statements the client emits that interfere with adaptive behaviors. One can also use the interview and imagery assessment techniques to determine the positive clinical potential of the client's imagery and self-instructional capabilities. Are there stressful situations in which the client is able to cope? What is the nature of the cognitive and behavioral coping mechanisms that are within the client's response repertoire? In other words, one can test the limits of the client's capabilities. Such an assessment serves several useful purposes: it communicates to the client areas of strength, and shifts the orientation of the assessment from pathology to capabilities and strengths; it provides the background for suggesting that the client may be able to employ such coping skills in the problem situation; and very specific images, and self-statements are suggested, which may be employed in therapy. For example, some time ago Chappell & Stevenson (1936) successfully treated peptic ulcer patients by having them imagine a pleasant scene whenever they experienced anxiety. Dorothy Yates (1946) offered a similar procedure of having clients enhance relaxation by thinking of a soothing word such as "calm" or a pleasant image. Many others have employed the client's imagery for the treatment of such varied problems as insomnia (Kahn, Baker & Weiss, 1968), pain (Turk 1975), depression (Beck 1970), avoidance behavior (Kazdin 1973), and other problems (Meichenbaum & Turk, 1975; Singer 1974, for a review of this imagery research). For now it is important to highlight that one can assess the clinical potential of the client's images and self-instructions as tools for use in the therapeutic process.

A Behavioral Test. There are other tools available to the clinician for eliciting and assessing his client's internal dialogue. One most useful procedure is the inclusion of a behavioral test. It is invaluable to have the client, wherever possible, actually engage in the referred problem or target behavior. For example, if he is interpersonally anxious the client can be asked to make a speech before a group, or, if phobic, to confront the phobic situation.

Following such a behavioral assessment the client can be encouraged to discuss his problem, not only in the context of general situations, and in historical terms, but also in terms of the specific assessment situation that he experienced. The client could explore in some detail his thoughts and feelings during the assessment situation. The clinician may try to have the client ascertain what were the particular aspects of the environment that triggered specific self-statements and images. At what point did the client begin to feel anxious? When was anxiety greatest? What were the self-statements and images that clients emitted at different points in the assessment? Having clients vicariously relive the behavioral assessment situation by means of the imagery procedure described above, will "pull" for his internal dialogue, and he can begin to explore the effects of such thought processes on his behaviors.

Another way to tap the client's cognitions is to videotape him while he undergoes the behavioral assessment or role playing, and is displaying the maladaptive behavior. Immediately after the taping, both client and therapist view the tape while the client tries to reconstruct the thoughts, and feelings he was experiencing on the tape. In this way, the therapist can use the client's videotape like a TAT card.

Following a discussion of the client's thinking process in the specific assessment situations, the client and therapist can explore the range of situations in which he has the same or comparable self-statements. Throughout the assessment, the therapist has to determine the degree to which the client's presenting problem is illustrative of a general thinking style. For example, in a recent case of a client who was obsessing and somewhat phobic about crossing streets, the therapist had to determine to what degree such indecisiveness was a characteristic thinking style evident in a variety of situations. The assessment will help the therapist in concluding whether to focus therapy on making the client aware of, and changing such a style, and/or focusing treatment on the specific presenting problem. A variety of factors influence this decision, including the severity, and duration of the presenting problem, goals of therapy, etc.

Throughout the assessment, the clinician provides the opportunity for the client to realize the irrational, self-defeating, and self-fulfilling aspects of his thinking style and self-statements and images.

A TAT-like Approach. Still another possible way to tap the client's internal dialogue, especially with children, is to employ TAT-like pictures related to the target behaviors. The pictures employed are *not* the standard Thematic Apperception Test pictures, but rather a set of pictures or slides that have been selected for the target population. For example, a set of slides of socially isolated children were used with withdrawn children. The withdrawn child is asked not only to report what is happening in the picture, the outcome, etc., but also to tell what the child in the picture is thinking and feeling, and what he can do to handle the situation. That is, an attempt is made to tap, by means of a projective device, the content of the client's internal dialogue. Interestingly, Meijers (1974) reports that such a projective device is effective in discriminating between socially withdrawn and socially outgoing children. The socially withdrawn children report a higher incidence of negative self-statements and images and the appraisal of more situations as personally threatening. These results take on particular significance in light of Meijers' (1974) finding that adult college students who identify themselves as having been a social isolate child report such experiences as the following:

> I used to watch the most popular child in the class, what she would do, who she would talk with. I used to read books on how to be popular and sometimes even practise in front of the mirror. But I know if I acted like her (the popular child), it wouldn't be me. I would be doing it for my mother or my teacher.

Although one has to treat such retrospective reports with caution, they do suggest the importance of assessing the client's internal dialogue (i.e., appraisals, attributions, self-evaluations) as well as the nature of the behavioral response repertoire.

Other Procedures. A number of other tests can be employed to tap the client's cognitions. For example, the instrument developed by Schwartz & Gottman (1974) was described earlier. It assessed the client's thinking processes following a role-playing situation. Other tests developed by D'Zurilla & Goldfried (1971), and Spivack & Shure (1974) have been offered to assess the client's problem-solving ability, his ability to identify problems and formulate solutions. Spivack & Shure developed a Means-Ends thinking test which presents the beginning of the problem and the end result, and the subject is asked to fill in the intermediary steps. Spivack and his colleagues (Shure, Platt & Spivack, 1972a, 1972b; Shure, Spivack & Jaeger, 1971; Spivack, 1972) have repeatedly found that problem children, adolescent, and adult psychiatric patients have manifested problem-solving deficits, most notably the absence of foresight in considering the possible consequences of various actions. Such tests may prove a useful adjunct in assessing the client's cognitions.

The Role of the Group in Assessing Cognitions. The focus of assessment thus far has been on the individual client and the format of assessment has been on a one-to-one individual basis. There are several advantages to consider in conducting assessment on a group basis, rather than on an individual basis. Besides the obvious saving in the clinician's time, perhaps the greatest benefit accrues if the group of clients have a similar referral problem. If all clients individually have to go through the same behavioral assessment, such as giving a speech, then they can subsequently examine as a group their common experiences. The therapist can explore the common behaviors, thoughts, and feelings. A shared exploration of the common set of self-statements, and images is invaluable in having the clients come to appreciate the role thoughts play in the behavioral repertoire. The recognition that other individuals have similar thoughts and feelings, similar internal dialogues, provides an additional impetus for self-examination and self-disclosure. The groups can examine the variety of situations in which they have similar self-statements, and images.

Another useful function of the group assessment is that the therapist can use the client's behavior in the group setting as an opportunity to analyze the client's internal dialogue. If a client is particularly quiet in the group the clinician can have the client examine his thinking processes about participating in the group. The clinician can have the clients explore the content of their internal dialogue as they experienced them in the behavioral assessment, in the group setting, and in other situations. Such a situational analysis of thinking processes provides fertile ground for assessment.

Note that the group provides a new potential for behavioral assessment procedures, in terms of fostering group identity, and cohesion. These elements can also be successfully employed as a basis for treatment.

The Role of Homework Assignments in Assessing Cognitions. As mentioned previously, one way of having the clients appreciate the role of negative self-statements is for the therapist to give a homework assignment of having clients listen to themselves with a "third ear." The purpose of the homework assignment is to strengthen the client's belief that self-statements, and images contribute to his problems. Clinicians differ in how demanding, and structured this assignment should be. Some clinicians encourage monitoring, recording, and graphing specific behaviors, thoughts, urges, moods, etc. How one proceeds depends in part upon how one views the role of cognitions. If one views them as behaviors *per se*, or reflections of irrational belief systems, etc., this will influence how explicit the homework assignment will be. My own approach is to request that the client note examples of negative self-statements, and images at the time when they occur or at the end of the day. These are discussed with the clinician the following week. The reason the client is not asked to keep a careful, detailed accounting of his cognitions or internal dialogue is because of the concern with what he might say to himself if he does not present a very detailed list of self-statements, and images. In other words, the therapist must have as much concern with what the client says to himself about the assessment procedures as with what he says about his presenting problem. Thus, by having the client comply with a general request to monitor his internal dialogue, he is likely to come to entertain the notion that part of his problem is the content of what he says to himself. Indeed, as the clients begin to report on the emission of self-statements in various situations, especially when conducting a group assessment, the therapist can begin to take a somewhat more passive role by asking (with some skill), "Are you trying to say that part of your problem is what you are telling yourself? How so?" At this point the patient or group of patients may try to convince the therapist as well as other members, and obviously themselves, that this is the case.

Two caveats are worth noting. First, the use of homework assignments should naturally evolve from the assessment procedures and from the group discussion. The clinician can solicit from clients' suggestions of what they think will be most helpful to try. In other words, it is made clear that the exploration, and examination of the clients' problems is a collaborative venture, of both clients and therapist. How the clients implement or fail to implement homework assignments provide a further basis for examining thinking styles.

A second caveat concerns the language, the words, the therapist employs in describing the homework assignment. Some clients, like some clinicians, may not respond favorably to the terms "self-statements" or "self-instructions." Instead, such phrases as thoughts about self, self-evaluations or self-concept may be used.

Summary

In summary, the clinician has a host of tools available, including interview and imagery procedures, behavioral assessments, videotaping, TAT-like tests, homework assignments, and group assessments in order to conduct a careful analysis of the client's self-statements and images. The purpose of the assessment is to record and analyze, as well as change, the client's internal dialogue about his presenting problem. In other words, it is strongly suggested that each time we subject a client to particular assessment devices we are also changing the way he views his own problem. Assessment and change are interdependent! Instead of this being a condition to decry, it is suggested that it should be recognized and maximally employed. How it is employed will depend upon how the clinician views his client's cognitions.

One consequence of taking a cognitive-behavioral orientation is that treatment generalization is built into the therapy package. The client's maladaptive behavior and thoughts become the cues, the reminders to employ the coping techniques which he learns in therapy. By making the client aware of his thoughts, images, behaviors, and those cues in the environment (especially the reactions of others) that trigger such cognitions, the client will come to use such behaviors as reminders to act differently. In short, the focus of assessment, and eventually therapy, is to influence what the client says to himself about his symptoms. Prior to assessment and therapy, each physiological attack, each set of catastrophizing ideation was a harbinger of further behavioral deterioration and emotional turmoil. By making the client aware of not only his physiological state, but what he says to himself about his arousal state, one provides the groundwork for change. In this way, treatment generalization is engineered into the therapy package.

A Cognitive-functional Assessment of Performance Deficits

Thus far, the focus of the assessment has been on what the client says to himself, that is, the commission of negative self-statements. However, the clinician must also be more directly concerned with what the client is *failing* to say to himself, that is, the failure to spontaneously produce the task-relevant cognitions that will aid in his performance of a task. The focus of the remainder of this chapter is how the clinician assesses performance deficit, especially on cognitive tasks.

The Comparative-Group Approach

Two strategies seem to characterize the study of psychological deficits. The first of these is a population comparison strategy, involving comparing the performance of a specific clinical population (e.g., schizophrenics, learning-disabled children, etc.) with a "normal" control group on a comprehensive battery of tests. Thus, one finds clinicians giving their clients a comprehensive battery of tests and noting performance relative to some normative population (e.g., Hamill, 1971; Vallett, 1969). As a result, not infrequently the clinician's report looks like a brochure for a Mental Measurement Yearbook. Illustrative of this approach is a study by Mykelbust, Bannochie, & Killen (1971) on learning-disabled children who were compared with "normal" controls on a comprehensive psychoeducational battery. The children were tested on the WISC, the Leiter International Performance Scale, the Oral Emergency Test, Healy Picture Completion Test I, Goodenough-Harris Drawing test, and eight subtests from the Detroit Tests of Learning Aptitude. The results of these tests were related to a host of academic achievement measures. One must admire the children's endurance in taking so many tests.

A fundamental question concerns the usefulness of such a comparative group approach, with its comprehensive battery of tests (i.e., a sort of "shot-gun" approach), for elucidating the precise nature of an individual's deficit. Whether one is working with learning-disabled children, schizophrenics, or some other population manifesting a behavioral or performance deficit, it is doubtful that a comparative-groups assessment approach will yield data of much scientific or clinical significance.

What we do learn from a battery of tests is that the target population as a group performs more poorly on assessment devices than do their normal counterparts—a rather underwhelming and non-informative finding. A deficient performance can arise for a variety of different reasons and a given level of performance may arise in many different ways. As Kinsbourne (1971) commented on the performance of schizophrenics:

> Subjects fail to focus attention on a task or situation if they lack interest in it, if they have emotional resistance toward participating, if they find that it makes excessive demands on their abilities, or if they are otherwise preoccupied. In the mere demonstration of a failure in selective attention, there is no discrimination between primary physiological causation and distractibility secondary to other causes, any or all of which might be applicable to a schizophrenic subject . . . rather than an independent manifestation of disturbed neuronal activity (p. 309).

Kinsbourne's comments highlight the fact that our client's manifestation of a particular performance deficit, especially on the highly demanding cognitive tasks employed in a comparative assessment battery, does not help us diagnose the psychological subprocesses contributing to the performance deficit. A cognitive-functional assessment approach, which analyzes psychological subprocesses, will be described momentarily.

The Specific-Deficits Approach

The comparative groups of "shot-gun" test battery is just one approach used by clinicians. A second assessment strategy employed is a specific-deficits assessment approach. In this instance the clinician hypothesizes that a particular type of deficit forms the basis of the client's deficient performance, and the clinician then attempts to assess that specific, hypothesized deficit through a battery of tests. This approach also typically involves the comparison of the client with a normative control group, but the focus is on a test battery designed to assess a specific deficit rather than a more global assessment battery.

The clinician thus proposes that a single deficiency underlies the client's problem and performance deficit. These specific deficits are usually labeled as problems in attention, or memory, etc. The clinician then selects a battery of tests to assess the specific deficit. For example, Kleuver (1971) hypothesized that a memory deficit contributed to children's poor reading ability. He then administered 16 memory tests, based on Guilford's (1967) structure of intellect model, to good and poor readers. He found that "normal" readers were superior to poor readers on several aspects of memory. However, Meachem (1972) conceptualized memory as an epiphenomenon consisting of various cognitive activities such as classifying, rehearsing, labeling, visual imagery, and sentence elaboration. Kleuver's results, then, tell us that learning-disabled children who are poor readers have a "memory" deficit relative to a control group, but in the light of Meachem's analysis of memory, this is not really a further specification of the nature of the psychological deficit. It simply amounts to a new label, rather than an explanation or definition of the problem. Salkind & Poggio (1975) reached a similar conclusion in a discussion of activity level in hyperactive children, as did Kopfstein & Neale (1972) in an examination of attention deficits in schizophrenics. In each case, the authors called for an explication of the number of different psychological subprocesses involved in fostering motoric or attentional controls. Memory, activity level, attention, and such processes should not be viewed as single or homogeneous phenomena. Rather, they are "chapter headings" which summarize psychological subprocesses.

Hypothetical Speculation

A consequence of following the comparative groups and specific deficits assessment approaches is premature model-building and neurologizing. An example taken from the work on psychological deficits with schizophrenics is revealing. A major source of theorizing in the area of schizophrenia derives from Broadbent's (1958) model of the human mind as an information channel of limited capacity. This model has led various investigators to attribute the schizophrenic performance deficit to: (1) a deficient attentional filter (Chapman & McGhie, 1962); (2) an input dysfunction (Venables, 1964); (3) a deterioration in channel capacity (Pishkin et al., 1962); (4) a failure in scanning processes (Silverman, 1964); (5) a slowness in processing data in the primary channel

(Yates, 1966); (6) defective programs (Callaway, 1970). The schizophrenic deficit has also been conceptualized in terms of neurological models. Thus, for instance, it has been hypothetically explained in terms of: (1) a primary deficit in central nervous system organization (Belmont et al., 1964); (2) a deficit in the cortical regulatory system (Venables, 1963); (3) a defect in excitatory modulation (Claridge, 1967) and others. One sees a similar trend to build models and neurologize the deficit with such other clinical populations as learning-disabled children.

Meichenbaum (1975a) and Meichenbaum & Cameron (1973b) argued that such hypothetical speculation, whether derived from an information-communication model or a neurological model, seems premature and essentially non-productive. They suggest that at present the focus of empiricism and theorizing may be more productively directed at a cognitive-functional approach to deficit analysis.

The Cognitive-Functional Approach

1. *The Analysis.* A cognitive "hyphen" functional analysis of a psychological deficit emphasizes both a task-analysis and an accompanying, psychological analysis of the cognitions (i.e., self-statements and images) that clients employ (or fail to employ) in order to do a task. The tradition of a functional analysis of behavior emphasizes a careful examination of environmental antecedents and consequents, as related to a given response repertoire. A functional analyst carefully defines the specific response class, notes its naturally occurring topography and frequency within various situational settings, and then systematically manipulates environmental events in order to describe a causal relationship. A *cognitive-functional* approach to psychological deficits is in the same tradition, but includes and emphasizes the role of the client's cognitions in the behavioral repertoire. In short, a functional analysis of the client's thinking processes, and a careful inventory of his cognitive strategies are conducted in order to determine which cognitions (or failure to produce which key cognitions), under what circumstances, are contributing to or interfering with adequate performance.

The cognitive-functional approach is concerned with the sequential psychological processes required to perform a particular task. The cognitive-functional analyst asks the question: "What psychological processes must the successfully achieving individual engage in, and which of these is my client failing to engage in?" In order to speculate about what leads to poor performance, the clinician should himself take the task or test on which his client manifested a performance deficit. Upon completion of the test, the clinician introspects about the thoughts, images, and behaviors he employed in order to perform adequately on the task. The clinician may wish to take the task once again, focusing on the cognitive and behavioral strategies he is employing. The clinician may have other individuals examine their strategies following performance on the task. During each performance the clinician is carefully watching for cues that may indicate the use of particular strategies. The clinician's concern is with the "process" variables, the "how" rather than merely the performance outcome.

Perhaps, our client's inadequate performance on the task results from his failure to spontaneously and appropriately engage in task-relevant cognitive and behavioral strategies, and/or from a number of client-generated task interruptions and distractions, and the way in which the client notices and copes with these interruptions. In short, a failure in the internal dialogue of the client, what he says or fails to say to himself prior to, accompanying, and following his performance on a task, become the focus of analysis. It is suggested that an analysis of such cognitive strategies will help elucidate the nature of the psychological deficit. As Gagne & Briggs (1974) have observed, an individual's performance is a reflection of the quality of his cognitive strategies, namely, the skill that governs the individual's own learning, remembering, and thinking behaviors. Characterized thus, cognitive strategies are similar to Skinner's (1968) self-management behaviors:

> A cognitive strategy is an internally organized skill that selects and guides internal processes involved in defining and solving novel problems. In other words, it is a skill by means of which the learner manages his own thinking behavior . . . Cognitive strategies have as their objects the *learner's own thought processes.* Undoubtedly the efficacy of an individual's cognitive strategies exerts a crucial effect upon the quality of his own thought (Gagne & Briggs, 1974, p. 48) (emphasis added).

A cognitive-functional approach is designed to ascertain the nature of the client's cognitive strategies and the role they play in contributing to the psychological deficit. Cognitive strategies are not "mythical" or merely hypothetical processes, but rather, can be viewed as sets of self-statements and images that clients emit while engaged in a task.

Thus, the "cognitive" portion of this hyphenated approach comprises describing the nature of cognitive strategies required to perform a task. By means of a logical analysis of the task demands, by taking the task oneself and introspecting on one's cognitive strategies, by observing and interviewing others who take the task, and finally, by systematically manipulating the task demands, one can better appreciate the sequential psychological processes required. This latter approach of manipulating the task demands leads us into our discussion of the functional aspects of the recommended diagnostic approach.

2. *Manipulation.* Just as the operant conditioner studying psychological deficits conducts a functional analysis by systematically manipulating environmental consequences, the cognitive-functional analyst notes the behavioral and performance changes that result from environmental manipulations. From such alterations in performance the clinician can readily infer the presence or absence of particular cognitive strategies. Three types of manipulations may be employed in a cognitive-functional approach. The first set of manipulations is directed to the task, thus affecting the psychological demands. These may be in the form of speeded performance requirements; increasing the rate of stimulus presentation, thus not permitting rehearsal processes to occur; presenting the task through another modality in order to infer at what particular phase of operation the deficit occurs; or making important cues in the stimulus more salient, in an attempt to elicit the solution strategy on a simpler task, then gradually returning to the more difficult tasks to see whether the client generalizes the solution strategy. Through this approach one can assess both the client's capabilities as well as his deficits, under which task parameters the client is able to demonstrate competence, and under which conditions the client's performance begins to deteriorate. By systematically manipulating the task demands, one can pinpoint the aspect of the client's response repertoire that is deficient. By having the client perform the same task over a number of trials, the clinician can note the changes in strategies with the development of proficiency at the task.

A second type of manipulation that can aid in investigating cognitive strategies is altering non-task, environmental variables. Assessment can be carried out in a room with few distracting stimuli present, or interpersonal factors may be arranged so as to reduce anxiety and so on. Through such means the clinician can learn whether the client is able to emit adequate cognitions "spontaneously" under ideal environmental conditions, and then proceed to determine what aspects of the situation cause a reinstatement of the deficit. Another source of such information is the client himself. Soliciting from the client his perception of the task, his description of his strategy, this appraisal of his performance, and his assessment of his own situation are key elements of a cognitive-functional analysis. Not infrequently, the client may offer a post-hoc strategy, which, if followed, would have led to adequate performance. That is, the client demonstrates that the correct strategy is within his repertoire, yet he fails to spontaneously and appropriately employ it. Flavell, Beach & Chinsky (1966) characterized such a deficit as a "production deficiency." It is suggested that our clients have something to tell us, if we would only ask and then listen.

The third manipulation employed by the cognitive-functional analyst is providing the client with supports in the form of: (1) direct task aides, such as memory prompts, descriptions of the task demands by breaking the stimuli into components, explicit feedback, opportunities for note taking; (2) instructional aides given to the client to help him appraise the task, focus attention, self-evaluate performance, etc. How a client's performance varies in response to such supports will help elucidate the nature of the deficits.

Vygotsky (1962) suggested that a most useful way to assess capabilities, especially in children, was to have the client perform a task and then note the degree, and kind of improvement that derives from the administration of instructions. For Vygotsky, the client's ability to employ and benefit from instructions was the best reflection of intellectual capabilities. This tradition of assessing capabilities as well as deficits, of testing limits, of systematically determining the conditions under which a particular deficit is manifested, has not been fully exploited by clinicians. But, in conducting such comparisons, an important caveat must be considered, especially when the cognitive-functional analyst compares his client's performance on the same task under varying conditions to a "normal" control group. Consider, for example, the situation in which clients are assessed on an attentional task under neutral and distracting conditions. The client group is found to be inferior to the matched normal control group under the distraction condition, but not under the neutral condition. Such a differential deficit may be due to an ability characteristic of the client *or* it may be attributable to the psychometric properties of the measurement instruments employed. Chapman & Chapman (1973) have pointed out that the magnitude of the performance deficit obtained by any generally less able group (clients) in comparison to another group (normals) is a direct function of the discriminating power of the test employed. A more discriminating test will reveal a larger discrepancy. Discriminating power is primarily a function of test reliability, and mean and variance of item difficulty. Oltmanns & Neale (1974) have indicated that differential deficits obtained may reflect statistical artifact of the measurement procedures rather than a specific deficit characteristic of the client group.

The cavaet for the cognitive-functional analyst is to be as concerned with the characteristics of his instruments as with the nature of the psychological deficit of the client. With this in mind we can begin to conduct a cognitive-behavioral assessment. Our focus is on the intellective activity, the constituent processes and the manner of their organization, the nature of our client's cognitive strategies, the content of his internal dialogue rather than merely the intellectual product or test score.

The Paradigm. The present cognitive functional assessment approach is in the tradition of M. B. Shapiro (1951) who has received insufficient attention, except for the efforts of James Inglis (1966) and Aubrey Yates (1970). In contrast to a test battery approach, Shapiro offered an experimentally oriented assessment approach in which the client's problems were formulated and specified into certain hypotheses. The clinician was encouraged to ask himself what effect the confirmation of each of his hypotheses would have on the treatment and disposition of the client. As Shapiro indicated, if any of these hypotheses are not likely to have an effect on treatment, the clinician should be disinclined to test them. The task for the clinician is to formulate and sequentially test various hypotheses. The client becomes the object of an experimental investigation, with the client often acting as his own control. In such a cognitive-functional experimental assessment approach, the distinction between assessment, and treatment becomes more obscure. A systematic experimental approach to a particular deficit will permit the clinician to make specific suggestions for remediation. Assessment of deficiencies and capabilities go hand-in-hand with remediation.

A somewhat different approach, of converging operations, offered by Garner, Hake, & Eriksen (1950), also provides a model for the cognitive-functional approach. Although the concept of converging operations was offered in the context of a debate about perception, the logic of the approach is applicable to any experimental investigation that is designed to elucidate the nature of psychological processes. By converging operations, Garner et al. meant any set of two or more independent experimental procedures that could explain or allow the selection or elimination of alternative hypotheses or concepts (i.e., establish a concept by ruling out alternative interpretations). The value of a set of operations depends less on the nature of the operations themselves than on the quality of the alternative hypotheses that are being considered.

Consequences of Adopting a Cognitive-Functional Assessment Approach

Meichenbaum (1975c) has examined several of the consequences of adopting a cognitive-functional assessment approach. These include the manner in which tests are used in assessment, the way treatment is conducted, and the way in which clinicians write their reports. It is the latter consequence that is most relevant for present purposes.

The adoption of a cognitive-functional assessment approach would have the impact of changing the way we write our diagnostic reports. At present, reading a case folder is usually a tedious task. One wonders what impact this has on those who have to write such reports.

> Test A was given; the scores indicated . . . This is consistent with Test B . . . and the teacher's report . . . etc., etc.

Such reports usually include a list of tests and a "cookbook" interpretation of each. Imagine instead a report in which the clinician shared with the reader his thinking processes, hypotheses, and attempts to test each of them, that is, the detective work. For example:

> The child was referred for this reason . . . After an examination of school records, interviews with teacher, parent, and child, the following tests were administered because . . . The performance level and profile was surprising in that the child demonstrated . . . In order to assess the reliability of these findings another test . . . which seems to assess the same psychological processes was administered under highly supportive conditions in order to assess the child's capabilities. These supportive conditions included . . . The performance deficit was still evident and seemed reliable, especially in light of the referral comments . . . In order to determine why the child did poorly on this task, the following functional operations were conducted sequentially . . . The logic and rationale for each of these is offered and the changes in the child's performance in response to each is described . . .

The administration of any psychological test such as the Wechsler intelligence scales should represent the beginning, not the end-product of our inquiry. The client's profile on the WAIS or some such test may serve as a clue for where to begin the experimental work, the exciting detective investigation, in order to pinpoint the nature of deficit.

Sleuthing

Shapiro & Ravenette (1959) remind us:

> Psychiatric patients suffer from a variety of disorders of affect, cognitions, and volition. A large number, if not the majority, of papers published by psychologists do not deal with these phenomena. Instead, they report upon the performance, by psychiatric patients, of a variety of tasks which might be described, without much loss of accuracy, as puzzles and indoor games. Examples are such tests as the pursuit rotor, the mirror drawing test, the block design test, the Rorschach test, and the Thematic Apperception Test (p. 296).

The present cognitive-behavioral assessment approach is designed to assess more directly our client's *affect*, *cognition*, and *volition*. Much work is required to more fully develop an assessment armamentarium to accomplish this. Perhaps one can learn from the superb cognitive-functional analyst, Sherlock Holmes . . . " 'Come, Watson. Come!' he cried. 'The game is afoot' . . ".

Summary

A cognitive-behavioral approach to the assessment of performance and behavioral deficits was described. The assessment approach was designed to determine the interdependence between the client's cognitions, and his behavioral repertoire. The client's cognitions are viewed as sets of self-statements and images, and as cognitive strategies which the client emits prior to, accompanying, and following his behavioral problem(s). The clinician determines what self-statements the client emits that interfere with the behavioral repertoire, and/or which self-statements the client is failing to emit, which, if emitted and complied with, would be incompatible with the maladaptive behaviors. A number of assessment devices, including interview, imagery and behavioral assessment, and homework assignments, conducted on both an individual and group basis, were offered as ways to assess the nature and content of the client's negative self-statements and images.

A cognitive-functional assessment approach was suggested to identify and explain the psychological subprocesses that underlie a particular performance deficit. To accomplish this, the clinician performs a psychological analysis of the task demands. By means of manipulating the task and environmental factors, and/or by providing the client with supports, the clinician can note the nature of the specific deficit. Several examples of this approach were offered.

In the same way that a cognitive-behavioral clinician performs an analysis of his client's cognitive strategies and internal dialogue, the present chapter summarized the cognitive strategies of clinicians as they perform assessments. What the clinician says to himself about his client's cognition influences the nature of the assessment procedure and the therapy regimen. But, no matter how the clinician conducts assessment, it should be underscored that one result of assessment is a change in what the client says to himself, and how he views his problem(s). By assessing the client's deficit we are changing it. The cognitive-behavioral assessment procedure attempts to capitalize upon this.

References

Beck, A. T. Cognitive therapy: Nature and relation to behavior therapy. *Behavior Therapy*, 1970a, **1**, 184–200.

Belmont, I., Birch, H., Klein, D., & Pollack, M. Perceptual evidence of CNS dysfunction in schizophrenia. *Archives of General Psychiatry*, 1964, **10**, 395–408.

Bergin, A. Cognitive therapy and behavior therapy: Foci for a multidimensional approach to treatment. *Behavior Therapy*, 1970, **1**, 205–212.

Berenson, B., & Carkhuff, R. R. *Sources of gain in counseling and Psychotherapy*. New York: Holt, Rinehart & Winston, 1967.

Braff, D., & Beck, A. Thinking disorder in depression. *Archives of General Psychiatry*, 1974, **31**, 456–462.

Broadbent, D. E. *Perception and Communication*. London: Pegamon Press, 1958.

Callaway, E. Schizophrenia and interference: An analogy with a malfunctioning computer. *Archives of General Psychiatry*, 1970, **22**, 193–208.

Chapman, L. J., & Chapman, J. Problems in the measurement of cognitive deficits. *Psychological Bulletin*, 1973, **79**, 380–385.

Chapman, J., & McGhie, A. A comparative study of disordered attention in schizophrenia. *Journal of Mental Science*, 1962, **108**, 487–500.

Chappell, M., & Stevenson, T. Group psychological training in some organic conditions. *Mental Hygiene*, 1936, **20**, 588–597.

Claridge, G. *Personality and arousal: A psychophysiological study of psychiatric disorder*. New York: Macmillan (Pergamon), 1967.

D'Zurilla, T., & Goldfried, M. Problem solving and behavior modification. *Journal of Abnormal Psychology*, 1971, **78**, 107–126.

Ellis, A. *Reason and emotion in psychotherapy*. New York: Lyle Stuart Press, 1961.

Feather, B., & Rhoads, J. Psychodynamic behavior therapy: I. Theory and Rationale. *Archives of General Psychiatry*, 1972, **26**, 496–502.

Flavell, J., Beach, D., & Chinsky, J. Spontaneous verbal rehearsal in a memory task as a function of age. *Child Development*, 1966, **37**, 283–299.

Gagne, R., & Briggs, L. *Principles of instructional design*. New York: Holt, Rinehart & Winston, 1974.

Garner, W., Hake, H., & Eriksen, C. Operationism and the concept of perception. *Psychological Review*, 1956, **63**, 149–159.

Glass, C. Response acquisition and cognitive self-statement modification approaches to dating behavior training. Unpublished doctoral dissertation, Indiana University, 1974.

Goldfried, M. R., Decenteceo, E. T., & Weinberg, L. Systematic rational restructuring as a self-control technique. *Behavior Therapy*, 1974, **5**, 247–254.

Gottman, J., Gonso, J., & Rasmussen, B. Social interaction, social competence and friendship in children. Unpublished manuscript, Indiana University, 1974.

Guilford, J. *The nature of human intelligence*. New York: McGraw-Hill, 1967.

Hamill, D. Evaluating children for instructional purposes. *Academic Therapy*, 1971, **6**, 343.

Homme, L. E. Perspectives in psychology: Control of coverants, the operants of the mind. *Psychological Record*, 1965, **15**, 501–511.

Inglis, J. *The scientific study of abnormal behavior*. Chicago: Aldine, 1966.

Kahn, M., Baker, B. L., & Weiss, J. Treatment of insomnia by relaxation training. *Journal of Abnormal Psychology*, 1968, **73**, 556–558.

Kinsbourne, M. Cognitive deficit: Experimental analysis. In J. McGaugh (Ed.), *Psychobiology*. New York: Academic Press, 1971.

Kopfstein, J., & Neale, J. A multivariate study of attention dysfunction in schizophrenia. *Journal of Abnormal Psychology*, 1972, **80**, 294–298.

Kazdin, A. The effect of model identity and fear relevant similarity on covert modeling. *Behavior Therapy*, 1974b, **5**, 624–636.

Kleuver, R. Mental abilities and disorders of learning. In H. Myklebust (Ed.), *Progress in learning disabilities*. (Vol. 2). New York: Grune & Stratton, 1971.

Mahoney, M. J. *Cognition and behavior modification*. Cambridge, Mass.: Ballinger Publishing Co., 1974.

Meachem, J. The development of memory abilities in the individual and society. *Human Development*, 1972, **15**, 205–228.

Meichenbaum, D. Cognitive modification of test anxious college students. *Journal of Consulting and Clinical Psychology*, 1972, **39**, 370–380.

Meichenbaum, D. *Cognitive behavior modification*. Morristown, N. J.: General Learning Press, 1974a.

Meichenbaum, D. Therapist manual for cognitive behavior modification. Unpublished manuscript, University of Waterloo, 1974b.

Meichenbaum, D. Self-instructional methods. In F. Kanfer, & A. Goldstein (Eds.), *Helping people change*. New York: Pergamon Press, 1975a.

Meichenbaum, D. Toward a cognitive theory of self-control. In G. Schwartz, & D. Shapiro (Eds.), *Consciousness and self-regulation: Advances in research*. New York: Plenum Press, 1975b.

Meichenbaum, D. Cognitive factors as determinants of learning disabilities: A cognitive-functional approach. Paper presented at the Nato Conference on "The Neuropsychology of Learning Disorders: Theoretical Approaches," Korsor, Denmark, June 1975c.

Meichenbaum, D., & Cameron, R. Stress inoculation: A skills training approach to anxiety management. Unpublished manuscript, University of Waterloo, 1973a.

Meichenbaum, D., & Cameron, R. Training schizophrenics to talk to themselves: A means of developing attentional controls. *Behavior Therapy*, 1973b, **4**, 515–534.

Meichenbaum, D., Gilmore, B., & Federovicius, A. Group insight *vs*. group desensitization in treating speech anxiety. *Journal of Consulting and Clinical Psychology*, 1971, **36**, 410–421.

Meichenbaum, D., & Turk, D. The cognitive-behavioral management of anxiety, anger, and pain. Paper presented at The Seventh Banff International Conference on Behavior Modification, 1975.

Meijers, J. A cognitive assessment of socially withdrawn children. Personal communication, 1974.

Murray, E., & Jacobson, L. I. The nature of learning in traditional and behavioral psychotherapy. In A. Bergin, & S. Garfield (Eds.), *Handbook of psychotherapy and behavior change*. New York: Wiley, 1971.

Myklebust, M., Bannochie, M., & Killen, J. Learning disabilities and cognitive processes. In H. Myklebust (Ed.), *Progress in learning disabilities*. (Vol. 2), New York: Grune & Stratton, 1971.

Novaco, R. A treatment program for the management of anger through cognitive and relaxation controls. Unpublished doctoral dissertation, Indiana University, Bloomington, Indiana, 1974.

Oltmanns, T., & Neale, J. Schizophrenic performance when distraction are present: Attentional deficit on differential task difficulty. Unpublished manuscript, State University of New York at Stony Brook, 1974.

Peterson, D. R. *The clinical study of social behavior*. New York: Appleton-Century-Crofts, 1968.

Pishkin, V., Smith, T., & Leibowitz, H. The influence of symbolic stimulus value on perceived size in chronic schizophrenia. *Journal of Consulting Psychology*, 1962, **26**, 323–330.

Platt, J., & Spivack, G. Problem-solving thinking of psychiatric patients. *Journal of Consulting and Clinical Psychology*, 1972a, **39**, 148–151.

Platt, J., & Spivack, G. Social competence and effective problem-solving thinking in psychiatric patients. *Journal of Clinical Psychology*, 1972b, **28**, 3–5.

Salkind, N., & Poggio, J. Hyperactivity: Theoretical and methodological concerns. Unpublished manuscript, University of Kansas, 1975.

Sarbin, T. Imagining as muted role-taking: A historical-linguistic analysis. In P. Sheelan (Ed.), *The function and nature of imagery*. New York: Academic Press, 1972.

Schwartz, R., & Gottman, J. M. A task analysis approach to clinical problems: A study of assertive behavior. Unpublished manuscript, Indiana University, 1974.

Shapiro, D. *Neurotic styles*. New York: Basic Books, 1965.

Shapiro, M. An experimental approach to diagnostic psychological testing. *Journal of Mental Science*, 1951, **97**, 748–764.

Shapiro, M., & Ravenette, E. A preliminary experiment on paranoid delusions. *Journal of Mental Science*, 1959, **105**, 295–312.

Shmurak, S. Design and evaluation of three dating behavior training programs utilizing response acquisition and cognitive self-statement modification techniques. Unpublished doctoral dissertation, Indiana University, 1974.

Shure, M., & Spivack, G. Means-ends thinking, adjustment and social class among elementary school-aged children. *Journal of Consulting and Clinical Psychology*, 1972, **38**, 348–353.

Shure, M., Spivack, G., & Jaeger, M. Problem-solving thinking and adjustment among disadvantaged preschool children. *Child Development*, 1971, **42**, 1791–1803.

Silverman, J. The problem of attention in research and theory in schizophrenia. *Psychological Review*, 1964, **71**, 352–379.

Singer, J. *Imagery and daydream methods in psychotherapy*. New York: Academic Press, 1974.

Skinner, B. F. *The technology of teaching*. New York: Appelton-Century-Crofts, 1968.

Spivack, G., & Shure, M. *Social adjustment of young children: A cognitive approach to solving real-life problems*. San Francisco: Jossey-Bass, 1974.

Turk, D. Cognitive control of pain: A skills training approach. Unpublished manuscript, University of Waterloo, 1975.
Vallett, R. *Programming learning disabilities.* Palo Alto, California: Fearon Publications, 1969.
Venables, P. Selectivity of attention, withdrawal, and cortical activation. *Archives of General Psychiatry*, 1963, **9**, 74–78.
Venables, P. Input dysfunction in schizophrenia. In B. Maher (Ed.), *Progress in experimental personality research.* (Vol. 1), New York: Academic Press, 1964.
Vygotsky, L. *Thought and Language.* New York: Wiley, 1962.
Yates, D. Relaxation in psychotherapy. *Journal of General Psychology*, 1946, **34**, 213–238.
Yates, A. J. Data processing levels and thought disorder in schizophrenia. *Australian Journal of Psychology*, 1966, **18**, 103–117.
Yates, A. J. *Behavior therapy.* New York: John Wiley, 1970.

PART THREE

Evaluation for Treatment Planning

CHAPTER 7

Assessment of Anxiety and Fear

JOHN R. LICK AND EDWARD S. KATKIN

State University of New York at Buffalo

Introduction

Our intention in this chapter is to discuss both techniques and methodological issues relevant to the assessment of fear and anxiety. We use the words fear and anxiety here as shorthand labels for a response complex consisting of verbal reports of anxiety and apprehension, physiological arousal involving the sympathetic branch of the autonomic nervous system, and behavioral phenomena such as avoidance and performance inefficiency. While we believe that most clients seeking help for anxiety-mediated distress show reactivity in all three of these response systems (cognitive, behavioral and physiological), there are circumstances under which these response components may be poorly correlated and may change at different rates (Hodgson & Rachman, 1974; Lang, 1969; Rachman & Hodgson, 1974). It is also clear that clients manifest anxiety reactions to a wide range of stimuli. Clients may be agoraphobic or snake phobic; they may be terrified of heart palpitations (cardiac neurosis) or heterosexual interactions (Marks, 1969). While the clinician might find a detailed discussion of special assessment problems associated with each of these phobic reactions useful, our goal here, given space limitations, is to focus on general principles of anxiety assessment which the clinician can then apply to his unique assessment needs.

We will begin this chapter by outlining the major issues and techniques relevant to assessment for planning therapeutic intervention and then discuss assessment strategies relevant to the evaluation of therapeutic outcome. Although these two assessment goals have overlapping concerns, greater emphasis is placed on theory when therapeutic planning is considered, whereas bias and quantification are stressed when outcome evaluation is discussed. These important differences justify their separate coverage. It should be obvious, however, that in clinical practice these two assessment goals intimately interact. One of the strengths of the behavioral approach to assessment is the emphasis placed on the evaluation of therapeutic change and the relationship that ideally exists between the clinician's monitoring of therapeutic progress and the application of therapeutic techniques. In this sense assessment for therapeutic planning is always an ongoing process strongly dependent on the evaluation of therapeutic outcome.

Evaluation for Therapeutic Planning

This phase of assessment is primarily concerned with acquiring detailed information about the "problems" with which the client wants help, and acquiring any other information which might suggest effective therapeutic techniques. Since most therapists rely quite extensively on the clinical interview for acquiring these data (at least with verbal clients), we will begin by discussing this assessment technique. Following our discussion of interviewing, we will outline other methods of acquiring data for therapeutic planning and conclude with a discussion of the utility of different types of clinical data for predicting therapeutic response to different treatment techniques.

The Clinical Interview

Preliminary stages. One of the first tasks of the interviewer is to create the nonspecific conditions that will maximize the chances of a client's honestly discussing his problems (Lazarus, 1971; Truax & Carkhuff, 1967). In this respect we have been concerned with the tendency of some inexperienced behavior therapists to "jump on" the first maladaptive anxiety reaction a client verbalizes, assuming that this is the focal issue with which the client really wants help. While many clients readily discuss their major concerns early in the assessment process, some clients will start out discussing a relatively unimportant "phobia," usually because of the excessive anxiety that would be engendered if they discussed fears of more central concern. Indeed, it is possible that behavior therapists are seeing a number of clients who want some kind of help but who are extremely threatened by discussing (at least in the initial stages of therapy) problems of central concern. It may be less distressing for clients like these to see a behavior therapist than a therapist of another theoretical persuasion because of the "objective-scientific "stereotype which surrounds behavior therapy (translation—the behavior therapist will hook me up to a machine and not upset me by probing into areas of my life that are very difficult to discuss). While we do not want to encourage behavior therapists to automatically discount the verbalized goals of clients on the assumption that these involve resistances against dealing with the *real* problem, we do believe that there are situations in which clients *do* initially show resistance (anxiety and avoidance) about discussing issues of critical concern. In these situations we believe the therapist should try to increase rapport and reduce the client's anxiety about self-disclosure (see Lazarus, 1971, for some useful suggestions) *before* rushing pell mell into detailed diagnosis and treatment of the client's presenting complaint. Of course, there will be times when a client will steadfastly insist that a circumscribed phobia is all he wants help with even though the therapist believes strongly that he has other problems which are much more distressing. In this case, the therapist should accept the client's goal at face value (if the therapist feels it is achievable) and help him work toward it, always being open, of course, to the possibility that during the course of therapy the client will discuss other difficulties he would like alleviated.

The detailed inquiry. Once the therapist identifies a fear reaction he would like to explore, the next step is to examine its antecedents and response components in as much detail as possible. Throughout this process the watch word is specificity. The therapist is interested in knowing exactly what the client means when he says he is "anxious." Does this refer to feelings of panic, heart palpitations, dizziness? How does the client react to these feelings? Does he avoid or confront situations that elicit anxiety? What are the precise situational cognitive or proprioceptive stimuli that are associated with anxiety reactions of varying intensity? In addition to relying on verbal interrogation to acquire this information, the therapist may employ imagery techniques and role-playing procedures. The imagery procedure can be useful in helping the client to make discriminations that are normally difficult under consulting room conditions. In this technique the client is asked to close his eyes and vividly imagine some past or future situation as if he were actually there. If the client can do this the therapist may then ask questions about aspects of the imagined stimulus situation, or the client's thoughts while in the situation, or the client's probable behavior. Role-playing can be useful in helping the therapist diagnose problems associated with interpersonal performance anxiety. For example, a male who reported experiencing a great deal of anxiety about approaching "eligible" women might be asked to role-play the initiation of a conversation with a woman. In this situation the therapist would play the role of the woman and the client would play himself. By observing the client's role-playing and subsequently discussing the experience with him, the therapist may be able to learn whether the client's difficulties in interacting with women are partly a function of inadequate knowledge about behavior which is likely to be reinforced; or (assuming that appropriate behavior is in the client's repertoire) whether anxiety interferes with performance to such an extent that current attempts at heterosexual interaction are unlikely to be successful.

Theoretical models of anxiety and the clinical interview. The clinical material we have discussed thus far would be grist for the mill of any behaviorally oriented therapist. There comes a point in the interview, however, where the therapist's theoretical *model* about the etiology, maintenance, and modification of fear plays an important role in shaping the conduct of the inquiry. We have identified three such "models" which seem to have some currency within what may be called the "broad spectrum" behavioral tradition. Although these models are discussed in separate paragraphs below they are not necessarily mutually incompatible and the clinician may simultaneously utilize features from any of them or switch from one to the other depending on the nature of the client and his anxiety complaints.

The most influential model in the behavioral assessment and treatment of anxiety is the classical S-R model which evolved from the work of Pavlov (1941), Hull (1943), and Wolpe (1958). Since this model basically argues that maladaptive anxiety is a classically conditioned response, assessment within the model is aimed at identifying the environmental, proprioceptive, or cognitive stimuli functioning as conditional stimuli for the anxiety responses. Once these stimuli have been identified the client's current anxiety reactions have been adequately "explained." However, the therapist is also interested in discovering the underlying dimensions that tie these stimuli together (see Wolpe, 1958; 1969, for clinical examples). This is particularly important, since therapeutic techniques based upon the model involve the systematic exposure of clients to fear-eliciting stimuli (either *in vivo* or imaginally). Without an understanding of the appropriate underlying dimensions this aspect of the task would be haphazard. Since the therapist cannot expose clients to all the unique stimuli that elicit fear reactions, he needs to expose them to a subset of stimuli (e.g., appropriate hierarchy) that has maximum relevance (generalizability) to their fears. The major therapeutic techniques developed from this model include systematic desensitization (Wolpe, 1958), implosive therapy (Stampfl & Levis, 1967), flooding (Watson, Gaind & Marks, 1972), graduated practice (Leitenberg & Callahan, 1973), and contact desensitization (Ritter, 1969).

Another model of anxiety, discussed at length by Meichenbaum in this volume, is the cognitive mediational model. This model assumes that cognitive activity associated with external stimuli plays an important role in producing and maintaining maladaptive anxiety. Thus, assessment within this model is aimed at understanding the cognitive activity intervening between anxiety-eliciting events and anxiety responses. Therapeutic approaches developed from this model include thought-stopping (Rimm, 1973; Wolpe, 1969), rational emotive therapy (Ellis, 1973; Goldfried, Decenteceo & Weinberg, 1974; Meichenbaum et al., 1971), and stress innoculation training (Meichenbaum, 1974; Meichenbaum & Cameron, 1973).

The last model of anxiety to be discussed in this section is what we have called the response-reinforcement model. This model has not been articulated well or extensively discussed in the literature; in fact, our current use of the words "response-reinforcement" may be the first effort at formally labelling it. The basic rationale of the model is that the *consequences* of a fear reaction (or some of its components) have important implications for the etiology and maintenance of the fear. These consequences may be either positively or negatively reinforcing and are often socially mediated. This notion bears much resemblance to the concept of "secondary gain" and may be clarified with a few clinical examples. Lazarus (1971), for instance, reported treating a 30-year-old male who had a bridge phobia. This phobia prevented the client from going to work at a time when increasing job demands were making him feel overwhelmed. Lazarus speculated that the phobia of bridges may have developed and been maintained through powerful negative reinforcement (e.g., the bridge phobia prevented him from going to work and helped him to avoid facing the anxiety of being overwhelmed on the job). In a similar vein, Fodor (1974) has suggested that some agoraphobic symptoms in women may develop and be maintained because they are successful in helping clients to avoid the anxiety that would be experienced if they engaged in behaviors contrary to certain sex-role stereotypes (e.g., had an affair or left their husbands). This model clearly calls for a thorough exploration of the possible positive and negative reinforcing values of an anxiety reaction as part of the assessment procedure. Should the therapist hypothesize that anxiety reactions are being positively or negatively reinforced, he should aim his intervention at reducing the reinforcement value of the anxiety responses.

Adjuncts to the Interview

While most clinicians use the interview as the primary data source for therapeutic planning, there will be times when this assessment tool may not provide sufficient information. Under these circumstances, the clinician may employ a variety of other assessment techniques including questionnaire measures, self-monitoring, behavioral observation, or physiological recording. Since these procedures will be described in detail in the section dealing with therapeutic outcome, we will merely mention some situations in which they may be profitably employed at this point.

The primary value of most questionnaires is that they may alert the therapist to areas of difficulty that may have been missed during the interview. Among the questionnaires used this way are various survey schedules and assertion inventories. While these instruments do not provide information that could not, in theory, be obtained from the interview, they take little time for clients to complete and may help the therapist avoid missing significant clinical material.

Self-monitoring can be useful when a client is unable to describe situational and/or cognitive antecedents of recurrent feelings of anxiety. By having the client keep a record of the situations and thoughts associated with these "anxious feelings," the therapist and client may be able to discover what stimuli trigger them.

Behavioral observation has its greatest diagnostic utility in situations where the client cannot describe important aspects of an anxiety-eliciting situation or his behavior in that context. This may occur with verbal clients who experience a breakdown in the ability to make discriminations when highly aroused, or in clients who have poorly developed verbal repertoires. Although physiological measurement is not commonly used in diagnostic assessments, it may have considerable value when the therapist is unsure about whether the client is reacting physiologically to phobic stimuli.

Predicting Response to Treatment

After the clinician has completed his interview(s) and any adjunct procedures, he usually makes a decision about what techniques to employ in the initial stages of therapy. Should he use systematic desensitization, thought-stopping, cognitive restructuring, flooding, reinforced practice, or some combination of the above? Diagnostic information that could indicate which therapy techniques would be most effective with different clients and various anxiety problems would be of enormous help. Unfortunately, although most of the techniques noted above have received a considerable amount of controlled investigation, the data obtained from such studies are often of minimal help to the clinician in making treatment decisions. An important reason for this is that much of the research has been of the "analogue" variety and has employed subject populations, treatment procedures, and therapists that deviate markedly from those usually involved in clinical practice (Bernstein & Paul, 1971). Furthermore, as we will discuss in the following section on therapeutic outcome, much research has tended to employ statistical definitions of treatment effectiveness (Lick, 1973) and outcome criteria with little demonstrable external clinical validity (Lick & Unger, 1975). Finally, there has been little research aimed at delineating technique x type of client interactions. This is unfortunate, since it is unlikely that any one fear reduction technique will be maximally effective across a range of therapists, clients, or anxiety problems (Bergin & Strupp, 1972; Lick, 1975; Smith & Nye, 1973). To facilitate thinking and research about possible technique x type of client interactions, we will discuss the possible prognostic significance of several client variables, including type of phobic disturbance, responses to personality inventories, and psychophysiological reactivity.

Type of phobia. It is likely that different fear reduction techniques are differentially effective with different types of phobic disturbance. Indeed, studies have generally indicated that *in vivo* exposure to phobic stimuli, either through flooding or reinforced practice, is superior to imaginal desensitization in the treatment of agoraphobia (Emmelkamp & Wessels, 1975) and animal phobia (Bandura, Blanchard & Ritter, 1969; D'Zurilla, Wilson & Nelson, 1973).[1] It is also likely that socially unskilled clients with interpersonal anxiety would benefit a great deal from skills training programs (Twentyman & McFall, 1975) in addition to or in lieu of therapeutic procedures designed to reduce fear directly.

Personality variables. Meichenbaum, Gilmore & Fedoravicius (1971) found that speech anxious subjects who obtained high scores on Watson & Friend's (1969) Social Avoidance and Distress Scale (a measure of generalized interpersonal anxiety) responded better to rational-emotive therapy than systematic desensitization, while the converse was true for clients who scored low on this measure. Two investigations (Reppucci & Baker, 1968; Baker, Cohen, & Saunders, 1973) have suggested that acrophobic subjects who resemble Leary's "autocratic personality" may do better with self-directed rather than therapist-directed desensitization. Several other studies (DiLoreto, 1961; Farmer & Wright, 1971) have found technique x personality interactions, suggesting that additional research along these lines may be profitable.

Physiological reactivity. While most clients seeking treatment for maladaptive anxiety show some physiological reactivity in the presence of phobic stimuli, there are individual differences in both the extent of this reactivity and subjects' perceptions of it. Borkovec (1973a, 1973b) has suggested that the efficacy of different treatment techniques may interact with this subject variable. Specifically, he suggested that treatment focusing on the manipulation of cognitions and expectancies may be effective with individuals showing minimal physiological arousal, but conditioning procedures (e.g., systematic desensitization) may be necessary to modify fear in subjects manifesting high levels of physiological distress. This position has yet to be confirmed empirically but data showing that subjects' scores on an Autonomic Perception Questionnaire (Mandler, Mandler & Uviller, 1958) interacted with fear responses to repeated presentations of phobic stimuli (Borkovec, 1973a; Stone & Borkovec, 1975) are consistent with it. Finally, there are some data (Lader, Gelder & Marks, 1967) suggesting that subjects' rates of physiological habituation to neutral stimuli (e.g., tones) are highly correlated with therapeutic response to systematic desensitization and fear reduction to films of fear-eliciting stimuli. If these findings are confirmed in other studies, they suggest that habituation rate to neutral stimuli or rate of spontaneous electrodermal fluctuations (which is highly correlated with habituation rate; see Katkin, 1975) may have considerable prognostic significance for the behavior therapist.

[1]We have yet to see published data indicating a superiority for imaginal desensitization over procedures employing *in vivo* exposure. This suggests that when it is feasible therapists should strongly consider using real as opposed to imaginal stimuli.

Evaluating Therapeutic Outcome

In this section we will discuss assessment approaches and methodological problems relevant to the evaluation of therapeutic outcome. We will begin the section by discussing self-report, since this is the first source of data the clinician or researcher usually relies upon in assessing therapeutic change. We will then discuss behavioral observation and physiological assessment, and conclude by discussing the therapeutic meaning of differing amounts of change in different outcome criteria.

The major assumption made here is that clients seeking treatment for maladaptive anxiety want to modify their reactions to a particular *population* of anxiety-eliciting stimuli that they may encounter in the natural environment. Clients do not, in our estimation, seek therapy to change responses on questionnaires, physiological and behavioral reactions to imagined animals, or unassertive responses to videotaped unreasonable requests. Regardless of the reliability of such measures or the thoroughness with which they assess behavioral, cognitive, and physiological reactions, they have little *clinical value* as outcome measures unless they correlate highly with a client's reactions to problematic stimuli encountered in the natural environment.

Self-report

It is common within the behavioral tradition to downplay the utility and validity of self-report as a method for acquiring data on the effectiveness of behavioral treatment (e.g., Ayllon & Azrin, 1968; Azrin, Holz & Goldiamond, 1961; Begelman & Hersen, 1971; Gordon, 1975; Simkins, 1971). In fact, an important source of motivation for the development of physiological and behavioral observation techniques over the past decade came from a desire to develop assessment techniques that were independent of self-report. While we generally endorse these latter developments, we are concerned that self-report has been rejected too quickly by some behaviorists and is not being given the attention it deserves as a useful methodological approach to assessment. Indeed, as continuing research demonstrates that the more "objective' behavioral and physiological approaches to assessment are also subject to artifacts, biases, and interpretive problems (e.g., Bernstein, 1973; Blom & Craighead, 1974; Johnson & Bolstad, 1973; Lick, 1973; Lick & Unger, 1975; Rachman, Marks & Hodgson, 1973), it appears that it is time to reconsider what self-report can and cannot do in providing useful information relevant to the evaluation of therapeutic outcome. A good place to begin this reappraisal is with a critical examination of some of the reasons for the behaviorist's aversion to self-report. We will then discuss self-report measures designed to assess general attitudes toward phobic stimuli, felt anxiety, and specific fear reactions, and conclude with a consideration of self-monitoring by clients.

The behavioral aversion to self-report: A critical examination. The behavioral attack on self-report has proceeded at both an empirical and theoretical level. Empirically, a number of studies, particularly in the area of fear assessment, have revealed low correlations between measures of fear obtained by self-report and those obtained by behavioral and physiological assessment (Hersen, Eisler, Miller, Johnson & Pinkston, 1973; Lang, 1969; Rutner, 1973). These data may suggest that certain types of self-report measures used in a certain manner have little predictive validity; however, it is important to realize that self-report is a flexible assessment technique that can be used to assess *cognitive*, *behavioral*, and *physiological* indices of anxiety. Clients can rate their cognitive fear of a situation before or after encountering it; they can record the frequency of avoidance and approach behaviors towards a fear-eliciting situation in the natural environment; and they can take their pulse before entering certain well-defined fearful situations. In most studies showing low concordance between behavioral and self report indices of fear, subjects have been asked to indicate how distressed they were while performing target behaviors, or they have been asked to rate their cognitive anxiety in response to a stimulus class (e.g., snakes) before being given a behavioral test (e.g., approaching a snake). Since cognitive anxiety is poorly correlated with overt fearful behavior and physiological arousal under certain circumstances, a self-report measure of cognitive arousal will sometimes correlate poorly with behavioral and physiological measures *even if the self-report instrument is a perfectly valid measure of cognitive anxiety*. The failure to distinguish between the method of self-report and the state of cognitive anxiety (Campbell & Fiske, 1959) has generated unnecessary pessimism about the validity of self-report. Actually, there are a wide range of behaviors relevant to anxiety assessment in addition to cognitive distress that can be assessed via self-report (e.g., dating frequency for someone with heterosexual anxiety; airplane trips for an acrophobic; camping trips and picnics for a snake phobic). While self-reports about these kinds of behavioral phenomena should not be automatically accepted as veridical, neither should they be discounted *a priori*. The accuracy of such self-reports is really an empirical question. At this juncture, however, it is worth noting that a number of studies have suggested close correspondence between self-reports of easily discriminable behavioral phenomena (e.g., number of dates) and the actual behaviors themselves (Hedquist & Weinhold, 1970; Lando, 1975; Lick & Sushinsky, 1975; Twentyman & McFall, 1975).

At the theoretical level behaviorists have objected to self-report because it is subject to wilful distortion and relies heavily on clients' ability to make verbal discriminations which break down under certain conditions (e.g., inattention, drugs, extreme stress) or not exist to begin with (e.g., in young children and some psychotics). This, of course, indicates the inappropriateness of self-report for certain client populations and target behaviors (e.g., subtle motor behaviors which may be difficult for clients to discriminate). However, the possibility of volitional bias does not contraindicate the use of self-report. While we agree that clients *can* bias self-reports to avoid disappointing themselves, the therapist, or researcher, the important questions concern the extent to which this actually happens, the situations in which it occurs, and what can be done to estimate or minimize the bias. Indeed, if the *possibility* of volitional bias constituted sufficient grounds to invalidate an assessment approach, virtually all reactive behavioral observation would have to be discounted, since it is usually based on behaviors that are at least partly under voluntary control. Actually, very little is known about the extent to which clients bias reports (or volitional behaviors on laboratory assessment tasks) of improvement in a therapy or research context. Virtually all of the research to date dealing with this issue has been concerned with analogue populations of fearful subjects and their performance on behavioral tests as a function of various instructional manipulations (Bernstein, 1973; Bernstein & Nietzel, 1973, 1974; Blom & Craighead 1974; Borkovec, Stone, O'Brien & Kaloupek, 1974; Miller & Bernstein, 1972; Smith, Diener & Beaman, 1974). What this research means for possible biases associated with self-report measurement is unclear. It should not be assumed, however, that whatever biases may be associated with demand characteristics will necessarily influence self-report measures more dramatically than other types of behavioral data. For example, under certain circumstances it may be less aversive for a client to exert extra effort on a behavioral approach test (e.g., approach closely to a snake even though this was very unpleasant) to show his therapist he has improved, than to lie about having engaged in certain easily discriminable behaviors relevant to his fear (e.g., about having gone on a picnic or a hike in the woods). Parenthetically, if demand characteristics exerted as potent an influence as some authors have suggested, it would be difficult to explain the relatively large number of fear reduction studies that have found no significant improvement for treated subjects on various self-report measures (e.g., Brown, 1973; Johnson & Sechrest, 1968; Lang, Lazovik & Reynolds, 1965; Lick, 1975; Rutner, 1973).

Standardized attitude measures. Several instruments employing Likert-type response formats have been developed to provide measures of general attitude towards fearful stimuli. These measures are usually filled out in the consulting room and have been used extensively in fear reduction research. The Fear Survey Schedules mentioned earlier fall into this category (Braun & Reynolds, 1969, Geer, 1965; Lang & Lazovik, 1963; Manosevitz & Lanyon 1965; Wolpe & Lang, 1964). These instruments ask clients to rate their overall fear of a wide variety of different experiences and situations on a five or seven point Likert scale (e.g., dogs, dead bodies, rejection, heart palpitations). A major problem with the fear surveys, however, is the fact that they were not designed to assess fear in specific situations. Indeed, several years ago one of the authors (Lick) saw a fear survey schedule in which a subject had given a number of fear ratings to the same stimulus item on a number of occasions in obvious violation of the instructions which asked for one fear rating per item. Closer examination revealed that the subject had filled in additional descriptive detail each time he gave more than one fear rating for a given item. For example, in responding to the item "snake," the student indicated "no fear" if the snake were harmless and caged, but "terror" if the snake were poisonous and encountered on a camping trip. This experience suggested that one of the reasons for the low correlations often reported between subjects' fear survey responses and other fear measures (see Hersen, 1973, for a review of this literature) concerns the ambiguity of the verbal stimuli on the FSS. To investigate this possibility, Lick and Sushinsky (1975) performed an experiment in which separate groups of college students rated their fear to a variety of self-report stimuli (e.g., "rats," "harmless white rat enclosed in a glass covered cage," "snakes," "a harmless three foot snake enclosed in a glass covered cage," etc.). A week later these subjects were asked to approach a rat or snake as in the standard behavioral approach test (Lang & Lazovik, 1963), and correlations were computed between self-reported fear towards each verbal stimulus and the amount of approach behavior subjects manifested on the behavioral approach test. The correlations indicated a greater degree of congruence between behavioral and cognitive fear when self-report stimuli accurately described the real stimuli subjects encountered on the behavioral approach test. These data suggest that attitude measures of fear should employ very specific descriptions of stimuli whenever possible (see Wicker, 1969; Fazio, 1969). Indeed, given the ambiguity of fear survey stimuli, it would appear that the major value of these instruments in outcome assessment is in providing suggestive data about possible "symptom substitution" or generalized improvement in fears not targeted for treatment. Other measures of general attitude that can be used with more specific self-report stimuli include the Semantic Differential (particularly the 11 bipolar adjectives reflecting the evaluative dimension) (Osgood, Suci & Tannenbaum, 1957) and the S-R Inventory of Anxiousness (Endler, Hunt & Rosenstein 1962). In addition to being readily adapted to assessing reactions to very specific self-report stimuli, these two measures employ more complex response formats than the five or seven point scales used with FSS items. While this may increase the reliability of measurement, research is needed to determine whether these more complex response formats increase predictive validity over that obtained with a single five or seven point Likert scale (Griffiths & Joy, 1971).

Measures of felt anxiety. From the client's perspective, one of the most important goals of treatment is a reduction in the feelings of tension, apprehension and panic often produced by fearful stimuli. Indeed, unless the phenomenal experience of anxiety is markedly reduced, many clients are unlikely to be pleased about treatment outcome, regardless of behavioral or physiological changes which may have occurred. Therefore, the measurement of a client's cognitive distress while he is in a fear-eliciting situation is important. To this end, a number of measures have been developed. One of the first and most widely employed is the Fear Thermometer (Walk, 1956). This is a ten-point scale in which 1 is usually defined as "completely calm" and 10 as "absolute terror." The client is asked to indicate how anxious he feels by placing a mark someplace on this scale. Another frequently employed measure is the Affect Adjective Check List (Zuckerman, 1960). This instrument consists of a variety of adjectives depicting various moods and feelings and instructs clients to check whatever adjectives describe their mood at the immediate moment. Maximum score on the instrument is 21 and it can be completed by clients in a few minutes. Two additional measures of cognitive distress which have received substantial use are the Anxiety Differential (Husek & Alexander, 1963) and the State-Trait Anxiety Inventory A-State Scale (Spielberger, Gorsuch & Lushene, 1970).

Specific fear measures. Most of these measures, which are listed in Table 1, have been developed for research purposes to facilitate subject screening and provide a paper and pencil measure of therapeutic change. These measures generally contain questions dealing with both cognitive, behavioral, and sometimes physiological manifestations of anxiety. Given the tripartite nature of the anxiety construct this is entirely appropriate. The important question for the clinician, of course, concerns the reliability and validity of these instruments. In discussing this question it is important to keep in focus one of their intended purposes: to reflect change in clinically relevant fear behavior.

TABLE 7.1

Self-report Measures of Specific Fears

Target Problem	Questionnaire Format	Reference
Fear of snakes	30 true-false items	Lang, Melamed & Hart 1970
Fear of spiders	30 true-false items	Lang, Melamed & Hart 1970
Fear of mutilation	30 true-false items	Hastings, 1971
Fear of heights	20 six pt. items	Baker, Cohen & Saunders, 1973
Fear of tests	19 five pt. items	Alpert & Haber, 1960
Fear of tests	21 true-false items	Sarason, 1957
Fear of heterosexual dating	20 seven pt. items	Twentyman & McFall, 1975
Assertive deficits	31 true-false items	Wolpe & Lazarus, 1966
Assertive deficits	30 six pt. items	Rathus, 1973
Assertive deficits	50 five pt. items	Galassi, Delo, Galassi & Bastien, 1974
Assertive deficits	40 five pt. items	Gambrill & Richey, 1975

As we pointed out earlier, this would require data showing that changes on these measures were highly correlated with changes in clients' behavior *vis à vis* anxiety-eliciting stimuli encountered in the natural environment. This is a particularly strenuous criterion which none of the above measures has met to any substantial extent. However, research does exist indicating reasonable reliability as well as some construct and criterion validity for most of the measures listed above. For example, Klorman, Weerts, Hastings, Melamed & Lang (1974) presented data on the reliability and validity of the measures in Table 7.1 dealing with fears of snakes, spiders, public speaking, and physical mutilation. It was concluded that these instruments have sufficient reliability and discriminant validity to recommend their use as screening and outcome measures in fear reduction research. While these data do not justify the use of any of these measures as primary outcome criteria, they do indicate that they are useful for subject screening and as ancillary outcome measures.

In concluding this section we would like to suggest that researchers developing new fear questionnaires deliberately employ items tapping all three anxiety response systems. A good example of this approach are the questionnaires developed by Baker *et al.* (1973) and Gambrill & Richey (1975). Their measures allow for a separate assessment of cognitive anxiety and behavioral inhibitions. Finally, we believe the validity of self-report measures would be enhanced if greater use were made of the "behavior analytic model" (Goldfried & D'Zurilla, 1969). Briefly, this model, in contrast to the "rational-intuitive" approach to questionnaire construction, emphasizes the importance of empirically determining the population of problematic situations in which clients manifest a particular difficulty in a *given environment*. Applied to fear assessment, this suggests that questionnaire items for fear inventories should be selected only after the researcher has surveyed the kinds of problematic situations which clients manifesting a particular type of phobia will encounter in a given environment (see, for example, Goldsmith & McFall, 1975).

Self-monitoring. It is reasonable to hypothesize that clients will be able to report their cognitive and behavioral reactions to fear-eliciting stimuli more accurately *after* they have just encountered these stimuli than while filling out questionnaires in the consulting room. It would also appear that the accuracy of self-report will be enhanced when the phenomena clients are asked to report about are specific and highly discriminable. These two principles coalesce in the concept of self-monitoring, a methodological approach to data acquisition becoming increasingly prominent in the behavioral literature on self-control (McFall, 1970; Johnson & White, 1971). In self-monitoring, the client is asked to keep a written record of discriminable behavioral phenoma (e.g., study time, cigarettes smoked, foods eaten). However, with the exception of a few recently reported studies (Hedquist & Weinhold, 1970; Twentyman & McFall, 1975), this procedure has been used infrequently in assessing therapeutic outcome in the area of anxiety. This is unfortunate, since self-monitoring might be useful in assessing behavioral, cognitive, and perhaps even physiological manifestations of anxiety. For example, in the area of motor behavior, clients could be asked to monitor certain predefined behaviors relevant to their target problem. Exactly what these behaviors would be is dependent on the nature of the client's fear reactions. A client with a cardiac neurosis (fear of heart attack), for example, might be asked to record the frequency with which he engaged in previously avoided activities that were "physically taxing" (e.g., running, sexual intercourse, climbing stairs); or, a client with a fear of dating might be asked to keep a record of all the social interactions he had with the opposite sex (see Twentyman & McFall, 1975).

While it is apparent that self-monitoring has the advantage of providing data on clients' reactions to fear-eliciting stimuli soon after they have been encountered in the natural environment, the reliability and reactivity of this approach should be examined before it is recommended. Although the reliability and reactivity of self-monitoring with a range of behaviors including smoking, eating, face touching, and studying have been investigated (Johnson & White, 1971; Lipinski & Nelson, 1974; Mahoney, Moore, Wade & Moura, 1973; McFall, 1970; Nelson, Lipinski & Black, 1975), little work with fear relevant behavior has been done in this area. However, research on the effects of feedback on fear behavior suggests that self-monitoring may be reactive and have a therapeutic effect on maladaptive anxiety (Emmelkamp, 1974; Hepner & Cauthen, 1975; Leitenberg, Agras, Allen, Butz & Edwards, 1975; Rutner, 1973). While this may be an asset for the clinician interested in maximizing therapeutic change, it is a potentially important confounding influence for the researcher. Although there is little hard data on the reliability of self-monitoring, we believe that the actual reliability of self-monitoring will depend upon two factors—saliency and client motivation. As Simkins (1971) has suggested, unless the focal behaviors are clearly and rigorously defined, reliability will suffer. It is also reasonable to expect that the reliability of self-monitoring will increase as the saliency of the behavior to be monitored increases. Thus, frequency of airplane trips, dates, earthquakes, and anxiety, for example, can probably be monitored more reliably than the frequency of face-touching or smoking behaviors which have relatively low saliency (at least within a certain frequency range). Indeed, it is doubtful whether clients can reliably discriminate small changes in subtle motor behaviors when they are highly aroused (e.g., eye contact, voice hesitations, hand movements).

With respect to motivation, it is probably true that for most clients self-monitoring is aversive, and unless the clinician or researcher insures that the reinforcement for careful monitoring exceeds its punishing quality, attention to the task is likely to lag and reliability may suffer (Lipinski & Nelson, 1974). This suggests that therapists should try to "sell" clients on the importance of accurate self-monitoring and be careful to avoid prescribing self-monitoring chores which will be excessively troublesome and time consuming (e.g., keeping track of multiple behaviors that have high base rates). For further discussion of self-monitoring, see Chapter 5.

Behavioral Observation

The direct observation of the client's behavior in the presence of fear-eliciting stimuli is the hallmark of the behavioral approach to assessment. Within this tradition assessment techniques have ranged from unobtrusive observation of the client in the natural environment, to direct observation of the client's behavior on standardized assessment tests performed in the clinic or laboratory. Indeed, the development of standardized laboratory assessment tasks constitutes a most significant methodological development in behavior therapy research and has played an important role in influencing behavioral thinking in the area of fear assessment. Consequently, we will begin this section by discussing those standardized tests. As we do this we will point out potential methodological problems and where appropriate, suggest ways in which the clinical utility of these instruments may be enhanced. We will then turn our attention to less structured assessment approaches involving both reactive and unobtrusive observation of the client's behavior in the natural environment. Throughout this discussion the reader should be aware that our focus will be on behavioral observation even though it is apparent that concurrent assessment of physiological and cognitive arousal is both desirable and feasible.

Behavioral approach test (*BAT*). This test was first introduced by Lang & Lazovik (1963) to provide a behavioral measure of snake fear. In this test subjects receive instructions to progressively approach, and if possible, handle a caged snake. The test is administered before and after treatment, and increases in approach behavior are interpreted as evidence of improvement. Since Lang & Lazovik's demonstration, literally hundreds of behavior modification investigations have employed the basic BAT paradigm to assess various animal fears as well as acrophobia (Ritter, 1969) and claustrophobia (Miller & Bernstein, 1972). It is not surprising, therefore, that the BAT has been the subject of considerable research. This research has focussed primarily on the effects that certain procedural variations and instructional manipulations have on approach behavior. For example, Borkovec & Craighead (1971) demonstrated equivalent avoidance behavior in fearful subjects regardless of whether they approached the phobic object or pressed a button bringing the phobic object closer to them. Bernstein & Nietzel (1973) found fearful subjects manifested significantly more approach behavior when instructions to approach were delivered sequentially by an experimenter rather than when they were delivered all at once by a tape recorder. Feist & Rosenthal (1973) found that a live snake produced significantly more avoidance than a preserved specimen, and a number of studies have found that instructions emphasizing the critical importance of maximum approach produce more behavioral approach on a BAT than instructions that ask for approach in a less demanding way (Bernstein, 1973; Bernstein & Nietzel, 1973, 1974; Miller & Bernstein, 1972; Smith, Diener & Beamen, 1974). These data have important implications for subject selection procedures in fear reduction research; however, their major significance has been to alert clinicians and researchers to the possibility that "objective" BAT data may be biased by demand characteristics. That is, subjects may respond to the implicit demand of the pre-and post- BAT assessments by exaggerating the extent of disturbance at pre-test and the amount of improvement at post-test. Thus, a portion of a subject's BAT improvement could reflect unusual effort to comply with the post-test demand for "improved behavior"—a demand that may not exist in the natural environment. The data cited above suggest that this could happen, since BAT performance is modifiable, within limits, by instructional and contextual variables. Unfortunately, whether clients actually do bias BAT performance enough to create the illusion of "improvement" is unknown.

While the possibility of "spurious" demand-induced improvement is probably the most widely publicized reason for exercising caution in interpreting the clinical significance of BAT data, it is not the only reason for such caution. Probably more important is the restricted range of fear-eliciting stimuli usually employed with the BAT and the "safe" environment within which it is conducted. Concerning the first point, subjects receiving the BAT are usually exposed to a very limited number of fear-eliciting stimuli. For example, in assessing snake fear, a subject would be asked to approach one, or at most two different snakes. The problem here is that clients do not typically have difficulty with one or two unique fear-eliciting stimuli, and unless the stimuli employed in the BAT are randomly sampled from the universe of stimuli capable of eliciting fear, the assessor does not know if a subject's BAT behavior will predict his reactions to the range of stimuli subjects are likely to encounter in the natural environment. This caution is reinforced by data showing that subjects will, under certain conditions, manifest more approach behavior to a snake they have seen before than to a new snake with different coloration (Bandura, Blanchard & Ritter, 1969; Bandura, Grusec & Menlove, 1967; Blanchard, 1970) and that the amount of generalization of improvement from a familiar to a novel snake interacts with the kind of treatment received (Blanchard, 1970; Bandura, Blanchard & Ritter, 1969). Another problem with the BAT concerns the "safe, predictable" environment associated with its administration. For example, in using the BAT to assess animal fear, subjects are frequently asked to approach a caged animal in systematic stepwise fashion and are informed that they can escape the situation by stopping the test if they desire. Furthermore, the presence of the experimenter and the general context (Orne, 1962) convey the impression that everything is "under control" and nothing dangerous or unpredictable will occur. This, of course, is in stark contrast to the natural environment which is frequently loaded with uncertainty and does not usually provide a convenient "panic button." Given this disparity in uncertainty between the BAT and natural environment we would expect that gains made on a "safe" BAT would sometimes fail to generalize to the natural environment. This suspicion was confirmed by Lick & Unger (1975), who described two animal phobic subjects who manifested a great deal of improvement on a laboratory BAT but did not show improved functioning in the natural environment. These two subjects could calmly touch their respective phobic objects (snake and spider) while they were housed in a glass aquarium; however, these same subjects reacted with a great deal of avoidance and behavioral distress when the phobic stimulus was taken out of the cage and placed on the floor 30 feet away from them. When asked about their divergent reactions in these two situations, both subjects said they felt in control when the phobic stimulus was in the aquarium even though they were touching it, but when the phobic object was outside the aquarium they felt that they were not in control and were terrified at the possibility of the snake or spider moving in an unpredictable fashion. Indeed, Unger & Lick[2] have found that animal phobics report being most afraid when confronting the fear-eliciting animal in situations in which they cannot predict how the animal will behave. Lick, Condiotte & Unger (1975) found that instructions influencing perceptions about the predictability of a rat's behavior had a potent effect on subjects' physiological and cognitive reactions to repeated rat exposures. Taken together, these data suggest that the variable of phobic stimulus uncertainty plays an important role in mediating fear behavior in phobic subjects and underscores the importance of considering this variable when interpreting the clinical relevance of "improvement" manifested on a traditional laboratory BAT.

Interpersonal performance test. One of the first tests in this category was developed by Paul (1966) to measure public speaking anxiety. The test involved having subjects give a short speech before a small audience during which trained observers rated the occurrence of visible manifestations of anxiety (e.g., trembling hands, speech blocks, throat clearings) on a timed behavioral checklist. Since then the paradigm has been modified to assess anxiety elicited by other types of interpersonal situations. For example, Borkovec, Stone, O'Brian & Kaloupek (1974) designed a performance test to assess anxiety associated with heterosexual interaction. In this test male subjects were asked to interact with a non-responsive female for a few minutes in an attempt to create a favorable impression. Variations of this heterosexual interaction

[2]Unger, T., & Lick, J. Unpublished data. State University of New York at Buffalo, 1975.

test have been used by a number of other investigators to assess competency and anxiety associated with heterosexual interaction (Arkowitz, Lichtenstein, McGovern & Hines, 1975; Glasgow & Arkowitz, 1975; Twentyman & McFall, 1975). While these tests allow for the convenient measurement of cognitive, behavioral, and physiological components of anxiety while subjects are engaged in fear-eliciting interpersonal situations, the important question for outcome assessment concerns their external validity. One of the few studies reporting data on this issue (Twentyman & McFall, 1975) found moderate correlations between cognitive and behavioral anxiety in the heterosexual performance test and the natural environment (as determined by self-monitoring of various aspects of everyday dating behavior).

A great deal more research needs to be done on the external validity of the interpersonal performance tests. In addition to evaluation anxiety, which may be an important variable influencing the generalizability of performance test data, we believe the restricted range of fear-eliciting situations usually employed in such tests attenuates their external validity. Consequently, we suggest that assessors using these measures employ as many different stimulus situations as possible (e.g., different speech topics, audience sizes, locations, speech lengths) at least until future research indicates how flat the generalization gradient is across variations in these types of stimuli.

Role-playing test. In this test clients are asked to role-play responses to prerecorded social stimuli presented on audio or video tape. The test was first developed to assess deficits in assertive behavior (McFall & Marston, 1970) but has also been used to assess anxiety and performance deficits associated with heterosexual interaction. When used to measure assertive deficits, clients listen to a series of recorded scenarios usually involving some kind of unreasonable request. Clients are asked to imagine that the recorded request is actually taking place and are instructed to respond as if they were actually in the situation described on the tape. For example, in a role-playing test for assertiveness one situation a client might be asked to imagine is that it is the end of a busy day at work and just as he is about to leave his boss asks him to stay and finish some extra work (scene from Eisler, Hersen, Miller & Blanchard, 1975). On the other hand, if the test were designed to assess heterosexual competency, a client might be asked to imagine that he asked a woman he saw at a party to dance and she responded that she was not much of a dancer (from Arkowitz *et al.*, 1975). Regardless of the eliciting stimuli, subjects' role-played responses can be evaluated along a variety of dimensions including response latency, voice loudness, speech duration, eye contact, etc.

One important advantage of the role-playing test, not shared by the performance tests discussed in the preceding sections, is the ease with which clients can be exposed to a wide range of different fear-eliciting interpersonal situations. Not surprisingly, the major drawback of the role-playing test is the possible lack of correspondence between role-played performance to imagined situations and actual behavior in those situations when they are confronted in the natural environment. Unfortunately, this critical question has received little research attention. While some studies have reported treatment effects on both role-playing tests and *in vivo* behavioral measures (Curran & Gilbert, 1975; Goldsmith & McFall, 1975; Twentyman & McFall, 1975), other investigations have failed to find treatment effects generalizing from role-playing to *in vivo* tests (e.g., Hersen, Eisler & Miller, 1974; Kazdin, 1974). The correlation between these two sets of measures is currently unknown.

Observation in the natural environment. Up to this point our discussion of observational techniques has been limited to contrived laboratory tests. A recurrent problem with this mode of assessment has been the restricted range of fear eliciting stimuli employed and the reactive nature of the observation. To some extent, the first problem can be minimized by accompanying the client and observing his/her behavior in the natural environment. For example, an acrophobic could be observed driving over bridges, looking out of sky-scrapers, or flying in an airplane. A snake phobic might be observed walking through tall grass in a park, or at a reptile exhibit in a zoo (Becker & Costello, 1975). While this mode of assessment is time consuming and provides data which may be difficult to quantify, it can yield useful information about the generalizability of laboratory based assessment. However, it does not address the problem of reactivity. In other words, even though the assessor can observe the client's behavior in a wide range of naturalistic situations, it is possible that his/her behavior in these situations would be different if he/she were not being observed. There are only two known ways of getting around this problem. The therapist can rely on "informers," or he can observe the client's behavior unobtrusively in either naturally occurring or contrived situations. The first approach presents fewer logistical problems, although it potentially raises difficulties concerning confidentiality and it is not always clear that other individuals are necessarily less biased in observing the client's behavior than the client himself. Still, this approach has merit, and there is no question that confidence in outcome data is increased when there is convergent agreement between the client and other observers about the existence of behavior change. Although unobtrusive observation may provide more reliable data, it is difficult to implement and presents a number of ethical problems. Thus, although we believe this technique can provide extremely important information, it is unlikely that it will ever be popularly employed as a major outcome measure.

Physiological Assessment

It is generally accepted that the experience of anxiety or fear is associated with autonomic nervous system discharge. This assumption has been incorporated into general theories of behavior and specific theories of emotion.

Wolpe (1971), in a discussion of his theory of psychotherapy by reciprocal inhibition has perhaps taken the strongest position concerning the relationship of autonomic arousal to fear by asserting that anxiety may be defined "as an organism's characteristic constellation of autonomic responses to noxious stimulation" (p. 341). In general, Wolpe's view is that phobic behavior is stimulated by the evocation of an anxiety (autonomic) response, which in turn drives the organism to escape from (or avoid) the anxiety eliciting stimulus. This view, it should be noted, is based on Mowrer's (1947) two-factor theory of avoidance learning, and it derives some theoretical support from the principle of anxiety conservation proposed by Solomon & Wynne (1954). The anxiety conservation view suggests that rapid avoidance of a noxious stimulus prevents the autonomic response from being fully elicited, and therefore prevents it from being extinguished. Although there has been considerable controversy over the validity of the principle of anxiety conservation, and the two factor theory from which it is derived (Costello, 1970; Herrnstein, 1969), there has not been any clear resolution of the issue. It remains evident that many therapists interested in the use of behavior therapy espouse the notion that an anxiety response, generally defined as possessing substantial autonomic nervous system correlates, lies at the core of avoidance behavior, and is the focal response which must be treated. It is no surprise, therefore, that a large literature has developed concerning the evaluation of autonomic responses with respect to behavior therapy.

Basic research on the relationship between sympathetic arousal and anxiety has been concerned with a variety of response systems, including the electrodermal, the cardiovascular, and the neuroendocrine systems. Since blood pressure recording requires sophisticated technology and catechol amine assessment involves biochemical assays, it is unlikely that such techniques would be of immediate relevance to clinicians who require simple and practical measures. Thus, the focus of this discussion will be upon measurements which can be taken from the skin surface of subjects relatively easily and with relatively simple technology. Therefore, this portion of the chapter will address itself to the assessment of *electrodermal activity* and *cardiac rate* as indexes of anxiety and fear.

Electrodermal measurement. The measurement of electrodermal activity, specifically the conductance of the skin (e.g., the reciprocal of apparent resistance) is easily achieved. Polygraphs are available from a number of commercial outlets and the most widely used electronic circuitry for the assessment of skin conductance has been described in detail (Lykken & Venables, 1971). These skin conductance circuits can be built by a competent technician for minimal cost or purchased directly from a number of polygraph manufacturers. Once the subject is properly connected to the polygraph (see Edelberg, 1967, for essential technical details), there are a range of phenomena to observe. First, proper calibration of the skin conductance circuit will indicate that a subject sitting at rest has a "resting" level of skin conductance (typically between 2 and 20 micromhos). There is a substantial literature showing that conductance level is directly related to sympathetic nervous system innervation of sweat glands, and it is tempting, but invariably misleading for the clinician to assume that the level of conductance is therefore a direct index of anxiety or fear. Indeed, it is frequently observed that some subjects during rest demonstrate considerably higher levels of conductance than other subjects during extreme fear. For this reason, skin conductance in fear assessment is usually defined in terms of the magnitude of a specific response to stimulation. That is, the presentation of a stimulus will invariably result in a specific transitory increase in skin conductance. Typically, the response is measured by measuring the skin conductance level prior to stimulus presentation and then again after the maximum conductance increase in response to the stimulus has been reached. The difference between these two points is, by convention, expressed as $\log^{11}$ post stimulus conductance level—$\log^{11}$ prestimulus conductance level.

Recently, much attention has been paid to the small changes in skin conductance level that occur in the absence of any stimulation. These fluctuations, seemingly spontaneous, are also likely to be of somewhat smaller magnitude than the specific responses elicited by stimulation, and are referred to either as "spontaneous fluctuations" or "nonspecific fluctuations." There is now a great deal of evidence to suggest that these small amplitude spontaneous fluctuations may be the clinician's simplest and most accurate physiological index of elicited anxiety.

In general, electrodermal measurements have proved to have some clinical significance as indices of therapeutic outcome. The use of electrodermal activity as an adjunct to the practice of behavior therapy (and especially systematic desensitization) has been reviewed exhaustively by Katkin & Deitz (1973). In their review they pointed out that in order for physiological assessment to have any utility at all the following demonstrations must be made: first, that fear eliciting stimuli should be capable of eliciting a physiological response; second, that the imagination of fear eliciting stimuli (at least in desensitization) should be capable of eliciting a physiological response, and finally, that the therapeutic procedures employed should result in a demonstrable reduction in the observed physiological response when compared to a suitable control procedure. For the time being we will ignore the critical issue of whether or not the elicited physiological response is correlated with verbal and motor indices of fear, and whether the reduction of such responses after treatment are correlated with verbal and motor indices of fear reduction. This issue, which is of fundamental importance, will be discussed later.

The data on specific utility of electrodermal measures for the assessment of fear are relatively clear. There seems little doubt that the specific electrodermal response to a stimulus provides an accurate index of a fear state. Phobic subjects give larger specific electrodermal responses to phobic stimulus objects than to nonphobic stimulus objects and they also show larger electrodermal responses to phobic objects than nonphobic subjects show to the same objects (Geer, 1966; Wilson, 1967). This relationship holds true for real stimulus objects (Barlow, Agras, Leitenberg & Wincze, 1970; Barlow, Leitenberg, Agras & Wincze, 1969); pictorial stimulus objects (Geer, 1966; Wilson, 1967); and for imagined stimulus objects, the type most frequently employed in clinical settings (Barber & Hahn, 1964; Craig, 1968; Lang, Melamed & Hart, 1970).

In addition to these results there is a burgeoning literature on the clinical significance of increases in the rate of spontaneous fluctuations in skin conductance level. In a series of experiments over the last decade, Katkin and his colleagues have demonstrated that although there is virtually no relationship between the frequency of spontaneous electrodermal fluctuations and self-report measures of anxiety, there is a clear and consistent relationship between the experimental induction of stress and the increase in rate of spontaneous fluctuations (Katkin, 1965, 1966, 1975; Rappaport & Katkin, 1972). These studies have demonstrated further that spontaneous fluctuation rate is a precisely time-locked index of the presence or absence of threat. Specifically, the following relationships have been delineated. When subjects are threatened with electric shock in a laboratory setting their tonic level of skin conductance *and* their rate of spontaneous fluctuations increases; however, when they are removed from the threat, and allowed to relax, the tonic level of skin conductance stays elevated, whereas the spontaneous fluctuation rate shows a rapid decline to the pre-stress level. Thus, it appears that spontaneous fluctuation rate may be a direct index of the transitory state of fear that is elicited by specific, threatening stimuli.

From the vantage of the active clinician who chooses to use physiological assessment, but who does not want to get overinvolved in technical and measurement problems, the use of the spontaneous fluctuation rate represents an excellent compromise. Scoring the measure requires little more effort than counting observable responses, which are usually defined as any response that is of some minimum magnitude criterion. Thus, this index of electrodermal activity can be quantified "on line," and does not require any time consuming measurement or transformation. For these, and other reasons, Szpiler & Epstein (in press) have termed it a "unique measure of anxiety."

Cardiac measurement. The assessment of cardiac activity has long been one of the fundamental techniques on psychophysiological research on stress and anxiety. It is generally accepted that when a subject is sympathetically aroused the rate at which his heart beats increases. Each beat of the heart generates electrical activity which can be detected from the surface of the body at various places, and displayed on a polygraph in the same manner as electrodermal activity. Most commercially available polygraphs for psychological research include appropriate couplers and transducers for the detection and amplification of cardiac rate. For a detailed description of the techniques of electrocardiography the interested reader should see Brener (1967). In this article Brener describes the most common techniques used for measurement of cardiac rate activity and discusses the importance of cardiotachometry in the assessment of heart rate responses to stimulation. A cardiotachometer provides the observer with a digital readout in beats per minute of the time interval between heartbeats. By properly calibrating a cardiotachometer one can adjust it so that, for instance, if the time interval between two beats is one second the tachometer gives a digital reading of 60 beats per minute. If the time interval between two beats were 0.5 seconds the tachometer would give a digital output of 120 beats per minute. In other words, the cardiotachometer allows the observer to observe the rate at which the heart is beating at each successive beat.

While the heart rate assessment is usually restricted to the clinic or laboratory, radio telemetry (see Wolff, 1967) allows a subject to move freely about his environment while connected to miniature electrodes and transmitters which send back physiological signals to a receiver at a remote station. This technique, which is more applicable to cardiac than to electrodermal measurement, could allow clinicians to assess the cardiac responses of phobic clients to fear-eliciting situations encountered in the natural environment. Although this has rarely been done because of the large expense involved, future technological advances may bring telemetric devices within a price range that will facilitate their widespread use. However, expensive, sophisticated electronic equipment is not the only way of monitoring heart rate. For centuries it has been known that an individual's heart rate could be monitored quite reliably by placing the fingers over the pulse of the wrist and counting the perceived beats. Indeed, this method of cardiac measurement has been used in a number of recent behavior therapy investigations (e.g., Borkovec, 1973a; Paul, 1966). Furthermore, in an interesting extension of this approach, Bell & Schwartz (1975) have shown that subjects can be taught to reliably monitor their own pulse rates during daily activities. These investigators found a high correlation between subjects' self-monitoring of *in vivo* pulse rates and heart rate measured in the laboratory with electronic equipment. This suggests that clients can be trained to monitor their pulse rates in the natural environment during periods of rest and perhaps before and/or during exposure to stressful stimuli.

Measurement of cardiac activity differs from measurement of electrodermal activity in many ways, but perhaps the most important is that the cardiac rate response to stimulation is sometimes accelerative and sometimes decelerative. The theoretical significance of differences between cardiac rate acceleration and cardiac rate deceleration has been discussed in some detail by Lacey (1967) and by Graham & Clifton (1966), who have suggested that deceleration represents the normal orienting response to external stimuli to which the subject wishes to attend, while acceleration represents a state of arousal associated with internal concentration or rejection of external stimulation. There has been considerable discussion about the relative merits of this analysis of what Lacey (1967) has called "directional fractionation," and there are serious implications for the use of cardiac rate measurement in the assessment of therapeutic outcome. For instance, if the Lacey hypothesis is upheld then one might assume that a fearful subject who shows cardiac rate acceleration to the presentation of a phobic object may be responding with some type of cognitive avoidance response of the phobic object associated with the rejection of the stimulus, whereas the subject who responds to a phobic stimulus object with cardiac deceleration may tend to cope with his phobia by attending to the object and focusing upon it. This hypothesis, while suggestive, reflects the fact that a simple interpretation of cardiac rate response as an index of fearfulness or anxiety is probably unjustified. Subjects who are equally aroused or fearful may show either cardiac rate increases or cardiac rate decreases to certain classes of stimulus objects. It is likely, however, that if the phobic stimulus object is sufficiently intense to elicit large general sympathetic responses that the cardiac rate associated with such responses would be accelerative in nature.

Clinical interpretation. While physiological assessment plays an important theoretical role in fear reduction research, its value in outcome assessment depends on the relationship between reductions in physiological arousal and concomitant changes in behavioral and cognitive responses to fearful stimuli. For example, a number of studies have found that phobic subjects give larger electrodermal responses to phobic than non-phobic stimuli and show larger responses to fearful stimuli than subjects who are not phobic (see Katkin & Deitz, 1973; Mathews, 1971). Furthermore, there are considerable data to indicate that subjects manifest an increased rate of "spontaneous" electrodermal responses when exposed to stressful stimuli (Katkin, 1965; 1966; 1975). However, there are also substantial data to indicate that specific electrodermal responses may habituate quite rapidly even though a subject continues to manifest fear in other response systems (Lomont & Edwards, 1967; Leitenberg, Agras & Barlow, 1969). Thus, it is difficult to interpret the clinical significance of attenuations in electrodermal responses to fear-eliciting stimuli, since such stimuli may continue to elicit fear reactions in other response systems. For this reason, some authors have suggested that heart rate may have more external validity than electrodermal measures as a physiological indicant of maladaptive fear (Lang, 1970; Hodgson & Rachman, 1974; Mathews, 1971). Indeed, Lang (1970) reported a correlation of 0.91 between heart rate reduction to phobic imagery and a composite measure of behavioral and self-reported reduction in fear. A large number of other studies have reported correlations between heart rate accleration to fear-eleciting stimuli and both behavioral and cognitive fear indicants (e.g., Borkovec, 1973a; Borkovec *et al.*, 1974; Paul, 1966). While these data support the use of heart rate acceleration as a physiological measure of fear, several considerations strongly suggest the use of electrodermal measurement as well. Lacey (1967) has demonstrated that subjects tend to show a unique pattern of autonomic responses to external stimuli. In other words, some subjects consistently respond to external events with cardiovascular reactions, while others typically respond with electrodermal responses. By measuring both response systems simultaneously, the clinician will maximize the sensitivity of physiological assessment. Thus, clinicians are well advised to employ both cardiac and electrodermal measurement simultaneously when recording physiological reactions.

A Note on Asynchrony Among Response Measures

Throughout this chapter we have discussed a range of assessment techniques for evaluating cognitive, behavioral, and physiological indices of anxiety. The need for this multi-dimensional approach to assessment arises, in part, from the observation that some clients respond to treatment by showing uneven changes across these three response systems (see Rachman & Hodgson, 1974). For example, a client may show behavioral changes but still manifest cognitive distress and physiological reactivity in fearful situations. What are we to make of this type of asynchrony? First, there is evidence (Hodgson & Rachman, 1974; Lang & Lazovik, 1963) to suggest that asynchronies that may exist at the end of therapy in response to fearful stimuli disappear with time. This implies that the most important response system is the one which maintains stability over time and consequently predicts the follow-up status of the other response systems. Unfortunately, there are no convincing data indicating which response system, if any, has preeminence in this respect. While Wolpe (1958) has suggested that reductions in the autonomic component of fear are often crucial for improvements to occur in other response systems, several studies have demonstrated that clients may make behavioral changes *before* evidencing reductions in physiological or cognitive distress (Leitenberg, Agras, Butz & Wincze, 1971; Watson, Gaind & Marks, 1972). Indeed, this pattern of change may occur more frequently than not (see Lick & Bootzin, 1975), and therefore place considerable emphasis on the behavioral fear component. However, the importance of carefully monitoring cognitive and physiological anxiety over time to determine if these response components are extinguishing, or if the asynchrony is being resolved by gradual behavioral deterioration cannot be minimized.

A Concluding Comment on Statistical vs. Clinical Significance

A major theme running through our discussion of outcome assessment has been the concern about the external validity of assessment techniques. The behavior therapy literature contains literally hundreds of studies which show "statistically significant" changes in treated as opposed to control subjects on self-report tests and laboratory measures of behavior change. While these data may have significant theoretical significance, unless the outcome criteria employed correlate highly with a client's behavior in the natural environment, they have little clinical utility. In this regard it is important for clinicians to be concerned about both the external validity of outcome measures and the amount of change treated subjects show on them. A number of authors (Bakan, 1966; Lick, 1973; Lykken, 1968) have cautioned that "statistical significance" does not imply clinical utility. Indeed, it is entirely possible for a group of treated subjects to show statistically significant changes which are clinically trivial. One way to minimize the tendency to equate statistical significance and clinical effectiveness is to employ a "normal" control group (or have access to normative data) and see how its members perform on the criterion measures used to assess the effects of therapy (Becker & Costello, 1975; Meichenbaum, *et al.*, 1971). The scores of the "normal "group are used as a standard against which to assess the clinical meaningfulness of changes manifested by treated subjects. While this strategy is useful, it does not protect against the use of clinically irrelevant outcome criteria. The only way this can be accomplished is by employing outcome measures that are directly linked to the behaviors the client wants to modify. If this is done, it will usually be easy to differentiate statistically significant changes that are trivial from clinically meaningful improvements. For example, if a treatment program is designed to increase dating frequency in heterosexually inhibited clients, it will be reasonably easy to assess its clinical utility if dating frequency is assessed. If this does not change, it is unlikely that the program has much clinical value, regardless of improvement that may have taken place on other laboratory assessment devices (Melnick, 1973). This argues, of course, for the use of outcome criteria closely tied to the important *in vivo* behaviors clients want to change.

References

Alpert, R., & Haber, R. M. Anxiety in academic achievement situations. *Journal of Abnormal and Social Psychology*, 1960, **61**, 207–215.

Arkowitz, H., Lichtenstein, E., McGovern, K., & Hines, D. The behavioral assessment of social competence in males. *Behavior Therapy*, 1975, **6**, 3–13.

Ayllon, T., & Azrin, N. H. *The token economy: A motivational system for therapy and rehabilitation.* New York: Appleton-Century-Crofts, 1968.

Azrin, N. H., Holz, W., & Goldiamond, I. Response bias in questionnaire reports. *Journal of Consulting Psychology*, 1961, **25**, 324–326.

Bakan, D. The test of significance in psychological research. *Psychological Bulletin*, 1966, **66**, 423–437.

Baker, B. L., Cohen, D. C., & Saunders, J. T. Self-directed desensitization for acrophobia. *Behaviour Research and Therapy* 1973, **11**, 79–89.

Bandura, A., Blanchard, E. B., & Ritter, B. The relative efficacy of desensitization and modeling approaches for inducing behavioral, affective and attitudinal changes. *Journal of Personality and Social Psychology*, 1969, **13**, 173–199.

Bandura, A., Grusec, J. E., & Menlove, F. L. Vicarious extinction of avoidance behavior. *Journal of Personality and Social Psychology*, 1967, **5**, 16–23.

Barber, T. X., & Hahn, K. W. Experimental studies in "hypnotic" behavior: Physiological and subjective effects of imagined pain. *Journal of Nervous and Mental Disease*, 1964, **139**, 416–425.

Barlow, D. H., Agras, W. S., Leitenberg, H., & Wincze, J. P. An experimental analysis of the effectiveness of "shaping" in reducing maladaptive avoidance behaviour: An analogue study. *Behaviour Research and Therapy*, 1970, **8**, 165–173.

Barlow, D. H., Leitenberg, H., Agras, W. S., & Wincze, J. P. The transfer gap in systematic desensitization: An analogue study. *Behaviour Research and Therapy*, 1969, **7**, 191–196.

Becker, H. G., & Costello, C. G. Effects of graduated exposure with feedback of exposure times on snake phobias. *Journal of Consulting and Clinical Psychology*, 1975, **43**, 478–484.

Begelman, D. A., & Hersen, M. Critique of Obler and Terwilliger's "Systematic desensitization with neurologically impaired children with phobic disorders." *Journal of Consulting and Clinical Psychology*, 1971, **37**, 10–13.

Bell, I. R., & Schwartz, G. E. Voluntary control and reactivity of human heart rate. *Psychophysiology*, 1975, **12**, 339–348.

Bergin, A. E., & Strupp, H. H. (Eds.). *Changing frontiers in the science of psychotherapy*. New York: Aldine-Atherton, 1972.

Bernstein, D. A. Situational factors in behavioral fear assessment: A progress report. *Behavior Therapy*, 1973, **4**, 41–48.

Bernstein, D. A., & Neitzel, M. T. Procedural variation in behavior avoidance tests. *Journal of Consulting and Clinical Psychology*, 1973, **41**, 165–174.

Bernstein, D.A., & Neitzel, M.T. Behavioral avoidance tests: The effects of demand characteristics and repeated measures on two types of subjects. *Behavior Therapy*, 1974, **5**, 183–192.

Bernstein, D. A., & Paul, G. L. Some comments on therapy analogue research with small animal "phobias." *Journal of Behavior Therapy and Experimental Psychiatry*, 1971, **2**, 225–237.

Blanchard, E. B. The generalization of vicarious extinction effects. *Behaviour Research and Therapy*, 1970, **8**, 323–330.

Blom, B. E., & Craighead, E. W. The effects of situational and instructional demand on indices of speech anxiety. *Journal of Abnormal Psychology*, 1974, **83**, 667–674.

Borkovec, T. D. The effects of instructional suggestion and physiological cues on analogue fear. *Behavior Therapy*, 1973a, **4**, 185–192.

Borkovec, T. D. The role of expectancy and physiological feedback in fear research: A review with special reference to subject characteristics. *Behavior Therapy*, 1973b, **4**, 491–505.

Borkovec, T. D., & Craighead, W. E. The comparison of two methods of assessing fear and avoidance behavior. *Behaviour Research and Therapy*, 1971, **9**, 285–291.

Borkovec, T. D., Stone, N. M., O'Brien, G. T., & Kaloupek, D. G. Identification and measurement of a clinically relevant target behavior for analogue outcome research. *Behavior Therapy*, 1974, **5**, 503–513.

Braun, P. R., & Reynolds, D. N. A factor analysis of a 100-item fear survey inventory. *Behaviour Research and Therapy*, 1969, **7**, 399–402.

Brener, J. Heart rate. In P. H. Venables, & I. Martin (Eds.), *A manual of psychophysiological methods*. New York: John Wiley, 1970.

Brown, H. A. Role of expectancy manipulation in systematic desensitization. *Journal of Consulting and Clinical Psychology*, 1973, **41**, 405–411.

Campbell, D. T., & Fiske, D. Convergent and discriminant validation by the multi-trait, multi-method matrix. *Psychological Bulletin*, 1959, **56**, 81–105.

Costello, C. G. Dissimilarities between conditioned avoidance responses and phobias. *Psychological Review*, 1970, **77**, 250–254.

Craig, K. D. Physiological arousal as a function of imagined, vicarious, and direct stress experiences. *Journal of Abnormal Psychology*, 1968, **73**, 513–520.

Curran, J. P., & Gilbert, F. S. A test of the relative effectiveness of a systematic desensitization program and an interpersonal skills training program with date anxious subjects. *Behavior Therapy*, 1975, **6**, 510–521.

DiLoreto, A. O. *Comparative psychotherapy*. New York: Aldine-Atherton, 1971.

D'Zurilla, T. J., Wilson, G. T., & Nelson, R. A preliminary study of the effectiveness of graduated prolonged exposure in the treatment of irrational fear. *Behavior Therapy*, 1973, **4**, 672–685.

Edelberg, R. Electrical properties of the skin. In C. C. Brown (Ed.), *Methods in psychophysiology*. Baltimore: Williams and Wilkins, 1967.

Eisler, R., Hersen, M., Miller, D. M., & Blanchard, E. B. Situational determinants of assertive behaviors. *Journal of Consulting and Clinical Psychology*, 1975, **43**, 330–340.

Ellis, A. *Reason and emotion in psychotherapy*. New Jersey: Lyle Stuart, 1973.

Emmelkamp, P. M. G. Self-observation versus flooding in the treatment of agoraphobia. *Behaviour Research and Therapy*, 1974, **12**, 229–237.

Emmelkamp, P. M. G., & Wessels, H. Flooding in imagination vs. flooding *in vivo*: A comparison with agoraphobics. *Behaviour Research and Therapy*, 1975, **13**, 7–15.

Endler, W. S., Hunt, J. McV., & Rosenstein, A. J. An S-R Inventory of anxiousness. *Psychological Monographs*, 1962, **76** (17, Whole No. 536).

Farmer, R. G., & Wright, J. M. C. Muscular reactivity and systematic desensitization. *Behavior Therapy*, 1971, **2**, 1–10.

Fazio, A. F. Verbal and overt-behavioral assessment of a specific fear. *Journal of Consulting and Clinical Psychology*, 1969, **33**, 705–709.

Feist, J. R., & Rosenthal, T. L. Serpent versus surrogate and other determinants of runway fear differences. *Behaviour Research and Therapy*, 1973, **11**, 483–489.

Fodor, I. G. The phobic syndrome in women: Implications for treatment. In V. Franks, & V. Burtle (Eds.), *Women in therapy*. New York: Brunner-Mazel, 1974.

Galassi, J. P.. Delo, J. S., Galassi, M. D., & Bastien, S. The college self-expression scale: A measure of assertiveness. *Behavior Therapy*, 1974, **5**, 165–171.

Gambrill, E. D., & Richey, C. A. An assertion inventory for use in assessment and research. *Behavior Therapy*, 1975, **6**, 550–561.

Geer, J. H. The development of a scale to measure fear. *Behaviour Research and Therapy*, 1965, **3**, 45–53.

Geer, J. H. Fear and autonomic arousal. *Journal of Abnormal Psychology*, 1966, **71**, 253–255.

Glasgow, R. E., & Arkowitz, H. The behavioral assessment of male and female social competence in dyadic heterosexual interactions. *Behavior Therapy*, 1975, **6**, 488–498.

Goldfried, M. R., Decenteceo, E. T., & Weinberg, L. Systematic rational restructuring as a self-control technique. *Behavior Therapy*, 1974, **5**, 247–254.

Goldfried, M. R., & D'Zurilla, T. J. A behavior analytic model for assessing competence. In C. D. Spielberger (Ed.), *Current topics in clinical and community psychology*. Vol. I New York: Academic Press, 1969.

Goldsmith, J. B., & McFall, R. M. Development and evaluation of an interpersonal skill training program for psychiatric inpatients. *Journal of Abnormal Psychology*, 1975, **84**, 51–58.

Gordon, S. B. Multiple assessment of behavior modification with families. *Journal of Consulting and Clinical Psychology*, 1975, **43**, 917–919.

Graham, F. K., & Clifton, R. K. Heart rate change as a component of the orienting reflex. *Psychological Bulletin*, 1966, **65**, 305–320.

Griffiths, R. D., & Joy, M. The prediction of phobic behavior. *Behaviour Research and Therapy*, 1971, **9**, 109–118.

Hastings, J. E. Cardiac and cortical responses to affective stimuli in a reaction time task. Unpublished doctoral dissertation. University of Wisconsin, 1971.

Hedquist, F. J., & Weinhold, B. K. Behavioral group counseling with socially anxious and unassertive college students. *Journal of Counseling Psychology*, 1970, **17**, 237–242.

Hepner, A., & Cauthen, N. R. Effect of subject control and graduated exposure on snake phobias. *Journal of Consulting and Clinical Psychology*, 1975, **43**, 297–304.

Herrnstein, R. Method and theory in the study of avoidance. *Psychological Review*, 1969, **76**, 49–69.

Hersen, M. Self-assessment of fear. *Behavior Therapy*, 1973, **4**, 241–257.

Hersen, M., Eisler, R. M., & Miller, P. M. An experimental analysis of generalization in assertive training. *Behaviour Research and Therapy*, 1974, **12**, 295–310.

Hersen, M., Eisler, R. M., Miller, P. M., Johnson, M. B., & Pinkston, S. G. Effects of practice, instructions, and modeling on components of assertive behavior. *Behaviour Research and Therapy*, 1973, **11**, 443–451.

Hodgson, R., & Rachman, S. Desynchrony in measures of fear. *Behaviour Research and Therapy*, 1974, **2**, 319–326.

Hull, C. L. *Principles of behavior*. New York: Appleton-Century-Crofts, 1943.

Husek, T. R., & Alexander, S. The effectiveness of the anxiety differential in examination stress situations. *Educational and Psychological Measurement*, 1963, **23**, 309–318.

Johnson, S. M., & Bolstad, O. D. Methodological issues in naturalistic observation: Some problems and solutions for field research. In L. A. Hamerlynck, L. C. Handy, & E. J. Mash (Eds.), *Behavior change: Methodology, concepts and practice*. Champaign, Ill.: Research Press, 1973.

Johnson, S. M., & Sechrest, L. Comparison of desensitization and progressive relaxation in treating test anxiety. *Journal of Consulting and Clinical Psychology*, 1968, **32**, 280–286.

Johnson, S. M., & White, G. Self-observation as an agent of behavioral change. *Behavior Therapy*, 1971, **2**, 488–497.

Katkin, E. S. Relationship between manifest anxiety and two indices of autonomic response to stress. *Journal of Personality and Social Psychology*, 1965, **2**, 324–333.

Katkin, E. S. The relationship between a measure of transitory anxiety and spontaneous autonomic activity. *Journal of Abnormal Psychology*, 1966, **71**, 142–146.

Katkin, E. S. Electrodermal lability: A psychophysiological analysis of individual differences in response to stress. In I. G. Sarason, & C. D. Speilberger (Eds.), *Stress and anxiety*. Washington, D. C.: Hemisphere Publishing Co., 1975.

Katkin, E. S., & Deitz, S. R. Systematic desensitization. In W. F. Prokasy, & D. Raskin (Eds.), *Electrodermal activity and psychological research*. New York: Academic Press, 1973.

Kazdin, A. E. Effects of covert modeling and model reinforcement on assertive behavior. *Journal of Abnormal Psychology*, 1974, **83**, 240–252.

Klorman, R., Weerts, T. C., Hastings, J. E. Melamed, B. G., & Lang, P. J. Psychometric description of some specific-fear questionnaires. *Behavior Therapy*, 1974, **5**, 401–409.

Lacey, J. I. Somatic response patterning and stress: Some revisions of activation theory. In M. Appley, & R. Trumbell (Eds.), *Psychological stress*. New York: Appleton-Century-Crofts, 1967.

Lader, M. H., Gelder, M. G., & Marks, I. M. Palmar conductance measures as predictors of response to desensitization. *Journal of Psychosomatic Research*, 1967, **11**, 283–290.

Lando, H. A. A comparison of excessive and rapid smoking in the modification of chronic smoking behavior. *Journal of Consulting and Clinical Psychology*, 1975, **43**, 350–355.

Lang, P. J. The mechanics of desensitization and the laboratory study of human fear. In C. M. Franks (Ed.), *Behavior therapy: Appraisal and status*. New York: McGraw-Hill, 1969.

Lang, P. J. Stimulus control, response control, and the desensitization of fear. In D. J. Lewis (Ed.), *Learning approaches to therapeutic behavior*. Chicago: Aldine Press, 1970.

Lang, P. J., & Lazovik, A. D. Experimental desensitization of a phobia. *Journal of Abnormal and Social Psychology*, 1963, **66**, 519–525.

Lang, P. J., Lazovik, A. D., & Reynolds, D. J. Desensitization, suggestibility and pseudotherapy. *Journal of Abnormal Psychology*, 1965, **70**, 395–402.

Lang, P. J., Melamed, B. G., & Hart, J. A psychophysiological analysis of fear modification using an automated desensitization procedure. *Journal of Abnormal Psychology*, 1970, **76**, 220–234.

Lazarus, A. A. *Behavior therapy and beyond.* New York: McGraw-Hill, 1971.

Leitenberg, H., Agras, W. S., Allen, R., Butz, R., & Edwards, J. Feedback and therapist praise during treatment of phobia. *Journal of Consulting and Clinical Psychology*, 1975, **43**, 396–404.

Leitenberg, H., Agras, W. S., & Barlow, D. H. Contribution of selective positive reinforcement and therapeutic instructions to systematic desensitization therapy. *Journal of Abnormal Psychology*, 1969, **74**, 113–118.

Leitenberg, H., Agras, S., Butz, R., & Wincze, J. Relationship between heart rate and behavioral change during the treatment of phobias. *Journal of Abnormal Psychology.* 1971, **78**, 59–68.

Leitenberg, H., & Callahan, E. J. Reinforced practice and reduction of different kinds of fears in adults and children. *Behaviour Research and Therapy*, 1973, **11**, 19–30.

Lick, J. R. Statistical vs. clinical significance in research on the outcome of psychotherapy. *International Journal of Mental Health*, 1973, **2**, 26–37.

Lick, J. R. Expectancy, false galvanic skin response feedback, and systematic desensitization in the modification of phobic behavior. *Journal of Consulting and Clinical Psychology*, 1975, **43**, 557–567.

Lick, J. R., & Bootzin, R. R. Expectancy factors in the treatment of fear: Methodological and theoretical issues. *Psychological Bulletin*, 1975, **82**, 917–931.

Lick, J. R., Condiotte, M., & Unger, T. Habituation to repeated presentations of a phobic stimulus as a function of uncertainty about phobic stimulus behavior. Unpublished manuscript, State University of New York at Buffalo, 1975.

Lick, J. R., & Sushinsky, L. Specificity of fear survey schedule items and the prediction of avoidance behavior. Unpublished manuscript, State University of New York at Buffalo, 1975.

Lick, J. R., & Unger, T. External validity of laboratory fear assessment: Implications from two case studies. *Journal of Consulting and Clinical Psychology*, 1975, **43**, 864–866.

Lipinski, D., & Nelson, R. The reactivity and unreliability of self-recording. *Journal of Consulting and Clinical Psychology*, 1974, **42**, 118–123.

Lomont, J. F., & Edwards, J. E. The role of relaxation in systematic desensitization. *Behaviour Research and Therapy*, 1967, **5**, 11–25.

Lykken, D. T. Statistical significance in psychological research. *Psychological Bulletin*, 1968, **70**, 151–159.

Lykken, D. T., & Venables, P. M. Direct measure of skin conductance: A proposal for standardization. *Psychophysiology*, 1971, **8**, 656–672.

Mahoney, M. J., Moore, B. S. Wade, T. C., & Moura, M. G. M. The effects of continuous and intermittent self-monitoring on academic behavior. *Journal of Consulting and Clinical Psychology*, 1973, **41**, 65–69.

Mandler, G., Mandler, J. M., & Uviller, E. T. Autonomic feedback: The perception of autonomic activity. *Journal of Abnormal and Social Psychology*, 1958, **56**, 367–373.

Manosevitz, M., & Lanyon, R. I. Fear survey schedule: A normative study. *Psychological Reports*, 1965, **17**, 699–703.

Marks, I. M. *Fears and phobias.* New York: Academic Press, 1969.

Mathews, A. M. Psychophysiological approaches to the investigation of desensitization and related procedures. *Psychological Bulletin*, 1971, **76**, 73–90.

McFall, R. M. Effects of self-monitoring on normal smoking behavior. *Journal of Consulting and Clinical Psychology*, 1970, **35**, 135–142.

McFall, R. M., & Marston, A. R. An experimental investigation of behavioral rehearsal in assertive training. *Journal of Abnormal Psychology*, 1970, **76**, 295–303.

Meichenbaum, D. *Cognitive behavior modification.* Morristown, New Jersey: General Learning Press, 1974.

Meichenbaum, D., & Cameron, R. Stress innoculation: A skills training approach to anxiety management. Unpublished manuscript. University of Waterloo, 1973.

Meichenbaum, D. H., Gilmore, F. B., & Fedoravicius, A. Group insight versus group desensitization in treating speech anxiety. *Journal of Consulting and Clinical Psychology*, 1971, **36**, 410–421.

Melnick, J. A comparison of replication techniques in the modification of minimal dating behavior. *Journal of Abnormal Psychology*, 1973, **81**, 51–59.

Miller, B. V., & Bernstein, D. A. Instructional demand in a behavioral avoidance test for claustrophobic fears. *Journal of Abnormal Psychology*, 1972, **80**, 206–210.

Mowrer, O. H. On the dual nature of learning—A re-interpretation of "conditioning" and "problem-solving." *Harvard Educational Review*, 1947, **17**, 102–148.

Nelson, R. O., Lipinski, D. P., & Black, J. L. The effects of expectancy on the reactivity of self-recording. *Behavior Therapy*, 1975, **6**, 337–349.

Orne, M. On the social psychology of the psychological experiment. With particular reference to demand characteristics and their implications. *American Psychologist*, 1962, **17**, 776–783.

Osgood, C. E., Suci, G. J., & Tannenbaum, P. H. *Measurement of meaning*. Urbana: University of Illinois Press, 1957.

Paul, G. L. *Insight vs. desensitization in psychotherapy: An experiment in anxiety reduction.* Stanford: Stanford University Press, 1966.

Pavlov, I. P. *Conditioned reflexes and psychiatry* (translated by W. H. Gantt). New York: International Publishers, 1941.

Rachman, S., & Hodgson, R. Synchrony and desynchrony in fear and avoidance. *Behaviour Research and Therapy*, 1974, **2**, 311–318.

Rachman, S., Marks, I. M., & Hodgson, R. The treatment of obsessive-compulsive neurotics by modelling and flooding *in vivo*. *Behaviour Research and Therapy*, 1973, **11**, 463–471.

Rappaport, H., & Katkin, E. S. Relationships among manifest anxiety, response to stress, and the perception of autonomic activity. *Journal of Consulting and Clinical Psychology*, 1972, **38**, 219–224.

Rathus, S. A. A 30-item schedule for assessing assertive behavior. *Behavior Therapy*, 1973, **4**, 398–406.

Reppucci, N. D., & Baker, B. L. Self-desensitization: Implications for treatment and teaching. In R. D. Rubin, & C. M. Franks (Eds.), *Advances in behavior therapy*. New York: Academic Press, 1968.

Rimm, D. C. Thought stopping and covert assertion in the treatment of phobias. *Journal of Consulting and Clinical Psychology*, 1973, **41**, 468.

Ritter, B. Treatment of acrophobia with contact desensitization. *Behaviour Research and Therapy*, 1969, **7**, 27–33.

Rutner, I. V. The effects of feedback and instructions on phobic behavior. *Behavior Therapy*, 1973, **4**, 338–348.

Sarason, I. G. Test anxiety, general anxiety, and intellectual performance. *Journal of Consulting Psychology*, 1957, **21**, 485–490.

Simkins, L. The reliability of self-recorded behaviors. *Behavior Therapy*, 1971, **2**, 83–87.

Smith, R. E., Diener, E., & Beaman, A. L. Demand characteristics and the behavioral avoidance measure of fear in behavior therapy analogue research. *Behavior Therapy*, 1974, **5**, 172–182.

Smith, R. E., & Nye, S. L. A comparison of implosive therapy and systematic desensitization in the treatment of test anxiety. *Journal of Consulting and Clinical Psychology*, 1973, **41**, 37–42.

Solomon, R. L., & Wynne, L. C. Traumatic avoidance learning: The principles of anxiety conservation and partial irreversibility. *Psychological Review*, 1954, **61**, 353–385.

Spielberger, C. D., Gorsuch, R. L., & Lushene, R. E. *Manual for the State-Trait Anxiety Inventory*. Palo Alto, California: Consulting Psychologist Press, 1970.

Stampfl, T. G., & Levis, D. J. The essentials of implosive therapy: A learning-theory based psychodynamic behavioral therapy. *Journal of Abnormal Psychology*, 1967, **72**, 496–503.

Stone, N. M., & Borkovec, T. D. The paradoxical effect of brief CS exposure on analogue phobic subjects. *Behaviour Research and Therapy*, 1975, **13**, 51–54.

Szpiler, J. A., & Epstein, S. Nonspecific electrodermal responses as a unique measure of anxiety. *Journal of Abnormal Psychology*, in press.

Truax, C. B., & Carkhuff, R. R. *Toward effective counseling and psychotherapy: Training and practice*. Chicago: Aldine, 1967.

Twentyman, C. T., & McFall, R. M. Behavioral training of social skills in shy males. *Journal of Consulting and Clinical Psychology*, 1975, **43**, 384–395.

Walk, R. D. Self-ratings of fear in a fear-invoking situation. *Journal of Abnormal and Social Psychology*, 1956, **52**, 171–178.

Watson, D., & Friend, R. Measurement of social-evaluative anxiety. *Journal of Consulting and Clinical Psychology*, 1969, **33**, 448–457.

Watson, J. P., Gaind, R., & Marks, I. M. Physiological habituation to continuous phobic stimulation. *Behaviour Research and Therapy*, 1972, **10**, 269–278.

Wicker, A. W. Attitudes versus actions: The relationship of verbal and overt behavioral responses to attitudinal objects. *Journal of Social Issues*, 1969, **25**, 41–78.

Wilson, G. D. GSR responses to fear-related stimuli. *Perceptual and Motor Skills*, 1967, **24**, 401–402.

Wolff, H. S. Telemetry of psychophysiological variables. In P. H. Venables, & I. Martin (Eds.), *A manual of psychophysiological methods*. New York: John Wiley, 1967.

Wolpe, J. *Psychotherapy by reciprocal inhibition*. Stanford: Stanford University Press, 1958.

Wolpe, J. *The practice of behavior therapy*. New York: Pergamon Press, 1969.

Wolpe, J. The behavioristic conception of neurosis: A reply to two critics. *Psychological Review*, 1971, **78**, 341–343.

Wolpe, J., & Lang, P. J. A fear survey schedule for use in behavior therapy. *Behaviour Research and Therapy*, 1964, **2**, 27–30.

Wolpe, J., & Lazarus, A. A. *Behavior therapy techniques*. New York: Pergamon Press, 1966.

Zuckerman, M. The development of an affective adjective checklist for the measurement of anxiety. *Journal of Consulting Psychology*, 1960, **24**, 457–462.

CHAPTER 8

Psychophysiological Measurement in Assessment[1]

LEONARD H. EPSTEIN

Department of Psychology
Auburn University
Auburn, Alabama

Introduction

The use of physiological responses as dependent measures in clinical research is well established (Averill & Opton, 1968; Lacey, 1959; Lang, 1971). Physiological behavior is particularly intriguing for clinical research, as quantitative and reliable measurement is possible. Recent developments in clinical treatment and assessment have stimulated additional use of physiological measurement. Of particular importance have been demonstrations of psychological interventions affecting physiological processes (Blanchard & Young, 1974), and a trend toward complete assessment of each behavioral disorder, including measurement of responses in the physiological, motoric, and self-report modalities (Lang, 1971).

This chapter describes procedures for utilization of psychophysiological measurement in clinical research and practice. As at least a cursory understanding of psychophysiology is necessary to discuss the appropriate use and interpretation of physiological measurement procedures, several basic principles will be presented in an introductory section. Also included in an introductory section are considerations in choosing the appropriate physiological dependent response(s), and a discussion of using physiological responses as indications of emotional behavior. The remainder, and bulk of the chapter, is devoted to a survey of physiological measurement procedures in clinical research and practice. The amount and variety of research done using physiological assessment precludes a comprehensive review of any particular content area. Thus, the reader will be exposed to a representative sample of the uses of physiological measurement. These uses have been organized into three areas: treatment evaluation, assessment, and design and execution of treatment.

[1]The author thanks Edward B. Blanchard and Michel Hersen for indicating the potential of psychophysiological measurement in clinical research, and to Jim McCoy, for his very constructive comments on an earlier version of this manuscript.

Characteristics of Physiological Responses

Reliable measurement of apparently significant clinical behavior is the tempting possibility that physiological measurement offers the empirically oriented clinician. However, in many cases it is difficult to evaluate physiological responding as one would evaluate motoric behavior. When assessing motoric behavior it is usually assumed that characteristics of responding are a function of specified environmental conditions. While constraints have recently been discussed (Bowers, 1973; Seligman, 1970), changes in motoric behavior are usually interpreted as a direct function of changes in some environmental event. There are, however, several psychophysiological principles that limit the utility of a simple, stimulus-response arousal model of physiological responding, and which should be considered in the interpretation of physiological responses. These principles indicate that it is difficult to assume parametric relationships between environmental events and levels of physiological responding.

One of the most important constraints on responding relates to the law of initial values (LIV) (Wilder, 1950), which states that the magnitude of a response will be a function of the prestimulus response level: the greater the prestimulus response level, the smaller the absolute response. Baseline levels and response amplitudes should be negatively correlated. Thus, an experimenter may observe only a small absolute heart rate change to an aversive stimulus when the baseline heart rate is greater than 100, as opposed to a baseline heart rate of 72. Likewise, the lower the baseline response level, the smaller the absolute response decrease. That is, biofeedback for heart rate decrease may produce a smaller absolute decrease when the baseline rate is 60, as opposed to 72. In the simplest sense, the LIV states that absolute response values within and between subjects are difficult to compare. Johnson & Lubin (1972) present numerous statistical procedures for analyzing degree of change as a function of different baseline values. For within subject analyses, procedural or experimental control of baseline differences is possible by requiring a long habituation period to establish reliable baseline estimates of resting responding. These baseline values should then be reliably reproducible in the baseline phase of each experimental session.

A second difficulty in interpreting physiological responses as parametric functions of environmental stimuli is the influence of homeostatic control on physiological response levels. That is, most autonomic responding is continually regulated by the generally antagonistic sympathetic and parasympathetic branches of the autonomic nervous system. And, as most stimuli activate both branches, oscillations around a stable mean value are produced. All homeostatic changes in responding are not, however, a function of parasympathetic activity, but in some cases may simply be due to a decrease in sympathetic functioning (Lang, 1972).

An example of a homeostatic mechanism is adaptation. After repeated stimulus presentations, an activated response will gradually return to baseline prestimulus levels. Adaptation occurs for most non-noxious (e.g., flashing lights) as well as some noxious events (e.g., shock). Adaptation should be evaluated during the initial stages of experimentation for two reasons. *First*, subjects should be thoroughly adapted to the measurement situation before baseline data are collected. If not, baseline values are likely to be high initially, as the subject has not adapted to the novelties of the measurement environment. Baseline measurement will then vary across sessions, as the subject begins to adapt. Certainly, studies designed to produce decreases in responding need to be especially careful of decelerating baselines. *Second*, when stimuli are initially presented in an experiment, responding may be partly due to the novelty produced by unadapted stimuli. This responding is often an organism's non-specific response to environmental change, and has been called an orienting response (Sokolov, 1963). Orienting responses should be ruled out before it is suggested that the stimuli themselves possess important activation characteristics for the subject. As Lang (1971) indicates, adaptation is often not a smooth and steady decline in rate or magnitude of response. Thus, a standard introductory session (or sessions) designed to adapt the subject to the experimental situation and stimuli is advisable to produce baselines.

Another homeostatic mechanism involves the concept of rebound. Rebound refers to the homeostatic reflex immediately following quick termination of stimulation which often produces post-stimulus levels lower than the prestimulus level. Consequently, variable baselines preceding and following responses are possible as a function of response magnitude.

Finally, the duration of response measurement is important, as latency and duration of physiological responses differ (Averill & Opton, 1968). While some systems respond quickly to stimulation (as heart rate), or intermediately (as GSR), others (as gastric motility), require a great deal of measurement time per unit response. Other physiological events (as endocrine responses), occur over even longer durations. These slow acting, long lasting responses are important as they may relate to development and/or maintenance of chronic psychological and physiological processes (Selye, 1950).

There are several additional areas in the basic science of psychophysiology that are important for the appropriate use of physiological measurement, but are beyond the scope of this chapter. One of these involves information about the mechanisms responsible for changes in activity levels or response characteristics of physiological responses. A second is a comparative analysis of the various procedures for recording a response. Both of these areas are covered, in any case, in several psychophysiology texts. Those who might be stimulated by the ideas presented in this chapter should see Brown (1967) or Venables & Martin (1967) for information on measurement considerations, and Greenfield & Sternbach (1972) for a comprehensive overview of the state of the art of psychophysiology, including detailed examination of the physiological mechanisms underlying the responses.

Selection of the Target Response

Measurement of an appropriate target response is important for the determination of treatment effects. For most psychophysiological disorders the response system to be assessed is indicated by the disorder. For example, blood pressure is an appropriate response for assessment of a hypertension patient, and frontalis and/or neck EMG responses are useful in assessing muscular contraction headaches. However, as is obvious from examining any of the methodological texts in psychophysiology, there is considerable discussion on the most appropriate way to measure each response system, and the best procedure for subsequently reducing the physiological data. The clinician using physiological measurement should be aware of the relative advantages and shortcomings with the various techniques of response measurement (Brown, 1967; Greenfield & Sternbach, 1972; Venables & Martin, 1967).

The use of the physiological response as the major target response does not preclude assessment of the motoric or self-report modalities. However, the determination that the physiological basis for a psychophysiological disorder has been modified requires physiological measurement. In many cases the physiological response does not serve as the major target, but is assessed to isolate the contribution of physiological processes to a selected behavioral or cognitive disorder. An excellent example of this is provided by Leitenberg, Agras, Butz, & Wincze (1971), who measured heart rate and motoric behavior during treatment of phobias. Their target measure was motoric behavior, but they were concerned with the contribution of, or necessity for, physiological change in producing modification in motoric behavior.

The careful selection of the appropriate target response is important because of the potential differences between individuals in their most reactive response systems. As Engel (1972) and Lacey *et al.* (1956) have indicated, an individual subject may have an idiosyncratic pattern of responding which is emitted to numerous environmental stimuli, and within this pattern, one particular system may reliably show a maximal response to various stimuli. The first principle is called response stereotypy, while the second is called response specificity or symptom specificity. These patterns have been replicated numerous times (see Engel, 1972 for a concise statement on specificities), but of course, do not predict responding of all subjects. These data do, however, suggest that the probability is slight that one particular response can be maximally sensitive when measured across different stimuli in several subjects.

Two strategies have been used when selecting the target physiological response to be measured. The first is to measure one selected response. Heart rate (Leitenberg, Agras, Butz & Wincze, 1969) and GSR (Barlow, Leitenberg, Agras & Wincze, 1969) are popular single responses. When only one response is measured, and this response has not been pre-determined for each subject, it is possibly a reactive response for some subjects and a relatively non-reactive response for others. Lack of responding for some subjects is not then sufficient to rule out a physiological contribution to the problem. This difficulty is well understood by many investigators (Leitenberg *et al.*, 1971), and limits the power of single response investigations.

A second approach is to measure several responses, which for example may include cardiovascular, respiratory, electrodermal, and muscular responses (Lang *et al.*, 1971). Concurrent measurement of numerous physiological responses has often been used to identify stimulus specificity, which is a consistent pattern of responding across several subjects produced by one stimulus. While general patterns are often shown across subjects, these analyses may be somewhat limited in clinical reasearch and treatment, as the properties of stimulus events for individual clinical subjects probably are best observed in terms of the response system in which the individual is most reactive.

Concurrent measurement of several responses can be used to provide a sample of responses for subsequent identification of response specificity as well as stimulus specificity. In that way, target responses can be determined individually for each subject in a group, and both stimulus and response specificity could be determined for several situations across subjects (Engel & Bickford, 1961). However, a possible problem (i.e., equating amplitudes of different responses across subjects) arises if individual target responses are chosen for each subject. For example, how comparable is a five beat per minute heart rate change with a two cycles per minute change in respiration? Lacey (1956) has discussed this problem in detail and developed autonomic lability scores to equate response amplitude across different systems. The autonomic lability scores take into account prestimulus levels, which are likely to be different across subjects and responses.

The reliability estimates of response specificity patterns within subjects has been mixed. While Lacey & Lacey (1967) demonstrated similar response patterns at four year retest, several other investigators (Johnson, Hord & Lubin, 1963; Oken, Grinker, Heath, Herta, Korchin, Sabskin & Schwartz, 1962) were unable to replicate stereotypy patterns at even one week or two day intervals. Likewise, Wieland & Mefferd (1970) showed intraindividual variation to several standard stimulus tasks over 120 days of measurement for three subjects. They indicate that various environmental and organismic variables can influence momentary responding. This variability may make determination of the appropriate target response difficult. It would appear essential that intra-individual stability of measurement should be established before a target response is chosen (Barlow & Hersen, 1973).

The selection of the appropriate target response to use for an individual subject requires obtaining a sample of several systems by initial measurement of several responses to the experimental stimuli. The stimuli Lacey (Lacey & Lacey, 1958) used in determining response specificity patterns are easily reproducable laboratory situations such as the cold pressor task, mental arithmetic, and word fluency tests. It is also possible to evaluate response patterns to specific stimuli that are very relevant to the client; Malmo, Shagass & Davis (1950), for example, used stimuli derived from case histories of muscular disorder clients.

Measurement of emotion

Emotion has been a central concept in the acquisition and maintenance of various behavior disorders for many theories of psychopathology. Consequently, a considerable amount of research has been performed to operationally define this construct.

The idea that particular physiological responses or response patterns are indicative of emotion and can then be used to define emotion has been a popular notion in psychology (Fehr & Stern, 1970; Goldstein, 1968). Investigations of this problem have typically involved the identification of specific responses that occur across subjects in response to one environmental (emotional) event. Investigations of this type relate to the principle of stimulus specificity (Engel, 1972; Lacey, Bateman & Van Lehn, 1953), which states that specific psychological stimuli produce specific physiological responses. The most often quoted evidence for specific physiological responses to specific psychological stimuli is provided by Ax (1953) and J. Schacter 1957). Ax's (1953) investigation involved the measurement of physiological responses during staged situations designed to produce fear and anger. The results indicated a reliable differentiation of response patterns to these two events. Ax (1953) interpreted the response patterns in fear to be consistent with an epinephrine activated response, while anger could be attributed to the combined effect of epinephrine and norepinephrine. These results were also obtained by J. Schacter (1957). However, Wenger, Clemens, Darsie, Engel, Estess & Sonnenschein (1960) demonstrated that simply producing these autonomic effects by infusion of epinephrine and norephinephrine was not sufficient to produce self-reports of fear and anger. This finding is consistent with the data reported by S. Schacter and Singer (1962), who indicated that both environmental and physiological variables are necessary for self-report of emotional behavior.

One major problem in defining emotion in terms of physiological responding stated cogently by Lang (1972), and reinforced by Rachman & Hodgson (1974) and Hodgson & Rachman (1974), is that the responses in the self-report, motoric, and physiological systems do not typically correlate highly.

Lang suggests that this may be because the environment can shape each system independently, with the effect that the response systems do not respond concordantly to a given stimulus. Extending Lang's hypothesis, Skinner (1975) argued that if concordance of responses do occur, it is not evidence for a basic inter-relation between response systems, but for similar environmental contingencies operating concurrently on more than one response system. In any case, no one has developed a procedure for determining which is the best measure of emotional behavior (i.e., self-report, motoric, or physiological). Thus, if attempts are necessary to operationalize the construct of emotion, referents should include, motoric, self-report, and physiological indices.

Physiological Responses in Treatment Evaluation

There are many physiological responses which are modifiable by psychologically based interventions and which can, therefore, serve as the target response for treatment evaluation. Blanchard and Young (1974) have presented several examples which include migraine headaches, hypertension, cardiac arrythmias, and Raynand's disease in the cardiovascular system; muscular contraction headaches, subvocal speech, and paralyses in the muscular system; stomach acid ph in the gastro-intestinal system; and cortical activity in the nervous system. These examples have in common direct measurement of a physiological response as the dependent variable, and a behavioral intervention as the independent variable. Measurement of a physiological response is necessary for the empirical demonstration of treatment effects for many disorders. The recent emphasis on modification of physiologically based disorders has led to the development of new and better techniques for measuring various responses. Examples include measurement of anal sphincter pressure (Kohlenberg, 1973), and beat-by-beat blood pressure recording (Tursky, Shapiro & Schwartz, 1972). These measurement procedures have provided researchers with the necessary fine-grained, continuous analyses that facilitate detection of subtle changes in the response, and provides increased opportunity for contact between the response and experimental contingencies.

Physiological responses can be measured when a physiological process is suspected to be involved in the acquisition or maintenance of the disorder even though the major target response is in another modality. In this case physiological measurement is useful for two reasons. *First*, people respond in three modalities; the cognitive, motoric, and physiological response systems (Hersen & Bellack, in press; Lang, 1971). Thus, an adequate assessment of many psychological disorders must include measurement in each system. For example, Borkovec *et al.* (1974) recently showed that deficits in interpersonal behaviors are often accompanied by cardiovascular arousal and self-reports of discomfort. Also, in a review, Borkovec (1973b) postulated that significant change of fear behavior is difficult if motoric and cognitive changes are attempted without physiological change. For example, after a selected behavioral treatment for a dog phobia, a client may approach and pet a dog reporting he is unafraid. However, Borkovec suggested that change in these modalities may not be maintained if physiological arousal remains high in the presence of the dog.

Second, the intensity of the responses in the three modalities is very different, such that inter-correlations are typically low. For one client a motoric response may provide a sensitive assessment measure, while for a second client a physiological response may be most sensitive. Such variance across individuals thus necessitates accurate measurements in all systems to identify the best dependent variable. The situation would be very different if correlations across systems were uniformly high, as then, measurement of either response system would be satisfactory. Numerous studies have measured physiological responses while the target response is in another modality. An exploratory examination of the relationship between heart rate (a physiological response), and approach to a phobic object (a motoric response) was performed by Leitenberg *et al.* (1971). Theories that stress the importance of anxiety defined by sympathetic nervous system responding (Wolpe, 1963) suggest that physiological responses must be suppressed for motoric behavior change to occur. Physiological and motoric behavior were recorded concurrently in treatment during the presentation of phobic objects. Results indicated that motoric change could occur without antecedent physiological change. In fact, this was observed for 7 of the 9 patients treated. Four patterns emerged across subjects; simultaneous heart rate increase, phobic behavior decrease; phobic decrease, heart rate increase; phobic decrease, stable heart rate; and heart rate decrease after phobic decrease. Differences were thus observed in the response of individual patients to treatment. It is most interesting that the behavior change reliably occurred independent of physiological change. While follow-up was not assessed, it is possible that maintenance of change would be inferior for subjects who demonstrated motoric but not physiological change. In contrast to the above results, Borkovec (1973a) investigated approach behavior to a feared snake after assessing autonomic activity. Increases in approach were greatest for subjects with an absence of strong pretest physiological arousal. As hypothesized by Borkovec, strong internal (physiological) fear responses could serve to maintain avoidance behavior. The above two studies indicate that the importance of physiological responses in the maintenance and modification of phobic behavior is undecided. However, physiological measurement is useful, if only to indicate the involvement or non-involvement of physiological processes for particular clients. As Hodgson & Rachman (1974) suggest, "It seems reasonable to assume that concordant changes should be the eventual aim of therapy and that a therapeutic intervention which alters only one measure (e.g., verbal or GSR) at a low level of stress, should be regarded with little enthusiasm."

While this discussion has dealt primarily with the use of physiological measurement in studies of fear modification, physiological measurement can be useful in studying other types of disorders. For example, Lewinsohn, Lobitz, & Wilson (1973) demonstrated that neurotically depressed subjects were physiologically more responsive than normals to mildly aversive events. Thus, a reduction in physiological responding to such stimuli may serve as an index of improvement. Schwartz (1975) indicated that responding of the facial musculature is different in depressed and non-depressed subjects. Responding of selected facial muscles may thus be useful in assessing treatment effects. Hare (1965) has shown that psychopaths typically underrespond to aversive events, so that increases in responding may be significant. Fenz & Steffy (1965) indicated changes in electrodermal responding to social stimuli parallelled changes in overt social behavior for a schizophrenic population.

Physiological responding can be related to motoric or self-report behavior change in two ways. *First*, changes in physiological responses may be necessary for behavior change, as indicated by Borkovec (1973b). Or *second*, physiological change may occur as a result of behavior change (Fenz & Steffy, 1965). In either case, measurement of physiological responses would be very useful in treatment outcome-evaluative studies.

Physiological Responses in Assessment. A common step in all types of assessment is the evaluation of organic impairment. This is typically carried out by a physician in the very early stages of assessment. The tests used will vary according to the physician and the laboratory facilitates available, but organic assessment may include a physical examination, review of systems, blood chemistry analyses, urinalysis, skull and chest x-rays. In addition, psychometric tests such as the Reitan neuropsychological battery are often used to assess organicity.

The initial assessment of organic impairment serves two purposes. *First*, it can indicate when the cause for the disorder is obviously organic and a medical procedure is indicated. *Second*, it may suggest the degree of organic impairment and the amount of behavior change feasible. These organic limitations are obvious in cases of brain damage or stroke related paralyses. However, initial organic involvement should by no means be used as an indication that significant behavior change can not be accomplished (Martin & Epstein, 1975). For example, Blanchard & Young (1974), in a review on biofeedback procedures, indicated significant clinical effects on numerous physiologically based disorders could be accomplished with reinforcement and feedback procedures. Also, Zlutnick, Mayville & Moffat (1975) modified organically based seizures in several youngsters by either breaking the response chain that occurs prior to the seizure, or by differentially reinforcing non-seizure behavior (DRO). Finally, Epstein, Hannay, & Looney (1975) investigated the modification, by fading procedures, of visual acuity in subjects with vision worse than 20/20.

In addition to identifying an organic basis for a disorder, a therapist often wants to rule out a suspected organic basis. This is most useful in conversion reactions, which can be defined as the exhibition of inappropriate behavior that the person attributes to a physical malfunction, when no organic basis exists. If the disorder is chronic, organic factors are often ruled out by a physician. However, numerous conversion disorders are episodic, or occur intermittently. Common examples seen by psychologists are conversion headaches. In these cases the organic involvement would be expected to occur, and thus could only be evaluated, during an attack. The evaluation would include measurement of physiological correlates of muscular contraction and vascular headaches. Assume a client is referred to a therapist for muscular contraction (tension) headaches, which are often diagnosed by the referral source on the basis of a self-report of symptoms. During an assessment period the client is instructed to call the therapist for physiological measurement whenever he has a moderate to severe headache. The therapist arranges for forehead and neck musculature measurement on five headache occasions, and finds very low muscle tension on each occasion. The therapist may then be able to rule out a physiological contribution, and should then pay major attention to variables maintaining self-report of headache.

Epstein & Abel (1975) used frontalis electromyogram recordings as part of the evaluation to assess clients for inclusion in a study investigating biofeedback treatment effects on muscular contraction headaches. Twenty-five clients were referred by physicians for "tension headaches" over an 18-month period. The assessment included: (a) frontalis EMG level greater than 10 microvolts during a headache, (b) history of symptoms consistent with muscular contraction headaches, (c) baseline self-report of headaches over a 2-week period indicating at least one headache every 2 days. Surprisingly, only six of the twenty-five referrals met these criteria. The other nineteen clients included subjects who had headaches for organic causes (e.g., a slipped disc), those who had very infrequent muscular contraction headaches, and also subjects who were reporting headaches without demonstrable muscular involvement. These latter referrals could be considered conversion reaction subjects, as their reports of physical symptoms were unrelated to physiological changes.

A potentially important area in assessment utilizing physiological measurement is the identification of people with a high risk of developing a psychophysiological disorder. Various factors have been discussed which may be important in developing a psychophysiological disorder, including response patterns which are specific to various psychological variables (Alexander, 1950; Grace & Graham, 1952); and predispositions to respond to a stressful stimulus within a particular organ system (Lacey, Bateman & Van Lehn, 1953). These factors can be classified by the concepts stimulus specificity for psychological factors, and response specificity for response dispositions. The factors that are responsible for the development of specificities are not known, but many consider stimulus-specific behavior innate, and specific behavior learned (Engel, 1972). Independent of the etiology of specificities, it may be possible to determine in a pre-morbid stage what disorder an individual is likely to develop. It is not known when this evaluation would be most predictive for each disorder, but there is evidence that for some disorders this may be possible at an early age as, for example, some children have psychophysiological skin disorders and allergies (Graham, 1972), and children who are hyperreactive blood pressure, responders to the standard pressor stimulus have parents with hypertension (Hines & Brown, 1932). Numerous studies have demonstrated that persons with psychophysiological disorders respond maximally to aversive stimuli in the system underlying the disorder (Engel & Bickford, 1961; Malmo & Shagass, 1949; Malmo *et al.*, 1950). But except for early work on prediction of hypertension, little has been done to identify high-risk persons in terms of response specific patterns and exposure to certain stressful environments. This is regrettable, as procedures are currently available for assessing both the environmental events and individual response specificities.

An important function of assessment can be to establish the relationship between changes in a physiological response and changes in psychological events as many psychiatric and medical disorders involve physiological changes to specific environmental stimuli. These stimuli can be organized at many levels, from establishing functional relationships between environmental events and specific responses, to assessing the psychosocial characteristics and organizational climate of a total human environment (Kiritz & Moos, 1974). The following section will deal with assessment procedures for events which are influencing the physiological responding of individual clients. The procedures will be discussed according to whether the important environmental events are self-reported or directly observed.

Self-report Methods. These procedures include standardized inventories to assess psychological and environmental stimuli, and procedures for self-monitoring important ongoing environmental events. The inventory procedures will be discussed first, followed by self-monitoring approaches.

An assessment of psychological-physiological relationships can be performed by relating gross changes in environmental events to changes in physiological responses. Standardized instruments for assessing the presence and magnitude of events that are associated with long and short-term physiological effects have been developed. Holmes & Rahe (1967) describe environmental changes as life events, and assume that both positive and negative events can affect physiological behavior. The changes are distributed across sleeping, eating, social, recreational, personal, and interpersonal behaviors. Changes in these behaviors are considered to reflect life changes, which are quantifiable by taking into account the magnitude of importance of each life event (Masuda & Holmes, 1967). When life events are summed they produce life change scores. These scores predict health changes as a function of experiences within the last year (Rahe, Mahan & Arthur, 1970), and as a function of daily events (Holmes & Holmes, 1970). The prediction of health changes from non-recent (within the last 6 months to year) changes is accomplished by the Social Readjustment Rating Scale, while daily events can be assessed using the Schedule of Recent Experiences, or the recently constructed Life Events Inventory, (Cochrane & Robertson, 1973).

These inventories could be quite useful in assessing the relationship between environmental events and physiological processes. The major use of these procedures in assessment and treatment is probably for episodic disorders, which could be reflected by daily changes in experiences. In these cases measurement of physiological responses could be obtained several times per week, and related to quantitative change in life event scores. In addition, the inventories may be useful in identifying standard situations which should then be individually assessed in more detail.

The second self-report method, self-monitoring, consists of the detection and recording of environmental events by the client himself. The recording system should be both convenient to carry and easy to use. Small spiral notebooks or 3 × 5 cards which have been arranged for recording of necessary information have been employed by the author. Self-monitoring can be used to generate hypotheses about important controlling environmental events. For example, a therapist might instruct a client to record all the activities he engaged in during each hour, and how he felt about them. Another strategy would be to record, from memory, all activities that preceded an attack of an episodic disorder (e.g., a headache) by 3 hours. For these analyses, or from daily use of a standardized inventory, events that are reliably related to the disorder could be identified, operationally defined, and then self-monitored to produce a fine-grained analysis of the relationship between specific events and the disorder. For example, an initial analysis may indicate that a secretary repeatedly develops a headache at lunchtime each day, after the morning's work. Components of her morning activities could be operationally defined and rated each hour. Activities might include meeting with her superior, typing, filing, etc. Each could be checked if it occurred, and rated accordingly.

Both of these self-report procedures can provide only correlative information on psychological and physiological interactions. When using life change inventories, the life changes may be influenced by many factors in addition to psychological events, such as weather, diet, or disease (Graham, 1972). Therefore, a correlation between life changes and physical disability may not mean the physiological response is a function of a psychological event, and can thus be misleading. A related difficulty is that life change can be a function of the disability itself. For example, as Graham (1971) states, loss of a job may be a function of a disability, as opposed to the job loss influencing the disability. Similar problems are evident when relating self-monitored environmental events to physiological responses. Correspondence in time between the event and the physiological response does not indicate that they are functionally related. It can *not* be over-emphasized that the relationship between self-reported life events and changes, and physical disability can only provide *correlative evidence.*

There are several available procedures which can provide evidence of functional relationships between events. As Baer, Wolf, & Risley (1968) state, a functional analysis requires manipulation of events that are "responsible for the occurrence or non-occurrence of that behavior." That is, the probability of the response is a direct function of the presence or absence of the stimulus. Functional analyses are typically used in treatment evaluation, but they can also serve to identify controlling relationships between events and responses. An intriguing example of a functional analysis in behavioral assessment was performed by Hersen, Miller, & Eisler (1973). The investigators video-taped social interactions between four alcoholics and their spouses. They experimentally manipulated the topic of conversation either alcohol or non-alcohol related in a reversal design. The results indicated that eye contact of the wife was a direct function of the topic of conversation. When alcohol was discussed the wife looked at her husband often, when it was not discussed she looked at him less. A reverse trend was observed for the alcoholic himself.

Thus, to determine casual relationships between certain events and physiological responses the event should be directly manipulated. Procedures for these types of assessment can be differentiated according to properties of the stimuli being assessed. The stimuli can vary from analogue to real-life events.

Experimentally Controlled Analogue Stimuli. This category includes assessment procedures that involve the use of stimuli that represent those which occur in the natural environment, but are presented in a laboratory environment. For the most part stimuli have been presented during structured interviews or by the use of audio-visual equipment.

An important early investigation utilizing the interview method was described by Malmo, Shagass, & Davis (1950). This study was an attempt to assess whether patients who report disorders related to muscle function actually respond to stressful stimuli by muscular responding. The study involved recordings from selected muscle groups in patients with a tension headache, a writing difficulty, and a head tic. Patients were exposed to a standard pain stimulus and then discussed events important in the acquisition and maintenance of their present disorder. Physiological data indicated striking changes in the involved muscle and self-report of the symptom during selected interview times when important material was presented. It is interesting that Malmo *et al.* (1950) report muscle tension changes during the standard painful stimulus, but no correlated symptom report. This represents yet another indication that physiological changes are not sufficient to account for a response in the self-report system. A prior investigation (Malmo & Shagass, 1949) indicated that patients with head pain complaints and heart complaints responded differentially to a standard painful stimulus. The head complainers showed maximal responsivity in the muscular system, while the heart complainers responded greatest in the cardiovascular system. In summary, Malmo demonstrated response specificity both across groups of subjects in response to a standard pain stimulus, and within subjects in relation to specific topics of conversation.

There are many similar investigations (i.e., Wolff, 1950) utilizing the experimental interview. However, these procedures are not without their problems (Lang, 1971). For example, there may be different stimulus intensities or different energy requirements of the stimuli presented to the subject that may influence physiological responding independently of the psychological effects. In addition, the use of experimental interviews is often complicated as the interpretation of psychological events are made *post hoc*, as defined by the physiological change. That is, after a session is terminated, an examination of the polygraph record is used to define psychological states during the sessions.

There have been several investigations of psychological variables performed in more controlled environments, which provide better estimates of psychological-physiological relationships. Prigatano & Johnson (1974) presented a variety of visual stimuli (slides) to spider phobic and non-spider phobic subjects. The stimuli included spider, sea-scape, and surgical scenes, thus sampling specific phobic, pleasant, and generally aversive scenes. Electrocardiogram, skin resistance, finger blood volume, and respiration were recorded. Results indicated differential changes only for the spider phobic subjects in the presence of spider slides. Changes occurred with cardiovascular and skin responses but not for respiration. Thus, this investigation indicated that controlled visual stimuli presented in a laboratory setting may produce differential changes in autonomic responding.

Lang, Melamed, & Hart (1970) used tape recorded scenes to present hierarchy items for assessment of the relationship between subjectively graded steps in an anxiety hierarchy and physiological responding. Spider phobic and public-speaking anxious subjects were tested. The results showed a linear relationship between heart rate and skin conductance measures and vividness of visualization of hicrarchy items. In general, the spider phobic subjects tended to become more aroused to the higher hierarchy items than the public-speaking anxious subjects. Grossberg & Wilson (1968) provided additional data on procedures for presenting stimuli. They compared physiological responses when stimuli were read to the subjects and when subjects were instructed to imagine stimuli. Results indicated a clear superiority in production of physiological arousal for the imagined over-the-tape recorded scenes. This indicates that while taped scenes can be used to facilitate imagery, subjects must visualize the appropriate stimulus during assessment. In this sense, visual stimuli may be preferred, as they may facilitate subject involvement more than auditory stimuli.

Motion pictures or videotapes present stimuli which are more realistic than slides or audiotapes. During one of twelve experimental interviews Malmo, Shagass, & Davis (1950) presented a film about a woman suffering from psychogenic headaches to a muscle contraction headache client, and observed a considerable increase in frontalis muscle tension. Regretably, Malmo *et al.* (1950) did not present neutral films to control for possible activation due to watching any movie. Lazarus (1967) has used various types of films to study psychological and physiological components of emotion. His work demonstrates the potential flexibility of films. He varied the soundtrack of the film, thereby manipulating instructional sets in combination with a common visual presentation. Videotape has also been increasingly used in studying behavior (Eisler, Hersen, & Agras, 1973). Videotape has the advantage of allowing the experimenters to develop scenes tailored to events unique in an individual's life, thereby further decreasing the gap between real life and laboratory stimuli.

Real Life Stimuli. The most valid stimuli to relate to physiological changes are those that occur in the environment. However, while generalization problems may decrease, problems in controlling parameters of the stimuli increase. Consequently, a trade off between lack of control and increase in representativeness of stimuli must be considered. An excellent example of assessment using naturalistic stimuli is provided by Purcell, Brady, Chai, Muser, Molk, Gordon, & Means (1969). These investigators evaluated the effects of separating asthmatic children from their natural parents. Measures of expiratory flow rate, clinical exams, daily observations of the child, and daily report of medication intake were recorded. Data were collected during baselines, experimental phases, and in return to baseline conditions. During the experimental period a "foster" parent was placed in the child's natural home, while the parents were removed. Dependent measures reflected a positive change during the experimental separation for the 13 subjects whose attacks were thought to be strongly influenced by psychological events, while minimal changes were observed in the 12 children whose asthma attacks were not believed to be a function of psychological events. This investigation provided clear evidence that parental-child interactions can be highly influential in stimulating asthma attacks in certain children.

An obvious difficulty when using real-life stimuli is accurate measurement of an episodic physiological response in the natural environment. For this reason several experimenters have not measured the physiological response itself, but the correlated behavioral effects of the disorder. This is the case with another investigation on psychological influences on asthma. The relationship between interactions with her mother and observed symptoms of physiological dysfunction in an asthmatic client was observed by Metcalfe (1956). She recorded daily activities and symptoms of asthma attacks in a 21-year old hospitalized woman. Post-discharge analysis indicated a strong correlative relationship between her attacks and interactions with her mother during her period of hospitalization. A subsequent separation from her mother after hospitalization resulted in a dramatic decrease in attacks, from a baseline of at least one attack per day for 24 months, to 9 attacks in 20 months post discharge. It should be noted that in this case the mother's behavior was not directly manipulated, which is a requirement for a functional analysis. However, the reliable observation of symptoms associated with the presence or absence of the mother provide a demonstration of the correlative relationship between the mother and her daughter's problem. Several of the examples which follow also do not involve direct manipulation of the independent variable, or psychological event in this case.

It may not always be necessary to measure physiological responses in the natural environment directly after manipulation of psychological events in order to assess effects of environmental stimuli. Many situations produce sustained changes which may be adequately assessed in the laboratory at a point removed from the actual experience with the environmental event. An example of this is the measurement of physiological responding preceding and following doctoral level oral exams. Smith & Wenger (1965) investigated autonomic responding the day of doctoral level oral exams, and one month after the exams. The measurements were designed to provide assessments of episodic (phasic) responding to an anxiety provoking situation. Data were presented in terms of autonomic balance scores, which indicate the dominance of the sympathetic or parasympathetic nervous systems. The results indicated relative sympathetic increase during the time just prior to the oral exam, compared with the control measurement. This finding is consistent with results obtained for subjects suffering from chronic anxiety states (Wenger, 1948).

Recent advances in technology have allowed for the detection of physiological activity in the natural environment. Telemetry has been instrumental in these applications (Mackay, 1967; Sandler, McCutcheon, Fryer, Rositano,

Westbrook & Hano, 1975). Telemetry involves the transmission of physiological signals from a subject outside a laboratory to a recorder or data storage unit in a laboratory. Telemetric recording provides for the on-line measurement of various physiological responses while the client is in the natural environment. A primary use of telemetry has been the monitoring of patients during or following surgery or acute care. As Mackay (1967) points out, this technology is also well suited to investigation of the influence of psychological events. An additional use for telemetry is the assessment of various treatment effects. For example, Weiss & Engel (1971) monitored selected extra-laboratory electrocardiogram activity in patients who were receiving laboratory biofeedback training for premature ventricular contractions.

Procedures have also been developed for direct measurement of physiological responding in the natural environment by portable detection and recording devices. Examples of this technology include portable EMG (Rugh & Solberg, 1974) detection and a portable and automated blood pressure detector and recorder (Schneider, 1969).

The use of a portable physiological detector is discussed by Rugh & Solberg (1974). They investigated variables influencing bruxism, which is excessive clenching and gnashing of teeth in response to environmental events. Clients were provided a portable EMG feedback device, which presented a tone when levels of jaw (masseter) muscle activity exceeded a preset criterion. The device was adjustable so that normal masseter movement in smiling and talking was not sufficient to elicit a tone. While no quantifiable data were presented, the authors reported that the device was helpful in teaching clients to identify situations in which bruxism occurred.

In addition, procedures for direct measurement of physiological events in the natural environment are available. These are relatively simple, and include pulse rate measurement (Bell & Schwartz, 1975), portable blood pressure measurement (Olmstead, 1967), observation of respiration rate, and a "sweat bottle" for assessing skin conductance (Straham, Todd & Inglis, 1974). In addition to direct measurement by an experimenter, such responses as pulse rate and respiration rate may be self-monitored after a client is trained to accurately observe these events. While this type of measurement procedure seems ideal for naturalistic assessment, two possible limitations should be noted. First, many important responses require considerable technology for detection of the relevant parameters. Second, measurement may involve a disruption of ongoing activity to obtain the physiological responses. These values may then be inconsistent with those obtained during the ongoing activity.

Physiological measurement in the design and execution of treatment

Physiological measurement can be useful in the design of treatment variables for individual clients. Lang *et al.* (1970) demonstrated that hierarchy items for desensitization can be ranked according to physiological responding of phobic subjects. Also, Barabasz (1974) reported that ordering of items in this objective fashion was helpful in desensitization with children. Likewise, physiological responses can be used to operationalize aversive stimuli. For example, if a treatment is designed using the classical conditioning paradigm, then the unconditioned stimulus must, by definition, reliably elicit physiological arousal prior to pairing of the events.

Physiological measurement can also be used to assist in the execution of treatment. In this way, the experimenter can study the process of therapy and make decisions about therapeutic variables according to objective criteria. Biofeedback treatments can be classified in this way, as changes in the physiological response are used to determine changes in treatment components. However, aside from current biofeedback approaches, Lang (1971) notes that relatively little work has been done using physiological responses in treatment execution. An interesting use of physiological measurement is reported by Lang & Melamed (1969), who used a punishment-escape paradigm to suppress ruminative vomiting in a 9-month old infant. The aversive stimulus (shock) was presented contingent upon vomiting, determined by an EMG response in the throat and by nurses' observations. The shock was terminated when vomiting behavior stopped. The treatment suppressed vomiting resulting in an increase in body weight. Kohlenberg (1970) notes that many therapists may not have physiological measurement equipment available for such response definition, and has developed procedures for accurate observational measurement of motoric vomiting behavior.

Numerous treatment studies have measured physiological responses during therapy (see Mathews, 1971, for a review of physiological measurement during desensitization). These measures typically are used to assess changes during or as a function of treatment, or as a pure outcome evaluative measure, and do not influence the execution of treatment. A unique use of physiological measurement would be to gauge treatment exposure. This assessment may be important for accurate determination of treatment effects. When a patient sample is exposed to a treatment or set of treatments, individual subjects are likely to respond to the same, or different treatments, at very different rates. Typically, treatments are equated in terms of the length of exposure to treatment, but they could also be equated in terms of similarity of physiological change, independent of the time required to equate the changes. Similar logic often is used in drug evaluation, where treatments are evaluated after a therapeutic dosage is evident, and in basic operant conditioning studies, where subjects are exposed to experimental conditions until the response to the condition is stable, indicating the condition is reliably controlling the behavior. Thus, treatment could be equated in terms of common behavioral criteria. One could then denote a therapeutic dosage of a specific treatment by equating degree of physiological change across subjects. If this is done, the experimenter must be careful to avoid using the physiological response as the target behavior to define treatment success. If he does this, he will have confounded the target response with the behavioral criteria used to equate exposure. He will then always be successful, as treatments will continue until modification of the target response is demonstrated. Analyses to objectively equate treatment experience would be interesting for the comparison of treatment effects per unit of therapist time, providing a cost-benefit analysis (Epstein & McCoy, 1975).

A related use for physiological measurement is to equate drug dosages by psychophysiological measurement (Stroebel, 1971). An excellent example of this is provided by Lader & Wing (1966) in an investigation of the pharmacological treatment of anxiety. They assessed drug dosages in terms of a behavioral criterion: habituation effects to an auditory click. Results showed that equivalent dosages of amorbarbital sodium and chlordiazepoxide had similar effects on several objective indices of anxiety, but varied greatly in cost of the drugs to produce equivalent effects.

Another use of physiological measurement would be to predict treatment success. If Borkovec's (1973) previously noted discussion of behavioral-physiological relationships is correct, then a client experiencing physiological arousal may do poorly in a shaping program, but might do better in desensitization which is supposed to operate directly on the physiological system. Mathews, Johnston, Shaw & Gelder (1974) investigated the predictive value of several assessment measures, including heart rate and skin conductance, which were collected during treatment evaluation of phobic subjects. The treatments were flooding, desensitization, and a non-specific control. Results indicated equivalent effects for desensitization and flooding, both of which were superior to the control condition. The authors then attempted to identify the variables which contributed to improvement across subjects. The results did not indicate that any physiological measure was among the dependent measures which accounted for the most variance in predicting improvement. Data for individual subjects were also examined across treatment sessions. Examination of within subject data indicated a general decrease in heart rate across the two sessions in which physiological measures were reported, independent of treatment. However, heart rate showed an increase during the first 10 minutes of the first treatment session for flooding, which then decreased over the remainder of the session. This result is particularly interesting as it is consistent with a finding reported by Lang, Melamed, & Hart (1970) in their psychophysiological investigation of phobic patients during desensitization. These authors found greatest post-treatment change for subjects experiencing high heart rates during initial presentation of fearful scenes. These subjects also showed high correspondence between physiological responses and verbal report. Thus, Lang *et al.* (1970) indicated that subjects who respond with increased physiological arousal during initial hierarchy steps, and who can verbally discriminate their physiological responses, are those subjects who are most likely to respond favorably to treatment. Extending these findings to Mathews *et al.* (1974), it would have been predicted that the subjects who were exposed to flooding would do best. While this hypothesis was not substantiated by Mathews *et al.* (1974), Marks, Boulougouris & Marset (1971) reported flooding to be superior to desensitization for agoraphobic clients.

The use of physiological assessment to predict the response to particular types of treatment seems very appropriate. The variability between physiological, motoric, and cognitive responses is great enough so that numerous arrangements of the response amplitudes across response modalities within a subject sample is possible. For example, consider a sample of phobics who will not approach a feared object. Within this sample, some subjects are likely to have a physiological component to the disorder, while others are not. In addition, distributed across this dimension, some of these subjects are likely to have great correspondence between verbal reports of motoric and/or physiological behavior, while others will not. Each of these types of clients may respond differentially to any one treatment. Or, the same treatment may work for each type of client, but may be much less efficient with one patient type than another.

Indirect Physiological Assessment Procedures

Previous discussion has emphasized direct physiological measurement. While direct measurement of physiological responses is preferable, there are instances when the physiological response cannot be directly measured. Two of these situations are when laboratory physiological measurement devices are not available and during assessment in the natural environment. Three procedures for indirect measurement of physiological responding will be mentioned: direct observation, outcome recording, and self-monitoring.

Many physiological responses have behavioral correlates which are directly measurable. For example, asthma attacks (Metcalfe, 1964), seizures (Zlutnick *et al.*, 1975), and vomiting (Kohlenberg, 1970) produce unique motoric response patterns and thus can be carefully observed. In addition, observation of complaints or reports of pain may reflect changes in a physiological response. The procedures for observation are standard behavioral observation procedures, with the motoric correlates of the physiological response as the target behavior. These procedures can not be used for physiological problems which do not have easily discriminable overt symptoms. Headaches and hypertension, for example, are problems that are difficult to directly observe.

In some cases the problem behavior produces permanent effects on the environment that can be readily measured. For example, amount of medication (Epstein, Hersen & Hemphill, 1974), amount of a standard task completed (Fordyce, Fowler, Lehmann, DeLateur, Sand & Trieschmann, 1973), and number of work or school days missed can be assessed. Each of these may be sensitive to changes in the underlying disorder. Any behavior that is disrupted when the person is ill may be useful dependent measure.

Finally, the client can be requested to detect and record occurrences of his problem (i.e., self-monitor his disorder). Self-monitoring is a complex process (Kazdin, 1974) which can effect the rates or topography of the response being observed. Also, reliability can be a function of the concurrent responses maintained by the environment (Epstein, Miller & Webster, 1975; Epstein, Webster & Miller, 1975), and the valence of the response (Kazdin, 1974). Results of numerous studies indicate that many easily definable, low or moderate frequency responses, such as cigarette smoking (Fredericksen, Epstein & Kovesky, 1975), can be reliably recorded. When discussing self-monitoring of physiological responses, one should differentiate between recording symptoms of the response and recording the response itself. The overt symptoms of many physiological abnormalities, such as asthma, are easily detectable by the client or by direct observation procedures. Some other disorders, such as headaches, present symptoms that are covert and only observable to the client. Self-monitoring, as opposed to direct observation, may then be necessary for measurement of the symptoms. Of course, the experimenter should be careful when obtaining reports of pain responses, as the pain report can be influenced by factors other than physiological change. For example, a tension headache client could report pain in the absence of muscle contraction in order to avoid an unpleasant event.

While symptoms of abnormal physiological processes may be detectable, it is unclear whether subjects can identify the actual physiological change which is the basis for the disorder. Most studies in which a self-report estimate of physiological response levels is recorded indicate low correlations between systems (Mandler & Kremen, 1959; Mandler, Mandler & Uviller, 1958). Several studies required subjects to make overt responses to changes in ongoing physiological responses using standard stimulus control paradigms. In general, these results indicate that untrained subjects cannot detect natural variation in the system, but training of physiological responses in humans can significantly improve a subject's detection. Detection has been assessed for heart rate (Brener & Jones, 1974; Epstein & McCoy, 1975; Epstein & Stein, 1975), brain wave activity (Stevens, 1967), and electrodermal measures (Stern, 1972). Research efforts to develop a technology to produce accurate discrimination of physiological events is relatively recent, and no studies have as yet assessed the detection of people experiencing a disorder involving physiological components. Thus, at present, when using indirect measurement, either direct observation or assessment of permanent effects are preferable.

Summary

Uses of physiological measurement in clinical research and practice were discussed. Potential uses in assessment and treatment are numerous. Physiological measurement seems ideally suited to behavioral research as data are collected automatically, apparently reliably, in a direct representation of underlying responding. In most cases, however, the potential for physiological measurement in clinical research has not been realized (Lang, 1971).

Two recent innovations have provided a strong impetus for physiological measurement. The first is bio-feedback, which has demonstrated that many physiological response systems can be influenced by psychological interventions. Bio-feedback stimulated the development of measurement procedures for using the physiological response as the primary target response. The second innovation relates to the recent emphasis in behavioral assessment for complete evaluation of each client. This assessment includes measurement of physiological, motoric, and self-report modalities, and has been used in evaluating the contribution of physiological processes for numerous behavior disorders. The emphasis on complete assessment has also resulted in a decrease in the use of one isolated response system as the single measure of a disorder. In particular, "emotional" behavior is typically not simply defined by physiological arousal, but by assessment including motoric and self-report measurement.

Several relatively new uses of physiological assessment were discussed. These include development of assessment procedures to identify patients with a high-risk of developing a psychophysiological disorder, prediction of success in therapy, the equating of therapy "exposure," and procedures for specifying environmental-physiological relations.

References

Alexander, F. *Psychosomatic Medicine: Its principles and applications.* New York: Norton, 1950.

Averill, J. R., & Opton, E. M. Psychophysiological assessment: Rationale and problems. In R. McReynolds (Ed.), *Advances in psychological assessment*: Volume I. Palo Alto: Science and Behavior Books, 1968.

Ax, A. F. The physiological differentiation between fear and anger in humans. *Psychosomatic Medicine*, 1953, **15**, 433–442.

Baer, D. M., Wolf, M. M., & Risley, T. R. Some current dimensions of applied behavior analysis. *Journal of Applied Behavior Analysis*, 1968, **1**, 91–97.

Barlow, D. H., & Hersen, M. Single-case experimental designs: Uses in applied clinical research. *Archives of General Psychiatry*, 1973, **21**, 319–325.

Barlow, D. H., Leitenberg, H., Agras, W. S., Wincze, J. P. The transfer gap in systematic desensitization: An analogue study. *Behaviour and Research and Therapy*, 1969, **7**, 191–196.

Barabasz, A. F. Quantifying hierarchy stimuli in systematic desensitization via GSR: A preliminary investigation. *Child Study Journal*, 1974, **4**, 207–211.

Bell, I. R., & Schwartz, G. E. Voluntary control and reactivity of human heart rate. *Psychophysiology*, 1975, **12**, 339–348.

Blanchard, E. B., & Young, L. D. Clinical applications of bio-feedback training: A review of evidence. *Archives of General Psychiatry*, 1974, **30**, 573–589.

Borkovec, T. D. The effects of instructional suggestion and physiological cues on analogue fear. *Behavior Therapy*, 1973a, **4**, 185–192.

Borkovec, T. D. The role of expectancy and physiological feedback in fear research: A review with special reference to subject characteristics. *Behavior Therapy*, 1973b, **4**, 491–505.

Borkovec, T. D., Stone, N. M., O'Brein, G. T., & Kaloupek, D. G. Evaluation of a clinically relevant target behavior for analogue outcome research. *Behaviour Therapy*, 1974, **5**, 503–513.

Bowers, K. S. Situationism in psychology: An analysis and a critique. *Psychological Review*, 1973, **80**, 307–336.

Brener, J., & Jones, J. M. Interoceptive discrimination in intact humans: Detection of cardiac activity. *Physiology and Behavior*, 1974, **13**, 763–767.

Cochrane, R., & Robertson, A. The life events inventory: A measure of the relative severity of psychosocial stressors. *Journal of Psychosomatic Research*, 1973, **17**, 135–139.

Eisler, R. M., Hersen, M., & Agras, W. S. Effects of videotape and instructional feedback on nonverbal marital interaction: An analog study. *Behavior Therapy*, 1973, **4**, 551–558.

Engel, B. T. Response specificity. In N. S. Greenfield, & R. A. Sternbach (Eds.), *Handbook of psychophysiology*. New York: Holt, Rinehart & Winston, 1972.

Engel, B. T., & Bickford, A. F. Response specificity. *Archives of General Psychiatry*, 1961, **5**, 478–489.

Epstein, L. H., & Abel, G. G. Bio-feedback effects on muscular contraction headaches. Unpublished manuscript, University of Mississippi Medical Center, 1975.

Epstein, L. H., Hannay, H. J., & Looney, R. L. Fading and reinforcement in the modification of visual acuity. Paper presented at Association for Advancement of Behavior Therapy, San Francisco, December, 1975.

Epstein, L. H., Hersen, M., & Hemphill, D. P. Music feedback in the treatment of tension headache: An experimental case study. *Journal of Behavior Therapy and Experimental Psychiatry*, 1974, **5**, 59–63.

Epstein, L. H., & McCoy, J. F. Heart rate as a discriminative stimulus. Unpublished manuscript, Auburn University, 1975.

Epstein, L. H., & McCoy, J. F. Issues in smoking control. *Addictive Behaviors*, 1975, **1**, 65–72.

Epstein, L. H., Miller, P. M., & Webster, J. S. The effects of reinforcing concurrent behavior on self-monitoring. *Behavior Therapy*, in press.

Epstein, L. H., & Stein, D. B. Feedback-influenced heart rate discrimination. *Journal of Abnormal Psychology*, 1974, **83**, 585–588.

Epstein, L. H., Webster, J. S., & Miller, P. M. Accuracy and controlling effects of self-monitoring as a function of concurrent responding and reinforcement. *Behavior Therapy*, in press.

Fehr, F. S., & Stein, J. A. Peripheral physiological variables and emotion: The James-Lange theory revisited. *Psychological Bulletin*, 1970, **74**, 411–424.

Fenz, W. D., & Steffy, R. A. Electrodermal arousal of chronically ill psychiatric patients undergoing intensive behavioral treatment. *Psychosomatic Medicine*, 1968, **30**, 423–436.

Fordyce, W. E. Fowler, R. S., Lehmann, J. F., DeLateu, B. J., Sand, P. L., & Trieschmann, B. L. Operant conditioning in the treatment of chronic pain. *Archives of Physical Medicine and Rehabilitation*, 1973, **54**, 399–408.

Fredericksen, L. W., Epstein, L. H., & Kosevsky, B. P. Reliability and controlling effects of three procedures for self-monitoring smoking. *Psychological Record*, 1975, **25**, 255–264.

Grace, W. J., & Graham, D. T. Relationship of specific attitudes and emotions to certain bodily diseases. *Psychosomatic Medicine*, 1952, **14**, 243–251.

Graham, D. T. Psychosomatic medicine. In N. S. Greenfield, & R. D. Sternbach (Eds.), *Handbook of Psychophysiology*. New York: Holt, Rinehart & Winston, 1972.

Goldstein, M. L. Physiological theories of emotion: A critical historical review from the standpoint of behavior theory. *Psychological Bulletin*, 1968, **69**, 23–40.

Grossberg, J. M., & Wilson, H. K. Physiological changes accompanying the visualization of fearful and neutral situations. *Journal of Personality and Social Psychology*, 1968, **10**, 124–133.

Hare, R. D. Temporal gradient of fear arousal in psychopaths. *Journal of Abnormal Psychology*, 1965, **70**, 442–445.

Hersen, M., & Bellack, A. S. Assessment of social skills. In A. R. Ciminero, K. S. Calhoun, & H. E. Adams (Eds.), *Handbook for Behavioral Assessment*. New York: John Wiley & Sons, in press.

Hersen, M., Miller, P. M., & Eisler, R. M. Interactions between alcoholics and their wives: A descriptive analysis. *Quarterly Journal of Studies on Alcohol*, 1973, **34**, 516–520.

Hines, E. A., Jr., & Brown, G. E. Standard stimulus for measuring vasomotor reactions. Its application in the study of hypertension. *Proceedings of the Staff Meeting of the Mayo Clinic*, 1932, **7**, 332–335.

Hodgson, R., & Rachman, S. II. Desynchrony in measures of fear. *Behaviour Research and Therapy*, 1974, **12**, 319–326.

Holmes, T. S., & Holmes, T. H. Short-term intrusions into the life style routine. *Journal of Psychosomatic Research*, 1970, **14**, 121–132.

Holmes, T. H., & Rahe, R. H. The social readjustment rating scale. *Journal of Psychosomatic Research*, 1967, **11**, 213–218.

Johnson, L. C., Hord, D. J., & Lubin, A. Response specificity for difference scores and autonomic lability scores. U.S. Navy Medical Neuropsychiatric Research Unit, Rep. 63–12, August 1963.

Johnson, L. C., & Lubin, A. On planning psychophysiological experiments: Design, measurement and analysis. In N. S. Greenfield & R. A. Sternbach (Eds.), *Handbook of Psychophysiology*. New York: Holt, Rinehart & Winston, 1972.

Kazdin, A. E. Self-monitoring and behavior change. In M. J. Mahoney & C. E. Thoresen (Eds.), *Self-control: Power to the person*. Monterey: Brooks/Cole, 1974.

Kiritz, S., & Moos, R. H. Physiological effects of social environments. *Psychosomatic Medicine*, 1974, **36**, 96–114.

Kohlenberg, R. J. The punishment of persistent vomiting: A case study. *Journal of Applied Behavior Analysis*, 1970, **3**, 241–245.

Kohlenberg, R. J. Operant conditioning of human anal sphincter pressure. *Journal of Applied Behavior Analysis*, 1973, **6**, 201–208.

Lacey, J. I. *The evaluation of autonomic responses: Toward a general solution*. Annals of the New York Academy of Science, 1956, **67**, 123–164.

Lacey, J. I. Psychophysiological approaches to the evaluation of Psychotherapeutic process and outcome. In E. A. Rubinstein, & M. B. Parloff (Eds.), *Research in psychotherapy*. Washington, D. C.: American Psychological Association, 1959.

Lacey, J. I., Bateman, D. E., & Van Lehn, R. Autonomic response specificity: An experimental study. *Psychosomatic Medicine*, 1953, **15**, 8–21.

Lacey, J. I., & Lacey, B. C. Verification and extension of the principle of autonomic response specificity. *American Journal of Psychology*, 1958, 71, 50–73.

Lacey, J. I., & Lacey, B. C. The law of initial value in the longitudinal study of autonomic constitution: Reproducibility of autonomic responses and response patterns over a four year interval. *Annals of the New York Academy of Sciences*, 1967, **38**, 1257–1290.

Lader, M. H., & Wing, L. *Physiological measures, sedative drugs, and morbid anxiety*. New York: Oxford University Press, 1966.

Lang, P. The application of psychophysiological methods to the study of psychotherapy and behavior modification. In A. E. Bergin, & S. L. Garfield (Eds.), *Handbook of Psycho-Therapy and Behavior change: An empirical analysis*. New York, Wiley, 1971.

Lang, P. J., & Melamed, B. G. Avoidance conditioning therapy of an infant with chronic ruminative vomiting. *Journal of Abnormal Psychology*, 1969, **74**, 1–8.

Lang, P. J., Melamed, B. G., & Hart, J. A psychophysiological analysis of fear modification using an automated desensitization procedure. *Journal of Abnormal Psychology*, 1970, **76**, 220–234.

Lang, P. J., Rice, D. G., & Sternbach, R. A. The psychophysiology of emotion. In N. S. Greenfield, & R. A. Sternbach (Eds.), *Handbook of Psychophysiology*. New York: Holt, Rinehart & Winston, 1972.

Lazarus, R. S. Cognitive and personality factors underlying threat and coping. In M. H. Apply, & R. Trumball (Eds.), *Psychological Stress: Issues in Research*. New York: Appleton-Century-Crofts, 1967.

Leitenberg, H., Agras, S., Butz, R., Wincze, J. P. Relationship between heart rate and behavioral change during the treatment of phobias. *Journal of Abnormal Psychology*, 1971, **78**, 59–68.

Lewinsohn, P. M., Lobitz, W. C., & Wilson, S. Sensitivity of depressed individuals to aversive stimuli. *Journal of Abnormal Psychology*, 1973, **81**, 259–263.

Mackay, R. S. Telemetry and telestimulation. In C. C. Brown (Ed.), *Methods in Psychophysiology*. Baltimore: Williams & Wilkins, 1967.

Malmo, R. B., & Shagass, C. Physiologic study of symptom mechanisms in psychiatric patients under stress. *Psychosomatic Medicine*, 1949, **11**, 25–29.

Malmo, R. B., Shagass, C., & Davis, F. H. Symptom specificity and bodily reactions during psychiatric interview. *Psychosomatic Medicine*, 1950. **12**, 362–376.

Mandler, G., & Kremen, I. Autonomic feedback: A correlational study. *Journal of Personality*, 1958, **26**, 388–399.

Mandler, G., Mandler, J. M., & Uviller, E. T. Autonomic feedback: The perception of autonomic activity. *Journal of Abnormal and Social Psychology*, 1958, **56**, 367–373.

Marks, I. M., Boulougouris, J., & Marset, P. Flooding versus desensitization in the treatment of phobic patients: crossover study. *British Journal of Psychiatry*, 1971, **119**, 353–375.

Martin, J. E., & Epstein, L. H. Evaluating treatment effectiveness in cerebral palsy: Single-subject designs. *Physical Therapy*, in press.

Masuda, M., & Holmes, T. H. Magnitude estimation of social readjustments. *Journal of Psychosomatic Research*, 1967, **11**, 219–226.

Mathews, A. M. Psychophysiological approaches to the investigation of desensitization and related procedures. *Psychological Bulletin*, 1971, **76**, 73–91.

Mathews, A. M., Johnston, D. W., Shaw, P. M., & Gelder, M. G. Process variables and the prediction of outcome in behavior therapy. *British Journal of Psychiatry*, 1974, **125**, 256–264.

Metcalfe, M. Demonstration of a psychosomatic relationship. *British Journal of Medical Psychology*, 1956, **29**, 63–66.

Oken, D., Grinker, R. R., Heath, H. A., Herta, M., Korchin, S. J., Sabshin, M., & Schwartz, N. B. Relation of physiological response to affect expression. *Archives of General Psychiatry*, 1962, **6**, 336–351.

Olmstead, F. Measurement of blood flow and blood pressure. In C. C. Brown (Ed.), *Methods in Psychophysiology*. Baltimore: Williams & Wilkins, 1967.

Prigatano, G. P., & Johnson, H. J. Autonomic nervous system changes associated with a spider phobic reaction. *Journal of Abnormal Psychology*, 1974, **83**, 169–117.

Purcell, K., Brady, K., Chai, H., Muser, J., Molk, L., Gordon, N., & Means, J. The effect on asthma in children of experimental separations from the family. *Psychosomatic Medicine*, 1969, **41**, 144–162.

Rachman, S., & Hodgson, R. Synchrony and desynchrony in fear and avoidance. *Behaviour Research and Therapy*, 1974, **12**, 311–318.

Rahe, R. H., Mahan, J. L., & Arthur, R. J. Prediction of near-future health change from subjects' preceding life changes. *Journal of Psychosomatic Research*, 1970, **14**, 401–406.

Rugh, J. D., & Solberg, W. K. The identification of stressful stimuli in natural environments using a portable bio-feedback unit. Paper presented at the Bio-feedback Research Society, Colorado Springs, February, 1974.

Sandler, H., McCutcheon, E. P., Fryer, T. B., Rositano, S., Westbrook, R., & Hano, P. Recent NASA contributions to biomedical telemetry, *American Psychologist*, 1975, **30**, 257–264.

Schacter, J. Pain, fear, and anger in hypertensives and normotensives. *Psychosomatic Medicine*, 1957, **19**, 17–29.

Schacter, S., & Singer, J. E. Cognitive, social and psychological determinants of emotional state. *Psychological Review*, 1962, **69**, 379–399.

Schneider, R. A. A fully automated portable blood pressure recorder. *Journal of Applied Physiology*, 1968, **24**, 115–118.

Schwartz, G. E. Bio-feedback, self-regulation, and the patterning of physiological processes. *American Scientist*, 1975, **63**, 314–324.

Seligman, M. E. P. On the generality of the laws of learning. *Psychological Review*, 1970, **77**, 406–418.

Selye, H. *Stress*. Montreal: ACTA, 1950.

Skinner, B. F. The steep and thorny way to a science of behavior. *American Psychologist*, 1975, **30**, 42–49.

Smith, D. B. D., & Wenger, M. A. Changes in autonomic balance during phasic anxiety. *Psychophysiology*, 1965, **1**, 267–271.

Sokolov, V. N. *Perception and the conditioned reflex*. New York: MacMillan, 1963.

Stern, R. M. Detection of one's own spontaneous GSR's. *Psychonomic Science*, 1972, **29**, 354–356.

Stevens, J. R. Endogenous conditioning to abnormal cerebral electrical transients in man. *Science*, 1962, **137**, 974–976.

Straham, R. F., Todd, J. B., & Inglis, G. B. A palmar sweat measure particularly suited for naturalistic research. *Psychophysiology*, 1974, **11**, 715–720.

Stroebel, C. F. Psychophysiological pharmacology. In N. S. Greenfield, & R. A. Sternbach (Eds.), *Handbook of Psychophysiology*. New York: Holt, Rinehart & Winston, 1972.

Tursky, B., Shapiro, D., & Schwartz, G. E. Automated constant cuff pressure system to measure average systolic and diastolic blood pressure in man. IEEE Transactions on Bio-medical engineering, 1972, **19**, 271.

Venables, P., & Martin, I. *A manual of psychophysiological methods*. New York: Wiley, 1967.

Weiss, T., & Engel, B. T. Operant conditioning of heart rate in patients with premature ventricular contractions. *Psychosomatic Medicine*, 1971, **33**, 301–321.

Wenger, M. A. Studies of autonomic balance in Army Air Forces personnel. *Comparative Psychology Monographs*, 1948, **19**, No. 4.

Wenger, M. A., Clemens, T. L., Darsie, M. L., Engel, B. T., Estess, F. M., & Sonnenschein, R. R. Autonomic response patterns during infusion of epinephrine and nonepinephrine. *Psychosomatic Medicine*, 1960, **22**, 294–307.

Wieland, B. A., & Mefferd, R. B., Jr. Systematic changes in levels of physiological activities during a four month period. *Psychophysiology*, 1970, **6**, 669–689.

Wilder, J. The law of initial values. *Psychosomatic Medicine*, 1950, **12**, 392–401.

Wolff, H. G. Life situations, emotions and bodily disease. In M. L. Regment (Ed.), *Feelings and Emotions: The Loosehart Symposium*. New York: McGraw-Hill, 1950.

Wolpe, J. Psychotherapy: The non-scientific heritage and the new science. *Behavior Research and Therapy*, 1963, **1**, 23–28.

Zlutnick, S., Mayville, W. J., & Moffat, S. Modification of seizure disorders: The interruption of behavioral chains. *Journal of Applied Behavior Analysis*, 1975, **8**, 1–12.

CHAPTER 9

Assessment of Depression

LYNN P. PEHM

University of Pittsburgh

Introduction

Depression is a fairly recent target of behavioral intervention. Although a variety of new and innovative behavioral models have been proposed (e.g., Beck, 1972; Ferster, 1973; Lewinsohn, 1969; Seligman, 1975), there is little agreement as to exactly what behavior is assessed or modified. Each theory focuses on a differently defined class of behavior as the primary symptoms. This diversity generally typifies the state of affairs in depression research. There is little agreement in the psychiatric and psychological literatures as to what constitute the phenomena of depression. At a broad conceptual level depression has been considered both as a single symptom and as a syndrome (e.g., Mendels, 1968). It is clearly something akin to the syndrome concept which behaviorists have addressed. That is, behavioral research has assumed that depression includes a number of correlated behaviors which may occur in various combinations. There is still a great deal of disagreement as to which behaviors are included and as to the significance of combinations.

Clinical texts on depression offer very different lists of symptoms of depression (e.g., Beck, 1972; Mendels, 1970; Woodruff, Goodwin & Guze, 1974). Many of these symptoms are not exclusive to depression. Harrow, Colbert, Detre & Bakeman (1966), for instance, found that only 11 of 24 hypothesized symptoms differentiated between depressed and schizophrenic patients in state hospital samples. It is also difficult to find a single symptom which is universally ascribed to depression. In a discussion of this problem in the context of assessment, Levitt & Lubin (1975) present a list of 54 symptoms, each of which is included in at least two of a group of 16 depression scales. Only the symptom, "self-devaluation," was represented on all 16 scales, and clinical descriptions of some apathetic depressed patients suggest that even this symptom may not be necessary in depression (e.g., Beck, 1972).

Attempts have been made to bring greater order to the phenomena of depression by identifying groups of symptom combinations. Diagnostic categorizations of various types have been proposed. The American Psychiatric Association's *Diagnostic and Statistical Manual of Mental Disorders* (DSM-II, 1968) lists three depressive diagnoses under Psychotic Disorders (Schizophrenia, schizo-affective type, depressed; Involutional melancholia; and Manic-depressive illness, depressed type), one depressive diagnosis under Psychoneurotic Disorders (Depressive neurosis), and one depressive diagnosis under Personality Disorders (Cyclothymic personality). One of the more frequently cited typologies distinguishes endogenous from reactive depression (e.g. Mendels & Cochrane, 1968). Recently Winokur (1973) has suggested a classification schema which consists of: (1) Normal Grief, (2) Secondary Depression, in which depression occurs with other non-affective pathology, and (3) Primary Affective Disorders. The latter category is further divided into unipolar versus bipolar depressions (Perris, 1966, 1968, 1969, 1971). All of these typologies are based largely on severity, accompanying nondepressive symptoms, and inferred etiology.

A complete review of the evidence for these various diagnostic distinctions and typologies is far beyond the scope of this chapter. Suffice it to say that although some promising lines of evidence are appearing, it is probably premature to distinguish among different depressive syndromes (Beck, 1972; Seligman, Klein & Miller, 1974; Stern, McClure & Costello, 1970), especially for the purposes of differential functional intervention.

From a behavioral perspective, a conventional framework for organizing and discussing the symptoms of depression is to classify symptoms by their mode of expression into verbal-cognitive, overt-motor, and physiological categories (Lang, 1968). This has been a fruitful approach in the area of anxiety research, but depression cannot be considered as a simple analogy to anxiety.

Depression, for instance, does not evidence quite the same situationality as anxiety. While mood varies as a function of various environmental events and contingencies (e.g., Lewinsohn & Graf, 1973; Lewinsohn & Libet, 1972), specific eliciting stimuli are not so easily identifiable. This fact has implications for assessment. Severity of depression is not measurable in terms of the number of situations in which it occurs, nor is it as feasible to assess overt-motor or physiological responsivity to some set of depression-eliciting stimuli. Depression is usually thought of as a pervasive "mood," which affects many kinds of responses in all situations. It is usually assumed to have a general effect on responding in one time period in contrast to a previous time period. Anxiety assessment tends to be made by inter-individual comparisons across a sample of situations (e.g. the Fear Survey Schedule; Wolpe & Lang, 1964) and by intra-individual comparisons between test- and control-stimulus situations (e.g., heart rate in presence and absence of a snake). Depression research tends to make inter-individual comparisons across a sample of response classes (e.g. reduced eating, reduced sexual behavior, reduced work activity, etc.) and by intra-individual comparisons between responding at different points in time (e.g. present versus "premorbid" activity level).

Further differences between anxiety and depression can be seen by comparing their symptoms in the verbal-cognitive mode of expression. Anxiety measurement usually assumes a single severity dimension, even though items on anxiety scales may sample both situations and response modes. Anxiety measurement usually includes items relating to the quality and extent of anxious affect in various situations, and may include self-report about overt-motor and physiological manifestations as well. In depression the analogous dimension would be one of "sad affect." Self-report depression instruments typically include items related to quality and quantity of depressive affect and self-report of (depressed) overt-motor and physiological behavior. But other kinds of items are included as well. Depression includes a number of verbal-cognitive behaviors which might be classed as beliefs, attitudes, and attributions. Depressed persons report such things as pessimism, guilt, sense of failure, hopelessness, self-hate, etc. These symptoms are not indications of sad affect *per se* and require some separate classification. This is particularly desirable since these classes of behavior may potentially become specific targets for behavioral intervention. The potential utility of an expanded consideration of cognitive variables in behavior modification has recently been suggested by a number of sources (e.g., Beck, 1970a; Mahoney, 1974; Meichenbaum, 1974). Cognitive distortion in depression is held to be important by a number of contemporary theorists including Beck (1970b, 1972), Ferster (1973), Lazarus (1974) and Seligman (1974).

A very similar contrast can be made between depression and anxiety with regard to overt-motor symptoms. Behavioral anxiety research usually conceptualizes anxious behavior as avoidance of a stimulus (e.g. behavioral avoidance tests) or as disruptions in ongoing behavior chains (e.g. speech disfluencies). Overt-motor indications of depression can be conceptualized as deceleration of a wide variety of responses in the person's repertoire and the accelerated occurrence of a few specifically depressive behaviors, especially crying. The deceleration of behavior in depression can be characterized by any of the measurement strategies traditionally associated with the concept of response strength. That is, in theory, depressed individuals can be contrasted with non-depressed individuals in terms of reduced probability, reduced frequency, reduced duration, reduced amplitude, and increased latency of responding. Responses of almost any description are potentially included in this conceptualization, including: psycho-motor behavior, verbal behavior, and behavior related to work, recreation, eating, and sex.

A comparison between anxiety and depression research is also instructive with regard to physiological indices. Anxiety research has employed a variety of indicants of physiological arousal (e.g. heart rate, respiration, GSR increases) in phobic stimulus situations. No parallel exists in depression research.

Psychiatric descriptions of depression place much emphasis on socalled "neuro-vegetative" symptoms: loss of appetite and weight, loss of libido, fatigability, and sleep disturbances. From a behavioral point of view these symptoms reduce to overt-motor and verbal-cognitive behaviors. Loss of appetite and libido translate to reduced frequency of eating and sexual behavior along with verbal-cognitive reports of loss of motivation. Fatigability parallels this translation but in terms of general activity and interest. Sleep disturbances are descriptively matters of overt-motor behavior as well. Physiological bases may be inferred from any of these classes of behavior but physiological measurement is, at best, at the experimental stage. Therefore, the above behaviors will be classed in other categories in this review.

A number of somatic complaints are also included in most lists of psychiatric symptomatology: headaches, constipation, and general reports of pain and aching. Again from a behavioral point of view, what is actually being described is a class of verbal-cognitive behavior which can be termed "hypochondriacal complaints."

A great deal of psychobiological research is, of course, going on in the area of depression (e.g., Williams, Katz & Shield, 1972). Investigations of EMG, EEG, sedation threshold, and endocrine, electrolyte, and amine metabolism have produced promising but somewhat inconsistent findings (Beck, 1972; Becker, 1974; Stern, McClure & Costello, 1970; Williams, Katz & Shield, 1972). It is probably safe to say that none of the methods has reached a point of consistent validity and reliability as to make it a potential criterion variable in depression assessment. As such, physiological measures are not included in this paper.

In summary and conclusion to the above discussion, depression can be considered to include the following classes of behavior in the verbal-cognitive area: (1) sad affect, (2) reports of decelerated behavior and lack of motivation to perform a variety of activity, (3) hypochondriacal complaints, and (4) distortions of experience in the form of guilt, negative self-evaluation, pessimism about the world and the future, etc. In the overt-motor area depression includes: (1) behavior of depressive typography such as a sad demeanor, head hanging, and crying, and (2) deceleration of activity level, which includes a variety of measures of motoric and speech activity.

A few additional comments are in order regarding this list of categories of depressed behavior. *First*, the list is admittedly somewhat arbitrary. It is an attempt to categorize the behaviors which appear to identify depression, as abstracted from the general depression literature; these include clinical description, experimental psychopathology research, and assessment research. Unavoidably the list also has some implicit theoretical characteristics which will become clearer as specific assessment methods are discussed. The list also involves some notable omissions. Suicide behavior is not included. Although suicide is often associated with depression, it is sufficiently different in a functional sense to merit independent evaluation and is thus felt to be beyond the scope of this chapter. *Second*, anxiety is not included. Although anxiety is one of the most frequently cited symptoms of the syndrome of depression, it is again sufficiently distinct to warrant separate evaluation. Behavioral assessments of anxiety is a separate, well developed methodology. *Third*, psychotic behavior is not explicitly included on the list. Delusions are definitive of psychotic depressions, but the assumption is being made here that the distinction is a quantitative one and that delusions may represent extremes of the cognitive distortions evidenced in most depressions.

With the above general considerations in mind, it is now possible to review existing methods of depression assessment. The review is organized more in terms of scale format than mode of symptom expression. In attempting to include assessment methods which have gained some currency in the depression literature generally, it is impossible to follow consistently the behavioral distinction between verbal-cognitive, overt-motor, and physiological measures.

Self-Report Depression Scales

Levitt and Lubin (1975) list 23 self-administered depression scales which have been described in the psychological literature. Most of these have achieved only limited use and have relatively little psychometric data available to support them. Only those scales which have achieved some empirical support will be reviewed here.

MMPI—Depression Scale

The MMPI (Hathaway & McKinley, 1951) is certainly the most widely used instrument which assesses depression. The D scale is composed of 60 true-false items. Forty-nine items were selected on the basis of differentiation between a group of normals and a group of hospitalized manic-depressive, depressed patients. Eleven items were selected on the basis of distinguishing between the depressed group and other psychiatric patients. Considerable psychometric data are available. Dahlstrom and Welsh (1960) present tables of reliability data suggesting moderate test-retest reliabilities, which the authors interpret as due to the scale's sensitivity to mood changes. Split-half reliabilities given in this source range from 0.35 to 0.84, with a median in the low 0.70's. The scale has been criticized for the heterogeneity of its items on factor analysis (e.g., Comrey, 1951). Harris & Lingoes (1955) grouped the items into 5 logical subscales which they termed *subjective depression*, *psychomotor retardation*, *complaints about physical malfunctioning*, *mental dullness*, and *brooding*. The first three subscales are quite consistent with other conceptions of depression. The latter two are less typical. Discriminant validity is only moderate, partly due to the fact that many items overlap with other MMPI scales. Concurrent validity is also moderate (see Table 9.1).

From the point of view of behavior therapy assessment the scale has little to recommend it beyond its familiarity. The empirical derivation of the items results in a very mixed group of statements, many of which are not very illuminating when analyzed separately (e.g., I sometimes tease animals; False). Attempts have been made to develop revised MMPI depression scales with greater internal consistency (Dempsey, 1964) and discriminant validity (Costello & Comrey, 1967), but these scales have the same drawback in terms

TABLE 9.1

Correlation between Self-rating Measures of Depression from Various Sources

Measure	SDS	DI	DACL	Psychiatric Ratings
MMPI–D	.58[a] .70[b]	.41[a] .75[c]	.31[d] .54–.57[e] .42–.55[f]	.11[a] .50[c]
Zung SDS		.83[a]	.53[g] .63[h] .58[i] .27–.38[j]	.20[a]
Beck DI			.66[d] .38–.50[j]	.19[a] .66[c] .65[k] .67[e]
Lubin DACL				.32–.38[j] .71[m] .61[m]

[a] Seitz (1970), $N = 30$, male, psychiatric patients, depressed.
[b] Zung, Richards, & Short (1965), $N = 152$, psychiatric patients, mixed.
[c] Nussbaum, Wittig, Hanlon, & Kurland (1968), $N = 19$, psychiatric patients, depressed.
[d] Nussbaum *et al.* (1963), $N = 66$, psychiatric patients, depressed, Form E.
[e] Lubin (1967), $N = 80$, psychiatric patients mixed, Forms E–G.
[f] Lubin (1967), $N = 97$, female, college students, Forms A–D.
[g] Levitt & Lubin (1975), $N = 51$, psychiatric patients, mixed, Form E.
[h] Levitt & Lubin (1975), $N = 54$, psychiatric patients, mixed, Form E.
[i] Levitt & Lubin (1975), $N = 47$, student nurses, Form E.
[j] Lubin (1967), $N = 36$, female, psychiatric patients, mixed, Forms A–D.
[k] Beck (1972), $N = 226$, psychiatric patients, mixed.
[l] Metcalfe & Goldman (1965), $N = 183$, psychiatric patients, mixed.
[m] Fogel, Curtis, Kordasy, & Smith (1966), $N = 73$, 39 males and 34 females, psychiatric patients, mixed.

of item pool while they lose the value of the data accumulated on the original scale.

Lewinsohn and his colleagues (Lewinsohn & Graf, 1973; Lewinsohn & Libet, 1972; Libet & Lewinsohn, 1973; MacPhillamy & Lewinsohn, 1974) have used a set of multiple MMPI criteria to define depressed populations for research. Shipley and Fazio (1973) and Fuchs (1975) used the MMPI as a dependent variable in behavioral group therapy outcome studies and found significant pre- to post-treatment decreases which were greater than changes for placebo and waiting list groups. These uses do provide comparability to other studies and populations where the MMPI has been employed. Until other scales are further developed the MMPI-D Scale will probably have its primary value in behavioral research as a kind of marker variable allowing comparisons between studies on a general dimension of self-reported severity of depression.

Zung Self-Rating Depression Scale (*SDS*)

The SDS (Zung, 1965; Zung, Richards & Short, 1965) consists of 20 self statements calling for a response of degree of agreement on a 4-point scale. Items were selected to sample diagnostic depressive symptoms and are grouped in three areas: Pervasive Affect—2 items, Physiological equivalents—8 items, and Psychological Equivalents—10 items. The latter category includes 2 items relating to psychomotor retardation or agitation and 8 items related to "ideation" (Zung, 1965). Scores are converted to percent of maximum score.

No data on reliability on internal consistency are presented in either of the Zung articles. Evidence for validity is offered in the following forms. *First*, outpatients who received an initial diagnosis of psychoneurotic depressive reaction had a mean SDS score of 64, which was significantly higher than the mean of 53 for a group receiving other diagnoses (Zung, Richards & Short, 1965). *Second*, a group of inpatients who received initial depressive diagnoses and retained the same diagnosis at discharge had SDS scores of 74 at admission and 39 at discharge. *Third*, patients in another group whose diagnoses were changed at discharge had a lower initial mean SDS score of 53 (Zung, 1965). Data on individual item differences are presented but no item analysis is performed. Concurrent validity, in terms of correlations with other depression scales, is shown in Table 9.1.

The SDS is psychometrically unsophisticated. It samples a variety of response classes and gives considerable weight to self-report of physiological dysfunction. However, the format does allow comparative analyses of item subsets. Although this scale is a quick, convenient means of assessing general reverity of depression and has achieved some popularity, use in behavioral practice and research is questionable pending stronger psychometric support.

Beck Depression Inventory (BDI)

The BDI consists of 21 items written to reflect 21 different specific manifestations of depression (Beck, 1972; Beck, Ward, Mendelson, Mock & Erbaugh, 1961). Each item consists of 4 or 5 statements ranked in order of severity of expression of the symptom. The examinee is to choose the statement which is closest to his or her present state. Each alternative is assigned a non-empirical weight of 0 to 3.

Internal consistency was demonstrated by significant relationships between each item and BDI total scores and by an odd-even item correlation of 0.86, Spearman-Brown corrected to 0.93 (Beck *et al.*, 1961). No test-retest reliability data are reported in the original reports but some data are available from other sources. A test-retest correlation of 0.75 after one month was obtained by the present author as part of some unpublished data from a pilot study with 23 normal undergraduates. Miller and Seligman (1973) report a test-retest reliability of 0.74 for 31 normal undergraduates with a 3-month interval.

A correlation of 0.67 between BDI change scores and changes in clinician's ratings was reported by Nussbaum, Wittig, Hanlon & Kurland (1963) in a drug study. Several pieces of evidence for the construct validity of the BDI are reviewed by Beck (1972). Evidence for discriminant validity of the BDI appears quite good. With a sample of 606 patients, Beck (1972) found a correlation of 0.72 between the BDI and clinicians' ratings of depression, but only 0.14 between the BDI and clinicians' anxiety ratings. Concurrent validity is moderate to good (see Table 9.1).

Factor analyses of the BDI have been done by Cropley & Weckowitz (1966), Weckowitz, Muir & Cropley (1967), and Pichot & Lempérière (1964), (the latter with a French translation of the instrument). The results of these analyses are inconsistent despite the fact that the first two studies employed overlapping populations.

The BDI has much to recommend for its use in behavior therapy. It is a relatively short instrument with a broad sampling of self-report response classes. In general its psychometric properties are very good, with its discriminant validity especially notable. It is probably most suited to clinical populations but also seems to be useful with subclinical populations. For instance, Miller & Seligman (1973) found predicted differences in expectancy shifts between groups of depressed and non-depressed college students, defined by a cut-off score of 9 on the BDI. This is notable since in the original Beck *et al.* (1961) sample, the group identified as "none" on depth of depression ratings had a mean BDI score of 10.9. Although it is sensitive to clinical change, the nature of the questions on the BDI probably makes this instrument most useful as a selection criterion for behavioral research or as a pre- and post-assessment measure. Rush, Khatami & Beck (1975) have used the BDI as a periodic measure in their case studies. Fuchs (1975) used the BDI as a pre- and post-therapy measure. In general this scale appears to be the best of presently available self-report measures of general depression severity.

Lubin Depression Adjective Check List (DACL)

The DACL check lists consist of 7 forms (A-G). Forms A-D consist of balanced sets of 22 positive and 10 negative adjectives from a pool of items which significantly differentiated between a group of 48 depressed female psychiatric patients and a group of 179 normal females. Forms E-G consist of balanced sets of 22 positive and 12 negative adjectives from a pool of adjectives which significantly differentiated between a group of 47 depressed male psychiatric patients and a group of 100 normal males.

Psychometric data are presented by Lubin (1967). Intercorrelations among the 7 forms are high, regardless of sex of subject group. Internal consistency indices range from 0.79 to 0.90, and split-half reliabilities range from 0.82 to 0.93 for normals and from 0.86 to 0.93 for patients. All forms were cross-validated in a large study using normals, and depressed and non-depressed patient groups. Correlations with other depression instruments are moderate (Table 9.1).

The DACL's have the advantage of rapid administration ($2\frac{1}{2}$ minutes for normals) and equivalent forms which make them ideal for purposes of frequent repeated assessment as is often called for in behavioral treatment. Normative data are excellent, especially for Form E which was administered to a cross-sectional sample of 3009 adults in a national survey (Levitt & Lubin, 1975).

Comment on Self-Report Depression Scales

It should be noted that the DACL taps a more limited range of depression behavior than the other measures reviewed above. The adjectives on these lists are all more or less synonyms or antonyms for "depressed." As such, the DACL measures depressed affect specifically. Each of the other scales includes items involving the self-report of overt-motor, physiological, and cognitive distortion behavior. This distinction may be particularly important for behavioral therapy approaches where specific response classes are targeted. It may be important to keep various classes of depressive behavior distinct on self-report instruments. Each type of instrument has its own value and specific uses. For instance, the DACL or similar instruments are particularly suited for assessing the relationship between depressed affect and other aspects of behavior (e.g., Lewinsohn & Graf, 1973; Lewinsohn & Libet, 1972a). A more general measure such as the BDI may be more useful in assessing initial severity of depression or long term improvement. When the latter type of instrument is used it might be of value for behavioral clinicians and researchers to examine specific item or subscale changes in order to illuminate specificity or generalization of therapy effects.

Although behaviorists generally prefer to keep verbal-cognitive, overt-motor, and physiological expressions of emotion distinct, it should be noted that inclusion of items relating to all three modes of expression has some logic for a self-report depression scale. Depression involves distortions of experience, and the self-report of these distortions of a number of specific behaviors has traditionally been seen as a part of depressive behavior. Thus for an individual to endorse the item on the BDI ("I wake up early every day and can't get more than 5 hours' sleep") should not be taken as an index of overt or physiological sleep behavior. It *should* be taken as an indication of cognitive-verbal concern and complaint about specific aspects of sleep behavior. This cognitive-verbal behavior may or may not be distorted, but in either case it is a component of depression. If overt or physiological sleep behavior is to be a specific target of intervention, it should surely be assessed more directly and objectively.

One further comment is called for regarding self-report measures of depression. Simple self-rating scales should not be overlooked. Although a measure such as the DACL is a fairly quick and direct method of assessing depressed affect, a simple self-rating of degree of subjective depression is even more rapid and direct. Aitken (Aitken, 1969; Aitken & Zealley, 1970) has reviewed some of the arguments for such scales and described their use in a clinical setting. The "Visual Analogue Scale" suggested by Aitken is simply a 100 mm graphic scale anchored only at the ends by "normal mood" and "extreme depression". A correlation of 0.79 with the Hamilton Rating Scale is reported. For many clinical and research purposes such a scale may well be sufficient. Rush, Khatami & Beck (1975) used this scale as one form of repeated assessment in three case studies. Data on the comparability of such a simple self-rating scale with other self-rating measures would be valuable.

Interviewer Rating Scales

In addition to the self-rating scales, a number of instruments have been developed which rely largely on self-report yet which depend on an interviewer to make the actual rating. The Beck Depression Inventory was initially administered in this way (Beck, 1972) but has more typically been used as a self-rating scale. The Hamilton Rating Scale and the Grinker Feelings and Concerns Check List are probably the most frequently used interviewer rating scales.

Hamilton Rating Scale

This instrument consists of 17 variables, each of which is rated on a 3- or 5-point scale (Hamilton, 1960, 1967). The 1967 version incorporates some minor revisions. Items vary in the specificity of anchoring. The content includes cognitive, behavioral, and physiological symptoms usually associated with depression and, in addition, some less usual symptoms such as derealization and depersonalization, paranoid symptoms, and obsessional symptoms. The scale is designed for use with patients already diagnosed as having a depressive disorder. Hamilton (1960) recommends summing the scores of two independent raters or doubling the score of one rater for numerical consistency. He also recommends that all available information on the patient be used in making the ratings. Hamilton (1960) reports an interrater reliability of 0.84 for 10 patients, which increased to 0.90 for a total of 70 patients as the raters conferenced successive groups of 10 patients. Inter-item correlations tend to be rather low. Hamilton (1960) argues that the range may be restricted by his use of a homogeneous depressed population, but this is the population for which the instrument was designed. No other reliability or validity data are presented. Two successive factor analyses have been performed (Hamilton, 1960, 1964) on 49 and 152 male depressed patients respectively. The factors obtained have been ambiguous and difficult to label.

The Hamilton Rating Scale is not well developed psychometrically. The items also mix cognitive-verbal and overt behaviors within the same dimension. For instance, the suicide rating is anchored by "feels life is worth living" and "attempts at suicide" in the 1960 Hamilton article. Unidimensionality here is questionable. Although it has gained some popularity, further development and refinement of the scale would be required before it could be recommended for clinical use.

The Feelings and Concerns Check List

This instrument is made up of 47 items selected and revised on the basis of pilot work (Grinker, Miller, Sabshin, Nunn & Nunally, 1962). Each item is rated on a 4-point scale, from 0 (not present) to 3 (markedly present). The content of the items is entirely cognitive. Five factors derived from a factor analysis of 96 depressed patients are scored separately. The factors are labeled: (I) dismal, hopeless, bad feelings, (II) projection to external events, (III) guilty feelings, (IV) anxiety, and (V) clinging appeals for love.

An average inter-rater reliability of ratings of the 47 items is 0.43 calculated over 23 patients. Inter-rater reliability for total scores is not presented. Internal consistency reliabilities based on single raters for the five factors ranged from 0.61 to 0.90. No internal consistency figures are given for total scores.

Grinker *et al.* (1961) also present data on a 139-item Current Behavior Check List. Ratings of present or absent are made for each item based on general ward observation and nursing chart data. Items for this scale were re-written after an earlier version failed to achieve sufficient inter-rater reliability. Items cover a wide variety of observable, overt behaviors, and physical symptomatology. The scale was intended as a supplement to the verbal-cognitive Feelings and Concerns Check List.

Ten factors were extracted in a factor analysis of the scale. Internal reliability ratings for the 10 factors ranged from 0.64 to 0.86. The scale differentiated poorly between depressed and control groups. Little other data on reliability or validity are presented. The authors are not very encouraging about this scale and it has been used infrequently.

These two scales represent an admirable attempt to assess separately different classes of depressive behavior, both in terms of the separate scales and factor scores. Unfortunately, the result is less than a complete success. Both scales have marginal reliability and have very limited (demonstrated) validity.

Comment on Interviewer Rating Scales

It is desirable in behavioral therapy or research to avoid relying entirely on self-report measures of depression. Interviewer rating scales offer one form of reliability check on self-report. In essence, these instruments represent a means of quantifying the opinion of a judge other than the depressed person himself. This is essentially the rationale behind Lewinsohn's use of four of the Feelings and Concerns Check List factors along with the MMPI for selection and definition of a research population. Unfortunately, although a second, presumably expert, observer is involved, the basic data being rated are essentially the same (i.e., the patient's verbal self-report). The use of a skilled interviewer may reduce some of the distortions and biases of the patient but at the expense of introducing the distortions and biases of the interviewer. Standard rating scales do not eliminate these distortions.

There are several potential purposes for interviewer rating scales, but for the most part these purposes can all be better achieved by other means. Hamilton (1960) notes that some depressed patients are unwilling or unable to fill out questionnaires. In such a case the assistance of an interviewer in filling out a self-report form such as the BDI serves as well as an interviewer rating. If the patient is mute, neither means of assessing verbal-cognitive symptoms will be of much use.

If the reliability of the patient's self-observations is at question, then the better solution would be to obtain a second rating on the same or a very similar instrument by an informant who knows the patient well (e.g., a spouse). Rush, Khatami, & Beck (1975) comment on differences between patient and spouse perceptions of the depressed person. Such an informant could rate from a much better sample of behavior than a 50-minute interview.

If the validity of the patient's self-report is questioned (i.e., is what the patient calls depression the same as what an expert calls depression?), then it is questionable again whether an interview represents the best form of data collection. This brings us back to issues of interviewer bias and inter-rater reliabilities. Interviewers may have a better perspective on issues of severity of certain symptoms (e.g., how long a sleep latency constitutes a deviation from the norm?). On the other hand, better anchored self-report instruments might eliminate this difficulty. Finally, if verbal-cognitive symptoms are considered, establishing validity through another rater makes little sense. Verbal-cognitive behavior is logically assessed by self-report methods. If overt-motor or physiological symptoms are considered, then from a behavioral point of view the best way to validate self-observations is to observe and measure the overt or physiological behavior directly. The value of interviewer rating scales is probably limited to situations where these alternatives are not available or practical. As direct assessment methods improve and develop, interviewer rating scales may ultimately be replaced in behavioral research and practice.

Assessment of Overt Verbal Behavior

A number of case studies have focused on specific aspects of depressed verbal behavior as targets for modification. Robinson and Lewinsohn (1973b) identified a slowed rate of speech as a target behavior in a chronically depressed psychiatric patient. Number of words per 30-second interval in therapy interviews were tabulated with a hand counter by an observer behind a one-way mirror. Rate of speech appeared to be a fairly stable response characteristic which was brought under reinforcement control. Ince (1972) used a verbal conditioning procedure to increase positive self-references over 17 therapy sessions. However, no reliability data are presented for the rating of positive self-statements. Aitken & Parker (1965) provided reinforcement contingencies for positive self-evaluation response choices to a written sentence completion task, but no reliability or validity data are presented.

Lewinsohn and his colleagues (Lewinsohn, 1968; Lewinsohn, Weinstein & Alper, 1970; Libet & Lewinsohn, 1973; Libet, Lewinsohn & Javorek, 1973; Rosenberry, Weiss & Lewinsohn, 1968) have evolved a method of coding the verbal interaction behavior of individuals in group and home settings. Pursuing the general hypothesis that depression represents a deficit in social skills, these researchers have attempted to validate a series of objective measures of social skill in verbal interactions.

Rosenberry, Weiss & Lewinsohn (1968) selected 32 depressed and 55 non-depressed undergraduate subjects on the basis of MMPI criteria. Subjects were asked to listen to two tape recorded speakers and respond with a button push whenever they would respond in any way in an effort to be helpful to the speaker. Contrary to the hypothesis, no differences were found on the mean number of responses emitted by depressed and non-depressed subjects. Depressed subjects were found to respond in a less stable and predictable fashion than non-depressed subjects, although these effects reached significance for only one of the tapes.

Lewinsohn, Weinstein & Alper (1970) selected depressed undergraduate subjects on the same MMPI criteria plus a set of criteria derived from the Grinker Feelings and Concerns Check List factors. Five female and four male subjects were seen for 18 sessions of group therapy. Interaction data on four social skill variables were collected by two observers at each session. These variables were: (1) total amount of behavior emitted by and directed towards each individual, (2) use of positive and negative reactions by each individual, (3) interpersonal efficiency ratio, defined as number of verbal behaviors directed toward an individual relative to the number of verbal behaviors the individual emits, and (4) range of interactions with others. Inter-rater reliabilities were stated to be satisfactory although figures are given only for numbers of actions ($r = 0.97$) and reactions ($r = 0.99$) given by an individual. Group treatment in this study consisted of weekly feedback to subjects of their coded interpersonal data from the prior week. These data served as a basis for discussion, goal formulation, and change efforts on the part of each subject. As such, the meaning of changes on these variables is difficult to interpret, and only representative graphs of selected variables for individual subjects are presented. Pre- and post-therapy scores on the MMPI and Grinker factors suggest improvement of depression but no statistical tests are presented.

Libet and Lewinsohn (1973) selected depressed, non-depressed "psychiatric," and normal control subjects on the basis of MMPI and Grinker interview criteria. Using a similar system, interpersonal verbal behavior was coded for two groups over a number of sessions. Inter-rater reliabilities ranged from 0.63 to 0.99. Depressed subjects were found to have lower total activity levels, although this effect was significant for only one group during its earlier sessions. Depressed subjects emitted fewer positive reactions to others but did not differ on negative reactions. No differences were found for the interpersonal efficiency measure. Interpersonal range was found to be narrower for depressed males only. An additional measure, action latency, indicated that depressed subjects were significantly slower in responding to another's reaction.

In an elaborate and statistically sophisticated study of social skill variables in group and home observation settings, Libet, Lewinsohn, & Javorek (1973) coded interpersonal behavior of depressed, non-depressed "psychiatric" and normal control subjects in five self-study groups and 18 visited homes. Again, subjects were identified on the basis of MMPI and Grinker interview criteria.

In addition, clinical referrals and subjects solicited by newspaper ads for this study were included. Nineteen social skill and six criterion variables were defined in this study. Inter-rater reliabilities were generally good although the authors note that temporal stability was low for many of the variables. Situational differences between the two settings were also apparent. In the groups, depressed males were found to emit and initiate fewer questions (a functionally reinforcing event), made fewer comments, and were slower in response to reactions. They were also affected more by aversive reactions and elicited fewer positive reactions. Results for females in the group were generally in the same direction but non-significant. At home, depressed males were found to emit fewer actions but to initiate *more* actions. This latter reversal was attributed to lesser participation in ongoing conversations initiated by others. In addition, depressed males were more silent, slower to respond to reactions, and elicited a lower rate of positive reinforcement. Depressed females were less active, slower to respond to reactions, and elicited a lower rate of positive reinforcement. Interestingly, the authors concluded on the basis of other analyses that social skill does not seem to be evidenced by higher ratios of positive to negative reactions elicited. This ratio tended to remain constant regardless of total number of reactions elicited. This finding may relate to the nature of the situations studied.

Lewinsohn and his colleagues have used their behavioral coding system as part of the assessment and evaluation in a series of clinical cases. As an assessment tool the method has been used to identify problem areas which then become targets for behavioral intervention. Sample problem areas in the case studies include generally low activity level in the family (Martin, Weinstein & Alper, 1968), few initiations by the client (Lewinsohn & Atwood, 1961; Lewinsohn & Shaffer, 1971), low rates of mutual reinforcement (Lewinsohn & Shaw, 1969), and negative reactions from the spouse (Lewinsohn & Shaffer, 1971). Lewinsohn & Shaffer (1971) point out that the use of home observations, as a basis for assessment, provide data that can be used as objective feedback to clients by focusing attention of the client and his family on their interpersonal behavior. In two controlled studies, Johansson, Lewinsohn, & Flippo (1969) and Robinson & Lewinsohn (1973a), the content categories in Lewinsohn's coding system were used as target response classes in an interview setting. In applications of this Premack Principle, high frequency response classes were made contingent on the prior occurrence of a low frequency response class.

As these methods are described they are somewhat cumbersome for most clinical uses, requiring multiple, well trained observers in home or group settings. McLean, Ogston, & Grauer (1973) describe a simplified method based on Lewinsohn's coding system. Patients were required to make ½-hour tape recordings of problem discussion with their spouses at home. These recordings were separated into 30-second intervals and coded for positive and negative initiations and reactions. Scores were calculated as proportions of interaction for both discussants. Inter-rater agreement ranged from 73% to 97%, with an average agreement of 88%. Couples in the experimental group, who received a behaviorally oriented training procedure, decreased significantly in negative reactions on post-test. A mixed control group did not change significantly on these measures.

Fuchs (1975) videotaped 10 minute segments of therapist-absent interaction among groups of depressed subjects in a therapy study. Number of statements in 10 minutes was counted as a simple assessment of verbal activity level. Inter-rater agreement from pre- to post-testing ranged from 83% to 100%, with a mean of 87%. Experimental subjects increased in verbal activity level significantly more than placebo therapy controls.

Comment on Assessment of Overt Verbal Behavior

Although the measures described here are relatively new, the general approach seems quite promising. Reliabilities of the measures appear to be good and validity data are accumulating. Replication and normative data are needed but evidence is sufficient at this point to warrant cautious use of some of these measures for certain purposes. Libet, Lewinsohn, & Javorek (1973) point out that their activity level measure, defined as the total number of verbal actions emitted per hour, best differentiates depressed subjects from normals. The verbal coding methods are, of course, limited to multiple (e.g., group, family, or couples therapy) foci. When therapy in any of these formats is to be considered, verbal interaction measures are certainly desirable. A cautionary note should be sounded by Libet, Lewinsohn, & Javorek's (1973) observations of situational effects on their measures. Such effects ought to be taken into account in any use (i.e., assessment should be in the same situation as the therapy intervention). Other situations may be samples as tests of generalization. Given that normative data are generally lacking on these measures they are most appropriate in cases where contrasts are presented (e.g., pre- to post-therapy assessment in clinical or research uses).

Assessment of Overt-Motor Depressive Behavior

Relatively little work has been done on the objective measurement of overt-motor depressive behavior. Reisinger (1972), in a single subject reversal design study, describes the use of token reinforcement and response cost to increase smiling and decrease crying behavior respectively. Careful behavioral definitions of the responses led to inter-rater reliabilities above 90% for observation periods of up to 2 hours.

Behavior Rating Scale

Williams, Barlow, & Agras (1972) describe the use of behavioral assessment procedures for ten depressed psychiatric inpatients. At randomly determined points during each half hour of the day from 8 a.m. to 4 p.m., a trained observer noted the presence or absence of each of the following four response classes: (1) talking, (2) smiling, (3) motor activity (10 subclasses further define this behavior), and (4) time out of room. Inter-rater reliability of 96% is reported. An analysis of the correlations among the four behavioral measures yielded a Kendall's coefficient of concordance of 0.70 ($P < 0.01$). On this basis scores were summed and treated as a single index of severity of depression. Comparisons were made between the behavioral index, BDI, and Hamilton Rating Scale at 3-day intervals during the course of patients' hospitalizations. Mean correlations (calculated with appropriate Fisher's z-transformations) between the measures were as follows: Beck & Hamilton $r = 0.82$, Hamilton and behavioral index $r = 0.71$, Beck and behavioral index $r = 0.67$. The authors discuss the manner in which data from the different sources supplement each other in characterizing the depressive behavior of specific patients. On the basis of follow-up information on five patients, the authors suggest that the course of overt-behavioral improvement during hospitalization is more predictive than either of the other instruments of post-hospitalization improvement. Hersen, Eisler, Alford & Agras (1973) used this behavior rating scale to assess improvement of three patients on a token economy ward. In three single-subject reversal designs, improvement on the behavior rating scale was demonstrated to occur when patients were under token reinforcement conditions. No self-report measures were taken.

This rating scale stands alone as an effort to develop a psychometrically sound measure of overt-motor depression behavior. Further data on its psychometric properties would be helpful. However, present evidence suggests that this instrument can be used profitably in inpatient settings. It would be recommended that this behavior rating scale be used in conjunction with a verbal self-report measure. It would be interesting to examine the four "sub-scales" separately as well as the total severity index.

Continuous Telemetric Monitoring

Kupfer, Detre, Foster, Tucker & Delgado (1972) describe an apparatus which permits 24 hour telemetric recording of activity in inpatient settings. A miniature transmitter containing a ferromagnetic ball in an inductance coil is encased in a cylinder 2.2 cm. in diameter and 6.7 cm. long. The transmitter is worn on a leather wrist band and has a range of 100 feet. Receivers transform data into pulses which are read out digitally as number of counts per minute.

A reliability of 91.7% agreement is reported for five subjects wearing transmitters on each wrist for one hour. Kupfer, Weiss, Foster, Detre, Delgado & McPartland (1974) report a 0.73 reliability for wrist and ankle transmitters. This research has shown correlations between activity level and various sleep parameters such as EEG movement, minutes awake, time asleep, REM time, and REM activity (Kupfer *et al.*, 1972; Kupfer & Foster, 1973; Weiss, Kupfer, Foster & Delgado, 1974). Kupfer *et al.* (1974) found differences between unipolar and bipolar depressives prior to drug treatment. Unipolars had much higher levels of activity. No drug effects were found but clinically improved unipolars ($N = 4$) decreased in activity level. This is the only study reporting relationships between the telemetered activity level and any conventional depression measure. No significant correlations were obtained with self-rating depression items on the KDS-1 (Kupfer & Detre, 1971), a general psychiatric self-report form. A correlation of 0.85 was found, however, with self-rated anxiety on the KDS-1 during drug treatment. This correlation is not surprising in light of the fact that a number of patients showed increased "agitation" during drug treatment; this was reflected in the anxiety ratings.

This assessment technique has a great deal of promise as a definitive measure of psychomotor activity. Hopefully, further validational evidence will be forthcoming in order to clarify relationships between retarded and agitated psychomotor activity and depression versus anxiety. The limited evidence so far suggests agitation is more closely related to anxiety. Correlations between telemetered psychomotor activity and other well validated measures of depression would also be helpful. Use of this method is likely to be limited to research settings due to the expense of the equipment.

Activity Schedules

The use of activity schedules in depression research deserves comment although it might be questioned whether these devices can be properly labeled depression assessment instruments. In general, what is involved is a self-recording of overt events or activities. In that depression involves decreased activity, these techniques do assess depression. However, there is usually an additional assumption that some specific activities or events are particularly important as determinants of depression. Therefore, it is sometimes the theoretical cause of depression rather than depression *per se* that is being assessed.

The best developed instrument of this type is the MacPhillamy & Lewinsohn (1971, 1972a, 1972b) Pleasant Events Schedule (PES). The PES is based on Lewinsohn's theoretical model of depression, which accounts for depression as a lack or loss of response contingent positive reinforcement. As such, the PES is intended to assess the amount of external positive reinforcement that the individual receives. The PES consists of 320 events generated from lists of positive events elicited from 66 subjects (MacPhillamy & Lewinsohn, 1972a). A revised Form III used another 70 subjects (Lewinsohn & Graf, 1973). The instrument is used in two ways: (1) as a retrospective report of the events of the last 30 days, and (2) as the basis for daily logs of ongoing behavior. As a retrospective instrument, subjects are first asked to indicate the frequency with which each item occurred within the last 30 days on a three point scale, 1—not happened, 2—a few (1-6) times, and 3—often (7 or more times). Subjects then go through the list a second time indicating how pleasant and enjoyable each event was or would be potentially, again on a three point scale (1—not pleasant, 2—somewhat pleasant, and 3—very pleasant). Three scores are derived from these ratings: (1) *Activity Level*—defined as the sum of the frequency ratings, (2) *Reinforcement Potential*—defined as the sum of the pleasantness ratings, and (3) *Obtained Reinforcement*—defined as the sum of the product of the frequency and pleasantness ratings for each item. Test-retest reliabilities for 37 subjects over a 4-8 week span were 0.85, 0.66, and 0.72 for the three respective scores (MacPhillamy & Lewinsohn, 1972a, 1972b). Alpha coefficients of internal consistency were 0.96, 0.98, and 0.97 for the same scores. Norms for male and female college students are given by MacPhillamy & Lewinsohn (1972b).

Evidence for the validity of the instrument is presented by MacPhillamy & Lewinsohn (1974). All three scores statistically differentiated between depressed individuals and both psychiatric and normal controls. These groups were defined by MMPI and Feelings and Concerns Check List factor ratings. The entire PES has also been used by Lewinsohn and his coworkers to generate shorter lists specific to individuals. Lewinsohn & Libet (1972) and Lewinsohn & Graf (1973) selected the 160 most pleasant items for individual subjects and had them use these lists as daily activity check lists for 30 days. Significant intra-individual correlations were found between number of pleasant events and mood as measured by the DACL. In the Lewinsohn & Graf (1973) study, depressed subjects were found to engage in fewer pleasant events.

The use of individualized PES's in therapy has been described by Lewinsohn (1973). Schedules of 160 items derived as above were kept for 30 days by 10 depressed patients. The 10 items most highly correlated with mood were then selected as targets for behavior change efforts and were reinforced with minutes of psychotherapy time. Target activities increased significantly more than a set of control activities.

Ad hoc activity schedules or logs have been reported in case studies by Lewinsohn & Atwood (1969) and Rush, Khatami, & Beck (1975). The latter report employed activity schedules as a part of the therapy program. The patients' daily logs served as a basis for correcting cognitive distortions of their own behavior. In a controlled psychotherapy outcome study, Fuchs (1975) employed an activity schedule procedure in a self-control oriented therapy program. Using the PES as an item pool, a shortened list of 20 classes of reinforcing behavior was constructed. Items on this list, termed the Positive Activities Schedule, were written to emphasize the active role of the subject in producing potential reinforcement. Experimental subjects kept daily activity logs using the Positive Activities Schedule as a guide. These logs served as a basis for: (1) attempts to modify distortions of self observations, (2) selection of target behaviors to be increased, and (3) selection of behaviors to be used as contingent self-reinforcement. In addition, this study used the PES as a pre- and post-therapy outcome measure in comparisons between the experimental group, placebo therapy, and waiting list controls. Increases in self-reported pleasant events over the last 30 days tended to be greatest for the experimental group.

There are several cautionary notes regarding the use of these instruments as methods of assessing overt depressive behavior. As these are retrospective instruments, the validity of the reports of overt behavior may be questioned. If cognitive distortion is an important aspect of depressive behavior, then recollected self-report may well be distorted. Wener & Rehm (1975) reported distorted underestimations of success experiences by depressed individuals in a laboratory task. Differences between frequencies of pleasant events in the past 30 days found between depressed and non-depressed individuals may be due as much to distorted recollections as to actual differences in behavior.

The problem of cognitive distortion is probably greatly diminished if not eliminated when the PES or a subset of its items are used as a daily log measure. Daily self-monitoring of discrete, well defined events tends to be fairly accurate (see Thoresen & Mahoney, 1974, for a review). The self-recording format, however, introduces another problem due to the reactivity of self-monitoring. Self-monitoring has been shown to influence a variety of behaviors being observed (e.g., Thoresen & Mahoney, 1974), and the therapy studies cited above suggest that depression may also be affected by self-monitoring. This may be especially true for an instrument such as the PES, since by definition it taps only pleasant activities. One might expect a shift of attention to pleasant events when they are to be explicitly monitored and a concurrent improvement in mood. Thus, although the PES may have considerable value and promise as a part of therapeutic interventions, its use as an independent measure of overt-motor activity in depression is questionable at this point.

Comments on Assessment of Overt-Motor Depressive Behavior

This is the most recent and most sparsely investigated area of depression. The work with greatest immediate applicability has been done with inpatients. Methods for use with outpatients are warranted.

Future Directions in Depression Assessment

Behavioral depression research is burgeoning. Further development and innovation in assessment can be expected. Behaviorists appear to be placing increasing emphasis on psychometric evaluation of their assessment techniques. While further information on issues of reliability, validity, and standardization of existing methods are forthcoming, new contents and formats may also be expected. Self-report measures of depression are by far the most developed forms of assessment, and they generally cover quite a range of verbal-cognitive behavior. Nevertheless, they are not very effective in assessing certain cognitive aspects of depression, which are of importance in contemporary theories of depression. Beck (1972), Ferster (1973), Lazarus (1974) & Seligman (1975) all suggest that depressed persons inaccurately perceive or process information about their experience. These distortions of experience are assessed to some extent by items on self-rating scales relating to guilt, pessimism, hopelessness, negative self-evaluation, etc. As specific formulations of the nature of cognitive distortion develop, more extensive, specific scales will become a necessity. One example of this kind of development is the recently published Hopelessness Scale (Beck, Weissman, Lester & Trexler, 1975). This 20-item true-false scale was developed out of Beck's cognitive approach to depression (Beck, 1970b, 1972). Hopelessness is defined as a person's negative expectancies concerning himself and his future life. Hopelessness is held to be a core characteristic of depression but is also implicated in other forms of pathology including suicide, schizophrenia, alcoholism, sociopathy, physical illness (Beck *et al.*, 1975). Thus the scale can be considered to be a means of assessing one cognitive component which may be important with respect to specific forms of therapeutic intervention (e.g., Beck's cognitive therapy).

The development of other scales assessing specific dimensions of verbal-cognitive aspects of depression can be expected. Helplessness is a likely candidate. Seligman's (1974, 1975) approach to depression suggests that a core characteristic is the perception of a non-contingent relationship between one's behavior and the outcome of that behavior. This dimension is again tapped incidently on self-report scales. No specific scale has been developed to assess this dimension. The Rotter Internal—External Locus of Control Scale (Rotter, 1966) has been used in this context as a measure of generalized expectation of response-reinforcement independence by Hiroto (1974), but Miller & Seligman (1973) dispute its value. Other more behavioral measures might be extrapolated from this research. For instance, helplessness has been assessed experimentally by failure to escape a loud noise in a finger shuttle box task (Hiroto, 1974) and slower solutions to an anagram task (Hiroto & Seligman, 1975). These tasks could conceivably be developed into standardized measures of helplessness. In general, the development of methods of assessing specific dimensions of cognitive deficit in depression are likely to be a valuable adjunct to the assessment of therapy from various orientations.

Although some excellent initial results have been achieved, further developments in the assessment of overt behavior deficits in depression can also be expected. For instance, given Lewinsohn's emphasis on social skill deficits in depression, it is somewhat surprising that more assessment methodology has not been borrowed from the social skill literature (e.g., Hersen & Bellack, in press). As an example, social skill has been assessed by eliciting role played responses to problem situations which are introduced and begun by a line of dialogue from another person. Presentations have been on tape (e.g., Rehm & Marston, 1968) or by a confederate (e.g., Eisler, Miller & Hersen, 1973). The dimensions scored on the social skills measures bear a great deal of similarity to the dimensions assessed in work with depression. Responses such as latency and duration of speech, smiling, and eye contact have been assessed as representing both social skill and, in other formats, depression. Other dimensions from the social skill literature, such as loudness and expressivity, may also be relevant to depression. This form of assessment also has the advantage of allowing for assessment representing different situations in a format applicable to outpatients without requiring groups or family members to participate.

Finally, the future of depression research is likely to incorporate refinements in physiological assessment as such measures become adaptable to clinical use. One possible avenue of development may be that so called "neuro-vegetative signs" of depression (sleep disturbance, loss of "libido," and loss of appetite and weight) will be assessed more carefully and directly by borrowing methods from the behavioral literature on insomnia, sexual orientation, and obesity. Some of these methods would represent substantial improvements over one or two item ratings on self-report scales.

Recommendations for the Present

At this stage in the development of behavioral assessment and therapy for depression, a few practical suggestions can be made. It perhaps goes without saying that depressive behavior from different modes of expression ought to be sampled by appropriate formats. Choices of methods for assessing at least verbal-cognitive and overt-motor channels are available. The value of combining measures for depression is discussed by Williams, Barlow & Agras (1972), who point out that the depressed behavior of individual patients is sometimes not describable in one mode alone. For instance, one patient's behavioral data changed markedly because she withdrew to her room during the hospital stay of a patient whom she feared. She resumed her usual ward activity when he was discharged. Her scores on the Hamilton and Beck scales reflected a more constant and balanced picture of her depression during this period. The Lewinsohn Pleasant Events Schedule research (Lewinsohn & Graf,

1972; Lewinsohn & Libet, 1972) suggests that overt activity and cognitive measures covary in depression, but whether or not behavior and cognition will change together as a result of therapy aimed at one or the other, remains an open question.

The choices of assessment method will depend in part on the purpose of the assessment. For the purpose of selecting and defining a depressed subject population for research, the usual practice in behavioral research has been to combine a self-report scale (e.g., MMPI-D or BDI) with a confirmation from a clinician (e.g., psychiatric diagnoses of depression or Hamilton Rating Scale). These criteria identify a research sample within the population traditionally conceptualized as depressed in the psychiatric and psychological literatures. Although it would be logical from a behavioral perspective to include a measure of overt behavior, no one measure can be recommended as definitive of depression at this point.

For the purpose of assessing treatment outcome, a good depression battery would include measures of cognitive-verbal, overt-verbal, and overt-motor behavior. The BDI, an adaptation of the Lewinsohn coding system such as the one used by McLean, Ogston & Grauer (1973), and the Williams, Barlow & Agras (1972) behavior rating scale would be ideal (though impractical for some settings). Since outcome evaluation is partly for the purpose of assessing transfer and generalization of effects, another recommendation is the greater use of subscales and individual item assessment. For instance, the BDI was constructed to tap 21 separate depressive symptoms. Examinations of which of these individual items change, in what order, and to what degree following some form of behavioral intervention could be very illuminating.

For the purpose of choosing targets for modification, assessment research in depression has relatively little to offer the behavioral clinician at this point. Some of the Lewinsohn case studies reviewed above describe examples of selecting targets for modification from verbal coding data. The Williams, Barlow, & Agras (1972) behavior ratings could well serve as a basis for interventions on the order of Reisinger's (1972) reinforcing the behavior of smiling. Beyond these suggestions, innovation and *ad hoc* assessment are still required in this area of behavioral assessment.

As in other areas of psychopathology, a "bootstrapping" effect can be observed in depression assessment. Advances in theory, psychotherapy, and experimental psychopathology are slowed by vague and unreliable assessment methods, but when such advances occur they feed back to assessment methods by suggesting ways of sharpening and stabilizing our measures. As yet we have not been lifted to great heights by our depression "bootstraps," but rapid and accelerating movement is underway.

References

Aiken, E. G., & Parker, W. H. Conditioning and generalization of positive self-evaluation in a partially structured diagnostic interview. *Psychological Reports*, 1965, **17**, 459–464.

Aitken, A. C. B. Measures of feeling using analogue scales. *Proceedings of the Royal Society of Medicine*, 1969, **62**, 989–993.

Aitken, R. C. B., & Zealley, A. R. Measurement of moods. *British Journal of Hospital Medicine*, 1970, **4**, 214–224.

American Psychiatric Association. DSM-II Diagnostic and statistical manual of mental disorders (2nd Ed.) Washington, D. C.: American Psychiatric Association, 1968.

Beck, A. T. Cognitive therapy: Nature and relation to behavior therapy. *Behavior Therapy*, 1970a, **1**, 184–200.

Beck, A. T. The core problem in depression: The cognitive triad. *Science and Psychoanalysis* 1970b, **17**, 47–55.

Beck, A. T. *Depression: Causes and treatment.* Philadelphia: University of Pennsylvania Press, 1972.

Beck, A. T., Ward, C. H., Mendelsohn, M., Mock, J., & Erbaugh, J. An inventory for measuring depression. *Archives of General Psychiatry*, 1961, **4**, 561–571.

Beck, A. T., Weissman, A., Lester, D., & Trexler, L. The measurement of pessimism: The hopelessness scale. *Journal of Consulting and Clinical Psychology*, 1974, **42**, 861–865.

Becker, J. *Depression: Theory and research.* Washington, D. C., Winston & Sons, 1974.

Comrey, A. L. A factor analysis of items on the MMPI depression scale. *Educational and Psychological Measurement*, 1957, **17**, 578–585.

Costello, C. G., & Comrey, A. L. Scales for measuring depression and anxiety. *Journal of Psychology*, 1967, **66**, 303–313.

Cropley, A. J., & Weckowicz, T. E. The dimensionality of clinical depression. *Australian Journal of Psychology*, 1966, **18**, 18–25.

Dahlstrom, W. G., & Welsh, G. S. *An MMPI handbook.* Minneapolis: University of Minnesota Press, 1960.

Dempsey, P. A. Undimensional depression scale for the MMPI. *Journal of Consulting Psychology*, 1964, **28**, 364–370.

Eisler, R. M., Miller, P. M., & Hersen, M. Components of assertive behavior. *Journal of Clinical Psychology*, 1973, **29**, 295–299.

Ferster, C. B. A functional analysis of depression. *American Psychologist*, 1973, **28**, 857–870.

Fogel, M. L., Curtis, G. C., Kordasy, F., & Smith, W. G. Judge's ratings, self-ratings, and checklist report of affects. *Psychological Reports*, 1966, **19**, 299–307.

Fuchs, C. Z. The reduction of depression through the modification of self-control behaviors: An instigation group therapy. Unpublished doctoral dissertation, University of Pittsburgh, 1975.

Grinker, R. R., Miller, J., Sabshin, M., Nunn, J., & Nunally, J. D. *The phenomena of depression.* New York: Harper, 1961.

Hamilton, M. A rating scale for depression. *Journal of Neurology, Neurosurgery and Psychiatry*, 1960, **23**, 56–61.

Hamilton, M. Development of a rating scale for primary depressive illness. *British Journal of Social and Clinical Psychology*, 1967, **6**, 278–296.

Harris, R. E., & Lingoes, J. C. Subscales of the MMPI: An aid to profile interpretation. Unpublished manuscript, University of California, San Francisco, 1955.

Harrow, M., Colbert, J., Detre, T. P., & Bakeman, R. Symptomatology and subjective experiences in current depressive states. *Archives of General Psychiatry*, 1966, **14**, 203–212.

Hathaway, S. R., & McKinley, J. C. *MMPI manual* (Revised 1951). New York: The Psychological Corporation, 1951.

Hersen, M., & Bellack, A. S. Assessment of social skills. In A. R Ciminero, K. S. Calhoun, & H. E. Adams (Eds.), *Handbook of behavioral assessment.* New York: Wiley, in press.

Hersen, M., Eisler, R. M., Alford, G. S., & Agras, W. S. Effects of token economy on neurotic depression: An experimental analysis. *Behavior Therapy*, 1973, **4**, 392–397.

Hiroto, D. S. Locus of control and learned helplessness. *Journal of Experimental Psychology*, 1974, **102**, 187–193.

Hiroto, D. S., & Seligman, M. E. P. Generality of learned helplessness in man. *Journal of Personality and Social Psychology*, 1975, **31**, 311–327.

Ince, L. P. The self-concept variable in behavior therapy. *Psychotherapy: Theory, Research and Practice*, 1972, **9**, 223–225.

Johansson, S., Lewinsohn, P. M., & Flippo, J. F. An application of the Premack principle to the verbal behavior of depressed subjects. Paper presented at the Meeting of the Association for Advancement of Behavior Therapy, Washington, D. C., 1969.

Kupfer, D. J., Detre, T. P. Development and application of the KDS-1 in inpatient and outpatient settings. *Psychological Reports*, 1971, **29**, 607–617.

Kupfer, D. J., Detre, T. P., Foster, F. G., Tucker, G. J., & Delgado, J. The application of Delgado's telemetric mobility recorder for human studies. *Behavioral Biology*, 1972, **7**, 585–590.

Kupfer, D. J., & Foster, F. G. Sleep and activity in a psychotic depression. *Journal of Nervous and Mental Disease*, 1973, **156**, 341–348.

Kupfer, D. J., Weiss, B. L., Foster, F. G., Detre, T. P., Delgado, J., & McPartland, R. Psychomotor activity in affective states. *Archives of General Psychiatry*, 1974, **30**, 765–768.

Lang, P. J. Fear reduction and fear behavior: Problems in treating a construct. In J. M. Shlien (Ed.), *Research in psychotherapy, Vol. 3*. Washington, D. C.: American Psychological Association, 1968.

Lazarus, A. A. Multimodal behavioral treatment of depression. *Behavior Therapy*, 1974, **5**, 549–554.

Levitt, E. E., & Lubin, B. *Depression: Concepts, controversies and some new facts*. New York: Springer, 1975.

Lewinsohn, P. M. Manual of instruction for the behavior ratings used for the observation of interpersonal behavior. Unpublished manuscript, University of Oregon, 1968 (Revised, 1971).

Lewinsohn, P. M. The use of activity schedules in the treatment of depressed individuals. Unpublished manuscript, University of Oregon, 1973.

Lewinsohn, P. M., & Atwood, G. E. Depression: A clinical research approach. *Psychotherapy: Theory, Research and Practice*, 1969, **6**, 166–171.

Lewinsohn, P. M., & Graf, M. Pleasant activities and depression. *Journal of Consulting and Clinical Psychology*, 1973, **41**, 261–268.

Lewinsohn, P. M., & Libet, J. Pleasant events, activity schedules and depressions. *Journal of Abnormal Psychology*, 1972, **79**, 291–295.

Lewinsohn, P. M., & Shaffer, M. The use of home observation as an integral part of the treatment of depression: Preliminary report and case studies. *Journal of Consulting and Clinical Psychology*, 1971, **37**, 87–94.

Lewinsohn, P. M., Weinstein, M. S., & Alper, T. A behavioral approach to the group treatment of depressed persons: Methodological contributions. *Journal of Clinical Psychology*, 1970, **26**, 525–532.

Libet, J. M., & Lewinsohn, P. M. Concept of social skill with special reference to the behavior of depressed persons. *Journal of Consulting and Clinical Psychology*, 1973, **40**, 304–312.

Libet, J. M., Lewinsohn, P. M., & Javorek, F. The construct of social skill: An empirical study of several measures on temporal stability, internal structure, validity, and situational generalizability. Unpublished manuscript, University of Oregon, 1973.

Lubin, B. Manual for the Depression Adjective Check Lists. San Diego: Educational and Industrial Testing Service, 1967.

MacPhillamy, D., & Lewinsohn, P. M. *The Pleasant Events Schedule*. Unpublished manuscript, University of Oregon, 1971.

MacPhillamy, D. J., & Lewinsohn, P. M. The measurement of reinforcing events. Paper presented at the 80th Annual Convention of the American Psychological Association, Honolulu, 1972a.

MacPhillamy, D. J., & Lewinsohn, P. M. The structure of reported reinforcement. Unpublished manuscript, University of Oregon, 1972b.

MacPhillamy, D. J., & Lewinsohn, P. M. Depression as a function of levels of desired and obtained pleasure. *Journal of Abnormal Psychology*, 1974, **83**, 651–657.

Mahoney, M. J. *Cognition and behavior modification*. Cambridge, Mass.: Ballinger, 1974.

Martin, M. L., Weinstein, M. S., & Lewinsohn, P. M. The use of home observations as an integral part of the treatment of depression: The case of Mrs. B. Unpublished manuscript, University of Oregon, 1968.

McLean, P. D., Ogston, K., & Grauer, L. A behavioral approach to the treatment of depression. *Journal of Behavior Therapy and Experimental Psychiatry*, 1973, **4**, 323–330.

Meichenbaum, D. *Cognitive behavior modification*. Morristown, New Jersey: General Learning Press, 1974.

Mendels, J. Depression: The distinction between syndrome and symptom. *British Journal of Psychiatry*, 1968, **114**, 1549–1554.

Mendels, J. *Concepts of depression*. New York: Wiley, 1970.

Mendels, J., & Cochrane, C. The nosology of depression: The endogenous-reactive concept. *American Journal of Psychiatry*, 1968, **124**, 1–11.

Metcalfe, M., & Goldman, E. Validation of an inventory for measuring depression. *British Journal of Psychiatry*, 1965, **111**, 240–242.

Miller, W. R., & Seligman, M. E. P. Depression and the perceptions of reinforcement. *Journal of Abnormal Psychology*, 1973, **82**, 62–73.

Nussbaum, K., Wittig, B. A., Hanlon, T. E., & Kurland, A. A. Intravenous nialamide in the treatment of depressed female patients. *Comprehensive Psychiatry*, 1963, **4**, 105–116.

Perris, C. A study of bipolar (manic-depression) and unipolar recurrent depressive psychoses. *Acta Psychiatrica Scandinavi*, 1966, **42**, 7–189.

Perris, C. Genetic transmission of depressive psychoses. *Acta Psychiatrica Scandinavica*, 1968, **42**, 45–52.

Perris, C. The separation of bipolar (manic-depressive) from unipolar recurrent depressive psychoses. *Behavioral Neuropsychiatry*, 1969, **1**, 17–25.

Perris, C. Abnormality on paternal and maternal sides: Observations in bipolar (manic-depressive) and unipolar depressive psychoses. *British Journal of Psychiatry*, 1971, **118**, 207–210.

Pichot, P., & Lempérière, T. Analyse factorielle d'un questionnaire d'auto-evaluation des symptoms dépressif. *Revue de Psychologie Appliquée*, 1964, **14**, 15–29.

Rehm, L. P., & Marston, A. R. Reduction of social anxiety through modification of self-reinforcement: An instigation therapy technique. *Journal of Consulting and Clinical Psychology*, 1968, **32**, 565–574.

Reisinger, J. J. The treatment of "anxiety-depression" via positive reinforcement and response cost. *Journal of Applied Behavior Analysis*, 1972, **5**, 125–130.

Robinson, J. C., & Lewinsohn, P. M. An experimental analysis of a technique based on the Premack principle for changing the verbal behavior of depressed individuals. *Psychological Reports*, 1973a, **32**, 199–210.

Robinson, J. C., & Lewinsohn, P. M. Behavior modification of speech characteristics in a chronically depressed man. *Behavior Therapy*, 1973b, **4**, 150–152.

Rosenberry, C., Weiss, R. L., & Lewinsohn, P. M. Frequency and skill of emitted social reinforcement in depressed and non-depressed subjects. Unpublished manuscript, University of Oregon, 1968.

Rotter J. B. Generalized expectancies for internal versus external control of reinforcements. *Psychological Monographs*, 1966, **80** (Whole No. 609).

Rush, A. J., Khatami, M., & Beck, A. T. Cognitive and behavior therapy in chronic depression. *Behavior Therapy*, 1975, **6**, 398–404.

Seitz, R. Five psychological measures of neurotic depression: A correlation study. *Journal of Clinical Psychology*, 1970, **26**, 504–505.

Seligman, M. E. P. Depression and learned helplessness. In R. J. Friedman & M. M. Katz (Eds.), *The psychology of depression: Contemporary theory and research*. New York: Winston-Wiley, 1974.

Seligman, M. E. P. *Helplessness: On depression, development and death*. San Francisco: Freeman & Company, 1975.

Seligman, M. E. P., Klein, D. C., & Miller, W. R. Depression. In H. Leitenberg (Ed.), *Handbook of behavior therapy*. Englewood Cliffs, New Jersey: Prentice Hall, in press.

Shipley, C. R., & Fazio, A. F. Pilot study of a treatment for psychological depression. *Journal of Abnormal Psychology*, 1973, **82**, 372–376.

Stern, J. A., McClure, J. N., & Costello, C. G. Depression: Assessment and etiology. In C. G. Costello (Ed.), *Symptoms of psychopathology: A handbook*. New York: Wiley, 1970.

Thoresen, C. E., & Mahoney, M. J. *Behavioral self-control*. New York: Holt, Rinehart & Winston, 1974.

Weckowicz, T. E., Muir, W., & Cropley, A. J. A factor analysis of the Beck Inventory of Depression. *Journal of Consulting Psychology*, 1967, **31**, 23–28.

Weiss, B. L., Kupfer, D. J., Foster, F. G., & Delgado, J. Psychomotor activity, sleep, and biogenic amine metabolites in depression. *Biological Psychiatry*, 1974, **9**, 45–53.

Wener, A., & Rehm, L. P. Depressive affect: A test of behavioral hypotheses. *Journal of Abnormal Psychology*, 1975, **84**, 221–227.

Williams, J. G., Barlow, D. H., & Agras, W. S. Behavioral measurement of severe depression. *Archives of General Psychiatry*, 1972, **27**, 330–333.

Williams, T. A., Katz, M. M., & Shield, J. A., Jr., (Eds.), *Recent advances in the psychobiology of the depressive illnesses*. Washington, D. C.: U. S. Government Printing Office, 1972.

Winokur, G. The types of affective disorders. *Journal of Nervous and Mental Disease*, 1973, **156**, 82–96.

Wolpe, J., & Lang, P. J. A Fear Survey Schedule for use in behavior therapy. *Behaviour Research and Therapy*, 1964, **2**, 27–30.

Woodruff, R. A., Jr., Goodwin, D. W., & Guze, S. B. *Psychiatric diagnosis*. New York: Oxford University Press, 1974.

Zung, W. A self-rating depression scale. *Archives of General Psychiatry*, 1965, **12**, 63–70.

Zung, W. W. K., Richards, C. B., & Short, M. J. Self-rating depression scale in an outpatient clinic. *Archives of General Psychiatry*, 1965, **13**, 508–516.

CHAPTER 10

Assessment of Psychotic Behavior

CHARLES J. WALLACE[1]

Camarillo-Neuropsychiatric Institute Research Program

and

The Program for Clinical Research
Camarillo State Hospital
Camarillo, California

Introduction

The first task in writing a review such as this is to selectively attend to what at first seems a vast amount of relevant literature. The topic of this chapter is psychotic behavior. Thumbing through a few years of the *Journal of Abnormal Psychology* yields dozens of potentially relevant articles, almost all of which are concerned with the assessment of cognitive deficit(s) in schizophrenia. But the focus of this book is practical behavioral assessment; assessment presumably used to evaluate the effects of behavior change procedures. Cognitive deficits are rarely the focus of such procedures and, as Chapman & Chapman (1973) point out, different characteristics of assessment measures lead to rather different definitions of the construct "cognitive deficit". Hence, this review will be oriented primarily to assessment techniques used in the modification of psychotic patients' behavioral excesses or deficits. The reader interested in measures of cognitive deficit is referred to the chapter by Meichenbaum in this book and to reviews by Payne (1970), Neale & Cromwell (1970), McGhie (1971), Reed (1970), Venables (1973), Maher (1972), Cromwell (1975), and Easterbrook (1970).

The second task in writing a review is to categorize the relevant material so that it can be presented to the reader in a useful fashion. Since the book's focus is on behavior change techniques, perhaps a look at a "typical" operant-conditioning-based treatment regimen may provide a starting point for categorizing assessment tools. The typical operant procedure involves the selection of a target behavior to change, definition and recording of the behavior, and programming of the environment to act (or refrain from acting) contingent

[1]The author thanks Robert Paul Liberman, M.D. for his kind and generous support.

upon the occurrence of the behavior. Assessment at this level is relatively easy; the target behavior is simply recorded and the clinical effectiveness of the procedure is reflected in the increase or decrease of the target behavior. Hersen & Barlow (1976) have described this as a "one-to-one" relationship between assessment and treatment. The information provided by the assessment is directly relevant to the decision to continue or to modify the treatment procedure.

The assessment process can become and often has been several steps removed from this simple but informative one-to-one relationship. Assessment has frequently involved people, places, and events that are different than those used during treatment; the assessment behavior has often been different than the targeted behavior (in spite of the use of the same label for both assessment and treatment behaviors). The difficulty with such indirect assessment procedures is that such information is not immediately relevant to treatment. Information that indicates no change may reflect a flaw in the assessment process rather than ineffective treatment.

Despite this interpretative difficulty, behavior change techniques have been evaluated with both direct and indirect assessment procedures. Hence, this review will examine three broad categories of the behavioral assessment of psychotic patients: the measurement and recording of targeted excesses and deficits; the measurement and recording of observed but non-targeted behaviors; and the measurement and recording of behavior using rating scales. Table 10.1 presents the classes to be discussed within each of the three broad categories, and also notes the areas of assessment for each of the relevant articles.

The third task in writing a review is to highlight those aspects of the relevant literature that may be particularly beneficial. It is the reviewer's assumption that the reader is at the point in treatment that he or she has selected a class of behavior to change and is now seeking a suitable definition and recording procedure. This review will attend to the definitions and recording procedures of past assessment techniques to aid the reader in consulting the relevant studies before implementing his or her own assessment strategy. Treatment procedures and their results will be deliberately given short shrift.

Targeted Deficits

Many of the studies to be reviewed in this section are reports of token economies conducted with chronic psychotics. Because these generally large-scale programs are reported in only a few pages, sufficient detail is often lacking to determine their exact assessment procedures. Therefore, these studies will be only briefly discussed.

Self-care skills

Table 10.1 lists the token economies that have targeted self-care skills. There is general agreement between studies about the various behaviors that constitute these skills (e.g., showering, brushing teeth, combing hair, maintenance of living areas and personal possessions, appropriate meal behaviors). Ayllon & Azrin (1965, 1968a) provide a relatively complete listing. They defined the self-care skills of their female patients as grooming (hair combed; wearing of dress, slip, panties, bra, stockings, and shoes), bathing at the designated time, participating in exercises, making beds, and cleaning around bed areas. Of course, each of these behaviors required further specification, but this was not reported.

The recording technique usually involved observing the behavior at a specified time and place. This made recording and reinforcement relatively convenient and hopefully more consistent. Again, Ayllon & Azrin (1965, 1968a) provide a relatively complete description of their recording process. Grooming was checked three times per day, bathing was checked at one designated time per week, tooth brushing at one designated time per day, exercises twice a day, and bed making once per day. Attendants apparently supervised the tasks and recorded patients' performance while distributing tokens.

Work skills

Table 10.1 list those token economies that have targeted on- and off-ward work. There have been wide variations in the behaviors that constitute such work, and not enough details are reported to resolve these differences. In fairness, most reports do indicate that extensive criteria were developed for each job (e.g., Hersen *et al.*, 1972) and were posted either at some central location or at the job site (e.g., Gripp & Magaro, 1971). Again, Allyon & Azrin (1965, 1968a) provide the most complete description of an on-ward work program; they established ten categories of on-ward work (e.g. grooming assistant, laundry assistant, and dietary assistant), with from three to eight jobs per category. Each job was defined in terms of the specific steps necessary for correct completion. For example, the job of oral hygiene assistant consisted of the following steps:

> Assembles toothpaste, toothbrushes, gargle solution and paper cups. Pours gargle into cups and dispenses toothpaste or gargle to all patients (1965, p. 372).

Other jobs were defined in similarly thorough fashion. The recording process was the same as that for self-care skills; the time and place for the jobs were specified, and attendants supervised the tasks, recorded performance, and distributed tokens.

TABLE 10.1

The Areas of Functioning Assessed by Studies Dealing with Behavioral Excesses and Deficits of Psychotic Patients

	Target Deficits[a]				Target Excesses[a]				Observed, Non-target[a]			
Study	Self Care	Work Skills	Therapy Activities	Inter-personal	Self Care	Delu-sional	Hallucin-ation	Verbal, Physical Abuse	Environ-ment	General-ization[b]	Out-come[c]	Rating Scales
Ayllon & Azrin (1965, 1968a, TE)	X	X	X		X						12	
Schaefer & Martin (1966, 1969)	X	X		X					X			
Atthowe & Krasner (1968 TE)	X	X	X	X	X	X					13, 14	Palo Alto Group Psycho-therapy Study
Heap *et al.* (1970, TE)	X	X	X	X		X					12, 14	
Winkler (1970, TE)	X[1]	X	X		X			X			12	
Lloyd & Garlington (1970, TE)	X										13	
Feingold & Migler (1972, TE)	X	X									13	
Shean & Zeidberg (1971, TE)	X	X	X	X							12, 14 & key press	MACC–11

TABLE 10.1—continued

	Target Deficits[a]				Target Excesses[a]				Observed, Non-target[a]			
Study	Self Care	Work Skills	Therapy Activities	Inter-personal	Self Care	Delu-sional	Hallucin-ation	Verbal, Physical Abuse	Environ-ment	General-ization[b]	Out-come[c]	Rating Scales
Maley *et al.* (1973, TE)	X			X							tasks	MACC–11
Paul *et al.* (1972, TE)	X	X		X					X			MSBS, IMPS, NOSIE–30, SBSG1
Glickman *et al.* (1973, TE)	X	X									12	
Greenberg *et al.* (1975, TE)	X	X		X							14	
Arann & Horner (1972, TE)		X									12	
McReynolds & Coleman (1972, TE)	X	X	X								12, 14	
Henderson & Scoles (1970, TE)		X	X	X							13	
Gripp & Magaro (1971, TE)		X				X		X	X			NOSIE, PRP, WAS, MSBS, ELGIN

TABLE 10.1—continued

	Target Deficits[a]				Target Excesses[a]				Observed, Non-target[a]			
Study	Self Care	Work Skills	Therapy Activities	Inter-personal	Self Care	Delu-sional	Hallucin-ation	Verbal, Physical Abuse	Environ-ment	General-ization[b]	Out-come[c]	Rating Scales
Lloyd & Abel (1970, TE)	X	X		X							Ward Status 14	
Pomerleau *et al.* (1972, TE)		X	X	X	X			X			14	WB1
Hersen *et al.* (1972, TE)	X	X	X	X	X						13	
Steffy *et al.* (1969, TE)	X				X			X			14	PRP, MSBS
Schwartz & Bellack (1975, TE)												NOSIE–30
Milby *et al.* (1975, TE)		X	X									COPES
Hollander *et al.* (1973, TE)		X										
Mitchell & Stofelmayer (1973)		X[1]										
Curran *et al.* (1973)			X									
McInnis *et al.* (1973)			X									

TABLE 10.1—continued

	Target Deficits[a]				Target Excesses[a]				Observed, Non-target[a]			
Study	Self Care	Work Skills	Therapy Activities	Inter-personal	Self Care	Delu-sional	Hallucin-ation	Verbal, Physical Abuse	Environ-ment	General-ization[b]	Out-come[c]	Rating Scales
Ayllon & Azrin (1968, b)			X									
Allen & Magaro (1971)			X									
Sobell *et al.* (1970)			X								2, 4, 7, 8, 10	
Wallace *et al.* (1973)			X[1]							2, 4, 7, 8, 10		
Wilson & Walters (1966)				X[1]						3, 4, 6, 9, 11		Own "talkative-ness"
Bennet & Maley (1973)				X[1]						3, 4, 6, 9, 11 3, 4, 6, 9, 11		MACC–11, PRP
Tracey *et al.* (1974)				X[1]						3, 4, 6, 9, 10 3, 4, 6, 9, 10		
Wallace & Davis (1974)				X[1]								
King *et al.* (1960)				X								EMIS
Liberman (1972)				X[1]						3, 5, 6, 9, 11		

TABLE 10.1—continued

	Target Deficits[a]				Target Excesses[a]				Observed, Non-target[a]			
Study	Self Care	Work Skills	Therapy Activities	Inter-personal	Self Care	Delu-sional	Halluci-nation	Verbal, Physical Abuse	Environ-ment	General-ization[b]	Out-come[c]	Rating Scales
Sabatasso & Jacobson (1970)				X						3, 4, 6, 8, 10 3, 5, 6, 9, 10 2, 4, 7, 8, 10		
Sherman (1968)				X								
Sherman (1965)				X								
Isaacs *et al.* (1960)				X								
O'Brien *et al.* (1969)				X[1]								
Kale *et al.* (1968)				X[1]						2, 5, 6, 8, 10 2, 4, 7, 8, 10		
Milby (1970)				X[1]								
Stahl *et al.* (1974)				X[1]								Own self-care & interpersonal
Roberts (1969)				X								
Liberman *et al.* (1974)	X	X			X	X	X	X				
Ayllon & Michael (1959)					X	X		X	X			
Ayllon & Haughton (1962)					X				X			

TABLE 10.1—continued

	Target Deficits[a]				Target Excesses[a]				Observed, Non-target[a]			
Study	Self Care	Work Skills	Therapy Activities	Inter-personal	Self Care	Delu-sional	Hallucin-ation	Verbal, Physical Abuse	Environ-ment	General-ization[b]	Out-come[c]	Rating Scales
Ayllon (1963)					X				X			
Paden *et al.* (1974)					X							
Upper & Newton (1971)					X							
Moore & Crum (1969)					X							
Harmatz & Lapuc (1968)					X							Own Semantic Differential
Atthowe (1972)					X							
Wagner & Paul (1972)					X							MSBS
Ayllon & Haughton (1964)						X						
Wincze *et al.* (1972)						X[1]				3, 5, 6, 9, 11 3, 5, 6, 9, 11		Own psychi-atric interview
Liberman *et al.* (1973)						X[1]				2, 5, 6, 9, 11 2, 5, 6, 9, 11		
Richardson *et al.* (1972)						X						
Sanders (1971)						X[1]						

TABLE 10.1—continued

	Target Deficits[a]				Target Excesses[a]				Observed, Non-target[a]			
Study	Self Care	Work Skills	Therapy Activities	Inter-personal	Self Care	Delu-sional	Halluci-nation	Verbal, Physical Abuse	Environ-ment	General-ization[b]	Out-come[c]	Rating Scales
Cayner & Kiland (1974)						X		X				
Rickard *et al.* (1960)						X						
Patterson & Teigen (1973)						X				2, 5, 7, 8, 10		
Rickard & Dinoff (1962)						X						
Bartlett *et al.* (1971)						X[1]						
Ullman *et al.* (1965)						X[1]				3, 4, 6, 9, 11 3, 4, 6, 9, 11		Welsh A & R
Meichenbaum (1969)						X[1]				3, 4, 6, 9, 11 3, 4, 6, 9, 11		
Meichenbaum & Cameron (1973)						X[1]				3, 4, 6, 9, 11 3, 4, 6, 9, 11		
Haynes & Geddy (1973)							X[1]					
Bucher & Fabricatore (1970)							X					
Nydegger (1972)							X			2, 5, 7, 8, 10		

TABLE 10.1—continued

	Target Deficits[a]				Target Excesses[a]				Observed, Non-target[a]			
Study	Self Care	Work Skills	Therapy Activities	Inter-personal	Self Care	Delu-sional	Halluci-nation	Verbal, Physical Abuse	Environ-ment	General-ization[b]	Out-come[c]	Rating Scales
Rutner & Bugle (1969)							X			3, 4, 6, 9, 11		
Moser (1974)							X			3, 4, 6, 9, 11 2, 5, 7, 9, 10		
Anderson & Alpert (1974)							X					
Lindsley (1959, 1963)							X				Lever	
Wallace *et al.* (1973)								X		2, 5, 7, 8, 10		
Hunter *et al.* (1962)									X[1]			
Harmatz *et al.* (Notel)									X[1]			
Mariotto & Paul (1974)									X[1]			IMPS, MSBS, NOSIE–30, SBSG1
Paul *et al.* (1973)									X[1]			
Holahan (1972)									X[1]		X	Own Semantic Differential

TABLE 10.1—continued

	Target Deficits[a]				Target Excesses[a]				Observed, Non-target[a]			
Study	Self Care	Work Skills	Therapy Activities	Inter-personal	Self Care	Delu-sional	Halluci-nation	Verbal, Physical Abuse	Environ-ment	General-ization[b]	Out-come[c]	Rating Scales
Holahan & Saegert (1973)									X[1]			Own attitude toward & environment
Ittelson *et al.* (1970)									X[1]			
DeRisi *et al.* (1975)									X[1]			
Higgs (1970)									X			BRPS
Esser (1965)									X			
Lindsley (1956, 1960)											Lever	
Lindsley (1962)											Con-jugate	
Nathan *et al.* (1964)											Con-jugate	
Lentz *et al.* (1971) (1973)												MSBS, SBSG1, NOSIE–30
Baker (1971)									X			

[a]1 = interrater reliability indicated.
[b]2 = same response for both generalization and treatment assessment.
3 = different response.

4 = same setting for both generalization and treatment assessment.
5 = different setting.
6 = same time for both generalization and treatment assessment.
7 = different time.
8 = same assessment technique for both.
9 = different assessment technique.
10 = same response measure (duration, frequency, etc.).
11 = different response measure.
The number of entries in the "generalization" column correspond to the number of generalization measures used in the study.
[c]12 = number of patients performing the task.
13 = number of tokens or points.
14 = discharge.

Ayllon & Azrin (1965, 1968a) also provided tokens for off-ward work. The description of this work is less complete than that of on-ward work except for a particularly well specified, 17 step procedure designed to shape five patients to become laundry assistants (1968a).

In marked contrast to the rather global reports provided by token economies is the specificity of the definition of work provided by Mitchell & Stoffelmayer (1973). They assessed the effects of sitting as a reinforcer for work output in two extremely inactive schizophrenics. Work was defined as coil-stripping, which was further defined as "holding the coil in one hand while pulling off the wire from the coil with the other hand" (p. 420). Patients were observed for 30-minute sessions divided into sixty 30-second intervals. "An instance of work was any occurrence of the defined behavior during a 30-second period" (p. 420).

Attendance at Therapeutic Activities

Many of the token economies targeted attendance at various therapeutic activities (Table 10.1). In addition to scheduled activities such as occupational therapy, gym class, homemaking class, automotive workshop, art clinic, and meals, behaviors such as piano playing, basketball playing, and the taking of medication were labelled "therapeutic activities." Unfortunately, the definition of attendance was not generally specified; attendance could have meant various combinations of appearing at the activity site, staying for a specified duration, or "actively" participating.

Another set of studies, specifically concerned with increasing patient use of therapeutic activities through reinforcer sampling and exposure procedures, defined attendance in terms of a very specific patient behavior which was easily observed and recorded. (Neither duration nor participation were part of the definition.) Curran, Lentz, & Paul (1973) and McInnis, Himelstein, Doty, & Paul (1974) defined attendance at evening activities as the asking for or purchase of a pass which was available for a limited period of time in the evening and which allowed entrance to the activity area. Ayllon and Azrin (1968b) defined participation as the paying of a token to go for a walk, listen to music, or view a movie. Wallace, Davis, Liberman, & Baker (1973) defined both staff and patient attendance at therapeutic activities as the number of individuals present at the activity site during each of 4 surreptious checks.

Interpersonal Skills

Table 10.1 lists the token economies which have targeted the increase of prosocial, interpersonal behaviors. The reports do not present definitions and recording methods in great detail.

Numerous other studies specifically concerned with an increase in interpersonal skills have taken far greater pains to specify the definition and recording of such skills. The most consistent element in all of these studies has been the inclusion of speech as part of the definition of interpersonal skills. There has been some disagreement, however, about the quantity and quality of speech that constitutes an interpersonal skill. Some studies have targeted an increase of any sound or speech irrespective of content (Liberman, 1972; Stahl, Thomson, Leitenberg & Hasazi, 1974; Wilson & Walters, 1966). Others have defined speech in terms of a very specific response such as "hello" or "food" (Isaacs, Thomas & Goldiamond, 1960; Kale, Kaye, Whelan & Hopkins, 1968; Sabatasso & Jacobson, 1970; Sherman, 1965). Still others have defined speech in terms of one or more response categories (Bennett & Maley, 1973; O'Brien, Azrin & Henson, 1969; Roberts, 1969; Tracy, Briddell & Wilson, 1974; Wallace & Davis, 1974).

The recording and reinforcement process is relatively straightforward when content is not part of the definition of speech. An observer can tally the number of words or sounds during a session (Liberman, 1972; Stahl *et al.*, 1974; Wilson & Walters, 1966), or automatic devices can be used (Wilson & Walters, 1966), particularly when the rate of speech is high enough to make hand tallying difficult.

The recording process is similarly straightforward when a specific response is the target. This is particularly evident in Sabatasso & Jacobson's (1970), Isaac *et al.*'s (1960), and Sherman's (1963, 1965) shaping of speech in mute psychotics. Assessment consists of matching the patient's response to the behaviors defined in the various steps of the shaping procedure. Kale *et al.* (1968) similarly provided an easily assessed behavior; the target response was "Hi" or "Hello", Mr. ——————" which was recorded based on scheduled, on-ward contacts.

The recording process is more difficult when speech is defined in terms of a class of responses. The observer has to decide that the patient's response is one of many which can be placed in the targeted categories. Generally, such studies have been performed in relatively controlled sessions, often with one or more observers using partially automated recording or reinforcement devices. The reader is urged to review these studies (Bennett & Maley, 1973; O'Brien *et al.*, 1969; Tracey *et al.*, 1974; Wallace & Davis, 1974) since, in spite of their many differences, they represent an equally high degree of "precision" in defining and measuring target behaviors.

In contrast to the use of speech as part of the definition of interpersonal skills, Milby (1970) defined interpersonal skills in terms of social interaction. Interaction was further defined as "talking to, working with, or playing with another patient or staff member" and was assessed in 12 daily 2-minute observations.

In a completely different approach, King, Armitage & Tilton (1960) increased "cooperation" among patients using the Multiple Operant Problem Solving Apparatus (MOPSA). Cooperation was defined as complex patterns of lever pulling which had to be coordinated between patients in order to earn reinforcement.

Targeted Excesses

This section includes studies whose purpose was to reduce behavioral excesses. These excesses were generally regarded as symptomatic.

Self-care

A relatively small number of token economies (Table 10.1) have targeted specific excesses such as frequent clothes changing (Winkler, 1970), urinating on the floor (Pomerleau, Bobrove & Harris, 1972), and wearing hospital clothes during the daytime (Hersen, Eisler, Smith & Agras, 1972). Several, non-token economy studies have targeted the reduction of classes of behavior such as inappropriate meal behaviors, incontinence, inappropriate wearing of clothes, and hoarding of various objects. Because these studies have little in common and are often reported in scant detail, their presentation, study-by-study, would be rather disjointed. Hence, the reader interested in targeting mealtime excesses is referred to studies by Ayllon & Michael (1959, two cases of refusal to eat); Ayllon & Haughton (1962, refusal to go to the dining room and refusal to leave the dining room); Ayllon (1963, food stealing); Ayllon & Azrin (1968a, refusal to eat decreased by a shaping program which is particularly well defined); Sobell, Schaefer, Sobell & Kremer (1970, chronic missing of meals); Harmatz & Lapuc (1968, obesity); Moore & Crum (1971, obesity); Upper & Newton (1971, obesity); and Paden, Himelstein & Paul (1974, assessment of correct behaviors). Enuresis was targeted by Atthowe & Krasner (1968); Atthowe (1972); and Wagner & Paul (1970, also day time incontinence). Ayllon (1963) and Liberman, Wallace, Teigen, & Davis (1974, 2 cases) targeted inappropriate use of clothing. Ayllon & Michael (1959) and Ayllon (1963) reported 5 cases in which hoarding was reduced.

Delusions

Because of its importance in diagnosing patients as psychotic, delusional speech has received a good deal of attention in the behavioral literature. (Unfortunately, this attention has not resulted in a standardized assessment techniques.) Delusions have been generally defined as speech whose content is at variance with reality. Since the content of one patient's delusions rarely matches the content of another patient's, most studies have gone through the laborious process of simply listening to patients and making a catalogue of delusional statements which can be grouped into larger categories (e.g., Ayllon and Haughton, 1964; Liberman *et al.*, 1974; Liberman, Teigen, Patterson & Baker, 1973; Wincze, Leitenberg & Agras, 1972).

Once defined, several investigators have then simply recorded the number or duration of delusional comments made by the patient during spontaneous interchanges (Cayner & Kiland, 1974, Case 1; Richardson, Karklas & Lal, 1972; Sanders, 1971). This assumes, of course, that the patient interacts at a high rate and will continue to do so during all of the treatment phases.

The majority of investigators, however, have chosen to approach the patient and assess delusional speech during the scheduled approaches. Liberman *et al.* (1974), Ayllon & Michael (1969), and Ayllon & Haughton (1964), for example, had nursing staff approach and interact with patients once every half hour for from 1 to 5 minutes. Numerous others have scheduled longer but less frequent approaches; i.e., interviews or sessions (Bartlett, Ora, Brown, & Butler, 1971; Liberman *et al.*, 1973, 1974; Patterson & Teigen, 1973; Rickard, Dignam & Horner 1960; Rickard & Dinoff, 1962; Wincze *et al.*, 1972).

Wincze *et al.*, 1972 and Patterson & Teigen (1973) then specified that the interviewers ask patients pre-determined, "delusion-eliciting" questions. This made observation fairly simple since any response to a question other than the correct one was recorded as delusional. Wincze *et al.*'s (1972) procedure was particularly involved; interviewers randomly selected 15 questions from a pool of 105 questions that had been separately constructed for each patient, and the measure of treatment effectiveness was the number of delusional answers.

The other studies using scheduled approaches and sessions have described the interviewer as being either "neutral" or "non-directive." In contrast to asking questions, this made recording more difficult since the observer had to decide that a particular verbalization fit one or more categories of delusions rather than merely recording the correctness of an answer to a specific question. These studies also showed a good deal of variation in their measure of treatment effectiveness. Ayllon & Michael (1959), Ayllon & Haughton (1964), and Liberman *et al.* (1974) used the number of delusional intervals as the measure of treatment effectiveness. Bartlett *et al.* (1971) and Liberman *et al.* (1974, case JP) divided sessions into intervals of arbitrary length and used the number of intervals with delusional speech as the measure of treatment effects. Rickard, Dignam & Horner (1960, experiment 2) and Rickard & Dinoff (1962) recorded the duration of rational speech during 10-minute intervals of a 30-minute interview. Liberman *et al.* (1973) recorded the duration of time during an interview to the onset of the first delusional statement.

Several studies have targeted categories of "sick" and "healthy" talk rather than patient-specific delusions (Meichenbaum, 1969; Meichenbaum & Cameron, 1973; Ullmann, Forsman, Kenny, McInnis, Unikel & Zeisset, 1965). Instances of healthy talk, defined as verbalization of comfort, liking, good physical and mental health, and personal assets were counted on tape recordings of highly structured interviews.

Hallucinations

Less attention has been given to the modification of hallucinations than to the modification of delusions. Perhaps this difference is due to the fact that hallucinations are extremely difficult to define. Haynes & Geddy (1973) defined hallucinations as "verbal, facial, and/or gestural responses to an unobservable stimulus" (p. 123). Of course, the difficulty has been the identification of a stimulus which cannot be observed. This paradox has been resolved in three ways. The patient has been frequently asked to report when he is aware of this stimulus (Anderson & Alpert, 1974; Bucher & Fabricatore, 1970; Liberman *et al.*, 1974, Case BR; Moser, 1974; Nydegger, 1972; Rutner & Bugle, 1969). Less frequently, the patient has been observed and behaviors presumably correlated with hallucinations have been noted (Anderson & Alpert, 1974; Liberman *et al.*, 1974). Or, the observational situation has been modified or the patient behavior so restricted that any response can be considered an indication of hallucinations (Haynes & Geddy, 1973; Lindsley, 1959, 1963).

The recording technique for self-report has generally been quite simple; the patient has been asked to record in a diary or book whenever there was an unobservable stimulus (most often voices and occasionally visions). This assumes that reporting the hallucinations to the therapist is not reinforcing (or punishing). Moser (1974) reduced the reinforcement value of reporting by having the patient drop the written record in a mailbox once every 2 weeks. Self report also assumes that the hallucinations occur infrequently enough that recording remains low in cost for the patient. Anderson & Alpert's (1974) patient had a rather high frequency of hallucinations; they had him record each hallucination during a limited time period (1 hour).

Two studies observed behaviors that were correlated with hallucinations. Patients were first interviewed for some time and those behaviors that appeared to covary with the self-report of hallucinations were identified. The two studies used different recording techniques; Liberman *et al.* (1974) tallied the behaviors during scheduled interviews while Anderson & Alpert (1974) rated the amount of hallucination-correlated behavior during breakfast and lunch.

The patient in the Haynes & Geddy (1973) study was so withdrawn that almost any verbal behavior was considered an indication of hallucinations. Lindsley (1959, 1963) observed patients in experimental rooms in which no one but the patient was present. Thus, any vocalization was defined as a "vocal hallucinatory symptom."

Physical and Verbal Abuse

In spite of their obvious importance, only a few studies have even mentioned physical or verbal abuse (Ayllon & Michael, 1959; Cayner & Kilard, 1974; Gripp & Magaro, 1971; Liberman *et al.*, 1974; O'Brien & Azrin, 1972; Pomerleau *et al.*, 1972; Steffy *et al.*, 1969; Wallace, Teigen, Liberman & Baker, 1973; Winkler, 1970). The reader is referred to Liberman *et al.* (1974) for a relatively complete description of verbal and physical abuse (seven cases of verbal abuse, six of assault, and five of property destruction) and to O'Brien & Azrin (1972) for the assessment of screaming.

Observed, Non-targeted Behaviors

This section catalogues methods of observing and recording behaviors which have not been targeted for modification. These methods can be grouped into three broad classes: observation and recording of behaviors of large groups of individuals in order to develop a "picture" of the living environment; observation and recording of behaviors to determine the generalization of treatment effects to various combinations of non-targeted behaviors, settings, and times; observation and recording of events which represent the outcome of an intervention but which themselves are not the targets of the intervention (e.g., the number of tokens earned, rates of discharges and readmission, and amount of medication prescribed).

Environment

Those instruments that have assessed psychiatric environments have had several elements in common. They have all used observers to periodically record an instantaneous picture of the environment using a pre-determined set of categories to code the observed behaviors. The prototypical instrument is Hunter, Schooler & Spahn's (1962) Location-Activity-Inventory (LAI).

The LAI categorized patient behavior on four major dimensions: location (14 ward locations), position (6 positions of the patient in relationship to the walls, such as against the wall, facing the corner), posture (6 categories such as sitting, walking), and activity (5 broad classes such as social activities, non-functional activities, no behavior). Based on examples provided in the report, thoroughly detailed definitions were made of each category.

Once each hour for 12 hours, an observer walked through the ward on a random routine, stopping at each of the locations, noting the number and identity of the patients, and observing each for 10 seconds. Behaviors were coded using one category for each of the four dimensions (if more than one category were observed, only the "most salient" was recorded). Observations were conducted after the patients had adapted to the observers and after the observers had practiced for an unspecified length of time.

All of the other instruments are variations on this basic theme. Table 10.2 lists the major dimensions, sampling frequencies, duration of observations, and the method of calculating interrater reliability for each instrument. These variations make comparisons among the instruments somewhat difficult. Nevertheless, there are certain similarities. Almost all of the observation categories are relatively simple and include on a few possible behaviors. Several investigators have combined categories to create dimensions which facilitate cross-study comparisons. For example, Harmatz, Mendelsohn & Glassman (1973) summed across various combinations of their 11 categories to obtain dimensions comparable to those of the LAI. Mariotto & Paul (1974) used combined categories in comparing the results of the TSBC with rating on the Impatient Multidimensional Psychiatric Scale.

A variation of the typical coding procedure is the use of "mutually exclusive" and "concomitant" dimensions of the BSF and BOI. The mutually exclusive dimension for both comprises five behaviors (running, walking, standing, sitting, and lying), only one of which can be coded during the observation interval. This, of course, is similar to the LAI. The concomitant dimension includes behaviors such as smoking, talking, watching television, washing self, and receiving medication. As many of these are coded as are observed during the interval. This is unlike the LAI, but is like all of the other coding systems.

Hunter *et al.* (1962) developed the LAI to obtain a "reliable and comprehensive description of the overt ward behavior of chronic schizophrenics" (p. 69). They question, however, the "usefulness of the instrument in measuring behavioral change. It is not known how sensitive it is to change; i.e., how acute the instrument is" (p. 73). As it turns out, these instruments have been used to evaluate the effects of several treatments. Schaefer & Martin (1966) used the BSF as the major assessment device in the evaluation of their token economy. They set out to determine if the token economy reduced patient "apathy." Apathy was defined as a single-entry code; i.e., there were no concomitant behaviors during the observation interval. The token economy was effective in

TABLE 10.2

Major Characteristics of Environmental Observation Instruments

Characteristics	Instrument			
Name and Authors	Behavior Study Form (BSF) - - - - - - - - - - - - - Schaefer & Martin (1966)	Behavior Mapping - - - - - - - - - - - - - Ittelson *et al.* (1970)	No name given - - - - - - - - - - - - - Holahan (1972)	No name given - - - - - - - - - - - - - Holahan & Saegert (1973)
Dimensions and Categories	(a) mutually exclusive (5 categories) (b) concomitant (13 categories) (c) Location	18 categories grouped into 6 "analytic," activity dimensions and location	(a) social (7 categories) (b) non-social (3 categories)	(a) social (3 categories) (b) non-social active (3 categories) (c) isolated passive (2 categories)
Sampling Frequency	Once every ½ hour	Varies but general once every 15 minutes	Once every 75 seconds during a 45 minute session	Once every 5 minutes for 74 minutes in morning and afternoon
Duration of Observation	Instantaneous	Instantaneous	Instantaneous	Instantaneous
Reliability	None indicated	% agreement + split-half	% agreement	Method not indicated but reported as 0.94 to 0.98
Name and Authors	Behavior Observation System (BOS) - - - - - - - - - - - - - Harmatz *et al.* (1973)	Staff-resident interaction chronograph (SRIC) - - - - - - - - - - - - - Paul *et al.* (1973)	Time sample behavior checklist (TSBC) - - - - - - - - - - - - - Paul *et al.* (1972) Mariotto & Paul (1974)	Behavior Observation Instrument (BOI) - - - - - - - - - - - - - DeRisi *et al.* (1975)
Dimensions and Categories	11 categories	(a) patient behavior (5 categories) (b) staff behavior (11 categories)	25 categories	(a) appropriate (b) inappropriate (c) neutral

TABLE 10.2—continued

Characteristics		Instrument		
Sampling Frequency	Not indicated	Not indicated	Once every hour	Variable; depending upon application
Duration of Observation	Not indicated	Each staff member for 10 minutes divided into 10, 1-minute intervals	2 seconds	5 seconds
Reliability	Method not indicated but reported to be "high"	Intraclass correlation coefficient	Intraclass correlation coefficient	(a) intraclass correlation coefficient (b) % agreement (c) Kappa
Name and Authors	No name given - - - - - - - - - - - - - Ayllon & Michael (1959) Ayllon & Haughton (1962) (1964) Ayllon (1963)	No name given - - - - - - - - - - - - - Moos (1968)	No name given - - - - - - - - - - - - - Esser *et al.* (1965)	Location-activity inventory - - - - - - - - - - - - - Hunter *et al.* (1962)
Dimensions and Categories	(a) appropriate (b) inappropriate (c) neutral	16 categories	(a) location (3′ × 3′ squares) (b) posture (c) activity (d) interaction	(a) location (b) position (c) posture (d) activity
Sampling Frequency	Once every ½ hour	Not indicated	Once every ½ hour	Once every hour
Duration of Observation	1 to 3 minutes	Instantaneous	Instantaneous	10 seconds
Reliability	None indicated	Correlation coefficient likely Pearson	Not indicated	(a) contingency coefficient (b) split half

increasing observations with multiple-code entries. Paul, Tobias, & Holly (1972) used the TSBC to evaluate the effects of dropping medication; Mariotto & Paul (1974) used the TSBC to validate the IMPS. Holahan (1972) found his time sampling measure to be sensitive to changes in seating array in an experimental dayroom, and Holahan & Saegert (1973) found changes in their measure as a result of remodeling the ward.

Generalization

Any treatment procedure represents a unique combination of five elements; a particular behavior is targeted for change in a particular setting at a particular point in time and is evaluated according to changes in a particular assessment technique using a particular response measure (frequency, duration, etc.). The generalization of treatment effects means that treatment-induced changes are not restricted to the unique combination in which they occur. Table 10.1 lists those studies that have evaluated both direct treatment and generalization effects, thus allowing a comparison between the two.

Perhaps the simplest measure of generalization is one in which everything is the same as treatment except that the response is assessed at a later point in time. For example, Wallace *et al.* (1973), after finding an increase in patient and staff attendance at therapeutic activities, reassessed attendance 6 weeks after discontinuing the original observations (code 2,4,7,8,10 in Table 10.1). Attendance was still high. Rickard & Dinoff (1962) observed the same patient's delusional speech using the same assessment technique as in the original study conducted 2½ years earlier (Rickard *et al.*, 1960).

The more typical follow-up study involves assessment of the target behavior in a different setting (aftercare) and at a different time than that of treatment. Patterson & Teigen (1973) had a different observer ask his patient the same questions in an aftercare facility as were originally asked in the inpatient setting (code 2,5,7,8,10 in Table 10.1). Treatment effects generalized to the aftercare facility. Several other studies which indicate a follow-up assessment do so in a rather anecdotal fashion, simply indicating that the effects of treatment persisted after its termination (e.g., Moser, 1974; Nydegger, 1972).

Generalization effects have been assessed concomitant to treatment using different settings, responses, assessment techniques, or response measures. Tracy *et al.* (1974), for example, kept all elements the same between generalization and treatment except the response and, necessarily, the assessment technique (code 3,4,6,9,10). They determined whether the increase in patients' positive statements about activities generalized to an increase in the actual use of the activities. They examined records ("escort slips") of the names of patients who participated in off ward activities, and they found a correlation between the increase in the number of positive statements and the increase in the number of patients using the activities.

Kale *et al.* (1968) assessed generalization with all elements the same except the setting. They initially increased greeting responses to one "experimenter" and then assessed the generalization of greeting response to several other "experimenters" (code 2,5,6,8,10 in Table 10.1). No generalization was found until the new "experimenters" employed the original treatment procedures. (Kale *et al.*, also mentions the "generalization" of treatment effects when a contingency is deliberately removed as part of a reversal or withdrawal experimental design. This is, in a sense, generalization across time. However, since this is an issue concerned with the procedures for demonstrating treatment effects and not with procedures for assessment, it will not be discussed here. The reader is referred to Hersen & Barlow (1976) for discussions of various experimental designs and to Hartmann & Atkinson (1973) for a discussion of difficulties in evaluating this type of generalization.)

Most studies have assessed generalization effects using a combination of different settings, responses, etc. For example, Bennett & Maley (1973) initially increased the duration of time that patients spent during sessions engaged in four interpersonal behaviors; talking and attending to another person, asking and answering questions, and working cooperatively. Generalization was assessed in two ways. Records of token earnings were examined to determine if there had been an increase in behaviors such as grooming. Generalization thus involved behaviors different than the targets, assessed in a different manner, and with a different response measure (duration versus number of tokens) than treatment (code 3,4,6,9,11 in Table 10.1). Secondly, 20 daily, randomly scheduled, 1-minute observations were conducted to determine if patients increased their audible verbalization to other patients; again, this was a different response from 3 of the 4 targets with a different assessment technique and response measure. Both assessment procedures indicated improvement, the several differences between generalization and treatment adding to one's confidence in the power of the treatment techniques.

Unfortunately, the use of these several differences makes interpretation difficult when there is no generalization. In spite of this, the choice of a particular means of assessing generalization may be most appropriately guided by clinical considerations such as the likely aftercare facility to which the patient will be sent, the likely behaviors that will return a patient to the hospital, etc. Liberman (1972), for example, first increased the number of verbalizations (irrespective of content) in a group of four psychotics, and then assessed generalization by having the patients work together to make their lunch in the hope "that the conversation would flow naturally from patient to patient as they communicated their desires, instructions, requests, and social amenities to one another. Nothing of the sort occurred" (p. 157). The lunch situations seem particularly relevant clinically; however, the lack of generalization can be attributed to the large differences in either behaviors or in settings between the treatment sessions and the lunch.

Outcome Measures

The typical measure of treatment effectiveness in a token economy has been the number or percentage of patients completing a scheduled task. Since this measure is obtained by summing across a group of patients, it masks individual differences which may be important in modifying treatment programs to achieve maximum success with all patients (Ayllon & Azrin, 1965; Shean & Zeidberg, 1971). Allen & Magaro (1971) addressed themselves to this issue in a study of the effects of being paid versus paying tokens on attendance at occupational therapy. The results for the entire group of 26 patients indicated a relatively constant rate of attendance which decreased considerably when patients were asked to pay to attend. However, inspection of individual patient records indicated that only 9 patients showed the effect. Since the other patients attended at a very low rate, if at all, the effects of the 9 responsive patients greatly influenced the summated measure. Some token economies do report individual data (e.g., Lloyd & Garlington, 1968) which also indicate the wide range of individual differences in patient responsiveness to treatment.

Several token economies have reported the number of tokens distributed (Atthowe & Kranser, 1968), the number of hours worked (Ayllon & Azrin, 1965), or an index reflecting a combination of behaviors (Greenberg, Scott, Pisa & Friesen, 1975). This is a summation across both patients and tasks and masks individual variation even more. This may be satisfactory if the focus is on program evaluation; it would be unsatisfactory if the focus were on individual patient responsiveness. This also assumes that records of token earnings and job completions are accurately maintained. For discussions of record keeping procedures, the reader is referred to articles by Milby, Willicutt, Hawk, MacDonald & Whitfield (1973), and Patterson (1975).

A difficulty with measures of earnings or performance is that they are subject to the influence of economic variables such as savings (Winkler, 1971, 1972). As a patient's savings of tokens tend to accumulate, task performance tends to deteriorate. An interpretation of such results in terms of the declining effectiveness of the contingencies would be incorrect since economic variables would be "at fault." Adjustment of the savings balance should increase performance.

In contrast to such in-house evaluation measures, Davison (1969) has argued that token economies ought to be evaluated based on "how effective the procedure is in changing the individual so that he can function as a 'normal' person in the outside world" (p. 278). Several studies have reported discharge rates (Atthowe & Krasner, 1968; Ayllon & Haughton, 1964; Greenberg *et al.*, 1975; Heap *et al.*, 1970; Lloyd & Abel, 1970; Shean & Zeidberg, 1971; Steffy *et al.*, 1969). However, the decision to discharge is subject to variables beyond the scope of most programs, and it has been argued that discharge is not an appropriate measure of effectiveness (Ayllon & Azrin, 1968a). Greenberg *et al.* (1975) reported an "out-hospital" measure which is somewhat less subject to these uncontrolled variables. They combined the number of days spent on a community job before discharge, the number of days spent on home visits, and the number of days spent in the community after discharge.

A rather different outcome measure, perhaps not truly classifiable as "outcome," was used by Maley *et al.* (1973). They compared token economy and control patients on a test battery consisting of 5 tasks: orientation (17 questions), spending (purchasing items and making change), discrimination (circles, squares, and triangles of different colors and sizes), commands (perform two actions per command without repetition of command), and a timed walk (80 yards). Token economy patients were superior to control patients on all measures except the timed walk. This superiority is somewhat difficult to interpret because the effects of the token economy on target behaviors were not evaluated, and the relationships of the 5 tasks to the specific contingencies of the token economy are not very clear. A similar measure was used by Shean & Zeidberg (1971); they had token economy and control patients tap a telegraph key for 5 minutes. However, the authors provide a rationale in terms of past studies for the use of key-tapping as an indicator of "motivation." Token economy patients improved significantly over the course of three testings.

Perhaps the historical basis for the use of such motor tasks is the work of Lindsley and his colleagues (Lindsley, 1956, 1960, 1963; Lindsley & Skinner, 1954). Lindsley had extremely chronic, regressed patients participate in as many as 500 daily, 1-hour sessions in which lever-pulling was reinforced with candy, cigarettes, etc. (1-minute VI schedule). He found that the rate of pulling varied as a function of such events as being given ground privileges, changes in medication, and the presence or absence of a therapist. He also found that the patients paused more in their responding than normals, and that this variability in the absence of external events could be labelled as psychotic incidents (short pauses), episodes (moderate length pauses), or cycles (long-term variations in rate). Psychotic incidents were often accompanied by vocal hallucinatory symptoms. Based on correlations with two rating scales (Mednick & Lindsley, 1958), Lindsley concluded that low rates of pulling reflected a high degree of pathology. Hutchinson & Azrin (1961) and King, Merrill, Loeringer & Denny (1957) used FR schedules and did not find the same results.

Lindsley and his colleagues then applied similar methodology to analyze social interactions. Using "conjugate reinforcement," each dyadic partner's rate of looking, listening, and talking could be measured. In two studies with chronic (Lindsley, 1962) and acute (Nathan, Schneller & Lindsley, 1964) psychotics, the rates of patients' looking. listening, and talking were affected by the content of the conversation, the type of partner (psychologist or fellow patient), and severity of psychopathology.

Rating Scales

Although some behavior modifiers have eschewed their use, several rating scales have proven to be sensitive to behavioral interventions, particularly token economies. This section will catalogue those several scales, discussing first the scales that assess multiple levels of functioning and then those made for the assessment of more specific areas. For general reviews of the use of rating scales with psychotics, the reader is referred to articles by Klett (1968) and Goldberg (1974).

Multiple Areas

Table 10.3 lists some of the characteristics of scales that have been used in at least two studies of behavioral interventions. Table 10.1 lists the studies that have used these and other ratings scales. Generally, work with the NOSIE-30, SBSGI, and IMPS has been done by Paul and his colleagues. Paul *et al.* (1972) used the SBSGI, NOSIE-30, IMPS, MSBS (see below) and TSBC to evaluate changes in functioning as the result of the withdrawal of maintenance doses of psychotropic medication. No medication-related changes were found on any of the measures. Correlations among the measures "supported the validity of the assessment instruments in measuring a common factor, but indicated that additional information is added by each instrument" (p. 112). Lentz, Paul & Calhoun (1971) used the SBSGI, NOSIE-30, and MSBS with 137 chronic patients who had been rejected for placement in the community. They found that all three scales were quite reliable and that the "significant correlations between total scores of all three instruments show that a common 'level of functioning' factor is assessed over raters, behaviors, situations, and instruments; however, the level of intercorrelations further indicates that each of the three instruments, contributes additional information on patient functioning as well" (p. 73).

Mariotto & Paul (1974) then assessed the validity of the IMPS through a multitrait-multimethod study using the NOSIE-30, SBSGI, MSBS, and TSBC, each administered at two points in time, 6 months apart. They again found that the IMPS was highly correlated with the other measures, and they conclude that the IMPS has excellent concurrent validity. However, the IMPS was not a very good predictor of changes. Interestingly, the authors conclude that this was most likely due to the more abstract and judgmental items of the IMPS which made the scale susceptible to rater bias; they suggest that the IMPS be

TABLE 10.3

Major Characteristics of Rating Scales used with Psychiatric Inpatients in Behaviorally Oriented Studies

	Scales							
Characteristics	Multiple Areas of Functioning					Specific Areas		
Name and Authors	Nurses observation scale for inpatients (NOSIE; NOSIE–30) Honingfield, *et al.* (1966)	Social breakdown syndrome gradient index (SBSG 1) Gruenberg *et al.* (1966)	Psychotic reaction profile (PRP) Lorr *et al.* (1960)	Inpatient multi dimensional psychiatric scale (IMPS) Lorr *et al.* (1962)	Mood, affect, communication cooperation (MACC–11) Ellsworth (1962)	Ward atmosphere scale (WAS) Moos & Hours (1968)	Minimal social behavior scale (MSBS) Farina *et al.* (1957)	Community oriented environment scale Form C (COPES) Moos (1972)
No. Items	30 or 65	23	85	75	16	120	32	102
Rated by	Ward staff	Ward staff	Ward staff	Interviewer	Ward staff	Staff and patients	Interviewer	Staff and patients
Rating Period	3 days before rating	7 days before rating	3 days before rating	After interview	Retrospective	Retrospective	After interview	Retrospective
Scores	Total assets; Social competence; Social interest Personal neatness; Irritability Manifest psychosis Retardation	Total only	Thinking Disorganization Withdrawal Paranoid belligerence Agitated depression	Excitement vs. retardation Schiz. disorganization Cognitive distortion Anxious intropunitiveness Total morbidity	Mood Affect Communication Cooperation	12 subscales such as: order variety clarity + "Halo" Scale	Total only	10 subscales such as: involvement; support control

restricted to cases in which the desired information is an ordinal ranking rather than an absolute level of functioning.

Other studies not done by Paul and his colleagues have all indicated that the various scales involved reflected the effects of behavioral interventions. Gripp & Magaro (1971) and Schwartz & Bellack (1975) found that the NOSIE-30 discriminated token economy from control patients as did the PRP (Gripp & Magaro, 1971; Steffy *et al.*, 1969). The PRP also indicated improvement for patients trained in interaction skills compared to those not trained (Bennett & Maley, 1973). The MQCC-II similarly reflected improvement for behaviorally treated patients (Bennett & Maley, 1973; Maley *et al.*, 1973; Shean & Zeidberg, 1971).

Specific Areas

Several rating scales have been developed to assess the social skills of psychotic patients. Baker (1971) used a simple scale to rate mute patients' replies to a verbally presented, 60 item questionnaire: 0 for no reply, 1 for a grunt, 2 for an inappropriate or imperfect reply, 3 for a perfect reply, and 4 for a perfect reply plus some extra speech. Wilson & Walters (1966) assessed ward-ward generalization of a laboratory generated increase in the speech of near-mute psychotics by having ward staff indicate the "talkativeness" of each patient on a 7-point scale.

By far the most frequently used scale for assessing social skills in lower functioning patients is the MSBS. The MSBS is not so much a rating scale as it is a rigidly structured interview in which the patient is presented with standard questions and "social situations." The situations include items such as the interviewer's offering to shake hands, offering the patient a cigarette, and then searching for matches to light his own cigarette (the matches having been deliberately placed close to the patient). Of the seven studies that have used the MSBS, all but one (Gripp & Magaro, 1971) have found it to reflect improvement with behavioral interventions and to be highly correlated with the SBSGI, NOSIE-30, IMPS, and other scales.

A number of social skills scales have been developed primarily to assess the effects of assertion training with higher functioning patients. These involve both self-report items and behavioral, role-played tasks. The latter are usually audio or video tape recorded and later rated for behaviors such as eye contact, fluency, and latency. Because these scales have been recently reviewed, they will not be discussed here. The reader is referred to the chapter by Eisler in this book and to the review by Hersen and Bellack (in press).

In a rather different vein, Moos and his colleagues (e.g., Moos, 1972) have developed a rating scale to assess patient and staff perception of ward "atmosphere." An initial version of the scale used a semantic differential technique which was revised to the true-false format of the WAS, Form B. Gripp & Magaro (1971) used the WAS, Form B in their comparison of a token economy with three control wards; they found a considerable number of positive changes for the token economy program compared to the control wards.

Moos (1972) revised the WAS, Form B and renamed it the COPES. Milby, Pendergrass & Clarke (1975) used the COPES to evaluate differences in ward atmosphere between token economy and control wards. They found that token economy patients saw themselves as more involved and as more encouraged than control patients.

Miscellaneous

There are a number of rating scales which, although not involved in the assessment of behavioral interventions, have been used extensively and which may be helpful to the reader. The review by Goldberg (1974) lists several interview-based scales which are part of complete assessment packages that attempt to standardize and automate all clinical records. These thoroughly researched scales have good reliability and validity, and cover extensive areas of function. Other well researched, interview-based rating scales include the Structured and Scaled Interview to Assess Maladjustment (Gurland, Yorkston, Stone, Frank, & Fleiss, 1972) and the Structured Clinical Interview (Burdock & Hardesty, 1968).

In addition, a scale by Hogarty and Ulrich (1972, the Discharge Readiness Inventory) may be particularly useful in circumventing the problem of factors other than clinical status influencing the decision to discharge a patient. The scale is based on interviews with the patient and staff, and yields both a total score and scores on four factors presumed to reflect discharge readiness (community adjustment potential, psychosocial adequacy, belligerence, and manifest psychopathology).

Alevizos & Callahan (1975) have developed the Behavioral Performance Test (BPT), an observation based test which assesses six areas of functioning (low frequency unusual behavior, aggressive incidents, self-care skills, work skills, high frequency unusual behavior, and verbal interaction). The BPT can be used by professional or ward staff, and can form the basis for either individual patient or program-wide evaluations.

An occasional problem in implementing a behavioral intervention is the selection of an event that may be a reinforcer. Cautela has developed two self-report scales (one for outpatients and one for inpatients) that ask patients to indicate the extent to which they like various items and activities (Cautela, 1972; Cautela & Kastenbaum, 1967). The outpatient scale is reliable and valid (Cautela, 1972). No data have been reported for the inpatient scale.

Discussion

In much the same way as for treatment procedures, assessment procedures represent specific combinations of the "observation of a given attribute (behavior) on a given occasion within a specified setting by certain observers employing certain instruments" (Wiggins, 1973, p. 292). Again in much the same way as for treatment procedures, the important concern is the degree to which the information developed from the assessment procedures can be generalized to other combinations of observers, occasions, etc. Indeed, Cronbach, Gleser, Nanda & Rajaratnan (1972) have defined the problem of the reliability of measurement as a problem of generalizability. Perhaps a discussion of the key elements of the assessment process may alert the reader to conditions that may limit the generalizability of the information.

Definition of the behavior

The definition of the behavior to be recorded or rated should be as specific and precise as possible. Ayllon & Azrin (1968a) state this succinctly in their "Dimensions of Behavior Rule: Describe the behavior in specific terms that require a minimum of interpretation" (p. 36). In effect, the less the observer has to interpret, the greater the confidence that can be placed in the generalizability of the results from observer to observer.

Behaviors as seemingly straightforward as, "clean dress, hair combed, and clean nails," can be extremely difficult to define and may lead to disagreement between observers (Feingold & Migler, 1972). Ayllon & Azrin (1968a) also present four cases in which an imprecise definition of a simple work behavior led to disagreement between observers about when the behavior had been performed.

In addition to problems of generalizability, incompletely specified definitions may add error to the assessment process, making the detection of a treatment effect more difficult. Sherman (1965) reported that he was unable to systematically increase voice volume in one patient because he could not accurately measure and hence consistently reinforce very small but increasing changes in volume.

Fortunately, there are several ways to sharpen the definition of a behavior, each of which ultimately reduces the difficulty of the observer's discriminations (interpretations that the behavior has or has not occurred). One way is to simply remove the observer from the entire assessment process by using completely automated assessment devices. This was, of course, the tack taken by Wilson & Walters (1966) with their speech rate meter and by Lindsley in both his work with chronic schizophrenics (Lindsley 1959, 1960, 1963) and in his assessment of social situations (Nathan *et al.*, 1964).

A second way is to focus on the "permanent products" of the behavior (i.e., permanent changes in the environment that occur as a result of the behavior). Ayllon & Azrin (1968a) state this in their "Behavior Effect Rule: Arrange the situation so that the behavior produces some enduring changes in the physical environment" (p. 127). Examples are the weight criterion of the obesity studies of Upper & Newton (1971), Moore & Crum (1969), and Harmatz & Lapuc (1968); the weight criterion of excessive clothes (Ayllon, 1963); the wetness criterion of enuresis (Atthowe, 1973; Wagner & Paul, 1970); and the job criteria of Ayllon & Azrin (1965).

A third way is to include in the definition such a narrow range of behavior that discrimination is relatively easy. This was the approach taken by Patterson & Teigen (1973) and Wincze *et al.* (1972) in their use of delusion-eliciting questions. All but the correct answers were labelled delusional, with the corect answers consisting of only a few words. The observer's task was simply to match the patient's answer to the few words of the "standard." A fourth way is, paradoxically, the opposite: define the response so broadly that the discrimination is easy. This was the approach taken by Wilson & Walters (1966) and by Liberman (1972) in defining speech as any audible verbilizations.

A problem to be aware of in specifying behavior is that the specifications should be guided by the "substantive" meaning of the class of behaviors being targeted. This simply means that the definition of the behavior should reflect what the investigator "meant" by the class of behavior he has targeted. An example is given by Kale *et al.* (1968). As indicated previously, they defined greeting responses as simply "Hi" or "Hello, Mr. ——————." One of the patients, rather than saying one of the two responses, began (in two sessions) immediately talking to the experimenter about relevant events. The experimenter continued to talk to the patient because the behavior was therapeutically desirable, but it could not be counted as a greeting response since the speech did not match either of the two responses that had been defined as greetings. Undoubtedly, most people would consider the patient's behavior as being an example of a reasonably appropriate greeting; nevertheless, the specificity of the response definition would not allow it to be counted as such. There is no easy solution to the dilemma; the assessor has to be aware of the problem and has to make a compromise between the need for assessment that is generalizable from observer to observer and the need to target a behavior that is "meaningful."

Observer

There are several specific qualities of the observer that may limit generalizability of the assessment information. These have been reviewed in detail by Johnson & Bolstad (1973), who also suggest several ways to strengthen generalizability. The reader is referred to their article since their discussion and suggestions will only be briefly summarized here.

Bias. Almost all of the studies cited in this review have used observers who were aware of the various phases and likely results of the treatment process. Such knowledge (experimenter bias) may lead to distortions in the assessment process, even to the point of blatant faking of the data (Azrin, Holz, Ulrich & Goldiamond, 1961). Bias may also affect the treatment process through verbal and non-verbal communication to the patient of the manner in which he is expected to behave. In that case, it may not be treatment per se that is effective; rather, it may be the combination of the expectancy and the treatment that is effective, much as in the sensizing manner of a pre-test in attitude research.

Johnson & Bolstad (1973) give several suggestions for reducing bias: (a) give as little information to the observer as possible about the treatment phases or about the assignment of patients to various conditions (e.g., Bartlett *et al.*, 1971; Bennett & Maley, 1973; Tracey, *et al.*, 1974); (b) continually check the observer (e.g., Tracey, *et al.*, 1974); (c) provide no payoff to the observers for obtaining particular patterns of results. It should also be noted that the more ambiguous the response definition the more likely are the effects of bias (Kent, O'Leary, Diament & Dietz, 1974).

Reactivity. Reactivity refers to the possibility that the observation process itself, apart from the effects of treatment procedures, may be responsible for changes in the observed behavior. This, of course, makes questionable the generalization of information from assessed to non-assessed times. Studies of reactivity have yielded somewhat contradictory results (see Johnson & Bolstad 1973 for a review). More recent studies have continued this contradictory "trend." Johnson & Bolstad (1975) found that families did not behave differently when observers were present than when observers were absent.

Hagen, Craighead, & Paul (1975) similarly took surreptitious audio recordings of staff behavior during a lunch routine; they found that the presence or absence of an observer did not significantly affect the quality or quantity of staff behavior. Moos (1968) found that patients' wearing of a wireless microphone did not, in general, lead to marked reactivity effects defined in terms of 16 simple behaviors such as looking, smiling, coughing, and talking.

However, this was true only for the group as a whole; individual patients showed large reactivity effects with the more disturbed patients showing larger effects. Unfortunately, the design of the experiment allows an alternate interpretation; individual reactivity effects may have simply reflected the greater variability of the more disturbed patients (no comparison was given of the same patients in the same setting and condition at different times).

Johnson & Bolstad (1973) suggest several ways to reduce reactivity, should it be a problem. The observation process should be as unobtrusive as possible (e.g., Hagen *et al.*'s (1970) tape recorder; Paul *et al.*'s (1973) having observers act as "pieces of furniture" with no eye contact to staff or patients, or at least a period of adaptation to the observer's presence should be allowed before information is gathered (e.g., Hunter *et al.*, 1962).

Certain types of observers may be associated with higher degrees of reactivity; for example, the presence of a "doctor" may elicit more somatic complaints and/or delusional statements than other types of observers. (Zarlock, 1966).

Perhaps the lowest degree of reactivity is obtained with measures focusing on the "outcomes" or products of the treatment process. For example, Palmer & McGuire (1973) developed a scale of 50 "unobtrusive" items that they believed were potentially related to patient rehabilitation on a state hospital ward. Those items included observations of the working condition of the washer and dryer, the number of pieces of incoming mail, and the number of referrals to vocational rehabilitation services. Holahan (1972), in addition to the time sampling measure of social interaction, recorded the number of cigarette butts left in the experimental dayroom after the sessions, the number of ounces of coffee consumed, and the number of minutes spent in the room after the announced end of the session. Interestingly, all three measures were positively correlated with the amount of social interaction.

Accuracy. There are two general procedures for determining the accuracy of observation: (a) the observer's recordings can be compared to a criterion set of recordings developed from known stimulus material; (b) the observer can be joined in the responding process by another observer with later comparison between the two recordings. The latter is the more typical way of assessing accuracy, and is most often labelled interrater reliability or interrater agreement. This, of course, is a direct attempt to measure the degree to which information can be generalized across observers and assumes that the observers will be completely independent of one another throughout the entire agreement process. Such a determination of accuracy is extremely important; without it, the adequacy of the information is much the same as that developed from a psychometric test of unknown reliability.

The most widely reported index of agreement simply divides the number of agreements by the sum of agreements plus disagreements, and then multiplies the result by 100 to achieve a % agreement figure (Tracey, *et al.*, 1974; Holahan, 1972; Wincze *et al.*, 1972). The use of this formula with behaviors that have either a very high or very low rate of occurrence, however, may lead to spuriously inflated agreement estimates. Hartmann (1972) and Hawkins & Dotson (1975) suggest corrective alterations of the index. If a behavior occurs at a very low rate, then only occasions during which either observer scored the behavior should be included in calculating the index (e.g., Wallace & Davis, 1974). If a behavior occurs at a high rate, then only occasions during which either observer did not score the behavior should be included in the calculations.

Interrater agreement can also be calculated in several other ways: Pearson (Lentz *et al.*, 1971), intraclass correlation coefficient (Paul *et al.*, 1973), contingency coefficient (Hunter *et al.*, 1962), phi coefficient (Winkler, 1970), kappa (Winkler, 1970), or weighted kappa (DeRisi *et al.*, 1975). Each of these involves summation across either time, patients, or behaviors. It is possible to have disagreement on numerous components of the summation and still have high agreement because of the "cancelling" effects of the summation. Although Johnson & Bolstad (1973) suggest that this may be acceptable if the only measure of evaluating treatment effects is a similar summation, it is possible to question the adequacy of a measure whose components are unreliable.

A difficulty in the measurement of interrater agreement is the reactivity of the agreement process. Several laboratory based studies (Kent *et al.*, 1974; O'Leary & Kent, 1973) have indicated that agreement may increase when the observer is aware that his agreement with an independent observer is being assessed. The implication is that data are different when the observer is being assessed than when he or she is not. To reduce this effect, it is possible to use either continuous agreement monitoring (Tracey *et al.*, 1974) or to randomly schedule frequent checks.

Methods of Observation and Recording

Perhaps the most convenient observation (as well as the lowest in reactivity) is the recording of the permanent products of a behavior. Assuming that the products last long enough, observations can be scheduled to suit the time and place of the observer.

Many behaviors, however, are not easily defined in terms of enduring environmental changes (e.g., delusions). These behaviors have to be directly observed and are usually recorded each time that they occur (e.g., Richardson *et al.*, 1972; Winkler's (1970) recording of noise and violence). If, however, the behavior occurs at either a very high or low rate, the observer may "miss" instances of the behavior. A solution to this is to schedule the time and place for the occurrence of the behavior, counting only during the scheduled observations (e.g., Ayllon & Haughton, 1964; Wincze *et al.*, 1972). Another solution is to divide the observation period into intervals and then record the occurrence or non-occurrence of the behavior during each interval, rather than counting the number of instances of the behavior (e.g., Mitchell & Stoffelmayer, 1973). Still another solution is to schedule brief observation periods as samples of a larger time block such as a day, noting the occurrence or non-occurrence of the behavior during each period (e.g., Hunter *et al.*, 1962; Schaefer & Martin, 1966).

A problem in scheduling observation periods and determining the length of intervals is that the observations may not be generalizable to the "true" rate of occurrence, "true" meaning the actual number of responses during the full unit of time from which the sample is drawn. Although the selection of a time-sampling strategy is eventually a "seat of the pants" process, it is likely that a frequently occurring behavior may need less observation than a low rate behavior, while behaviors of long duration may require fewer samples than the number required for short duration behaviors. In effect, the more that the to-be-sampled-time block is "filled" with the behavior, the less time that has to be sampled in order to use the obtained proportion of occurrence as an estimate of the true occurrence. However, the less the total amount of observation time, the less sensitive is the dependent measure to reflecting treatment changes.

Once the amount of sampling time has been determined, it then has to be scheduled. Thomson, Holmberg & Baer (1974) found that the lowest error rate was achieved with a sampling strategy that scheduled frequent but brief observations. They observed two behaviors of three school teachers, but their results may not be applicable beyond the school situation. In any event, a good deal of work still needs to be done to determine the most accurate and/or efficient strategy for various applications.

Validity

The question of the validity of behavioral measures has rarely been considered. Johnson & Bolstad (1973) have a cogent discussion of the issues involved, and the reader is urged to consult their article. Briefly, concurrent validity refers to the generalization of information from one method of measuring a construct to another method of measuring the same construct. This implies that behavioral assessments are concerned with constructs rather than discrete, unitary behaviors. Indeed, as seemingly simple a label as self-care skills encompasses a large array of discrete behaviors and is best considered a construct rather than a "behavior." This is even more the case for labels such as interpersonal skills or delusional speech.

Only one study (Mariotto & Paul, 1974) represents a particularly well executed, concurrent validity study. Several methods (interview-based rating scales, ward rating scales, and observational measures) were used to assess a set of traits defined by the IMPS. As indicated previously, concurrent validity of the IMPS was quite good, although it was not a valid measure of change. The few other studies that could be classed as validity studies were concerned with assessing the generalization of treatment effects. Many of these confounded changes in both the definitions of the targeted constructs and the method of assessment. For example, Bennett & Maley's (1973) use of token earnings to evaluate the effects of increasing four interpersonal behaviors involved different assessment methods and constructs. As such, it could be considered a study of construct rather than concurrent validity; however the lack of a "theory" to connect the constructs (Kerlinger, 1973) makes it difficult to interpret either positive or negative results in spite of the clinically encouraging increase that was found in both constructs. Clearly, there is a good deal of work yet to be done concerning the content, concurrent, and construct validity of behavioral assessments.

References

Alevizos, P. N., & Callahan, E. J. Behavioral assessment of psychosis. In A. R. Ciminero, K. S. Calhoun, & H. E. Adams (Eds.), *Handbook for behavioral assessment*. New York: Wiley, in press.

Allen, D. J., & Magaro, P. A. Measures of change in token economy programs. *Behaviour Research and Therapy*, 1971, **9**, 311–318.

Anderson, L. T., & Alpert, M. Operant analysis of hallucination frequency in a hospitalized schizophrenic. *Journal of Behavior Therapy and Experimental Psychiatry*, 1974, **5**, 13–19.

Atthowe, J. M. Controlling nocturnal enuresis in severely disabled and chronic patients. *Behavior Therapy*, 1972, **3**, 232–240.

Atthowe, J. M., & Krasner, L. Preliminary report on the application of contingent reinforcement procedures (token economy) on a "chronic" psychiatric ward. *Journal of Abnormal Psychology*, 1968, **73**, 37–43.

Arann, L., & Horner, V. M. Contingency management in an open psychiatric ward. *Journal of Behavior Therapy and Experimental Psychiatry*, 1972, **3**, 31–37.

Ayllon, T. Intensive treatment of psychotic behaviour by stimulus satiation and food reinforcement. *Behaviour Research and Therapy*, 1963, **1**, 53–61.

Ayllon, T., & Azrin, N. H. The measurement and reinforcement of behavior of psychotics. *Journal of the Experimental Analysis of Behavior*, 1965, **8**, 357–383.

Ayllon, T., & Azrin, N. H. *The token economy: A motivational system for therapy and rehabilitation*. New York: Appleton-Century-Crofts, 1968a.

Ayllon, T., & Azrin, N. H. Reinforcer sampling: A technique for increasing the behavior of mental patients. *Journal of Applied Behavior Analysis*, 1968b, **1**, 13–20.

Ayllon, T., & Haughton, E. Control of the behavior of schizophrenic patients by food. *Journal of the Experimental Analysis of Behavior*, 1962, **5**, 343–352.

Ayllon, T., & Haughton, E. Modification of symptomatic verbal behaviour of mental patients. *Behaviour Research and Therapy*, 1964, **2**, 87–97.

Ayllon, T., & Michael, J. The psychiatric nurse as a behavioral engineer. *Journal of the Experimental Analysis of Behavior*, 1959, **2**, 323–334.

Azrin, N. H., Holy, W., Ulrich, R., & Goldiamond, I. The control of the content of conversation through reinforcement. *Journal of the Experimental Analysis of Behavior*, 1961, **4**, 25–30.

Baker, R. The use of operant conditioning to reinstate speech in mute schizophrenics. *Behaviour Research and Therapy*, 1971, **9**, 329–336.

Bartlett, D., Ora, J. P., Brown, E., & Butler, J. The effects of reinforcement on psychotic speech in a case of early infantile autism, age 12. *Journal of Behavior Therapy and Experimental Psychiatry*, 1971, **2**, 145–149.

Bennett, P. S., & Maley, R. F. Modification of interactive behaviors in chronic mental patients. *Journal of Applied Behavior Analysis*, 1973, **6**, 609–620.

Bucher, B., & Fabricatore, J. Use of patient-administered shock to suppress hallucinations. *Behavior Therapy*, 1970, **1**, 382–385.

Burdock, E. I., & Herdesty, A. S. Psychological test for psychopathology. *Journal of Abnormal Psychology*, 1968, **73**, 62–69.

Cautela, J. R. Reinforcement survey schedule: Evaluation and current applications. *Psychological Reports*, 1972, **30**, 683–690.

Cautela, J. R., & Kastenbaum, R. A reinforcement survey schedule for use in therapy, training, and research. *Psychological Reports*, 1967, **20**, 1115–1130.

Cayner, J. J., & Kiland, J. R. Use of brief time out with three schizophrenic patients. *Journal of Behavior Therapy and Experimental Psychiatry*, 1974, **5**, 141–145.

Chapman, L. J., & Chapman, J. P. Problems in the measurement of cognitive deficit. *Psychological Bulletin*, 1973, **79**, 380–390.

Cromwell, R. L. Assessment of schizophrenia. *Annual Review of Psychology*, 1975, **26**, 593–621.

Cronbach, L. J., Gleser, G. C., Nanda, H., & Rajarantnam, N. *The dependability of behavioral measurements*. New York: Wiley & Sons, 1972.

Curran, J. P., Lentz, R. J., & Paul, G. L. Effectiveness of sampling-exposure procedures on facilities utilization by psychiatric hard-core chronic patients. *Journal of Behavior Therapy and Experimental Psychiatry*, 1973, **4**, 201–207.

Davison, G. C. Appraisal of behavior modification techniques with adults in institutional settings. In C. M. Franks (Ed.), *Behavior Therapy: Appraisal and status*. New York: McGraw-Hill, 1969.

DeRisi, W. J., Alevizos, P., Eckman, T., Callahan, E. J., & Liberman, R. P. The Behavior Observation Instrument: I. Direct Observation for program evaluation in applied settings. Unpublished manuscript, 1975. (Available from the authors, Camarillo State Hospital, Box A, Camarillo, CA 93010).

Easterbrook, J. A. Disorders of attention. In C. G. Costello (Ed.), *Symptoms of psychotherapy: A handbook*. New York: Wiley, 1970.

Ellsworth, R. B. The MACC behavioral adjustment scale, Form II. Beverly Hills, California: Western Psychological Services, 1962.

Esser, A. H., Chamberlain, A. S., Chapple, E. D., & Kline, N. S. Territoriality of patients on a research ward. *Recent Advances in Biological Psychiatry*, 1965, **7**, 36–44.

Farina, A., Arenberg, D., & Guskin, S. A scale for measuring minimal social behavior. *Journal of Consulting Psychology*, 1957, **21**, 265–268.

Feingold, L., & Migler, B. The use of experimental dependency relationships as a motivating procedure on a token economy ward. In R. D. Rubin, H. Fensterheim, J. D. Henderson, & L. P. Ullmann (Eds.), *Advances in behavior therapy*. New York: Academic Press, 1972.

Goldberg, L. R. Objective diagnostic tests and measures. *Annual Review of Psychology*, 1974, **25**, 343–367.

Greenberg, D. J., Scott, S. B., Pisa, A., & Friesen, D. D. Beyond the token economy: A comparison of two contingency programs. *Journal of Consulting and Clinical Psychology*, 1975, **43**, 498–503.

Gripp, R. F., & Magaro, P. A. A token economy program evaluation with untreated ward comparisons. *Behaviour Research and Therapy*, 1971, **9**, 137–149.

Gruenberg, E. M., Brandon, S., & Kasius, R. D. Identifying cases of the social breakdown syndrome. In E. M. Gruenberg (Ed.), *Evaluating the effectiveness of community mental health services*. New York: Milbank, 1966.

Gurland, B. J., Yorkston, N. J., Stone, A. R., Frank, J. D., & Fleiss, J. L. The structured and scaled interview to assess maladjustment (SSIAM). *Archives of General Psychiatry*, 1972, **27**, 259–263.

Hagen, R. L., Craighead, W. E., & Paul, G. L. Staff reactivity to evaluative behavioral observations. *Behavior Therapy*, 1975, **6**, 201–206.

Harmatz, M. G., & Lapuc, R. Behavior modification of over-eating in a psychiatric population. *Journal of Consulting and Clinical Psychology*, 1968, **32**, 583–587.

Harmatz, M. G., Mendelsohn, R., & Glassman, M. L. Behavioral observation in the study of schizophrenia. Paper read at the Annual Meeting of the American Psychological Association, Montreal, 1973.

Hartmann, D. P. Notes on methodology: On choosing an interobserver reliability estimate. Unpublished manuscript, University of Utah, 1972.

Hartmann, D. P., & Atkinson, C. Having your cake and eating it too: A note on some apparent contraditions between therapeutic achievements and design requirements in $N = 1$ studies. *Behavior Therapy*, 1973, **4**, 589–591.

Hawkins, R. P., & Dotson, V. A. Reliability scores that delude. In E. Ramp, & G. Semb (Eds.), *Behavior analysis: Areas of research and application.* Englewood Cliffs, New Jersey: Prentice-Hall, 1975, in press.

Haynes, S. N., & Geddy, P. Suppression of psychotic hallucinations through time-out. *Behavior Therapy*, 1973, **4**, 123–127.

Heap, R. T., Boblitt, W. E., Moore, C. H., & Hord, J. E. Behavior-milieu therapy with chronic neuropsychiatric patients. *Journal of Abnormal Psychology*, 1970, **76**, 349–354.

Henderson, J. D., & Scoles, P. E., Jr. Conditioning techniques in a community-based operant environment for psychotic men. *Behavior Therapy*, 1970, **1**, 245–251.

Hersen, M., & Barlow, D. H. *Single case experimental designs: Strategies for studying behavior change.* New York: Pergamon Press, 1976.

Hersen, M., & Bellack, A. S. Assessment of social skills. In A. R. Ciminero, K. S. Calhoun, & H. E. Adams (Eds.), *Handbook for behavioral assessment*. New York: Wiley, in press.

Hersen, M., Eisler, R. M., Smith, B. S., & Agras, W. S. A token reinforcement ward for young psychiatric patients. *American Journal of Psychiatry*, 1972, **129**, 228–233.

Higgs, W. J. Effects of gross environmental changes upon behavior of schizophrenics: A cautionary note. *Journal of Abnormal Psychology*, 1970, **76**, 421–422.

Hogarty, G. E., & Ulrich, R. The discharge readiness inventory. *Archives of General Psychiatry*, 1972, **26**, 419–426.

Holahan, C. J. Seating patterns and patient behavior in an experimental dayroom. *Journal of Abnormal Psychology*, 1972, **80**, 115–124.

Holahan, C. J., & Saegert, S. Behavioral and attitudinal effects of large-scale variation in the physical environment of psychiatric wards. *Journal of Abnormal Psychology*, 1973, **82**, 454–462.

Hollander, M., Plutchik, R., & Horner, V. Interaction of patient and attendant reinforcement programs: The "piggyback" effect. *Journal of Consulting and Clinical Psychology*, 1973, **41**, 43–47.

Honigfeld, G., Gillis, R. O., & Klett, C. J. NOSIE—30: A treatment-sensitive ward behavior scale. *Psychological Reports*, 1966, **19**, 180–182.

Hunter, M., Schooler, C., & Spohn, H. E. The measurement of characteristic patterns of ward behaviors in chronic schizophrenics. *Journal of Consulting Psychology*, 1962, **26**, 69–73.

Hutchinson, R. R., & Azrin, N. H. Conditioning of mental-hospital patients. *Journal of the Experimental Analysis of Behavior*, 1961, **4**, 87–93.

Issacs, W., Thomas, J., & Goldiamond, I. Application of operant conditioning to reinstate verbal behavior in psychotics. *Journal of Speech and Hearing Disorders*, 1960, **25**, 8–12.

Ittelson, W. H., Rivlin, L. G., & Proshansky, H. M. The use of behavioral maps in environmental psychology. In H. M. Proshansky, W. H. Ittelson, & L. G. Rivlin (Eds.), *Environmental Psychology*. New York: Holt, Rinehart & Winston, 1970.

Johnson, S. M., & Bolstad, O. D. Methodological issues in naturalistic observation: Some problems and solutions for field research. In L. A. Hamerlynck, L. C. Handy, & E. J. Mash (Eds.), *Behavior Change: Methodology, Concepts, and Practice.* Champaign, Ill.: Research Press, 1973.

Johnson, S. M., & Bolstad, O. D. Reactivity to home observation: A comparison of audio recorded behavior with observers present or absent. *Journal of Applied Behavioral Analysis*, 1975, **8**, 181–187.

Kale, R. J., Kaye, J. H., Whelan, P. A., & Hopkins, B. L. The effects of reinforcement on the modification, maintenance, and generalization of social responses of mental patients. *Journal of Applied Behavior Analysis*, 1968, **1**, 307–314.

Kent, R. N., O'Leary, K. D., Diament, C., & Dietz, A. Expectation biases in observational evaluation of therapeutic change. *Journal of Consulting and Clinical Psychology*, 1974, **42**, 774–781.

Kerlinger, F. N. *Foundations of behavioral research*. New York: Holt, Rinehart & Winston, 1973.

King, G. F., Armitage, S. G., & Tilton, J. R. A therapeutic approach to schizophrenics of extreme pathology: An operant-interpersonal method. *Journal of Abnormal and Social Psychology*, 1960, **61**, 276–286.

King, G. F., Merrell, D. W., Lovinger, E., & Denny, M. R. Operant motor behavior in acute schizophrenia. *Journal of Personality*, 1957, **25**, 317–326.

Klett, C. J. Assessing change in psychiatric patients. In P. McReynolds (Ed.), *Advances in psychological assessment*. Palo Alto, CA: Science and Behavior Books, 1968.

Lentz, R. J., Paul, G. L., & Calhoun, J. F. Reliability and validity of three measures of functioning with "hard core" chronic mental patients. *Journal of Abnormal Psychology*, 1971, **78**, 69–76.

Liberman, R. P. Reinforcement of social interaction in a group of chronic mental patients. In R. D. Rubin, H. Fensterheim, J. D. Henderson, & L. P. Ullmann (Eds.). *Advances in behavior therapy*. New York: Academic Press, 1972.

Liberman, R. P., Teigen, J., Patterson, R., & Baker, V. Reducing delusional speech in chronic, paranoid schizophrenics. *Journal of Applied Behavior Analysis*, 1973, **6**, 57–64.

Liberman, R. P., Wallace, C. J., Teigen, J., & Davis, J. R. Interventions with psychotic behaviors. In K. S. Calhoun, H. E. Adams, & K. M. Mitchell (Eds.), *Innovative treatment methods in psychopathology*. New York: Wiley, 1974.

Lindsley, O. R. Operant conditioning methods applied to research in chronic schizophrenia. *Psychiatric Research Reports*, 1956, **5**, 118–139.

Lindsley, O. R. Reduction in rate of vocal psychotic symptoms by differential positive reinforcement. *Journal of the Experimental Analysis of Behavior*, 1959, **2**, 269.

Lindsley, O. R. Characteristics of the behavior of chronic psychotics as revealed by free-operant conditioning methods. *Diseases of the Nervous System*, 1960, **21**, 66–78.

Lindsley, O. R. Direct behavioral analysis of psychotherapy session by conjugately programmed closed-circuit television. Paper read at the Annual Meeting of the American Psychological Association, St. Louis, 1962.

Lindsley, O. R. Direct measurement and functional definition of vocal hallucinatory symptoms. *Journal of Nervous and Mental Disease*, 1963, **136**, 293–297.

Lindsley, O. R., & Skinner, B. F. A method for the experimental analysis of the behavior of psychotic patients. *American Psychologist*, 1954, **9**, 419–420.

Lloyd, K. E., & Abel, L. Performance on a token economy psychiatric ward: A two year summary. *Behaviour Research and Therapy*, 1970, **8**, 1–9.

Lloyd, K. E., & Garlington, W. K. Weekly variations in performance on a token economy psychiatric ward. *Behaviour Research and Therapy*, 1968, **6**, 407–410.

Lorr, M., & Klett, C. J. *Inpatient multidimensional psychiatric scale*. Palo Alto, California: Consulting Psychologists Press, 1966.

Lorr, M., O'Connor, J. P., & Stafford, J. W. The psychotic reaction profile. *Journal of Clinical Psychology*, 1960, **16**, 241–245.

Maher, B. A. The language of schizophrenia: A review and interpretation. *British Journal of Psychiatry*, 1972, **120**, 3–17.

Maley, R. F., Feldman, G. I., & Ruskin, R. S. Evaluation of patient improvement in a token economy treatment program. *Journal of Abnormal Psychology*, 1973, **82**, 141–144.

Mariotto, M. J., & Paul, G. L. A multimethod validation of the Inpatient Multidimensional Psychiatric Scale with chronically institutionalized patients. *Journal of Consulting and Clinical Psychology*, 1974, **42**, 497–509.

McGhil, A. Attention and perception in schizophrenia. In B. A. Maher (Ed.), *Progress in experimental personality research*. New York: Academic Press, 1971.

McInnis, T., Himelstein, H. C., Doty, D. W., & Paul, G. L. Modification of sampling-exposure procedures for facilities utilization by chronic mental patients. *Journal of Behavior Therapy and Experimental Psychiatry*, 1974, **5**, 119–129.

McReynolds, W. T., & Coleman, J. Token economy: Patient and staff changes. *Behaviour Research and Therapy*, 1972, **10**, 29–35.

Mednick, M. T., & Lindsley, O. R. Some clinical correlates of operant behavior. *Journal of Abnormal and Social Psychology*, 1958, **57**, 13–16.

Meichenbaum, D. H. The effects of instructions and reinforcement on thinking and language behavior of schizophrenics. *Behaviour Research and Therapy*, 1969, **7**, 101–114.

Meichenbaum, D. H., & Cameron, R. Training schizophrenics to talk to themselves: A means of developing attentional controls. *Behavior Therapy*, 1973, 4, 515–534.

Milby, J. B. Modification of extreme social isolation by contingent social reinforcement. *Journal of Applied Behavior Analysis*, 1970, **3**, 149–152.

Milby, J. B., Pendergrass, P. E., & Clarke, C. J. Token economy versus control ward: A comparison of staff and patient attitudes toward ward environment. *Behavior Therapy*, 1975, **6**, 22–30.

Milby, J. B., Willicutt, H. C., Hawk, J., MacDonald, M., & Whitfield, K. A system for efficiently recording individualized behavioral measures. *Journal of Applied Behavior Analysis*, 1973, **6**, 333–338.

Mitchell, W. S., & Stoffelmayer, B. C. Application of the Premack principle to the behavioral control of extremely inactive schizophrenics. *Journal of Applied Behavioral Analysis*, 1973, **6**, 419–425.

Moore, C. W., & Crum, B. C. Weight reduction of a chronic schizophrenic by means of operant conditioning procedures: A case study. *Behaviour Research and Therapy*, **7**, 129–131.

Moos, R. H. Behavioral effects of being observed: Reactions to a wireless radio transmitter. *Journal of Consulting and Clinical Psychology*, 1968, **32**, 383–388.

Moos, R. H. Assessment of the environments of community-oriented psychiatric treatment programs. *Journal of Abnormal Psychology*, 1972, **79**, 9–18.

Moos, R. H., & Houts, P. S. Assessment of the social atmospheres of psychiatric wards. *Journal of Abnormal Psychology*, 1968, **73**, 595–604.

Moser, A. J. Covert punishment of hallucinatory behavior in a psychotic male. *Journal of Behavior Therapy and Experimental Psychiatry*, 1974, **5**, 297–301.

Nathan, P. E., Schneller, P., & Lindsley, O. R. Direct measurement of communication during psychiatric admission interviews. *Behaviour Research and Therapy*, 1964, **2**, 49–57.

Neale, J. M., & Cromwell, R. L. Attention and schizophrenia. In B. A. Maher (Ed), *Progress in experimental personality research*. New York: Academic Press, 1970.

Nydegger, R. V. The elimination of hallucinatory and delusional behavior by verbal conditioning and assertive training: A case study, *Journal of Behavior Therapy and Experimental Psychiatry*, 1972, 3, 225–227.

O'Brien, F., & Azrin, N. H. Symptom reduction by functional displacement in a token economy: A case study. *Journal of Behavior Therapy & Experimental Psychiatry*, 1972, **3**, 205–207.

O'Brien, F. Azrin, N. H., & Henson, K. Increased communications of chronic mental patients by reinforcement and response priming. *Journal of Applied Behavior Analysis*, 1969, **2**, 23–31.

O'Leary, K. D., & Kent, R. N. Behavior modification for social action: Research tactics and problems. In L. A. Hamerlynck, L. C. Handy, & E. J. Mash (Eds.), *Behavior change: Methodology, concepts, and practice*. Champaign, Ill.: Research Press, 1973.

Paden, R. C., Himelstein, H. C., & Paul, G. L. Videotape versus verbal feedback in the modification of meal behavior of chronic mental patients. *Journal of Consulting and Clinical Psychology*, 1974, **42**, 623–624.

Palmer, J., & McGuire, F. L. The use of unobtrusive measures in mental health research. *Journal of Consulting and Clinical Psychology*, 1973, **40**, 431–436.

Patterson, R. L. *Maintaining effective token economies*. Springfield, Ill.: Charles C. Thomas, 1975.

Patterson, R. L., & Teigen, J. R. Conditioning and post-hospital generalization of non-delusional responses in a chronic psychotic patient. *Journal of Applied Behavior Analysis*, 1973, **6**, 65–70.

Paul, G. L., McInnis, T. L., & Mariotto, M. J. Objective performance outcomes associated with two approaches to training mental health technicians in milieu and social-learning programs. *Journal of Abnormal Psychology*, 1973, **82**, 523–532.

Paul, G. L., Tobias, L. L., & Holly, B. L. Maintenance psychotropic drugs in the presence of active treatment programs. *Archives of General Psychiatry*, 1972, **27**, 106–115.

Payne, R. W. Disorders of thinking. In C. G. Costello (Ed.), *Symptoms of psychopathology: A handbook*. New York: Wiley, 1970.

Pomerleau, O. F., Bobrove, P. H., & Harris, L. C. Some observations on a controlled social environment for psychiatric patients. *Journal of Behavior Therapy and Experimental Psychiatry*, 1972, **3**, 15–21.

Reed, J. L. Schizophrenic thought disorder: A review and hypothesis. *Comprehensive Psychiatry*, 1970, **11**, 403–432.

Richardson, R., Karkalas, Y., & Lal, H. Application of operant procedures in treatment of hallucinations in chronic psychotics. In R. D. Rubin, H. Fensterheim, J. D. Henderson, & L. P. Ullman (Eds.), *Advances in behavior Therapy*. New York: Academic Press, 1972.

Rickard, H. C., Dignam, P. J., & Horner, R. F. Verbal manipulation in a psychotherapeutic relationship. *Journal of Clinical Psychology*, 1960, **16**, 364–367.

Rickard, H. C., & Dinoff, M. A follow-up note on "verbal manipulation in a psychotherapeutic relationship". *Psychological Reports*, 1962, **11**, 506.

Roberts, A. E. Development of self-control using Premack's differential rate hypothesis: A case study. *Behaviour Research and Therapy*, 1969, **7**, 341–344.

Rutner, I. T., & Bugle, C. An experimental procedure for the modification of psychotic behavior. *Journal of Consulting and Clinical Psychology*, 1969, **33**, 651–653.

Sabatasso, A. P., & Jacobson, L. I. Use of behavioral therapy in the reinstatement of verbal behavior in a mute psychotic with chronic brain syndrome. *Journal of Abnormal Psychology*, 1970, **76**, 322–324.

Sanders, R. M. Time-out procedure for the modification of speech content—A case study. *Journal of Behavior Therapy and Experimental Psychiatry*, 1971, **2**, 199–202.

Schaefer, H. H., & Martin, P. L. Behavioral therapy for "apathy" of hospitalized schizophrenics. *Psychological Reports*, 1966, **19**, 1147–1158.

Schaefer, H. H., & Martin, P. L. *Behavioral therapy*, New York: McGraw Hill, 1969.

Schwartz, J., & Bellack, A. S. A comparison of a token economy with standard inpatient treatment. *Journal of Consulting and Clinical Psychology*, 1975, **43**, 107–109.

Shean, G. D., & Zeidberg, Z. Token reinforcement therapy: A comparison of matched groups. *Journal of Behavior Therapy and Experimental Psychiatry*, 1971, **2**, 94–105.

Sherman, J. A. Reinstatement of verbal behavior in a psychotic by reinforcement methods. *Journal of Speech and Hearing Disorders*, 1963, **28**, 398–401.

Sherman, J. A. Use of reinforcement and imitation to reinstate verbal behavior in mute psychotics. *Journal of Abnormal Psychology*, 1965, **70**,155–164.

Sobell, L. C., Schaefer, H. H., Sobell, M. B., & Kremer, M. E. Food priming: A therapeutic tool to increase the percentage of meals bought by chronic mental patients. *Behaviour Research and Therapy*, 1970, **8**, 339–345.

Stahl, J. R., Thomson, L. E., Leitenberg, H., & Hasazi, J. E. Establishment of praise as a conditioned reinforcer in socially unresponsive psychiatric patients. *Journal of Abnormal Psychology*, 1974, **83**, 488–496.

Steffy, R. A., Hart, J., Craw, M., Torney, D., & Marlett, N. Operant behavior modification techniques applied to a ward of severely regressed and aggressive patients. *Canadian Psychiatric Association Journal*, 1969, **14**, 59–67.

Thomson, C., Holmberg, M., & Baer, D. M. A brief report on a comparison of time-sampling procedures. *Journal of Applied Behavior Analysis*, 1974, **7**, 623–626.

Tracey, D. A., Briddell, D. W., & Wilson, G. T. Generalization of verbal conditioning to verbal and nonverbal behavior: Group therapy with chronic psychiatric patient dyads. *Journal of Applied Behavioral Analysis*, 1974, **7**, 391–402.

Ullmann, L. P., Forsman, R. G., Kenny, J. W., McInnis, T. L., Unikel, I. P., & Zeisset, R. M. Selective reinforcement of schizophrenics' interview responses. *Behaviour Research and Therapy*, 1965, **2**, 205–212.

Upper, D., & Newton, J. G. A weight reduction program for schizophrenic patients on a token economy unit: Two case studies. *Journal of Behavior Therapy and Experimental Psychiatry*, 1971, **2**, 113–115.

Venables, P. H. Input regulation and psychopathology. In M. Hammer, K. Salzinger, & S. Sutton (Eds.), *Psychopathology: Contributions from the behavioral and biological sciences*. New York: Wiley, 1973.

Wagner, B. R., & Paul, G. L. Reduction of incontinence in chronic patients: A pilot project. *Journal of Behavior Therapy and Experimental Psychiatry*, 1970, **1**, 29–38.

Wallace, C. J., & Davis, J. R. The effects of information and reinforcement on the conversational behavior of chronic psychiatric patient dyads. *Journal of Consulting and Clinical Psychology*, 1974, **42**, 656–662.

Wallace, C. J., Davis, J. R., Liberman, R. P., & Baker, V. Modeling and staff behavior. *Journal of Consulting and Clinical Psychology*, 1973, **41**, 422–426.

Wallace, C. J., Teigen, J. R., Liberman, R. P., & Baker, V. Destructive behavior treated by contingency contracts and assertive training: A case study. *Journal of Behavior Therapy and Experimental Psychiatry*, 1973, **4**, 272–274.

Wiggins, J. S. *Personality and prediction.* New York: Addison-Wesley, 1973.

Wilson, F. S., & Walters, R. H. Modification of speech output of near mute schizophrenics through social learning procedures. *Behaviour Research and Therapy,* 1966, **4**, 59–67.

Wincze, J. P., Leitenberg, H., & Agras, W. S. The effects of token reinforcement and feedback on the delusional verbal behavior of chronic paranoid schizophrenics. *Journal of Applied Behavior Analysis*, 1972, **5**, 247–262.

Winkler, R. C. Management of chronic psychiatric patients by a token reinforcement system. *Journal of Applied Behavior Analysis*, 1970, **3**, 47–55.

Winkler, R. C. The relevance of economic theory and technology to token reinforcement systems. *Behaviour Research and Therapy*, 1971, **9**, 81–88.

Winkler, R. C. A theory of equilibrium in token economies. *Journal of Abnormal Psychology*, 1972, **79**, 169–173.

Zarlock, S. P. Social expectations, language, and schizophrenia. *Journal of Humanistic Psychology*, 1966, **6**, 68–75.

CHAPTER 11

Assessment of Addictive Behavior

MARK B. SOBELL

Department of Psychology
Vanderbilt University

and

LINDA C. SOBELL

Dede Wallace Mental Health Center

and

Department of Psychology
Vanderbilt University

Introduction

The chapter reviews present methods of behaviorally assessing addictive behaviors. Therefore, the following discussion focuses largely upon methodologies, their rationale, and adequacy. As the term *addiction* has often been used indiscriminately, some basic definitions are in order. Throughout this review, we will use the term *addiction* in a conservative and technical sense, as defined by Einstein (1975): "Addiction is considered to be a physiological state that arises from the use of opium and its derivatives and synthetic narcotics (heroin, morphine, demerol, methadone), alcohol, and barbiturates. It is the body's way of adapting to these substances" (p. 9). If any of these substances is consumed in sufficient amounts over continuous and sufficient periods of time, *tolerance* and *physical dependence* will result, followed by *withdrawal* symptoms upon the cessation of drug use.

Tolerance refers to the fact that with continuous use, an addicting drug must be taken in increasing amounts in order to manifest the same degree of response as was formerly displayed using lesser amounts. The mechanisms responsible for tolerance are unknown, possibly involving an adaptation of cellular metabolism such that one's body becomes dependent upon a certain minimum level of a specific drug at any given time. *Physical dependence* is used to describe an assumed habituation of bodily functions to an extent that when the drug is no longer consumed, withdrawal symptoms will occur. *Withdrawal*, which can include a variety of symptoms (psychomotor agitation, hallucinations, seizures, etc.), involves a presumed readaptation to normal physiological functioning (i.e., functioning without presence of the drug in the body). *Habituation* is often used synonymously with *psychological dependence* and describes repeated use of a drug to the point where an individual feels uncomfortable when not using that substance (independent of physical symptoms), or continues to use the drug despite incurring serious adverse consequences.

Colloquially, a wide variety of substances, such as tobacco, coffee, food, etc., have sometimes been referred to as "addicting." This review will consider only those substances (specifically—alcohol, opium, opium derivatives, and barbiturates) which have been demonstrated to sometimes result in *physically addictive processes* to be "addicting" drugs. In order to become addicted, one must continuously and repeatedly engage in drug taking behavior. The *behaviors which constitute patterns which can potentially result in physical addiction* are our concern in this chapter—these *are the addictive behaviors.*

As our major concern is with behavioral assessment, this discussion will emphasize attempts to derive observable and quantifiable measures of alcohol and drug use, determinants of those behaviors, and the interpretation of such measures. Treatment procedures and results will not be addressed unless relevant to assessment issues. Reviews of behavioral treatment studies are readily available (e.g., Bridell & Nathan, 1976; Cautela, 1975; Droppa, 1973; Elkins, 1975; Hamburg, 1975; Miller, 1973, 1975; Nathan & Bridell, in press). Finally, when considering determinants of alcohol and drug use, we will primarily be concerned with studies that have used alcohol and drug use as *dependent variables* and have operationally specified their independent variable manipulations.

Drinking and drug use are relatively easy behaviors to define, identify and quantify, and there are many obvious potential social and cultural antecedents and consequences of such behaviors. Despite these facts, behavioral research regarding alcohol and drug use has only recently been initiated: mostly within the past decade. Furthermore, when alcohol studies are excluded, only a paucity of behavioral research remains. Perhaps this is related to certain political and sociocultural influences which promote an avoidance of research or clinical work in these areas by many professionals (Cahn, 1970). However, to assert that little behavioral drug research has been conducted is not meant to excuse this neglect. By the end of this review, it will be readily apparent that there exists a critical need for further behavioral research in these areas.

Before proceeding, two caveats are in order. *First*, even in the experimental laboratory, few behaviors occur in a vacuum. The behaving organism and its environment interact continuously, and a change in one domain usually affects the structure of the other. Thus, we cannot adequately examine alcohol and drug consummatory behavior without also attending to the environment in which that behavior occurs. *Second*, assessment is a necessary ingredient for planning and verifying the effectiveness of *any* treatment, whether or not that treatment is behavioral in nature.

Traditional Methods and Traditional Problems

The primary behaviors which alcohol and drug abuse treatments are intended to change are observable and subject to verification by chemical test. It is ironic, therefore, that diagnostic and treatment outcome assessment of alcohol and drug problems has been in a state of perpetual confusion for many years. In large part, these conceptual confoundings are more prevalent in the alcohol than the drug literature, but this may simply reflect a greater concentration of clinical research in that area. Also, a contributory factor may reside in the social controls which differentiate the various substances. Simply put, the non-prescription use of hard drugs (e.g. heroin and its derivatives) and barbiturates is distinctly illicit. Applying this arbitrary societal definition, any use of these substances can technically be considered as abusive and aberrant.

Similar to the World Health Organization (Eddy, Halsbach, Isbell & Seevers, 1965), the *Diagnostic and Statistical Manual of Mental Disorders, Second Edition* (DSM-II) of the American Psychiatric Association (1968) diagnostically defines *drug dependence* simply by the type of substance involved. The major criteria for this diagnosis are that the drug is not being used as medically prescribed and that the individual is "dependent" on the substance, having demonstrated either "habitual use or a clear sense of need for the drug" (p. 45). Alcoholism is more extensively defined in the *DSM-II*, yet also retains a non-specificity. In essence, "alcoholism" is diagnosed when one suffers adverse consequences as a result of his/her personal alcohol intake (Keller, 1960). The *DSM-II* diagnostic system includes categories of *episodic excessive drinking* and *habitual excessive drinking*, defined by the highly arbitrary criterion of the number of times that a person becomes "intoxicated" per year. A final category of *alcohol addiction* is defined by the appearance of withdrawal symptoms or presumptive evidence of impending withdrawal. An earlier and highly popular alcoholism diagnostic system was formulated by Jellinek (1960), and labeled various types of alcohol problems with Greek letters. Jellinek only defined five such "species," although he felt additional varieties could be described. His definitional criteria basically involved distinctions between psychological and physical consequences of alcohol use and physical dependence on alcohol.

More recently, the National Council on Alcoholism (1972) proposed a check list of over 90 possible diverse symptoms for diagnosing various levels of alcoholism. This proposed system is so bulky in its formulation that it does not appear likely to gain wide acceptance as a diagnostic tool. Other attempts to evaluate alcohol and drug addicts have involved the analysis of personality correlates measured by psychological tests (see Barry, 1973, for a review).

Considered as a whole, traditional methods of assessing alcohol and drug problems and treatment outcome have suffered from two major problems: (1) a lack of adequate specificity, and (2) a lack of empirical foundation. A number of reviews of alcoholism and drug treatment outcome evaluations have addressed these deficiences (Crawford, Chalupsky & Hurley, 1973; Droppa, 1972; Emrick, 1973; Hill & Blane, 1967; Miller, 1973a, 1973b; Miller, Pokorny, Valles & Cleveland, 1970; Morell, 1975; Savada, 1975; Sobell, 1975; M. Sobell & L. Sobell, 1975b; Voegtlin & Lemere, 1974).

Behavioral Assessment of Addictive Behaviors

Our consideration of assessment methods will be facilitated by classifying studies according to their primary research orientation and the setting in which they were conducted. In the following discussion, studies are considered as representing either a basic research (defining the basic nature of addictive behaviors and relationships between components of those behaviors and other environmental, physiological, or personal events) or an applied research (developing effective methods for changing addictive behaviors) orientation. Additionally, the settings in which research studies are performed are important for determining the generalizability of results. Thus, studies are further classified as having been performed in either: (1) a well controlled laboratory or inpatient setting, or (2) a less controlled natural or outpatient setting. Controlled settings are research environments structured such that fine precision of measurement can be achieved and alternative explanations of results minimized. However, caution must be used when generalizing the results of studies conducted in a controlled setting to behavior as it would occur in the natural environment. Those studies conducted in environments where the investigators have rather limited control over occurrences of extraneous events shall be considered as having been conducted in a natural or a less controlled setting. Such studies obviate some problems of generalizability, but often involve less precise measurement of variables and less certain attribution of effects.

Basic Research Conducted in a Controlled Setting

With rare exceptions, behavioral investigations of alcohol and drug use have been conducted only within the past 15 years. For instance, in the early 1960s it was still speculated that the mere consumption of one or two drinks by a chronic alcoholic would cause the onset of physical dependence on alcohol, followed by alcohol withdrawal symptoms upon the cessation of drinking (Jellinek, 1960). It was only with the innovation of giving alcohol to alcoholics within a controlled research setting (i.e., Mendelson, 1964) that empirical tests of the effects of alcohol on alcoholics and studies of the nature of deviant drinking patterns became possible. This type of research, closely supervised and conducted within a controlled setting, has produced a plethora of valuable information about the nature of alcohol intoxication and alcoholics, but has been a source of controversy since its inception. It is argued, for example, that alcoholics are incapable of granting a truly informed consent to experimental procedures involving consumption of alcohol (Mann, 1974), and that administration of alcohol to such individuals can have only damaging consequences. The former objection is a topic for philosophical debate, while the latter is refuted by several recent reports (Faillace, Flamer, Imber & Ward, 1972; Gottheil, Murphy, Skoloda & Corbett, 1972; Paredes, Hood, Seymour & Gollob, 1973; M. Sobell & L. Sobell, 1972, 1973a, 1973b, in press) demonstrating that alcoholics administered alcohol in research studies function at least as well upon leaving the controlled setting (usually a hospital) as alcoholics who were not allowed access to alcohol. No major behavioral studies have yet been reported which involve the experimental administration of addicting drugs other than alcohol. This situation may well exist because of the illicit nature of drugs other than alcohol. While recent behavioral research has investigated non-addicting drugs, such as marijuana (Cappell & Pliner 1974), a consideration of that research is beyond the purview of this chapter.

The behavioral assessment of addictive behaviors can be accomplished using measures of observable behaviors (i.e., amount of alcohol consumed, sip rate, response latency, etc.), physiological state (i.e., breath test for blood alcohol concentration, urinalysis, pulse rate, galvanic skin response, etc.), or verbal (but verifiable) self-reports of behavioral functioning (i.e., amount of alcohol or drugs consumed outside the research setting, time spent in non-drinking environments, drug-related incarcerations, etc.). While the first two types of measures provide direct assessments, verbal reports should only be used when they can be adequately corroborated. Studies often use a combination of different measures within a single investigational procedure. For that reason, we will consider measures as they relate to various types of assessment procedures.

Operant Procedures

Operant procedures were among the earliest used to investigate alcohol drinking behavior. A variety of techniques have been used in these studies, all sharing the feature that a subject has the opportunity to emit a specified criterion response (usually pressing a button, lever, or key) which, under appropriate conditions, will produce a small amount of alcoholic beverage as a reinforcer. Mendelson & Mello (1966), for example, had alcoholic subjects work for alcohol or money on a key-pressing task. A subject-controlled on-off switch, an alcohol or money reinforcement selector switch, a counter to record reinforcement occasions, and a circular translucent response key illuminable in several colors were mounted on a tilted panel. Above the panel within easy reach of the subject was a tumbler into which 10 cc of 86-proof bourbon could be dispensed. Subjects were adult male alcoholics incarcerated for drunkenness, and although maintaining their blood alcohol concentrations (BAC) between 0.15% and 0.30% (0.10% = 100 mg alcohol/100 cc blood), no subject proved unable to work at the operant task because of intoxication. Dependent variable measures included the number of work sessions in which subjects engaged, average session length in minutes, amount of beverage alcohol dispensed, periodic breath tests for BAC, the number of times each subject removed his glass from the dispenser to drink, and the number of reinforcement points earned each day.

A good example of the use of multiple measures has been provided by Nathan, Titler, Lowenstein, Solomon, & Rossi (1970), who used an operant apparatus to investigate the drinking behavior and correlates of drinking behavior of incarcerated male alcoholic subjects. A criterion response occurred when the subject used his finger to interrupt an electric eye light beam. A computer automatically recorded and summarized operant responding as well as temporal and quantitative aspects of each subject's drinking behavior. Also, six times daily the behavior of each subject was observed for 5 minutes and categorized according to specific activities in which he was engaged (i.e., his locus on the ward, his persistence, whether he was engaging in behavioral anomalies, his physical appearance, and his social interactions). Physiological measurements obtained throughout the study included BAC determined by Breathalyzer, and periodic monitoring of subjects' temperature, pulse rate, blood pressure, rate of respiration, and three indices of physical ataxia. Using this battery of measures, they concluded that their chronic alcoholic subjects behaved as though they preferred social isolation to socialization, whether they were drunk or sober. O'Brien (1972) and Nathan, Goldman, Lisman & Taylor (1972) used similar apparatus to investigate socialization differences between alcoholics and non-alcoholics, drinking decisions by alcoholics, and effects of alcohol on short-term memory of alcoholics. Commercial devices (i.e., the BRS-Lehigh Valley Modular Test System) are also available for studying operant drinking tasks with human subjects, and have been used in studies by Mello & Mendelson (1971), Miller, Hersen, Eisler & Elkins (1974), and others.

Finally, operant tasks may hold promise for use in determining the relative reinforcing value of alcohol for subjects. In this regard, Cannon, Ross & Snyder (1973) used a progressive ratio schedule of reinforcement (where reinforcement is contingent upon a gradually increasing number of responses) with alcohol as a reinforcer, and found that alcohol was not a more powerful reinforcer for alcoholics than for non-alcoholics once drinking was underway.

Baseline Drinking Procedures

"Drinking behavior" is a summary phrase used to describe a class of responses. Amazingly, it is only within the present decade that various components of drinking behavior have been measured. Drinking behavior was first studied in a simulated bar and cocktail lounge environment (Schaefer, Sobell & Mills, 1971a; Sobell, Schaefer & Mills, 1972) as an alternative to naturalistic observation. These studies were conducted in a large remodeled dayroom at a state hospital. The setting included a padded and varnished bar with a full-length mirror and bottle display, barstools, tables and chairs, music, and dim lighting. Groups of either three to four hospitalized alcoholics or normal drinkers were allowed to drink freely (to a limit of 16 drinks), and observers recorded each drink ordered, the type of drink, number of sips taken, total time (sec) per drink, and intersip intervals (sec). Within this setting, state hospital alcoholics ordered more drinks, preferred straight drinks, took larger sips and drank faster, but took a longer time between sips than did normal drinkers (Sobell *et al.*, 1972). For the alcoholics (the only subjects serving in a second session), the various components of drinking behavior were found to be highly reliable. For instance, Figs 11.1 and 11.2 display the close similarity for mean time per drink and mean time between sips found over sessions 1 and 2. Nathan & O'Brien (1971) also found chronic alcoholics to prefer straight drinks and to tend to gulp rather than sip their drinks. More recently, Williams & Brown (1974) investigated baseline drinking of hospitalized alcoholics and normal drinkers in New Zealand and found a

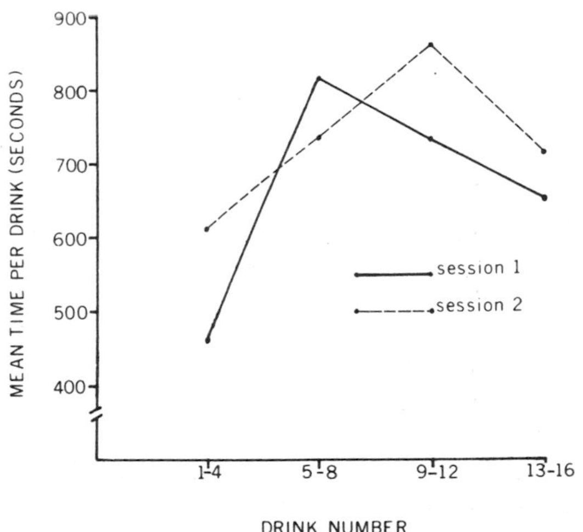

Fig. 11.1. Mean time (sec) per drink as a function of drink number and session number for 26 chronic alcoholics in two baseline drinking sessions. Means were computed from individual subject medians. Reprinted from: *Behaviour Research and Therapy*, 1972, **10**, 257–267. Reprinted with permission of Pergamon Press, Inc.

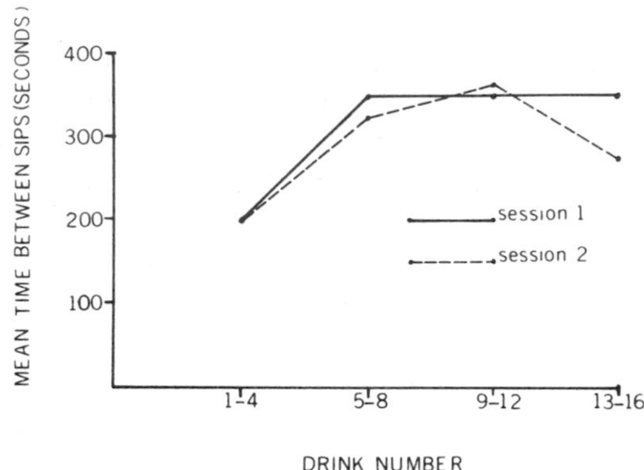

Fig. 11.2. Mean time (sec) between sips as a function of drink number and session number for 26 chronic alcoholics in two baseline drinking sessions. Means were computed from individual subject medians: Reprinted from: *Behaviour Research and Therapy*, 1972, **10**, 257–267. Reprinted with permission of Pergamon Press, Inc.

great congruence with the American results, except that New Zealand drinkers tended to prefer weaker drinks which they consumed in larger gulps.

In the only study to date investigating baseline drinking behaviors of female (middle-class) alcoholics, Tracey, Karlin, & Nathan (1974) found that all subjects prefered mixed drinks, and that mean intersip interval, drink consumption time, and sip size were similar to values previously found for male normal drinkers. The authors cautioned, however, that these differences may have resulted from social class distinctions. Goldman (1974) added a group decision making requirement to the baseline procedure and found that the group decision requirement tended to delay initiation of drinking by chronic alcoholic males and to lower their overall alcohol consumption during a period of prolonged drinking. Despite the susceptibility of baseline drinking to such procedures, Mello & Mendelson (1970) compared programmed administration of alcohol with free availability using chronic male alcoholic subjects. They concluded that baseline procedures had greater generality for describing addictive drinking.

The Taste Test: An Unobtrusive Measure of Consumption

When attempting to measure alcohol consumption in an experimental setting, a basic problem is that the subjects' awareness of what is being measured may be reactive with experimental procedures. That is, subjects may drink differently when they are aware their consumption is being measured. An ingenious method for avoiding the problem of reactivity was simultaneously developed by Marlatt, Demming, & Reid (1973) and by Miller & Hersen

(1972), each group basing their procedure on Schacter's (1971) investigations of obesity. In the Marlatt *et al.* procedure, subjects are told they will be participating in a beverage tasting experiment. They are seated at a table on which are placed three beverage decanters and glasses. A standard manually operated memory drum is on the table, as well as rating forms to be filled out by the subject. Beverages can be alcoholic or non-alcoholic in nature and similar or dissimilar in appearance. The subject is instructed to sample the beverages as necessary in order to rate each on a semantic differential scale in terms of a series of adjectives (i.e., "bitter," "strong," "mellow," etc.) displayed on the memory drum. Typically, the task is terminated after 15 minutes, long before the subject has finished comparing the beverages. While subjects' belief that they have been engaged in a taste comparison test has been verified by post-experimental inquiry, the real dependent variable measure with this procedure is the total amount of beverage consumed by the subject during the test. In addition, sip rate is monitored through a one-way window and BAC is often measured by breath test. This procedure has been useful in studying determinants of alcohol consumption and treatment effectiveness.

Contingency Management Procedures

Another useful assessment procedure involves modifying reinforcement contingencies within a controlled environment and measuring the effects of those manipulations on drinking behavior. For instance, Cohen, Liebson, Faillace & Allen (1971) used contingency management procedures and a within-subject experimental design to study five chronic alcoholics. Subjects had the option of drinking up to 24 ounces of 95-proof ethanol on weekdays for 5 consecutive weeks. During alternate weeks, if the subject drank 5 ounces or less of the beverage in a given day he was maintained in an enriched environment. If he drank over 5 ounces, he was maintained in an impoverished environment for the remainder of that day plus 24 hours. All subjects were found to conform to the contingencies during these weeks, whereas they typically drank more than five ounces daily during intervening non-contingency weeks. A great many additional studies of this variety have been performed at the Baltimore City Hospital. For example, it has been found that chronic alcoholics will moderate their drinking in order to be allowed to stay in an enriched environment (Cohen, Liebson & Faillace, 1973) and to obtain monetary rewards (Cohen, Liebson & Faillace, 1971).

Balanced Placebo Designs

While it is often assumed that the effects of alcohol on behavior are all mediated by physiological processes, intoxicated behavior is a function not only of alcohol, but also of a person's past learning and expectations regarding how alcohol should affect him. In order to separate learned from physiological determinants of the effects of alcohol on behavior, Marlatt *et al.* (1973) used a taste test procedure coupled with a balanced placebo design. Through pre-testing, it was determined that a 1:5 mixture of vodka to tonic water (quinine), highly chilled, was indistinguishable from tonic water alone. Using groups of 32 male alcoholics and 32 male normal drinkers as subjects, one-half of the subjects in each group were adminstered a taste test comparing decanters containing only tonic water, while the remaining subjects compared decanters containing a mixture of vodka and tonic. Within each beverage administration condition, however, one-half of the subjects were told that they were comparing mixtures of vodka and tonic, while the other subjects were instructed that they were simply comparing three different types of tonic water. This procedure, diagrammed in Table 11.1, is a balanced placebo design and allows the differentiation of learned and physiological effects of alcohol. For instance, in this study the only significant determinant of beverage consumption was the instructional set—what the subjects thought they were drinking—and not the actual alcoholic content of the drink. This design has value in investigating determinants of alcohol consumption in both alcoholics and non-alcoholics, as will be reviewed next.

TABLE 11.1

Balanced Placebo Experimental Design

		Subjects are Administered	
		Real Drug	Placebo
Subjects are told they received	Real Drug	Combined Effects of Drug and Expectations	Effects of Expectation only (learned factors)
	Placebo	Effects of Drug only (physiological factors)	Effects of Placebo

Procedures for Investigating Determinants of Alcohol Consumption

Using taste test procedures, Higgins & Marlatt (1973, 1975) and Marlatt, Kosturn & Lang (1975) assessed the effects of stress on drinking of alcoholics and normal drinkers. Their results, taken *in toto*, suggest that social stress could induce drinking in non-alcoholics, as long as opportunities to cope with the stressful situation prior to drinking were precluded, while physical stress was found ineffective in eliciting drinking. This interpretation was supported in a study reported by Miller, Hersen, Eisler & Hilsman (1974). In that study eight alcoholic and eight non-alcoholic inpatients served as subjects in ten minute operant sessions where lever presses earned alcohol reinforcement (5 cc of alcohol mixture) on an FR-50 schedule. A within-subject counter-balanced design was used, with each subject participating in both a stressed and no-stressed condition prior to operant responding. The social stress condition consisted of role-playing in five situations requiring assertive responses. For instance, subjects were asked to role-play how they would respond if a gas station attendant had installed an entire set of new tires on their car when they had simply requested that one tire be installed. No matter how subjects responded, their performance was criticized as unassertive. Under the stress conditions, it was found that alcoholics emitted a greater number of operant responses to obtain alcohol than normal drinkers. Another assessment of the stress manipulation indicated that both alcoholics and normal drinkers significantly increased their pulse rate in the stress condition.

In a recent study by Caudill & Marlatt (1975), male normal drinker subjects performed a wine taste test under one of three experimental conditions: a confederate of the experimenter performed the test simultaneously with the subject and was a "heavy" consumer of wine, the confederate was a "light" consumer of wine, or there was no confederate present at all. While subjects who had either a low consumption model or no model at all did not differ significantly from one another in total wine consumed, those subjects exposed to the heavy drinking model drank significantly more alcohol than subjects in either of the other groups.

Brown & Williams (in press) extended the taste test procedure to involve the use of non-alcoholic beverages. Three groups of male alcoholics ($n = 20$), male psychiatric patients ($n = 20$), and non-hospitalized males ($n = 20$) participated in a tea-tasting test. This task was used to investigate the relative degree of control exercised over drinking in these individuals by internal cues (i.e., physiological state) and external cues (in this case, whether or not tea was a preferred variety by the individual). A within-subject design was used, and on some occasions subjects were preloaded (having already consumed 500 ml of tea) prior to participating in the taste test. This procedure was intended to provide a strong internal cue intended to inhibit drinking. Preloading reliably inhibited drinking in the non-alcoholic subjects, but did not affect the alcoholics' intake. Although not responding to the internal cue of preloading, alcoholics drank significantly more of the blend of tea they preferred most (an external cue) and less of a non-preferred drink (water) than did non-alcoholics. While Brown & Williams interpreted their findings as suggesting that alcoholics are less responsive to internal cues and more responsive to external cues than non-alcoholics, data reported by Miller, Hersen, Eisler, Epstein, &

Wooten (1974) indicate that non-alcoholics were differentially responsive to external visual cues (bottles of liquor, pictures of alcoholic beverages) while performing a lever pressing task to obtain alcohol, but alcoholic subjects were not differentially responsive. They hypothesized that the excessive drinking of alcoholics may be more a function of internal cues than of external cues. Additional studies appear necessary in order to clarify these contradictory results.

Blood Alcohol Concentration (BAC) Discrimination Training

Lovibond & Caddy (1970) first trained alcoholic subjects to discriminate their own BAC. Subjects were administered alcohol, received electric shocks at BACs above 0.0065%, and were also instructed in how to determine their probable BAC induced by various amounts of alcohol consumed over various time intervals. In this regard, Bois & Vogel-Sprott (1974) were able to teach nine non-alcoholic subjects to self-titrate their own alcohol consumption so as to accurately achieve various low BACs. In later sessions, these subjects learned to estimate their own BACs rather accurately, even though limited to internal cues (i.e., unaware of the actual amount of alcohol they had consumed). In contrast, Silverstein, Nathan & Taylor (1974) found that alcoholics could only learn to accurately estimate their BACs if provided with feedback training (information about the accuracy of their estimates and how much alcohol they had consumed). Procedures used in these studies typically involve various methods (i.e., Bois & Vogel-Sprott used a Body Sensation Check List) to direct subjects' attention to physical and cognitive effects of alcohol intoxication, and then compare subjects' BAC estimates with breath test readings of actual BAC.

Basic Research Conducted in a Natural Setting

Baseline Drinking Behavior

Kessler & Gomberg (1974) conducted a field investigation of barroom drinking behavior. Pairs of observers entered 15 local bars, ordered drinks, and then began recording observations about the next male customer to enter the bar. They continued the recording until the patron had left. Observers independently recorded the time when the subject entered and left the bar, whether or not the subject was alone, the type of clothing worn, estimated age, height and weight of the subject, number and type of drinks ordered, number of sips taken per drink, and total time taken to consume each drink. The 53 subjects were unaware that they were being observed. Agreement between observers was either above 88% or above a Pearson r of 0.81 for all variables except height and weight, which were more moderately correlated. They found number of sips per drink to be a relatively stable measure and that subjects predominantly ordered either beer or mixed drinks. Surprisingly, the type of bar was not a substantial determinant of drinking patterns. These findings are at some variance with similar studies of normal drinking behavior in controlled settings (Schaefer, Sobell & Mills, 1971a; Sobell, Schaefer & Mills, 1972; Williams & Brown, 1974). Several factors (i.e., paying for drinks vs. free drinks, available companionship, subject factors, etc.) might account for these differences. Whereas baseline studies conducted in experimental settings allow a controlled assessment of the influence of many environmental factors, studies conducted in a natural setting should provide data truly representative of drinking as it naturally occurs. Studies conducted in the natural setting could benefit from: (1) including measurements of subjects' BACs, (2) interviewing subjects and (3) tracking subjects through a variety of settings. Further, both approaches to studying baseline drinking behavior would do well to extend the experimental environment to include a greater variety of settings. Finally, ethical requirements of obtaining prior informed consent from subjects may, if carried to an extreme, preclude use of naturalistic observation as a research technique. The naturalistic observation of illicit drug use involves even more serious ethical and legal problems, and it is no surprise that the literature lacks such reports.

Determinants of Alcohol Consumption

Relatively few studies have used behavioral assessment techniques to examine determinants of alcohol consumption in the natural environment. An interesting naturalistic study of modeling effects on drinking has been reported by Reid (1975) and was conducted at a local tavern. A researcher would engage a bar patron in discussion and then proceed to consume either a great deal or very little of an alcoholic beverage while sitting next to the subject. The subject's drinking was monitored by observers also present in the bar. It was found that bar patrons exposed to a high consumption model consumed significantly more alcohol than subjects exposed to a low consumption model. Present ethical guidelines concerning research performed with human subjects would appear to greatly limit the feasibility of designing such experimental studies to be conducted in the natural environment.

Physiological Measures of Alcohol or Drug Use

A number of commercial devices (Erwin, Greenberg & Minzer, 1972) can be used to analyze breath samples for BAC. Although often somewhat costly, breath analysis enables an accurate and rapid physiological assessment of degree of alcohol intoxication. Instruments using gas chromatography analysis are currently among the most widely used devices. Several portable and inexpensive devices for breath testing are also available. One of these, the Mobat, was evaluated by Sobell & Sobell (1975a) as having relatively good accuracy for clinical applications, although being too imprecise for strict research use. At the present time, however, precise measurement of BAC can only be obtained with a substantial investment ($1,000 - $3,000) in breath analysis equipment, or through the laboratory analysis of blood samples. Currently, we, and others, are investigating the validity of self-reports of drinking by comparing subjects' expected BACs (based on their reports) with their physiologically assessed BAC. Results of those investigations are not presently available.

An early method used to determine whether persons were under the influence of heroin or similar opiates was the administration of Nalline. Nalline is a synthetic opiate which when administered in small doses will induce dilation of the pupils in individuals who are under the influence of heroin or similar opiates (Terry & Braumoeller, 1956). The Nalline test, however, is often haphazard and unpredictable, with side effects of nausea, irritability, headaches and dizziness, and is susceptible to false readings induced by emotional stress (Lewis, Pollack, Petersen & Geis, 1973).

Modern physiological surveillance for use of heroin or similar substances is predominantly performed by gas-liquid or thin-layer chromatography analysis of urine specimens (Dole, Kim & Eglitis, 1966; Mule, 1969). Using well controlled laboratory procedures, these methods have been demonstrated to be quite reliable for urine collected within 12 hours of drug intake (Parker, Hine, Knomof & Elliott, 1966). Recent evidence, however, suggests that even major processing laboratories are often highly inaccurate in their analysis procedures. For instance, Gottheil, Caddy & Austin (1975) sent artificially prepared (spiked) urine specimens for analysis to two government approved laboratories. One laboratory was aware that spiked samples would be processed, but still correctly identified only 53.8% of those samples. The other laboratory, which was unaware of the experimental test, only identified 49.4% of the test samples. On the other hand, the laboratory unaware of the test reported 66.3% false positives, whereas the laboratory aware that their work was being scrutinized reported only 3.8% false positives. The authors suggested that satisfactory performance by laboratories on "blind" proficiency tests should be a mandatory requirement for federal licensing. Trellis, Smith, Alston & Siassi (1975) performed a similar study, and found regular laboratory analysis to provide an incidence of false positive reports as high as 15%, although this proportion decreased markedly when laboratories were informed of their performance.

Veracity of Self-Reports

Self-reports of alcohol and other drug use have served for years as a basis for diagnosis, treatment decisions, and follow-up evaluations of treatment effectiveness. Despite this pronounced dependency on self-reports, evaluations of self-report reliability and validity have only recently been undertaken. In an experimental situation, Miller & Epstein (1975) evaluated the effect of self-monitoring and self-reinforcement on the drinking patterns of two alcoholics. Subjects participated in a sequence of daily taste rating tests and were observed through a two-way mirror. Subjects were instructed to monitor and record their sip frequency. During a baseline period, both subjects accurately reported their sips. When subjects were then instructed to increase their sipping, one subject accurately reported his sipping, while the other subject continued to sip at the same rate as before, but reported himself as taking more sips. In a succeeding phase, these subjects were instructed not only to diminish their frequency of sipping, but also to reinforce themselves with a hospital canteen booklet contingent upon complying with the instructions. During this phase, both subjects' self-reports were highly reliable. This study is important because: (1) it demonstrates the great variability which may exist among subjects in their accuracy of self-reports and, therefore, suggests that one should seek to corroborate self-reports and use caution in generalizing results from investigations using very few subjects, and (2) it suggests that even though some subjects may react to perceived demand characteristics by providing fraudulent self-reports of their drinking behavior, appropriate programming of consequences may produce more accurate self-reporting.

An ideal corroboration of self-reports of drinking or drug use can be obtained by in-field verification via breath testing or collection of urine specimens. Random urine checks are frequently conducted both by drug treatment programs and by probation or parole officers. For unknown reasons, however, the use of breath analysis in alcohol treatment programs has been rare, and data are similarly lacking on the validity of alcoholics' self-reports about their drinking. At least one study is currently in progress to determine the validity of self-reports of drinking by alcoholics by obtaining in-field breath samples (Sobell, VanderSpek & Sobell 1975), but that investigation is not yet completed.

An indirect assessment of the validity of self-reports can be obtained from determining the validity of self-reported drinking or drug use histories. Ball (1967) interviewed 59 ex-convict narcotic addicts regarding their arrest history and current use of drugs, and then verified their reports by checking hospital records, arrest records, and urine specimens collected at the time of the interview. Thirty-two percent of the subjects accurately reported their total number of arrests, 29% under-reported, and 38% over-reported their past arrests. This finding led Ball to question the completeness of arrest records.

Five of the seven subjects who were using heroin reported that fact in the interview. Stephens (1972) mailed questionnaires regarding drug use, work experience, and encounters with police to 100 former narcotic addicts and to their conselors and relatives. Subjects' answers agreed with their counselors 82% of the time and with their relatives 89% of the time. Finally, Petzel, Johnson & McKillip (1973) used an interesting ploy in assessing the validity of self-reports by 628 high school students in a survey of drug use. A bogus drug, arbitrarily named "Bindro," was included in a checklist where students reported drugs they had used. They found that 24 (3.8%) of the respondents indicated they had actually used the drug "Bindro."

Ball's finding that official records of arrests might be incomplete has been supported in the alcohol literature. Three studies (Guze, Tuason, Stewart & Picken, 1963; L. Sobell & M. Sobell, 1975; Sobell, Sobell & Samuels, 1974) have similarly found that alcoholics tend to overestimate their arrest history as compared to official records. In the Sobell *et al.* (1974) study, interviews were conducted with state hospital chronic alcoholics who were unaware that their answers would later be verified using official arrest records. The Pearson correlation coefficient between self-reports of arrests and official records was 0.65. The subjects were accurate in 37% of the cases, they overestimated arrests in 39% of the cases, and arrests were underestimated in 24% of the cases. In the L. Sobell and M. Sobell (1975) study, outpatient alcoholics in a community alcoholism treatment program were initially interviewed, and three weeks later were administered an additional interview containing 16 embedded drinking history items repeated from the first interview. Interview responses were verified using driver records, arrest records, and local and state hospitalization records. The inter-interview reliability (percent agreement) for all subjects over all items was 91.98%. It was found that 85.99% of all answers were correct, 9.2% were overestimated as compared to official records, and only 4.8% were underestimated. While these results generally support the use of self-reports, until additional research has determined the conditions conducive to valid self-reports, it is suggested that self-reports should be corroborated by *at least* interviewing significant others, obtaining in-field breath or urine samples, and verifying history data via available official records. In this regard, L. Sobell & M. Sobell (in press) recently determined that drivers' records are readily available throughout the United States and most of Canada at little or no cost and could be obtained for 90.4% of 500 consecutive admissions to an alcoholism treatment program.

Applied Research Conducted in a Controlled Setting

Within-Treatment Assessments of Aversion Therapy

Aversion therapy has been a primary focus for applied research studies conducted in controlled settings. In aversion therapy, aversive events (either electrical, chemical, or imaginal) are repeatedly paired with the sight, smell, thoughts, taste, etc. of either alcohol or drug administration on the theoretical basis that these stimuli will come to elicit a conditioned aversive response which will counter drug-taking behaviors. Reviews of aversive conditioning are provided by Rachman & Teasdale (1969), Cautela & Rosenstiel (1975), and Elkins (1975).

Hallam, Rachman, & Falkowski (1972) investigated electrical aversion therapy with 10 of 18 alcoholic inpatients, the remaining patients serving as a control group. Painful but harmless electrical shocks were administered to the arm of subjects while they tasted, smelled, and looked at alcoholic drinks, while they watched slides of drinking-related stimuli, and while subjects fantasized themselves drinking. Assessments conducted before and after treatment included physiological measures of heart rate, pulse volume, and galvanic skin resistance to slide presentations and fantasies of alcohol and non-alcohol related stimuli. Contrary to expectations, aversion therapy was not found to increase the size of autonomic responses to drinking stimuli. Miller & Hersen (1972a) reported a single case study of aversion therapy using a taste test involving a choice between alcoholic and non-alcoholic beverages. The test was administered before and during electrical aversion conditioning, and a follow-up taste test was conducted 6 months after treatment. In this case, electrical aversion produced marked decreases in the amount of alcohol consumed in the taste test. A later study using a similar choice taste test (Miller, Hersen, Eisler & Hemphill, 1973) contradicted this early finding. Thirty inpatient male alcoholics were randomly assigned to one of three treatments: aversion conditioning (500 total trials), an aversion conditioning control procedure (shock set below pain threshold), and group psychotherapy. Significant between group differences in amount of alcohol consumed in the taste test were not obtained.

Wilson, Leaf, & Nathan (1975) used a cross-over experimental design with four inpatient chronic alcoholics to evaluate aversion therapy. Treatment effectiveness was evaluated with a baseline (*ad libitum*) drinking situation imposed for three days prior to and immediately following treatment. Using measures including the frequency, duration, and distribution of each subject's baseline drinking and thrice daily breath analyses for BAC, they found that aversion therapy did not substantially reduce the amount of alcohol consumed by subjects.

The effectiveness of aversion therapy with alcoholics was also assessed by Marlatt (1975). Before and after treatment, subjects were engaged in a "beverage preference test"—slides of alcoholic and non-alcoholic beverages were presented to the subjects, and they indicated whether or not they would "like to have" what was pictured on the slide. Besides assessing beverage preferences, an unobtrusive measure of decision latency was also recorded. A behavioral observation assessment was also conducted. The subject was left alone in a waiting room where both alcoholic and non-alcoholic beverages were present, ostensibly for temporary storage. He was observed for 10-second time samples through a disguised one-way mirror, and a series of scores were recorded, such as the subject's direction of gaze, position in the room with respect to beverages, and reaching and touching at bottles. These measures each showed predicted changes as a result of aversion therapy, although statistical analyses were not performed. Considering the evidence as a whole, it seems likely that if aversion therapy is a successful treatment, the success is not based on a counterconditioning process.

Behavioral assessment has also been used to monitor the effectiveness of aversion therapy for narcotic and methadrine addicts. Liberman (1968) treated two narcotic addicts via aversion therapy using apomorphine, a non-addictive, centrally acting emetic. During treatment sessions, subjects were randomly confronted with the necessity to choose between morphine and more socially appropriate items such as coffee, soft drinks, cigarettes, and candy. If the subject chose the socially appropriate items, this led to a waiting period and no conditioning trials. Unfortunately, specific data were not reported for this study. Spevack, Pihl, & Rowan (1973) treated three male adolescent intravenous methadrine users by electrical aversion therapy. Dependent variable measures included the subjects' self-reported frequency of thoughts about (injection) ritual-related stimuli, self-reports of drug use, and examination of subjects' arms for injection tracks. The measurement of self-reported frequency of specific drug related thoughts has been used relatively often in drug research, but has never been assessed for reliability or validity, nor is it clear how such assessment would be performed. Recording of alcohol-related thoughts has apparently not been used in alcohol treatment evaluation studies.

Other Within-Treatment Assessments

Several other methods for behaviorally assessing treatment effectiveness have also been used with alcoholics. Steffen (1975), for instance, found that alcoholics could attain greater decreases in muscle action potentials when given electromyographic feedback as part of relaxation training, than when participating in an attention placebo training procedure. Schaefer, Sobell, & Mills (1971b) investigated the effects of videotape self-confrontation with drunken behavior on alcoholics when they were sober. Subjects participated in from one to five experimental drinking sessions which were videotaped. Self-confrontation play-back sessions, interposed between drinking sessions, were expected to decrease alcohol consumption over the course of sessions. While subjects' verbal behavior testified to a strong impact by the videotapes, their drinking behavior remained relatively unchanged throughout the sessions.

Mills, Sobell & Schaefer (1971) attempted to shape the drinking behavior of inpatient chronic alcoholics to approximate the drinking of normal drinkers. Electric shock avoidance contingencies were arranged such that subjects would be shocked only if they ordered straight drinks, gulped their drinks, ordered too quickly, or ordered greater than three drinks per session. With this method, nine alcoholic subjects learned to nearly totally avoid shocks while still consuming a limited amount of alcoholic drinks. As part of a broad spectrum, multi-component behavioral treatment program for chronic alcoholics, M. Sobell and L. Sobell (1972, 1973a) incorporated avoidance contingencies similar to those used by Mills *et al.* (1971) in shaping the drinking of 20 subjects. Also, three "probe" sessions, during which subjects were aware they would receive no shock regardless of their drinking behavior, were interspersed among contingent shock sessions. As a group, subjects emitted a significantly greater number of inappropriate drinking behaviors during probe sessions than during shock contingency sessions. However, a more detailed examination of the data indicated that this probe session increase could not be attributed to any particular subject or small group of subjects. Subjects had been verbally instructed about the contingencies and only received a combined total of 30 shocks throughout the experiment. Because few shocks were delivered during the experiment and probe session excesses could not be attributed to particular subjects, the authors suggest that differences between probe session and contingency session drinking behaviors may have reflected planned experimentation by subjects (i.e. seeing how five drinks would affect them).

Miller, Becker, Foy, & Wooten (1975) investigated interrelationships among components of the drinking behavior of three male alcoholic inpatients. A multiple baseline single case experimental design (Barlow & Hersen, 1973) was used, and subjects were videorecorded while they were sequentially instructed to modify various components of their drinking behavior in a baseline situation. Following each session, the total amount of alcohol consumed by the subject, the strength of drinks (both liquor and mixers were available), and mean sip size were calculated. Two judges rated videotapes for number of sips and intersip intervals, demonstrating good inter-judge reliability (sips $r = 1.00$, intersip interval $r = 0.95$). While instructional control was demonstrated over each component of drinking behavior for all subjects, two subjects also displayed a reciprocal relationship among components. For example, as their sip size decreased, their intersip interval also decreased so that they drank more rapidly. This study demonstrates the importance of monitoring a number of components of drinking behavior when attempting to modify that behavior.

In a final study of interest, Miller, Hersen, Eisler, & Elkin (1974) examined the relationship between drinking of alcoholics as assessed by an operant task and a taste test during inpatient treatment, and subsequent post-treatment abstinence. On both measures, subjects who were functioning successfully at follow-up had consumed significantly less alcohol during the inpatient tests. This study suggests that behavioral assessment procedures might be of significant value in predicting post-treatment functioning.

Applied Research Conducted in a Natural Setting

Assessment in Inpatient Treatment

Gottheil, Corbett, Grasberger & Cornelison (1972) describe the use of a drinking decisions model. In this program, alcoholic inpatient males were given their option to drink up to 2 ounces of 40% alcohol each hour for 12 hours each day, 5 days per week. Alcohol intake, blood alcohol levels, eating, sleeping, working, and socializing behavior were regularly assessed. This procedure provided a viable research setting as the subjects did not become grossly inebriated, did not experience severe hangovers or withdrawal symptoms, and constituted no management problems. One-third of the 29 subjects never drank throughout the 4-week drinking decisions program, one-third began drinking but stopped, and one-third drank throughout the program. The authors suggest that this method might be an efficient technique for the controlled study of determinants of drinking within an inpatient environment.

Assessment in Outpatient Treatment

Miller (1972) reported a case study involving the outpatient use of behavioral contracting with an alcoholic and his wife. The subject maintained a daily record of his alcohol consumption before and throughout treatment and for a 10-day probe interval 6 months after treatment. The subject's self-reports were corroborated by his wife and friends. Using reciprocal contingency contracts involving privileges and fines, the subject's drinking was reduced from an average of 7 to 8 drinks ($1\frac{1}{2}$ oz hard liquor or equivalent) per day to a range of from 0 to 3 drinks per day.

Daily drinking records as an adjunct to outpatient treatment of alcoholics were also investigated by L. Sobell & M. Sobell (1973). Alcohol Intake Sheets recording the date, specific type of drink, percentage alcohol content, time the drink was ordered, number of sips per drink, amount of the total drink consumed, and the environment where the drinking occurred were maintained for a minimum of 5 months by six alcoholic outpatients while they attended weekly sessions of behaviorally oriented group therapy. When self-damaging drinking was reported, subjects were reinforced for recording their drinking, but it was simultaneously made salient that such behavior was likely to have self-destructive long-term consequences. Validity of the self-reported drinking behavior was corroborated through a number of sources. They suggested that self-monitoring of drinking by alcoholics during out-patient treatment has three major benefits: (1) it encourages subjects to be constantly aware of drinking which occurs and to analyze their environment for situations which might lead to problem drinking, (2) it encourages within-treatment discussion of drinking situations and drinking which actually occurs, and (3) it can facilitate early treatment intervention by identifying the onset of problem drinking.

Earlier in this chapter, use of an inexpensive, portable breath testing device with alcoholics in outpatient treatment was discussed (M. Sobell & L. Sobell, 1975a). Miller, Hersen, Eisler & Watts (1974) have used a similar device to advantage in a case study investigation of outpatient treatment of a chronic male alcoholic by means of contingent reinforcement of lowered blood alcohol levels.

The outpatient use of behavioral assessment techniques in drug studies has varied widely, Polakow & Doctor (1973) reported on the use of contingency contracting with a young male daily barbiturate user. The subject was required to participate in an agreed-upon-number of "non-drug related activities per week," and such activities had to be verifiable. Twelve-month follow-up assessment included self-reports of drug usage, checks on the subject's employment, reports of marital difficulties by the subject and his wife, and checks of police and court records. In a further study, Polakow (1975) treated a female barbiturate addict probationee through similar methods. Follow-up of 18 months' duration yielded self-reports of maintained employment and no arrests or drug usage. These reports were verified with the employer and by checking police and court records. In each of these cases, subjects were probationees, and this may have facilitated the gathering of corroborative information.

Boudin & Valentine (1973) described a broad spectrum outpatient behavioral treatment program for drug addicts, which used contingency contracting as a central element. Subjects were provided with wrist counters (Lindsley, 1968) used for the daily recording of "behavioral pinpoints." "Pinpoints" for individual subjects were selected by the program staff and defined as behaviors which were functionally related to that subject's drug use. Definitions were either operational or subjective, including such measures as number of cigarettes smoked, number of marijuana "tokes," frequency of sexual relations, drug urges, urges to escape from the program, thoughts about making or breaking the contingency contract, and number of times able to relax during a day, etc. In addition, clients were contractually required to contact a paraprofessional staff member by telephone every 3 waking hours daily. This procedure allowed a daily monitoring of the clients' activities, and also gathered data regarding the number of telephone contacts made as scheduled. Although specific results were not presented, an interesting aspect of this program is that a strong emphasis was placed on evaluating functional relationships between measures, as well as between measures and significant events in the clients' daily functioning. Individual charts summarizing behavioral pinpoints on a number of variables for a given subject were routinely examined for significant accelerations, decelerations, continuations, and/or cyclic effects. The report includes two case examples demonstrating that behavior *patterns* might be more indicative of an impending crisis (high probability of drug use) than single measures.

Assessment in Follow-up

Treatment outcome evaluation is one area where behavioral assessment of addictive behaviors has substantially changed traditional, often archaic, assessment procedures. Lovibond & Caddy (1970) evaluated a treatment procedure aimed at training alcoholics to become non-problem drinkers by means of BAC discrimination training combined with extensive behavioral counseling. Post-treatment follow-up for intervals ranging from 16 to 20 weeks found experimental subjects to demonstrate significantly less post-treatment alcohol intake than control subjects. Follow-up data were gathered by interview with the subjects and were corroborated by interviews with other informants. The primary outcome measure was subjects' self-reports about the number of drinking occasions when their blood alcohol concentration had exceeded a level of 0.07%. As discussed earlier, there currently exists considerable ambiguity regarding the ability of alcoholic subjects to reliably estimate their BAC over an extended period of time, even after initial training.

In a follow-up assessment of the efficacy of aversion therapy with alcoholics, Marlatt (1973) used subjects' self-reports corroborated by reports of significant others. His primary measure of drinking behavior was the amount of pure alcohol (in order to standardize across beverages with different alcohol contents) subjects consumed per day, and average weekly consumption rates were reported for subjects.

M. Sobell & L. Sobell (1972, 1973a, 1973b, in press) tested a broad spectrum behavioral treatment for chronic alcoholics. Seventy state hospital chronic alcoholics were assigned to a treatment goal of either complete abstinence or controlled drinking (operationally defined as alcohol ingestion equal to or less than 6 oz of 86-proof liquor, or equivalent, per day). Within each goal condition, subjects were then randomly assigned to either the behavioral treatment program or the conventional state hospital treatment program. The multiple treatment components were highly complex and will not be described here. Dependent variable measures of treatment outcome were the most extensive used to date in behavioral assessment of alcoholism treatment, and complete 2-year follow-up data were reported for 69 of the 70 subjects. Data obtained from subjects' self-reports were corroborated by interviews with many collateral information sources, such as relatives, friends, employers, welfare agencies, etc. Both subjects and collaterals were interviewed every 3 to 4 weeks over the 2-year period, and arrest records, drivers records, and hospital records were routinely used as data sources. Daily drinking dispositions for each day were coded as abstinent, controlled drinking, drunk, incarcerated in jail, or incarcerated in hospital for alcohol-related reasons. Other outcome measures included evaluations by collaterals of subjects' general adjustment to interpersonal relationships and stressful situations, the nature of subjects' vocational activities, residential status and stability, use of outpatient therapeutic supports, and a physical health evaluation conducted at the end of the second year of follow-up. The second-year outcome report for this project (M. Sobell & L. Sobell, in press) also provides individual subject drinking profiles which describe in detail each of the 69 subjects' drinking patterns during follow-up. Presentation of individual subject outcome profiles helps circumvent the problems inherent in presenting grouped subject data for a large number of subjects. Also, the use of multiple measures of treatment outcome allows a comparison of the relationship between changes in drinking behavior and changes in other areas of life functioning. For instance, second-year results found that behaviorally treated subjects with a controlled drinking goal functioned significantly better than their respective control subjects on a variety of measures, including drinking behavior. On the other hand, differences in drinking behavior between experimental and control subjects with a non-drinking treatment goal approached statistical significance ($0.10 < p < 0.05$), but this tendency was not supported by other adjunctive measures of treatment outcome. Thus, the lack of a statistically significant difference between these groups did not appear to be coincidental.

Hunt & Azrin (1973) found good evidence of effectiveness for a community-reinforcement approach to alcoholism which stressed the re-arrangement of alcoholics' community reinforcers, such as their job, and family and social relations, so that drinking would result in a time-out from reinforcement. Eight subjects were treated by the community-reinforcement method, and eight were treated in a traditional treatment program. Primary measures of treatment outcome included number of days unemployed, number of days when drinking occurred (all subjects had a goal of abstinence), and number of days spent away from home. Weekly follow-up interviews were conducted for the first month following discharge, then extended to bi-monthly and later to monthly contacts. Corroboration by a family member was sought during the interviews. Also, an independent 6-month outcome evaluation was performed by an assistant not associated with the counseling program. The Pearson correlation between outcome data obtained from regular interviews and the independent interview was 0.95.

A novel element was used in outcome assessment by Miller (1975), who evaluated the short term effects of a reinforcement contingency management system for chronic public drunkenness offenders. Local "Skid Row" helping agencies participated in a program whereby 10 randomly selected chronic inebriates received goods and services contingent upon their sobriety, and another 10 received routine services from these agencies. Using randomly administered breath tests with SM-7 Sober Meters, BACs were sampled within consecutive 5-day intervals. Comparing pre- and post-treatment data, subjects in the contingency management group were found to have significantly decreased arrests and alcohol consumption, and to have spent significantly more hours employed than control subjects. The use of random breath analysis for BAC, a direct indicant of recent drinking, should be included in alcoholism treatment assessment whenever possible.

Vogler, Compton, & Weissbach (1975) evaluated a behavioral treatment program for chronic alcoholics which combined components of the programs developed by Lovibond & Caddy (1970) and by M. Sobell & L. Sobell (1972). The primary outcome measure used to compare two comparison groups of subjects was average number of gallons of absolute alcohol consumed per subject per year. While differences were demonstrated using this measure, the presentation of grouped data over such a long interval would seem to have limited utility. Measures of daily drinking disposition, number of days lost from work, amount of money spent on alcohol per month, and several scales relating drinking companions and environment were also used in this study, but no significant differences between groups were obtained.

Aside from urine surveillance, treatment outcome assessment in addictive drug research would seem to be in its infancy. Procedures used by Polakow (1975) and Polakow & Doctor (1973) have already been reviewed. O'Brien, Raynes, & Patch (1972) evaluated the effects of electrical aversion therapy, relaxation training, and systematic desensitization with two heroin addicts. Follow-up was obtained by searching subjects for track marks (puncture scars), and gathering self-reports of drug use substantiated by family reports. In an extension of the work reported by Boudin & Valentine (1973), Boudin, Valentine, Ingraham, Brantley, Ruiz, Smith, Catlin & Regan (in press) included a treatment outcome report for 23 subjects who had been in treatment for a minimum of 15 days during a 15-month interval. Dependent variables included tri-weekly urinalysis during treatment status plus random weekly urinalysis after treatment, self-reports, reports by significant others and official agencies, number of days gainfully employed and/or enrolled in school as validated by employer and/or school personnel, and personal/social adjustment determined from assessment of each client's "pinpoint" data and treatment, and post-treatment records. The small number of negative case outcomes precluded statistical contrasts of negative and positive case outcomes. However, despite the limited data available, this array of treatment outcome measures represent by far the most comprehensive and empirical assessment of drug treatment outcome now available in the literature. As an additional part of that study, Boudin *et al.* also related subject history characteristics and treatment program performance with treatment outcome. It was found that degree of success in the program was significantly related to the number of years previously addicted to heroin, previous cost of the habit, and number of times previously enrolled in methadone programs. Follow-up reports sometimes include retrospective analyses of subject or treatment characteristics found to be associated with treatment outcomes. The use of such post-treatment autopsy techniques can provide valuable suggestions concerning factors associated with success; however, the *post hoc* analyses used to obtain these findings might reflect either true associations or clusterings which have occurred by chance. Therefore, such hypotheses should not be considered as demonstrated until later confirmed by empirical test.

The State of the Art

An Overview of Alcohol Studies

The work reviewed in this chapter represents the beginning stages of applying behavioral methods to problems of addictive behavior, with the great majority of studies only having been reported during the past 5 years. Nevertheless, in the area of alcohol problems the advances provided by behavioral investigations have already compelled a sweeping reconsideration of traditional concepts (Pattison, Sobell & Sobell, in press). While it is still too early to accurately determine exactly how traditional views of alcohol problems will be altered, the evidence clearly demonstrates that changes are now in progress.

The use of behavioral assessment in alcohol studies has been largely concentrated in basic research and research conducted in controlled setting. While the value of this research has been repeatedly demonstrated, large scale empirical tests of the effectiveness of treatment techniques based on knowledge provided by basic research have been rare. When conducted, clinical tests have frequently involved very few subjects, although several studies reviewed in this chapter have reported substantial individual differences among subjects. The promising results of the few large-scale clinical tests thus far reported surely emphasize the need for similar research. Other areas of alcohol problems needing behavioral assessment research are readily apparent: (1) very few studies have used female subjects, even though the few existing studies of female drinking behavior have typically found results quite different from those obtained using male subjects, (2) research should be performed using subjects manifesting varying severities of drinking problems, rather than primarily using chronic, often "Skid-Row," alcoholics, (3) more studies should be conducted in outpatient settings, because such treatment settings are becoming increasingly popular, and because of the limited amount of control that the experimenter (or therapist) has over extraneous variables in such settings, and (4) more measurement procedures with demonstrated generalizability to the subject's natural environment need to be developed—while unobtrusive measures, such as the taste test, are undoubtedly a major advance in methodology, one can not help but wonder whether the entire situation of an alcoholic individual being invited to serve in a taste test might at least seem strange, if not artificial, to that person.

An Overview of Studies with Addicting Drugs other than Alcohol

Reports of behavioral assessments of drug taking and associated behaviors are rare in the literature. It is somewhat of an enigma that, to the authors' knowledge, no studies involving the actual experimental administration of such drugs in controlled laboratory settings have yet been reported. Instead, drug studies have tended to be performed as treatment case studies and typically emphasize description of treatment procedures rather than assessment of treatment effects. Another problem with existing studies of behavioral treatment of drug addicts is that they have typically involved only one or two subjects. For instance, Cautela & Rosensteil (1975) reviewed 18 such studies where the sample size was stated, and only six of those studies involved three or more subjects. Overall, the predominant need in this area is for increased research, *per se*.

Assessment of Addictive Behaviors: Future Needs

Research on the behavioral assessment of addictive behaviors has proliferated substantially in recent years. The following is but a short list of suggested directions that further research might pursue so as to maximize practical benefits:

1. A greater array of unobtrusive or non-reactive measures need to be developed, particularly concerning drugs other than alcohol.

2. An increased amount of large sample behavioral treatment outcome studies are needed to validate techniques.

3. Major efforts need to be directed toward delineating determinants of valid self-reports.

4. Intensive research on the reliability, validity, and interrelations of dependent variable measures used for assessing treatment effectiveness should be conducted. Such an effort might encourage at least some standardization among measures. Comparability between data obtained from different studies is presently quite limited.

5. More research is needed investigating how subject characteristics (i.e., demographic factors, performance on behavioral tests, etc.) interact with various treatment approaches, and how subject and treatment factors combine to predict treatment effectiveness.

6. Whenever possible, investigators should use a battery of assessment techniques and draw conclusions based on the interrelation of those measures. This approach is somewhat akin to developing construct validity for outcome conclusions. Outcome measures may include physiological assessments, assessments based on motor behavior, self-reports, reports by collateral informants, and any available documentation.

7. Extremely few studies using behavioral assessment with polydrug problems have been conducted, although polydrug use is quite common (i.e., Freed, 1973).

8. Intensive research regarding assessment *procedures* is needed. For example: How frequently should follow-up contacts be made with subjects? How should interview questions be phrased, how are group results affected when subjects are lost for follow-up?

Before closing, two additional points deserve mention. While behavioral assessment is one way of measuring addictive behaviors, it is only one of many possible approaches. In many ways, the new behavioral measures are superior to what has been available, but it would be foolhardy to ignore all former work in these areas. Thus far, few efforts have been made toward integrating knowledge gained from behavioral approaches to addictive behaviors with other empirical findings.

Lastly, we must address the often unpalatable but nevertheless mandatory need to balance pragmatism and precision in performing behavioral assessments of addictive behaviors. In clinical practice, for instance, it is seldom necessary to determine BAC with accuracy to the nearest 0.01 %, and it would be impractical to invest $3,000 in a gas chromatograph for that purpose, when adequate screening testers can be purchased for less than $1.00 each. Which procedures are to be used for behavioral assessment remains the province of those implementing the assessment and will to some extent reflect their research and/or clinical agendas. In our opinion, the best way for one to ensure both, that satisfactory assessments are accomplished and that assessment performed by others is appropriately interpreted, is to be knowledgeable about available methods and procedures.

References

American Psychiatric Association. *Diagnostic and statistical manual of mental disorders* (2nd edition). Washington, D. C.: American Psychiatric Association, 1968.

Ball, J. C. The reliability and validity of interview data obtained from 59 narcotic drug addicts. *American Journal of Sociology*, 1967, **72**, 650–654.

Barlow, D. H., & Hersen, M. Single–case experimental designs uses in applied clinical research. *Archives of General Psychiatry*, 1973, **29**, 319–325.

Barry, H. B. III. Psychological factors in alcoholism. In B. Kissin & H. Begleiter (Eds.), *The biology of Alcoholism, Volume 3: Clinical pathology*. New York: Plenum Press, Inc. 1974.

Bois, C., & Vogel-Sprott, M. Discrimination of low blood alcohol levels and self-titration skills in social drinkers. *Quarterly Journal of Studies on Alcohol*, 1974, **35**, 86–97.

Boudin, H. M., & Valentine, V. E. III. Behavioral techniques as an alternative to methadone maintenance. Paper presented at the 6th Annual Meeting of the Association for Advancement of Behavior Therapy, New York, 1972.

Boudin, H. M., Valentine, V. E. III, Inghram, R. D., Jr., Brantley, J. M., Ruiz, M. R., Smith, G. G., Catlin, R. P. III, & Regan, E. J., Jr. Contingency contracting with drug abusers in the natural environment. *International Journal of the Addictions*, in press.

Briddell, D. W., & Nathan, P. E. Behavior assessment and modification with alcoholics: Current status and future trends. In M. Hersen, R. M. Eisler, & P. M. Miller (Eds.), *Progress in behavior modification: Volume 2*. New York: Academic Press, 1976.

Brown, R. A., & Williams, R. J. Internal and external cues relating to fluid intake in obese and alcoholic subjects. *Journal of Abnormal Psychology*, in press.

Cahn, S. *The treatment of alcoholics: An evaluation study*. New York: Oxford University Press, 1970.

Cannon, D., Ross, S. M., & Snyder, E. The reinforcing effects of alcohol as measured by a progressive ratio schedule. Paper presented at the 53rd Annual Meeting of the Western Psychological Association, Anaheim, California, April 1973.

Cappell, H., & Pilner, P. Cannabis intoxication: The role of pharmacological and psychological variables. In L. L. Miller (Ed.), *Marijuana: Effects on human behavior*. New York: Academic Press, 1974.

Caudill, B. D., & Marlatt, G. A. Modeling influences in social drinking: An experimental analogue. *Journal of Consulting and Clinical Psychology*, 1975, **43**, 405–415.

Cautela, J. R., & Rosenstiel, A. K. The use of covert conditioning in the treatment of drug abuse. *International Journal of the Addictions*, 1975, **10**, 277–303.

Cohen, M., Liebson, I. A., & Faillace, L. A. The modification of drinking in chronic alcoholics. In N. K. Mello & J. H. Mendelson (Eds.), *Recent advances in studies of alcoholism*. Washington, D. C.: U. S. Government Printing Office, 1971.

Cohen, M., Liebson, I., & Faillace, L. Controlled drinking by chronic alcoholics over extended periods of free access. *Psychological Reports*, 1973, **32**, 1107–1110.

Cohen, M., Liebson, I. A., Faillace, L. A., & Allen, R. P. Moderate drinking by chronic alcoholics: A schedule-dependent phenomenon. *Journal of Nervous and Mental Disease*, 1971, **153**, 434–444.

Crawford, J. J., Chalupsky, A. B., & Hurley, M. M. The evaluation of psychological approaches to alcoholism treatments: A methodological review. Final Report, AIR-96502-3/73-FR, American Institutes for Research, Palo Alto, California, 1973.

Dole, V. P., Kim, W. K., & Eglitis, I. Detection of narcotic drugs, tranquilizers, amphetamines, and barbiturates in urine. *Journal of the American Medical Association*, 1966, **198**, 349–352.

Droppa, D. C. Behavioral treatment of drug addiction: A review and analysis. *International Journal of the Addictions*, 1973, **8**, 143–161.

Eddy, N. B., Halsbach, H., Isbell, H., & Seevers, M. Drug dependence: Its significance and characteristics. *Bulletin of the World Health Organization*, 1965, **32**, 721–733.

Einstein, S. *Beyond drugs*. New York: Pergamon Press, 1975.

Elkins, R. L. Aversion therapy for alcoholism: Chemical, electrical, or verbal imagery. *International Journal of the Addictions*, 1975, **10**, 157–209.

Emrick, C. D. A review of psychologically oriented treatment of alcoholism. *Quarterly Journal of Studies on Alcohol*, 1974, **35**, 523–549.

Erwin, R. E., Greenberg, L. A., & Minzer, M. K. *Defense of drunk driving cases* (3rd ed., 1972 Suppl.). New York: Matthew Bender, 1972.

Faillace, L. A., Flamer, R. N., Imber, S. D., & Ward, R. F. Giving alcohol to alcoholics: An evaluation. *Quarterly Journal of Studies on Alcohol*, 1972, **33**, 85–90.

Freed, E. X. Drug abuse by alcoholics: A review. *International Journal of the Addictions*, 1973, **8**, 451–473.

Goldman, M. S. Drink or not to drink—experimental analysis of group drinking decisions by 4 alcoholics. *American Journal of Psychiatry*, 1974, **131**, 1123–1130.

Gottheil, E., Caddy, G. R., & Austin, D. L. Clinical significance of urine drug screens. Paper presented at the Canadian Psychiatric Association Annual Meeting, Banff, Canada, September 25, 1975.

Gottheil, E., Corbett, L. O., Grasberger, J. C., & Cornelison, F. S. Fixed interval drinking decisions. I. A. research and treatment model. *Quarterly Journal of Studies on Alcohol*, 1972, **33**, 311–324.

Gottheil, E., Murphy, B. F., Skoloda, T. E., & Corbett, L. O. Fixed interval drinking decisions. II. Drinking and discomfort in 25 alcoholics. *Quarterly Journal of Studies on Alcohol*, 1972, **33**, 325–340.

Guze, S. B., Tuason, V. B., Stewart, M. A., & Picken, B. The drinking history: A comparison of reports by subjects and their relatives. *Quarterly Journal of Studies on Alcohol*, 1963, **24**, 249–260.

Hallam, R., Rachman, S., & Falkowski, W. Subjective, attitudinal and physiological effects of electrical aversion therapy. *Behaviour Research and Therapy*, 1972, **10**, 1–13.

Hamburg, S. Behavior therapy in alcoholism, a critical review of broad-spectrum approaches. *Journal of Studies on Alcohol*, 1975, **36**, 69–87.

Higgins, R. L., & Marlatt, G. A. The effects of anxiety arousal on the consumption of alcohol by alcoholics and social drinkers. *Journal of Consulting and Clinical Psychology*, 1973, **41**, 426–433.

Higgins, R. L., & Marlatt, G. A. Fear of interpersonal evaluations and situational control as determinants of alcohol consumption in social drinkers. *Journal of Abnormal Psychology*, 1975, in press.

Hill, J. M., & Blane, H. T. Evaluation of psychotherapy with alcoholics: A critical review. *Quarterly Journal of Studies on Alcohol*, 1967, **28**, 76–104.

Hunt, G. M., & Azrin, N. H. A community-reinforcement approach to alcoholism. *Behaviour Research and Therapy*, 1973, **11**, 91–104.

Jellinek, E. M. *The disease concept of alcoholism.* New Brunswick, New Jersey: Hillhouse Press, 1960.

Keller, M. Definition of alcoholism. *Quarterly Journal of Studies on Alcohol*, 1960, **21**, 125–134.

Kessler, M., & Gomberg, C. Observations of barroom drinking: Metholodology and preliminary results. *Quarterly Journal of Studies on Alcohol*, 1974, **35**, 1392–1396.

Lewis, V. S., Pollack, S., Petersen, D. M., & Geis, G. Nalline and urine tests in narcotic detection: A critical overview. *International Journal of the Addictions*, 1973, **8**, 163–171.

Liberman, R. P. Aversive conditioning of drug addicts: A pilot study. *Behaviour Research and Therapy*, 1968, **6**, 229–231.

Lindsley, O. R. A reliable wrist counter for recording behavioral rates. *Journal of Applied Behavior Analysis*, 1968, **1**, 77–78.

Lovibond, S. H., & Caddy, G. R. Discriminated aversive control in the moderation of alcoholics' drinking behavior. *Behavior Therapy*, 1970, **1**, 437–444.

Mann, M. Presentation as part of a panel discussion on Human Subjects for Alcoholism Research: Ethical and Legal Considerations. Meeting of the Alcohol and Drug Problems Association, San Francisco, December 1974.

Marlatt, G. A. A comparison of aversive conditioning procedures in the treatment of alcoholism. Paper presented at the annual meeting of the Western Psychological Association, Anaheim, California, April 1975.

Marlatt, G. A., Demming, B., & Reid, J. B. Loss of control drinking in alcoholics: An experimental analogue. *Journal of Abnormal Psychology*, 1973, **81**, 233–241.

Marlatt, G. A., Kosturn, C. F., & Lang, A. R. Provocation to anger and opportunity for retaliation as determinants of alcohol consumption in social drinkers. Unpublished manuscript, 1975.

Mello, N. K., & Mendelson, J. H. Experimentally induced intoxication in alcoholics: A comparison between programmed and spontaneous drinking? *Journal of Pharmacology and Experimental Therapeutics*, 1970, **173**, 101–116.

Mello, N. K., & Mendelson, J. H. A quantitative analysis of drinking patterns in alcoholics. *Archives of General Psychiatry*, 1971, **25**, 527–539.

Mendelson, J. H. (Ed.), Experimentally induced chronic intoxication and withdrawal in alcoholics. *Quarterly Journal of Studies on Alcohol*, 1964, Supplement No. 2.

Mendelson, J. H., & Mello, N. K. Experimental analysis of drinking behavior of chronic alcoholics. *Annals of the New York Academy of Sciences*, 1966, **133**, 828–845.

Miller, B. A., Pokorny, A. D., Valles, J., & Cleveland, S. E. Biased sampling in alcoholism treatment research. *Quarterly Journal of Studies on Alcohol*, 1970, **31**, 97–107.

Miller, P. M. The use of behavioral contracting in the treatment of alcoholism: A case report. *Behavior Therapy*, 1972, **3**, 593–596.

Miller, P. M. Behavioral treatment of drug addiction: A review. *International Journal of the Addictions*, 1973, **8**, 511–519.

Miller, P. M. Behavioral assessment in alcoholism research and treatment: Current techniques. *International Journal of the Addictions*, in press.

Miller, P. M., Becker, J. B., Foy, D. W., & Wooten, L. S. Instructional control of the components of alcoholic drinking behavior. Unpublished manuscript, 1975.

Miller, P. M., & Epstein, L. H. An experimental analysis of the effects of self-management procedures on the drinking behavior of chronic alcoholics. Unpublished data, University of Mississippi Medical Center, 1975.

Miller, P. M., & Hersen, M. Quantitative changes in alcohol consumption as a function of electrical aversive conditioning. *Journal of Clinical Psychology*, 1972, **28**, 590–593.

Miller, P. M., Hersen, M., Eisler, R. M., & Elkin, T. E. A retrospective analysis of alcohol consumption on laboratory tasks as related to therapeutic outcome. *Behaviour Research and Therapy*, 1974, **12**, 73–76.

Miller, P. M., Hersen, M., Eisler, R. M., Epstein, L. H., & Wooten, L. S. Relationship of alcohol cues to the drinking behavior of alcoholics and social drinkers: An analogue study. *Psychological Record*, 1974, **24**, 61–66.

Miller, P. M., Hersen, M., Eisler, R. M., & Hemphill, D. P. Electrical aversion therapy with alcoholics: An analogue study. *Behaviour Research and Therapy*, 1973, **11**, 491–497.

Miller, P. M., Hersen, M., Eisler, R. M., & Hilsman, G. Effects of social stress on operant drinking of alcoholics and social drinkers. *Behaviour Research and Therapy*, 1974, **12**, 67–72.

Miller, P. M., Hersen, M., Eisler, R. M., & Watts, J. G. Contingent reinforcement of lowered blood/alcohol levels in an outpatient chronic alcoholic. *Behaviour Research and Therapy*, 1972, **12**, 261–263.

Mills, K. C., Sobell, M. B., & Schaefer, H. H. Training social drinking as an alternative to abstinence for alcoholics. *Behavior Therapy*, 1971, **2**, 18–27.

Morell, J. Outcome and evaluation research in drug abuse rehabilitation—A critical analysis. Unpublished manuscript, The Hahnemann Medical College and Hospital, 1975.

Mule, S. J. Identification of narcotics, barbiturates, amphetamines, tranquilizers, and psychotomimetics in human urine. *Journal of Chromatography*, 1969, **39**, 302–311.

Nathan, P. E., & Briddell, D. W. Behavioral assessment and treatment of alcoholism. In B. Kissin, & H. Begleiter (Eds.), *The biology of alcoholism, Vol. 5*. New York: Plenum Press, in press.

Nathan, P. E., Goldman, M. S., Lisman, S. A., & Taylor, H. A. Alcohol and alcoholics: A behavioral approach. *Transactions of the New York Academy of Sciences*, 1972, **34**, 602–627.

Nathan, P. E., & O'Brien, J. S. An experimental analysis of the behavior of alcoholics and nonalcoholics during prolonged experimental drinking: A necessary precursor of behavior therapy? *Behavior Therapy*, 1971, **2**, 455–476.

Nathan, P. E., Titler, N. A., Lowenstein, L. M., Solomon, P., & Rossi, A. M. Behavioral analysis of chronic alcoholism. *Archives of General Psychiatry*, 1970, **22**, 419–430.

National Council on Alcoholism. Criteria for the diagnosis of alcoholism. *American Journal of Psychiatry*, 1972, **129**, 127–135.

O'Brien, J. S. Operant behavior of a chronic alcoholic under fixed ratio and fixed interval schedules of reinforcement using alcohol as a reinforcer. *British Journal of Addiction*, 1972, **67**, 167–176.

O'Brien, J. S., Raynes, A. E., & Patch, V. D. Treatment of heroin addiction with aversion therapy, relaxation training and systematic desensitization. *Behaviour Research and Therapy*, 1972, **10**, 77–80.

Paredes, A., Hood, W. R., Seymour, H., & Gollob, M. Loss of control in alcoholism: An investigation of the hypothesis, with experimental findings. *Quarterly Journal of Studies on Alcohol*, 1973, **34**, 1146–1161.

Parker, K. D., Hine, C. H., Knomof, N., & Elliott, H. W. Urine screening techniques employed in the detection of users of narcotics and their correlation with the nalorphine test. *Journal of Forensic Science*, 1966, **11**, 11–20.

Pattison, E. M., Sobell, M. B., & Sobell, L. C. (Eds.), *Emerging concepts of alcohol dependence*. New York: Springer, in press.

Petzel, T. P., Johnson, J. E., & McKillip, J. Response bias in drug surveys. *Journal of Consulting and Clinical Psychology*, 1973, **40**, 437–439.

Polakow, R. L. Covert sensitization treatment of a probationed barbiturate addict. *Journal of Behavior Therapy and Experimental Psychiatry*, 1975, **6**, 53–54.

Polakow, R. L., & Doctor, R. M. Treatment of marijuana and barbiturate dependency by contingency contracting. *Journal of Behavior Therapy and Experimental Psychiatry*, 1973, **4**, 375–377.

Rachman, S., & Teasdale, J. *Aversion therapy and behavior disorders: An analysis*. Florida: University of Miami Press, 1969.

Reid, J. B. Observational studies of alcohol consumption in natural setting. Paper presented at the Conference of Behavioral Approaches to Alcoholism and Drug Dependencies, University of Washington Alcoholism and Drug Abuse Institute, Seattle, July 1975.

Savada, S. W. Research approaches in illicit drug use: A critical review. *Genetic Psychology Monographs*, 1975, **91**, 3–59.

Schacter, S. Some extraordinary facts about obese humans and rats. *American Psychologist*, 1971, **26**, 129–144.

Schaefer, H. H., Sobell, M. B., & Mills, K. C. Baseline drinking behaviors in alcoholics and social drinkers; Kinds of drinks and sip magnitudes. *Behaviour Research and Therapy*, 1971a, **9**, 23–27.

Schaefer, H. H., Sobell, M. B., & Mills, K. C. Some sobering data on the use of self-confrontation with alcoholics. *Behavior Therapy*, 1971b, **2**, 28–39.

Silverstein, S. J., Nathan, P. E., & Taylor, H. A. Blood alcohol level estimation and controlled drinking by chronic alcoholics. *Behavior Therapy*, 1974, **5**, 1–15.

Sobell, L. C. Empirical assessment of alcoholism treatment evaluation: Past, present and future. In P. E. Nathan & G. A. Marlatt (Eds.), *Behavioral assessment and treatment of alcoholism*. New Brunswick: Rutgers Center for Alcohol Studies, in press.

Sobell, L. C., & Sobell, M. B. A self-feedback technique to monitor drinking behavior in alcoholics. *Behaviour Research and Therapy*, 1973, **11**, 237–238.

Sobell, L. C., & Sobell, M. B. Outpatient alcoholics give valid self-reports. *Journal of Nervous and Mental Disease*, 1975, **161**, 32–42.

Sobell, L. C., & Sobell, M. B. Driver records: An aid in follow-up tracking and verification of self-reports of alcoholics. *International Journal of the Addictions*, in press.

Sobell, L. C., VanderSpek, R., & Sobell, M. B. Unpublished data, Vanderbilt University, 1975.

Sobell, M. B., Schaefer, H. H., & Mills, K. C. Differences in baseline drinking behavior between alcoholics and normal drinkers. *Behaviour Research and Therapy*, 1972, **10**, 257–267.

Sobell, M. B., & Sobell, L. C. Individualized behavior therapy for alcoholics: Rationale, procedures, preliminary results and appendix. *California Mental Health Research Monograph, No.* 13, Sacramento, 1972.

Sobell, M. B., & Sobell, L. C. Alcoholics treated by individualized behavior therapy: One year treatment outcome. *Behaviour Research and Therapy*, 1973a, **11**, 599–618.

Sobell, M. B., & Sobell, L. C. Individualized behavior therapy for alcoholics. *Behavior Therapy*, 1973b, **4**, 49–72.

Sobell, M. B., & Sobell, L. C. A brief technical report on the Mobat: An inexpensive portable test for determining blood alcohol concentration. *Journal of Applied Behavior Analysis*, 1975a, **8**, 117–120.

Sobell, M. B., & Sobell, L. C. The need for realism, relevance and operational assumptions in the study of substance dependence. In H. D. Cappell & A. E. LeBlanc (Eds.), *Biological and behavioral approaches to drug dependence.* Toronto: Addiction Research Foundation, 1975b.

Sobell, M. B., & Sobell, L. C. Second year treatment outcome of alcoholics treated by individualized behavior therapy: Results. *Behavior Research and Therapy*, in press.

Sobell, M. B., Sobell, L. C., & Samuels, F. H. Validity of self-reports of alcohol-related arrests by alcoholics. *Quarterly Journal of Studies on Alcohol*, 1974, **35**, 276–280.

Spevack, M., Pihl, R., & Rowan, T. Behavior therapies in the treatment of drug abuse: Some case studies. *Psychological Record*, 1973, **23**, 179–184.

Steffen, J. J. Electromyographically induced relaxation in the treatment of chronic alcohol abuse. *Journal of Consulting and Clinical Psychology*, 1975, **43**, 275.

Stephens, R. The truthfulness of addict responses in research projects. *International Journal of the Addictions*, 1972, **7**, 549–558.

Terry, J., & Braumoeller, F. L. Nalline: An aid in detecting narcotic users. *California Medicine*, 1956, **85**, 299–308.

Tracey, D. A., Karlin, R. B., & Nathan, P. E. An experimental analysis of the behavior of female alcoholics. Paper presented at the 8th Annual Meeting of the Association for Advancement of Behavior Therapy, Chicago, November 1974.

Trellis, E. S., Smith, F. F., Alston, D. C., & Siassi, I. The pitfalls of urine surveillance: The role of research in evaluation and remedy. *Addictive Behaviors*, 1975, **1**, 83–88.

Voegtlin, W. L., & Lemere, F. The treatment of alcohol addiction: A review of the literature. *Quarterly Journal of Studies on Alcohol*, 1942, **2**, 717–803.

Vogler, R. E., Compton, J. V., & Weissbach, T. A. Integrated behavior change techniques for alcoholics. *Journal of Consulting and Clinical Psychology*, 1975, **43**, 233–243.

Williams, R. J., & Brown, R. A. Naming mixed drinks: Alcoholics vs. social drinkers. *Psychological Reports*, 1974, **35**, 33–34.

Wilson, G. T., Leaf, R. C., & Nathan, P. E. Aversive control of excessive alcohol consumption by chronic alcoholics in laboratory setting. *Journal of Applied Behavior Analysis*, 1975, **8**, 13–25.

CHAPTER 12

Assessment of Behavior of the Mentally Retarded

ALAN E. KAZDIN AND MARGARET KLEIS STRAW

The Pennsylvania State University

Introduction

Traditionally, conceptualizations of mental retardation have focused upon defects and deficits in the individual.[1] In some types of retardation, specific organic aberrations and diseases such as mongolism, phenylketonuria, congenital rubella, and others have been shown unambiguously to be associated with retarded development. However, in the majority of cases of retardation, organic anomalies are not actually detected. In these cases, physiological and psychological abnormalities and dysfunctions such as brain damage, learning disability, low mental functioning, and a host of other factors are hypothesized to account for retarded behavior. A common characteristic of hypothesized accounts of retarded behavior is that they focus on internal states of the individual. Behavior of the retardate is regarded as an inexorable result of these internal conditions or aberrations.

A major hypothetical construct that has been essential to the definition of retardation is intelligence. Intelligence is viewed as a mental ability that accounts for a wide range of behaviors across diverse situations. Level of tested intelligence has been used to classify individuals whose development is retarded and even to establish degrees of retardation (severely, profoundly, moderately, and mildly retarded). The implication of a classification schema heavily dependent upon intelligence is that individuals are assumed to have fixed ability levels. Indeed, it is likely that individuals have some upper limit on the level of functioning that can be achieved with respect to a given behavior. However, it is presumptuous to assume that test performance reflects these limits. As ordinarily used, tests of current performance are mistakenly assumed

[1]The term "mental retardation" in many ways violates the general approach advocated in the present chapter. The notion focuses on internal mental states rather than upon overt behavior. While aspects of "mental" development (e.g., intellective functioning) may be retarded, these are inferred from "behavioral" retardation, i.e., performance that lags behind normative levels on various tasks.

to reflect an individual's potential in a variety of situations (i.e., primarily those involving intellective or cognitive functioning). While test performance does predict performance on a variety of tasks, it does not necessarily provide a preview of the level of competence one can achieve as a function of concentrated training.

Despite theoretical debates about the actual and supposed etiologies of retarded development and about the criteria for classification, there is unified concern about what can be done to treat and to rehabilitate individuals whose behavior is retarded. The behavioral approach has attempted to provide a conceptualization of retarded behavior that is oriented toward designing effective treatment interventions (Gardner, 1971; Thorne, 1970). The approach focuses on environmental factors and learning experiences to explain how particular behaviors may have developed or have failed to develop (cf. Bijou, 1966).

From a treatment perspective, the behavioral approach concentrates on the *behaviors* that need to be changed and the *environmental conditions* that can be altered to effect change. Rather than focusing upon etiological considerations and internal states to which retardation might be attributed, the main interest is in current factors which can be utilized to alter behavior. The behavioral approach *is* concerned with causes of retarded behavior in the sense that current environmental events can be shown to relate causally to behavior change. However, this focus can be distinguished from a concern with original traumatic or chronic developmental events that led to the behavior.

The behavioral approach does not ignore physiological, psychological, or sociocultural determinants of retarded behavior. These determinants provide the limiting conditions in a person's physiological and environmental make up, presumably some of which cannot be overcome. For example, it may not be possible to train certain motor skills because of aberrations in gross anatomy or physiological functioning. Also, the effect of certain stimuli on behavior may be limited because of sensory or perceptual defects. Yet, physiological, psychological, and sociocultural impediments to development should not on *a priori* grounds be presumed to restrict performance under special conditions of training. As with intelligence, developmental abnormalities do not unambiguously specify the behavioral capabilities and limitations of a given individual.

It retardation is viewed from the standpoint of behavior rather than from unique physical and psychological characteristics, the role of general principles of behavior in rehabilitation becomes clearer. From a behavioral standpoint, the issue is not that the individual is retarded but only that his behavior in ordinary circumstances fails to attain normative levels (Lindsley, 1964). The focus of rehabilitation is to restructure the contingencies and perhaps other features of the environment to develop specific behaviors (Bijou, 1971).

Among the behavioral techniques available, those based upon operant conditioning have been relied upon heavily in programs for the mentally retarded. Using procedures based upon reinforcement, extinction, and punishment, diverse behaviors have been developed including grooming, toileting, walking, academic performance, language and speech, social interaction, job-related behaviors, and responsiveness to various stimuli (e.g., instructions, approval) in the environment (cf. Forehand & Baumeister, 1976; Gardner, 1971; Haring & Lovitt, 1967; Kazdin, 1975a; Kazdin & Craighead, 1973; Watson, 1967). The operant approach encompasses particular strategies of assessment, treatment, and experimental validation of treatment.

The present chapter focuses on the behavioral approach toward assessment in operant programs for the mentally retarded. The topics covered include the assessment of responses that are to be changed and of events in the environment that may influence those responses, strategies of assessing behavior, the criteria which dictate selection of a particular strategy, the reliability of assessment, and special considerations in assessing behaviors of the retarded. The general approach towards assessment and the specific methods described apply broadly to diverse client populations rather than to the retarded alone. Thus, to illustrate application of the methods with the retarded, behavioral programs that have focused exclusively on this population will be discussed. Examples of the assessment methods utilized across diverse behaviors altered in programs for the retarded will be detailed.

Behavioral Assessment

Behavior of the mentally retarded, and indeed other populations as well, has been viewed in terms of general categories such as behavioral deficits or excesses, socially aversive (undesirable) behaviors, problems of stimulus control, lack of responsiveness to events that ordinarily serve as reinforcers, and others (cf. Bandura, 1968; Bijou & Redd, in press; Ferster, 1965; Gardner, 1971). These categories provide a way of discussing behavior in general terms. The categories suggest how specific behavioral problems might have developed and the kinds of changes that need to be effected with treatment. For example, in the case of behavioral deficits such as lack of self-care, social, or language skills, an intervention must focus on developing new behaviors not previously in the repertoire of the client. In the case of behavioral excesses, such as excessive talking or aversive behaviors such as aggressive acts, the behavior must be decreased or eliminated altogether. For problems in stimulus control, such as unresponsiveness to instructions or responses performed at inappropriate times or places, behaviors must be developed in the presence of specific antecedent events. Finally, lack of responsiveness to events such as praise signals that treatment must focus on developing the reinforcing capacity of various stimuli, perhaps as a precondition for developing other behaviors.

From the standpoint of assessment and treatment, global categories of behavior are not sufficiently precise to be useful. The behavior that needs to be altered (i.e., the target behavior), must be carefully specified. Thus, the most important feature of the behavioral approach is overt response assessment.

Response Assessment

The purpose of assessing behaviors is three-fold. *First*, assessment reveals the extent to which the target behavior is performed. Assessment reflects performance prior to the intervention or treatment. The preprogram rate of behavior is often regarded as unnecessary because individuals familiar with the client attest to performance. Yet, reliance upon human judgment rather than upon objective assessment may distort the extent to which the behavior is actually performed. Human judgment or global impressions of behavior often do not correspond to the actual information obtained from assessing behavior objectively (cf. Kazdin, 1973d; Schnelle, 1974). Second, pretreatment assessment is always advisable because of the reactive nature of assessment. Mere observation of behavior may temporarily change behavior (Kazdin, 1974; Webb, Campbell, Schwartz & Sechrest, 1966). If assessment and treatment are introduced at the same point in time, it is impossible to determine whether behavior changes observed are the function of the assessment or of the program being instituted. A *third* reason that assessment of behavior is required is to reflect behavior change after treatment is implemented. Behavior during the program must be compared with the baseline level of performance. Thus, careful assessment is essential.

The selection of a target response is the initial step in developing a behavior modification program. This step is much more difficult than it might seem. Usually, there is a tendency to refer to response areas in global terms that are not appropriate for behavioral assessment. For example, clients will be referred to as having reading deficits, excessive aggressiveness, withdrawal, autistic behavior, and inadequate language skills. Global labels and ambiguous terms are inadequate for beginning assessment. Behavior needs to be described in terms so that few or no inferences are required to detect a response.

The initial response or responses to which the general labels refer must be observed carefully prior to deciding upon the response definition. Before developing the precise definition of behavior, the client can be observed informally. Notes of the behaviors that occur and the events associated with the behaviors can serve as a basis for the subsequent definition that will be used for assessment. For example, a retarded child who is labeled as unresponsive to others may, through an informal evaluation, appear to respond slowly to commands and instructions. The specific target behaviors (e.g., latency to respond to commands or compliance with instructions) serve to operationalize the global concept. These behaviors become the object of assessment and behavior change rather than the global concept.

Some examples of behavioral definitions derived from global concepts with the retarded illustrate the extent to which the responses must be operationalized. Repp & Dietz (1974) focused upon the aggressive and attacking behaviors of a 12-year old institutionalized retardate. The specific behaviors assessed included biting, hitting, scratching, and kicking others. Barton (1970) decreased inappropriate speech of a severely retarded institutionalized child. The child frequently gave random verbal responses that appeared unrelated to stimuli previously presented. To assess inappropriate speech, the client was asked questions about various pictures. Inappropriate responses were those that did not include answers pertaining to the content of the pictures. O'Brien, Azrin, & Bugle (1972) focused upon crawling with retarded children in a day-care nursery school program. Crawling was defined as uninterrupted movements across the floor for at least three seconds with the knees in contact with the floor. Redd (1969) altered the cooperative play of severely institutionalized children. Cooperative play was defined as manipulating a toy while in physical contact with another child. These descriptions show how the response can be defined concretely to conduct behavioral assessment.

As a general rule, a response definition should have three characteristics: objectivity, clarity, and completeness (Hawkins & Dobes, 1975). To be *objective*, the definition should refer to observable characteristics of behavior or environmental events. Definitions should not refer to inner states of the individual or to teleological terms which are not properties of the behavior itself. Thus, expressing anger, attempting to achieve a goal, or being hyperactive are not "responses" satisfactory for behavioral assessment. To be *clear*, the definition should be so unambiguous that it could be read, repeated, and paraphrased accurately. To be *complete*, the boundary conditions of the definition must be delineated so that the responses to be included and excluded are enumerated.

The completeness of the definition is a prerequisite to the objectivity of the response. If the range of responses included in the definition is not described carefully, observers have to infer whether the response has occurred. For example, consider an objective and clear target response such as waving one's hand to greet someone (cf. Stokes, Baer & Jackson, 1974). In most instances, when the individual's hand is fully extended and moving back and forth, there would be no difficulty in agreeing that the individual is waving. However, ambiguous instances may require judgments on the part of observers. For example, the child might move his hand once (rather than back and forth) while his arm is not extended, or move all fingers on one hand up and down as if to say good-bye. These latter responses are instances of waving to individuals who reciprocate with similar greetings. Yet, for assessment purposes, the response definition must specify whether these and related variations of waving are to be included.

In practice, completeness of a definition derives from applying the definition to the client's behavior on a preliminary basis and then making rules to handle ambiguous instances of scoring. For example, for the relatively simple response of waving, one would specify all the instances where the response is not obvious or requires judgment. For responses that are more complex such as verbal interaction, cooperative tasks, compliance with instructions, and creative writing or speaking, the boundary conditions become increasingly complex and increasingly important to specify.

The extent to which a response definition is objective, clear, and complete determines, in part, whether observers agree in scoring behavior. Also, these conditions determine whether the subject's behavior or the observers' judgments are changing over the course of a project (Baer, Wolf & Risley, 1968; Hawkins & Dotson, 1975). Precise criteria for a maximally objective, clear, and complete definition have not been specified. A rigorous test might be to provide two observers who are unfamiliar with the client, behavior, or setting with a written description of the target response. If, from the description alone, observers agree in scoring the response without communicating about the client's behavior, this would strongly suggest that the definition has met the criteria adequately (cf. Hawkins & Dobes, 1975).

Frequently, the behaviors of interest are complex and include several topographically distinct responses. It is not always essential to assess each behavior of interest. Indeed, practical constraints often limit the number of behaviors that can be assessed. Usually, staff members in an institution or rehabilitation setting are responsible for completing the assessment. Because of their time limitations, only one or a few responses can be observed at a given time.

Assessment and treatment of several behaviors simultaneously is not essential for another reason. Often altering one behavior influences other responses that are not focused upon directly (Kazdin, 1973c, 1975b). Responses topographically similar to the target response are altered. Behaviors that share similar components with the target response would be expected to change along with the target response (cf. Schick, 1971). For example, changing one social response (e.g., approaching other individuals) is likely to affect other responses as well (e.g., talking to others) (cf. Buell, Stoddard, Harris & Baer, 1968).

In some cases, altering one behavior is associated with changes in other behaviors that are topographically dissimilar. For example, reducing uncooperative child behavior in the home (not complying with commands, hitting, yelling, and so on) has been associated with a reduction in the frequency of bedwetting and stuttering even though these latter behaviors were not focused upon directly (Nordquist, 1971; Wahler, Sperling, Thomas, Teeter & Luper, 1970). Similarly, decreasing a boy's inappropriate talking at school was associated with an increase in social behavior, an increase in disruptive behavior, a decrease in attentive behavior in a group situation, and a decrease in the use of "girl's" toys (Sajwaj, Twardosz & Burke, 1972, Exp. 1). In addition, punishing self-stimulatory responses of children increased both the use of toys during free play and appropriate verbalizations (Epstein, Doke, Sajwaj, Sorrell & Rimmer, 1974). Topographically distinct behaviors sometimes go together or cluster across settings and over time for a given individual (Wahler, 1975). Thus, change in one behavior influences other behaviors with which it has been associated.

For purposes of assessment, the generalized effects of an intervention across behaviors not focused upon has two implications. Initially, various practical constraints may limit the number of responses that can be observed at one time. If several behaviors are of interest, only one or two of them may be assessed at a time. After these behaviors are focused upon, the others might then be altered. Of course, in some cases changes due to treatment of the target behavior may be so broad that the new behaviors no longer require an intervention. A second point is that if resources are available, multiple reponses might be assessed even if the focus is only on one or two responses (Kazdin, 1973c). Because the effects of an intervention sometimes are broad, other responses of interest can be assessed. The responses assessed should be determined by examining areas related to the client's adequate functioning in a given setting such as self-care, work, and academic skills, social interaction, verbalizations, and so on. These areas might reveal side effects of a given intervention and influence areas selected for subsequent treatment decisions.

Stimulus Assessment

Although the assessment of target responses is necessary, it is not always sufficient. Assessing stimulus events contributes to the program. Stimulus events, as discussed here, refer to antecedents and consequences that may be associated with a target behavior.

The assessment of stimulus events is important for two reasons. *First*, in many programs for the retarded treatment focuses on a response in relation to particular stimuli. Performing the target response *per se* may not be of interest unless some event has preceded it. For example, behaviors such as compliance to commands, instructions, or directions refer to responses in relation to particular antecedent events. Similarly, social responses such as cooperative behavior, conversation, and answering questions may be of interest only after other events have occurred. Thus, with many target responses, observation of stimulus events is an integral part of assessment.

In one sense, of course, the stimulus conditions are always important in a behavior program. Behavior change is always sought in some setting (e.g., classroom, ward, home) or in the presence of some individuals. Yet, assessment of stimulus conditions is only important when the conditions vary in a given setting and the responses of interest must be performed in relation to a particular aspect of the stimulus conditions.

A *second* reason for assessing stimuli associated with the target behavior pertains to the evaluation of the program. In programs for the mentally retarded, antecedent events and consequences are manipulated to alter behavior. Often, responses of individuals who influence the client's behavior such as attendants, parents, teachers, and peers are the antecedents and consequences that are manipulated. For example, in an institution, attendants may provide verbal statements (e.g., instructions or praise), gestures (e.g., physical contact, motions, or nonverbal directives), expressions (e.g., smiles, frowns), or tangible events (e.g., money) to alter behavior. Data on the delivery of these antecedent events and consequences, particularly if they are manipulated, are essential to evaluating the program.

The failure to observe events designed to alter a client's behavior can make the basis for behavior change unclear. For example, praise by a ward attendant may be used to alter a resident's social behavior (talking with others). If the attendant's behavior is not assessed, the causes of change in resident social interaction may be ambiguous. Unless the attendant's behavior is observed, whether his or her behavior changed in the intended direction is unknown. Moreover, if the resident's social behavior does not change this may have resulted from the attendant's failure to implement the intended contingency or from a failure of the correctly administered contingency to affect resident behavior. Observation of the target response and of the events manipulated to influence that response is essential to isolate the source of change.

Methods of Assessment

The methods of assessment refer to how observed responses are scored and converted into data. Assessment of behaviors of clients or of individuals who influence the clients can be achieved by different methods. The four strategies usually used in applied operant work include frequency, interval, duration, and the number of individuals who perform a response.

Frequency Measure

Frequency or the number of times that the response occurs in a given period is extremely simple to use because the observer merely tallies response occurrences. A frequency measure is usually used when the target response is discrete and has a relatively constant duration. A discrete response has a clear beginning and end, so that a distinct instance can be counted (Skinner, 1966). The response should consume a relatively constant amount of time so that the tallied units are comparable. Ongoing behaviors such as smiling, talking, resting, and studying usually are not easily recorded as frequencies because they are not sufficiently discrete or because their duration varies widely. For example, scoring talking with a frequency measure might be difficult because a given conversation may include long or short pauses in speech, interruptions of other individuals, whispers, and so on. Also, a person may speak to one individual for 10 seconds and to another individual continuously for several minutes. Because talking of this kind has no clear beginning or end unless precise definitions are given and because talking episodes may vary in duration, frequency measures might be inappropriate.

Frequency measures have been used for such diverse behaviors as the number of: correct academic responses (Harris & Sherman, 1974), aggressive acts (Horton, 1970), speech disfluencies (Kazdin, 1973a), self-abusive responses (Tanner & Zeiler, 1975), greeting responses (Kale, Kaye, Whelan & Hopkins, 1968), stealing episodes (Azrin & Wesolowski, 1974), units of work completed (Zimmerman, Overpeck, Eisenberg & Garlick, 1969), and epileptic seizures (Zlutnick, Mayville & Moffat, 1975), among others.

Frequency measures merely require noting response instances. Usually, behavior is observed for a constant amount of time each day (or session) so that the frequencies across days are directly comparable. Yet, constant time periods across days are not necessarily essential because frequency is easily converted into rate of responding (by dividing response frequency by minutes of observation). Response rates are comparable across different durations of observation.

Frequency measures have several advantages (cf. Bijou, Peterson & Ault, 1968; Skinner, 1953). *First*, response frequency is easily recorded by individuals who work in naturalistic settings (e.g., parents, teachers, ward attendants). Counting can be facilitated further by various devices, such as golf counters worn as wrist watches. *Second*, frequency measures readily reflect changes over time. Response frequency or rate is sensitive to alterations of the contingencies of reinforcement. The principles of operant conditioning are based upon changes in response frequency, so it is desirable to observe frequency or rate directly. *Third*, frequency expresses the amount of behavior, which is usually of concern to individuals in rehabilitation and educational settings. Interventions are implemented to decrease or increase the number of times a certain response occurs, so frequency provides a direct measure of most program goals.

Interval Recording

Assessment is often based upon units of time rather than upon discrete response units. One time-based method is used to record behavior during short intervals. Typically, interval recording samples behavior for a single block of time such as 30 or 60 minutes, once per day. The block of time is divided into shorter intervals (e.g., each interval equal to 10 or 15 seconds). During each interval of observation, the target response is scored as having occurred or not occurred. If a discrete behavior such as hitting someone occurs one or more times in a single interval, the response is scored merely as having occurred. Several response occurrences within an interval are not counted separately. If the behavior is ongoing with an unclear beginning and end, or occurs for a long period of time, it is scored in each interval in which it appears. Interval recording has been used for a variety of behaviors including appropriate mealtime responses (Barton, Guess, Garcia & Baer, 1970), social responses (O'Connor, 1969), and uncooperative child behavior in the home (Wahler, 1969). Investigations in special education and "normal" classroom settings have relied heavily upon interval recording to score whether students are working on classroom assignments, paying attention, sitting in their seats, and performing other appropriate classroom behaviors (cf. Kazdin, 1975a; O'Leary & O'Leary, 1972).

In one variation of interval recording, the intervals during which clients are observed are spread over periods throughout the day rather than occurring continuously for a single time block. This variation, sometimes referred to as *time sampling*, involves observing at several different moments separated in time. As with interval recording, behavior is classified as occurring or not occurring at a given time. Yet, time sampling scores the behavior on the basis of performance at the *end* of an interval rather than on the basis of performance throughout the interval. For example, whether individuals engage in the target response may be observed hourly. At the end of the hour, someone observes and records whether the target response is occurring. The observations are made again an hour later. Behavior occurring during the intervening period before the next observation is conducted is not assessed. Thus, the main differences between interval and time sampling methods is whether the periods of observation occur in immediate succession or are separated in time, and whether the period is scored on the basis of performance during the interval or at the end of the interval. (In some studies the distinction breaks down because some time (e.g., a few seconds) is allotted between intervals.) Time sampling has been used for scoring behaviors such as inactivity or social interaction (e.g., talking to, or working or playing with someone) (Milby, 1970; Schaefer & Martin, 1966).

Interval recording is probably the most frequently used strategy in applied behavior analysis. This strategy is widely used for at least four reasons. *First*, it is very flexible because any observable response can be recorded with this strategy. Whether a response is discrete, varies in duration, is continuous, or is sporadic, it can be classified as occurring or not occurring during a specific time interval. *Second*, several different responses can be scored simultaneously. During a given interval, an observer can score whether any of the several different responses has or has not occurred (cf. Hart, Reynolds, Baer, Brawley & Harris, 1968; Madsen, Becker & Thomas, 1968). *Third,* the results of interval scoring are easily communicated to others. The proportion of intervals in which the target response is performed can be converted into a percentage which provides a simple measure of the amount of the response. *Finally,* interval recording is consistent with the goal of many programs that attempt to increase the amount of time a response such as studying, working, and socializing is performed. The percentage of intervals in which the response occurs reflects this goal directly.

Duration

Another time-based method of observation is response duration. Duration is used for a target response that is continuous rather than one that is discrete or of exceedingly short time periods. For example, scoring an instance of greeting someone, making a gesture, or other acts that may be performed quickly are not usually amenable to duration measurement. Duration has been used for a variety of responses such as the amount of time individuals speak rationally (Liberman, Teigen, Patterson & Baker, 1973), remain in a situation in which they are afraid (Leitenberg, Agras, Thompson & Wright, 1968), spend returning from school and errands (Phillips, 1968), engage in play and social responses (Redd, 1969; Whitman, Mercurio & Caponigri, 1970), and work on classroom assignments (Surratt, Ulrich & Hawkins, 1969).

Assessment of response duration merely requires starting and stopping a stop-watch or noting the time at which a response begins and ends. If the beginning and end of the response are not carefully defined, duration is difficult to measure. For example, a child may cry continuously for several minutes, whimper, whine, or moan for short periods, cease all noises for a few seconds, and begin intense crying again. To handle changes in the intensity of responses (e.g., crying to whining) and pauses (e.g., periods of silence), a decision has to be reached whether they are included in or excluded from the response definition.

Response duration is appropriate where the goal is to increase or decrease the length of time a response lasts. In most programs, the goal is to increase or decrease the frequency of a response rather than its duration. Even when the goal is to alter response duration, interval recording is often selected because it is so flexible.

Number of Individuals

In some rehabilitation programs, the number of individuals who perform a given response is assessed. The measure does not analyze the individual client's response. Each individual is scored as having performed or not having performed the response. Counting the number of individuals is a discrete measure that is easily recorded. It has been used in a number of situations where the goal is to increase the number of individuals who perform a response in a group situation. For example, investigators have assessed the number of individuals who use eating utensils rather than their hands to eat (Ayllon & Azrin, 1964), brush their teeth (Lattal, 1969), participate in or attend various activities (Colman & Boren, 1969; Miller & Miller, 1970), and complete homework (Harris & Sherman, 1974).

Generally, the number of individuals, as a measure of program effectiveness, is not ideally suited to treatment and rehabilitation where the careful analysis of individual behavior is important. As noted earlier, operant principles are directed at frequency of a given individual's responses. Performance of the individual, however, is lost when the number of individuals is used as a measure of behavior change. Whether the number of individuals who engage in a response is measured depends upon the goal of the program.

Criteria for Selecting an Assessment Method

Selecting an assessment method is dictated by such factors as the goals of the program, the behaviors observed, the rate of responding, the ease with which the response can be detected, and a variety of practical exigencies. Two major considerations are the characteristics of behavior and practical resources available for observation. The characteristics of the behavior usually make one or two of the strategies particularly appropriate. For example, behaviors such as responding to an instruction, taking a spoonful of food without spilling, headbanging, and attending an activity are discrete responses and are easily observed with a frequency measure. In contrast, behaviors such as talking, engaging in a tantrum, and working on a job are ongoing events and are more likely to be assessed by interval or duration measures. Although some behaviors are more or less well suited to a particular strategy of assessment, usually more than one method is available.

A second consideration which dictates the assessment strategy is pragmatic. The strategy used often depends upon the resources available to assess behavior. The strategy has to be convenient, so that teachers or attendants in a classroom or institution can easily incorporate assessment into their routine activities. As noted earlier, the frequency method of assessment usually is the easiest strategy to use. However, it is sometimes difficult to ensure that staff assesses behavior and records each occurrence, particularly in a situation where there is a low staff-client ratio. Thus, to ensure that behavior is assessed, one may use a time-sampling procedure where the client is checked periodically and behavior is recorded as occurring or not occurring at specific points in time.

Even though the behavior could be readily assessed with a frequency measure, the time-sampling procedure might be used to ensure that staff members regularly assess the behavior. Each staff member could have specific preselected times that he or she was assigned to observe behavior for a short period (e.g., 2 minutes). The different times spread across several staff members would make assessment relatively easy. Also, any assessment period that was missed could easily be traced to a specific staff member so that failure to observe could be readily corrected.

Interobserver Agreement (or Reliability)

In some programs with the retarded, the target response is recorded automatically and mechanically. Automatic recordings minimize or eliminate human judgment from scoring the response. A variety of devices have been used such as automatic signaling devices that detect toileting accidents (Azrin & Foxx, 1971), circuits to record work performance and job completion (Schroeder, 1972), stabilimetric devices attached to one's seat to record movements related to attentive behavior (Edelson & Sprague, 1974), a scale to weigh the amount of work completed (Logan, Kinsinger, Shelton & Brown, 1971), a sound-level meter to record noise level (Schmidt & Ulrich, 1969), and others. The advantage of automated devices derives not only from their convenience but also from their precision. In the absence of human observers to record behavior, the consistency with which behavior is observed is maximized by automated data collection. Yet, the majority of programs with the retarded rely on human observers to record behavior. Typically, an observer scores a client's behavior using one of the methods described earlier. Although the observer adheres to a prespecified code, scoring behavior requires that the observer make judgments about the occurrence of the response. The diversity of responses observed and altered in rehabilitation and educational settings usually precludes automated recording. Thus, the extent to which behavior is observed consistently by observers is a major issue.

Independently of the assessment method selected, steps need to be taken to ensure that the behaviors are recorded consistently. To assess the consistency with which observations are made, two observers must simultaneously but independently record behavior for a given client on some occasions. Interobserver agreement or reliability of measurement is central in assessing and evaluating behavior-change programs for two reasons. Initially, agreement reflects the extent to which the target response is well defined. Lack of agreement can signify that the response definition is unclear or incomplete and that the behavior must be redefined. Thus, the extent of agreement achieved is, in part, a test of the adequacy of the response definition.

Interobserver agreement also is important to determine whether the client's behaviors are observed accurately. With low agreement, the data may differ greatly depending upon who is scoring behavior. Variation in the data due to the observer adds to any variability in client behavior and obscures actual performance. Evaluating the intervention depends upon data that are relatively stable. Measurement error contributes to variability and makes subsequent evaluation more difficult than would otherwise be the case. Indeed, if the variability due to assessment error is extremely large, establishing a stable baseline rate of behavior and evaluating the intervention may be delayed.

Methods of Calculating Reliability

Reliability provides an estimate of observers' agreement in scoring behavior. To estimate reliability, at least two observers are required who simultaneously score a given individual's behavior. Their scores are compared to determine the extent of agreement. Separate methods of calculating agreement may be distinguished depending on the strategy of assessment employed (Kazdin, in press).

Total Frequency, Number of Individuals, and Duration. When frequency, the number of individuals, or response duration is assessed, a comparison is usually made between the totals of the observations of each observer for an observation period. For a frequency measure (or a tally of the number of individuals), observer agreement is assessed by computing the extent to which observers agree on the total count for a given observation period. Often the two observers do not agree perfectly in the totals. Agreement is computed by dividing the smaller total by the larger total. The proportion usually is multiplied by 100 to form a percentage. For example, two attendants might count the frequency of aggressive responses for an institutionalized retardate in a 1-hour period. One observer may obtain a total of 10 responses while the other might record 8 responses for the same time period. Dividing the smaller number (8) by the larger number (10) and multiplying by 100 yields 80% agreement on the total frequency. (When the number of individuals who perform a response is counted, the same formula is applied.)

Agreement on the total frequency does not indicate that observers agree a given percentage of the time. The percentage is deceptive in that it is possible for observers not to record the same response and yet have high total frequency agreement. Because there is no assurance that the observers agree on specific instances, high agreement on the total may be achieved without consistent agreement on response occurrences.

When response duration is assessed, calculation of agreement is similar to that of frequency assessment. Two observers record response duration in a given session. The shorter duration is divided by the longer duration and multiplied by 100 to form a percentage. Agreement so calculated refers to the total time (accumulated on a timer or stop watch) rather than to identical scoring at any given moment in time. If duration is used for an ongoing response and the watch or time is not repeatedly turned on and off, the likelihood of disagreement at any given point in time is probably minimal.

Interval-by-Interval Agreement. With interval or time-sampling assessment strategies, reliability is calculated differently from that of total frequency. With interval assessment, the extent to which observers agree interval-by-interval can be calculated. Agreement is usually computed by determining the number of intervals upon which two observers agree on the occurrence of the target response (Bijou *et al.*, 1968). An agreement is counted if the two observers record the response as occurring in the same interval. Disagreement is counted for a given interval when one observer scores a response as occurring and the other does not. Reliability equals the number of agreements divided by the number of agreements plus disagreements, multiplied by 100. For example, two observers who record study behavior for 100 10-second intervals in a classroom situation may achieve 40 agreements and 10 disagreements. Reliability would be $40/(40 + 10) \times 100$ or 80% agreement. Agreement refers to the percentage of identical intervals that the observers scored the response.

Level of Agreement

Agreement between observers has to reach an acceptable level before and throughout data collection. No single criterion for an acceptable level of agreement can be stated formally. The level required in a given program depends upon many factors such as the variability of the observed behavior, the strength of the intervention, and the frequency of responding. For example, an intervention that drastically changes behavior may be only partially obscured by fluctuations in the data from inconsistent observations. In contrast, weak effects of an intervention might be completely hidden by only moderately unreliable recording.

Although no universal criterion for agreement can be set, convention dictates that agreement should fall between 80 and 100%. Reliability lower than 80% suggests moderate error in recording that calls for training observers more thoroughly or clarifying the response definition. Although the majority of reliability estimates in the literature fall within the above range, the actual consistency of observations probably is substantially lower. Agreement between observers depends upon the conditions under which reliability is assessed. Many of the conditions, such as observer awareness that reliability is assessed and working with an observer with whom idiosyncratic definitions of behavior may have developed, can inflate reliability. For an extended discussion of reliability and sources of bias that can influence reliability assessment several other sources may be consulted (Bijou *et al.*, 1968; Hersen & Barlow, 1976; Johnson & Bolstad, 1973; Kazdin, 1976; Lipinski & Nelson, 1974; O'Leary & Kent, 1973).

Responses Focused Upon with the Mentally Retarded

The methods of assessment apply widely across treatment populations. Thus, it is important to illustrate the behavioral focus of programs with the mentally retarded and the methods used to assess their behavior. The behaviors focused upon in programs for the retarded vary widely depending upon the setting in which the program is conducted (e.g., institution, daycare facility, classroom, sheltered workshop, or the home) and the level of functioning of the individual at the time the program is begun. Behaviors commonly focused upon with the retarded include self-care, classroom behaviors, verbal responsiveness and language development, social responses, work-related behaviors, and disruptive behaviors. The present section samples select studies in each of these areas to illustrate the methods of assessment that are used.

Self-Care

Teaching self-care skills to the severely and profoundly retarded has been the focus of much behavioral research. The skills most commonly taught include toileting, feeding, grooming, and ambulation. Diverse methods have been used to assess these behaviors.

Azrin & Foxx (1971) used automated procedures to develop appropriate toileting by having individuals wear training pants which set off an alarm when wet and by putting fixtures in toilets that signalled successful toileting. The number of accidents was assessed by having an attendant check hourly whether pants were wet or dry for 8 hours a day. During the training phase of the study, all accidents were signalled and could be recorded as they occurred. During post training and a long-term follow-up, attendants again checked each subject regularly.

An interesting and somewhat indirect method of assessment was used to evaluate the effects of another operant toilet-training program (Dayan, 1964). Although the training procedure appeared to be effective, no direct supporting data were gathered. However, Dayan reasoned that if the toilet training had been successful, the amount of laundry cleaned for the cottage in which the new technique had been used would have decreased. Since the institution recorded the number of pounds of laundry cleaned for each unit each month, it was possible to compare amount of laundry cleaned before and after the introduction of the program. A reduction in laundry was associated with the toilet-training program.

Another self-care behavior often focused upon is feeding. O'Brien, Bugle & Azrin (1972) worked with a 6-year old profoundly retarded child who ate with her hands and spilled a great deal of food. A program was devised to develop appropriate eating responses, operationally defined as taking food from her plate, using a spoon, and putting the food in her mouth without spilling it. Each response was recorded as correct or incorrect. Similarly, Nelson & Hanson (1975) focused on correct handling of utensils. They recorded correct utensil, incorrect utensil, and other behavior using a time-sampling procedure.

Barton *et al.* (1970) also attempted to improve mealtime behavior in a retarded population. They developed a checklist of frequently occurring categories of mealtime behavior including stealing, eating with fingers, messy utensils, neat utensils, "pigging," and other behaviors. Subjects were observed six to twelve times per meal until one of the defined behaviors occurred or until 10 seconds had elapsed. Data were presented in terms of the percentage of occurrences of each class of behaviors.

O'Brien *et al.* (1972) reported an interesting program for increasing walking in profoundly retarded children. The children were coaxed across the room by trainers with candy. During training, the children were restrained if they crawled and later were also primed to walk. That is, after restraint, the trainer raised the child to his feet. Two observers in separate observation rooms depressed a button for the duration of each response. Data were presented in terms of both crawling as percentage of total time in locomotion and as mean number of crawls.

The methods of assessment of self-care skills vary greatly according to the target behavior. They have ranged from almost completely automated techniques as in toilet training to simple checklists as in feeding. The common element in this area is that most of the behaviors lend themselves to careful operational definition and, as such, are relatively straightforward to assess.

Classroom Behavior

Many training programs and institutions for the mentally retarded provide classroom instruction. These programs may focus on practical activities such as telling time, making change, and other basic living skills or upon attending to the session, working on an assignment, or completing tasks in specific subject areas.

The majority of the classroom studies with retardates have focused on attending or on-task behavior (cf. Baker, Stanish & Fraser, 1972; Broden, Bruce, Mitchell, Carter & Hall, 1970; Dalton, Rubino & Hislop, 1973; Kazdin, 1973b; Osborne, 1969; Zimmerman, Zimmerman & Russell, 1969). In these studies, child behavior typically is observed with an interval assessment strategy in which attentive behavior is scored as occurring or not occurring across several intervals. For example, Kazdin & Klock (1973) observed educably retarded children in a classroom for fifty 15-second intervals and classified their behavior as attentive or inattentive. To meet the criteria of on-task behavior, the child who was observed had to be attentive for the entire interval. Any off-task time caused the interval to be classified as inattention. In this study, the teacher's contingent verbal and nonverbal approval was also recorded by the same interval procedure.

In one of the few automated procedures used to measure attending, Edelson & Sprague (1974) had children sit on stabilimetric cushions which had built-in microswitches that measured any movement of 1.6 mm or more. The movement closed the circuit and automatically advanced the counter. If no movements were recorded during a 30-second interval, a rear light on the child's chair flashed to signal that he had earned two pennies. After every 30-second period the teacher recorded the number of movements for each subject and reset the counter.

Aside from on-task behavior, investigators have focused upon mastery of specific academic tasks. Knapczyk & Livingston (1973) measured accuracy of performance on a reading task in a junior high school class of educably retarded students by simply having teachers grade and record all classroom exercises during a token reinforcement program designed to increase reading skill.

Many subjects taught to the retarded emphasize practical areas rather than traditional academic tasks. For example, Wunderlich (1972) used automated instruction on the identification of coinage and coin equivalencies for retarded children enrolled in a day-care program. Children worked at a programmable panel which presented master slides of coins and slides of correct and incorrect monetary equivalents. Correct responses (identifying the slides which were monetarily equivalent to the master slides) were automatically reinforced with candy. The numbers of correct and incorrect responses were automatically recorded.

In a practical classroom exercise, Clark, Boyd & Macrae (1975) taught six mildly retarded and/or delinquent teenagers how to fill out nine basic items found on most job application forms including phone number, birthdate, and other personal information. Assessment was accomplished by giving subjects unfamiliar applications to complete after various phases of training. Each response was scored as correct, attempted but incorrect, or not attempted.

As with self-care, many behaviors of interest in the classroom have been quite amenable to behavioral assessment. The major behaviors of interest are acedemic performance or completion of some practical tasks. The percentage of correct responses on the task (e.g., reading comprehension, arithmetic problems, printing letters) is used to reflect behavior change.

Verbal Responsiveness and Language Development

A wide range of behaviors related to language have been focused upon with the retarded. The behaviors have ranged from developing responsiveness to instructions to training receptive and productive language.

In an effort to develop very basic instruction-following skills in the severely and profoundly retarded, Kazdin & Erickson (1975) reinforced the completion of components of a simple ball play activity upon instruction. Scores of zero to three were assigned to behaviors ranging from failing to sit when instructed to catching the ball and rolling it back to the instructor. In those cases when the child had to be physically guided to complete the task, the response was not scored as complete.

An interesting variation in the assessment of instruction following was developed in a study with an 8-year-old boy who had not yet completed first grade (Fjellstedt & Sulzer, 1973). The boy had academic difficulty because he responded extremely slowly to instructions. During daily sessions, the experimenters instructed him to perform school-related tasks such as putting work materials away or starting to work, and recorded response latency as the dependent measure. The child was reinforced for decreasing the duration of inappropriate responding.

Zimmerman, Zimmerman & Russell (1969) used a token program to increase instruction following in a group of seven retarded children. A list of 30 instructions ranging from pointing to one's nose to drawing geometric figures or counting was prepared. Observers merely tallied the number of instructions that were correctly followed.

A large number of programs for the retarded have focused upon language acquisition. Diverse responses have been developed such as the use of verbs, plural nouns, past and present tenses, adjectives, subject-verb agreement, question asking, and others (e.g., Baer & Guess, 1971; Barton, 1970; Guess, Sailor, Rutherford & Baer, 1968; Lutzker & Sherman, 1975; Martin, 1975; Peine, Gregerson & Sloane, 1970; Schumaker & Sherman, 1970; Twardosz & Baer, 1973). Typically, authors record correct responses in the presence of various stimuli designed to evoke the target response. For example, Guess (1969) developed receptive language in two 13-year-old Mongoloid males. Subjects were taught to discriminate singular and plural words and to respond by pointing to pictures of one or more of the appropriate stimulus items. Responses were recorded as correct or incorrect for each trial.

Another aspect of language training is the elimination of inappropriate speech. For example, Kazdin (1971) used response cost (withdrawal of tokens) to suppress a retarded woman's talking to herself while working. Instances of talking to herself aloud were recorded for approximately four hours daily. Butz & Hasazi (1973) used differential reinforcement of other behavior to eliminate perseverative speech in a retarded boy. The behavior was assessed by scoring whether perseverative speech occurred in a 30-second recording interval across 40 intervals per session. The percentage of intervals containing perseverative speech was then calculated.

Social Responses

Social response deficits such as lack of or minimal social interaction and the absence of cooperative play frequently distinguish retarded persons. Despite the importance of social behaviors with retarded subjects, relatively few studies have focused on the wide range of skills that might be included here.

To teach a greeting response (handwaving), Stokes *et al.* (1974) reinforced retarded children for waving when the trainer came within 3 feet of the children. Greetings to the trainers were classified as spontaneous, prompted, or incorrect. After training in different locations with two trainers, individuals not involved in training approached the subjects to test for generalization. Data were presented in terms of the correct percentage of greeting responses. After varying amounts of training across trainers, the responses generalized to other individuals.

Kazdin & Polster (1973) increased the frequency of social interactions during work breaks among two adult male retardates in a sheltered workshop. At the end of each break, each client received a token for each person with whom he had conversed. The number of individuals with whom each client conversed changed as a function of token reinforcement.

Redd (1969) developed a program to increase cooperative play in two retarded boys and also to evaluate the degree to which the boys' behavior came under stimulus control of the reinforcing agent. Observers recorded entrance and exit of the adult who administered reinforcement, occurrence of cooperative play, and delivery of reinforcement on a multiple-pen event recorder. The final data were presented in cumulative time units of cooperative play. These data could also have been converted to frequency to cooperative play by, counting each onset of play as recorded on the event recorder.

Other authors in the area have studied smiling (Hopkins, 1968; Reisinger, 1972), and cooperative play (Redd, 1970; Redd & Birnbrauer, 1969; Whitman *et al.*, 1970). Most data have been obtained as frequency or duration of the response.

Work-Related Behavior

For the mildly retarded client, treatment often focuses on work-related behaviors. Many behaviors taken for granted in industry have been developed with the retarded such as punctuality, consistent work attendance, and job productivity.

Production rate has been focused upon almost exclusively as a dependent measure. Under laboratory conditions, Evans & Spradlin (1966) compared production rates under salaried versus piece-rate systems. Using an electronic programmable panel, plunger-pulling responses were automatically recorded. Tokens (backed by pennies) were given after every five pulls on the plunger in the piece rate condition and noncontingently in the salaried condition.

In a series of experiments varying the parameters of reinforcement, Schroeder (1972) used a unique automated procedure to assess productivity of six adult retardates. The tools (such as soldering irons and wire cutters) used to complete the assigned tasks were wired so that a circuit was completed whenever they were appropriately used. Because the assigned tasks were relatively simple (e.g., cutting wires into prescribed lengths), a single response always indicated completion of the task and could be automatically recorded to give an exact frequency count of the units completed.

Other authors have developed automated devices to record production rates (Cotter, 1971; Greene & Hoats, 1969; Screven, Strata & LaFond, 1971; Tate, 1968). Automated recording has the advantages of being completely reliable, not requiring human observers for long periods of observation, and permitting the programming of consequences for specified response units. However, because of the expense involved and the difficulty in adapting many tasks to automated recording, authors have relied heavily upon human observers. Sometimes frequency data can be gathered using other measures. For example, Logan *et al.* (1971) reinforced mildly retarded adolescent males with praise or money to increase productivity at a drill press. Productivity was measured by the number of rivets drilled. Because counting would be a lengthy and tedious procedure, the rivets were weighed after each work period and converted from weight to numbers via a conversion table.

Work behavior has also been assessed with a duration measure. Bateman (1975) reinforced a lower preference task (e.g., winding wool into balls, plug assembly), with higher preference task (e.g., sewing bathmats, sealing bags). Productivity was assessed by recording total time spent on each task and on irrelevant behaviors for two retarded adults. Of course, this measure is not a direct assessment of completion of work units but might be useful in situations where rate *per se* is not as crucial as the manner in which work is performed.

Zimmerman, Stuckey, Garlick & Miller (1969) reinforced productivity of retardates in a sheltered workshop (for assembling and packing Western Electric terminal boards). After a box of units was filled, the subject marked his production sheet and turned it in to a handler who also recorded its completion. The supervisor compared these two work records at the end of each day. In most cases, a system similar to this could be easily adapted to workshop and industry programs. Not only would careful records insure accuracy of recording, but they would also provide daily feedback on production rate for the worker, which might increase his production rate in and of itself (cf. Jens & Shores, 1969).

Disruptive Behaviors

Disruptive behaviors are frequently focused upon, particularly among institutionalized retardates. These behaviors may range from tantrums and verbal abuse of staff to serious aggressive acts directed toward others or oneself (cf. Forehand & Baumeister, 1976; Smolev, 1971). Decreasing disruptive behavior often is a prior condition to developing adaptive behaviors. Self-destructive behaviors such as head banging, limb biting, gouging, or nail and hair pulling have received considerable attention.

Lovaas & Simmons (1969) recorded both duration and frequency of self-destructive behaviors for three institutionalized retarded children. A multiple-pen event recorder was used to record each occurrence of the target behavior as well as withdrawal and whining during the punishment (shock contingent on hitting) phase of the study. Corte, Wolf & Locke (1971) also decreased the frequency of self-injurious behaviors including slapping, hair pulling, hand chewing, and face gouging in four retarded institutionalized adolescents. Both differential reinforcement of other behaviors (food reinforcement after 15-seconds of no self-destructive behavior) and shock were used to control these behaviors. Response frequency was used as the assessment strategy.

Aggressive acts toward others have also been focused upon with the retarded. Clark, Rowbury, Baer & Baer (1973) used time out (at least 3 minutes in an isolation booth) to control choking and armwraps, other attacks on people such as pouncing on them, and destruction of equipment in an 8-year-old mongoloid girl. An interval assessment strategy was used. The occurrence or nonoccurrence of these behaviors was recorded for 10-second intervals over a one and one-half hour recording session.

Vukelich & Hake (1971) also used time out to control aggression in an 18-year-old 170 pound retarded female who was continually restrained prior to the program. Frequency of choking and grabbing was recorded by the experimenter or an aide during each of four nonrestrained 45-minute sessions per day, as was the time of occurrence and the name of the person toward whom the attack was directed. Whenever the target behavior occurred the subject was restrained in a chair in the day room and the session was terminated.

An interesting assessment method was used with a 58-year-old retarded wheel chair patient who was extremely loud and abusive on the ward (Bostow & Bailey, 1969). Vocal responses were automatically recorded on a voice-operated portable tape recorder. Whenever the noise level went above a predetermined threshold, the recorder was activated and produced a distinctive sound on the tape. After sessions were complete, observers listened to the tapes and merely counted the number of sounds on the tapes indicating an above threshold noise level. Thus, a target behavior which would have been difficult to quantify subjectively was easily objectified.

Burchard & Barrera (1972) recorded frequency of a variety of target behaviors ranging from swearing to personal assault in a group of mildly retarded males. They included the practical feature of having the aide and the subject fill out forms giving information on the time of the incident, the behavior being punished, and the punishment given (either a fine of 5 to 30 tokens or time out of 5 to 30 minutes). At the end of each day, aide and subject forms could be compared to provide interjudge agreement data.

Considerations in Assessing Behaviors of the Retarded

As noted earlier, the methods of behavioral assessment do not apply uniquely to the retarded. The methods refer to techniques of assessing behavior and apply independently of the specific overt behavior assessed and the population treated. However, applying these methods across diverse behaviors and populations is not always associated with the same obstacles and problems. Assessment of retarded behavior sometimes requires special considerations because of the characteristics of the target behavior or of the program. Two general considerations that arise in many programs for the retarded are the effects of observing low rates of responding and the impact of shaping some terminal response.

Low Rate of Responding. Many behaviors developed with the retarded may initially occur at an extremely low rate or not at all. Behaviors such as attending to a task, working on a job, grooming, interacting socially, and others may not be in the repertoire of the client and need to be developed. Low rates of responding can present practical problems in both the selection of an assessment strategy and the design of treatment interventions. Indeed, as noted earlier, sometimes actual assessment is preceded by informal observation, so that the investigator can select the strategy best suited to the behavior. If the behavior is rarely performed, there might be some difficulty in deciding the best way to measure it. For example, if the goal is to increase talking to peers and the individual does not talk at all, some measure must be selected without the benefit of seeing in advance the communication patterns of this individual.

In many cases, the low frequency target response is a behavior that needs to be eliminated. For example, in institutional or classroom settings, fighting is often a response investigators wish to change. From the standpoint of assessment, the problem with fighting is that it may occur infrequently, but when it occurs its consequences can be severe. It is often difficult to assess fighting in such a way as to establish a clear rate of behavior. The relatively low rate at which fighting usually occurs makes it difficult to reflect behavior change in the program. The low base-rate data do not provide a level upon which change can be clearly shown for a given client.

There is another problem associated with low rates of responding that warrants mention. It is sometimes difficult to assess interobserver agreement when the target behavior occurs infrequently. For example, if observers record attentive behavior on an interval assessment method, only a small proportion of intervals of attentive behavior may be scored. If there is only one interval of attentive behavior out of 100 intervals observed, agreement between observers (given the formula provided earlier for interval reliability) could only be 0% or 100%. Low rates of responding do not provide a sample of the behaviors upon which interjudge agreement can be adequately based (cf. Hawkins & Dotson, 1975; Kazdin, in press).

The frequent need to focus on responses of relatively low rates in retardates need not impede assessment or behavioral intervention. Whether the low frequency behavior is to be increased (e.g., appropriate feeding) or decreased (e.g., aggressive acts), usually some related response that has a higher frequency can be assessed to avoid problems associated with low frequency response assessment. For example, if the purpose of the program is to eliminate fighting, other responses can be observed such as cooperative social interaction, aggressive verbalizations that usually precede fighting, arguments and, similar behaviors that probably occur at a higher frequency than the low frequency target response. Fighting can still be observed. Yet, the effect of the program on other responses can be evaluated as well. (Although beyond the scope of the present chapter, there would be treatment benefits of focusing upon some prosocial behavior that could be reinforced rather than merely eliminating fighting. The focus of treatment would be on increasing some existing response that eventually could occur at a high rate rather than on low frequency fighting [cf. Kazdin, 1975a].)

Shaping and Behavioral Assessment. An obstacle in behavioral assessment of retardates sometimes may occur when behaviors have to be shaped. In developing behaviors to overcome a response deficit, a response definition is selected. The response definition usually is based upon the terminal goal. For example, in developing self-care behaviors such as dressing oneself, the response of interest may be dressing oneself completely in the morning and perhaps changing into nighttime attire in the evening. Observations would sample two periods (morning and evening) and indicate whether the individual dressed or not. Alternatively, the number of garments (e.g., shirt, socks, shoes) put on without the aid of an attendant may be recorded. If a client does not dress him or herself at all, it is difficult to assess *any* behavior at the early stage of a treatment program. Even if the program is progressing, it is difficult to see change in the data because the response has to be shaped. For example, in scoring whether the garment is put on without assistance, the client is likely to be scored as not putting on a particular garment by himself for several sessions even after training has begun. However, a shaping procedure may be used to develop components of the response (e.g., putting an arm through the sleeve). From the standpoint of assessment, the problem is that progress may be made as the behavior is shaped although this is not reflected in the data until training has advanced considerably.

When a response has to be shaped, as is often the case in developing skills with the retarded, it is important to delineate the components of the response both from the standpoint of assessment and treatment (cf. Horner & Keilitz, 1975). Thus, to record dressing behavior where the terminal response must be shaped, the components of dressing should be assessed, rather than the overall response of dressing or not dressing. For example, for putting on each garment, subcomponents might be delineated such as picking up the garment, placing it over one's head, pulling the head through, putting one arm through, and so on. The component responses can be quantified so that, for example, a point is given for each correct component completed. Shaping can focus on the components as needed for any individual subject or garment. However, the data will reflect the stage of progress generally to a greater extent than a dichotomous rating of whether the individual dressed appropriately or placed a given garment on correctly.

With many responses, shaping presents no particular problem from the standpoint of assessment because the terminal response merely represents *more* of the early responses already in the client's repertoire. For example, for attending to a task, shaping merely focuses upon increasing the amount of time spent attending. The final response resembles the components that were shaped so the same measure is easily used to reflect progress toward the terminal goal and attainment of the goal. However, the other responses, shaping must develop behaviors that will no longer be in the response repertoire once the final goal is achieved. For example, in developing complex speech, early sounds (e.g., pronunciation of components of a word) that are reinforced differ from the terminal goal. When the terminal goal is achieved, (e.g., speaking in sentences), the early components are no longer present as specific response units. Assessment must be designed so that progress can be reflected while shaping is conducted before the final target response is achieved.

Conclusion

Behavioral assessment is designed specifically to meet the requirements of a given client and treatment program. There is no single method to assess particular behaviors. There are no inventories of retarded behavior that are routinely used when specific areas such as self-care skills, language acquisition, social interaction, and other areas are focused upon in behavior modification. Behaviors given the same label (e.g., aggressive acts) may differ widely across individuals. Thus, generically one must speak of assessment strategies rather than measures of specific behaviors. The measures described were frequency, interval, duration, and number of individuals performing some response. The method selected depends upon characteristics of the response for a given client and upon demands of the setting in which the individual is functioning. Typically, more than one strategy can easily be adopted to assess the particular response. Thus, the investigator can make decisions on the basis of practical constraints that abound when working in applied settings.

Several examples of programs with the retarded were outlined. These examples illustrated the flexibility of behavioral observation. Any given method of observation can be applied to any of the response categories focused upon with the retarded. In some cases, the responses are observed through some automated means. More commonly, human observers are involved in judging whether the behavior was performed. The use of human observers, of course, introduces a source of variation into the data that must be checked. Assessment of interjudge agreement, in part, determines the consistency with which these observations are conducted.

Assessment of retarded behavior presents relatively few unique problems. The problems in assessment result from specific characteristics of behavior rather than from individuals who are labeled retarded. Two areas in which problems sometimes arise in assessment of retarded behavior were addressed briefly, namely, assessment of responses with low rates and of component responses when a terminal response has to be shaped. While these problems may arise in programs for the retarded, they occur as a function of response characteristics or of the program focus rather than the population.

Behavioral assessment represents a way to evaluate treatment interventions, in general. Obviously, the methods of assessment have been used extensively to evaluate programs where the treatment interventions are based upon behavior modification. It is somewhat unfortunate that the methods of evaluation are commonly seen as inextricably bound with substantive positions about treatment strategies. Although there is some basis for such connections, the methods detailed in the present chapter need not be restricted to behavioral interventions. The goal of most training programs for the retarded is to alter some behavior. This is the goal independently of the orientation selected for designing treatments. Behavioral assessment may prove to be a useful adjunct to determine whether treatment is having a direct impact on behavior independently of the treatment used.

References

Ayllon, T., & Azrin, N. H. Reinforcement and instructions with mental patients. *Journal of the Experimental Analysis of Behavior*, 1964, **7**, 327–331.

Azrin, N. H., & Foxx, R. M. A rapid method of toilet training the institutionalized retarded. *Journal of Applied Behavior Analysis*, 1971, **4**, 89–99.

Azrin, N. H., & Wesolowki, M. D. Theft reversal: An overcorrection procedure for eliminating stealing by retarded persons. *Journal of Applied Behavior Analysis*, 1974, **7**, 577–581.

Bandura, A. A social learning interpretation of psychological dysfunctions. In P. London, & D. Rosenhan (Eds.), *Foundations of abnormal psychology*. New York: Holt, Rinehart & Winston, 1968.

Baer, D. M., & Guess, D. Receptive training of adjectival inflections in mental retardates. *Journal of Applied Behavior Analysis*, 1971, **4**, 129–139.

Baer, D. M., Wolf, M. M., & Risley, T. R. Some current dimensions of applied behavior analysis. *Journal of Applied Behavior Analysis*, 1968, **1**, 91–97.

Baker, J. G., Stanish, B., & Fraser, B. Comparative effects of a token economy in nursery school. *Mental Retardation*, 1972, **10**, 16–19.

Barton, E. S. Inappropriate speech in a severely retarded child: A case study in language conditioning and generalization. *Journal of Applied Behavior Analysis*, 1970, **3**, 299–307.

Barton, E. S., Guess, D., Garcia, E., & Baer, D. M. Improvements of retardates' mealtime behaviors by timeout procedures using multiple baseline techniques. *Journal of Applied Behavior Analysis*, 1970, **3**, 77–84.

Bateman, S. Application of Premack's generalization on reinforcement to modify occupational behavior in two severely retarded individuals. *American Journal of Mental Deficiency*, 1975, **80**, 604–610.

Bijou, S. W. A functional analysis of retarded development. In N. R. Ellis (Ed.), *International review of research in mental retardation, Volume 1*. New York: Academic Press, 1966.

Bijou, S. W. Environment and intelligence: A behavioral analysis. In R. Cancro (Ed.), *Intelligence: Genetic and environmental influences*. New York: Grune & Stratton, 1971.

Bijou, S. W., Peterson, R. F., & Ault, M. H. A method to integrate descriptive and experimental field studies at the level of data and empirical concepts. *Journal of Applied Behavior Analysis*, 1968, **1**, 175–191.

Bijou, S. W., & Redd, W. H. Behavior therapy for children. *Handbook of American psychiatry*. New York: Basic Books, in press.

Bostow, D. E., & Bailey, J. B. Modification of severe disruptive and aggressive behavior using brief timeout and reinforcement procedures. *Journal of Applied Behavior Analysis*, 1969, **2**, 31–27.

Broden, M., Bruce, C., Mitchell, M. A., Carter, V., & Hall, R. V. Effects of teacher attention on attending behavior of two boys at adjacent desks. *Journal of Applied Behavior Analysis*, 1970, **3**, 199–203.

Buell, J., Stoddard, P., Harris, F. R., & Baer, D. M. Collateral social development accompanying reinforcement of outdoor play in a preschool child. *Journal of Applied Behavior Analysis*, 1968, **1**, 167–173.

Burchard, J. D., & Barrera, F. An analysis of timeout and response cost in a programmed environment. *Journal of Applied Behavior Analysis*, 1972, **5**, 271–282.

Butz, R. A., & Hasazi, J. E. The effects of reinforcement on perseverative speech in a mildly retarded boy. *Journal of Behavior Therapy and Experimental Psychiatry*, 1973, **4**, 167–170.

Clark, H. B., Boyd, S. B., & Macrae, J. W. A classroom program teaching disadvantaged youths to write biographic information. *Journal of Applied Behavior Analysis*, 1975, **8**, 67–75.

Clark, H. B., Rowbury, T., Baer, A. M., & Baer, D. M. Timeout as a punishing stimulus in continuous and intermittent schedules. *Journal of Applied Behavior Analysis*, 1973, **6**, 443–455.

Colman, A. D., & Boren, J. J. An information system for measuring patient behavior and its use by staff. *Journal of Applied Behavior Analysis*, 1969, **2**, 207–214.

Corte, H. E., Wolf, M. M., & Locke, B. J. A comparison of procedures for eliminating self-injurious behavior of retarded adolescents. *Journal of Applied Behavior Analysis*, 1971, **4**, 201–213.

Cotter, V. W. Effects of music on performance of manual tasks with retarded adolescent females. *American Journal of Mental Deficiency*, 1971, **76**, 242–248.

Dalton, A. J., Rubino, C. A., & Hislop, M. W. Some effects of token rewards on school achievement of children with Down's syndrome. *Journal of Applied Behavior Analysis*, 1973, **6**, 251–259.

Dayan, M. Toilet training retarded children in a state residential institution. *Mental Retardation*, 1964, **2**, 116–117.

Edelson, R. I., & Sprague, R. L. Conditioning of activity level in a classroom with institutionalized retarded boys. *American Journal of Mental Deficiency*, 1974, **78**, 384–388.

Epstein, L. H., Doke, L. A., Sajwaj, T. E., Sorrell, S., & Rimmer, B. Generality and side effects of overcorrection. *Journal of Applied Behavior Analysis*, 1974, **7**, 386–390.

Evans, G. W., & Spradlin, J. E. Incentives and instructions as controlling variables of productivity. *American Journal of Mental Deficiency*, 1966, **71**, 129–132.

Ferster, C. B. Classification of behavioral pathology. In L. Krasner, & L. P. Ullmann (Eds.), *Research in behavior modification*. New York: Holt, Rinehart & Winston, 1965.

Fjellstedt, N., & Sulzer-Azaroff, B. Reducing the latency of a child's responding to instructions by means of a token system. *Journal of Applied Behavior Analysis*, 1973, **6**, 125–130.

Forehand, R., & Baumeister, A. A. Deceleration of aberrant behavior among retarded individuals. In M. Hersen, R. M. Eisler, & P. M. Miller (Eds.), *Progress in behavior modification: Volume 2*. New York: Academic Press, 1976.

Gardner, W. I. *Behavior modification in mental retardation*. Chicago: Aldine, 1971.

Green, R. J., & Hoats, D. L. Reinforcing capabilities of television distortion. *Journal of Applied Behavior Analysis*, 1969, **2**, 139–141.

Guess, D. A functional analysis of receptive language and productive speech: Acquisition of the plural morpheme. *Journal of Applied Behavior Analysis*, 1969, **2**, 55–64.

Guess, D., Sailor, W., Rutherford, G., & Baer, D. M. An experimental analysis of linguistic development: The productive use of the plural morpheme. *Journal of Applied Behavior Analysis*, 1968, **1**, 299–306.

Haring, N. G., & Lovitt, T. C. Operant methodology and educational technology in special education. In N. G. Haring, & R. Schiefelbusch (Eds.), *Methods in special education*. New York: McGraw-Hill, 1967.

Harris, V. W., & Sherman, J. A. Homework assignments, consequences, and classroom performance in social studies and mathematics. *Journal of Applied Behavior Analysis*, 1974, **7**, 505–519.

Hart, B. M., Reynolds, N. J., Baer, D. M., Brawley, E. R., & Harris, F. R. Effect of contingent and non-contingent social reinforcement on the cooperative play of a preschool child. *Journal of Applied Behavior Analysis*, 1968, **1**, 73–76.

Hawkins, R. P., & Dobes, R. W. Behavioral definitions in applied behavior analysis: Explicit or implicit. In B. C. Etzel, J. M. LeBlanc, & D. M. Baer (Eds.), *New developments in behavioral research: Theory, methods, and applications. In honor of Sidney W. Bijou*. Hillsdale, New Jersey: Lawrence Erlbaum Associates, in press.

Hawkins, R. P., & Dotson, V. A. Reliability scores that delude: An Alice in Wonderland trip through the misleading characteristics of inter-observer agreement scores in interval recording. In E. Ramp, & G. Semb (Eds.), *Behavior analysis: Areas of research and application*. Englewood Cliffs, New Jersey: Prentice-Hall, 1975.

Hersen, M., & Barlow, D. H. *Single case experimental designs: Strategies for studying behavior change*. New York: Pergamon, 1976.

Hopkins, B. L. Effects of candy and social reinforcement, instructions and reinforcement schedule leaning on the modification of maintenance of smiling. *Journal of Applied Behavior Analysis*, 1968, **1**, 121–129.

Horner, R. D., & Keilitz, I. Training mentally retarded adolescents to brush their teeth. *Journal of Applied Behavior Analysis*, 1975, **8**, 301–309.

Horton, L. E. Generalization of aggressive behavior in adolescent delinquent boys. *Journal of Applied Behavior Analysis*, 1970, **3**, 205–211.

Jens, K. G., & Shores, R. E. Behavioral graphs as reinforcers for work behavior of mentally retarded adolescents. *Education and training of the Mentally Retarded*, 1969, **4**, 21–28.

Johnson, S. M., & Bolstad, O. D. Methodological issues in naturalistic observation: Some problems and solutions for field research. In L. A. Hamerlynck, L. C. Handy, & E. J Mash (Eds.), *Behavior change: Methodology, concepts, and practice*. Champaign, Illinois: Research Press, 1973.

Kale, R. J., Kaye, J. H., Whelan, P. A., & Hopkins, B. L. The effects of reinforcement on the modification, maintenance, and generalization of social responses of mental patients. *Journal of Applied Behavior Analysis*, 1968, **1**, 307–314.

Kazdin, A. E. The effect of response cost in suppressing behavior in a prepsychotic retardate. *Journal of Behavior Therapy and Experimental Psychiatry*, 1971, **2**, 137–140.

Kazdin, A. E. The effect of response cost and aversive stimulation in suppressing punished and nonpunished speech disfluencies. *Behavior Therapy*, 1973a, **4**, 73–82.

Kazdin, A. E. The effect of vicarious reinforcement on attentive behavior in the classroom. *Journal of Applied Behavior Analysis*, 1973b, **6**, 71–78.

Kazdin, A. E. Methodological and assessment considerations in evaluating reinforcement programs in applied settings. *Journal of Applied Behavior Analysis*, 1973c, **6**, 517–531.

Kazdin, A. E. Role of instructions and reinforcement in behavior changes in token reinforcement programs. *Journal of Educational Psychology*, 1973d, **64**, 63–71.

Kazdin, A. E. Self-monitoring and behavior change. In M. J. Mahoney, & C. E. Thoresen (Eds.), *Self-control: Power to the person*. Monterey, Calif.: Brooks/Cole, 1974.

Kazdin, A. E. *Behavior modification in applied settings*. Homewood, Ill.: Dorsey, 1975a.

Kazdin, A. E. Recent advances in token economy research. In M. Hersen, R. M. Eisler, & P. M. Miller (Eds.), *Progress in behavior modification, Volume 1*. New York: Academic Press, 1975b.

Kazdin, A. E. Methodology of applied behavior analysis. In T. Brigham, & A. C. Catania (Eds.), *Applied behavioral research: The analysis of social and educational processes*. New York: Irvington/Naiburg—Wiley, in press.

Kazdin, A. E., & Craighead, W. E. Behavior modification in special education. In L. Mann, & D. A. Sabatino (Eds.), *The first review of special education, Volume 2*. Philadelphia: Buttonwood Farms, 1973.

Kazdin, A. E., & Erickson, L. M. Developing responsiveness to instructions in severely and profoundly retarded residents. *Journal of Behavior Therapy and Experimental Psychiatry*, 1975, **6**, 17–21.

Kazdin, A. E., & Klock, J. The effects of nonverbal teacher approval on student attentive behavior. *Journal of Applied Behavior Analysis*, 1973, **6**, 643–654.

Kazdin, A. E., & Polster, R. Intermittent token reinforcement and response maintenance in extinction. *Behavior Therapy*, 1973, **4**, 386–391.

Knapczyk, D. R., & Livingston, G. Self-recording and student teacher supervision: Variables within a token economy program. *Journal of Applied Behavior Analysis*, 1973, **6**, 481–486.

Lattal, K. A. Contingency management of tooth-brushing behavior in a summer camp for children. *Journal of Applied Behavior Analysis*, 1969, **2**, 195–198.

Leitenberg, H., Agras, W. S., Thompson, L. D., & Wright, D. E. Feedback in behavior modification: An experimental analysis in two phobic cases. *Journal of Applied Behavior Analysis*, 1968, **1**, 131–137.

Liberman, R. P., Teigen, J. R., Patterson, R., & Baker, V. Reducing delusional speech in chronic, paranoid schizophrenics. *Journal of Applied Behavior Analysis*, 1973, **6**, 57–64.

Lindsley, O. R. Direct measurement and prosthesis of retarded behavior. *Journal of Education*, 1964, **147**, 62–81.

Lipinski, D., & Nelson, R. Problems in the use of naturalistic observation as a means of behavioral assessment. *Behavior Therapy*, 1974, **5**, 341–351.

Logan, D. L., Kinsinger, J., Shelton, G., & Brown, J. M. The use of multiple reinforcers in a rehabilitation setting. *Mental Retardation*, 1971, **9**, 3–5.

Lovaas, O. I., & Simmons, J. Q. Manipulation of self-destruction in three retarded children. *Journal of Applied Behavior Analysis*, 1969, **2**, 143–157.

Lutzker, J. R., & Sherman, J. A. Producing generative sentence usage by imitation and reinforcement procedures. *Journal of Applied Behavior Analysis*, 1974, **7**, 447–460.

Madsen, C. H., Becker, W. C., & Thomas, D. R. Rules, praise and ignoring: Elements of elementary classroom control. *Journal of Applied Behavior Analysis*, 1968, **1**, 139–150.

Martin, J. A. The control of imitative and nonimitative behaviors in severely retarded children through "generalized-instruction following". *Journal of Experimental Child Psychology*, 1971, **11**, 390–400.

Milby, J. B. Modification of extreme social isolation by contingent social reinforcement. *Journal of Applied Behavior Analysis*, 1970, **3**, 149–152.

Miller, L. K., & Miller, O. L. Reinforcing self-help group activities of welfare recipients. *Journal of Applied Behavior Analysis*, 1970, **3**, 57–64.

Nelson, G. L., & Hanson, C. R. Training correct utensil use in retarded children: Modeling vs. physical guidance. *American Journal of Mental Deficiency*, 1975, **80**, 114–122.

Nordquist, V. M. The modification of a child's enuresis: Some response–response relationships. *Journal of Applied Behavior Analysis*, 1971, **4**, 241–247.

O'Brien, F., Azrin, N. H., & Bugle, C. Training profoundly retarded children to stop crawling. *Journal of Applied Behavior Analysis*, 1972, **5**, 131–137.

O'Brien, F., Bugle, C., & Azrin, N. H. Training and maintaining a retarded child's proper eating. *Journal of Applied Behavior Analysis*, 1972, **5**, 67–72.

O'Connor, R. D. Modification of social withdrawal through symbolic modeling. *Journal of Applied Behavior Analysis*, 1969, **2**, 15–22.

O'Leary, K. D., & Kent, R. N. Behavior modification for social action: Research tactics and problems. In L. A. Hamerlynk, P. O. Davidson, & L. E. Acker (Eds.), *Critical issues in research and practice*. Champaign, Illinois: Research Press, 1973.

O'Leary, K. D., & O'Leary, S. G. (Eds.), *Classroom management: The successful use of behavior modification*. New York: Pergamon, 1972.

Osborne, J. G. Free time as a reinforcer in the management of classroom behavior. *Journal of Applied Behavior Analysis*, 1969, **2**, 113–118.

Peine, H. A., Gregersen, G. F., & Sloane, H. A program to increase vocabulary and spontaneous verbal behavior. *Mental retardation*, 1970, **8**, 38–44.

Phillips, E. L. Achievement place: Token reinforcement procedures in a home-style rehabilitation setting for "pre-delinquent" boys. *Journal of Applied Behavior Analysis*, 1968, **1**, 213–223.

Redd, W. H. Effects of mixed reinforcement contingencies on adults' control of children's behavior. *Journal of Applied Behavior Analysis*, 1969, **2**, 249–254.

Redd, W. H. Generalization of adult's stimulus control of children's behavior. *Journal of Experimental Child Psychology*, 1970, **9**, 286–296.

Redd, W. H., & Birnbrauer, J. S. Adults as discriminative stimuli for different reinforcement contingencies with retarded children. *Journal of Experimental Child Psychology*, 1969, **7**, 440–447.

Reisinger, J. J. Treatment of "anxiety depression" via positive reinforcement and response cost. *Journal of Applied Behavior Analysis*, 1972, **5**, 125–130.

Repp, A. C., & Deitz, S. M. Reducing aggressive and self-injurious behavior of institutionalized retarded children through reinforcement of other behaviors. *Journal of Applied Behavior Analysis*, 1974, **7**, 313–325.

Sajwaj, T., Twardosz, S., & Burke, M. Side effects of extinction procedures in a remedial preschool. *Journal of Applied Behavior Analysis*, 1972, **5**, 163–175.

Schaefer, H. H., & Martin, P. L. Behavioral therapy for "apathy" of hospitalized schizophrenics. *Psychological Reports*, 1966, **19**, 1147–1158.

Schick, K. Operants. *Journal of the Experimental Analysis of Behavior*, 1971, **15**, 413–423.

Schmidt, G. W., & Ulrich, R. E. Effects of group contingent events upon classroom noise. *Journal of Applied Behavior Analysis*, 1969, **2**, 171–179.

Schnelle, J. F. A brief report on invalidity of parent evaluations of behavior change. *Journal of Applied Behavior Analysis*, 1974, **7**, 341–343.

Schroeder, S. R. Parametric effects of reinforcement frequency, amount of reinforcement, and required response force on sheltered workshop behavior. *Journal of Applied Behavior Analysis*, 1972, **5**, 431–441.

Schumaker, J., & Sherman, J. A. Training generative verb usage by imitation and reinforcement procedures. *Journal of Applied Behavior Analysis*, 1970, **3**, 273–287.

Screven, C. G., Straka, J. A., & Lafond, R. Applied behavioral technology in a vocational rehabilitation setting. In W. I. Gardner (Ed.), *Behavior modification in mental retardation*. Chicago: Aldine, 1971.

Skinner, B. F. Some contributions of an experimental analysis of behavior to psychology as a whole. *American Psychologist*, 1953, **8**, 69–78.

Skinner, B. F. What is the experimental analysis of behavior? *Journal of the Experimental Analysis of Behavior*, 1966, **9**, 213–218.

Smolev, S. R. Use of operant techniques for the modification of self-injurious behavior. *American Journal of Mental Deficiency*, 1971, **76**, 295–305.

Stokes, T. F., Baer, D. M., & Jackson, R. L. Programming the generalization of a greeting response in four retarded children. *Journal of Applied Behavior Analysis*, 1974, **7**, 599–610.

Surratt, P. R., Ulrich, R. E., & Hawkins, R. P. An elementary student as a behavioral engineer. *Journal of Applied Behavior Analysis*, 1969, **2**, 85–92.

Tanner, B. A., & Zeiler, M. Punishment of self-injurious behavior using aromatic ammonia as the aversive stimulus. *Journal of Applied Behavior Analysis*, 1975, **8**, 53–57.

Tate, B. G. An automated system for reinforcing and recording retardate work behavior. *Journal of Applied Behavior Analysis*, 1968, **1**, 347–348.

Throne, J. M. A radical behaviorist approach to diagnosis in mental retardation. *Mental Retardation*, 1970, **8**, 2–5.

Twardosz, S., & Baer, D. M. Training two severely retarded adolescents to ask questions. *Journal of Applied Behavior Analysis*, 1973, **6**, 655–661.

Vukelich, R., & Hake, D. F. Reduction of dangerously aggressive behavior in a severely retarded resident through a combination of positive reinforcement schedules. *Journal of Applied Behavior Analysis*, 1971, **4**, 215–225.

Wahler, R. G. Setting generality: Some specific and general effects of child behavior therapy. *Journal of Applied Behavior Analysis*, 1969, **2**, 239–246.

Wahler, R. G. Some structural aspects of deviant child behavior. *Journal of Applied Behavior Analysis*, 1975, **8**, 27–42.

Wahler, R. G., Sperling, K. A., Thomas, M. R., Teeter, N. C., & Luper, H. L. The modification of childhood stuttering: Some response–response relationships. *Journal of Experimental Child Psychology*, 1970, **9**, 411–428.

Watson, L. S. Application of operant conditioning techniques to institutionalized severely and profoundly retarded children. *Mental Retardation Abstracts*, 1967, **1**, 1–18.

Webb, E. J., Campbell, D. T., Schwartz, R. D., & Sechrest, L. *Unobtrusive measures: Nonreactive research in the social sciences*. Chicago: Rand McNally, 1966.

Whitman, T. L., Mercurio, J. R., & Caponigri, V. Development of social responses in two severely retarded children. *Journal of Applied Behavior Analysis*, 1970, **3**, 133–138.

Wunderlich, R. A. Programmed instruction: Teaching coinage to retardated children. *Mental Retardation*, 1972, **10**, 21–23.

Zimmerman, J., Overpeck, C., Eisenberg, H., & Garlick, B. J. Operant conditioning in a sheltered workshop. *Rehabilitation Literature*, 1969, **30**, 326–334.

Zimmerman, J., Stuckey, T. E., Garlick, B. J., & Miller, M. Effects of token reinforcement on productivity in multiply handicapped clients in a sheltered workshop. *Rehabilitation Literature*, 1969, **30**, 34–41.

Zimmerman, E. H., Zimmerman, J., & Russell, C. D. Differential effects of token reinforcement on instruction-following behavior in retarded students instructed as a group. *Journal of Applied Behavior Analysis*, 1969, **2**, 101–112.

Zlutnick, S., Mayville, W. J., & Moffat, S. Modification of seizure disorders: The interruption of behavioral chains. *Journal of Applied Behavior Analysis*, 1975, **8**, 1–12.

CHAPTER 13

Behavioral Assessment of Social Skills

RICHARD M. EISLER

Veterans Administration Center, and
University of Mississippi Medical Centre
Jackson, Mississippi

Introduction

The importance of effective interpersonal behavior has been stressed by nearly all philosophical and scientific theorists concerned with the nature of human social relationships. While our secondary schools and universities have focused almost exclusively on teaching the requisite academic and technical skills to function in increasingly complex work environments, social interpersonal skills are rarely taught. At best they are earned unsystematically from family and peer groups.

One of the earliest modern day theorists to emphasize the crucial role of the interpersonal environment in determining human behavior was Harry Stack Sullivan (1892–1949). Sullivan was an analytically trained psychiatrist who believed that "personality" was purely a hypothetical entity which could not be studied apart from interpersonal situations (see Hall & Lindzey, 1957). Unlike some of his contemporaries, Sullivan felt that the basic unit for studying human behavior was the interpersonal transaction as opposed to intrapsychic events. The gamut of so-called mental disorders was viewed in the Sullivanian framework as a reflection of inadequate or inappropriate interpersonal relationships. The individual's predisposition to respond to others in a hostile or loving way was the result of a socially acquired "dynamism" or habit.

Empirical verification of the relationship between impairment of interpersonal functioning and various behavior disorders was demonstrated in a series of studies carried out by Zigler & Phillips and their colleagues (Levine & Zigler, 1973; Phillips & Zigler, 1961, 1964; Zigler & Phillips, 1960, 1961). Research by these investigators with psychiatric patients showed that the level of social competence, based on global measures of educational, vocational, and marital attainment, was related to the degree of psychiatric impairment.

In general, less social competence was associated with more severe symptomatology. Further, within a group of psychiatrically disturbed individuals, those who evidenced greater competence (social skill) were found to have a better prognosis than less socially skillful individuals.

Unfortunately, these rather impressive diagnostic findings did not immediately give rise to treatment strategies specifically designed to improve the social skills of psychiatric patients or individuals who were regarded as socially deviant. Similarly, there was little attempt, until recently, to develop procedures aimed at the assessment of interpersonal abilities and deficits as opposed to the traditional assessment of symptom patterns (e.g., anxiety, depression, psychosis, etc.).

However, more recent application of social learning principles to clinically relevant problems in human behavior has given a new impetus to the study of the ability of individuals to maintain or attempt to change the behavior of others in various interpersonal relationships. While human social interaction is an incredibly complex process with major affective, cognitive, and behavioral components, there appears to be a renewed interest in studying this basic human process from an empirical point of view. The rationale for the clinical application of social skills training is covered extensively in numerous recent works (Alberti & Emmons, 1974; Goldstein, 1973; Lazarus, 1971; Rimm & Masters, 1974; Wolpe, 1969; Wolpe & Lazarus, 1966). In addition, there are several reviews of the literature on experimental methodology and clinical techniques (Hersen & Bellack, 1976; Hersen, Eisler & Miller, 1973).

At present there are no generally agreed upon definitions of social skills which apply to all interpersonal situations. Most clinicians and researchers have relied on clinical intuition and definitions appropriate to their specific objectives. The purpose of the present chapter is to discuss the various methods of social skill assessment which have been used and to propose some practical guidelines.

Rationale

Social skills training has been used successfully with a wide diversity of clinical populations ranging from relatively well adjusted college students who report discomfort in various social situations, to chronic psychiatric patients who are unable to function outside of an institution.

In contrast to treatment strategies which have attempted to remove various target symptoms, the objective of social skills training is to teach individuals more effective ways of interacting with other people. The major assumption of the skills model is that maladaptive behaviors will gradually be replaced by the acquisition, performance, and reinforcement of more adaptive social behavior. In some instances, the goal of social skills training is to help an individual develop more functional response repertoires in dealing with specific individuals in his environment such as his spouse, employer, or his parents. In other cases, training is focused on developing greater competence in certain classes of interpersonal situations. For example, an individual may be taught various sequences of behavior to perform while on a date, how to refuse the unreasonable requests of others, or how to express appreciation or affection appropriately.

Skill versus Performance Deficit

There has been controversy in the literature as to whether the observed failure of an individual to exhibit socially skillful behavior results from his never having acquired the requisite behavior, or his fear that exhibiting certain kinds of behavior might lead to aversive consequences. Wolpe & Lazarus (1966) have argued that for some individuals, interpersonal relationships evoke anxiety which consequently inhibit their expression of normal feelings and the performance of adaptive social behavior. Based on this formulation, Wolpe and Lazarus advocated encouraging individuals so afflicted to assert their natural impulses which would "reciprocally inhibit" anxiety. In fact, numerous authors have suggested that "systematic desensitization" or other methods of anxiety reduction be employed so that the individual becomes less timid in exhibiting previously acquired social behavior.

Perhaps some empirical support for the anxiety inhibition hypothesis may be found in the recent work of Arkowitz and his colleagues with college students. For example, Arkowitz, Lichtenstein, McGovern & Hines (1975) compared high and low frequency daters on a variety of self-report, peer ratings, and behavioral measures of social competence in heterosocial interactions. While self-report and peer ratings of social anxiety differentiated the two groups during semi-structured interactions, behavioral measures of the interaction did not. In contrast, Eisler and his colleagues (Eisler, Hersen & Miller, 1973; Eisler, Hersen, Miller & Blanchard, 1975), utilizing a hospitalized psychiatric population, have consistently noted a number of behavioral differences between those patients who were judged to be "very assertive" as compared to those who were rated "very unassertive." In the latter study the high assertives were found, paradoxically, to evidence more speech disruptions, which are symptomatic of anxiety, than the lows. Weinman, Gelbart, Wallace & Post (1972) compared the effects of behavioral treatment (socio-environmental therapy) with systematic desensitization and relaxation training in inducing assertive social behavior using groups of schizophrenic patients. While *all* treatments reduced anxiety, only the behavioral treatment produced an improvement in the interpersonal behavior of chronic patients.

Thus, it appears that with the more clinically malfunctioning individual, anxiety is not the sole basis for his lack of socially skilled performance. In all probability, some empirical findings will support the skill deficit hypothesis and some the anxiety inhibition hypothesis, depending on the particular characteristics of the target population, method of assessment, and definition of social skill. Whether or not one wishes to assess degree of subjective anxiety or physiological arousal in social situations, it would appear that the major task of social skill assessment will be to focus on observable measures of social interaction.

Parameters of Social Skill

An initial step in the assessment of a social skills training program is to arrive at definitions of target behaviors which comprise the skill. At first glance, this would seem to be a relatively straightforward task since most of us presume to "intuitively" identify individuals who demonstrate socially adept behavior in contrast to those who appear relatively unskilled. Once these behaviors have been defined it would appear that self-report measures could be constructed that ask individuals how they respond to others in a broad sample of interactive situations. In addition, overt behavioral measures should be developed which reflect the observed absence or presence of the target behaviors in varying degrees during social interaction.

However, this reasoning is deceptively oversimplified and may obscure more complex issues in defining and assessing social skills. For example, in the case of self-report measures, asking an individual how anxious he becomes on a date may be much easier for him to respond to than asking him what behaviors he engages in on that date to elicit favorable responses from the girl. The verbal and non-verbal behavioral sequences emitted and responded to during interpersonal interactions are far more difficult to define and measure than counting steps walked toward a phobic object, or recording the frequency of pronouns emitted during a verbal conditioning experiment.

An additional problem in the assessment of social skill concerns variations in the social-interpersonal context of the emitted behaviors. For example, a recent study by Eisler *et al.* (1975) showed that a group of male subjects consistently emitted behavior which was judged to be more "assertive" when they were interacting with women than with men. They were also more assertive when interacting with relatively unfamiliar persons (e.g., waitress) than with familiar persons (e.g., spouse).

There are social norms governing what is considered to be appropriate social behavior in different situations. For instance, an individual who exhibits a specific sequence of behaviors when interacting with certain individuals under specified circumstances may be judged to evidence highly skilled behavior. If he exhibits the *same* sequence of behaviors to different individuals (e.g., boss versus friend) or to the same individual under different circumstances (e.g., at a party versus at work), observers might conclude that he was relatively unskilled. Additionally, various groups of individuals with different social norms may view the same interaction differently. For example, a father observing his son interact with a prominent person in the community might rate the son's behavior as socially maladaptive, whereas a peer observing the same interaction might rate it as skillful.

Thus, it is not only the observed behaviors which must be judged as relatively skilled or unskilled, but the interaction of those behaviors within a specific interpersonal context. These judgments are further influenced by the values and norms held by specific groups of observers. While assessment procedures have not as yet been tailored to all of these issues, they should be kept in mind in judging the relative merit of assessment techniques used thus far. In the next section we will briefly report on some of the definitions and techniques used in various investigations concerned with social skill assessment.

Relevant Research

While there will be no attempt to review all the literature involving the assessment of social skills, the reader should be familiar with some of the definitions and assessment procedures employed by others before we consider some practical guidelines to be used in social skill assessment.

Assertive Behavior

One of the first conceptual areas to be delineated for interpersonal skills training was developed under the rubric of assertive behavior (Wolpe, 1958, 1969). Assertiveness training was a therapeutic technique designed for individuals who appeared passive and/or anxious during interpersonal encounters. Unassertive individuals have been described as lacking in spontaneity, or being inadequate, inhibited, emotionally constricted, etc. However, these descriptions and Wolpe's (1969) definition of "assertive as the outward expression of practically all feelings other than anxiety" (p. 61) have not led to easily quantifiable measures of assertive behavior. In fact, assertiveness has been and still is confused with the expression of socially maladaptive hostility and aggression.

McFall and his colleagues (McFall & Marston, 1970; McFall & Lillesand, 1971; McFall & Twentyman, 1973) initiated the empirical assessment of the effects of various behavioral treatments designed to improve an individual's ability to make assertive statements. McFall and Marston (1970), using a role playing format, constructed a series of behavioral assessment situations in which unassertive college students rehearsed assertive responses to pre-recorded audio stimuli. For example, the subject listened to the description of an interpersonal scene as follows:

Narrator: Imagine this morning that you took your car to a local Standard station and you explicitly told the mechanic to give your car a simple tune up. The bill should have been about $20. It's now later in the afternoon and you're at the station to pick up your car. The mechanic is walking over to you.

Mechanic: "Okay, let me make out a ticket for you. The tune up was $12 for parts and $8 for labor. Uh, grease and oil job was $6. Antifreeze was $5. Uh, $4 for a new oil filter. And, uh, $5 for rotating the tires. That's $40 in all. Will this be cash or charge?"

Assessment of the subject's audiotaped responses to 16 such role played situations pre-and post-training was rated by 5 "blind" judges. The raters were asked which response of a paired sample of a subject's responses was "more assertive." Unfortunately, there was no attempt to assess the *degree* of agreement among the raters which would have provided some consensual evidence that raters had defined assertion skill in a similar manner. The only other "behavioral" measure of assertion in those scenes was response latency to scene descriptions. In addition, subjects were asked to supply self-report ratings of their anxiety and degree of satisfaction with their response on global scales. Pre- and post-pulse measures were taken, presumably to provide physiological evidence of changes in anxiety. Also administered to assess anxiety were the Taylor Manifest Anxiety Scale (Taylor, 1954) and the Wolpe-Lang (1964) Fear Survey Schedule. Finally, to assess generalization of training, subjects were subsequently exposed to a bogus telephone call by an experimenter posing as a magazine salesman. Measures of subjects' ability to refuse the sales pitch included total time subjects stayed on the phone, elapsed time before the subject made his first refusal, and a global judgment by raters regarding the subject's "social skill" in handling the call.

Thus, in a well controlled experiment it should be noted that many behavioral measures of social skill were not objectively defined, but rather left primarily to the subjective impressions of the raters. It was also interesting to note that many of the measures employed dealt with the degree of the subject's anxiety (subjective anxiety report, standardized anxiety rests, and physiological pulse measures). Whether physiological activity (i.e., anxiety) has a specific or unique relationship to the performance of socially skilled acts has yet to be convincingly demonstrated. On the other hand, the use of standardized role played scenes requiring assertive responses appeared to be an excellent method of obtaining behavioral data on social performance.

Eisler *et al.* (1973), utilizing a series of fourteen role playing situations similar to those devised by McFall & Marston (1970), attempted to identify specific verbal and non-verbal behaviors which were related to global judgments of assertiveness. In order to make the role played situations more natural, live respondents prompted subjects' responses. In addition, the interactions were videotaped to permit judges to respond to visual as well as auditory cues. Groups of psychiatric patients who were rated either above or below the median on a five point scale of global assertiveness were compared on nine behavioral measures and the Wolpe-Lazarus Assertiveness Questionnaire. It was found that patients judged to be highly assertive on the global measures evidenced more pronounced affect, lengthier responses, louder speech, and shorter response latencies relative to the lows. With respect to verbal content, it was found that the highs exhibited a lower frequency of compliant statements, and were more likely to request that the interpersonal respondents change their behavior than the lows. In addition, the Wolpe-Lazarus questionnaire was found to differentiate between high and low assertive subjects. In a series of treatment analogue studies, these behavioral measures were used to assess the effects of various treatment procedures on assertiveness (Eisler, Hersen & Miller, 1973; Hersen, Eisler, Miller, Johnson & Pinkston, 1973). Also, using single subject designs, it was observed that training subjects to exhibit more of these component behaviors led to higher global assertiveness ratings (e.g., Eisler, Hersen & Miller, 1974). Thus, while at least some components of the complex interpersonal behaviors labeled assertiveness were identified, it remained unclear as to the relative importance each specific behavior contributed to the global judgment of assertive skill. Additionally, it remained for further research to determine whether these components were relevant to all situations requiring assertive behavior.

It is unlikely that all behaviors which are judged to be associated with assertiveness or skillfulness in one interpersonal context will be necessary or sufficient in other interpersonal situations. It is obvious, for example, that if one is waiting in line to purchase a ticket to a ball game and someone cuts in line in front of him, the appropriate assertive response will differ depending on whether that person is a middle-aged man, an old woman, or a young child.

Some evidence for the situational determinants of assertiveness was provided by Eisler *et al.* (1975). Role playing scenes were constructed which required male subjects to interact with both male and female respondents (sex condition). A second aspect of social context which was varied was familiarity. In one condition the subject interacted with individuals he was presumed to have frequent interactions with such as his spouse or employer (familiar condition). Responses to familiar individuals were compared to responses to unfamiliar individuals, with whom it was presumed the subject would have less frequent contact (unfamiliar condition). With this particular subject population, it was found that subjects behaved more assertively toward women than to other men. Also, they were more assertive when interacting with unfamiliar persons of both sexes than toward familiar persons. The implications for social skills training are obvious in that quite different interpersonal behaviors may be required when one is interacting with different individuals. Thus, socially skilled individuals must discriminate what responses in their repertoires should be differentially emitted to a variety of individuals. It would also seem that a socially skilled individual would have to be adept at monitoring the responses of his interpersonal partner, and then be capable of changing his own behavior accordingly.

Social Skills and Depression

In a series of theoretical and empirical articles, Lewinsohn and his co-workers have examined the relationships between social skills and depression. (Lewinsohn, 1975; Lewinsohn & Shaffer, 1971; Lewinsohn, Weinstein & Alper, 1970; Libet & Lewinsohn, 1973). In discussing the etiology of depression, Lewinsohn has theorized that depressed individuals obtain little positive reinforcement from their interpersonal and family relationships. This lack of social skill is hypothesized as one of the antecedent conditions which produce the low rate of positive reinforcement. For Lewinsohn, the operational definition of social skill is the ability of the individual to emit behaviors which in turn are positively reinforced by others (Lewinsohn, 1975, p. 41).

Rather than using role playing situations to assess interpersonal interaction, Lewinsohn and his colleagues have used home observations of family interaction (Lewinsohn & Shaffer, 1971) and observation of behavior in group therapy (Libet & Lewinsohn, 1973). Measures of social skill were theoretically and empirically linked to the probability that the behaviors would elicit positive interpersonal expressions (actions) from others, e.g., affection, approval, interest, agreement, etc. Some of the derived measures of social skill which were found to differentiate depressed from non-depressed individuals were: (1) the total amount of verbal behavior expressed toward others (activity level); (2) number of times the individual initiated behavior that could not be classified as a reaction to someone else's behavior (initiation level); (3) the degree to which the individual distributed his/her behaviors equally toward a group of others (interpersonal range); (4) the amount of elapsed time before the individual responded to the behavior of another individual (action latency); and (5) the rate of positive or reinforcing behaviors the individual expressed toward others.

These measures do not include all those utilized by Lewinsohn, but they are representative of behavioral-interaction measures in which he demonstrated a functional relationship between the behaviors emitted by an individual and the consequent reactions they elicit from others during interpersonal exchanges. Thus, social skills were not conceptualized as a specified set of behaviors emitted by the individual alone, but also in terms of the actual and expected social consequences of those behaviors.

While Lewinsohn has convincingly demonstrated a relationship between interpersonal deficits on measures of social skill and the clinical phenomenon of depression, there is every reason to suspect that other forms of behavior disorder may result from inadequate social skill. Argyle (1969) has discussed social skill deficits as antecedent to a variety of clinical syndromes. While various writers have described the styles of interaction common to disordered groups, e.g., schizophrenics in global categories such as "withdrawn," Argyle (1969) has attempted to define the behavioral aspects of social withdrawal in terms of infrequent eye contact, low rates of interrupted speech, and atypical postures.

Heterosocial Skills

Parallel to the increased growth of assessment of interpersonal deficits in traditional psychiatric populations, there has been a rapid growth of research on the heterosocial skills of college students. This is not surprising in view of the fact that, historically, human psychological research conducted in university settings has relied upon the availability of subjects in close proximity to the investigators who also tend to be college professors. This is not to deny that lack of heterosocial skills represents a significant problem for college age adults who have been variously described as shy, lonely, or socially anxious. In fact, there is reason to expect that treatment and assessment models developed for studies of interpersonal problems with college students might be applied to other populations with different interpersonal problems. However, it should be remembered that college students as a group are atypical of the general population in that they tend to be younger, brighter, more verbally facile, and have distinctive social norms. Therefore, assessment procedures designed to reflect social skills of college students will probably differ in some respects from procedures applicable to more clinically disturbed populations.

For the most part, criterion measures used in identifying students who are presumably low in heterosocial skills are based on self-reports of minimal dating. Most studies have been concerned with evaluating various treatment procedures with respect to improving the social skills of low frequency daters, or comparing high and low frequency daters on a variety of self-report, behavioral, and physiological measures. Stimuli used to elicit interpersonal behavior have ranged from audiotape presentation of hypothetical social situations requiring the subject to respond to single stimulus prompts (Rehm & Marston, 1968), to live heterosexual situations whereby subjects were instructed to "get to know" his female partner (Arkowitz, *et al.*, 1975). However, even in the "in vivo" elicitation methods described in the latter study, the situations suffered from a certain degree of artificiality in that: (a) subjects were pretending they were in a real social situation, and (b) the female confederates were programmed to respond in a standardized manner.

There have been two somewhat different theoretical positions which have been presented to account for low frequency dating behavior. To some extent these different orientations have been reflected in a choice of assessment measures. For example, some investigators, including Borkovec, Stone, O'Brien & Kaloupek (1974) have assumed that a high degree of social anxiety inhibits performance. These authors employed self-report measures of anxiety and subjective awareness of internal autonomic cues. In addition, behavioral measures of speech disfluences were taken from subjects' verbalizations. Finally, autonomic activity was monitored by recording the subjects' heart rate before and after the social interaction.

In contrast to the conditioned anxiety hypothesis of minimal dating, Twentyman & McFall (1975) have suggested that non-daters may avoid heterosocial encounters because they lack the requisite interpersonal skills. These investigators employed a social skills training program for shy males. In addition to self-report and physiological indicators of anxiety, behavioral measures of the subjects' frequency and duration of interactions with females outside the experimental situation were obtained pre- and post-training. The results indicated that subjects who had received skill training showed less physiological responsivity to test stimuli and changed more than control subjects on frequency and duration of heterosocial interactions.

Most studies reviewed in the area of heterosocial competence have relied heavily on self-report measures of social anxiety and interpersonal behavior. When objective measures have been employed, judges are typically asked to make *global ratings* of the subject's assertiveness, social appropriateness, or other social skills. While interjudge reliabilities of these global ratings are often high, the behavioral elements comprising socially skilled behavior have remained obscure.

In an attempt to develop specific behavioral measures which would define heterosocial competence in college males, Arkowitz *et al.* (1975) compared high and low frequency daters on a number of specific behavioral measures of social performance in addition to the usual battery of self-report instruments and global social skill ratings by observers and peers. The seven behavioral components presumed to reflect the subject's social skill during an "in vivo" conversation with a female confederate were: (a) talk time, (b) number of silences, (c) number of verbal reinforcements, (d) number of head nods, (e) number of smiles, (f) time gazing at partner, and (g) several measures of pro-social speech content.

The results indicated very few behavioral differences between the two groups on social performance tasks involving live interaction with the female confederate. The high frequency daters did exhibit fewer "silences" and were rated higher in social skill than their low dating frequency counterparts, but none of the other expected behavioral differences materialized. Thus, while there were obvious differences in social skill detected by self-report, peer, and observer ratings, the specific behavioral components of those skills were not identified. The authors concluded: "One promising direction for future research would be the study of social skill differences based on behavioral measures which take into account the reciprocal and interactive characteristics of the dyadic interaction" (Arkowitz, *et al.*, 1975, p. 11).

It would seem apparent from the above studies that both measures of social anxiety and social performance are relevant to the assessment of minimal dating. The behavioral *complexity* of what has been labeled social skill in this relatively circumscribed area of minimal dating has been underscored by the extensive reliance of global measures and the negative results obtained with more specific behavioral assessment measures.

Self-Report Assessment Techniques

There are several methods of eliciting self-report information from an individual as to how he typically thinks, feels, or behaves when confronted with various interpersonal situations. These include: (1) structured paper and pencil inventories, (2) semi-structured interviews, and (3) self-monitoring techniques.

Structured Inventories. An increasing number of self-report instruments that assist individuals in reporting their responses to social situations are presently available. Most of these instruments sample a universe of interpersonal situations which typically elicit a specific class of responses of interest. For example, the Rathus Assertive Schedule (RAS) (Rathus, 1973) was designed to measure changes in assertive behavior. The RAS is a 30-item inventory in which the respondent is asked to indicate how "characteristic" the following statements are of his behavior, e.g., "I often have a hard time saying no," or "When I am given a compliment I sometimes just don't know what to say."

Two scales of social-evaluative anxiety were constructed by Watson & Friend (1969). The Social Avoidance and Distress Scale (SAD) was designed to measure the experience of distress, discomfort, and anxiety in social situations. The second instrument, the Fear of Negative Evaluation (FNE) scale was designed to assess the degree to which the respondent was apprehensive about receiving social disapproval by others in social situations.

With the RAS, SAD, and FNE, high intra-test reliabilities were established which indicated that scale items were measuring relatively homogeneous behavior dimensions. As is typical with most self-report inventories, much validating evidence was obtained by correlating the social behavior measures with other well established scales including personality inventories, measures of social anxiety, and other self-report questionnaires. The difficulties involved in validation with self-report measures are well known. All self-report measures are subject to biases relating to how the individual would like to present himself on the questionnaires. Secondly, while correlations between self-report measures may be high, the ability of these measures to predict an individual's behavior in any specific situation may frequently be extremely low.

With some social behavior inventories, the normative population on which the scale was derived and validated is specified. For example, the rather sophisticated Assertive Inventory (AI) developed by Gambrill & Richey (1975) reports norms for Berkeley, California and Seattle, Washington undergraduate males and females separately. However, this measure, as well as those previously discussed, was established on relatively intelligent college students, who presumably have similar socio-economic backgrounds and cultural values. The application of these tests to more clinically disordered populations, or to those of different ages and socio-economic status must be made with caution. The reader is referred to Hersen & Bellack (in press) for more inclusive descriptions of self-report measures of social behavior for use with different populations.

The following is a discussion of some of the advantages and disadvantages of using structured self-report inventories. These instruments are economical of time in that the examiner need not be present while they are being completed. The majority of these instruments are scored objectively so that meaningful comparisons may be made among individuals on specific variables. In this respect, self-report inventories have great utility for the preliminary screening of individuals who may have social skills deficits. With respect to clinical evaluation, questionnaires may help identify broad problem areas, which then can be scrutinized more carefully by the examiner in a more detailed inquiry. Finally, repeated administrations of self-report questionnaires represent a relatively easily attainable and quantifiable source of data on changes in an individual's perception of his social behavior over time, or in comparing the individual's pre-treatment and post-treatment perceptions of his behavior.

All self-report instruments of social skill have important limitations which must be kept in mind for various assessment situations. Assuming that the respondent is motivated to respond frankly about his interpersonal behavior, several problems become apparent. The first is that the respondent may or may not be able to *accurately* identify relevant aspects of his social behavior. Remembering the previous discussion, it was noted that interpersonal behavior consists of many verbal and non-verbal responses emitted simultaneously during an interaction sequence. Therefore, it may be difficult for a respondent to judge whether he was, for example, assertive or aggressive in a particular situation. In addition, some individuals tend to be more aware than others of how specific aspects of their behavior might be regarded by others. Another factor which enters into the validity of self-report data is the ability of the respondent to accurately assess the behavior of the other person to whom he is responding. For example, if an individual indicates that he usually expresses "resentment there and then when a friend criticizes him unjustly" (item on the Wolpe-Lazarus Questionnaire, Wolpe & Lazarus, 1966), he must be able to discriminate when friends do in fact criticize him. To the extent that respondents cannot accurately assess their own behavior or the behavior of others in relation to themselves, it is difficult to assess the validity of their verbal report of the interaction.

A final problem to be discussed in relation to self-report inventories is that items tend to be phrased in general terms, i.e., do you "usually," "sometimes," "never" do thus and so. This poses a problem for respondents since they are forced to "average" their behavior across situations. It also detracts from their ability to report how they behave in specific kinds of situations. Thus, an individual may have little difficulty in saying "no" to a salesman, but may rarely be able to say "no" to his father or to his girlfriend.

In summary, then, structured self-report measures represents a convenient quantifiable and economical means of collecting data on how individuals perceive their social behavior. To the extent that they are inaccurate in the assessment of various aspects of their own behavior and the behavior of others in interpersonal situations, the validity of their self-observations may be open to question.

Focused Clinical Interview

The focused clinical interview offers a very good way of eliciting social-interpersonal data from individuals or clients who are able to report on their own behavior with reasonable accuracy. As is true with all clinical interviews, those which focus on the person's behavior with others depends upon the establishment of rapport. Since most clients will initially begin to talk about personal problems in terms of anxiety, depression, marital unhappiness, etc., rather than their inability to handle social relationships, it is important for the interviewer to structure the interview around their specific interpersonal relationships.

In the initial phase of the interview, the interviewer should begin to elicit a "history" of typical interpersonal response patterns the client has evidenced throughout his life. For example, was he shy and inhibited around people, or did he manifest signs of a belligerent, hostile mode of response when growing up? Were there different patterns of response toward parents when compared with peers or siblings? The interviewer will also want to elicit information as to how successfully the client was able to master relatively common interpersonal tasks. A partial list of interpersonal behavior situations that might be explored by the clinician is as follows:

1. The ability to express contrary opinions to peers and instructors.
2. The ability to ask favors of someone.

3. The ability to initiate conversations with peers or strangers.
4. The ability to refuse unreasonable requests from strangers or friends.
5. The ability to request appointments or dates with someone.
6. The ability to compliment someone.
7. The ability to negotiate in "give and take" with family, friends, or spouse.
8. The ability to apply successfully for a job.
9. The ability to ask for help in solving problems.
10. The ability to resist pressure from others to behave in a manner contrary to one's beliefs.

The purpose of the "interpersonal history" is not to give the client insight into his interpersonal problems, but rather to more specifically determine the nature and extent of his interpersonal assets and liabilities. For example, the interviewer may wish to determine whether the client has had pervasive problems with many relationships, or if his interpersonal problems are confined to a few individuals or classes of individuals, e.g., employers, or heterosexual relationships. For instance, if it became obvious that the client never was able to obtain a second date with a girl after numerous first dates, it is likely he is lacking in heterosocial skills which must be delineated in subsequent interviews. The client's history of interpersonal behavior also gives the behavioral clinician clues as to what kinds of interpersonal behavior models the client has been exposed to, and the nature of the interpersonal reinforcement he has received to maintain various aspects of both his maladaptive and adaptive social behavior.

Following the historical aspects of the client's social interaction, the behavioral clinician should request that the client elaborate on his/her current interpersonal behavior. For this purpose, it is generally best to have the client describe in detail how he interacts with those individuals he sees on a frequent basis, i.e., employers, spouse, teachers, friends, etc. The description of interaction with present interpersonal partners then leads to a data-based formulation of the adaptiveness of the client's current social behavior.

Most individuals describe their interpersonal life in very general nonbehavioral terms which is of very little value in assessment of their social abilities. Frequently, a client will tell an interviewer that he is "anxious" in interpersonal situations. Behaviorally, this could mean that in interpersonal situations: (1) he is silent; (2) he talks about himself without pause; (3) he stammers and stutters a great deal; (4) his heart beats rapidly and his stomach feels queasy; or (5) he feels stupid and inept but can offer no concrete evidence that he in fact lacks social ability.

At this point, the interviewer should request that the client describe in behavioral terms exactly what he says and does during interpersonal encounters. Frequently, the client has incorrectly labeled many aspects of his interpersonal behavior and only a relatively exact replication of his extra-office social behavior will assist the clinician in assessing the nature and degree of his social deficits. To facilitate assessments, non-verbal aspects of the interaction should be queried regarding the client's posture, voice qualities, eye contact, handshake, etc., in addition to the content of *what* he says. Role playing, which will be discussed in a later section, is an alternative method of obtaining a closer approximation of the client's interpersonal behavior during actual encounters.

In summary, assessment of the appropriateness and effectiveness of the client's interpersonal behavior will depend on:

1. Precise knowledge of the client's actual interpersonal behavior with others including verbal and non-verbal components.

2. Knowledge of the social-interpersonal context of the client's interactions and characteristics of his interpersonal partners.

3. Precise knowledge of the nature and form of the interpersonal partners' responses to the client.

4. The clinician's awareness of the social interpersonal norms governing the specific interactions described by the client.

The latter is necessary to assess the degree to which the client's behavior is likely to elicit favorable consequences from the interpersonal environment, and the degree to which the client has exercised discriminative skill and judgment in utilizing his repertoire of social behaviors.

Conjoint Interviews

An additional means by which the behavioral clinician can "zero in" on the client's social behavior in his natural environment is to include real-life interpersonal partners in conjoint interviews. For instance, the author has on more than one occasion discovered significant discrepancies in the way that a client described himself by comparing his self-report with those of his spouse. Very often these disagreements in perception may be reduced by conjoint discussion to the point whereby both partners can agree on what behavior has taken place in a particular situation. Conjoint interviews also provide the clinician with more objective evidence on how others receive and interpret the client's social responses. Further suggestions on how to assess conjoint interviews will appear in the section on behavioral evaluation.

Self-Monitoring

An additional self-report method of assessing interpersonal behavior is that of self-monitoring. In contrast with the other self report methods previously discussed, self-monitoring requires the individual to record his behavior at specified intervals in a highly systematic manner.

Kazdin (1974) has discussed self-monitoring as a method of observing and reporting one's own observable (public) behavior or private events (cognitions). A major advantage of self-monitoring as an assessment technique is that it permits access to data that otherwise would not be readily available. Obviously, an individual's internal cognitions and perceptions of social-environmental events are not subject to public scrutiny. Perhaps less obvious, it is almost equally difficult to obtain data on an individual's day to day social interaction except through highly systematic self-report procedures.

Self-monitoring tends to be favored by behavioral clinicians over global self-report techniques because measures of behavior self-assessed prior to treatment (baseline conditions) are identical to measures used to assess changes in behaviors during treatment and also following the completion of treatment. Thus, there is a closer relationship between target behaviors selected for therapeutic change and assessment of those changes than with the more traditional psychometric inventories such as the MMPI.

Additionally, behavioral clinicians are enthusiastic about the therapeutic possibilities of self-monitoring techniques because they set the stage for "self-control" treatment strategies. In other words, when an individual is able to identify the frequency with which he engages in therapeutically "desirable" or "undesirable" behaviors, he is then in a position to instigate behavior change on his own initiative.

One factor which purportedly affects the reliability of self-monitoring has been referred to as the "reactivity" of the measurement technique. That is, once an individual begins to reflect on the extent to which he engages in a particular behavior, depending on whether he views that behavior as desirable or undesirable, the rate of that behavior will tend to either increase or decrease (see McFall, 1970, with respect to the reactivity of self-monitoring on cigarette smoking). In fact, self-monitoring has often been used precisely because it is expected that the reactive effects will result in behavior change in a therapeutically desirable direction.

As with all self-assessment techniques, it would be unwise to depend on data obtained by self-monitoring alone without convergent measures to substantiate the accuracy of self-report. One possibility would be to have an outside observer independently monitor the target social responses of an individual who was learning to monitor specific aspects of his own behavior. Simple correlations between the two reports would provide some evidence for the reliability of self-observation. To the extent that the subject was an inaccurate observer of his own behavior, feedback could then be employed to increase the accuracy of his self-observations.

The bulk of studies utilizing self-monitoring assessment procedures have, for the most part, dealt with relatively unambiguous covert or instrumental responses such as frequency of obsessional thoughts (Mahoney, 1971), number of cigarettes smoked (McFall, 1970), amount and kinds of foods eaten (Stollak,

1967), frequency of psychogenic tics emitted (Thomas, Abrams & Johnson, 1971). More recently, however, there have been attempts to employ similar monitoring procedures with more complex interpersonal behaviors. For example, Wills, Weiss & Patterson (1974) have developed measures of "affectional" behavior for married couples. Spouses were asked to monitor their partners' "pleasurable" and "displeasurable" behavior over a period of two weeks. In this procedure various areas of instrumental marital behavior were outlined for couples, e.g., spouse took out the garbage. Provisions were made for recording the daily frequency of these behaviors, as well as ratings of how pleasing the behaviors were to the spouse.

At this point, some specific guidelines can be offered as to how self-monitoring procedures might be employed to assess changes in frequency of interpersonal behavior:

1. Relevant target social behaviors to be increased or decreased should be identified by the trainer and discussed with the client. These could be non-verbal behaviors such as smiling or making appropriate gestures, etc. or verbal behaviors such as number of compliments issued during social interaction. Target behaviors should be defined as unambiguously as possible, with numerous examples given. In some cases it will be necessary for the trainer to provide coaching or modeling so that the client can reliably reproduce the response to be monitored.

2. Hypothetical role playing situations may be constructed during which the client will be expected to emit the desired responses. This could be role played situations with an employer, spouse, or in a dating situation.

3. Extra-office interpersonal situations may be planned where the emissions of the specified social behavior will be appropriate. For example, the client could be required to monitor his emission of positively reinforcing statements during nightly conversations with his spouse. In other situations it may be more feasible to have the client monitor the frequency of specific behaviors across a variety of social situations on a daily basis.

4. The client should be trained in self-recording procedures. He may accomplish this by using unobtrusive counters, or simple behavior checklists. In the case of relatively high frequency social behaviors, it is probably better to have these monitored by an unobtrusive counter while he is in the social situation. When this is not feasible, checklists can be filled out immediately following relevant interactions.

In summary, self-monitoring may be useful for assessing a few specific aspects of an individual's social behavior since he is unlikely to be able to consistently attend to more than one or two of his behaviors during social interaction. It also represents a good way of combining treatment with assessment procedures since self-monitoring depends upon training an individual to accurately discriminate important aspects of his social behavior, which he then both influences and assesses himself.

Physiological Assessment

There is some difference of opinion regarding the utility of psychophysiological measures in the assessment of social skills. With respect to the studies reviewed earlier, heart rate or pulse measures were employed to assess "social anxiety" in relation to its possible inhibitory effect on interpersonal performance (Borkovec *et al.*, 1974; Twentyman & McFall, 1975). This assumes that there is some direct relationship between a particular emotional state and behavioral performance. While Borkovec *et al.* (1974) found that a group of subjects who scored high on two self-reported items of social anxiety had higher mean heart rates than a group of low anxiety subjects, intercorrelations of the physiological measures with self-reported anxiety and autonomic perception, speech disfluencies, speaking time, and confederate ratings of anxiety indicated no significant relationships. Thus, the physiological measures employed were largely unrelated to self-report and behavioral measures in other response systems.

While the bulk of psychological research has supported the contention that physiological arousal mediates diverse forms of emotional behavior, Bandura (1969), in a review of the literature, has pointed out that the varied emotions which individuals experience phenomenologically (e.g., anger, fear, pleasure) are not accompanied by a corresponding diversity of physiological response patterns. Further, it appears that different emotional states are cognitively identified and discriminated primarily in terms of the external social situation rather than internal somatic cues. Finally, in assessing physiological responsivity to specific stimuli, correlations among physiological indicators tend to be quite low.

The implications of these findings for social skills assessment are:

1. There is no necessary relationship between general physiological arousal and self-report of specific emotional states. Some individuals may label their physiological arousal in interpersonal situations as anxiety, others may label it as pleasurable excitement, or still others as anger.

2. Some individuals may behave, to all outward appearances, in a highly socially skilled manner under conditions of high physiological arousal, while others may appear equally skilled under conditions of low or moderate arousal.

3. Individual differences in patterns of physiological arousal in response to interpersonal situations may lead to similar or different behavior patterns depending upon how they are interpreted by the person.

4. Of measures in all response systems, physiological indicators would appear to be among the least reliable in terms of predicting complex social behaviors.

In summary, physiological measures appear to lack validity with respect to assessment of social behavior. In addition, they are difficult to obtain since special apparatus is required which may be unavailable to many investigators. Finally, procedures involved in obtaining physiological measures are typically intrusive with regard to the "natural quality" of social interaction for which many investigators have striven. Therefore, if physiological measures are used to assess the emotional concomitants of social behavior, the results should be interpreted with caution. They may be used advantageously, however, in group analogue studies where individual differences in response to experimental conditions are relatively unimportant, and the artificiality of their presence can be tolerated.

Behavioral Assessment Techniques

As alluded to earlier in the chapter, the behavioral complexities of social skill present formidable assessment problems for the behavior analyst in comparison to the assessment of behaviors which allow for greater specification such as psychogenic tics, handwashing rituals, school absences, etc. Because socially important behaviors have many verbal and non-verbal components of differing relevances in different social situations, the specification of behavioral referents for any social skill is difficult to obtain. In addition, demonstration of the social significance or social validity of the specified behaviors is a necessary task.

Subjective versus Objective Measures

In this section, two somewhat overlapping definitions for specifying referents and validation procedures for assessing social skill will be discussed. For convenience, they will be referred to as objective and subjective definitions. In reality, objectively and subjectively defined social behaviors are on a continuum. To the extent that interpersonal behaviors can be precisely specified to outside observers in advance of the rating procedures, the measurement process is objective. To the extent judges decide for themselves whether the observed behaviors reflect various definitions of social skill, the process is subjective.

Objective Definitions

These definitions typically relate to components of social behaviors which can be precisely specified. For example, Eisler, Hersen & Agras (1973a) objectively defined interpersonal "looking" and "smiling." Looking was defined in terms of the subject turning his head 45 degrees toward his interpersonal partner, with eyes focused between the top of the head and chin. Smiling was defined as a 45° crease in the subject's cheek with teeth showing.

Other social interactional variables which may be defined with a high degree of objectivity would be duration of silence, length of utterance, duration of speech, interruptions, questions, or physical contact. Measurement of these relatively simple social responses is accomplished in a straightforward fashion by timing with a stop watch or counting frequency of their occurrence during specified interaction intervals.

Subjective Definitions

These definitions relate to more global aspects of social behavior which cannot be precisely specified. Examples of highly subjective definitions of social skill would be "masculine assertiveness," "empathetic listening," or "vocal affective tone." With these definitions, raters are asked to observe various segments of social interaction, and then make ratings of their impressions on global numerical scales indicating to what degree the variables were present.

In addition, a number of conversational content variables which have a high degree of subjectivity may be rated on similar global scales, e.g., "reinforcing comments" or "negotiation statement." However, it may be possible to increase the objectivity of these ratings by specifying classes of statements to be rated under a specific definitional category. For example, Lewinsohn (1975) specified that statements of affection, approval, agreement, and interest, etc. would be considered positive interpersonal reactions.

It is sometimes possible to use subjectively defined concepts of social skill to help specify more objective component behaviors. For example, Eisler *et al.* (1973) obtained global ratings of assertiveness in a series of analogue interactions. High and low assertive subjects identified by the global assertiveness ratings were compared on emission of specific behaviors which could be specified objectively and then rated reliably. Some of the component behaviors which distinguished the high and low assertive individuals were duration of reply, speech latency, and interpersonal request statements. Further validation that these component behaviors were related to subjective judgments of assertiveness would require that global ratings be again obtained on the unassertive individuals after they had been trained to decrease their speech latency, increase their duration of speech, and make additional interpersonal requests. An increase in assertiveness following changes in the specified target behaviors would provide evidence that the component behaviors were measuring assertiveness.

In most assessment situations requiring behavioral measures of social skill, it is probably better to use a combination of objective and subjective measures rather than relying on either type alone. While it is generally more difficult to obtain high interjudge agreement with subjective measures, they appear to possess greater social validity than any single objective behavioral measure of social skill. This is probably due to the fact that raters respond to subtle behavioral cues and social contextual variables, which usually cannot be specified with objective measures. In order to enhance the reliability of subjective measures, it would be highly desirable to demonstrate numerous examples of the subjectively defined social skills to raters as well as provide them with considerable practice in making ratings.

When using the more highly specified objective measures, it is necessary to demonstrate that the measured behaviors bear significant relationships to the skill which is being assessed. This may be accomplished through either correlational analysis, or the measure's ability to statistically discriminate between groups of individuals who appear to have the skill versus those who do not.

Development of Social Assessment Situations

There are several methods of eliciting social-interpersonal performances for behavioral assessment. In some instances, it is possible to require a subject to imagine that he is in a particular situation and then ask him what response he would give if he were really there. This is analogous to data that may be obtained during interviews, except that it stresses the exact form and content of the response. However, this method provides little direct indication as to how the other person in the social situation will respond.

Situations which most closely approximate the subject's real life situations are more likely to elicit his actual interpersonal response. This objective can be attained by either: (a) role playing social situations, or (b) involvement of the individual's real life interactional partners in the assessment situation. With respect to the latter, it is possible to obtain interactional data in either the office or laboratory, or in the natural environment setting. While some have argued that obtaining measures in the natural environment (e.g., at home) represents the "purist" sample of the individual's actual social behavior, it is possible that the presence of raters or recording equipment has "reactive" effects which may detract from the validity of the performance. In addition, the collection of data in the individual's natural environment will usually be too difficult or costly to obtain in most instances. Thus, the following guidelines are suggested in obtaining social interaction data by means of role playing or by observation of natural environment partners.

Role Playing

In order to maximize elicitation of the person's probable real life interpersonal responses, the following criteria should be observed prior to role playing:

1. Scenes of the target person's interaction with specific individuals should be recreated as vividly as possible. Attention should be paid to details leading up

to the interaction, the environmental surroundings of the interaction, e.g., in a department store or at home, etc. In addition, the client should be queried as to how he was feeling, and how he thought the other person was feeling. Sometimes it is possible to allow the person to take the role of the real life respondent in order to help the role played respondent deliver responses more similar to those the client interacts with in his natural environment.

2. A variety of scenes should be obtained which sample various dimensions of interpersonal difficulties. In order to obtain a broad perspective of the individual's social skills in a variety of interpersonal situations, scenes may be constructed which sample the person's behavior with several different respondents or different situations with the same respondent. For example, if it is desired to obtain assessment data on an individual's heterosocial skills, several simulated dating situations could be constructed. These would include role played scenes such as asking a girl for a date, greeting the girl at the door, and conversations with the girl during the date. Additional scenes could be devised which deal with the target individual's ability to interact with females who differ in age and familiarity to the client, e.g., girlfriend, cashier, or waitress.

Once relevant scenes have been identified, role playing procedures are introduced to the individual by his therapist or technician. Frequently, the target individual will complain that the role playing seems silly or unnatural. The therapist must counter with how much more useful this information is than "talking" about his interpersonal problems. Usually after three or four role played scenes, the client will feel free to respond naturally with little difficulty.

There are several ways in which the role played respondent can interact with the target individual. To a large extent this depends on the purpose of the assessment. For research purposes, it is best to have the respondent deliver relatively standardized replies, prepared in advance, so that the subject's performance over several baseline sessions is not affected by changes in the respondent's behavior. This rationale also applies when trying to standardize the role playing situations with groups of subjects. Unfortunately, the standardization of respondent behavior creates a somewhat artificial atmosphere for the interaction and should not be employed when one is attempting to achieve maximum therapeutic benefit. In clinical assessment situations, the therapist should attempt to respond as he thinks the real life or anticipated natural environment partners would respond.

Natural Environment Partners

In some cases it is possible to assess an individual's social skill by observing interaction with his natural environment partners. This may obviate the need for or supplement role playing. Assessment of natural interactions are possible when an individual's spouse, friends, or member of his family can be utilized in the assessment. This procedure is most often followed when it is expected that the assessment will lead to modifying the social interaction pattern of both partners. That is, the social skill of both individuals may be assessed in relation to the response pattern of the other.

When natural environment partners are available, assessment situations may be developed in several ways. In the first, it is possible to elicit particular kinds of interactional situations from both partners. For example, the therapist may want to assess how skillfully the couple negotiates common conflict situations. Sample situations might then be constructed to evaluate how the couple interacts when presented with critical life situations such as how to discipline the children, deal with financial problems, or regulate their sexual life. The identification and description of scenes are obtained in a manner similar to that described under role playing. To the extent possible, the couple is instructed to interact as if they were at home with respect to the key problem issues in a semistructured time limited manner.

A less structured format may be used when the couple has difficulty in identifying important issues that relate to their interaction. In these instances, instructing the couple to interact for longer periods of time concerning topics of their choice has merit. It must be stressed, however, that the therapist or other observers should not take part in the interaction, but merely observe it.

Observing and Recording Interaction

In observing both role played and natural environment partner interactions, it is desirable to have the observers as unobtrusive as possible since their presence may inadvertently influence the course of the observed interaction. One-way mirrors and television monitoring are two methods which permit observation of verbal and nonverbal social interaction which virtually eliminate most sources of observer influence. Of course, the fact that the individual(s) know that they are being observed may affect their "typical" interaction to some extent. However, these reactive effects appear to be relatively minor.

In clinical situations where the therapist employs himself as both role played respondent and observer, it is clear that he will, to some degree, alter the usual course of his client's performance. However, this should not present the therapist with an insurmountable obstacle in using role playing as an assessment procedure since the results will probably be more enlightening than the more traditional therapist-client discussions of his social behavior.

As has been stressed throughout the chapter, social interaction is a complex process with numerous behaviors being emitted, reciprocated, and exchanged during relatively brief time intervals. This presents a serious problem for a single observer or even several observers who cannot record all that is transpiring. One possibility is to pre-select specific interpersonal behaviors of interest and record them on a frequency of occurrence basis. The reader should be cautioned that reliability of ratings tend to drop drastically whenever a single observer attempts to record three or more behaviors simultaneously.

Videotape recordings of interpersonal interaction represent an alternative to live observation for both the clinician and researcher. Previous research has shown that observation from videotape is as reliable as live observation (Eisler, Hersen & Agras, 1973b). The advantage of videotape is that the observer can focus on different aspects of the social interaction during subsequent replays. This permits the researcher to more precisely examine specific social behaviors and sensitizes the clinician to aspects of social performance which would not be possible during one observation.

Summary and Conclusions

Behavioral approaches to the assessment and training of social skill is a relatively recent development. Assessment techniques based on the traditional conceptualization of underlying personality dynamics which attempted to quantify personality dimensions have little functional relevance to the measurement of interpersonal skills. Despite the sophistication of these measures, scores on objective tests and clinical interpretations of refined psychometric instruments failed to predict how an individual would behave under a given set of social-environmental circumstances.

The predictive failure of traditional assessment appears to result from several misconceptions. *First*, the generality of social behavior across situations was presumed to result from hypothetical personality constructs which were conceptualized as having etiological significance. In short, "personality" was presumed to cause certain kinds of interpersonal behavior. The possibility that the individual's behavior might, in part, be determined by the social environment was neglected. *Second*, the personality variables were defined in such global terms that classification of interactional observations could not be accomplished with any degree of accuracy or reliability. *Finally*, most psychometric instruments relied almost entirely on the self-report of the subject. We now know that subjects purposively or without awareness may not discriminate or accurately report on many of their activities, especially when these are complex social behaviors.

The assessment of social skill is still in its infancy. The recent attempts to delineate specific behaviors which comprise social skill has met with some success. The general application of specific behavioral skill measures to all populations in varying social situations seems doubtful. It may be that some identified behavioral measures will reflect social competence in a variety of interactive situations, while others will apply to relatively few situations.

Global measures of social skill presently appear to possess a high degree of consensual validity in that observers can agree that a particular individual in a given situation possesses a certain degree of social skill. In all probability, they are attending not only to the behavior of the actor whose skill they are assessing, but also to the responses elicited from the respondents. In fact, it may be possible to assess an individual's social skill by assigning him certain interpersonal tasks, e.g., to elicit praise, agreement, and cooperation, etc., from a series of respondents. The assessment of the individual's social skill would thus be accomplished by measuring the degree to which he elicited these behaviors from the respondents.

One final speculative notion should be mentioned. Perhaps the enumeration of various social skills including the ability to negotiate conflicts, the ability to monitor the non-verbal communications of others, and the ability to vary one's response repertoire depending on the responses of another can be specified and measured with greater precision than at present.

References

Alberti, R. E., & Emmons, M. L. *Your perfect right: A guide to assertive behavior*. San Luis Obispo: Impact, 1974.

Argyle, M. *Social interaction*. Chicago: Aldine, 1969.

Arkowitz, H., Lichtenstein, E., McGovern, K., & Hines, P. The behavioral assessment of social competence in males. *Behavior Therapy*, 1975, **6**, 3–13.

Bandura, A. *Principles of behavior modification*. New York: Holt, Rinehart & Winston, 1969.

Borkovec, T. D., Stone, N. M., O'Brien, G. T., & Kaloupek, D. G. Evaluation of a clinically relevant target behavior for analog outcome research. *Behavior Therapy*, 1974, **5**, 503–513.

Eisler, R. M., Hersen, M., & Agras, W. S. Videotape: A method for the controlled observation of nonverbal interpersonal behavior. *Behavior Therapy*, 1973a, **4**, 420–425.

Eisler, R. M., Hersen, M., & Agras, W. S. Effects of videotape and instructional feedback on nonverbal marital interaction: An analogue study. *Behavior Therapy*, 1973b, **4**, 551–558.

Eisler, R. M., Hersen, M., & Miller, P. M. Effects of modeling on components of assertive behavior. *Journal of Behavior Therapy and Experimental Psychiatry*, 1973, **4**, 1–6.

Eisler, R. M., Hersen, M., & Miller, P. M. Shaping components of assertive behavior with instructions and feedback. *American Journal of Psychiatry*, 1974, **131**, 1344–1347.

Eisler, R. M., Hersen, M., Miller, P. M., & Blanchard, E. B. Situational determinants of assertive behavior. *Journal of Consulting and Clinical Psychology*, 1975, **43**, 330–340.

Eisler, R. M., Miller, P. M., & Hersen, M. Components of assertive behavior. *Journal of Clinical Psychology*, 1973, **29**, 295–299.

Gambrill, E. D., & Richey, C. A. An assertion inventory for use in assessment and research. *Behavior Therapy*, 1975, **6**, 550–561.

Goldstein, A. P. *Structured learning therapy: Toward a psychotherapy for the poor*. New York: Academic Press, 1973.

Hall, C. S., & Lindzey, G. *Theories of personality*. New York: John Wiley & Sons, 1957.

Hersen, M., & Bellack, A. S. Assessment of social skills. In A. R. Ciminero, K. S., Calhoun, & H. E. Adams (Eds.), *Handbook for behavioral assessment*. New York: John Wiley & Sons, in press.

Hersen, M., Eisler, R. M., & Miller, P. M. Development of assertive responses: Clinical, measurement, and research considerations. *Behaviour Research and Therapy*, 1973, **11**, 505–521.

Hersen, M., Eisler, R. M., Miller, P. M., Johnson, M. B., & Pinkston, S. G. Effects of practice, instructions, and modeling on components of assertive behavior. *Behaviour Research and Therapy*, 1973, **11**, 443–451.

Kazdin, A. E. Self monitoring and behavior change. In M. J. Mahoney, & C. E. Thoresen (Eds.), *Self control: Power to the person*. Monterey: Brooks-Cole, 1974.

Lazarus, A. A. *Behavior therapy and beyond*. New York: McGraw-Hill, 1971.

Levine, J., & Zigler, E. The essential-reactive distinction in alcoholism: A developmental approach. *Journal of Abnormal Psychology*, 1973, **81**, 242–249.

Lewinsohn, P. M. The behavioral study and treatment of depression. In M. Hersen, R. M. Isler, & P. M. Miller (Eds.), *Progress in behavior modification, Vol. 1*. New York: Academic Press, 1975.

Lewinsohn, P. M., & Shaffer, M. Use of home observations as an integral part of the treatment of depression. *Journal of Consulting and Clinical Psychology*, 1971, **37**, 87–94.

Lewinsohn, P. M., Weinstein, M. S., & Alper, T. A behavioral approach to the group treatment of depressed persons: A methodological contribution. *Journal of Clinical Psychology*, 1970, **26**, 525–632.

Libet, J., & Lewinsohn, P. M. The concept of social skill with special references to the behavior of depressed persons. *Journal of Consulting and Clinical Psychology*, 1973, **40**, 304–312.

Mahoney, M. J. The self-management of covert behavior: A case study. *Behavior Therapy*, 1971, **2**, 575–578.

McFall, R. M. The effects of self-monitoring on normal smoking behavior. *Journal of Consulting and Clinical Psychology*, 1970, **35**, 135–142.

McFall, R. M., & Lillesand, D. B. Behavior rehearsal with modeling and coaching in assertion training. *Journal of Abnormal Psychology*, 1971, **77**, 313–323.

McFall, R. M., & Marston, A. R. An experimental investigation of behavioral rehearsal in assertive training. *Journal of Abnormal Psychology*, 1970, **76**, 295–303.

McFall, R. M., & Twentyman, C. T. Four experiments on the relative contributions of rehearsal, modeling, and coaching to assertion training. *Journal of Abnormal Psychology*, 1973, **81**, 199–218.

Phillips, L., & Zigler, E. Social competence: The action-thought parameter and vicariousness in normal and pathological behaviors. *Journal of Abnormal and Social Psychology*, 1961, **63**, 137–146.

Phillips, L., & Zigler, E. Role orientation, the action-thought dimension, and outcome in psychiatric disorder. *Journal of Abnormal and Social Psychology*, 1964, **68**, 381–389.

Rathus, S. A. A 30-item schedule for assessing assertive behavior. *Behavior Therapy*, 1973, **4**, 398–406.

Rehm, L. P., & Marston, A. R. Reduction of social anxiety through modification of self-reinforcement: An instigation therapy technique. *Journal of Consulting and Clinical Psychology*, 1968, **32**, 565–574.

Rimm, D. C., & Masters, J. C. *Behavior therapy: Techniques and empirical findings*. New York: Academic Press, 1974.

Stollak, G. E. Weight loss obtained under different experimental procedures. *Psychotherapy, Theory, Research and Practice*, 1967, **4**, 61–64.

Taylor, J. A. A personality scale of manifest anxiety. *Journal of Abnormal and Social Psychology*, 1953, **48**, 285–290.

Thomas, E. J., Abrams, K. S., & Johnson, J. B. Self-monitoring and reciprocal inhibition in the modification of multiple tics of Guilles de la Tourette's syndome. *Journal of Behavior Therapy and Experimental Psychiatry*, 1971, **2**, 159–171.

Twentyman, G. T., & McFall, R. M. Behavioral training of social skills in shy males. *Journal of Consulting and Clinical Psychology*, 1975, **43**, 384–395.

Watson, D., & Friend, R. Measurement of social-evaluative anxiety. *Journal of Consulting and Clinical Psychology*, 1969, **33**, 448–457.

Weinman, B., Gelbart, P., Wallace, M., & Post, M. Inducing assertive behavior in chronic schizophrenics: A comparison of socio-environmental, desensitization, and relaxation therapies. *Journal of Consulting and Clinical Psychology*, 1972, **39**, 246–252.

Wills, T. A., Weiss, R. L., & Patterson, G. R. A behavioral analysis of the determinants of marital satisfaction. *Journal of Consulting and Clinical Psychology*, 1974, **42**, 802–811.

Wolpe, J. *Psychotherapy by reciprocal inhibition*. Stanford: Stanford University Press, 1958.

Wolpe, J. *The practice of behavior therapy*. New York: Pergamon Press, 1969.

Wolpe, J., & Lang, P. J. A fear survey schedule for use in behavior therapy. *Behaviour Research and Therapy*, 1964, **2**, 27–30.

Wolpe, J., & Lazarus, A. A. *Behavior therapy techniques: A guide to the treatment of neuroses*. New York: Pergamon Press, 1966.

Zigler, E., & Phillips, L. Social effectiveness and symptomatic behaviors. *Journal of Abnormal and Social Psychology*, 1960, **61**, 231–238.

Zigler, E., & Phillips, L. Social competence and the process-reactive distinction in psychopathology. *Journal of Abnormal and Social Psychology*, 1962, **65**, 215–222.

CHAPTER 14

Assessment of Marital Dysfunction

THEODORE JACOB
University of Pittsburgh

Introduction

As noted throughout this volume, the behavioral assessment of any problem behavior rests on a common set of assumptions and principles. Of particular importance, assessment is viewed as integral to and often indistinguishable from intervention, in that both activities are part of an entire process requiring the ongoing measurement of behavior in contexts (Weiss, 1968). This ongoing assessment process, in turn, is fundamentally dependent on functional analyses of antecedent-behavior-consequence sequences. As noted by Peterson (1965), "the major task . . . (of assessment) . . . is to identify the stimuli involved in functional relationships with the behavior under consideration, and then, by systematic alteration in stimulus-response regularities, to modify behavior in whatever direction is desired" (p. 39). Stated otherwise, behavioral assessment is most accurately defined in terms of ongoing, functional analyses of distressful behavioral sequences and of more satisfying alternative interactions, and by necessity involves the identification, description and systematic evaluation of: (1) problem behaviors and desired alternatives, (2) events and behaviors which are functionally related to problem and to desired interactions, and (3) strategies for rearranging behavioral sequences so as to increase the frequency and magnitude with which desired behaviors occur.

Because of this intimate relationship between behavioral assessment and therapy, it is literally impossible to describe assessment procedures and techniques without reference to the rationale and characteristics of the overall treatment program within which assessment occurs. Therefore, a brief overview of behaviorally oriented marital therapy will be presented, with the aim of highlighting the major characteristics, goals, and strategies of such a treatment program. Hopefully, this general framework will aid the reader in understanding the purpose of particular assessment procedures that are subsequently discussed. After describing the various assessment procedures, this chapter will conclude with a discussion of salient issues, problems, and future research needs involved in the assessment of marital dissatisfaction.

Behavioral Marital Therapy

During the past decade, a number of clinicians and researchers have been actively involved in the development and evaluation of behavioral treatment approaches for marital dysfunction. Foremost among such efforts are those of Stuart (1969), Azrin (Azrin, Naster & Jones, 1973), and Patterson and Weiss (Patterson & Hops, 1972; Weiss, Hops & Patterson, 1973). Although differences across these presentations are evident, all have drawn heavily (if not exclusively) on a behavioral model in the generation of treatment rationales, objectives, and procedures. The following description of behavioral marital therapy will highlight the major characteristics of this treatment model, which of necessity, must be presented in a rather brief manner. Given the limited space that can be devoted to this description, together with the acknowledged differences reflected across the several variants of this model, the reader is encouraged to consult original sources for more detailed discussion.

From the very first contact with the presenting couple, the clinician begins teaching the clients a behavioral framework and associated vocabulary by which their difficulties can be understood and resolved. Implicitly and explicitly by words and by actions, the clinician attempts to explain and shape a behavioral orientation and vocabulary necessary for the effective modification of the dissatisfying relationship. Specifically, the clinician aids the clients in translating reported dissatisfactions, complaints, and unhappiness into specific, objective descriptions of behaviors and behavioral sequences. Slowly but consistently the clinician moves the clients from vague and global descriptions of dissatisfaction which emphasize the partner's motives and traits, to specific behavioral statements which define what each partner desires for himself and from his spouse. Of particular importance, each partner is helped to specify what *positive* behavioral changes from himself and from his partner are desired and would result in that member's increased satisfaction with his spouse and marital relationship. At the beginning of this specification procedure, the therapist first obtains information relevant to general areas and then to specific behaviors and interactions, all the while emphasizing the importance of stating positive and specific behaviors that one desires to increase versus negative and general behaviors that one desires to decrease. For example, a husband may initially describe a general dissatisfaction with his marriage, citing an absence of "love" and "affection" as major concerns. Through continued discussion and probing, the couple's sexual relationship becomes defined as a major problem area which the husband associates with persistent frustration and lack of fulfillment. With further questioning and description, the sexual difficulties are defined as the absence of sexual intercourse during the week; finally, the positive behavior that the husband desires and which would be associated with his increased satisfaction with the marital relationship is having sexual intercourse with his wife at least once during the weekend and at least twice during the week. Throughout this process, the clinician supports the clients in their concerns yet challenges them to be specific, positive, and behavioral, continuing to ask each partner: "what could your spouse do that would increase your satisfaction with him (her) and with your relationship?"

Having defined and described what each partner desires in specific, positive, behavioral terms, the clinician aids the couple in identifying behaviors and events that each spouse views as reinforcing, rewarding, and pleasurable. This step requires the clinician to define and catalogue events as potential positive reinforcers, which can be employed subsequently in the maintenance of desired relationship behaviors which were previously defined and described. Most obviously, events that each partner defines as positively reinforcing can be directly emitted behaviors from his (her) spouse, including both affectional behaviors (e.g., initiating sexual relationships, greeting the spouse with a hug and kiss upon returning home, talking about the day's events, sharing thoughts and feelings about various experiences, etc.), and instrumental behaviors (e.g., preparing meals on time, keeping the house neat and orderly, regular maintenance of automobile and yard, etc.). In addition, there are events which are reinforcing for each partner that involve persons other than the spouse and/or participation in activities not including the spouse (e.g., going bowling "with the boys," having private time on weekends, etc.). Although participation in such activities may be pleasurable, the reaction of the partner to the spouse's involvement could either increase or decrease the probability of repeated involvement, and hence, future level of pleasurable experiences. Imagine, for example, a husband returning home after an enjoyable evening "with the boys" and being greeted by a wife who expressed disapproval and anger versus interest and warmth. As such, the clinician would not only seek to identify such nonspouse reinforcers, but to specify those spouse behaviors (preceding and following the partner's involvement in an activity) which serve to enhance versus reduce the pleasure that the partner experiences.

Having defined and translated problem behaviors into their desirable positive counterparts (e.g., no sexual relationship versus sexual intercourse two times per week) and having identified and catalogued spouse and nonspouse events which are pleasurable and rewarding for each partner, the clinician aids the couple in negotiating and implementing a behavioral contract which specifies those spouse behaviors requested by each partner from the other, as well as spouse and nonspouse behaviors that each spouse finds rewarding. In general, each partner commits himself to certain performances independent of his spouse's performance of similarly requested behavior[1]. For example, the wife is asked to initiate sexual relations with her husband during the week, whereas the husband is asked to spend 1 hour per evening talking with his wife about the

[1]This approach is referred to as the "good faith" (versus the "quid pro quo") model of contingency contracting; the reader is referred to Weiss, Birchler & Vincent (1974) for an excellent discussion and analysis of several contrasting models.

day's events and activities. If the wife does initiate sexual activity, the husband will suggest an evening out together at a movie, restaurant, or play. Conversely, if the husband talks with his wife 1 hour per night throughout the week, the wife will take the children to a movie on Sunday afternoon while her husband watches a football game on television at home. To be noted, the above described contingencies involve the accrual of a reinforcing event (dinner out and watching television alone) contingent upon performance of requested behavior (intercourse and evening talks), whereas each partner commits him (her) self to perform the requested behavior whether or not the spouse performs the parallel requested behavior. In the previous example, the wife would only be obliged to take the children out on Sunday afternoon if her husband talks with her throughout the week, although she would still be obliged to initiate sexual activity whether or not her husband spoke with her every evening. Given this paradigm, the ability to identify and incorporate meaningful and potent reinforcers for each spouse will be very important insofar as increasing the probability that requested behavior will be performed and maintained—an issue that underscores the importance of clearly defining reinforcing behavior as previously described. Finally, initially stated contracts must be continually evaluated, refined, and revised in order to assure that desired behaviors are of current importance to the spouses, that each spouse understands and can perform the requested behavior, and that additional contracts can be added and monitored as treatment continues.

Finally, several workers have described training partners in general communication and problem solving skills which will help them generalize from specific issues dealt with during treatment to other difficulties that can (and most likely will) arise in the future. Although much of this training by necessity is occurring throughout previously described activities, it is not uncommon to include a focused intervention designed to consolidate previous learning and to increase the couple's future coping skills. Focusing on behaviors which directly relate to "negotiation and problem solving skills" as well as behaviors "which serve an en route function" (Weiss *et al.*, 1973), couples will practice and learn to communicate positive messages, to express requests rather than condemnations, to listen and grasp the partner's entire communication before responding, to positively reinforce (both verbally and nonverbally) the partner for constructive problem solving behavior, and to discuss and generate rules and guidelines which specify how, when, and under what conditions new as well as previously established contracts can be negotiated.

Marital Assessment Procedures

Having described the major objectives and strategies of behavioral marital therapy, relevant assessment procedures will now be presented. In the interests of clarity, the various assessment techniques will be discussed in terms of two major groupings: (1) reports of the marital relationship based upon perceptions of past behavior and events, and (2) observations of the marital relationship based upon the systematic monitoring of ongoing (current) behavior and events—these observations including: (a) spouse's self observations, (b) spouse's observations of partner, and (c) trained others' observations of current marital interaction. Within each of these groupings and subgroupings, various procedures will be described so as to highlight the quantity and quality of information that is obtained, the treatment objective or strategy that is advanced by obtaining and using such information, and relevant reliability and validity data associated with the various procedures or instruments.

Spouses' Reports of Self and Partner

Marital Precounseling Inventory (*MPI*). Stuart's (Stuart & Stuart, 1972) inventory represents the most systematically organized and comprehensive data collection procedure within this grouping. Overall, nine categories are assessed: Goals for Behavior Change, Resources for Change, Degree of Marital Understanding, Power Distribution, Congruence of Priorities, Communication Effectiveness, Sexual Satisfaction, Congruence in Child Management, and General Marital Satisfaction. After completing a basic information sheet and a family locator, the client answers a variety of questions—the common theme being the continued request for specific, behaviorally oriented information regarding the individual's reports and desires for self, spouse, and the marital relationship. The three general uses for the inventory are described as providing early socialization into the treatment model by structuring and directing the clients' attention toward positive behavioral statements and translations; providing a highly organized, comprehensive set of information directly related to treatment at the very onset; and providing a means for periodic evaluations by systematic comparisons among reports gathered before treatment (baseline), during treatment, and after treatment (outcome). Item B, for example, asks the client to "Please list three things which you would like your spouse to do more often. In answering this question, please be positive and specific. For example, write 'During dinner, ask me how I spent the day' instead of 'Be less preoccupied with himself all the time we are together' (negative and vague). How often did he or she do each of these things in the last 7 days? How important are each of these things to you?"

For each item of the questionnaire, the accompanying manual clearly and succinctly provides the rationale and use for each separate item and the associated information. For example, in describing the information obtained from the previously cited item, Stuart comments as follows: "This list serves to provide the therapist with a more focused description of exactly what changes each spouse would like to see in the behavior of the other . . . (and) . . . can be viewed as the benchmarks of how the husband and wife expect each other to act. A large proportion of the time in treatment can then be devoted to facilitating the exchange of these behaviors each of which is valued by the other. In addition, client estimates of the extent to which each has received desired responses from the other during the past week serve as a rough retrospective baseline and ratings of the importance of the goals suggest an intervention hierarchy for the therapist." (Stuart & Stuart, 1972, p. 6). Although Stuart recommends that clients complete the inventory prior to the first meeting with the therapist, alternative procedures can be adopted. For example, given the inventory's considerable length together with motivational characteristics of particular clients, the therapist might ask the clients to complete the inventory (in full or modified form) after the first meeting—a procedure which might increase the probability that the form is carefully completed so as to be maximally useful.

Information regarding the inventory's reliability and validity characteristics has not been obtained with the exception of Stuart's brief reference to MPI data collected from a 400 couple sample. Specifically, when asked to indicate who *has* decision making responsibility (from "almost always husband" to "almost always wife") in 11 different areas and who *should have* such responsibilities (Item G), "wives generally started treatment with discrepancy scores averaging 10.8 and terminated treatment with scores averaging 2.6, whereas husbands generally began treatment with average scores of 11.0 and terminated treatment with average scores of 0.9" (Stuart & Stuart, 1972, p. 10). Similarly, ratings of general marital satisfaction (Item L) for ten areas (each rated from "95% happy or satisfied" to "5% happy or satisfied") indicated that "starting assessments typically fell at overall men ratings of 38% for women and 30% for men with post-treatment means reaching 81% for both sexes." (Stuart & Stuart, 1972, p. 16).

Marriage Inventory (*MI*). Although similar in structure and aim, Knox's (1971) form is much less comprehensive and systematically constructed than that of Stuart. As such, less time is required to complete the inventory although the loss of information and specificity is considerable. The form first asks for basic demographic information ("General") and then requests the individual to complete an adjective check list aimed at describing both mood and overt behavior characteristics of the respondent ("Clinical"). The third section lists nine problem areas in marriage (Sex, Communication, Money, In-laws, Religion, Recreation, Friends, Alcohol, Children) as well as specific problems within each of the major domains (e.g., specific problems regarding Friends include "different friends," "time with," "confidences to friends," "too few friends," "too many friends," and "other"). Within each major category, the individual is asked to indicate specific problems that "you have had or are having in your marriage". The remaining six questions ask the individual to indicate behaviors emitted by self that are pleasing to his spouse, spouse behaviors that are pleasing to him, and self and spouse behaviors that one wishes to increase. No reliability or validity data have been reported for this instrument.

Marital Adjustment Scale (MAS). Of the various "report" procedures, the Locke-Wallace scale represents the best-known measure of general marital satisfaction which has been involved in various reliability and validity studies during the past 15 years (see Kimmel & van der Veen, 1974; Locke & Wallace, 1959). In its most recent form, the individual is asked to indicate his overall satisfaction with his current marriage along a 7-point scale ("very unhappy" to "perfectly happy") and the extent of agreement with his spouse ("always agree" to "always disagree") within eight areas of marriage (e.g., handling family finances, sex relations, etc.). The last six items request ratings relating to how disagreements end, mutual engagement in outside interests, and the like. In general, this form is not particularly useful in its original form and/or without the inclusion of other assessment procedures. Azrin *et al.* (1973), however, used a similar form and collected daily ratings from each spouse, using such information as a general baseline by which therapeutic interventions were assessed. Weiss *et al.* (1973) on the other hand, include such a scale in their assessment package in order "to allow coordination between our sample of cases and others reported in the literature". In sum, the MAS seems to bc of greatest value as an overall, general estimate of one's attractiveness to the current marriage as a rough screening device in selecting experimental and control groups for research activities and with some modification, as a general index of day-to-day fluctuations in one's degree of marital satisfaction.

Areas of Change Questionnaire (A-C). Another assessment procedure from the Oregon group (Weiss *et al.*, 1973), the A-C, was developed to pinpoint particular conflict areas. Specifically, this 34-item form asks the individual to indicate: (a) whether he wants his spouse to change certain behaviors, and if so, in what direction ("much less" to "much more"), (b) whether his partner would be pleased if he changed certain behavior, and if so, in what direction. Specific areas include decisions about spending money, spending time with children, sexual needs, etc. "By comparing the congruence between 'I want my partner to (change) . . .' and 'It would please my partner if I (changed)' between husband-wife and wife-husband combinations of these two modes, conflict agreement-disagreement scores are obtained." (Weiss & Margolin, 1975, p. 32). For example, if the husband indicates that he wants his wife to have meals on time "much more" and the wife indicates that her husband would be pleased if she had meals on time "much more", disagreement as to goals and/or objectives would be nonexistent, although there may be disagreement (conflict) regarding the "means" by which goals should be implemented. As noted by the authors, the A-C seems to be most useful "in providing a starting ground for the spouse to pinpoint instances of conflict about changing the behavior of the other." (Weiss *et al.*, 1973, p. 313).

Although reliability and validity data are far from extensive, several recent studies support the potential utility of this instrument. Specifically, Weiss *et al.* (1973) obtained an internal consistency index of 0.89 for the A-C scale, and correlations of —0.70 between wives' (and husbands') A-C scores and the Locke-Wallace Marital Adjustment Scale (n = 86), whereas Birchler and Webb (1975) found A-C mean scores to be 28.0 and 6.9 for distressed and nondistressed couples respectively (*n* = 100).

Marital Conflict Form (*MCF*). Similar to and overlapping previously described techniques, the MCF (Weiss & Margolin, 1975) attempts to aid the clients and therapist in the identification and specification of marital problem behavior. With this procedure, the client is presented with a list of 26 potential problem areas within marriages which can be subsumed within the domains of Family Living (e.g., finances, husband's work, friendships), Value and Philosophy (e.g., education, religion, etc.), Personal Factors (e.g., temperament and personality differences, sexual adjustment, personal habits, etc.), and Kinship Responsibilities (e.g., husband's mother, wife's mother, etc.). After identifying the three most problematic and the three most satisfying areas within his marriage, the individual is asked to indicate what his partner does that pleases *and* displeases him within each of the six designated areas. Accompanying instructions encourage the individual to be as specific as possible and provide examples of useful and informative kinds of responses that are desired. Finally, the individual is asked to rank the three problem areas (—1, —2, —3) and the three satisfying areas (+1, +2, +3) so as to indicate "how strongly you feel about each of the three Satisfying areas and the three Problem areas". Such data are not only useful in identifying and specifying relevant target behaviors, but can be valuable in selecting marital issues that the couple is asked to discuss during videotaped interactions at baseline (preintervention) and at termination.

Spouses' Observations of Self and Partner

Pleasant Thoughts (*PT*). First introduced by Patterson & Hops (1972) in an attempt to assess cognitive (versus motoric or verbal) correlates of marital relationship behavior, each individual is asked to monitor and record the frequency of pleasant thoughts about his (her) spouse. Depending on the therapist's desire for specificity, the client may also be asked to maintain a daily diary in which he would record spouse behavior associated with each pleasant thought and/or the context in which each thought occurred (e.g., time of day, other people present, physical setting, etc.). Such recordings would be requested throughout the treatment program and would aid the clinician in evaluating the effects and effectiveness of various treatment interventions. As with all observation (versus report) procedures, the client is asked to attend to and systematically monitor current ongoing interactions in as specific a manner as possible.

Although based on but two case studies, changes in the frequency with which spouses report pleasant thoughts have been clearly associated with corresponding changes in observer rated aversive interactions in the home (Patterson & Hops, 1972), and with spouses' observation of affectional interchanges (Weiss & Margolin, 1975).

Marital Activities Inventory—Together, Other, Alone (*MAITOA*). Although this instrument actually falls somewhere between report and observation procedures (Weiss refers to the technique as quasi-observational), it has been included in this grouping because of the demand for specific behavioral information regarding *very recent* events (Weiss *et al.*, 1973). Specifically, the inventory lists 100 potentially rewarding activities in which a person might engage (e.g., playing a musical instrument, sun bathing, having a snack, having a drink, kissing and hugging, visiting a friend, etc.). First, the respondent is asked to indicate those activities in which he participated or was involved during the past 4 weeks and with whom he participated (i.e., alone, with spouse only, with family members only, with spouse and other adults, with nonfamily, others). Next, the individual is asked to indicate those activities he would like to increase in frequency or try for the first time *and* with whom he wants to do so. In essence, this inventory "samples the range of activities available to the spouses and provides an indication of the relative amount of time spent in mutually satisfying activities versus that time spent in activities by self and with nonspouse others." (Weiss *et al.*, 1973). As a pretreatment measure, the MAITOA can be helpful in defining potentially rewarding spouse and nonspouse interactions, whereas comparison between pre- and post-treatment responses can aid in evaluating intervention effects; that is, by assessing change in the frequency of specific shared activities previously defined as "desired" behaviors, as well as the overall increase in number of shared activities.

Although no reliability data are presently available, recent findings provide initial support for the instrument's construct validity. That is, guided by the assumption that "aversiveness of one's partner is an essentially negative-going relationship, it was predicted, and found that distressed partners would avoid one another by engaging in a greater frequency of nonspouse events and sharing significantly fewer recreational events with spouse." (Birchler, Weiss & Vincent, 1975, p. 356).

Spouse Observation Checklist (*SOC*). The SOC (Weiss *et al.* 1973) consists of approximately 400 discrete behaviors which can be performed by either one spouse or both together, and are experienced as having positive or negative reinforcement value for the partner—that is, pleasing (P) or displeasing (D) consequences for the recipient. Overall, twelve areas of marital interaction are defined (Companionship, Affection, Consideration, Sex, Communication Process, Coupling Activities, Child Care and Parenting, Household Management, Financial Decision Making, Employment-Education, Personal Habits and Appearance, and Self and Spouse Independence), and within each area a great variety of P and D behaviors are enumerated; for example, we went for a ride, spouse asked me how my day was, spouse said my jokes are stupid, spouse interrupted me, spouse helped with cooking, spouse left a sink full of dishes, and spouse wrote a check without recording it[2].

The recording of Ps and Ds is performed daily by each spouse, using either the entire 400 item form or a modified form specific to a particular couple. As with other instruments, the SOC can be used to define "target" behaviors and potential reinforcers at the onset of treatment and to assess intervention effects via changes in daily ratings that span different points in therapy.

Regarding the instrument's reliability and validity characteristics, several studies can be noted. First, Birchler *et al.* (1975) reported a P/D ratio of 4.3 for distressed couples and 29.7 for nondistressed couples; based upon this same sample, Weiss *et al.* (1973) reported a correlation of 9.54 between P/D ratio scores and the Locke Wallace Marital Adjustment Scale. Second, Wills *et al.* (1974) reported a multiple $R = 0.508$ between the criterion variable of daily ratings of marital satisfaction and the five predictor variables of daily recordings of instrumental and affectional Ps and Ds and daily ratings of the quality of outside events. In addition, Ds accounted for greater criterion variance than Ps, and a sex difference emerged regarding the importance of

[2]Originally, Ps and Ds were categorized as instrumental and affectional behaviors, the former represented by a list of discrete behaviors which were to be rated daily as to frequency and degree of "pleasingness" to the recipient; that is, from -3 (strongly displeasing) to a $+3$ (strongly pleasing). In contrast, affectional behaviors referred to overt displays of love and affection of relatively short duration and were recorded as they occurred, with the use of mechanical counters. During the past two years, an extensive list of affectional behaviors has been defined and incorporated into the above described inventory, primarily within the areas of Companionship, Affection, and Consideration.

instrumental versus affectional Ps "with husbands emphasizing instrumental and wives emphasizing affectional behavior". Finally, subject recording accuracy was assessed by requesting husbands (without informing the wives) to increase their output of affectional behavior on two specified days and then assessing the wives' report of pleasurable affectionate behaviors. As noted, "the observed change in wives' reports was statistically significant and the average percentage was close to the targeted figure of 100%." (Wills *et al.*, 1974, p. 806).

Spouse Observations of Videotaped Interactions. In contrast to the three previously described techniques (MAITOA, PT, and SOC), several workers have attempted to create laboratory procedures whereby each partner can monitor and label ongoing self and spouse behaviors of relevance to problem definition and positive behavior change. Primarily taking place within treatment modules concerned with enhancing effective communication skills, the couple observes a videotape of their previously recorded interaction and each partner is asked to identify desirable self and spouse behaviors. Weiss and Margolin (1975), for example, asked each partner to track spouse behavior that was facilitating or helpful. Simultaneously, each spouse tracked his (her) own behavior and indicated when he (she) made a facilitating response—a procedure which provided information about the extent to which spouses agreed in the definition and identification of helpful (facilitating) behavior. (As reported by these investigators, the rate by which couples identified and tracked facilitating behavior was higher after a communication training intervention than at baseline.) Not only are such procedures unique in their ability to define target behavior precisely and immediately, but they are more closely integrated with ongoing intervention activities than are most other procedures. (see Carter & Thomas, 1973; Thomas, Carter & Gambrill, 1971 for further discussion of related procedures.)

Trained Others' Observations of Marital Interaction

In contrast with self-spouse reports and observations, the observation of a couple's behavior by a trained other represents the most potentially reliable data that the clinician can obtain. Notwithstanding the extremely important issues of validity and generalizability (issues which will be discussed in the final section of this chapter), the direct observation of marital interaction by trained others is indispensible to the clinician's understanding (assessment) and attempted modification of dysfunctional relationships. In brief, the clinician can never rely entirely on what couple's report about self and spouse (be it spouse perceptions or observations), but must at some level observe the couple's interactions directly in an attempt to identify functional relationships and to evaluate the effects of his intervention. At the simplest level, such observation occurs during the first contact a clinician has with the couple. Throughout this (and subsequent) meetings, the clinician attempts to construct a behavioral model for understanding the couple's distress, and in so doing, he not only listens to what the clients say (report) but he necessarily attends to *how they are currently behaving vis-à-vis* one another. Beyond such clinical observation, however, the therapist can collect observation data of a more precise, comprehensive and usable nature. That is, systematic observation can be undertaken in either the clinic (laboratory) or the home, and depending upon therapeutic objectives and technical resources, structured tasks, audio-video recordings, and/or trained observers can be introduced.

Overall, assessment of marital behavior can be based on observing the couple as they negotiate a structured task or as they engage in an ópen ended, more "naturalistic" dialogue. In either case, the ensuing interchange can be assessed along various interactional dimensions of relevance. The ostensible advantages to the structured task situation are that: (a) the therapist can create interactions of particular importance rather than waiting for such interchanges to occur "naturally", and (b) certain structured tasks are associated with objective, non-inferential outcome measures whereas one must rely entirely on observer ratings with interaction of a strictly verbal nature. To the extent that structured tasks are artificial and/or "game like", however, one can question the correspondence between behavior observed in such a situation and interchanges that occur in more naturalistic contexts.

Conflict—Resolution Tasks. Originating with the highly influential research of Strodbeck (1951), the revealed difference technique has been used (with and without modifications) in a great variety of family research efforts throughout the past 20 years (Jacob, 1975). In its original form, each family member privately read a series of items which described interpersonally relevant and/or problem situations, and for each item, the individual was asked to select the best solution or the preferred action from several alternatives. For example, "Suppose that you discovered a pack of cigarettes in the room of your 12-year-old son. Would you: (a) not say anything to your child, (b) ask your child to explain before you take any action, (c) tell your child that you discovered the cigarettes and that he will be grounded for 3 weeks." The investigator then selected several items which reflected disagreement among certain family members, brought those members together, told them about the different choices each had selected, and asked them to discuss these issues and to resolve the disagreements. Since the original form appeared, alternative formats have been suggested in which the item content includes both neutral and "charged" issues. Selection of choices can involve ranking choices from "most preferred" to "least preferred," selecting the three most preferred choices from a list of ten possibilities, or bringing members together for the joint discussion phase and not revealing the specific individual choices that each member made—this format referred to as an "unrevealed difference technique." (see Ferreira & Winter, 1968; Jacob, 1974; Winter, Ferreira & Bowers, 1973). Regardless of the specific form adopted, the RDT can provide a wealth of potentially important information. Specifically, not only can the joint discussion phase be assessed by means of a relevant coding system (see below), but data can be obtained regarding: (a) initial agreement among members (that is, similarity between the individually completed forms), and (b) influence of one member *vis-à-vis* another (that is, similarity between each member's individually completed form and the final joint form). As with most other procedures that have been discussed, RDT-generated interaction can be included as: (1) a means of specifying initially presented problems; (2) providing feedback to the couple during a communication training intervention; and (3) evaluating change in interaction from pretreatment (baseline) to termination[3].

Marital Interaction Coding System (*MICS*). The MICS (Hops, Wills, Patterson & Weiss, 1972) consists of a 29 item behavioral coding system aimed at assessing marital interactions associated with functional adaptive relationships. Modeled after Patterson's family coding system (Patterson *et al.*, 1969), the MICS contains 11 nonverbal and 18 verbal codes, which are subsumed within the four larger categories of Problem Solving Behaviors ("accept responsibility," "compromise," and "problem solving"); Problem Description Behaviors ("negative solution," "problem description," and "past solution"); Positive Exchanges (e.g., "agree," "approval," "assent," "smile"); and Negative Exchanges (e.g.. "complaint," "criticize," "no response," "turn off"). The Oregon group typically videotapes a 10-minute husband-wife interaction before treatment (baseline) and after treatment—these interactions involving the couple's attempt to solve problems selected from previously collected self-report data. Trained coders then score the videotapes along the 29 codes and, similar to other data, MICS information can be used in identifying and specifying target behaviors, providing feedback

[3]An important variant of the conflict resolution task was introduced by Olson & Ryder (1970) and was referred to as the Inventory of Marital Conflicts (IMC). Briefly, each partner privately reads 18 short vignettes describing a problematic marital interaction, and for each situation, the individual is asked to indicate who (that is, the husband or the wife) was responsible for the problem. Unbeknown to the couple, 12 of the 18 vignettes are constructed so that "the husband received information slanted to make the wife appear at fault and the wife received information which makes the husband appear as the guilty party" (Olson & Ryder, 1970). As with the RDT, the partners are subsequently brought together and asked to jointly discuss the vignettes and resolve any disagreements.

to the couple during communication training, and evaluating pre-intervention —post-intervention change.

Considerable work has been done with the MICS insofar as developing rater training procedures which yield high interjudge agreement and deal effectively with the issues of observer bias, and "decay" of observer accuracy (Johnson & Bolstad, 1973; Jones, Ried & Patterson, 1975; Ried, 1970; Ried & DeMaster, 1972). In addition, validity studies of the MICS have demonstrated that nondisturbed couples make significantly greater use of problem solving and positive exchange behaviors than do disturbed couples during a conflict resolution task (Birchler, Weiss & Vincent, 1975; Vincent, Weiss & Birchler, 1975), and that distressed couples engage in significantly more constructive problem solving behaviors at post-intervention versus pre-intervention (Patterson, Hops & Weiss, 1975).

3. *Home Observation.* Given sufficient resources, a couple can be observed and assessed at their home in exactly the same manner as clinic-laboratory assessments are performed. That is, it is possible to audiotape (or even videotape) a couple's home interaction during an assigned conflict resolution task or a less structured discussion, and then to assess these recordings in terms of various outcome measures or with the MICS. Home observations, however, seem to hold most promise insofar as obtaining minimally obtrusive and maximally naturalistic observations of marital interaction. Several family researchers, for example, have placed audio recorders in families' homes which are either activated automatically at predetermined times during the week or turned-on by the family during particularly important episodes (Bernal *et al.*, 1971; Johnson & Bolstad, 1974; Martin, Johnson, Johansson & Wahl, 1975; Purcell & Brady, 1965). Although such techniques could be adapted to the assessment of marital (versus parent-child) behaviors, the writer is not aware of any published studies describing such a procedure with couples. Finally, home observations can be obtained by having couples tape-record "practice" sessions or "exercises" from one week to the next—a procedure which not only can yield a sample of husband-wife interaction without the therapist (physically) present but can also aid in generalizing therapy gains to the more natural (home) environment (see Stuart, 1970, for an interesting example of an assessment-intervention procedure adapted for home use).

Discussion

The preceding section described a variety of report and observation techniques that may be used in the evaluation and modification of distressful marital relationships. As seen, most of these procedures have been developed very recently, and as such, critical data regarding reliability, validity, reactivity effects, and cross-measure relationships are extremely limited[4]. In addition, each procedure reflects certain assets and liabilities of obvious and immediate relevance for the practicing clinician in his day-to-day activities. In the following discussion, each group of measures will be briefly evaluated with the aim of highlighting salient strengths and weakness of clinical as well as theoretical-methodological significance.

Client report procedures represent extremely attractive assessment options for the harried, overextended clinician, in that a wealth of treatment-relevant data can be obtained with relatively little time investment from the therapist. In particular, such information can not only aid the clinician in achieving usable descriptions of client desires but in obtaining suggestions for communication training interventions as well as baseline data for relevant target behaviors. In addition, client report procedures (using the Marital Precounseling Inventory as a prototype) may hasten the client's socialization into a behavioral treatment framework and/or direct the individual's attention toward issues that he was previously unable to articulate. At the same time, it must be acknowledged that all such procedures assume that people are willing and/or able to recall and report accurately—an assumption that takes on special significance when the behaviors in question are intimately associated with the intense and far reaching affective components of marital distress. For most *traditional* self-report procedures (e.g., the Locke-Wallace Marital Adjustment Scale), it is also clear that social desirability effects are extremely influential determinants of client responses. In that most of the client report procedures previously reviewed require specific, clearly circumscribed responses, it might be assumed that such response biases would be less important factors to consider. Nevertheless, until further research addresses these issues, one must consider such potential distortions in evaluating information obtained from the various client report measures.

Between client reports and trained others' observations, one finds information that is based upon the client's observations of self and spouse. Reflecting the strengths of both client reports and trained others' observations, self and spouse observations yield specific behavioral data concerning current,

[4]Although reliability and validity data were reported in the previous section, information regarding relationships among the various measures was not presented. Of particular importance, Patterson *et al.* (1975) reported a positive relationship between spouses' P and D rates at home and trained others' ratings of facilitating behaviors (using the MICS) within a semistructured clinic interaction; Weiss *et al.* (1973) reported a correlation of −0.70 between Areas of Change scores and the Locke Wallace scale, a correlation of 0.54 between P/D ratio scores and the Locke-Wallace scale, and a correlation of 0.56 between P/D ratio scores and the intake interviewer's ratings of marital distress; Patterson and Hops (1972) reported a significant relationship between the frequency with which spouses recorded "pleasant thoughts" and trained others' ratings of aversive behaviors (using the MICS) within a semi-structured clinic interaction; and Weiss & Margolin (1975) reported a positive relationship between "pleasant thoughts" and spouses' observations of affectionate events.

ongoing events; they are obtained within natural versus simulated settings (e.g., laboratory observations); they do not rely on the clients' ability to accurately recall past events and interactions; and they require relatively little investment of clinician time and resources. In addition, such procedures allow for the collection of relatively private and/or fleeting interactions which may not be accurately described by clients' retrospective reports or easily accessible to "outside" observers. Notwithstanding such positive attributes, self and spouse observations may be extremely reactive measures, and as a result may yield information of questionable reliability and validity. On the one hand, self-observations (sometimes referred to as self-monitoring) provide the individual with continued, clear-cut feedback about his own behavior, as researchers in other areas have demonstrated (Lipinski & Nelson, 1974; Nelson, Lipinski & Black, 1975). Self-monitoring has also been shown to decrease the frequency of smoking, disruptive talking in a classroom, reported hallucinations, mouth biting, inappropriate motor behaviors, whinning, and vocal tics, and to increase the frequency of studying, participation in class discussions, swimming practice attendance, time spent in a room by a claustrophobic client, and parental attention to appropriate child behaviors. No less problematic is the interpretation of spouse observation data, whereby the individual must monitor his spouse's ongoing behavior and simultaneously act as a participant. In essence, the individual is required to observe behaviors which he strongly desires to eliminate or enhance and which he appropriately or inappropriately attempts to influence. Together with the potential confounds of "instrument decay" (Johnson & Bolstad, 1973) and the impact of differential "demand characteristics" at various stages of the treatment program, interpretation of spouse observation data becomes problematic indeed. Somewhat more encouraging, Wills *et al.* (1974) recently reported that P and D frequencies (from the Spouse Observation Checklist) did not change significantly over 12 days of observation, suggesting that "observer drift" was not in effect. In addition, when husbands doubled their emission of P's on two specified days (without informing the wives), changes in wives' reports were "close to the targeted figure of 100% . . . (suggesting) . . . that subjects were reasonably accurate observers even after 12 consecutive days of recording". Studies such as these are of critical importance in achieving a firm understanding of the significant parameters characterizing self and spouse observations, and at a minimum, future research should attempt to provide information regarding: (a) the relationship (correspondence) between self-spouse observations, self-spouse reports, and trained others' observations of spouses; and (b) variables influencing there liability of self-spouse observations such as differences in the couple's material circumstances and psychological sophistication, the quantity and quality of behaviors to be observed, and the type of training and monitoring provided during the treatment program. In the meantime, the practicing clinician would be encouraged to adopt the following guidelines if he should employ self and spouse observation procedures: (a) define target behaviors precisely in order to reduce the likelihood that changes in the affective quality of a couples' relationship will lead to changes in the criteria by which spouses acknowledge and record target behaviors; (b) monitor and collect client data on a daily basis in order to provide the couple with guidance, structure and encouragement; (c) collect baseline data for at least one week in order to increase the likelihood of obtaining stable and representative information; and (d) clearly and repeatedly convey to clients the importance of obtaining such data and how it will be of value in reaching treatment goals.

At least potentially, the final group of procedures (referred to as trained others' observations of spouses) represents the most reliable and important information that one might use in assessing and modifying dysfunctional interactions. Given sufficient resources (and herein lies the reason for saying "at least potentially" rather than "in actuality"), individuals other than the clients can be trained to be reliable, unbiased coders of significant ongoing interactions. Also, clients can be unobtrusively observed by placing multiple audio-recorders (or even video-recorders) in their homes for *extended* periods of time, thereby minimizing observer effects and maximizing the representativeness of the sampled behaviors. Realistically, however, such elaborate and extensive assessment procedures are virtually impossible to implement, requiring as they do the expense of supporting an ongoing group of highly trained raters as well as the purchase of fairly expensive recording equipment. Given such realities, one can collect trained others' observations by generating and videotaping relevant, treatment-related interactions in the clinic—a procedure which requires considerably less time than monitoring "naturalistic" (home) interactions for days or even weeks. In addition, such laboratory procedures can provide behavioral indices other than those obtained from ratings of verbal interchanges (e.g., the outcome measures associated with certain conflict resolution tasks). They also reflect greater precision than procedures associated with a more naturalistic (yet less controlled) observational context and can often be integrated directly into the ongoing treatment program (e.g., using videotaped interaction within communication training interventions). With any such simulation, however, observer and setting effects can obviously exert a considerable influence on emergent behavior, and to the extent that such influences occur, generalizations from the clinic to the natural environment become increasingly difficult (Johnson, Bolstad, & Lobitz, 1974; Martin *et al.*, 1975; O'Rourke, 1963). Although recent data are encouraging in suggesting a reasonable degree of correspondence between trained others' observations in a clinic setting and clients' observations in their homes (Patterson *et al.*, 1975; Patterson & Hops, 1972), continued evaluation of such procedures must attempt to clarify and specify: (a) the magnitude and direction of observer effects as related to the number and length of observations, and to the type of tasks (problems) used to generate interactions; and (b) the degree of correspondence between various kinds of observations by trained others and data obtained from client reports and client observations.

Conclusion

1. The behavioral assessment of marital dysfunction is an extremely recent undertaking and, as a result, the practicing clinician will be unable to identify any procedure of unquestioned clinical utility and/or empirical validity. Given this state of affairs, the interested practitioner would be advised as follows:

(a) Adopt those procedures which seem most relevant to and practical for your client population and clinical setting.

(b) Whenever appropriate and possible, obtain information from all three data sources—clients' reports, clients' observations, and trained others' observations.

(c) Question carefully and evaluate systematically the effects and effectiveness of your interventions.

(d) Continue to monitor recent developments and data in the field.

2. All of the empirical studies directly concerned with developing and evaluating behavioral assessment procedures for marital disturbance would fill little more than a page of references. Furthermore, most of these studies have been conducted within the past 5 years by one research group within one laboratory (Weiss *et al.*, 1973; Weiss & Margolin, 1975). Given the relative paucity of data and active investigators, it seems accurate indeed to characterize this research domain as barely beyond its infancy. At the same time, however, major research needs seem to be definable *and* attainable, and from this writer's perspective, would include the following:

(a) Major attention should be directed toward replicating (and extending) findings from the Oregon group by investigators working in different laboratory settings with similar and dissimilar client populations.

(b) Available procedures must be systematically evaluated as to basic psychometric characteristics, and if found to be lacking by current test construction standards they must be revised or discarded. Specifically, basic reliability and validity information as well as normative data based upon representative samples have only started to emerge for several procedures; for other instruments, such information is virtually nonexistent.

(c) The relationships among different procedures, both within and between major groupings, must be evaluated empirically and parametrically. At a minimum, attempts must be made to describe the degree of measure correspondence as related to: (1) the source of the reported data (i.e., client's self reports, client's spouse reports, client's self observations, client's spouse observations, and trained others' observations); and (2) the nature of the reported data (affect-laden versus "neutral" events, verbal versus nonverbal behaviors, affectional versus instrumental responses, etc.).

(d) Reactivity effects continue to be of major importance for behavioral marital assessment—whether observations are obtained from the client, the client's spouse, or a trained other. Intimately related to issues of reliability and validity, further research efforts should be aimed at clarifying the *magnitude and direction* of such influences as related to type of observer (client, client's spouse, and trained other), nature of observational context (e.g., clinic versus home interactions), and quality and quantity of behavior to be recorded.

(e) Finally, additional assessment procedures are very much needed in order to determine what sample, situational, and treatment variations are associated with what degree of treatment success as evaluated by what types of assessment procedures.

References

Azrin, N., Naster, B., & Jones, R. Reciprocity counseling; A rapid learning based procedure for marital counseling. *Behaviour Research and Therapy*, 1973, **11**, 365–382.

Bernal, M., Gibson, D. M., Williams, D. E., & Pesses, D. I. A device for automatic audio tape recording. *Journal of Applied Behavior Analysis*, 1971, **4**, 151–156.

Birchler, G. R., & Webb, L. Discriminant self reported measures of happy and unhappy marriages: A social learning formulation. Unpublished manuscript, 1975.

Birchler, G. R., Weiss, R. L., & Vincent, J. P. A multimethod analysis of social reinforcement exchange between maritally distressed and nondistressed spouse and stranger dyads. *Journal of Personality and Social Psychology*, 1975, **31**, 349–360.

Carter, R. D., & Thomas, E. J. A case application of a signaling system (SAM) to the assessment and modification of selected problems of marital communication. *Behavior Therapy*, 1973, **4**, 629–645.

Ferreira, A. J., & Winter, W. D. Decision making in normal and abnormal two-child families. *Family Process*, 1968, **7**, 17–36.

Hops, H., Wills, T. A., Patterson, G. R., & Weiss, R. L. Marital Interaction Coding System. Unpublished manuscript, University of Oregon Research Institute. See NAPS Document No. 02077 for 29 pages of supplementary material.

Jacob, T. Patterns of family conflict and dominance as a function of child age and social class. *Developmental Psychology*, 1974, **10**, 1–12.

Jacob, T. Family interaction in disturbed and normal families: A methodological and substantive review. *Psychological Bulletin*, 1975, **82**, 33–65.

Johnson, S. M., & Bolstad, O. D. Methodological issues in naturalistic observation: Some problems and solutions for field research. In L. A. Hamerlynck, L. C. Handy, & E. J. Mash (Eds.), *Behavior change: Methodology, concepts and practice: Proceedings of the Fourth Banff International Conference on Behavior Modification*. Champaign, Illinois: Research Press, 1973.

Johnson, S. M., & Bolstad, O. D. Reactivity to home observation: A comparison of audio recorded behavior with observers present or absent. *Journal of Applied Behavior Analysis* 1975, **8**, 181–185.

Johnson, S. M., Bolstad, O. D., & Lobitz, G. K. Generalization and contrast phenomena in behavior modification with children. In L. A. Hamerlynck, L. E. Handy, & E. J. Mash (Eds.), *Parenting: Directions, change and maintenance of healthy family behavior*. 1975, in press.

Jones, R. R., Reid, J. B., & Patterson, G. R. Naturalistic observation in clinical assessment. In P. McReynolds (Ed.), *Advances in psychological assessment. Vol.* 3. San Francisco: Jossey-Bass 1975, in press.

Kimmel, D., & van der Veen, F. Factors of marital adjustment in Locke's marital adjustment test. *Journal of Marriage and the Family*, 1974, **36**, 57–63.

Knox, D. *Marriage happiness: A behavioral approach to counseling*. Champaign, Illinois: Research Press, 1972.

Lipinski, D. P., & Nelson, R. The reactivity and unreliability of self recording. *Journal of Consulting and Clinical Psychology* 1974, **42**, 118–123.

Locke, H. J., & Wallace, K. M. Short marital adjustment and prediction tests: Their reliability and validity. *Marriage and Family Living*, 1957, **21**, 251–255.

Martin, S., Johnson, S. M., Johansson, S., & Wahl, G. The comparability of behavioral data in laboratory and natural settings. In L. A. Hamerlynck, L. C. Handy, & E. J. Mash (Eds.), *Parenting: Directions change and maintenance of healthy family behavior*. 1975, in press.

Nelson, R. O., Lipinski, D. P., & Black, J. L. The effects of expectancy on the reactivity of self recording. *Behavior Therapy*, 1975, **6**, 337–349.

Olson, D. H., & Ryder, R. G. Inventory of marital conflicts (IMC): An experimental interaction procedure. *Journal of Marriage and the Family*, 1970, **32**, 443–448.

O'Rourke, V. Field and laboratory: The decision making behavior of family groups in two experimental conditions. *Sociometry*, 1963, **26**, 422–435.

Patterson, G. R., & Hops, H. Coercion, a game for two: Intervention techniques for marital conflict. In R. E. Ulrich, & P. Mountjoy (Eds.), *The experimental analysis of social behavior*. New York: Appleton-Century-Crofts, 1972.

Patterson, G. R., Hops, H., & Weiss, R. L. Interpersonal skills training for couples in early stages of conflict. *Journal of Marriage and the Family*, 1975, **37**, 295–303.

Peterson, D. R. *The clinical study of social behavior*. New York: Appleton-Century-Crofts, 1968.

Purcell, K., & Brady, K. Adaptation to invasion of privacy: Monitoring behavior with a miniature radio transmitter. *Merrill-Palmer Quarterly*, 1965, **12**, 242–254.

Reid, J. B. Reliability assessment of observation data: A possible methodological problem. *Child Development*, 1970, **41**, 1143–1150.

Reid, J. B., & De Master, B. The efficacy of a spot-check procedure in maintaining the reliability of data collected by observers in quasi-natural setting: Two pilot studies. *Oregon Research Institute Bulletin*, 1972, **12**, Number 8.

Strodbeck, F. L. Husband-Wife interaction over revealed differences. *American Sociological Review*, 1951, **16**, 468–473.

Stuart, R. B. Operant interpersonal treatment for marital discord. *Journal of Consulting and Clinical Psychology*, 1969, **33**, 675–682.

Stuart, R. B. A cueing device for the acceleration of the rate of positive interaction. *Journal of Applied Behavior Analysis*, 1970, **4**, 257–260.

Stuart, R. B., & Stuart, F. *Marital Pre-Counseling Inventory*. Champaign, Illinois: Research Press, 1972.

Thomas, E. J., Carter, R. D., & Gambrill, E. D. Some possibilities of behavioral modification with marital problems using "SAM" (signal system for the assessment and modification of behavior). In R. D. Rubin, H. Fensterheim, A. A. Lazarus, & C. M. Franks (Eds.), *Advances in Behavior Therapy*. New York: Academic Press, 1971.

Vincent, J. P., Weiss, R. L., & Birchler, G. R. A behavioral analysis of problem solving in distressed and nondistressed married and stranger dyads. *Behavior Therapy*, 1975, **6**, 475–487.

Weiss, R. L. Operant conditioning techniques in psychological assessment. In P. W. McReynolds (Ed.), *Advances in psychological assessment*. Palo Alto: Science and Behavior Books, 1968.

Weiss, R. L., Birchler, G. R., & Vincent, J. P. Contractual models for negotiation training in marital dyads. *Journal of Marriage and the Family*, 1974, **36**, 321–330.

Weiss, R. L., Hops, H., & Patterson, G. R. A framework for conceptualizing marital conflict, a technology for altering it, some data for evaluating it. In F. W. Clark, & L. A. Hamerlynck (Eds.), *Critical issues in research and practice: Proceedings of the Fourth Banff International Conference on Behavior Modification.*, Champaign, Illinois: Research Press, 1973.

Weiss, R. L., & Margolin, G. Marital conflict and accord. In A. R. Ciminero, K. S. Calhoun, & H. E. Adams (Eds.), *Handbook for behavioral assessment.* New York: John Wiley, 1975, in press.

Wills, T. A., Weiss, R. L., & Patterson, G. R. A behavioral analysis of the determinants of marital satisfaction. *Journal of Consulting and Clinical Psychology*, 1974, **42**, 802–811.

Winter, W. D., Ferreiria, A. J., & Bowers, N. Decision making in married and unrelated couples. *Family Press*, 1973, **12**, 83–94.

CHAPTER 15

Assessment of Sexual Dysfunction

SALLIE SCHUMACHER,

and

CHARLES W. LLOYD,

Department of Psychiatry
Western Psychiatric Institute and Clinic
University of Pittsburgh School of Medicine
Pittsburgh, Pennsylvania

Introduction

The purpose of this discussion is to present a working plan for the clinical assessment of problems of sexual dysfunction. This plan has been developed within a context that recognizes the study of sexual behavior as a relatively new area of scientific inquiry with only a small body of information, limited and undeveloped theoretical bases, and no organized training or professional development programs. The method of approach is behavioral in orientation and emphasizes the importance of interdisciplinary involvement in the treatment of sexual dysfunction and in the development of the study of sexual behavior in general. Our goal is to provide the reader with information relevant for practical application, and, at the same time, alert him or her to the limitations of present techniques for the assessment and treatment of sexual dysfunction.

Problems in Diagnosing Sexual Dysfunction

Some of the problems related to the diagnosis of sexual dysfunction resolve around inconsistencies in the definition of terms and variations in diagnostic concepts. For many years impotence and frigidity have been general terms used to describe the major categories of sexual dysfunction in males and females. However, specific subcategories of dysfunction have been defined differently by different investigators and clinicians according to their experience, training, and theoretical orientation (Freud, 1950; Hastings, 1963; Johnson & Masters, 1964; Kinsey, Pomeroy & Martin, 1948). While some effort has been made to resolve this problem by replacing or limiting the use of the terms impotence and frigidity, and using instead more descriptive terms such as erectile or ejaculatory difficulties and orgasmic dysfunction (Ellis, 1961, 1966; Kaplan, 1974; Masters & Johnson, 1970), inconsistencies still exist. For example, primary impotence is the term used to describe the presenting complaint of a male by Cohn (1974) if he "has never been able to have an erection," by Masters & Johnson (1970) if he has never been able "to accomplish coital connection successfully," and by Walker (1947) if his impotence is psychogenic.

A standard way of classifying sexual dysfunction relates diagnosis to etiology and implies general treatment orientation. The most common, fundamental divisions in this scheme are dysfunctions associated with organic factors, individual psychological factors, and relationship factors, or some variation thereof (Ellis, 1966; Lansing, 1974; Oliven, 1955; Roen, 1965). Since one purpose of diagnosis is to identify factors presumably responsible for the presenting difficulty, this seems like a useful and logical approach to classification. However, major problems continue to arise because of the tendency to look at these divisions as discrete categories, to consider one category as more or less important than another, and to focus on diagnostic criteria that fit a specific frame of reference, sometimes to the exclusion of other relevant criteria.

In the present classification system of the American Psychiatric Association (APA, 1968), sexual dysfunction is classified as a psychophysiologic disorder, which by definition is a physical disorder "in which emotional factors play a causative role." The frequent association of psychological events with physical distress has been noted for many years and is the logical basis for the psychosomatic approach in medicine. The traditional psychosomatic research model requires study of the relationships between life situations, emotional response, and physical illness.

Results of extensive clinical experience and research in this area of medicine over the past 35 years have led some investigators to question the assumption that the basic disorder in psychosomatic illness is primarily psychologic and that an understanding and modification of the psychological process or situation will automatically result in a reversal of the physical complaint (Engel, 1967; Grinker, 1953; Lipowski, 1968; Margolin & Kaufman, 1948). As methods of measuring biological phenomena have improved, increasing emphasis has been placed upon studies to clarify the relationships between somatic and psychological events associated with disordered behavior (Mendels, 1973).

These changes in approach in no way negate the importance of consideration and analysis of psychological processes in assessment, nor do they suggest that treatment be less concerned with modification of behavior or behavioral situations. Instead, they offer another dimension of approach to clinical and research evaluation.

The criteria for diagnosing sexual dysfunction vary with those factors being stressed. Also, diagnosis varies with different ways of organizing information. While we may expect differences of opinion in definitions and in the meanings of diagnostic concepts, failure to understand these differences and their background can lead to confusion in diagnosis and less than effective treatment.

Approaches to Problems of Sexual Dysfunction

Differences between the psychodynamic and behavioral approaches to therapy in general are reflected in the therapy of sexual dysfunction. In the psychodynamic model specific sexual dysfunction is conceptualized as a symptom of unconscious conflict resulting from some arrest or disturbance in personality development. Treatment is directed toward the reorganization of personality, generally through the technique of free association and the phenomenon of transference. In the behavioral model, specific sexual dysfunction is viewed as a learned response pattern resulting from faulty conditioning. Therapy consists primarily of unlearning and relearning, usually by the method of systematic desensitization based on the principle of reciprocal inhibition (Dengrove, 1967; Eysenck, 1960; Rachman, 1961; Wolpe, 1958).

Neither approach, of course, can be summarized in a few sentences and neither can be considered a distinct entity. Both approaches share common elements and there are differences within each general approach that in some instances are as great as differences between approaches (Breger & McGaugh, 1965; Grossberg, 1964; Marks & Gelder, 1966).

Historically, there seems to be a mixed tradition in the treatment of sexual dysfunction, with evidence of certain discrepancies between theoretical beliefs advocated and the therapeutic courses actually pursued. For example, one finds psychoanalysts using simple explanation and suggestion in the therapy of certain potency disorders (Stekel, 1927), treating "fears of failure" by providing information to remove "wrong notions about sex" (Karpman, 1933), and, as a treatment technique, initially forbidding sexual intercourse (Kraines, 1948). On the other hand, one finds behaviorists emphasizing the importance of interpersonal relationships (Wolpe, 1958), utilizing fantasy material (Marquis, 1970), and making suggestions and interpretations continually (Lo Piccolo, Stewart & Watkins, 1972; Obler, 1973).

Marmor (1971) considers the Masters & Johnson approach to problems of sexual dysfunction a combination of both behavioral and psychodynamic approaches. As he points out, Masters & Johnson focus directly on the patient's presenting symptom, and utilize desensitization procedures to alleviate performance anxiety. At the same time, they recognize the importance of the influence of both interpersonal and intrapersonal dynamics on problems of sexual dysfunction. This is why they insist on treating both persons involved in a sexually distressed relationship and why they accept only referred patients who have been screened, at least in theory, by a referring authority. In addition, patients accepted for treatment by Masters & Johnson are evaluated carefully during the initial sessions and are refused treatment if a significant psychological disorder is present.

Marmor also feels that in utilizing a male/female therapy team approach, Masters & Johnson reflect their sensitivity to transference phenomena, and, in their roles as sexually permissive parent-surrogates, they facilitate behavioral changes by means of compassion and understanding as well as technical advice.

We feel there are elements in the Masters & Johnson approach to problems of sexual dysfunction that define this approach as original, rather than as a fusion of psychodynamic understanding and behavioral technique. Masters & Johnson do not apply psychiatric labels to their patients, nor do they focus on defense mechanisms or psychodynamic insights, either in theory or in practice. One might even say that their approach is relatively uncontaminated by psychodynamic language, a language which is heavily negative in tone, and which sets the traditional psychotherapist apart from other persons (Henry, Sims & Spray, 1973).

Similarly, Masters & Johnson, who have had no in-depth training in learning theories and behavior therapy, do not conceive of sexual dysfunction as a neurotic or psychotic disorder or as a learned, maladaptive behavior without regard for physiological and anatomical alteration. They do not speak or think in terms of aversive conditioning, primary or secondary reinforcement, or systematic desensitization, all of which focus on sex as performance. The Masters & Johnson approach is behavior therapy because it is explicit, not because elements corroborate existing behavior theory. Its value lies in its effectiveness, not in its validity with reference to theory.

Basically, Masters & Johnson consider sexual functioning as a natural physiologic process which is present in infancy and evolves throughout the lifetime of an individual in relation to the totality of his or her existence. Basic to their therapeutic approach is the premise that sexual dysfunction is primarily the result of disregarding or interfering with the naturalness of sexual expression though lack of information and/or an abundance of misinformation in regard to both sexual physiology and human interaction. Misunderstanding of the nature of sexual functioning leads directly to fear of sexual failure, the major psychological component of sexual inadequacy. Unrealistic cultural demands for effectiveness of performance have placed emphasis on sexual response as something to be skillfully accomplished, thereby removing sexual function from its natural context as a way of being, expressing, and sharing oneself.

Masters & Johnson are sensitive to actual and potential coping behaviors of individuals. Their assessment and therapeutic procedures, therefore, have a problem-solving orientation. Emphasis is upon ways of reversing a particular distress rather than on reasons or explanations for the distress. Assessment focuses on coping behaviors of the distressed patient as an individual and of the distressed couple as a unit, as well as the degree and kind of dysfunction present.

Our approach to problems of sexual dysfunction is based directly on that of Masters & Johnson. Our orientation, however, as stated previously, is interdisciplinary and this has led to different approaches to diagnosis, and to more extensive evaluations of assessment and therapeutic procedures, and therapeutic results.

General Assessment Procedure

Adequate sexual functioning is responding appropriately to internal and external sexual stimuli, usually within a relationship, and including orgasmic release. Sexual dysfunction, then, is defined in terms of specific conditions or states which interfere with sexual response and lower an individual's personal feeling of competence, lead to unhappiness, or threaten a valued relationship. It is common for differences in initial evaluation or perspective to occur between patient and therapist, even at a descriptive level. It is important that diagnostic terms and concepts be understood clearly by both.

Adequate assessment of sexual dysfunction involves clear description of the specific sexual problem by the dysfunctional individual and by his or her partner if the distress occurs within a relationship. This includes a definition of what the problem is, information about its onset, course, and duration, how the particular individuals involved feel about it, how they have tried to cope with it, and what its effect has been upon the relationship. The most common mistake made by the inexperienced therapist is to plunge into specific or non-specific treatment programs without enough information about the problem and without the awareness that the information is incomplete.

The systematic assessment of sexual dysfunction requires collection of data from several sources in order to provide an effective base for treatment. Although the importance of assessing as many relevant factors as possible in the diagnosis of behavior disorder has been noted by several investigators (Davison, 1969; Goldfried & Kent, 1972; Lazarus, 1973), present arguments concerned with psychodynamic versus behavior therapies, or medical versus behavioral approaches emphasize a narrow view of sexual behavior with consequent assessment and treatment along one dimension or another. Most clinicians today, whether of psychodynamic or behavioral orientation, still, by tradition, emphasize the importance of psychological factors in sexual behavior almost to the point of failure to recognize the possible contribution of physiological factors. We recommend a multidimensional approach with attention to cognitive, affective, and physiological factors, all of which play a role in determining sexual behavior patterns.

An important factor directly related to the kind of patient who seeks help for sexual dysfunction and, therefore, related to assessment procedure, is the specific clinical setting. Lief (1974) reports that 75% of couples who seek counseling from a marital or family therapy clinic have significant sexual problems. In only 15% is the sexual problem the major cause of marital distress. In the remaining 60%, sexual problems are the result rather than the cause of marital conflict. Frank, Anderson & Kupfer (in press) looked at similarities and differences between couples who sought therapy and couples who sought treatment for sexual dysfunction in a university setting which provided both therapies in separate speciality clinics. They found that the couples were very similar with respect to demographic data and the frequency of sexual problems. They also found that the couples differed significantly with respect to general marital compatibility and level of problem solving. Couples who sought treatment for sexual dysfunction were found to be more compatible, less conservative in general, and more thoughtful in their approach to life and problem solving than couples who sought treatment for marital problems.

These data suggest that the clinical setting determines in part the selection of patients with regard to some crucial variables related to diagnosis, treatment and outcome. While our experience has been in three different geographic areas, it nevertheless has been limited to that of specific clinical settings for the treatment of sexual dysfunction. This bias must be borne in mind.

Assessment at a very general level means forming impressions and making decisions about others (Jones, 1970). This includes organization and interpretation of data as well as routine collection of data. Sexual dysfunction results from a series of events that determine its onset and continuation. These events, internal and external, specific and nonspecific, do not suddenly end as a result of diagnosis and the initiation of treatment, but continue to occur and continue to be modified by new events. Adequate assessment, therefore, is a continuing process and essentially, there is no gap or break between assessment and treatment.

For example, the diagnosis of impotence may be made in a male who complains of repeated failure to obtain or maintain an erection, and immediate treatment may be directed toward alleviating his sexual performance anxiety. In the majority of cases, the patient will respond favorably and show initial, sometimes dramatic, improvement. However, also in the majority of cases, this initial improvement is not maintained. Continued treatment procedures depend upon further information from a comprehensive medical evaluation as well as information about the onset, course, circumstances, and duration of the impotence. In addition, ongoing evaluation must be made of the physiological and psychological responses to treatment in both the patient and his partner.

According to even the most recent texts (Ard, 1974; Cohn, 1974; Kaplan,

1974), the characteristic symptom of psychological impotence is that it is selective; that is, it occurs under one set of circumstances but not another. The reasoning seems to be that if a male is impotent in one circumstance but not another, the cause of this selective impotence must be psychological in nature and not due to physical changes, disease, or drugs. It has been suggested that there is no point in putting such a male through a series of examinations and tests to discover the cause since it is obvious that no abnormalities will be found to explain the impotence, because the patient has demonstrated adequately that his anatomy and physiology of erection are intact.

This is an example of a "hand-me-down" concept that has appeared in the literature through the years (Crider, 1946; Hastings, 1963; Stekel, 1927; Tuthill, 1955) and has never been supported by scientific inquiry. This kind of conclusion ignores all of the known evidence concerning diurnal variations within our internal environment, and disregards present information about certain disease processes and normal aging. Our data indicate that males with specific organic disease often demonstrate selective impotence directly related to fluctuations in physical status.

Standardized Psychological Test Measures

There is little in the literature concerning the use of psychological tests and inventories in the assessment of psychological factors associated specifically with sexual dysfunction. Hartman & Fithian (1972) administer a battery of psychological tests which includes the Minnesota Multiphasic Personality Inventory (MMPI), the Taylor-Johnson Temperament Analysis, the Draw-a-Person Test, and the Luscher Color Test. They utilize information from these tests to document clinical evaluation and as a clinical tool. However, they have not presented, as yet, a systematic, definitive evaluation of their data.

Derogatis (in press) presented a preliminary report on the use of the SCL-90, an extended version of the Hopkins Symptom Checklist (Derogatis, Lipman, Rickels, Uhlenhuth & Covi, 1974), as a screening device for coexisting symptomatology in patients with sexual dysfunction. He found that, when compared to psychiatric outpatients, patients with sexual disorder reported more distress on selected symptoms even though they had lower global levels of psychopathology. However, this report was on a limited population and any interpretation or discussion awaits further information and analysis.

We analysed MMPI data on 302 patients with sexual distress and did not find the data predictive of specific distress, intensity of distress, or treatment outcome. We feel that while the MMPI may be a relevant and sensitive instrument in the assessment of sexual distress, its present use is limited by our lack of knowledge of some of the complexities of sexual functioning and our present inadequate classification of sexual dysfunction. From another point of view, we have found the MMPI useful for clinical purposes. In spite of its limitations, the test does serve as an additional source of information concerning the psychological status of patients. Patients with several scale T scores of 70+ do behave differently than those with lower scores. In addition, patients with high scores on some scales handle information quite differently than those with high scores on other scales.

Several investigators have been concerned with the development of sexual experience scales (Brady & Levitt, 1965; Podell & Perkins, 1957; Zuckerman, 1973) and their possible use as clinical and research tools in the assessment and treatment of sexual dysfunction (Bentler, 1968a, 1968b; Derogatis, in press). These scales are based on the concept that sexual experiences occur in hierarchical sequence and, therefore, can be evaluated using Guttman scaling procedures (Guttman, 1950). Although it is assumed that information about an individual's sexual experience is important in the assessment of sexual distress, the usefulness of sexual experience scales remains to be demonstrated. On the basis of our clinical experience we question the appropriateness of structuring behaviors as varied and complicated as those involved in sexual expression into a simplistic, hierarchical sequence of "less advanced" and "more advanced" behaviors and choosing the sexually active, American male college student as the standard bearer.

The association between emotional and sexual disturbance has been verified clinically many times (Barnett, 1973; Cooper, 1970; O'Connor & Stern, 1972; Winokur, 1963). However, the assumption that all sexual problems are the result of major underlying psychological conflict has been challenged by clinicians and investigators involved in direct, problem-oriented approaches to problems of sexual dysfunction. There is an obvious flaw in reasoning, however, when a screening procedure is utilized to select only patients free of major psychopathology, and then the generalization is made that the majority of patients do not evidence major psychiatric problems (Masters & Johnson, 1970). It must be borne in mind that most of the reported high success utilizing behavioral techniques in the treatment of sexual dysfunction has been with very select populations (Kaplan, 1974). Some authors report an initial rejection of 50 to 70% of patient referrals (LoPiccolo & Lobitz, 1972; Obler, 1973).

Lazarus (1969) estimates that one-fifth of sexually inadequate people need extensive treatment for psychological disturbance. We have found that approximately one-fourth of our patient population has major psychological disturbance. For this reason we recommend that the HSCL and the MMPI be utilized for the assessment of related symptomatology and psychological disturbance in patients with problems of sexual dysfunction. Except in rare cases, we do not reject patients with psychological or marital disturbance, but instead refer them for appropriate treatment either concurrently with, or following our treatment.

The Clinical Interview

Masters & Johnson (1970) introduce their procedure for obtaining a sex history by pointing out that such a history is relatively meaningless if it is not correlated with other aspects of an individual's existence. This is perhaps the major reason why present psychological tests are inappropriate, or, at best, provide us with a minimum of information, that may be related only partly to actual sexual behavior. Sexual functioning occurs within the context of the whole person and his or her environment and is partially defined and qualified by that context. At present, we feel that the clinical interview, involving both partners in a sexually distressed relationship and a male/female therapy team, is the most powerful tool in the assessment of sexual dysfunction.

In our program we use therapy teams that include a physician and a psychotherapist. Treatment sessions are usually scheduled at weekly intervals and the average duration of therapy is ten sessions. When therapy is ended, patients are seen for follow-up in 3 months, 6 months, and 1 year.

In the initial interview session the therapy team interviews the sexually distressed couple to explore the nature of the presenting distress and to define preliminary objectives and goals of treatment. Interviewing both partners together helps to eliminate any pretense, intentional or unintentional, and brings out into the open similarities and differences in perception of the problem and any misconceptions that either partner may have about himself/herself or the other.

During the next two sessions, each therapist interviews each partner individually to obtain a complete medical-psychosocial history, with special emphasis upon sexual development and patterns of sexual behavior. Specific history taking procedures and a complete summary of the content of the interviewing schedule that we follow are provided by Masters & Johnson (1970), and need not be reviewed here. Also, some general principles involved in taking a sex history are reviewed by Green (1975), and the Group for the Advancement of Psychiatry (1974). An excellent behavioral diagnostic system that can be adapted for specific assessment of sexual dysfunction is provided by Kanfer & Saslow (1969).

In every clinical interview we employ a basic exploratory strategy to obtain information which helps us, as well as the patients, to define rather than interpret problems and to clarify alternatives rather than direct or suggest solutions. The basic data for assessment are verbalized self-reports of each patient and the physiological measurements described in the next section.

Because sexual functioning, for the most part, involves interaction between two people, successful treatment of sexual dysfunction is based upon adequate assessment of the two people involved in terms of their background, their personalities, and their personal philosophies and life styles. In addition, each couple, as a unit, has a specific background, personality, and working philosophy of its own which is not predictable on the basis of knowledge about either individual alone. The primary assessment task, then, is to obtain information about the specific sexual problem within a combined as well as within each individual's own framework of reference. The purpose in obtaining this information is to determine therapy procedures appropriate for a particular couple.

Assessment of Physiological Factors

A postulate that we find useful in assessing the factors that contribute to sexual dysfunction is that in the body's economy, sex is treated as a luxury. Certain functions such as respiration or vascular circulation are vital; without them, the body does not survive. On the other hand, sex is not essential for life or reasonable health. Under stress produced by physical or psychological factors, a less essential function such as sex may be sacrificed to maintain efficiency of those that are more critical. Thus, a meticulous search in depth for both physical and psychological components is important to make a reasonably precise diagnosis of possible causes of a sexual distress.

A complete medical history is obligatory. This should include details of all serious illnesses, in particular those that bear a temporal relationship to the onset of the sexual dysfunction. A thorough dietary history sometimes suggests poor eating habits that contribute to feelings of fatigue and general dysphoria. Included in the dietary history should be a careful estimation of intake of alcohol. Alcoholism can seriously impair sexual function in both men and women.

It is important to obtain details of medications patients are taking or have taken during the time that sexual dysfunctions have developed. Any relationship the patient thinks the therapy may have had to the dysfunction should be fully investigated. All medications that alter autonomic nerve transmission can alter sexual function. Among these compounds are tranquilizers, agents that elevate mood such as the tricyclic drugs and monoamine oxidase inhibitors, some antihypertensive compounds such as methyl dopa, and anticholinergic agents.

Estrogen given to men for treatment of carcinoma of the prostate markedly depresses sexual drive as do cyproterone acetate, which is sometimes used in Europe for treatment of dangerous sexual offenders, and progestational agents, which have been used in the USA for the same purpose. In women using an oral contraceptive, there may be a decrease in sexual drive. Sometimes this relates to the type of gestagen in the oral contraceptive, and it is therefore useful for the physician to inquire about the brand of estrogen-gestagen contraceptive being used. Changing the ratio of estrogen and gestagen can sometimes alter sexual interest.

There are anecdotal reports that heavy smoking of tobacco can decrease potency though no unequivocal proof. There are also anecdotal reports that the use of marihuana can increase sexual enjoyment but this, too, has not been supported. Narcotics can depress sexual function.

The medical history should include careful search for family histories of diabetes mellitus, vascular disease, mental illness, and other illnesses that may have a genetic component. A convenient time to obtain information about the relationship of the parents of the patient and the general pattern of family life in which the patient matured, is during discussion of family history. The developmental history should encompass both physical and psychosocial growth. The correlation of physical and behavioral sexual maturation and the ways in which the patient reacted to these events give important leads that improve understanding of attitudes the patient has as an adult.

Ever since there has been a serious interest in treatment of sexual dysfunction, there has been a wide belief that almost all of the problems in this area are of psychogenic origin. The most recent reports still attribute at least 90% of sexual distress to psychological origin (American Medical Association, 1972; Ard, 1974; Hastings, 1967; Kaplan, 1974; Katchadourian & Lunde, 1972; Masters & Johnson, 1970). However, evidence is increasing that there are many cases of sexual dysfunction in which physical derangement play a primary or at least a secondary causal role.

We have made a detailed analysis of findings on physical and laboratory examinations of 286 couples treated for sexual dysfunction at the Human Sexuality Center, Long Island Jewish-Hillside Medical Center, and at the Center for Study of Human Sexual Behavior at the University of Pittsburgh School of Medicine. The majority of these patients had no prior diagnosis of illness and no complaints of disability. The findings on physical and laboratory examinations, however, indicated that 51% of patients had abnormal findings. The possible significance of some of these results will be discussed after we have described our examination procedures.

It is essential for anyone contending with problems of sexual dysfunction to have a complete physical examination. In our program, in most cases, husband and wife are examined in the presence of one another. This conjoint physical examination has two purposes. The more important is, of course, detection of medical abnormalities. The other function is as a teaching procedure since the physician uses each part of the examination to educate and instruct patients about the human body in general, and the anatomy and physiology of the genitalia in particular.

While the examination is as thorough as possible in all patients, particular attention is paid to all approachable areas of the vascular system in men with problems of erectile efficiency. In both men and women with complaints of difficulties with orgasm, responsiveness of the genitalia to several vibration and tactile sensation stimuli is examined.

In a couple whose marriage is unconsummated, it is particularly important to estimate the tension of musculature around the vaginal introitus in the woman. Spasm of these muscles is a frequent cause of vaginismus, which can be a major factor in preventing successful intromission. In cases in which there does not seem to be discomfort during pelvic examination, there can still be vaginismus under the psychological threat of an attempt at penile penetration. A clue to this possibility can sometimes be obtained by prescribing the use of vaginal dilators at home. The inability or unwillingness of the patient to insert the dilators suggests that muscle spasm may be occurring in an environment where sexual relations could occur, even if no vaginismus occurs in the sexually unthreatening environment of the examining room.

In our assessment procedure, each patient also is subjected to an extensive laboratory work-up which includes: complete blood count, urinalysis, biochemical screen, which includes estimates of electrolytes and tests for hepatic and renal function, plasma cholesterol and triglycerides, and indices of thyroid function.

In women with evidence from history and physical examination of less than optimal ovarian function, estimation of estrogen by use of a vaginal smear technique and of plasma or urinary gonadotrophins (both FSH and LH) is helpful. Suggestions of decreased estrogen and increased gonadotrophins reinforce clinical impressions of intrinsic ovarian failure, whereas lowered levels of estrogen and of gonadotrophins make probable a diagnosis of ovarian failure because of decreased pituitary stimulation.

We have routinely measured total plasma testosterone in all men. Almost all of the values fall in the normal range, which is extremely wide, from 250 to 1500 mcg/dl. Very few men who are not obviously hypogonadal have plasma testosterone values below this range. Differences in values within the normal range do not seem to relate to sexual function in normal or dysfunctional men. Such lack of correlation may be because the level of this steroid is dependent on the amount of steroid binding protein present. The biologically effective moiety of the steroid is that fraction which is not bound. The specimen with high total testosterone, which is elevated because of the high concentration of binding protein, may actually be less effective biologically than the specimen with less binding protein and more free steroid. In addition to this influence of binding on the effectiveness of testosterone, there is the problem introduced in estimation of the effective level of testosterone by the episodic secretion of this steroid. In normal men, testosterone is secreted in bursts throughout both daylight and night so that major variations are introduced by the timing of the sampling. For this reason, we require that specimens of plasma be obtained at approximately 8:00 a.m. from all subjects.

If there is question of effectiveness of testicular secretion even in the presence of testosterone concentrations in the normal range, further information can be obtained by measuring gonadotrophins, particularly LH, in plasma or a

24-hour urine collection. Elevation of the LH above normal limits is evidence of a possible decrease in feedback effect of the androgen on the hypothalamico-pituitary system and, therefore, of less than optimal biological effects of the androgen.

In some women who have decreased sexual interest or suboptimal orgasmic response, particularly in cases following oophorectomy and replacement therapy with estrogen, testosterone levels may be decreased. Since the concentration of testosterone in women is normally slight, recognition of decreased levels may be difficult if not impossible. In such patients, the only way presently to determine if androgen therapy is useful is a trial of treatment. Small amounts of androgen given either orally or systemically can sometimes considerably increase sexual interest (Greenblatt, Mortara & Torpin, 1942).

The findings on physical and laboratory examinations in our patients are now being summarized and analyzed, so all of the specific data are not yet available. One of the most consistent findings is the high frequency of abnormalities of glucose metabolism in men with impotence (Schumacher & Lloyd, 1974). Some of these men had frank diabetes mellitus. The majority did not have an abnormality sufficient to warrant this diagnosis. It has been known for many years that diabetes mellitus itself is related to impotence. However, the observation that impotent men who have no signs of diabetes mellitus can have abnormal glucose tolerance curves has not been emphasized previously. The relationship of glucose tolerance abnormalities to impotence is not understood, but we believe this is an important finding to be explored further because we find no greater incidence of this type of abnormality in any of the other types of sexual dysfunction than is found in the normal population (Schumacher & Lloyd, 1975).

In our experience impotence is the most frequently seen sexual distress and the least responsive to therapeutic intervention (Schumacher, 1974). In this regard, our experience is similar to that of Cooper (1968, 1969, 1971) and Johnson (1965). Present methods of treatment are directed primarily towards reducing the patient's sexual performance orientation. This often results in decreasing his anxiety and the frustration or anger of his partner because of his failure. Therapy produces understanding of the problem by other partners and adaptation to it. It rarely results in complete restoration of potency in the distressed male to the level that it was before he developed thc problem. We are convinced that the reason for these less than optimal results is lack of understanding of the mechanisms that produce the difficulty.

Other significant abnormalities that have been observed on physical examination of men with erectile difficulties are: significant hypertension, arteriosclerotic heart disease with cardiac failure, arteriosclerotic changes in retinal vessels, hypothyroidism, Parkinsonism, hepatomegaly, prostatic hypertrophy, small and underdeveloped secondary sexual structures, hydrocele, varicocele, Peyronie's disease, and unilateral orchidectomy followed by irradiation therapy. The following abnormalities have been observed in sexually distressed women: significant hypertension, hypothyroidism, small and underdeveloped secondary sexual structures, prolapsed uterus, painful vaginal or perineal scars, vaginal mucosal atrophy, and imperforate hymen. In the laboratory examination we have found a significant incidence of elevated triglycerides, and decreased hepatic and renal function in impotent males. Several male and female patients have had abnormal indices of thyroid function.

The data we have accumulated so far lead us to conclude that the causes of sexual dysfunction include ignorance, negative attitudes, psychological factors, physical disease, and combined organic and psychological factors. We believe that a careful evaluation of all of the factors involved in determining sexual response is critical for a useful diagnosis of the type of dysfunction of which the patients complain, of possible causal agents, and to develop a reasonable approach to treatment.

Some Problems and Difficulties

Most present reports of behavioral approaches in the treatment of sexual dysfunction claim high success rates and emphasize the ease with which behavior change occurs as the result of educative procedures and certain therapy techniques. However, as in psychotherapy in general, the practice of sex therapy is running far ahead of any scientific evidence for the effectiveness of the various treatment approaches. In addition, all of the problems involved in the evaluation of psychotherapy in general are present also in the evaluation of sex therapy (Bergin & Strupp, 1972; Kiesler, 1973; Meltzoff & Kornreich, 1970).

The basic premise of the present behavioral approach to sexual dysfunction is the assumption that anxiety, fear, and lack of information are the causes of most sexual discomfort and distress. Reports in the literature in support of this assumption are all based upon data obtained from highly selected populations characterized by high motivation and cooperation, and an absence of serious neurotic conflict. In some studies, most of the "clients" were young college students.

We also find that fear of sexual failure and anxiety about one's adequacy as a sexual partner are major psychological components of sexual dysfunction. However, in some cases, anxiety and fear seem to be results rather than causes of sexual dysfunction and, in these situations, treatment too often results only in temporary improvement.

Current popular and professional interest in sex therapy and research seems to be increasing at a rapid pace, with major discussion and effort directed toward therapy procedure. Rapid and impressive treatment results often do occur and, in some situations, treatment procedure is relatively simple.

Emphasis upon dramatic results, however, has led to oversimplification in interpretation of actual results, of treatment procedure, and of sexual behavior itself. We believe that direct discussion of sexual functioning with the people involved is a more efficient and productive approach to problems of sexual dysfunction than individual treatment or indirect discussion of the problem. We also believe that many research questions are still to be asked and that many of the answers will be found through better assessment techniques and procedure.

References

American Medical Association. *Human sexuality.* Chicago: American Medical Association, 1972.

American Psychiatric Association. *Diagnostic and statistical manual of mental disorders* (2nd ed.). Washington, D. C.: American Psychiatric Association, 1968.

Ard, B. N., Jr. *Treating psychosexual dysfunction.* New York: Aronson, 1974.

Barnett, J. Sexuality in the obsessional neuroses. In E. G. Witenberg (Ed.), *Interpersonal explorations in psychoanalysis.* New York: Basic Books, 1973.

Bentler, P. M. Heterosexual behavior assessment: I. Males. *Behaviour Research and Therapy,* 1968, **6**, 21–25.

Bentler, P. M. Heterosexual Behavioral assessment: II. Females. *Behaviour Research and Therapy,* 1968, **6**, 27–30.

Bergin, A. E., & Strupp, H. H. *Changing frontiers in the science of psychotherapy.* Chicago: Aldine-Atherton, 1972.

Brady, J. P., & Levitt, E. E. The scalability of sexual experiences. *Psychological Record,* 1965, **15**, 275–279.

Breger, L., & McGaugh, J. L. Critique and reformulation of "learning-theory" approaches to psychotherapy and neurosis. *Psychological Bulletin,* 1965, **63**, 338–358.

Cohn, F. *Understanding human sexuality.* Englewood Cliffs, N. J.: Prentice-Hall, 1974.

Cooper, A. J. A factual study of male potency disorders. *British Journal of Psychiatry,* 1968, **114**, 719–731.

Cooper, A. J. Disorders of sexual potency in the male: A clinical and statistical study of some factors related to short-term prognosis. *British Journal of Psychiatry,* 1969, **115**, 709–719.

Cooper, A. J. Treatments of male potency disorders: The present status. *Psychosomatics,* 1971, **12**, 235–244.

Crider, B. Situational impotence. *Journal of Clinical Psychology,* 1946, **2**, 384–389.

Davison, G. C. Appraisal of behavior modification techniques with adults in institutional settings. In C. M. Franks (Ed.), *Behavior therapy: Appraisal and status.* New York: McGraw-Hill, 1969.

Dengrove, E. Behavior therapy of the sexual disorders. *Journal of Sex Research,* 1967, **3**, 49–61.

Derogatis, L. R. Psychological assessment of the sexual disabilities. In J. K. Meyer (Ed.), *Clinical management of sexual disorders.* Baltimore: Williams & Wilkins, in press.

Derogatis, L. R., Lipman, R. S., Rickels, K., Uhlenhuth, E. H., & Covi, L. The HSCL: A self-report symptom inventory. *Behavioral Science,* 1974, **19**, 1–15.

Ellis, A. Frigidity. In A. Ellis, & A. Abarbanel (Eds.), *The Encyclopedia of sexual behavior,* Vol. 1. New York: Hawthorn, 1961.

Ellis, A. *The art and science of love* (Rev. ed.). New York: Lyle Stuart, 1966.

Engel, G. L. The concept of psychosomatic disorder. *Journal of Psychosomatic Research,* 1967, **11**, 3–9.

Eysenck, H. J. Personality and behaviour therapy. *Proceedings of the Royal Society of Medicine,* 1960, **53**, 504–508.

Frank, E., Anderson, C., & Kupfer, D. J. Arenas of conflict: Marriage and the marriage bed. *American Journal of Psychiatry*, in press.

Freud, S. Contributions to the psychology of love. In *Collected Papers* (Vol. IV). London: Hogarth Press, 1950.

Goldfried, M. R., & Kent, R. N. Traditional versus behavioral personality assessment: A comparison of methodological and theoretical assumptions. *Psychological Bulletin*, 1972, **77**, 409–420.

Green, R. Taking a sex history. In R. Green (Ed.), *Human sexuality*. Baltimore: Williams & Wilkins, 1965.

Greenblatt, R. B., Mortara, F., & Torpin, R. Sexual libido in the female. *American Journal of Obstetrics and Gynecology*, 1942, **44**, 658–663.

Grinker, R. R., Sr. *Psychosomatic research*. New York: Norton, 1953.

Grossberg, J. M. Behavior therapy: A review. *Psychological Bulletin*, 1964, **62**, 73–88.

Group for the Advancement of Psychiatry. *Assessment of sexual functioning: A guide to interviewing* (GAP Rep. 88). New York: Group for the Advancement of Psychiatry, 1973.

Guttman, L. The basis for scalogram analysis. In S. A. Stouffer, L. Guttman, E. A. Suchman, P. F. Lazarsfeld, S. A. Star, & J. A. Clausen (Eds.), *Measurement and prediction*. Princeton, N. J.: Princeton University Press, 1950.

Hartman, W. E., & Fithian, M. A. *Treatment of sexual dysfunction*. Long Beach, California: Center for Marital and Sexual Studies, 1972.

Hastings, D. W. *Impotence and frigidity*. Boston: Little-Brown, 1963.

Henry, W. E., Sims, J. H., & Spray, S. L. *Public and private lives of psychotherapists*. San Francisco: Jossey-Bass, 1973.

Johnson, J. Prognosis of disorders of sexual potency in the male. *Journal of Psychosomatic Research*, 1965, **9**, 195–200.

Johnson, V. E., & Masters, W. H. Sexual incompatability: Diagnosis and treatment. In C. W. Lloyd (Ed.), *Human reproduction and sexual behavior*. Philadelphia: Lea & Febiger, 1964.

Jones, H. G. Principles of psychological assessment. In P. Mittler (Ed.), *The psychological assessment of mental and physical handicaps*. London: Methuen, 1970.

Kanfer, F. H., & Saslow, G. Behavioral diagnosis. In C. M. Franks (Ed.), *Behavior therapy: Appraisal and status*. New York: McGraw-Hill, 1969.

Kaplan, H. S. *The new sex therapy*. New York: Brunner/Mazel, 1974.

Karpman, B. Psychic impotence. *Psychoanalytic Review*, 1933, 20, 274–303.

Katchadourian, H. A., & Lunde, D. T. *Fundamentals of human sexuality*. New York: Holt, Rinehart & Winston, 1972.

Kiesler, D. J. *The process of psychotherapy*. Chicago: Aldine, 1973.

Kinsey, A. C., Pomeroy, W. B., & Martin, C. E. *Sexual behavior in the human male*. Philadelphia: Saunders, 1948.

Kraines, S. H. *The therapy of the neuroses and psychoses*. Philadelphia: Lea & Febiger, 1948.

Lazarus, A. A. Modes of treatment for sexual inadequacies. *Medical Aspects of Human Sexuality*, 1969, **3**, 53–58.

Lazarus, A. A. Multimodal behavior therapy: Treating the "basic id". *Journal of Nervous and Mental Disease*, 1973, **156**, 404–411.

Lief, H. I. Sexual functions in men and their disturbances. In S. Arieti (Ed.), *American Handbook of psychiatry* (Vol. 1; 2nd ed.). New York: Basic Books, 1974.

Lansing, C. The significance of sexual complaints. In D. W. Abse, E. M. Nash, & L. M. R. Louden (Eds.), *Marital and sexual counseling in medical practice*. New York: Harper & Row, 1974.

Lipowski, Z. J. Review of consultation psychiatry and psychosomatic medicine—III. Theoretical issues. *Psychosomatic Medicine*, 1968, **30**, 395–422.

LoPiccolo, J., & Lobitz, W. C. Behavior therapy of sexual dysfunction. In L. A. Hamerlynck, L. C. Handy, & E. J. Mash (Eds.), *Behavior change*. Champaign, Ill.: Research Press, 1973.

LoPiccolo, J., Stewart, R., & Watkins, B. Treatment of erectile failure and ejaculatory incompetence with homosexual etiology. *Journal of Behavior Therapy and Experimental Psychiatry*, 1972, **3**, 233–236.

Margolin, S. G., & Kaufman, M. R. What is psychosomatic medicine? *Medical Clinics of North America*, 1948, **32**, 609–610.

Marks, I. M., & Gelder, M. G. Common ground between behaviour therapy and psychodynamic methods. *British Journal of Medical Psychology*, 1966, **39**, 11–23.

Marmor, J. Dynamic psychotherapy and behavior therapy. *Archives of General Psychiatry*, 1971, **24**, 22–28.

Marquis, J. N. Orgasmic reconditioning: Changing sexual object choice through controlling masturbation fantasies. *Journal of Behavior Therapy and Experimental Psychiatry*, 1970, **1**, 263–271.

Masters W. H., & Johnson, V. E. *Human sexual inadequacy*. Boston: Little-Brown, 1970.

Meltzoff, J., & Kornreich, M. *Research in psychotherapy*. New York: Atherton, 1970.

Mendels, J. (Ed.). *Biological psychiatry*. New York: Wiley, 1973.

Obler, M. Systematic desensitization in sexual disorders. *Journal of Behavior Therapy and Experimental Psychiatry*, 1973, **4**, 93–101.

O'Connor, J. F., & Stern, L. O. Developmental factors in functional sexual disorders. *New York State Journal of Medicine*, 1972, **72**, 1838–1843.

Oliven, J. F. *Sexual hygiene and pathology*. Philadelphia: Lippincott, 1955.

Podell, L., & Perkins, J. C. A Guttmen scale for sexual experience—a methodological note. *Journal of Abnormal and Social Psychology*, 1957, **54**, 420–422.

Rachman, S. Sexual disorders and behavior therapy. *American Journal of Psychiatry*, 1961, **118**, 235–240.

Roen, P. R. Impotence. *New York State Journal of Medicine*, 1965, **65**, 2576–2582.

Schumacher, S. Treatment of sexual dysfunction. Paper presented at the Human Sexuality Seminar, Long Island Jewish-Hillside Medical Center, New York, April 1974.

Schumacher, S., & Lloyd, C. W. Interdisciplinary treatment and study of sexual distress. Paper presented at the meeting of the International Congress of Medical Sexology, Paris, July 1974.

Schumacher, S., & Lloyd, C. W. Physiological and psychological factors in male sexual dysfunction. Unpublished manuscript, 1975.

Stekel, W. *Impotence in the male*. Vol. I. New York: Liveright, 1927.

Tuthill, J. F. Impotence. *Lancet*, 1955, *I*, 124–128.

Walker, K. The causation and treatment of impotence. *The Practitioner*, 1947, **158**, 289–294.

Winokur, G. Sexual behavior: Its relationship to certain affects and psychiatric diseases. In G. Winokur (Ed.), *Determinants of sexual behavior*. Springfield, Ill.: Thomas, 1963.

Wolpe, J. *Psychotherapy by reciprocal inhibition*. Stanford: Stanford University Press, 1958.

Zuckerman, M. Scales for sex experience for males and females. *Journal of Consulting and Clinical Psychology*, 1973, **41**, 27–29.

CHAPTER 16

Assessment of Sexual Deviation in the Male[*]

GENE G. ABEL

Department of Psychiatry
University of Tennessee Center for the Health Sciences, and
Tennessee Psychiatric Hospital and Institute
Memphis, Tennessee

Introduction

The behavioral assessment of sexual deviations has reached a fairly sophisticated level within the last 10 years. Three factors appear to have contributed significantly to these advancements. *First*, traditional means of evaluation and treatment have not been particularly effective. In hopes of finding a more successful approach, deviates have been referred for newer treatment modalities, such as behavior modification. The availability of sexual deviates for assessment has led to concentrated efforts regarding their evaluation and treatment as opposed to other categories of psychological problems. *Second*, sexual activities such as exposing oneself or voyeurism are specific, easily identifiable acts that lend themselves to behavioral observation. Since accurate identification of the behavior to be changed is the hallmark of the behavioral approach, the overt nature of deviant sexual acts has assisted in their more thorough behavioral assessment. *Third*, rapid progress has been made in the physiologic measurement of sexual arousal patterns, allowing further objectivity to be brought to the assessment techniques for sexual deviates.

The following schema of assessment for sexual deviates assumes that to be relevant, the assessment procedures must be simple enough to be understood and applied by both the therapist and client. In order to facilitate understanding of what is basically a complicated issue (i.e., deviant sexual behavior), the complete assessment has been broken down into its four major components (Abel, Blanchard & Becker, in press; Barlow, 1974; Barlow & Abel, in press): (1) the extent of deviant arousal, (2) the amount of heterosexual arousal, (3) the adequacy of heterosocial skills, and (4) the appropriateness of gender role behavior.

*This work was supported in part by National Institute of Mental Health Grant MH27724.

These four components were arrived at empirically by assessing a variety of sexual deviates from the vantage point of their clinical needs, and then identifying what appeared to be the common components of these treatment needs, irrespective of diagnostic categories. The schema makes no pretense at being the "final word" on the areas of behavior needing assessment. Quite the contrary, it is expected that greater understanding of the treatment needs of sexual deviates will demand further elaboration and refinement of these and other components. At this time, however, the schema appears to assess the major areas that may or may not need treatment for all varieties of sexual deviates.

Under each of the four components are identified the self report, physiologic, and motor responses specific to that component. It is suggested that by integrating these three measures as they apply to the four major components, we will then begin to arrive at a thorough understanding of any specific excesses or deficits of behavior which contribute to the client's overall deviant behavior pattern.

Deviant Sexual Arousal

Abnormal arousal patterns have traditionally been viewed as the only component of behavior needing correction in sexual deviates. This simplistic view assumed that correction of the abnormal arousal pattern alone would lead to rehabilitation of the client. Subsequent discussion will demonstrate that this treatment alone is usually insufficient.

Deviant sexual arousal patterns include arousal to inappropriate objects (e.g., in pedophilia, homosexuality, bestiality, and fetishism) or inappropriate behaviors (e.g., in sadism, voyeurism, exhibitionism, and rape). The pedophile, for example, desires to hold, caress, have genital contact, and establish an emotional relationship with another person, but his choice of a young child to carry out this behavior frequently leads to his arrest. The voyeur, by contrast, usually selects an appropriate object (an adult female), but his behavior towards that female is inappropriate. Instead of attempting to develop a relationship, date, and possibly become sexually involved with her, he watches her through a window, usually fantasizing sexual behavior with her. Such inappropriate behavior (observing without consent) leads to his arrest.

Self Report. Assessment of deviant behavior usually begins with self report data obtained from the client. Obtaining information about deviant sexual behavior is usually hampered by both client and therapist characteristics. Many deviates are ashamed and feel quite guilty about their deviant sexual behavior after its commission. To relay such experiences to the therapist is to potentially incur even further ridicule and criticism. The therapist may himself harbor severe sanctions against such behaviors as rape, bestiality, or pedophilia. A thorough assessment, however, demands a complete understanding of exactly what deviant behaviors occur and what internal cues are associated with that behavior. The therapist should thus convey, in a concerned manner, his desire to assist the client in identifying antecedents and concomitants of the deviant acts. If the therapist, due to his belief system, is unable to maintain objectivity, he should identify this to the client and refer him to a therapist whose personal attitudes will allow a more accurate assessment.

To assess the client's self report of his deviant behavior, the therapist might begin by asking a general question, with an exhibitionist, for example, he might say: "Tell me in 10 or 15 minutes about what you do that leads to your arrest." If the client glosses over specific details, the therapist might ask him to slow down and describe things as they occur, step-by-step. The therapist should be especially attentive to the client's words and descriptive phases. Later during treatment, the therapist may have to recreate in imagery the exhibitionistic experience for the client. Using his words and his phrases facilitates his ability to recall and revisualize those experiences. The therapist improves his own comfort and ease with this vocabulary by actually using the client's language in the process of obtaining self report information. As the exhibitionist says "and as I come up to her, I pull my zipper down, pull it out, and flash her," the therapist responds, "so then you pull it out and flash her, and then what do you do?" Using this technique, the client and therapist both become more comfortable with the deviant's language, as it is spoken by both.

Quantifying the client's deviant behavior is also helpful, since it allows the therapist to identify high frequency behaviors that will probably need greater treatment than other, less frequent deviant behavior. Questions such as "How many times per day do you think about exposing yourself? How many times per week will you cruise areas to expose yourself? How many times per week do you actually expose yourself?" will all help clarify high frequency behaviors.

A more systematic means of collecting self report data is by a frequency count. In the early stages of evaluation, the client is asked to record three times per day (lunch, supper, and bedtime) how often he has fantasies of exposing himself and how often he actually exposes himself. The client carries a pocket-size notebook, and at the appropriate mealtime, tabulates the frequency of these experiences since the last reporting. Although still self-report data, such frequency counts represent a somewhat more systematic collection of information. By the time assessment has been completed, considerable data will have accumulated to identify the high frequency behaviors to be reduced. Such quantification is of some prognostic value as well, since Evans (1970) has reported that a high frequency of deviant behavior and a high frequency of deviant fantasies both identify those individuals who will need more extensive treatment.

Individually tailored "card sorts" offer another means of collecting self report information. Brief phrases are developed from the deviate's descriptions of highly erotic, deviant experiences he has had or would like to have. For example, two phrases developed for an exhibitionist included: (a) "I have an erection; I'm masturbating in front of an attractive 12-year-old girl; she's fascinated by my penis;" and (b) "It's in the afternoon; the two girls on the motor scooter are looking at my penis; they are really excited."

The client rates each phrase daily on a 7-point scale where —3 indicates the phrase was sexually repulsive, 0 sexually neutral, +3 high sexually erotic and —2, —1, +1 and +2 falling between. By tabulating the total arousal value of such deviant scenes on a daily basis, the client provides the therapist with an ongoing confirmation of his arousal pattern. Card sorts and frequency counts can also provide ongoing assessment of treatment, with gradual reduction of sexual arousal to such scenes and a lower frequency of deviant acts and fantasies to be expected as treatment progresses.

It is also important to understand not only the terminal behavior that the deviate executes (e.g., exposing his genitals to the female for the exhibitionist) but also the entire chain of behaviors that precede or follow that event. Therapy will probably be directed at *all* the behaviors along that chain, not just the terminal one (Mandel, 1970), and the therapist needs an understanding of all elements in the chain. For example,

Therapist: "Well, what exactly occurred the day you were arrested?"

Exhibitionist: "Not much, I just found a girl and exposed myself."

Therapist: "Tell me how you got to that final point of exposing yourself. What happened each step of the way?"

Exhibitionist: "Well, it started when I blew up at my wife. I got in the car and just planned to drive around a little. Then, I started looking for college girls, you know, short dresses. I really wasn't thinking about exposing myself. Then, I saw this real sharp one and young, so I slowed down to look. Then, I started thinking about exposing myself, and I circled the block and parked the car in front of her, like I usually do, and leaned over towards the sidewalk side of the car — — —."

Here, we are beginning to see not just the final cues active at the time the client exposed himself, but those early behaviors that, although not immediately active at the time of the exposure, still played a role in the chain of events that culminated in exposure. Improving the client's marital relationship, disrupting his avoidance of his wife after fights, blocking his solitary rides in the car, stopping his looking at attractive college girls (even though he perceives no urges to expose himself), etc., are all elements of the chain that will probably need disruption.

Finally, self report measures should include information about covert events occurring near or during the deviant behavior. Such internal cues play a vital role in the arousal patterns of deviates (Abel & Blanchard, 1974; McGuire, Carlisle & Young, 1965). For example, a 27-year-old rapist describes having raped over 50 women. By his report and available information from his defence lawyer, he has never injured his victims. When questioned about his fantasies during the rapes, he reports imagining beating and "cutting-up" his victim with a knife. If the therapist relies only on what the client reports as his overt behavior, internal cues also occurring at the time of the rape would be omitted from the behavioral analyses. In light of the above, treatment should be directed at these reported fantasies in addition to the actual behaviors involved in the rapes.

Self report provides considerable rapid, specific information regarding the client's deviant arousal pattern at minimal expense. Relying exclusively on such client controlled information, however, has its limitations, since such information may be misperceived, not recalled, or at times concealed by some clients.

Physiological Measures. Major advancements have occurred in assessing sexual arousal, and in the development of physiological devices that accurately record sexual arousal in males (Barlow, Becker, Leitenberg & Agras, 1970; Zuckerman, 1971) and females (Sintchak & Geer, in press). The details of how such instrumentation is applied to the physiological assessment of sexual deviates has recently been reviewed by Bancroft (1971) and Abel & Blanchard (in press).

The most valid measure of sexual arousal in male deviates is direct calibration of penile erection as recorded by the penile transducer (Zuckerman, 1971). This apparatus encircles the penis and generates an electrical signal as erection occurs. This signal is in turn displayed by a pen recording polygraph. By comparing partial erection measures to those recordings obtained during full erection, the client's physiologic erection during sexual stimulus presentation can be quantified as percent of a full erection. Such transducers are currently available[1] commercially and have brought a new objectivity to the assessment of deviant arousal.

In addition to choosing from a variety of transducers (Abel & Blanchard, in press), the therapist must also determine: (1) the modality of stimulus presentation during physiologic recording of erection, (2) the content displayed by that modality, and (3) the instructional set given the client during such recording. The deviant stimuli presented during erection measurement can be displayed by video tape clips, movies, slides, audio descriptions, written

[1] Farrall Instrument Company, P.O. Box 1037, Grand Island, Nebraska 68801.

descriptions, or by simply having the client fantasy his deviant experiences. A comparison of the effectiveness of different modalities at generating erections in homosexuals, voyeurs, pedophiliacs, exhibitionists, sadists, and rapists (Abel, Barlow, Blanchard & Mavissakalian, in press; Abel & Blanchard, in press) indicates that video tapes, slides, audio descriptions, and client's fantasies are most successful at producing erection responses in decreasing order of effectiveness. Since the therapist is attempting to evaluate the client's physiological arousal to deviant cues, and video clips produce the largest of such responses, this modality should be selected if available. Usually, 2-minute selections are sufficient for measurement, since longer selections fail to produce erections of significantly greater magnitude.

The therapist next selects the content displayed by the chosen modality. The deviant content should capture as closely as possible these environmental conditions, people, and acts that the client's self-report identified as most erotic. Sometimes, video clips for common deviant arousal patterns are commercially available (e.g., male homosexuality). Less common arousal patterns are not always as available in the video modality or 35mm slides[2]. Consequently, audio descriptions or free fantasy must be used. Audio descriptions appear to be especially effective for presenting idiosyncratic, bizarre sexual scenes (Abel, Blanchard, Barlow & Mavissakalian, 1975) or scenes that are technically or ethically impossible to present by other methods, such as incest or rape (Abel & Blanchard, in press). Evaluation of results using such accurate measures of physiologic arousal and precise control of stimulus content have demonstrated that, although verbal report sometimes correlates with physiologic measures of deviant erotic preferences, at times there is marked disparity between these two assessment strategies.

Abel *et al.* (1975), for example, explored the physiologic arousal response of a client who reported a fetish for women's sandals. Using audiotaped descriptions, the authors isolated sandal cues only. When such stimuli were presented, however, the client developed minimal physiological arousal. Assuming that the client's arousal must be in some way related to sandals, another audio description was developed to isolate cues specific to a woman's foot, devoid of sandal references. Contrary to the client's verbal report, foot stimuli generated marked erections. Using a single case experimental design, repeated measures confirmed these findings. This and other examples described by the authors substantiate that frequently, self report alone is insufficient to identify deviant arousal patterns. A thorough assessment of deviant arousal patterns requires the integration of information from all three sources (i.e., self-report, physiologic, and motor responses).

A final issue to be determined by the therapist during erection measures is the instructional set given the client. Deviates (Abel, Barlow, Blanchard &

[2]Farrall Instrument Company, P.O. Box 1037, Grand Island, Nebraska 68801.

Mavissakalian, in press), like normal males (Henson & Rubin, 1971; Laws & Rubin, 1969) have a certain degree of control over their erections during such measurement situations. Evidence suggests that the client's control of attention to the deviant stimuli is probably the technique by which such control is possible (Geer, 1974). This means that physiologic measures of deviant arousal should be conducted with cooperative clients who are not attempting to conceal their true arousal patterns. Since suppression of erections to sexual cues is far easier than generating false responses (Henson & Rubin, 1971; Laws & Rubin, 1969), when possible the therapist should give greater weight to *positive* erection measures, as opposed to drawing conclusions about arousal pattern based on the client's failure to develop erections to deviant stimuli. For example, erection responses to exhibitionistic cues should be accepted as a more valid finding indicating a client's deviant arousal than assuming that no erections to exhibitionistic cues indicates he is no longer aroused to such cues.

Abel & Blanchard (in press) also suggest that measurement of *both* the client's ability to be aroused by deviant cues and his ability to suppress that arousal be evaluated. Erection measures under both instructional sets allow the therapist to judge the client's ability to voluntarily influence the objectivity of such measures, and thus the therapist has a better understanding of the validity of the erection measures he is relying on. As data accumulate regarding the use of the penile transducer as an assessment instrument, the influence that instructional sets have on the validity of these physiologic measures should become more apparent.

Motor Responses: A client's motor behavior is not particularly helpful in identifying his deviant sexual preferences, although it is extremely helpful in identifying that component of overall deviant sexual arousal referred to as gender role behavior (see below). Actual deviant motor behavior is sometimes role played by the client during treatments such as electrical aversion or shame aversion (Serber, 1970), but visualizing deviant behaviors for assessment is usually not indicated.

Heterosexual Arousal

The second and frequently overlooked area of assessment is the client's arousal to adult heterosexual cues (sexual arousal to a mutually consenting adult homosexual would be equally as appropriate if selected by the client). Adequate arousal to appropriate sexual objects has been a frequently neglected area of assessment. It was assumed that clients who have suppressed their deviant arousal and have good social skills would "naturally" develop arousal to adult females. When such arousal was not forthcoming, the need for assessing heterosexual arousal became apparent (Abel & Blanchard, in press; Barlow, 1973; Barlow & Abel, in press).

Assessing the presence of heterosexual arousal is also of prognostic value. Feldman and MacCulloch (1971) identified the absence of prior heterosexual arousal as a means of identifying those clients who would not respond to their anticipatory avoidance treatment for male homosexuals. Barlow (1973) stresses how the presence of heterosexual arousal has also been viewed in the psychoanalytic literature as a good prognostic sign in treating deviates.

Assessment of this area closely follows the procedures outlined under deviant sexual arousal, since the only major difference is the gender of the chosen sexual object.

Self Report. Self report is usually rapid and fairly accurate at identifying heterosexual arousal. The client should indicate how old he was when heterosexual arousal began, his early and later dating patterns, the characteristics of the female or heterosexual behaviors he preferred. If the client denies heterosexual arousal, the therapist should determine *if at anytime* in the past the client did have some heterosexual arousal. Frequently that arousal pattern was present, but subsequent deviant arousal has been so strong that heterosexual arousal patterns have been almost forgotten, If such heterosexual arousal was present, the therapist should identify the exact cues that were most erotic at the time, since their incorporation into treatment to redevelop heterosexual arousal may be critical.

It is especially helpful to explore fantasies occurring during apparent heterosexual involvements or masturbation to supposed heterosexual cues.

Example. A 27-year-old male reports sexual arousal to homosexual themes, but also says he has had sexual intercourse with women on three occasions. His description of his heterosexual encounter suggests that he may have adequate heterosexual arousal. When questioned about his sexual fantasies during heterosexual intercourse, his true arousal pattern became more apparent. In all three circumstances he took great pains to fantasy that the women he was having intercourse with were actually men. Rather than having penile-vaginal intercourse, in his "mind's eye" he saw himself having anal intercourse with the fantasized male. In real life he put his arms around the woman and embraced her, but in imagination he visualized himself holding, embracing a man. In this case, relying exclusively on the overt behavior reported would have ignored significant internal cues.

The frequency reports and card sort techniques described under deviant sexual arousal can also be easily adapted to the evaluation of heterosexual arousal. The client self reports three times per day either heterosexual fantasies or actual heterosexual behaviors in the same small notebook used for deviant reporting. The card sort method is also adapted so that —3 (sexually repulsive) through +3 (highly sexually erotic scores are given to heterosexual phrases such as: (a) "I'm in a room with Alice; I have my arms around her; I feel her breast rubbing up against my chest, and (b) I'm naked, in bed with Jean; she's feeling my penis with her hand as she tells me how much she loves me." As with deviant arousal, frequency reports and card sort techniques allow a systematic means of collecting information about sexual preference for assessment value, but these measures are also used to assess the effects of treatment.

Physiological Measures. Physiologic techniques for the assessment of heterosexual arousal are almost identical to those for assessing deviant arousal. Use of the penile transducer, the modality used during the presentation, and instructional sets, remain the same. The major change is the selection of content to be presented during such measurement sessions.

Although recent work has identified the specific heterosexual movie content most erotic to non-deviates (Sanford, 1974), the therapist should be careful in selecting content that superficially might appear to be nondeviant. Mavissakalian, Blanchard, Abel, & Barlow (1975) presented strictly heterosexual and strictly homosexual males, video clips of a seductive, single girl, two lesbians, a heterosexual couple, and a male homosexual couple engaged in genital activity. Only the male homosexual couple (responded to by the homosexual group) and the lesbian couple clips (responded to by the heterosexual group) discriminated between the groups. The homosexual group reported responding to the heterosexual couple scenes by imaging sexual activity with the male participant. These findings demonstrate the importance of content selection for erection measures. Here, a scene depicting heterosexual intercourse was responded to as a homosexual cue by the homosexual group, thus stressing the need for careful content selection.

Similar care must be taken while evaluating other arousal patterns. Transvestites may interpret a slide of a female as actually a deviant cue (e.g., seeing himself really dressed well in women's clothes). A male to female transsexual may interpret a slide of a naked woman as deviant, allowing the woman to represent the kind of body he would want to have. Similar issues regarding stimuli selection are discussed by Abel & Blanchard (in press), and Abel *et al.* (1975).

Finally, the heterosexual stimulus for assessing arousal should be carefully selected. Pictures frequently chosen for presentation depict women from Playboy type magazines. In the client's world, however, the woman he is likely to meet and have the opportunity to become aroused to is not usually a Playboy type, but a girl from the office or "down the block." Erection measures should thus determine arousal to women more commonly seen in real life, rather than the atypical, infrequently encountered women displayed in popular magazines.

Discrepancies between physiologic measures and self report are seen during the assessment of heterosexual arousal, as in assessing deviant arousal. *Example:* A 27-year-old male reported that although married for 3 years he had no arousal to women, but extensive arousal to males. When questioned about ever having had minimal arousal to women, he denied the same. When further questioned about the woman he was least repulsed by, he described the pleasing personality of a female social worker he had been seeing weekly for almost 2 years. He was then asked to describe her in detail, and seemed to enjoy describing the texture and color of her skin.

Physiologic assessment included the development of audio scenarios of a few of the women he had described. The description of his social worker, outlining in detail her skin, was immediately associated with a marked increase in erection to greater than 50%. When questioned at the time, he denied any sexual arousal. Repeated presentation of cues depicting the same social worker with further elaboration of her physical characteristics continued to produce marked erections. Here the client's physiologic measures conflicted sharply with his self report, suggesting that he experienced significant physiologic arousal beyond what he reported. Further assessment of this client confirmed the validity of the erection measures.

Motor Responses. Motoric responses do not contribute significantly to the identification or the extent of heterosexual arousal and will not receive further elaboration.

Heterosocial Skills

Historically, behavioral treatments were first directed towards decreasing deviant arousal and increasing heterosexual arousal. However, it became clear that many of the clients were lacking in some of the basic heterosexual skills required. Such clients were no longer preoccupied with excessive deviant arousal, were sexually aroused by adult females, but reported they did not know how to interact socially with women.

Problems of interacting with females appear to exist along a continuum extending from social, to heterosexual, to explicit sexual interactions. On one end of the spectrum is the inability to carry out even rudimentary *social skills* with either males or females (e.g., not maintaining eye contact, appropriate body position, or flow of conversation with another individual). This general area is reviewed in Chapter 13, Assessment of Social Skills.

At the opposite end of this spectrum are specific *sexual skills* (i.e., the client lacking the specific behaviors needed to carry out explicit sexual activity with his partner). This general area is reviewed in Chapter 15, Assessment of Sexual Dysfunction. Midway between these two extremes are deficits in *heterosocial skills* (i.e., those social behaviors antecedent to explicit sexual activity). These latter complex behaviors normally develop on a trial and error basis during the course of early dating. By learning from our own successes and failures and modeling after others, most males learn to date, flirt, and communicate a desire for further intimacy with a female partner. When inadequate opportunity, practice, and modeling, or the client's deviant arousal pattern removes him from the possibility of relating socially to females (e.g., exclusively male homosexuals and pedophiliacs), it is not at all surprising that such clients have significant heterosocial deficits. Earlier, more simplistic treatments assumed that such skills would have to appear due to the socialization process, but experience strongly suggests that this is not always the case. Heterosocial skills must, therefore, be assessed from the usual self report, physiologic, and motoric elements.

Self Reports. The male deviate should be questioned about his past history of dating (e.g., age of onset, frequency, and information reflecting his adeptness). The therapist should identify what are the usual environments, people, and situations in which he excels or fails heterosocially. Are his heterosocial deficits occurring on approaching and first meeting a female (or preferred partner), initiating conversation with her, asking her for a social date, flirting, or during the more intimate exchanges just antecedent to sexual contact?

A common error in such assessment is the therapist's insensitivity to the client's real world of heterosexual interaction. If the therapist and client are from different social environments, the situations, opportunities, and style of heterosocial interacting may be entirely different. To ask the client how he approaches or interacts with women on coke dates and fraternity parties may have little relevance when his culture leads to heterosocial interactions at bars and bowling alleys.

Physiologic Measures. Eisler, Miller, Hersen & Alford (1974), Hersen (1973), Hersen, Eisler & Miller (1973), and Hersen & Miller (1974) have stressed the value of appraising the client's physiologic responses during his heterosocial performance. The therapist must not only be aware of his client's actual skills, but also the extent of anxiety, nervousness, tachycardia, diaphoresis, and tremor, etc., associated with these skills. If the client's heterosocial performance is flawless and yet he displays and describes excessive physiological responses, assessment must identify these factors for inclusion in the client's total treatment.

Directly monitoring such physiological responses with instruments, although possible, is usually not needed. Most therapists directly observe the client for such physiologic responses during role playing of his heterosocial skills as described below. In addition to therapist observation, the client should self-report his own anxiety during role playing by using the subjective unit of disturbance scale (SUDS) described by Wolpe & Lazarus (1966). The most severe anxiety experienced by the client is rated as 100; absolute calm is zero. After each role-playing scene, the client reports the greatest degree of anxiety or discomfort he experienced during the scene on the scale of zero to 100. The therapist also needs to know exactly which segment of his client's performance was associated with peak anxiety.

Motor Responses. Some clients can accurately recall and assess their heterosocial skills and concurrent physiologic responses, but most of us fail miserably at such a task. Therefore, the best means of evaluation is by actually observing the client's motor skills during heterosocial interactions. In this fashion the therapist observes and can confirm the client's self report. Although many authors use social skills training and report it as extremely helpful and effective with clients lacking skills (Clark & Arkowitz, 1975; Goldsmith, 1973; MacDonald, Lindquist, Kramer, McGrath & Rhyne, 1973; McGovern, Arkowitz & Gilmore, 1975), developing a means of quantifying heterosexual performance has been quite difficult.

Motor assessment should involve the client role playing scenes depicting those very situations he must deal with in real life. To insure that the therapist is evaluating an adequate sampling of such situations, the client should role play at least three different scenes. It is most helpful if a female assistant, of a similar age and unknown to the client, can role-play the part of the female to increase the validity of the situation. Three scenes might include the following: (1) the client enters a bar where a woman is sitting alone; he tries to introduce himself and strike up a conversation, (2) the client is at a small restaurant where he has eaten before; he tries to ask a familiar waitress for a date while she is serving him, and (3) the client has been invited to his date's apartment; he tries to flirt, discussing her personality, appearance, clothes, and his attraction to her.

Since mental health workers are usually heterosocially adept, the female assistant may have a tendency to lead the conversation in such scenes and inadvertently assist the client in his performance. Since the goal of this assessment is to evaluate his heterosocial performance, his performance is best taxed by cautioning the female confederate to avoid initiating conversation, to limit her verbal response to five words or less, and to avoid excessive reinforcement during the scene (either verbal or non-verbal).

Once the scene is established, heterosexual performance can be quantified by the use of an appropriate scale. Although a scale for assessing all categories of heterosocial behavior is not available, Barlow, Abel, Blanchard, Brostow & Young (1975) have recently developed a check list of three heterosocial behaviors that discriminate males with successful heterosocial skills from sexual deviates without these skills. Appropriate heterosocial motor skills in these three areas of performance include:

voice
- sufficiently loud, without breathy overtones,
- lower in pitch than female role player,
- no excessive inflection,
- no dramatic affect

form of conversation
- introduces, initiates conversation,
- responds at least once to female's vocalizations,
- allows no pauses—5 seconds or longer in conversation,
- comments reflect interest in the female

affect
- facial expression appropriate to conversation's content,
- eye contact occurs five seconds per 30 seconds of conversation,
- laughter is without giggling or high pitch

Usually $2\frac{1}{2}$ minutes of social interaction in each of three role-playing situations is observed. The client's performance is rated in 30-second blocks for the presence or absence of each subcategory under voice, form of conversation, and affect. The percent of appropriate behavior is calculated and compared with the client's self report of his heterosocial skills. This information is then combined with self report and evaluations of the client's physiologic responses during such role play, to pinpoint exactly what heterosocial deficits exist (i.e., those that need appropriate intervention). This assessment technique, as with the previously mentioned erection measures, can provide the therapist with a repeated assessment of the effects of treatment interventions in the heterosocial skills area.

Example. A male seeking treatment to reduce the occurrence of homosexual fantasies reports he also has marked difficulty trying to date women. Up to the present he has avoided dating. When simply near women, he feels nervous, anxious, and uncomfortable. The three role-playing situations mentioned above are described to him and he is instructed to be as socially adept as possible during the scenes. Although he displayed fair social skills during his interview with a male therapist, his performance is quite different in the heterosocial role playing scenes with a female. His voice assessment is extremely good (i.e., 90% appropriate). His form of conversation, however, is extremely poor, (e.g., he initiates conversation only twice in 3 minutes, he does not respond to the woman's replies, he allows some 50-second pauses to occur in conversation, and makes no comments reflecting interest in the woman). His affect performance is equally poor. His subjective units of disturbance are 75 to 100 during the three scenes.

This case highlights the value of the motor assessment of heterosocial skills and its relationship to self report and physiological assessment. Although the client displayed some deficits in the clinical interview, when faced with an actual woman in the role-playing situation his heterosocial skills deficits became obvious. His self report of heterosocial deficits, however, was only partially correct. Actual assessment of his voice performance indicated no significant deficits. His form of conversation and affect, however, were extremely poor and consistent with his self report.

These findings point out the added value of breaking down evaluation processes into subparts. Heterosocial skills are usually evaluated by global, unquantified assessment methods that fail to identify specific areas of competency or deficits. When complex behaviors are divided into subparts, some areas (such as this individual's voice assessment) turn out to be very appropriate, not needing treatment. Such discrimination of treatment needs allows the therapist to concentrate on the precise deficits needing remediation, with a more efficient use of therapist-client time.

The reliability of this heterosocial motor scale is relatively high when rating videotaped recordings of role playing scenes, but reliability is also a function of the specific behavior being observed. The reliability coefficient for the affect scale is 86-91%, the form of conversation scale 94-96%, and the voice scale 94-97%, when calculated by comparing agreement and disagreement of independent judges rating 30-second blocks of behavior.

The major relevance of such motor assessment is its validity. On the basis of self report, the therapist might assume that the client's heterosocial skills are adequate or deficit. However, we no longer have to make such speculations since role-playing heterosocial scenes allow us to actually observe and quantify performance. If physiologic concomitants of such skills occur, we can actually view the tremor or hear the client's inappropriate voice inflections. If the client's discomfort is not observable (such as feeling anxious or upset during such scenes), his self report of that disturbance (SUDs) can be more closely associated with the specific tasks that make such discomfort higher or lower, rather than relying on his recall of distant events (which are frequently distorted).

In spite of the initial success with this scale, numerous problems suggest it should only be considered a rudimentary first start at quantifying assets and deficits. It is already apparent (Barlow *et al.*, 1975) that the scale's validity does not hold up when used with age groups, races, and socioeconomic groups other than the original sample. Clinical experience also strongly suggests that the three heterosocial behaviors are but a small fraction of the total repertoire of behaviors needed for good heterosocial functioning, and thus the scale needs to be expanded. We will also need to integrate heterosocial skills assessment with the evaluation of the general, social, and specific sexual skills mentioned earlier, to arrive at a more comprehensive assessment of any one deviate's entire skills repertoire. A final issue needing exploration is how does in-office role-playing relate to heterosocial skills performance in the real world? It might be expected that a client's performance with our female confederate in the office would be considerably easier than a heterosocial encounter in a bowling alley with an unknown woman. Only further research in this area can answer these rather complicated problems.

Gender Role Behavior

The final component of assessing sexual deviations is gender role behavior, the most recently investigated and probably least understood of the four components. Our confusion regarding gender role behavior has probably evolved from our assumption that sexual identity and gender role are always positively correlated. As each of us develop, we acquire a sense of sexual identity (e.g., I am a male or I am a female). Assessment of this behavior is described under deviant sexual or heterosexual arousal.

Separate from one's sexual identity is how we represent ourselves to the environment (i.e., our gender role). If we represent the characteristics traditionally associated with males, our gender role would be viewed as masculine. Confusion has developed when it was assumed that sexual identity and gender role behaviors had to be similar. The effeminate homosexual, however, exemplifies how this is not always the case. The effeminate homosexual may sit, stand, walk, and dress in a fashion traditionally ascribed to females. When asked whether he considers himself a man or a woman, he replies (rather affronted), "Well, I'm a man, of course." We may be confused by his reply because although he reports he is a male (male sexual identity), we have interpreted that he represents himself as a female (female gender role behavior).

Furthermore, our diagnostic classification systems have also viewed sexual identity or gender role behavior as either masculine *or* feminine rather than such characteristics residing on a continuum. To underscore this issue, let us examine the gender role continuum and the associated clinical conditions seen along the continuum. To the far right might be the masculine homosexual and masculine heterosexual diagnostic categories. Their sexual identity is male; gender role behavior masculine. Further to the left is the effeminate homosexual, effeminate heterosexual, and transvestite diagnostic categories. In all three cases the gender role is becoming more feminine but elements of masculine gender role are still present. Sexual identity is predominately male, but in some cases sexual identity is blending into a female identity. Further to the left on the continuum would be the transsexual whose sexual identity and gender role is female and feminine respectively.

The important thing to note is that our current nomenclature (DMS II) simply does not fit the clinical conditions seen because: (a) gender roles exist on a continuum, (b) sexual identity exists on a continuum, and (c) gender role and sexual identity are not consistently correlated across clients. At present, it is best to analyze gender role behavior as a completely separate component of a sexual deviation.

Self Report. The client is asked how he "comes across to others" (i.e., masculine or feminine). The therapist needs to be especially sensitive to exactly what his client is seeking. If he is a male homosexual who desires to be more feminine and believes he "comes across" quite feminine, but motor evaluation (see below) confirms strong masculine role behaviors, treatment is indicated in this particular area A further check on the success of his gender role behavior is how others have responded to his role behavior performance.

Example. A 26-year-old biologic female (presurgical female to male transsexual) recently moved to a new town and began living completely as a male. The client reports that a female fellow worker is trying to arrange a date for the client with a girlfriend (assuming that the client was a man), and the client was recently propositioned by a female prostitute. In both circumstances, the female to male transsexual was related to as if she/he were a male. Since this is the gender role behavior the client has chosen to display, verbal report confirms adequate male gender role behavior.

Systematic self report measures are also possible with gender role behavior. Bem (1974) has recently developed an attitudinal measure that attempts to quantify characteristics usually identified with masculine or feminine roles. Bem's masculine and feminine scales have been developed to be independent of each other, and thus allow measurement of masculine and feminine characteristics exclusive of one another. A final refinement of the scale is that it quantifies the extent to which the client reports being able to diverge from typical sex-typed standards (e.g., reflecting the rigidity of the client's sex typing). Such a scale may offer considerable assistance in the evaluation of gender role behaviors if adequate standardization can be established for the culture from which the client emanates.

Frequency reports and card sorts are also possible when adapted to gender role behaviors. For example, masculine gender role cards might include: (a) I want my sexual partner to see me as a real "take charge person," (b) I want my sexual partner to feel that I really protect him/her, and (c) I want people to see me as truly masculine. Tabulation of such frequency reports or card sorts is identical to that described earlier and can likewise be used for evaluative purposes or as a measure of treatment progress.

Physiologic Measures. The client's assessment of internal states, such as anxiety and discomfort, should be assessed using the SUDs method as described under heterosocial skills, with visible physiologic responses monitored by the therapist during the client's actual performance of gender role behaviors described below.

Motor Responses. Barlow (1973) measured the motor performance of a group of males and females, identifying those modes of sitting, standing, and walking specific to traditional male or female gender role behaviors. These components are listed below:

Gender Role Behavior	Masculine	Feminine
Sitting:		
buttocks position from back of chair	distant	close
legs uncrossed, knees	apart	close
legs crossed	foot on knee	knee on knee
arm movement from	shoulder	elbow
fingers	together and straight	relaxed
wrist action	firm	limp
Standing:		
feet apart	greater than 3 inches	less than 3 inches
arm movements from	shoulder	elbow
hand motion	minimal or in pocket	greater than 4 movements per minute
wrist action	firm	limp
strides	long	short
hip "swish"	absent	present
arm movement from	shoulder	elbow
wrist action	firm	limp
arm to trunk relationship	free and swinging	close and non-swinging

Although the validity and reliability of these measures have not been reported, their use in single case experiments (Barlow, Reynolds & Agras, 1973) add support to their discriminatory value.

Assessment begins by asking the client to behave as masculine as possible (or feminine, depending on his goal of preferred gender role behavior), while he sits, stands, and walks. His performance is videotaped and rated as to the presence or absence of the gender role behaviors described above per unit of time. The percent appropriate (to gender role goal) behavior is then calculated in each of three motor behavior areas. These results are then integrated with self report and physiologic observations and compared with the client's treatment goals. If the client is directly seeking gender role behavior change (an infrequent request) or his gender role behavior is inconsistent with his sexual preference choice, specific treatments can be offered (Barlow *et al.*, 1973).

The assessment of gender role behaviors will not routinely apply to all clients, but should be applied in those cases where sexual identity and gender role behaviors may be at issue (e.g., homosexuality, transsexualism, and transvestitism). Assessment should also occur in those situations where the therapist sees disagreement between the client's reported sexual identity and his observed sex role behaviors. Examples of the latter might include a heterosexual male whose gross gender role behavior appears quite feminine or a masculine homosexual seeking more feminine gender role behaviors. As with the other major components of treatment, self report, physiologic, and motoric responses frequently correlate, but not absolutely. This is especially the case when the client is in the process of change (e.g., a transsexual begins to enact the gender role behaviors that he feels are consistent with his sexual identity).

Summary and Conclusions

Psychiatrists and psychologists have traditionally viewed sexual deviates as a heterogeneous group of individuals who can be subgrouped on the basis of similar deviant arousal patterns. Clinicians have been taught to identify these subgroups and to seek out the similarities between those with similar diagnostic labels. As greater numbers of deviates have been examined, other behavior excesses or deficits have been noted in addition to excessive deviant arousal. It has finally become apparent that relying on the single criterion of deviant arousal is insufficient in evaluating any one client, since other components of the client's sexual being need to be evaluated. It now appears warranted to discard the older diagnostic system, relying instead on the more detailed and more specific evaluation of deviant arousal, heterosexual arousal, heterosocial skills, and gender role behaviors.

This new, four-component assessment makes no presupposition that any one client must have difficulties in one-, two-, three-, or even in all four-component areas. Whether such excesses or deficits exist are conclusions arrived at only after an appropriate assessment of each of the four areas, rather than being based on what most homosexuals, for example, "usually" show.

Within the assessment of any one of the four components, the self report, physiologic, or motoric element may be especially valid for that component of sexual assessment. It should be pointed out that which of the three elements is most valid usually depends on which most accurately generates an observable response closely associated to the component being measured. For example, physiologic responses (erections) are especially effective at measuring deviant sexual arousal, since erections can be closely associated with the sexual cues presented. Heterosexual skills are most validly measured by the motoric response element, since these behaviors are immediately associated with adequate or inadequate heterosexual role playing.

This is not to say that the other elements can be excluded from the assessment. On the contrary, proper evaluation demands the inclusion of the most valid element with the integration of the other two elements. The examples mentioned above demonstrate the pitfalls of relying exclusively on either the self report, physiologic, or motoric element to the exclusion of the other two.

Probably the greatest advantage of this assessment scheme is that it remains fluid. The system documents where any one client stands along a continuum in each of the four component areas. Whether the client moves from that position, in which direction, and how far, remains a decision for the client to make. He may wish to increase or decrease his deviant or heterosexual arousal, increase or decrease his heterosocial skills, or he may wish to develop more masculine or feminine gender role behaviors. Although it is the therapist's responsibility to identify to the client where he stands on each of these continua, where he goes from there is a decision that must remain with the client. In any event, these assessment techniques will provide tracking of that movement during treatment, irrespective of the client's final choice.

Finally, the fluidity of such an assessment schema appears to fit quite well with the delicate ethical issues related to working with sexual deviates (Davison, 1974), such as: who really speaks for the client's best interests and is it the client or society that needs change? Since assessment and treatment fit on continua in each of the four areas, the client can have the opportunity to identify exactly what his goal will be. Rather than the male homosexual, for example, having to make a decision as to whether he wants to be homosexual or heterosexual, he can now identify that he wishes to maintain his arousal to males and his moderately feminine gender role behavior, but to develop greater heterosexual arousal and better heterosocial skills. Such precision of assessment, when supported by a concurrent treatment that is equally precise, provides a more humane approach to the modification of sexual deviation, an attitude long overdue in our society.

References

Abel, G. G., Barlow, D. H., Blanchard, E. B., & Mavissakalian, M. Measurement of sexual arousal in male homosexuals: The effect of instructions and stimulus modality. *Archives of Sexual Behavior*, in press.

Abel, G. G., & Blanchard, E. B. The role of fantasy in the treatment of sexual deviation. *Archives of General Psychiatry*, 1974, **30**, 467–475.

Abel, G. G., & Blanchard, E. B. The measurement and generation of sexual arousal in male sexual deviates. In M. Hersen, R. M. Eisler, & P. M. Miller (Eds.), *Progress in behavior modification: Volume II*. New York: Academic Press, in press.

Abel, G. G., Blanchard, E. B., Barlow, D. H., & Mavissakalian, M. Identifying specific erotic cues in sexual deviation by audiotaped descriptions. *Journal of Applied Behavior Analysis*, 1975, **3**, 58–71.

Abel, G. G., Blanchard, E. B., & Becker, J. V. Psychological treatment of rapists. In M. Walker, & S. Brodsky (Eds.), *Rape: Research, prevention, action*. Lexington, Massachusetts: Lexington Books, in press.

Barlow, D. H. Sexual deviation. Workshop presented at the meeting of the Association for Advancement of Behavior Therapy, New York, December 1972.

Barlow, D. H. Increasing heterosexual responsiveness in the treatment of sexual deviation: A review of the clinical and experimental evidence. *Behavior Therapy*, 1973, **4**, 655–671.

Barlow, D. H. The treatment of sexual deviation: Towards a comprehensive behavioral approach. In K. S. Calhoun, H. E. Adams, & K. M. Mitchell (Eds.), *Innovative treatment methods in psychopathology*. New York: John Wiley & Sons, 1974.

Barlow, D. H., & Abel, G. G. Recent developments in assessment and treatment of sexual deviation. In E. Craighead, A. Kazdin & M. Mahoney, (Eds.), *Behavior modification: Principles, issues and applications*. Boston: Houghton Mifflin, in press.

Barlow, D. H., Abel, G. G., Blanchard, E. B., Brostow, A., & Young, F. A heterosocial skills behavior checklist for males. Unpublished manuscript, 1975.

Barlow, D. H., Becker, J., Leitenberg, H., & Agras, W. S. Mechanical strain gauge recording of penile circumference change. *Journal of Applied Behavior Analysis*, 1970, **3**, 73–76.

Barlow, D. H., Reynolds, E. J., & Agras, W. S. Gender identity change in a transsexual. *Archives of General Psychiatry*, 1973, **28**, 569–576.

Bancroft, J. Application of psychophysiological measures to the assessment and modification of sexual behavior. *Behaviour Research and Therapy*, 1971, **9**, 119–130.

Bem, S. L. The measurement of psychological androgyny. *Journal of Consulting and Clinical Psychology*, 1974, **42**, 155–162.

Clark, J. V., & Arkowitz, H. The behavioral treatment of a social inhibition: A case report. Unpublished manuscript, 1975.

Davison, G. C. Homosexuality: The ethical challenge. Paper presented at the meeting of the Association for Advancement of Behavior Therapy, Chicago, November 1974.

Diagnostic and Statistical Manual of Mental Disorders, (2nd ed.). American Psychiatric Association, 1968.

Eisler, R. M., Miller, P. M., Hersen, M., & Alford, H. Effects of assertive training on marital interaction. *Archives of General Psychiatry*, 1974, **30**, 643–649.

Evans, D. Subjective variables and treatment effects in aversive therapy. *Behaviour Research and Therapy*, 1970, **8**, 147–152.

Feldman, M. P., & MacCulloch, M. J. *Homosexual behavior: Therapy and assessment*. New York: Pergamon Press, 1971.

Geer, J. H. Cognitive factors in sexual arousal—Toward an amalgam of research strategies. Paper presented at the American Psychological Association, New Orleans, September 1974.

Goldsmith, J. Training inpatients in interpersonal skills. Paper presented at the American Psychological Association, 1973.

Henson, D. E., & Rubin, H. H. Voluntary control of eroticism. *Journal of Applied Behavior Analysis*, 1971, **4**, 37–44.

Hersen, M. Self-assessment of fear. *Behavior Therapy*, 1973, **4**, 241–257.

Hersen, M., Eisler, R. M., & Miller, P. M. Development of assertive responses: Clinical, measurement, and research considerations. *Behaviour Research and Therapy*, 1973, **11**, 505–521.

Hersen, M., & Miller, P. M. Social skills training for neurotically depressed clients. Unpublished manuscript, 1974.

Laws, D. R., & Rubin, H. H. Instructional control of an autonomic sexual response. *Journal of Applied Behavior Analysis*, 1969, **2**, 93–99.

MacDonald, H. L., Lindquist, C. V., Kramer, J. A., McGrath, G. A., & Rhyne, L. L. Social skills training: The effects of behavior rehearsal in groups on dating skills. Unpublished manuscript, 1973.

Mandel, K. H. Preliminary report of a new aversive therapy for male homosexuals. *Behaviour Research and Therapy*, 1970, **8**, 93–96.

Mavissakalian, M., Blanchard, E. B., Abel, G. G., & Barlow, D. H. Responses to complex stimuli in homosexual and heterosexual males. *British Journal of Psychiatry*, 1975, **126**, 252–257.

McGovern, K., Arkowitz, H., & Gilmore, S. The evaluation of social skills training programs for college dating inhibitions. *Journal of Counseling Psychology*, in press.

McGuire, R. J., Carlisle, J. M., & Young, B. G. Sexual deviation as conditioned behavior: A hypothesis. *Behaviour Research and Therapy*, 1965, **2**, 185–190.

Sanford, D. Patterns of sexual arousal in heterosexual males. *Journal of Sex Research*, 1974, **10**, 150–155.

Serber, M. Shame aversion therapy. *Journal of Behavior Therapy and Experimental Psychiatry*, 1970, **1**, 213–215.

Sintchak, G., & Geer, J. H. A vaginal plethysmograph system. *Psychophysiology*, in press.

Wolpe, J., & Lazarus, A. A. *Behavior therapy techniques: A guide to the treatment of neuroses.* New York: Pergamon Press, 1966.

Zuckerman, M. Physiological measures of sexual arousal in the human. *Psychological Bulletin*, 1971, **75**, 297–329.

CHAPTER 17

Assessment of Behavioral Excesses in Children

RONALD A. MANN

Santa Ana Psychiatric Center
Santa Ana, California

Introduction

This chapter will be limited primarily to the assessment of behavioral excesses in children. Initially, however, some problems and misconceptions that have surrounded the mental health field as a whole will be presented; particularly, since those problems have influenced the treatment and assessment of children as well as adults. The problems, most of which could be minimized by the introduction of empirical assessment procedures, are as follows: First, it is generally the case that most therapists, irrespective of their proclaimed theoretical orientation, be it psychodynamic, organic, behavioral, or eclectic, etc., will insist that their type of therapy usually is effective. Indeed, many of their clients (or patients) would support their claims. And yet, reason would suggest that neither all therapists nor all modalities of treatment are equally effective, if effective at all. Certainly, many theoretical assumptions from which differing treatment interventions are derived, contradict one another. Furthermore, treatment techniques as well as therapists' skills vary greatly. In brief, it is obvious that the majority of claims of treatment efficacy have not been supported adequately by evaluative data.

A second problem, often encountered, is the notion that therapeutic or treatment interventions can result in only one of two possible outcomes: First, the treatment can result in producing a therapeutic or beneficial change in an individual's behavior; or secondly, the treatment can result in producing no effect at all. Nevertheless, another possibility, often overlooked by many therapists, is that a particular treatment intervention can result in a detrimental or counter-therapeutic outcome. Accordingly, rarely do therapists take credit for this third possibility. It is suggested that with the use of appropriate assessment procedures, a therapist could monitor many of his client's behaviors before, during, and after treatment. Thus, he could obtain necessary feedback of relevant changes in behavior occurring at these times. Such feedback could indicate whether a particular treatment was correlated with producing either therapeutic effects, no effects, or effects detrimental to the client's welfare.

A fourth problem, if not in word, then in practice, is the fact that many therapists do not explicitly specify or delineate treatment goals in a manner amenable to empirical evaluation. Thus, their assessment criteria for improvement, if any, often are vague and rely frequently on "clinical judgment" or "clinical intuition." The establishment of objective treatment goals is, necessarily, a prerequisite to any assessment procedure, regardless of type of treatment. Certainly, without objective treatment goals, adequate accountability of therapists' practices by the client, the public, or social agencies is difficult at best.

Finally, a most intriguing problem in the mental health field is the fact that there exists no mutually agreed-upon definition of the basic dependent variable (i.e., behavior). This lack of a common agreement of the nature of behavior has helped to generate disagreement in the mental health field with respect to both the treatment and the assessment of client's problems.

In brief, many problems surrounding the mental health field have differentially influenced the treatment and assessment of both children and adults. It is suggested that a relevant factor common to those problems is a deficit in the use of empirical assessment procedures by which to evaluate the effectiveness of different therapeutic interventions. Clearly, any therapist, teacher, or parent attempting to change demonstrably the behavioral excesses of children must, initially, develop a program not only of treatment but assessment as well, regardless of their theoretical orientation. Without demonstrable assessment, treatment effectiveness remains at best, testimonial. And, the exclusive use of testimonials to support treatment efficacy has for years been the hallmark of palm readers, faith healers, and snake oil salesmen.

Accordingly, assessment procedures will be presented in this chapter which have been well described (Bijou, Peterson & Ault, 1968; Hersen & Barlow in press; Sidman, 1960) and empirically tested (*Journal of Applied Behavior Analysis*, 1968). They are procedures that have been developed, taught, and used extensively by operant psychologists for a number of years in the experimental analysis of behavior (Bijou & Baer, 1967; Journal of the Experimental Analysis of Behavior; Keller & Schoenfeld, 1950; Skinner, 1938). More recently, these procedures have been refined for use by applied behavior analysts (Baer, Wolf & Risley, 1968) who have demonstrably changed and assessed a variety of socially relevant behaviors of diverse populations in varied settings such as in the home (Christophersen, Arnold, Hill & Quilitch, 1972; Herbert & Baer, 1972), half-way houses (Phillips, 1968; Phillips, Phillips, Fixsen & Wolf, 1971), schools (Barrish, Saunders & Wolf, 1968; Lahey, McNees & McNees, 1973), hospitals (Ayllon & Azrin, 1968; Hersen, Eisler, Smith & Agras, 1972; Mann & Moss, 1973), and experimental communities (Miller & Feallock, 1975).

Although these assessment procedures derive mainly from the operant behavior modification literature, clearly, these procedures are not limited to any specific theoretical approach. Indeed, many of the assessment procedures to be presented will be useful not only to measure, document, and evaluate children's behavioral excesses, but also the effectiveness of numerous types of treatment interventions ranging from drug treatments to psychodynamic therapies to behavior therapies as well.

In summary, the purpose of this chapter will be, hopefully, to diminish some of the problems surrounding the mental health field by presenting guidelines both on the scientific study of behavior and on the implementation of tested behavioral assessment procedures. Accordingly, such guidelines will be useful to evaluate effectively both behavioral excesses in children and any changes in those behavioral excesses that could occur as a function of differing treatments.

The Study of Behavior

The study and assessment of behavior becomes scientific only when an objective response definition can describe the behavior in a reliable manner. The behavior then can be studied functionally if it can be shown to change when other observable variables are manipulated systematically. These are, of course, the minimal criteria for any experimental science.

In order to obtain an objective response definition, most behavioral phenomena first are clinically identified and isolated through careful observation. The isolated behaviors are then precisely and explicitly described before they are studied. For example, to behaviorally analyze a retarded child, specific behaviors of interest would be isolated first. These very likely could include appropriate behaviors such as talking to other children or playing on playground equipment, and inappropriate behaviors such as self-stimulatory behaviors or self-destructive behaviors. Self-destructive behavior, for instance, could be described as "any self-directed slap or hit to the face with open hand or clenched fist." Each such slap or hit could be observed and recorded as a discrete occurrence.

Many behaviors of children are defined and quantified in such a discrete manner. A response definition may be considered discrete if the behavior's topography is described or defined so that it can be observed either to occur or not to occur. Typically, behaviors are defined in terms of such discrete occurrences for purposes of convenience and objectivity. Thus, in the example above, "each slap or hit to the face" by the retarded child would be considered the discrete response definition of "self-destructive" behavior so that each episode could be recorded, and its rate of occurrence could then be a natural measure.

Whether behavior is or is not ("in reality") discrete cannot be considered an important issue, paradoxical as this may seem. If the observable properties of behavior can be described to form an objective response definition which yields data suitable for control and prediction, then it is those properties which become the object of any scientific analysis or understanding that results. In effect, they are the "reality" that science can know. Thus, the major difficulty in the study and assessment of behavior is the problem of discovering appropriate defining properties that are both reliably measurable and sensitive to systematic changes in the environment.

Behavior: An Empirical Definition

The concepts of the nature of behavior, its causes, and the methods for its study vary greatly in the social sciences. Thus, it is no surprise that the term "behavior" has many different definitions, depending on the specific orientation of the various individuals who make up the mental health field. Since this chapter will deal with the assessment of behavior (i.e., children's behavioral excesses), a definition of the term "behavior" will be presented. This will be followed by a definition of children's behavioral excesses.

From a scientific and therefore empirical point of view, *behavior* may be defined as *any measurable or observable change or activity of an organism.* Thus, head banging, smiling, talking, hitting, spitting, and running are all behaviors. Similarly, physiological functions such as body temperature, EEG's, blood pressure, pupilary constriction, and heart rate are behaviors, since they are measurable. On the other hand, "happiness", "hallucinations", "anxiety," "attitudes," "emotions," and "dreams" are not behaviors, by definition. They are neither measurable nor observable, but rather inferred (usually from other behaviors). This does not mean that such inferred phenomena do not exist. It means, simply, that since they are not directly measurable they cannot be directly studied or assessed reliably. Nevertheless, an individual's verbal report describing these often inferred phenomena is a behavior. Thus, it would be empirical to record in a patient's hospital chart, for example, that the patient reported "hallucinating," "seeing objects," "hearing voices," or "feeling anxious," etc. Nevertheless, it would not be empirical to record that the patient was, in fact, hallucinating, seeing objects, hearing voices, or feeling anxious.

In brief, the scientific study and assessment of behavior requires that behavior be either measurable or observable. Such an empirical definition of behavior makes it amenable to public and scientific scrutiny and thus facilitates an objective and systematic analysis of the effectiveness of various therapists and therapeutic interventions.

Behavioral Excesses of Children

Behavioral excesses of children may be defined as any child's behavior whose rates of occurrence and/or duration of occurrence exceed socially defined standards of acceptability, desirability, or appropriateness within a given context.

Similarly, a behavior may be considered undesirable or inappropriate on the basis of deviant topographical characteristics even though other aspects of the behavior's rate and/or duration are normal. For instance, a child who is verbally adept with respect to conversational skills may have a noticeable lisp. The lisp provides an example of an undesirable topographical characteristic which is superimposed on speech; speech whose rate or duration is otherwise normal. Still, it could be argued that topographical anomalies could be subsumed, for purposes of quantification, under rate or duration.

Many behaviors which meet the above criteria are considered excessive or inappropriate by different members of society for a variety of reasons. For example, a child's behavior may be considered excessive because it is dangerous to himself or to others. Self-destructive or self-mutilating behaviors exhibited by some autistic children (Lovaas & Simmons, 1969), suicidal attempts or gestures of adolescents, and physical aggressiveness or assaultive behaviors often exhibited by delinquent children are some examples (Bernal, Duryee, Pruet & Burns, 1969; LeBlanc, Busby & Thomson, 1974).

Other behaviors may be judged undesirable or excessive simply because they can interfere with the desired behaviors or activities of others. For example, out-of-seat behaviors or excessive noise making by a child in a classroom are defined as inappropriate by teachers because they are disruptive and can interfere with the teaching of other children (Barrish, Saunders & Wolf, 1969; McArthur & Hawkins, 1974.)

Still, other behaviors of children may be considered socially undesirable because when they occur they provoke undesirable responses in others. Such behaviors include bizarre mannerisms and repetitive stereotypic gestures (i.e., self-stimulatory behaviors) sometimes exhibited by developmentally retarded, schizophrenic, and at times even normal children (Lovaas, Litrownick & Mann, 1971). Indeed, these types of behaviors can cue responses in others such as teasing from other children, name-calling, and being labeled as "strange," "retarded," or "crazy" by peers or adults. Similarly, such bizarre behaviors may be considered undesirable because the child who engages in them may cause other children or adults to avoid him. Certainly, such social avoidance by others could reduce seriously the identified child's learning of necessary social skills because of the minimized social interaction.

In addition, legal systems and social norms of communities define through their laws a large number of behaviors as excessive because they are considered to be either immoral or illegal. Excessive behaviors are judged illegal, ideally, when they cause harm to self, to others, or to other's property. When such behaviors occur, they are likely to cue police, juvenile authorities, or other social agencies to arrest, incarcerate, detain, or institutionalize those individuals engaging in those excessive behaviors.

Further, behaviors may be judged as excessive or inappropriate simply because they violate religious beliefs, cultural customs, or norms of a specific sub-culture or group. For example, many Black ghetto children are taught that it is absolutely necessary and appropriate to physically defend oneself if attacked. That is, physical defense is considered to be normal and often is highly adaptive in a "tough neighborhood." On the other hand, many suburban middle-class white parents teach their children that it is "wrong" to fight, and, to walk away or avoid a fight if possible. Thus, what may be considered excessive by one group, may be considered necessary and adaptive by another group.

Finally, it should be emphasized that a behavior socially defined as acceptable in one situation or context may be labeled as "bizarre" or inappropriate in another situation or context. For example, a child sitting in a stationary, straight-back chair and rocking back and forth for extended periods of time would appear to many observers to be engaging in psychotic-like self-stimulatory behavior. Such rocking can be observed commonly in retarded, autistic, or schizophrenic children. And yet, the same behavior occurring within the context of a child rocking in a rocking chair likely would not draw the attention of anyone, and if noticed, would be considered socially acceptable.

In summary, behaviors are defined as excessive or inappropriate by various members of society such as parents, teachers, sub-cultures, law enforcement agencies, and peers. Frequently occurring or excessive behaviors are labeled as inappropriate when they exceed the standards of acceptability within a given context or community.

Behavior: Social versus Scientific Definition

It is usual for children's behavioral excesses to be reported to therapists by parents, teachers, or members of social agencies such as juvenile authorities. Such reports (or presenting complaints), typically, are what may be considered to be "social definitions" of excessive behavior. As such, they are reported by scientifically unsophisticated and untrained observers. Thus, a social definition of behavior is usually a label, an anecdotal report, or a lay description of behavior. Although social definitions are considered important by members of society, such definitions often lack the objectivity, detail, and precision of scientific definitions of behavior. And yet, a scientific definition of behavior is a prerequisite to any accurate behavioral assessment procedure. Thus, the therapist-researcher is confronted with a seemingly serious problem. The problem is one of apparent conflict between the importance of social versus scientific definitions of behavior. Indeed, social definitions are important because it is society and not exclusively the small scientific community that ultimately determines the relevance of behavioral excesses. Accordingly, in order for behavioral assessment to be relevant to most members of society, scientific definitions must take into consideration the importance of social definitions. Thus, social definitions of behavior must be transposed into scientific definitions in a manner that can be useful both for a systematic analysis or assessment of behavior, and which can be understood and acceptable to *all* members of society. In other words, scientific definitions of behavior must be made to overlap sufficiently with social definitions in order to be relevant to both the social and the scientific communities.

Transposing Social into Scientific Definitions

Through careful discussion with the individual reporting a child's behavioral excesses and careful observation of the behaviors reported, the therapist can transpose the social definition of behavior into a more rigorous scientific one. For example, suppose a teacher reported to a therapist that an identified child in her class often said obscene words excessively. "Obscene words" is an example of a social definition. It is simply a label and lacks clarity and specificity, and thus, it is open to interpretation with respect to what is meant by "obscene." Accordingly, if two independent judges were to observe and record the number of times the child said "obscene words," very likely they could measure, record, and obtain different results. That is, what one observer considered obscene, might not be considered obscene by the other observer. Thus, to reliably assess the exact number (i.e., daily rate) of obscene words said by the child, it would be necessary, initially, to transpose the social definition, "obscene", into a scientific one. Typically this is done, first, by obtaining the anecdotal report (often in the form of a presenting complaint) from the individual reporting the problem behavior (e.g., the teacher). In the example above, the teacher could be questioned with respect to what she specifically meant by "obscene words." For instance, the teacher could be requested to write a list of each word she considered obscene which was emitted by the identified child. Then, if the therapist was in agreement, that list of specific words would become the scientific definition of obscene words. On the other hand, the therapist could observe the child and record each word he considered obscene. He then could determine whether his list of obscenities was congruent with the teacher's list. Finally, if it were, the agreed-upon list of words would be considered the scientific definition of "obscene words." Accordingly, each of the listed words, when repeated by the identified child, could be counted reliably, and a daily record kept before, during, and after treatment for assessment purposes. Thus, the definition of "obscene" would be relevant to both the scientific and social communities because it would meet the requirements necessary for reliable assessment and would be understood by all members of society.

In addition, it should be stressed that scientific definitions typically are tailored to describe the specific idiosyncratic behaviors of different children. For example, the scientific definition of "obscene words" likely could be different with a different child if that child emitted a different repertoire of obscenities. Accordingly, the list of words defining one child's "obscene word" behavior could be totally different than the list of words defining another child's "obscene word" behavior. In brief, the general principle of tailoring scientific definitions to each child's own characteristic behavioral excesses applies to other socially defined behaviors as well. This includes behavioral excesses such as "insulting", "aggressive", "uncooperative", and "self-stimulatory." This point was made clear in a recent study with autistic children in which "self-stimulatory behavior was defined individually for each child because each child's self-stimulation was highly idiosyncratic, ranging from behaviors as subtle as saliva swishing to others as obvious as body rocking" (Koegel, Firestone, Kramme & Dunlap, 1974, p. 523).

Planning the Assessment Program

Once a target behavior has been isolated and identified as excessive, and an objective response definition has been formulated, a program can be implemented to assess the progress of the behavior before, during, and after treatment. When planning a behavioral assessment program, a number of important problems must be taken into consideration:

First, the therapist should attempt to determine (by questioning parents, teachers, etc. and/or by direct personal observation) the conditions under which any excessive behavior occurs both most frequently and least frequently, or, those conditions under which the behavior does not occur at all. With this information, the therapist can arrange to have the problem behavior observed, measured, and recorded at the places and times the behavior is most likely to occur. Further, such information could provide clues for assessing environmental conditions or events which could differentially affect the behavior under study.

Second, the therapist should select an appropriate measurement procedure to help facilitate an accurate assessment of the target behavior. Often the measurement procedure selected will be determined, in part, by the nature and characteristics of the behavior being assessed.

Third, the primary observer responsible for observing and recording behavioral data should be specified, and, if necessary, trained in the use of an appropriate measurement procedure. This could be the therapist, a teacher, or a parent, depending on the conditions under which the excessive behavior is occurring, the convenience or inconvenience involved when measuring, or the expertise required to measure certain types of behaviors. For example, some extreme behavioral excesses such as self-destructive behaviors necessarily are assessed and treated, initially, under controlled hospital conditions. Certain types of behaviors, such as speech disfluencies, often are assessed most accurately by experts in a specific area, for example, a speech pathologist. Finally, many behavioral excesses such as tantrums, thumbsucking, excessive television viewing, eating too fast, and noise making can be observed and recorded by parents or teachers. In addition, if reliability determinations are to be used, the therapist should both arrange to have a second observer record the target behavior and specify procedures describing how the reliability determinations will be computed.

Fourth, the therapist should arrange with the primary observer where and when each observation session will be conducted. Further, the duration of each observation session should be specified. The length of each observation session will vary depending on the nature and characteristics of the target behavior. For example, behaviors which occur infrequently often are observed and measured during sessions that can last many hours. On the other hand, frequently occurring behaviors such as "nervous tics" can be assessed using shorter observation sessions. Finally, behaviors such as self-destructive behaviors or assaultive behaviors typically are measured during short observation sessions because of the potential risk involved if allowed to occur for long periods of time.

Fifth, during or after an initial pre-treatment assessment of a target behavior has been established, and before a treatment procedure has been introduced, therapeutic goals should be specified. Typically, treatment goals with children's behavioral excesses, by definition, will be aimed at either reducing the frequency or duration of target behaviors, or, eliminating them altogether.

Finally, an appropriate treatment assessment procedure should be implemented to provide the therapist with feedback on the function or magnitude of effectiveness of the treatment during and after its implementation.

The following sections of this chapter will address themselves to the above problems; procedures necessary for planning an effective assessment program will be presented.

Selecting a Measurement Procedure

There are numerous procedures for observing, measuring, and recording behavior which can facilitate an accurate assessment of children's behavioral excesses. Often, the procedure chosen will be determined, in part, by the nature and type of behavior being assessed and by practical as well as ethical limitations. Four commonly used measurement procedures will be presented. They include one in which the target behavior is not directly observed, namely, the direct measurement of permanent products. The other three measurement procedures require the direct observation of the behaviors under study. The observational procedures are: event recording, duration recording, and interval recording.

Direct Measurement of Permanent Products

There are numerous behaviors that children engage in which can result in what is known as "permanent products." A permanent product is any measurable or observable trace, artifact, or change in the environment which is the result of a specifiable behavior. Such a result or product of a behavior may be permanent or short-lived. Nevertheless, when such results or products are observed, it can be inferred reliably that a specifiable behavior has (or has not) occurred.

The examples of permanent products are many. For instance, a piece of cake missing from the refrigerator or cake crumbs on the kitchen floor are both permanent products and can suggest to a mother that her child has engaged in cake-eating behavior. Other examples of permanent products include written words and solved arithmetic problems. For instance, school teachers often use the direct measurement of permanent products when they evaluate their pupils by giving them tests or quizzes. That is, the teacher does not necessarily observe the children studying or doing their homework assignments. Rather, the teacher evaluates each student's studying behavior by assessing the differential results the students obtain on their quizzes. This is measured in terms of number of math problems solved without errors or the number of words spelled correctly, etc.

Other examples of permanent products include dirty footprints or mud on a recently cleaned floor. Such a product can suggest that a child has not wiped his shoes off properly on the door mat. A bedroom previously littered with toys which subsequently have been cleaned up and put away can indicate that a child has followed a parental request and cleaned up his room. Crayon markings on the wall, money missing from a purse, bitten fingernails, wet or soiled pants, and even a bed that has been made are other examples of permanent products. All can be used to assess the occurrence of some specifiable behavior. For instance, if a mother wanted to assess how often her child made his bed each week, it would not be necessary to observe directly the child making the bed. All that would be necessary would be to observe systematically whether or not the bed was, in fact, made to some criterion each morning. The made-up bed (e.g., sheets tucked in and bedspread neatly in place, etc.) is a permanent product, the result of the child engaging in bed making behavior.

Finally, a photograph, a movie, a videotape of a child's activities (Nordquist, 1971), or a tape recording of a child playing, talking, crying, screaming, or using obscenities are other examples of permanent products. For instance, if a speech pathologist wanted to assess the number or types of speech disfluencies emitted by a child, he could tape record either the child's conversation or the child's reading of a passage (Bennett, 1974). The tape then could be played back at a later time in order to facilitate a more precise and detailed analysis.

Clearly, in all of the above examples, what is measured or observed is not, in fact, the actual target behavior. Rather, the occurrences of a specifiable behavior are *inferred* from the direct observation or measurement of the behavior's known permanent products. Moreover, because the occurrences of a behavior are inferred rather than being directly observed using this method, care should be exercised with respect to what kinds of conclusions can be made from permanent products. This is especially true when more than one individual has been in the proximity of a permanent product. For example, if a mother wanting to assess bedmaking behavior had two children sharing a room, the observation that two beds had been made each morning could indicate that each child made his own bed. Or, it could indicate that one child made both beds. It is clear that someone made the beds. Who actually made each bed can become another problem. Similarly, when quizzes are given to large classes of students, care is usually taken to insure that students do not exchange answers (i.e., cheat) with each other. To the extent that such insurance is maintained, then quiz results (i.e., permanent products) are more likely to reflect each student's own studying behavior.

In brief, the direct measurement of permanent products is a useful measurement technique with a number of advantages: *First*, observers do not have to spend valuable time observing many behaviors of interest. Some behaviors like cleaning up a toy-littered room can consume far more time than the observation time required to verify the result of such behavior. *Second*, permanent products can be quantified for evaluation purposes. For example, the number of times a child makes his bed each week, the number of chores completed each day, the number of new words spelled correctly, and the number of times a child wets his bed are all examples of measures which can be used to assess children's behaviors before, during, and after any treatment intervention. *Finally*, the use of this technique is relatively easy to implement, requires no special instruments, and can be taught easily to parents, professionals, and paraprofessionals alike.

Event Recording

Event recording is a method of measurement whereby an observer records each occurrence of a target behavior during some specified unit of time (e.g., minutes, hours, days, weeks, etc.) in order to establish its frequency. This is done simply by counting each occurrence of the behavior under study. Often a tally-sheet (on which observers make checkmarks each time the behavior occurs), a wrist counter (Lindsley, 1968), or a hand counter, and a wristwatch or clock are the measurement instruments used with this type of procedure.

Counting the number of times that a target behavior occurs requires an accurate and objective definition or description of the behavior such that each occurrence (or non-occurrence) can be ascertained reliably (i.e., a discrete response definition). Thus, once the target behavior has been so defined, each occurrence is counted during specified observation sessions. Typically, each observation session is of a fixed and specified duration of time so that the frequency of the behavior can be established. For example, in order to establish the average frequency of a target behavior during each observation session, the time duration of the observation session (i.e., number of minutes, hours, etc.) is divided into the number of times the behavior occurred during that session. Thus, if a target behavior were observed to occur 30 times in a 2-hour session, its average frequency for that session would be equal to 30 divided by 2, yielding an average frequency of 15 occurrences per hour.

Each observation session can last for a period of time ranging from 10 minutes to 1 hour to 1 day to a full week and more, depending on the estimated frequency of the behavior under study. Typically, a series of observation sessions are used to obtain repeated measures of a target behavior. This is done to assess the variability and establish a trend in the behavior over many days or weeks. In general, a frequently occurring behavior requires shorter observation sessions, while infrequently occurring behaviors require longer observation sessions. For example, if a child in a classroom setting were observed to shove other children approximately one or twice per day (i.e., a low rate behavior), each observation session likely would last the better part of a school day (e.g., 4 hours). A 1-hour observation session each day might not be sufficient to detect the occurrences of this low-rate behavior. On the other hand, a frequently occurring behavior such as "nervous tics" could be observed and recorded during shorter observation sessions, for example, 1 hour per day.

In brief, event recording is a common method of measuring and assessing children's behavioral excesses. Further, it is a procedure which is relatively easy for parents to learn and use effectively. Usually, it is used to assess the frequency of episodic or short-duration behaviors such as hitting, kicking, spitting, hugging, stealing, saying "obscene words," "nervous" tics, and wetting pants. This method has the advantage of being a convenient, easy to implement procedure, and typically provides high inter-observer reliability.

Duration Recording

Duration recording is a method of measuring the time interval (i.e., duration) between the onset and termination of a target behavior. Typically, a stopwatch, a wristwatch with a sweep second hand, or a clock are used as measurement instruments with this type of measurement procedure. During observation sessions, observers note both the time of onset and the time of termination of each occurrence of the target behavior. The difference between the time of onset and termination yields the duration (in seconds, minutes, or hours) of each occurrence of the behavior under study. Thus, to use duration recording, the observer must be able to discriminate reliably the occurrence and non-occurrence of the target behavior. In a manner similar to event recording, an objective and discrete response definition of the target behavior is a prerequisite. In contrast to event recording, duration recording is used to measure relatively longer lasting behaviors such as whining, crying, or tantrums, eating too fast or too slow, staying awake for long periods of time after bedtime, excessive television viewing, thumbsucking, etc.

With event recording, the total number of occurrences of a target behavior are summed to obtain a frequency count of the behavior during each observation session. With duration recording, the duration of each occurrence of the target behavior is recorded during observation sessions. Each of those durations can then be summed to obtain a cumulative measure expressed as the total number of minutes (or hours) that the target behavior was occurring during each observation session. For example, if whining, crying, or mouthing objects were the excessive behaviors of interest, a mother, therapist, or teacher could record the duration of each episode occurring during a day. All of the recorded durations of any of those behaviors could then be summed at the end of each day. This would yield a cumulative record of the total number of minutes that the child engaged in whining (or crying or mouthing objects) on each day he was observed. The same data could be expressed as the percentage of time that the child engaged in a specified target behavior. This can be computed by dividing the number of minutes (or hours) that an observation session lasted into the cumulative number of minutes that the target behavior was occurring and multiplying by 100.

In brief, both event recording and duration recording require that a discrete response definition be used to describe the target behavior under study. With event recording, frequency or rate of the target behavior is the dependent variable. With duration recording, cumulative duration or percentage of time that the behavior was occurring is the dependent variable. Further, it should be noted that these two types of measurement procedures are not mutually exclusive. That is, both the frequency of a behavior (event recording) and the time duration of a behavior (duration recording) can be measured concurrently. Thus, an observer could measure and record, for example, the number of tantrums that a child engaged in daily and the duration of each of those tantrums. By totaling the tantrums, the daily rate would be obtained and by totaling the durations of each tantrum, the total daily time expended in tantrumous behavior would be obtained.

Interval Recording

Many behaviors that children can engage in are difficult to describe using a discrete response definition. That is, it is difficult for observers to specify with accuracy when such behaviors begin and when they terminate. And yet, it is often easy to ascertain reliably when those same behaviors are in progress. For example, the complex behaviors of a child playing with blocks or attempting to put together a puzzle usually can be observed and recorded reliably while those behaviors are in progress. However, the onset and termination of such behaviors often have vague boundaries and thus are difficult to assess accurately using discrete behavior measurement procedures such as event or duration recording. Indeed, playing with blocks or putting a puzzle together often includes a number of pauses and moments of inactivity. These pauses and moments of inactivity are interspersed, intermittently, between the active behaviors of handling the blocks or puzzle pieces and placing them in various positions. Thus, it is difficult to assess, specifically, whether such complex play behaviors begin and then stop repeatedly, or, whether such ongoing play (i.e., including both pauses and handling) is one continuous activity. Complex play behavior can become even more difficult to assess when using discrete measurement procedures if more than one child is involved in the interaction.

Accordingly, interval recording is the method of measurement which can be used to record objectively definable target behaviors which, otherwise, are difficult to describe and measure using a discrete response definition. In other words, this method can be used to measure behaviors whose onset and termination is difficult to ascertain, but whose occurrence while in progress can be described, observed, and recorded reliably.

With interval recording, each observation session is divided into equal time duration intervals. For example, if each observation session were $\frac{1}{2}$-hour long, it could be divided into 30 1-minute intervals, 60 $\frac{1}{2}$-minute intervals, 120 15-second intervals, or 180 10-second intervals. Each interval usually is displayed as consecutive blocks of time on special data recording sheets. An example of an interval recording sheet is presented in Fig. 17.1. In this figure, the data sheet has been designed for a $\frac{1}{2}$-hour observation session. Each minute of the session has been divided into six 10-second intervals. Typically, a data sheet such as this is placed on a clipboard which has a special mount (at the top) to hold a stopwatch. When an observer is ready to begin recording a target behavior, he starts the stopwatch and begins his observations. The observer must frequently keep an eye on the stopwatch as well as the child's behavior. The sweep second hand of the stopwatch indicates to the observer when to proceed to each succeeding interval for scoring the behavior. For example, during the first interval of time (in this case, during each 10-second interval), the observer either makes a checkmark to indicate the target behavior

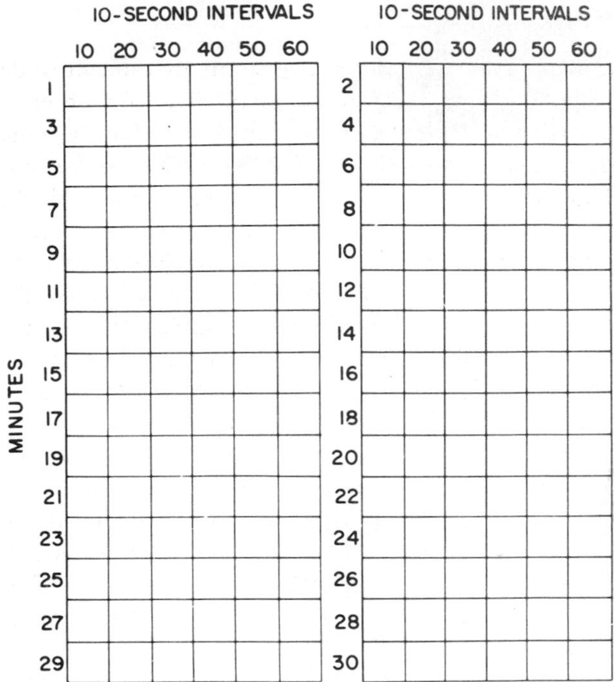

Fig. 17.1. An example of an interval recording data sheet which has been designed for a ½-hour observation session. Each minute of the session has been divided into six 10-second intervals.

was occurring or makes a zero to indicate the target behavior was not occurring. The observer then moves his pen or pencil to the next interval box and observes the child for another 10 seconds. Again, if the target behavior either is in progress from the preceeding interval, or, if the target behavior begins to occur anytime during the present interval, it is scored with a checkmark. On the other hand, if the target behavior were never in progress during the present interval, it is scored with a zero. This procedure is repeated again during each consecutive 10-second interval until the observation session has been terminated.

Interval recording can also be used to measure more than one target behavior simultaneously during an observation session. Two types of interval recording data sheets for measuring two or more behaviors simultaneously are presented in Fig. 17.2. In the first type of data sheet (top), each consecutive 10-second interval is displayed with three blocks or boxes for recording whether Behaviors A, B, and C are or are not occurring. With this type of data sheet, the observer simply makes a checkmark or a zero in each of the three boxes of each 10-second interval to indicate which behavior was or was not occurring.

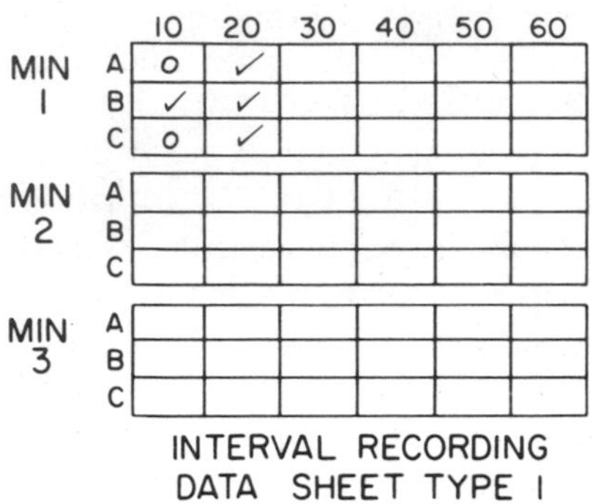

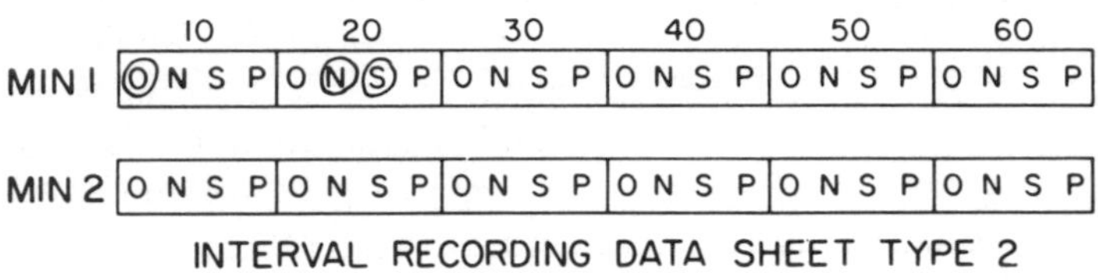

BEHAVIOR CODE

O NO PROBLEM BEHAVIORS
N NOISES, DISRUPTIVE SOUNDS, GRUNTS
S SELF-STIMULATORY BEHAVIOR
P PUSHING OR SHOVING OTHER CHILDREN

Fig. 17.2. Examples of two types of interval recording data sheets for measuring two or more target behaviors concurrently. In the first type of data sheet (top), each consecutive 10-second interval is displayed with three boxes for recording whether Behaviors A, B, and C are or are not occurring. A checkmark indicates which behavior was occurring during each 10-second interval and a zero indicates which behavior was not occurring. In the second type of data sheet (bottom), each 10-second interval box contains letter codes corresponding to a specific target behavior. When any of the coded target behaviors occur during an interval, the observer simply circles the appropriate letter code.

In this example, during the first 10-second interval, Behavior B was occurring; Behaviors A and C were not occurring. During the next 10-second interval, all three behaviors (i.e., Behaviors A, B, & C) were scored as occurring.

In the second type of data sheet (Fig. 17.2, bottom), each 10-second interval box contains a number of different letters (in this case, four letters). Each letter is a code for a specific target behavior. When any of the coded target behaviors occur (or are in progress) during an interval, the observer simply circles the letter code corresponding to that specific target behavior. Thus, in this example, the child of interest was not engaging in any problem behaviors during the first 10-second interval. During the next 10-second interval, the child was scored as engaging in self-stimulatory behavior and making noises, but not pushing or shoving other children.

When using interval recording, if a target behavior is occurring during the full interval or is occurring only during a small fraction of the interval, it is still scored the same. Thus, data derived from interval recording may not always reflect accurately the behavior under study, even when inter-observer reliability is high (cf. Hawkins & Dotson, 1975). Furthermore, when using this method, its sensitivity to subtle changes in behavior is determined in part by the length of each interval. For example, assume 30-second intervals were used to measure assaultive behaviors of a child and the child hit someone only once during the first minute of observation. The recorded data would indicate that the child had engaged in assaultive behavior for a period of 30 seconds even though the assaultive act may have lasted for no more than 1 or 2 seconds. Certainly, the use of a much shorter interval would have more accurately reflected assaultive behaviors of short duration and infrequent occurrence. On the other hand, 30-second intervals could be an appropriate interval to record the behaviors of children who engage in excessive television viewing because such behavior usually is of longer duration.

In general, the shorter the duration of each interval, the more sensitive it will be to subtle changes in the behaviors under study. Nevertheless, the duration of the interval selected for interval recording should depend in part on the characteristics of the target behavior. Specifically, short duration behaviors such as making excessive noises, pushing other children, mouthing objects, or self-stimulation, require shorter duration intervals. Long duration behaviors such as arguing excessively with children or teachers, excessive television viewing, and sleeping in the classroom can be measured effectively using longer duration intervals. Although short duration intervals can be used effectively to measure *both* short and long duration target behaviors, long duration intervals can be used effectively *only* to measure long duration target behaviors.

In a manner similar to duration recording, interval recording measures can be computed to obtain either the total duration of time that a behavior was occurring or the percentage of time that the target behavior was occurring during each observation session. For example, if 10-second intervals were used during a $\frac{1}{2}$-hour observation session, 180 consecutive intervals would be used to record whether the target behavior was or was not occurring. Assume that an observer recorded that a target behavior occurred during 60 of those intervals. In order to compute the percentage of time that a child engaged in that target behavior, the total number of intervals used in a session (e.g., 180 intervals) would be divided into the number of intervals which indicated the behavior had occurred. The quotient would then be multiplied times 100 yielding the percentage of time the target behavior was occurring during the session. In the example above, 180 would be divided into 60 and multiplied times 100 to equal $33\frac{1}{3}\%$ of the session.

When two observers are used to obtain reliability determinations (i.e., measures of inter-observer reliability), both observers must begin their observations and recordings at precisely the same time. This is accomplished by having both observers start their stopwatches at exactly the same time while maintaining independent observations. Or, if both observers remain in a stationary position during the full observation session, one large clock with a sweep second hand on an opposite wall facing both observers may be used equally well. Often, one of the observers will say, "one, two, three, begin," to indicate when to start either the stopwatches or to observe the clock and begin observations and recordings.

In brief, the advantages of interval recording are that it can be used to measure both a number of different target behaviors simultaneously and behaviors which are difficult to measure using discrete behavior measurement procedures. Further, this procedure can be used to measure discretely defined target behaviors as well. Nevertheless, it is more effective to use event recording with target behaviors that occur infrequently. The primary disadvantage of this method is that it requires the intense and constant attention of observers. This often has a fatiguing effect on observers when they record behaviors over an extended period of time and can contribute to lowered reliability. Finally, care should be taken when using intervals with durations shorter than 10 seconds since such short intervals can facilitate lowered inter-observer agreement.

Reliability

Accuracy in the recording of target behaviors is a prime concern in any behavioral assessment procedure, be it with children or adults. And yet, it is usually difficult to measure directly the accuracy of recorded data. Nevertheless, an assessment of accuracy may be obtained indirectly by employing a reliability determination procedure. Such a procedure involves comparing the recorded data of two independent observers. The comparison assesses to what extent both observers are in agreement with respect to their observations of the same target behavior. The greater the degree of correspondence (i.e., agreement) between both observer's data, the greater is the level of confidence in the reliability of these data.

Without employing a reliability determination procedure, it would be difficult to establish if an observer's recorded data of a child's behavior were accurate or to what degree they were accurate. For example, if only one observer recorded some specified behavior of a child, it would be difficult to assess whether observer bias or misinterpretation of the response definition influenced the obtained data. Similarly, it would be difficult to assess whether one observer's data were influenced by inconsistent observations during an observation session.

However, if two independent observers recorded a child's behavior, a reliability determination could be made by comparing both observer's recorded data. For example, if two observers were in agreement, and thus obtained the same or similar results, confidence in the accuracy of their data would be enhanced. Accordingly, a reliability determination would indicate a numerically high percentage of agreement. On the other hand, if there was excessive disagreement between the two observer's recorded data, a reliability determination would indicate a low percentage of agreement and thus reduce the level of confidence in the reliability of the obtained data.

At times, a low percentage of agreement can indicate that an observer was either inconsistently observing the target behavior or inconsistently recording the data. Often, it can suggest that the response definition of the target behavior may need to be revised and described in more objective terms. Indeed, the more objective the terms used to describe the target behavior, the less amenable the response definition will be to interpretation. Typically, this type of problem is resolved by questioning the two observers with respect to what, in fact, they each were observing and measuring. If a discrepancy is discovered, the behavior under study can be redefined (or better described) to help minimize misinterpretation, and the two observers again can measure the behavior. Reliability determinations can then be employed again to establish if the new definition of the target behavior is adequate for a reliable measurement.

In brief, a reliable observation and measurement of behavior implies that first, there is an objective and therefore scientific definition of the target behavior, and secondly, different observers using that definition have obtained similar results while independently observing and measuring the same target behavior. The extent to which two or more observers independently observe and record a target behavior and obtain the same or similar results determines the extent to which one has confidence in the reliability of their observations. Thus, accuracy in the recording of target behaviors is substantiated.

Computing Reliability

A reliability determination procedure requires two observers, a primary observer and a reliability observer. The primary observer independently observes a target behavior and records the data during *all* observation sessions. The reliability observer independently observes that same target behavior only during a portion of those observation sessions and records the data. The recorded data of the two observers are then compared in order to assess to what extent they both are in agreement with respect to their observations.

The degree to which both observers obtain the same or similar results can be computed and then expressed numerically as a percentage of agreement ranging from 0 to 100%. A high percentage of agreement between two observers indicates that both observers are in agreement and thus have obtained a reliable measurement of the target behavior they have been observing. Typically, inter-observer reliabilities of 90% or higher are considered quite acceptable by most researchers. However, percentages of agreement as low as 80 are acceptable when new response definitions are used or when complex behaviors such as psychotic speech are being studied.

To determine inter-observer reliability with interval recording procedures, the records of both the primary observer and the reliability observer are compared interval by interval. An example of such a comparison with a 2-minute observation session and 10-second intervals is presented in Fig. 17.3.

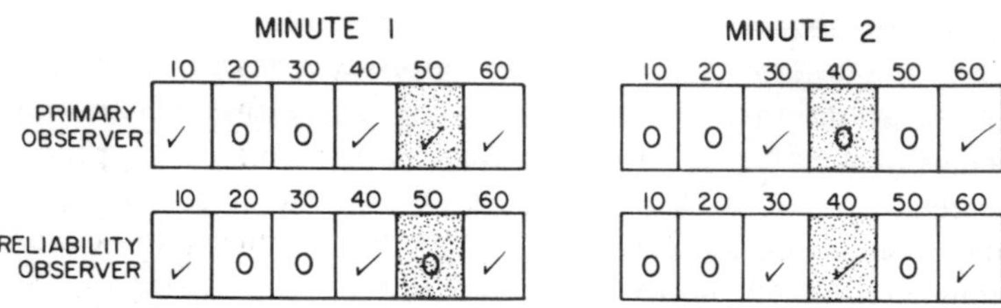

Fig. 17.3. A comparison of the recorded data of both a primary observer and a reliability observer from a 2-minute observation session using 10-second interval recording. Each interval in which both observers have not agreed has been shaded. All the other intervals indicate agreement.

In this example, each interval in which both observers have *not* agreed has been shaded. All of the other intervals indicate agreement. In order to compute the reliability, all of the intervals in which both observers agree that the target behavior has occurred *and* has not occurred are added to obtain the number of agreements (e.g., 10 agreements). The agreements are then divided by the sum of the disagreements (e.g., 2 disagreements) plus the agreements (i.e., 2 + 10). The quotient is then multiplied times 100, yielding the inter-observer reliability expressed as the percentage of agreement. The formula for computing reliability also can be expressed as $(A \times 100)/(D + A) = \%$ of agreement, where A equals the number of agreements and D equals the number of disagreements. Note, the sum of the agreements and disagreements always equals the total number of intervals used in a session. Thus, in the example of Fig. 17.3, (10 times 100) divided by (2 plus 10) equals 83.3%.

To determine inter-observer reliability with the other measurement procedures (i.e., permanent products, event recording, and duration recording), the recorded data of both the primary and reliability observers are compared. In order to compute reliability, the observer's data with the highest numerical figure is divided into the observer's data with the lower numerical figure. The quotient is then multiplied times 100, yielding the percentage of agreement. For example, assume while using event recording, that the primary observer recorded a child picking his nose ten times during a 1-hour observation session. And, assume the reliability observer recorded nose-picking nine times during that same session. The inter-observer reliability for that session would be 9 divided by 10 or 9/10 multiplied times 100. Thus, the percentage of agreement for that session would be 90. In a similar manner, assume two parents recorded whether their child had or had not made his bed each morning during one week of observations using the direct measurement of permanent products. Assume both the mother and the father each recorded independently that the bed had been made 7 times. The inter-observer reliability for that week would be 7 divided by 7 or 7/7 times 100. Thus, the percentage of agreement for that week would be 100.

When reliability determinations are computed for a number of different observation sessions, either the reliability for each session can be specified or the average reliability for all sessions can be computed and specified. The average reliability of all sessions can be computed simply by totaling the percentages of agreement of each session and dividing that sum by the number of sessions assessed.

In general, reliability determinations can be computed for one, many, or all observation sessions. The number of sessions in which two observers are used for reliability determinations can depend in part on practical limitations such as the availability of a second observer. It also can depend on the complexity of the target behavior being measured. For example, relatively unambiguous behaviors such as "hitting" or weight measurements may require few reliability checks to provide convincing evidence of the reliability of the assessment procedure. On the other hand, complex behavioral repertoires such as "psychotic speech" could require many more reliability checks to provide convincing evidence of reliability. Equally important, reliability determinations are typically made for some portion of the observation sessions used during pre-treatment (i.e., baseline conditions), treatment, and post-treatment conditions.

In summary, the data derived from the primary observer are the data which are normally used in the actual assessment of behavior. It is those data which are displayed graphically and analyzed before, during, and after treatment. On the other hand, the data derived from the reliability observer are obtained usually for only a portion of the total observation sessions. These data are used to establish an estimate of the reliability of the primary observer's data. In effect, the reliability observer's results are a replication of the primary observer's results when both of their data are similar. Thus, the greater the degree of correspondence between both observer's obtained data, the greater the level of confidence in the reliability of the assessment procedure's findings since, in effect, that assessment has been partially replicated.

Analysis of Data

Typically, a behavior under study is repeatedly observed and measured during pre-arranged observation sessions. The collected measurements of each observation session are recorded and then displayed as data points on a graph to facilitate analysis. As a result, the graphed representation of the behavior provides a clear and precise visual record of the magnitude, variability, and progress of the behavior over time.

Graphing

When either recording or analyzing data points on a graph, the vertical axis of the graph (i.e., the ordinate) is used to indicate the level or magnitude of the target behavior. The magnitude of the behavior can be expressed in terms of frequency (e.g., with event recording), total duration of time or percentage of time that a behavior was occurring (e.g., with duration recording and interval recording), and numerous other measures of magnitude such as weekly quiz grades, calories consumed, weight in pounds, or chores completed (e.g., with direct measurement of permanent products). The horizontal axis of the graph (i.e., the abscissa) is used to indicate the time base in specified units such as hours, days, weeks, or number of consecutive observation sessions. Data points are displayed usually as black dots connected by solid lines. Each data point indicates the magnitude of the target behavior during each unit of time that the behavior was measured.

An example of a target behavior is displayed graphically in Fig. 17.4. This graph presents the number of times (i.e., frequency) that an identified child hit a peer during daily 1-hour play periods in school. Specifically, these data indicate that the child hit a peer three times on Day 1, eight times on Day 2, five times on Day 3, and four times on Day 4, etc. Thus, it is evident that when a behavior is graphed, it is amenable to a relatively rapid visual analysis.

Baseline Analysis: Pre-treatment Assessment and Prediction of Behavior

A baseline is a record of repeated measures of a specified behavior over some period of time prior to any treatment intervention. Usually, each repeated measure of the baseline is graphed. Each data point of the graph visually

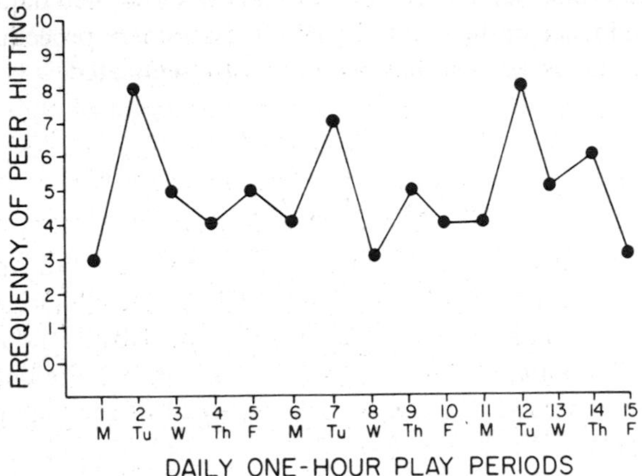

Fig. 17.4. Frequency of peer hitting during daily 1-hour play periods in school.

displays a precise record of the magnitudes of the behavior from observation session to observation session. Thus, when a sufficient number of data points have been recorded, the graph also provides a record of the variability or range in the magnitude of the behavior over time. For example, the baseline in Fig. 17.4 indicates that peer-hitting during daily play periods ranged from 3 to 8 times over a 3-week period.

An additional function of a baseline is that it can facilitate the detection of systematic changes in behavior that could occur prior to treatment. For example, Fig. 17.4 indicates that peer-hitting systematically occurred most frequently on Days 2, 7, and 12, or every Tuesday. If this were an actual baseline, it could be important for a therapist to determine if anything either happened or was different on Tuesdays in contrast to the other days. In brief, the detection of systematic changes or patterns in a target behavior could provide valuable clues to the discovery of relevant environmental events which could differentially affect the behavior under study.

Typically, behavioral data are graphed until a stable baseline has been established. Stability of a baseline is best characterized as that number of graphed data points which is sufficient to allow the prediction of the approximate future trend of a specified behavior.

In order to obtain a stable baseline, some general principles can be followed: *First*, the longer the period of time that a baseline is taken (i.e., the more data points), the more likely any systematic changes or predictable patterns will become visible in the behavior under study. *Second*, the greater the level of variation between data points, the more observations and recorded data points that will be necessary to establish stability. *Third*, if the variation in the level of behavior is relatively small, then a relatively short baseline with fewer data points may be all that is necessary to establish stability. *Finally*, and by definition, an unstable baseline is a baseline from which the future trend of a specified behavior cannot be predicted. Accordingly, when a baseline is unstable (i.e., unpredictable), it indicates that more data points may be required to establish its stability.

In effect, a stable baseline (as a pretreatment analysis) provides the basis for predicting what the level or magnitude of a specified behavior will be in the future, given that no treatment procedure is introduced (Risley, 1970). Figure 17.5 presents graphs of four general types of baselines to illustrate this point more clearly. Graph 1 illustrates an unstable baseline. In this graph, it is difficult to predict the future level or trend of the measured behavior. On

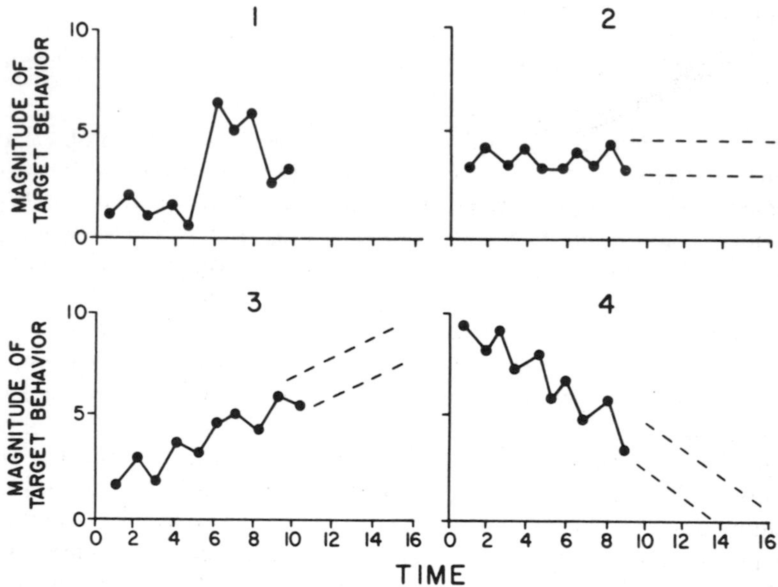

Fig. 17.5. Graphs of four general types of baselines. Graph 1 illustrates an unstable baseline. Graphs 2, 3, and 4 illustrate a flat-slope baseline, an ascending-slope baseline, and a descending-slope baseline respectively. Pairs of dotted lines have been extended beyond these three types of stable baselines to indicate the predicted future trends in the levels of the target behaviors.

the other hand, Graphs 2, 3, and 4 illustrate a flat-slope baseline, an ascending-slope baseline, and a descending-slope baseline respectively. In all three of these graphs, the baselines may be considered to be stable. That is, these graphs provide enough information to allow the prediction of the future trends of the measured behaviors. Pairs of dotted lines have been extended beyond each of these baselines to indicate the approximate future levels, range of variability, and thus future trend of the behaviors, given no treatment intervention is introduced.

In summary, obtaining a stable baseline is a necessary condition of most single-subject assessment procedures and can provide a therapist with the following information: *First*, a graphed baseline can present a documented and accurately measured visual record of the periodic magnitudes (and thus variability) of a target behavior over a specified period of time. *Second*, data are presented in a manner which facilitates the detection of systematic changes in behavior. *Third*, a baseline provides a basis for predicting a trend in the level of future occurrences of the target behavior. *Finally*, a baseline provides a projected reference against which the magnitude of any therapeutic change in behavior can be compared should a treatment intervention be introduced at some later time.

Treatment Analysis: Baseline-Treatment Design

After a stable baseline of the target behavior has been established, the treatment intervention can be introduced. Repeated measures of the target behavior are continued during the treatment condition, often until stability during this condition has been established. Any change in the level of the target behavior during treatment can then be compared with the level of behavior which would have been predicted from the baseline data. This type of comparison indicates if a change in the target behavior has occurred congruent with the introduction of the treatment and establishes the magnitude of that change.

Fig. 17.6 presents graphically an example of a baseline-treatment design. The first eight data points represent the baseline. The set of dotted lines extending past the baseline indicates the level of behavior which would have been predicted had the treatment intervention not been introduced. Data points 9 through 20 represent the change in the level of behavior during the treatment condition. The difference between the level of behavior predicted from the baseline, and the level of behavior occurring during treatment, represents the magnitude of change which has occurred congruent with the introduction of treatment variables.

Thus, with the use of appropriate measurement procedures, a baseline-treatment design can provide necessary feedback to a therapist of relevant changes in behavior that can occur before and during treatment. Such feedback could indicate whether a particular treatment was correlated with producing either therapeutic effects, no effects, or effects detrimental to a child's welfare. For example, should a target behavior remain unchanged congruent with the introduction of treatment, and continue unchanged over an extended period

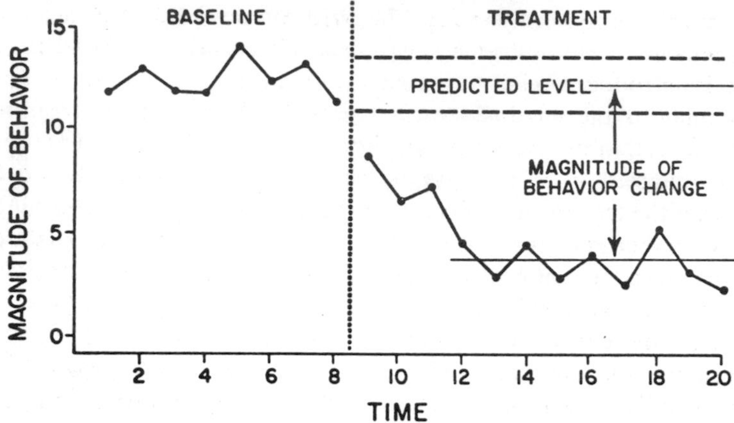

Fig. 17.6. An example of a baseline-treatment design. The first eight data points represent the baseline. The set of dotted lines extending past the baseline indicates the predicted future level of the target behavior, given that no treatment had been introduced. The difference between the predicted level of behavior and the level during treatment indicates the magnitude of behavior change occurring congruent with the introduction of treatment.

of time, such feedback would indicate to the therapist that the presently used treatment was ineffective. Thus, the therapist could try a different approach.

Further, should the treated behavior become worse congruent with the introduction of a particular treatment, that feedback could indicate a need to withdraw the treatment. If the treatment were withdrawn and the once worsening behavior reversed and returned to its original baseline level (i.e., pretreatment level), such feedback would suggest strongly that the treatment which had been used was having a deleterious causal effect.

On the other hand, should the target behavior improve congruent with the introduction of treatment, the magnitude of that improvement could be determined to ascertain if it were a socially significant improvement. Nevertheless, the baseline-treatment design does not provide adequate information to establish that a therapeutic change in the level of behavior, if any, were due to the treatment procedure. For example, a therapeutic change in behavior correlated with the introduction of the treatment procedure could have been coincidental. A more convincing demonstration of treatment causality can be obtained by using a single-subject reversal design.

Assessment of Causality: Single-Subject Reversal Design

The single-subject reversal design is an elaboration of the baseline-treatment design and is used to establish causality of the treatment variables (Baer, Wolf & Risley, 1968; Risley, 1970). An example of a single-subject reversal design is presented graphically in Fig. 17.7. With this design, a baseline level of the target behavior is established through repeated measures and the treatment procedure is introduced while repeated measurements are continued (in a manner similar to the baseline-treatment design). If during the treatment condition, the level of behavior changes significantly from the level that would have been predicted from the baseline, this change lends support to the *possibility* that the treatment is effective. Nevertheless, the prediction that the baseline level of behavior would have remained unchanged had the treatment not been introduced, has not been confirmed. And, any statement of treatment causality (i.e., effectiveness) is based on the accuracy of the baseline prediction. Indeed, the future level of behavior predicted from the baseline could have been inaccurate. Or, the therapeutic change in behavior correlated with treatment could have been a coincidental effect of unknown variables.

Accordingly, the treatment procedure can be withdrawn temporarily to ascertain its function in maintaining the therapeutic change in behavior. If the treatment procedure is withdrawn and the level of behavior returns to the level predicted by the baseline, then that reversal in the level of behavior supports the previous effectiveness of the treatment and supports the accuracy of the initial baseline prediction.

Typically, the treatment procedure is reintroduced after the reversal to establish a therapeutic change in the behavior again (see Fig. 17.7). If the level of the behavior changes again in a therapeutic direction, this second change

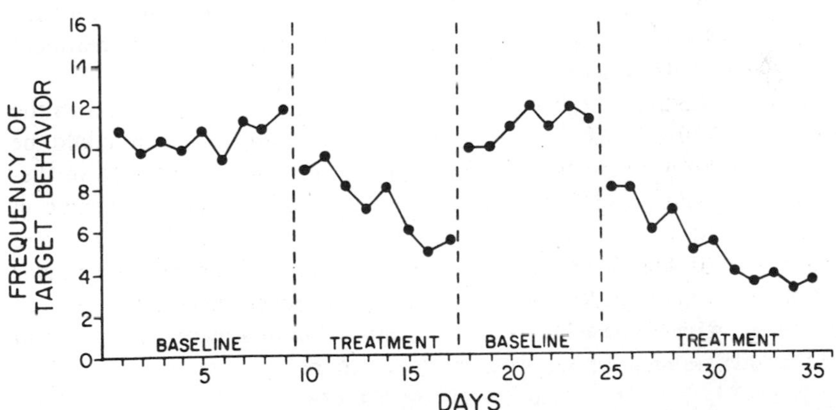

Fig. 17.7. An example of the data presentation of a single-subject reversal design. The frequency of a target behavior has been measured repeatedly to establish a stable baseline. Treatment is then introduced to determine if the behavior improves with reference to the baseline prediction. If the behavior does improve, the treatment can be withdrawn temporarily to see if the behavior reverses (i.e., during second baseline condition) in order to assess that treatment's previous function in maintaining therapeutic change. The treatment procedure is then reintroduced.

lends even greater support to the treatment procedure's effectiveness. In other words, each manipulation of the treatment procedure which produces a therapeutic change in behavior increases the confidence in the effectiveness of the treatment.

Thus, the advantage of a single-subject reversal design is that it can be used to assess the effectiveness of a specific treatment procedure on a particular target behavior of a given child (i.e., an intra-subject replication of treatment function). Equally important, if the same treatment procedure remediates similar problem behaviors in more than one child, such inter-subject replication increases the confidence in the generality of the treatment across different children.

The disadvantages of a reversal design are as follows: *First*, such a design requires developing a response definition of the target behavior and establishing a baseline; both of which take time and neither of which contribute to therapeutic changes in behavior. *Secondly*, the temporary removal of a treatment procedure (i.e., during the reversal condition) is at times undesirable. For example, some behaviors, such as assaultiveness and self-destructive behaviors, may be considered too dangerous to allow them to recover again during a reversal condition. Further, reversal conditions, like baseline conditions, use up time which does not always contribute to behavior change. *Finally*, some behaviors, once they have been therapeutically changed, will not reverse when treatment procedures have been withdrawn. Specifically, after the level of some behaviors have changed to some critical level during treatment, environmental variables can then maintain that change, even after the specific treatment that initially produced the change has been withdrawn. Consequently, single-subject reversal designs may not be suitable to assess the effectiveness of treatment procedures on certain types of behaviors that a therapist suspects will not reverse.

Assessment of Causality: Multiple Baseline Design

An alternative to the single-subject reversal design is the multiple baseline design (cf. Baer, Wolf & Risley, 1968; Risley, 1970). The multiple baseline design can be useful to assess the effectiveness of treatment procedures when the treatment effects either would appear to be irreversible or when the effects would be inappropriate to reverse. An example of a multiple baseline design is presented graphically in Fig. 17.8. In this example, each of the dotted vertical lines indicates the point at which the treatment procedure has been applied sequentially to each of the measured excessive behaviors in order to reduce frequency of occurrence.

With the multiple baseline design, two or more behaviors of a single child are defined and repeatedly measured for a period of time to establish stable

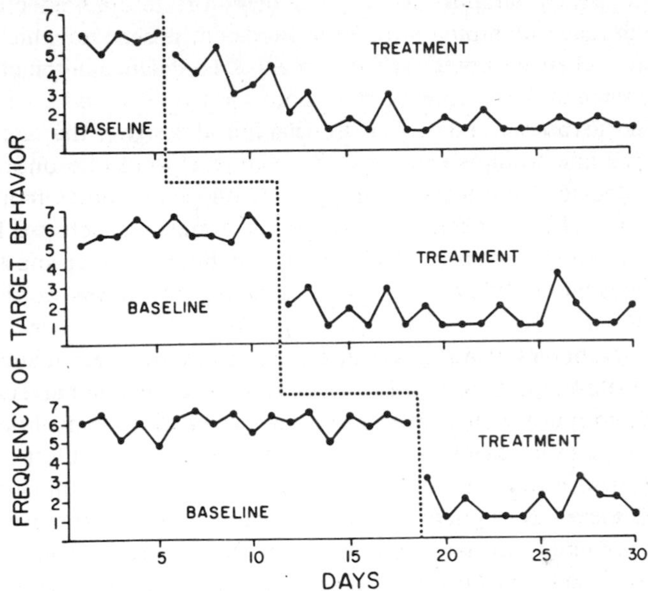

Fig. 17.8. An example of the data presentation of a multiple baseline design. Two or more different behaviors of a single individual, or the same type of behavior of two or more individuals are measured repeatedly to establish stable baselines. Treatment is then applied first to only one behavior, and then sequentially to the other behaviors to assess the effectiveness of a particular treatment.

baselines. After stable baselines have been established, the treatment procedure is applied, first to only one behavior and then sequentially to the other behaviors. Repeated measurements of all the behaviors are continued. If the level of the first behavior to which the treatment procedure is applied changes in a therapeutic direction, and if the level of the other behaviors continue relatively unchanged, then the treatment is applied to the second behavior, and so on. Each behavior change congruent with the sequential application of the treatment procedure provides additional evidence for the effectiveness of that treatment with a particular child. That is, each therapeutic change in behavior is a demonstrated replication of the effectiveness of the applied treatment procedure.

The logic of the multiple baseline design is based on two assumptions (Risley, 1970). *First*, each stable baseline provides a basis for predicting the future trend of the target behavior, given that no treatment intervention is introduced. This assumption is similar to that of the reversal design. *Second*, each of the measured behaviors is sensitive to the same variables.

The assumption that the first baseline would have continued unchanged had the treatment not been introduced is supported if the second baseline has continued unchanged (i.e., after a demonstrated behavior change has occurred in the first baseline). In other words, if the change in the level of the first behavior were caused by unknown variables occurring coincidental with the application of the treatment, then those variables should have also affected the second baseline since it is assumed that it is sensitive to the same variables. This second assumption is supported if the level of the second behavior is demonstrated to change significantly only when the same treatment procedure is applied to it. This logic holds for each successive change in behavior which occurs congruent with the application of the treatment procedure.

A multiple baseline design can also be used with two or more children who exhibit the same type of problem behavior. With this design, the same target behavior of different children is defined and repeatedly measured for a period of time to establish stable baselines. After stable baselines have been established, the treatment procedure is applied only to the behavior of the first child, and then sequentially to the behaviors of the other children. If the first child's behavior changes in a therapeutic direction, and if the behaviors of the other children continue unchanged, then the treatment is applied to the behavior of the second child, and so on. Each therapeutic change in the target behavior of the specific child to which the treatment has been applied adds confidence in the effectiveness of that treatment. Furthermore, such effectiveness demonstrates the generality of that specific treatment on the same type of problem across different children.

Still, multiple baseline designs have some disadvantages. *First*, the multiple baseline design, in a manner similar to the reversal design, requires developing response definitions and establishing stable baselines. This takes time and does not contribute to therapeutic change. Nevertheless, it is a requirement for a pretreatment analysis and demonstration of treatment efficacy. *Second*, only one target behavior at a time can be treated with a single individual. Thus, other target behaviors continue for some period of time without treatment, even after stability of those behaviors has been established. *Finally*, when the same type of target behavior is assessed with different children, the treatment is applied only to the behavior of one child at a time. Thus, the other children, whose behaviors are being assessed, remain temporarily untreated.

Nevertheless, the advantages of a multiple baseline design are many. *First*, such a design allows a therapist to assess the effectiveness of a particular treatment on two or more behaviors of a single individual. Further, the magnitude of the effect of that treatment can be ascertained for each of the assessed behaviors with a given child. *Second*, in order to demonstrate causality between a particular treatment procedure and target behaviors, it is not necessary to withdraw the treatment. Thus, in contrast to reversal designs, therapeutic changes in behavior can continue unchanged. *Finally*, when the same type of target behavior is assessed with more than one child, a demonstration of treatment effectiveness also establishes the generality of the treatment's effect on a specific target behavior across different children.

In brief, either a baseline-treatment design, a reversal design, or a multiple baseline design can be used to provide valuable feedback to a therapist on the progress of a child's behavioral excesses before, during, and after treatment. All three of these designs provide information on the magnitude of behavior change which can occur congruent with the introduction of a treatment procedure. Nevertheless, *only* the reversal design and the multiple baseline design can be used effectively to both assess and demonstrate a particular treatment's causal effect on target behaviors.

Summary

In summary, this chapter has attempted to point out some of the misconceptions and problems that have surrounded the mental health field; problems which have influenced the treatment and assessment of children as well as adults. It was suggested that a relevant factor common to those problems is a deficit in the use of empirical assessment procedures by which to evaluate behavior and the efficacy of different therapeutic interventions. Accordingly, this chapter presented guidelines both on the scientific study of behavior and on the implementation of behavioral assessment procedures.

Although the behavioral assessment procedures presented derive mainly from the operant behavior modification literature, it was stressed that these procedures are not limited to any specific theoretical approach or modality of treatment. In fact, the behavioral assessment procedures which have been presented in this chapter are adequate not only to measure, document, and evaluate children's behavioral excesses, but also the effectiveness of numerous therapies ranging from psychodynamic therapies to chemotherapies to behavior therapies as well. In addition, it should be noted that many of these procedures can be used effectively to assess both normal behavior and many types of behavior deficits in children and adults.

In conclusion, it is hoped that this chapter has provided a small foundation for the better understanding, prediction, and control of socially relevant behaviors. Presumably, through public awareness and more professional use of empirical assessment procedures there will occur both better treatment and a more adequate accountability of therapists' practices by clients, the public, colleagues, and social agencies.

References

Ayllon, T., & Azrin, N. *The token economy: A motivational system for therapy and rehabilitation.* New York: Appleton-Century-Crofts, 1968.

Baer, D. M., Wolf, M. M., & Risley, T. R. Some current dimensions of applied behavior analysis. *Journal of Applied Behavior Analysis*, 1968, **1**, 91–97.

Barrish, H. H., Saunders, M., & Wolf, M. M. Good behavior game: Effects of individual contingencies for group consequences on disruptive behavior in a classroom. *Journal of Applied Behavior Analysis*, 1969, **2**, 119–124.

Bennett, C. W. Articulation training of two hearing-impaired girls. *Journal of Applied Behavior Analysis*, 1974, **7**, 439–445.

Bernal, M. E., Duryee, J. S., Pruett, H. L., & Burns, B. J. Behavior modification and the brat syndrome. *Journal of Consulting and Clinical Psychology*, 1968, **32**, 447–455.

Bijou, S. W., & Baer, D. M. *Child development: Readings in experimental analysis*. New York: Appleton-Century-Crofts, 1967.

Bijou, S. W., Peterson, R. F., & Ault, M. H. A method to integrate description and experimental field studies at the level of data and empirical concepts. *Journal of Applied Behavior Analysis*, 1968, **1**, 175–191.

Christophersen, E. R., Arnold, C. M., Hill, D. W., & Quilitch, H. R. The home point system: Token reinforcement procedures by parents of children with behavior problems. *Journal of Applied Behavior Analysis*, 1972, **5**, 485–497.

Hawkins, R. P., & Dotson, V. A. Reliability scores that delude: An Alice in Wonderland trip through the misleading characteristics of interobserver agreement scores in interval recording. In E. Ramp, & G. Semb (Eds.), *Behavior analysis: Areas of research and application*. Englewood Cliffs, New Jersey: Prentice-Hall, 1975.

Herbert, E. W., & Baer, D. M. Training parents as behavior modifiers: Self recording of contingent attention. *Journal of Applied Behavior Analysis*, 1972, **5**, 139–149.

Hersen, M., & Barlow, D. H. *Single-case experimental designs: Strategies for studying behavior change*. New York: Pergamon Press, 1976.

Hersen, M., Eisler, R. M., Smith, B. S., & Agras, W. S. A token reinforcement ward for young psychiatric patients. *American Journal of Psychiatry*, 1972, **129**, 228–233.

Journal of Applied Behavior Analysis. Bloomington: Society for the Experimental Analysis of Behavior, 1968–.

Journal of the Experimental Analysis of Behavior. Bloomington: Society for the Experimental Analysis of Behavior, 1957–.

Keller, F. S., & Schoenfeld, W. N. *Principles of psychology*. New York: Appleton-Century-Crofts, 1950.

Koegel, R. L., Firestone, P. B., Kramme, K. W., & Dunlap, G. Increasing spontaneous play by suppressing self-stimulation in autistic children. *Journal of Applied Behavior Analysis*, 1974, **7**, 521–528.

Lahey, B. B., McNees, M. P., & McNees, M. C. Control of an obscene "verbal tic" through timeout in an elementary school classroom. *Journal of Applied Behavior Analysis*, 1973, **6**, 101–104.

LeBlanc, J. M., Busby, K. H., & Thomson, C. L. The functions of time-out for changing the aggressive behaviors of a preschool child: A multiple baseline analysis. In R. Ulrich, T. Stachnik, & J. Mabry (Eds.), *Control of human behavior* (Vol. 3). Glenview, Illinois: Scott, Foresman, & Company, 1974.

Lindsley, O. R. A reliable counter for recording behavior rates. *Journal of Applied Behavior Analysis*, 1968, **1**, 77–78.

Lovaas, O. I., Litrownik, A., & Mann, R. A. Response latencies to auditory stimuli in autistic children engaged in self-stimulatory behavior. *Behaviour Research and Therapy*, 1971, **9**, 39–49.

Lovaas, O. I., & Simmons, J. Q. Manipulation of self-destruction in three retarded children. *Journal of Applied Behavior Analysis*, 1969, **2**, 143–157.

Mann, R. A., & Moss, G. R. The therapeutic use of a token economy to manage a young and assaultive inpatient population. *Journal of Nervous Mental Disease*, 1973, **1**, 1–9.

McArthur, M., & Hawkins, R. B. The modification of several classroom behaviors of an emotionally disturbed child in a regular classroom. In R. Ulrich, T. Stachnik, & J. Mabry (Eds.), *Control of human behavior* (Vol. 3). Glenview, Illinois: Scott, Foresman, & Company, 1974.

Miller, L. K., & Feallock, R. A behavioral system for group living. In E. Ramp. & G. Semb (Eds.), *Behavior analysis: Areas of research and application.* Englewood Cliffs, New Jersey, Prentice-Hall, 1975.

Nordquist, V. M. A method for recording verbal behavior in free-play settings. *Journal of Applied Behavior Analysis*, 1971, **4**, 327–331.

Phillips, E. L. Achievement Place: Token reinforcement procedures in a home-style rehabilitation setting for "pre-delinquent" boys. *Journal of Applied Behavior Analysis*, 1968, **1**, 213–223.

Phillips, E. L., Phillips, E. A., Fixsen, D. L., & Wolf, M. M. Achievement Place: Modification of the behaviors of pre-delinquent boys within a token economy. *Journal of Applied Behavior Analysis*, 1971, **4**, 45–59.

Risley, T. R. Behavior modification: An experimental-therapeutic endeavor. In L. A. Hamerlynck, P. O. Davidson, & L. E. Acker (Eds.), *Behavior modification and ideal mental health services.* Calgary, Alberta, Canada: University of Calgary Press, 1970.

Sidman, M. *Tactics of scientific research.* New York: Basic Books, 1960.

Skinner, B. F. *The behavior of organisms.* New York: Appleton-Century-Crofts, 1938.

CHAPTER 18

Assessment of Children's Behavioral Deficits

LARRY A. DOKE*

Moccasin Bend Psychiatric Hospital
Chattanooga, Tennessee

Introduction

Recent developments in programs for children have prompted increased attention to procedures for assessing behavioral effects of remedial techniques. To place the content of this chapter in better perspective, these recent developments will be reviewed.

First, limitations on available funds for educating and treating handicapped children have led federal, state, and private funding agencies to insist upon more accountability data from service programs. Although considerable sums of service money have been and continue to be distributed to programs with political backing, increasing competition is coming from programs with clearly specified goals and documentation of progress toward those goals. These data-based programs have a distinct advantage over programs based entirely on promises, rational arguments, and testimonials. Thus, the growing interest in behavioral assessment may be explained in part by the cliché "there's money in it".

Second, educators and therapists have recently come to view handicapped children from a new perspective. Although children with handicaps and behavioral deficits are abnormal in a statistical sense, more and more research is showing that handicaps and behavioral deficits can be remediated via training procedures that would be used with *normal* children. In addition, educators and therapists have become more aware of the effects of early childhood experiences for normal and abnormal children. Re-education is no longer seen as a strategy that applies only to the normal school-aged child. The recognition that young handicapped children respond favorably to relatively "normal" training routines has led to the development of infant care, parent training, and daycare/treatment programs. Although they realize that active and early intervention can result in important changes,

*The author expresses thanks to Kathy Roberson, Kevin Hickey, Sherrie Doke, and Marge Loughman who assisted in preparing this manuscript.

an increasing group of educators and mental health workers are also seeing the broad gaps in what is now known about treating young children with behavioral deficits. In addition, these professionals are finding that the replicable techniques tend to be those that have been very clearly described and shown to have measurable and reliable effects. The growth of treatment programs for young handicapped children has indeed exposed a need for more information on the measurement of children's responses to innovative training techniques.

Third, many service programs are assuming *broad*, as well as *local* service responsibilities. It is becoming increasingly obvious that the large numbers of handicapped children will not be adequately served by the limited number of special schools, hospitals, and clinics. It is not unusual to find an area with over a thousand handicapped children being "served" by a special project for 35 children. In too many instances, noble efforts are not satisfying the broad service needs. This unpleasant observation is changing the perceived relationship between service and research. In the past, research has been primarily left to the universities whose role has been to develop techniques to be "plugged" into service programs. However, it is becoming increasingly obvious that researchers in academic settings often do not have access to children who exhibit the more perplexing clinical problems. A further concern is that techniques and demonstration programs that are developed in academic and research settings may be of limited generality, because of differences in the funding, staffing, and administrative organization of research (vs. service) projects. Hence, more programs are assuming what Risley (1969) has termed "experimental-therapeutic" responsibilities. As Risley has pointed out, programs that view service as an experimental-therapeutic endeavor do not delegate research responsibilities to one group and service responsibilities to another group. Instead, everyone is responsible for seeing that the effects of his service activities are clearly documented. If this development continues, service programs stand to be important contributors to the therapeutic and training technologies, as well as consumers of these technologies. Consequently, they will be indirectly serving a very broad group of handicapped children, in addition to their local clientele. However, in order for this development to continue, direct service personnel need to become familiar with the stringent criteria of applied behavior analysis and procedures for documenting treatment and training effects.

The developments described above have influenced all psychological service programs (hospitals, regular daycare programs and schools, nursing homes, prisons, etc.), not just programs for children with behavioral deficits. Fortunately, the information on behavioral assessment that is needed by these diverse types of programs is essentially uniform. In other words, most of the necessary measures and experimental procedures can be adapted readily across populations, settings, and types of behavior disorders. Much of the material in this chapter will, therefore, overlap with material in other chapters, although the procedures and issues presented in this chapter will be discussed as they relate to children with behavioral deficits. The general applicability of behavioral assessment techniques may be viewed as a factor arguing most strongly for their dissemination.

It would obviously not be difficult to measure the vocabulary of a child who has never learned to speak. This child's total vocabulary would number zero, and his speaking rate would be zero words per minute. However, special problems are encountered in measuring behaviors that frequently change form, that occur at unpredictable time, or that occur very seldomly. For example, suppose the task is to measure the vocabulary of a child who mutters, runs words together, uses words, but sometimes mispronounces them; combines nonsense words with real words; or speaks, but at unpredictable times. In such instances the observer of behavior needs to be familiar with the dimensions of behavior that are measurable, the measures of behavior that are at his disposal, and guidelines on how to collect, keep, and summarize behavioral data. Such information may be found in this chapter, along with examples of applications to various childhood behavior deficits.

Prior to this discussion, it is necessary to define a "behavioral deficit." On one hand, a child may be said to have a deficit if he lacks a skill that is required in daily living, socialization, or task performance. Or, a child may be described as having a behavioral deficit if he is slower than other children in learning a new skill. That is, if one child in a group does not exhibit a behavior that is exhibited by others in the group, then this child may be said to have a behavioral deficit. Furthermore, the term "deficit" need not only apply to behaviors that are unlearned. It may also apply to behaviors that have been learned, but are not exhibited well enough or frequently enough (i.e., low-probability behaviors).

The term "deficit" will not be used in this chapter to refer to or indicate organic or psychic problems. This restriction in the use of the term simplifies the measurement of deficits by directing attention to phenomena that can be seen and that occur under conditions that can be reconstructed. For the most part, these phenomena will be behavior problems that are encountered in educational, habilitative, and rehabilitative programs where the central objectives are to develop new skills or to teach children to use skills that they have already acquired.

Preliminary Guidelines

Some general guidelines apply to all types of behavioral assessment. The first of these guidelines, in fact a prerequisite to measurement, is to define what is to be measured. The adequacy of a measurement operation will in large part depend upon how well the target problem has been described. This description rests in turn upon an early decision regarding what one expects or desires to change. Suppose that the program objective is to develop a child's "social competence." The problem, thus defined, would be rather difficult to measure. We might first consider looking for a standardized test of "social competence," or we might ask judges to repeatedly rate the child's "social competence." Or, finding these methods to be unreliable, we might seek out a more direct measure of one of the possible referents (components) of "social competence": speaking up when addressed, starting conversations, wearing clothes appropriate to the situation, looking other people in the eye when talking, approaching strangers at social gatherings, using polite gestures, or a combination of these phenomena and others. Measurement procedures often become obvious when an apparently complex problem is described in terms of its observable referents (components).

Once a problem is defined, care should be taken to record the definition, so that it may be reviewed from time to time and accurately communicated to new observers. Constancy in the definition of behaviors is highly critical to measurement reliability, which will be discussed in greater detail at the end of this chapter. Measurement operations may often change if they are not described in writing or otherwise recorded when observations are first begun. This is especially true of definitions of low-probability behaviors, since records of these behaviors encompass relatively long training periods. When behavior definitions are written, they are easier to remember, much less likely to "drift" if new but similar behaviors should appear, and much easier to communicate to new or substitute observers. Each of these benefits contributes to improved measurement reliability.

Another important consideration is to choose the *easiest* possible measure for a problem. We would think it ridiculous to see a contractor measuring lots in a housing development with a 6-inch ruler. Yet parallels may often be seen in attempts at observing and measuring human behavior. Programs exist that employ teams of technicians to record behaviors for hours on end, when periodic 20-minute samples of the same behaviors would yield representative data. Children's motoric behaviors are sometimes recorded in laboratory settings with expensive electromechanical devices, despite the fact that representative data on the same phenomena could be obtained in natural environments and much less expensively using direct measurement by human observers. When conducting behavioral observations one should frequently ask whether the present measurement procedures and devices are the best ones for the job.

Much of the future growth of a technology for managing behavior is certain to depend upon demonstrations that behavior changes persist across settings and/or result in systematic changes in other important (non-target) behaviors. Hence, another general recommendation is to measure the generality and concurrent effects of changes in target behaviors. For example, initial measures in a therapeutic program might be directed at the duration of eye contact for a severely disturbed young child. However, the therapist may notice shortly after starting a treatment program that the child not only shows more sustained eye contact, but also looks at and touches objects in his environment more frequently. This observation should clue the therapist to start measuring this child's interaction with objects, and to include such measures earlier when assessing the progress of future children in similar training programs. By the same token, behavioral observers should be sensitive to undesirable side-effects of training programs, so that measures of these phenomena can also be started as early as possible in training.

Multiple measures can show important inter-relationships among behaviors. However, observers need to be advised to discontinue measures when they have been carried out for long enough periods of time to show that they are not yielding meaningful data. Many observers and programs waste large amounts of time and money collecting data that no one will ever have time to review. Behaviors and environmental events that are thought to be important before measurement has begun often prove to be unimportant. Although the thrust of this book is to encourage professionals to conduct systematic observations of behavior, observers also need to be cautioned to spend their time and efforts productively.

Therapists and educators often make the mistake of collecting data only during training sessions or only during times of the day when it is most convenient to observe a child. Yet, recent studies of generality (Lovaas, Koegel, Simmons & Long, 1973; Redd, 1970; Stokes, Baer & Jackson, 1974) have shown that training effects do not invariably transfer to new settings. Hence, consideration should be given to conducting routine measures of the target problems in different situations and at various times of day. Otherwise, it will be difficult to draw conclusions about the generality of training or treatment effects.

Whether assessing the direct or generalized effects of training, it is necessary to consider the optimal time(s) to observe. Obviously, one would not gather data on a child's social interaction skills when the child is working at a task that must be done independently. Nor would it be wise to schedule observations of toy play during a time of the day when the child's favorite television programs are aired. The task of scheduling observations when the target behavior can (or may) occur is often difficult. This problem typically presents itself when the objective of training is to develop a skill that will occur infrequently or intermittently, even after it has been learned to criterion. For example, compliance with adults' instructions is a skill that can only occur when adults give instructions. Since instructions from adults are usually (ideally) intermittent and infrequent, it may be necessary to obtain records on a child's compliance in standard pre-arranged test situations: a prepared list of instructions might be given during an observation period that might otherwise have passed without the child's ever receiving an instruction. At the end of each of these observation periods, the observer would simply record the percentage of the "staged" instructions that were followed. Training, of course, need not occur during these observation periods.

One of the most difficult initial tasks for an observer is to record the behavior of other people without interacting with them. For the individual who enjoys interacting with others, it is usually very uncomfortable to watch someone else closely over a long period of time without responding to his comments, without maintaining eye contact, without changing expression, or without providing any distractions.

The task of remaining unobtrusive when observing children with behavioral deficits can be even more difficult. An observer who is dedicated to helping others will wish to applaud and show approval when he sees a child exhibiting new forms of appropriate behavior. Most human observers will feel like shouting encouragement as the child struggles to emit even a response that turns out to be incorrect. Yet competent observers avoid doing these things.

The popular perception of scientific approaches to human problems is probably based in large part upon the cold, impersonal appearance of skilled and unobtrusive observers. Yet, observers do not need to be unfeeling and uncompassionate in order to learn to avoid interacting with children. In fact, the converse may be true. The observer who is interested in reliably documenting the effects of a training procedure can quickly learn to control his own behavior without ceasing to enjoy the benefits of training. Thereby, he may encounter new reinforcers in the form of his important contribution to the development of an expanded and more refined training technology.

Still, attention should be given to the ethical defensibility of behavioral measures. Before starting any form of behavioral assessment the nature and purpose of proposed measures should be described to the child's parent or legal guardian. Measurement should not proceed until permission has been granted by the parent or legal guardian, who should be assured that: (1) the behavioral data will be used solely for the purpose of evaluating the effectiveness of therapeutic or education techniques, and (2) the child's anonymity will be maintained in published accounts of the experimental-therapeutic findings. Of course, when potentially harmful measurement procedures are being considered, authorization should come from an independent review body (see, for example, the guidelines set by the American Psychological Association, 1973).

Though this hypothesis has never been verified, most experienced observers of behavior will agree that their data eventually become strong conditioned reinforcers (or punishers). Most behavior therapists and behavior analysts will also admit with some pride that their own behavior is controlled by their data. If this contention is correct, then it should be very important that a therapist or educator review the results of his work as often as possible. Hence, another general guideline in measuring behavior is to monitor data frequently, until they show that the behavior problem has been solved. (The problem solution, parenthetically, is probably the event from which data take on whatever conditioned reinforcing properties they might have.)

Many therapists and investigators complain of technicians who "do not stick to it." This observation is not particularly surprising, when one considers the conditions under which many observers are trained. Too often, observer training is conducted out of context. Observers may be taught in an artificial setting to measure one or more behaviors. After a few weeks of doing this reliably they may win the title of "trained observer" and obtain their course credit. At this point these observers may have the necessary skills, but they often lack the motivation to record routinely and consistently. Hence, it is recommended that observers be trained in a context where they will see changes in the behaviors they are recording. The initial target behaviors during training should therefore be relatively simple, in order to maximize the likelihood that trainees will see how data can guide the therapist or educator in resolving a behavior problem. Observers who have been trained in a complete and realistic problem-solving context should have fewer problems in following behavioral assessment routines.

In order to continue to contact whatever reinforcers might lie in the data, it is also important to keep up-to-date summaries of the data and to review these on a regular basis. Experienced therapists, investigators, and educators have probably heard technicians ask: "Now tell me again why we're taking data on that?" or "Didn't you tell me to stop keeping records on that 2 months ago?" Questions like these can best be avoided by reviewing records routinely. Otherwise, the technician may be placed on extinction, possibly also delaying the child's progress.

All of the foregoing guidelines apply to the measurement operations that will be described later. The inexperienced observer is encouraged to review them when he is ready to begin observing and recording behavior.

Some Measureable Dimensions of Behavior

Behavior is multi-dimensional. That is to say, there is more than one way to measure it. The measure(s) that will be selected in any given investigation will depend upon which dimension(s) of behavior one sets out to quantify. Hence, before listing specific measurement operations, it would be profitable to review some of the elementary parameters of behavior which are observable and quantifiable.

Unity

Distinct units of behavior may be defined in terms of response onsets and offsets that occur sequentially, and may therefore be counted. The fact that a ratio scale may be used to quantify behaviors makes it possible for behavioral scientists to calculate "rates" (i.e., the number of response units divided by the total observation time). It should be noted that rate is not a fundamental measure of behavior, but is derived from response counts and values along the temporal dimension. A child's rate of initiating requests may be assessed as three requests per day. A young cerebral palsy victim entering therapy may be determined to have a walking rate of six steps per minute. A student who shows delays in reading may have a reading rate (from a standard primer) of five pages per hour. Descriptions such as these may be made as long as behaviors are discrete; that is, the beginning and end of each response unit can be clearly specified.

Duration

Every behavior also has a duration which may be expressed as the period of time covered by a response or as the amount or percentage of time that a response is observed to occur over a relatively long sampling period. Following are sample expressions of duration data: Michael's episodes of sustained eye contact with his speech therapist range from 2 to 20 seconds, averaging 6 seconds. He maintained eye contact for a total of 10 minutes during a 30-minute speech therapy session last Tuesday. In other words, he maintained eye contact for 33% of this therapy session.

Inter-response time

Some behavioral deficits can be described in terms of amounts of time separating one response from the next. This dimension is referred to as "pausing time" or "inter-response time." For example, a child may enter therapy in order to gain control over long and rhythmic gaps in his speech. Although his rate of speech might be within normal limits, his within-sentence pauses might average 2 seconds in length, ranging from zero to 7 seconds. An objective of therapy might be to narrow the range of inter-response times for this child.

It should be noted that abnormal inter-response times may be observed for behaviors whose rates or durations are unremarkable. In other words, measures of inter-response times are not necessarily correlated with other measures.

Latency

A closely related dimension of behavior refers to the amount of time that passes between the presentation of a stimulus, signal, or cue, and the occurrence of a behavior that is appropriate in the presence of this event. This stimulus response lag is termed "latency." If, in considering the inter-response time dimension, one regards each response as a stimulus for the next, then inter-response times and latencies may be regarded as synonymous. To give an example of latency data, a child may be observed to comply reliably with adult instructions, but may not respond *promptly* to instructions. This child's latency in responding to instruction might initially be found to average around 10 seconds. A training program directed at improving this child's reaction time may be described as being concerned with decreasing his latency in complying with instructions.

Intensity

A dimension of behavior that has not received much attention from applied behavior analysts is response "intensity," or "amplitude." When values are assigned along this dimension, they are typically described as the product of the distance through which a response moves[1] and the mass that is moved (in grams, pounds, tons, etc.). This dimension of behavior is most likely to be of interest to persons who are working in the fields of physical therapy or kinesthesiology. Measures along this dimension typically require instrumentation (see the later discussion of automatic measures). Behavioral intensity will certainly receive much attention in applied behavior analysis as more convenient techniques are developed for measuring it.

Topography

A fundamental dimension of behavior is its "topography" or "form." Behavioral topography is typically denoted using everyday language to specify types of movement and parts of the body that are involved in a response. Thus, specific behaviors or clusters of behaviors are differentiated from other behaviors or clusters. In other words, behaviors are classified or defined by their topographies. For example, "raising one's hand to get the teacher's attention" may be given the following precise topographical description: "The right hand is raised, fingers extended upward, so that the butt of the

[1]Distance (or extensity) may be regarded as an independent dimension of behavior. For example, one may measure the daily distance that a child crawls, swims, or walks, throwing distance, kicking distance, jumping distance, etc.

palm is higher than the base of the right ear lobe. The arm or hand may not be touching the head, moving up and down, or moving back and forth." As seen in this and the following examples, precise topographical descriptions often include information about the *spatial direction(s)* of the target behavior(s): staggering to the left, weaving back and forth, hopping up and down, rocking forward and backward, etc.

Clearly, the topography of a behavior is the primary dimension of the behavior upon which we focus when developing a thorough definition of the behavior. As will be seen later in this chapter, information on response topography is particularly important when the effects of behavior shaping programs are being assessed.

These brief descriptions of the basic behavioral dimensions of unity, duration, inter-response time, latency, intensity, and topography have been presented to set the stage for later decisions regarding which measurement procedures are most appropriate. By conceptualizing behavior in terms of these dimensions the reader should be better able to understand the steps involved in measurement procedures to be described in the next section. At this point it is appropriate to note that measurement may be made concurrently along several behavioral dimensions, and that the outcome of one measure may not necessarily correlate with the outcome of another measure. The fact that behavioral dimensions and measurement procedures are described separately in this chapter is not meant to imply that measures should be made along one dimension at a time. In fact, it is sometimes the case that the phenomenon of interest is best described in terms of two or more dimensions; for example, measuring rates and durations of topographically-different physical exercises.

Types of Measures

Records of frequency or rate

As noted earlier, rate data are obtained by counting the number of discrete responses that occur over fixed or variable observation periods, then dividing this number by the duration of the observation period. At first glance, it might be difficult to see how frequency records (or any other records for that matter) can be obtained on behavioral deficits, since a deficit is usually thought of as the "absence" of one response or another. On the other hand, reliable information that a behavior has *never* occurred provides us with the ideal baseline. With this information, we need not be concerned over whether the effects of a training procedure will be confounded by unexpected baseline instability or trends in the pre-training data. If a child has never exhibited or learned a behavior, then by definition the rate of that behavior will be zero. Even in this case, however, the observer may obtain non-zero data if the target behavioral deficit is re-defined in terms of simpler, prerequisite forms that now occur and can be quantified.

The most important requirement in gathering rate or frequency data is that each response "unit" be well described. In other words, it must be possible to clearly identify the onset and offset of each response and the critical interval after which a new response will be recorded. This requirement is not always easily met. Consider, for example, the task of measuring the rate of eye contact for a child who has ocular convergence problems and whose eye contact is erratic: sometimes very brief, sometimes prolonged. Or, consider the task of establishing a vocalization rate for someone who holds vowel sounds for long periods, blends vowels together, and breathes irregularly during episodes of vocalization.

Once the units of behavior have been clearly defined, and once it has been decided that rate is the measure of choice, the actual mechanics of data collection are typically easy. Various ways have been used to count the occurrences of behavior: tallying by hand on a blackboard or on paper; advancing a hand or wrist counter; counting via electro-mechanical devices operated either by the target child or by an observer; counting behavioral products at the end of sampling periods (for example, worksheets completed, items assembled, foot prints, amounts of some substance used), etc. The time records that enter into rate computations can be easily obtained using a standard watch or wall clock. This part of the recording procedure can, of course, be further simplified by equating durations of sampling periods and by perhaps using an inexpensive but reliable signaling device (for example, a standard kitchen timer).

A hypothetical problem will show how rate data might be collected and summarized. In working with a speech-deficient child a need might arise for repeated records of speech rate. Before counts could be started, it would be necessary to define the response unit; for example, "any audible and recognizable word, regardless of whether it is pronounced correctly or has been emitted previously." An observer would then choose a situation and a time of the day when interruptions are unlikely and when the child is relatively free to engage in conversation. Later observations would be made at this standard time and under these same conditions. As illustrated in the top half of Fig. 18.1, the observer would record the "start time" of the observation period, then begin counting the child's words. If the child's speech rate were low, then it might be possible to tally the occurrences of each word with pencil and paper. Or, if possible, each word might be written down (see Hart & Risley, 1968, 1974) so that later analyses could be made regarding rates for old and new words, word combination rates, rates of correct word pronunciation, etc. Then, at the end of the observation period the observer would record the "stop time" and determine the total duration of the observation. The sample record in Fig. 18.1 shows that 27 words were heard over a 40-minute observation period from 9:05 a.m. to 9:45 a.m. Dividing the number of words (27) by the sample duration (40 minutes), one may obtain the rate of speech for that observation (0.68 words-per-minute). Out of context this rate figure is usually meaningless, since most individuals are not accustomed to thinking about words (or most other units of behavior) in fractional parts. However, it does become meaningful when used for the purpose of comparing the strength of the target behavior for this particular child from one standard observation period to the next.

The bottom half of Fig. 18.1 shows how the rate index derived above might be included in a graphic summary of this child's progress. Such a visual record often shows changes that would otherwise be difficult to detect. This feedback may direct the therapist or educator to continue or to stop what he has been doing about the problem. Hence, the recommendation is again made to keep graphs and summary charts up to date and to review them frequently.

In certain cases, rate data may be based upon the number of behavioral *products* per unit of time; for example, the number of correct math problems

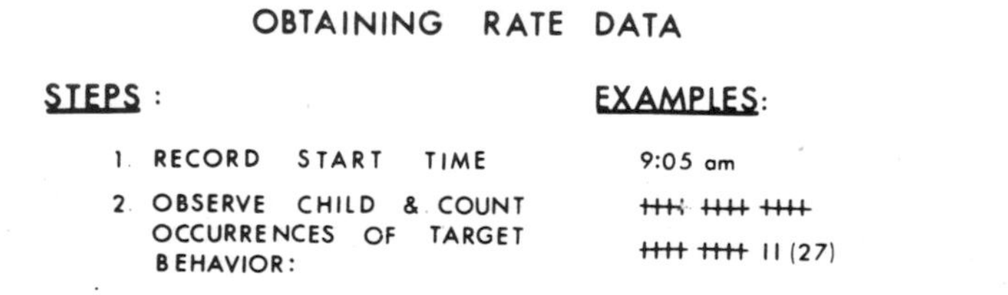

OBTAINING RATE DATA

STEPS:	EXAMPLES:
1. RECORD START TIME	9:05 am
2. OBSERVE CHILD & COUNT OCCURRENCES OF TARGET BEHAVIOR:	卌 卌 卌 卌 卌 II (27)
3. RECORD STOP TIME:	9:45 am
4. DIVIDE # OF OCCURRENCES BY TOTAL OBSERVATION TIME:	27 (WORDS) ÷ 40 (MINS.) = .68 WORDS PER MINUTE
5. CONSTRUCT GRAPHIC RECORD OF RATES FOR FREQUENT REVIEW:	

SPONTANEOUS SPEECH (WORDS PER MINUTE)
1.0
.5
0

Fig. 18.1. Steps in collecting and computing rate data. The lower half of the figure shows how the derived value might be included in a graphic summary of rates across sessions, days, weeks, or some other unit of time that would be labeled on the horizontal axis.

per hour, the number of clothing items found out of place each day, the quantity of a particular food substance consumed per week, etc. Rate data based upon product counts are most convenient, of course, when low-rate and intermittent behaviors are being studied.

When observing behaviors that do not noticeably alter the environment nor occur very often, it is usually advisable to seek ways to rearrange things so that these behaviors *do* produce changes in the environment, or leave traces. The crafty foreign agent is doing just this, when he affixes an inconspicuous piece of tape to his hotel door and door jam to detect subtle intrusions that are only likely to occur when he is not present. A residential program for children might use a similar tactic to monitor "rates" at which children use soap in hygenic activities. By installing calibrated mechanical dispensers of liquid soap, it might be easier (than if bar soap were used) to record amounts of soap used per day. Rates of soap usage could be obtained without having to watch children in the bathroom all day. Instead, an observer could simply measure soap levels in the dispensers at spaced intervals. (Refer to the discussion of automatic measures later in this section for further examples of product records.)

Timing measures

Measures of response latency, inter-response time, and response duration all involve recording the amount of time that passes between two events. These measures in clinical and educational settings can typically be obtained with enough precision using a stopwatch, a regular wristwatch, or a clock. Audio signals may also be recorded and played back in situations where visual observations cannot be interrupted by glances back and forth from a watch or clock to the child.

The following material pertains to measures of response latency and response duration. At the end of this section a method for measuring inter-response time will be presented as an example of how different types of measures may be used together.

Data on response *latency* may be useful in evaluating structured activities such as language or reading lessons, imitation training sessions, discussion periods, games with time limits, etc. Each timing of response latency begins with the presentation of a stimulus for a behavior and ends with the onset of the appropriate response. The length of each stimulus-response interval is then recorded, to be summarized later in the form of a central tendency figure or distribution of latencies per session. Obviously, it would not be possible to obtain a latency value on trials where no response occurred. Hence, additional information would be needed regarding the number or percentage of stimuli to which the child responded.

Duration data are also quite useful in remedial work with children. For example, after teaching a child to dress without assistance, one might wish to help the child increase his speed of getting dressed. Measures of time taken to dress would require that the dressing task be described clearly enough to allow an observer to determine the beginning and end of each dressing episode. Once the response has been clearly defined, timing might be done by using a standard wall clock and recording the times between the beginning and end of each dressing episode.

To give another example, a treatment objective might be to increase the durations of a child's eye contact with other people. One simple way to collect duration data on this behavior would be to time only the first instance of eye contact at fixed intervals (e.g., every 5 minutes). A stopwatch could be started when the child first makes eye contact and stopped the first instant he looks away; 5 minutes later the next episode of eye contact could be thus recorded and so forth[2].

These basic timing procedures can yield useful quantitative records on a variety of other behaviors that might need to be strengthened; for example, time on task in standard academic activities, balancing time on a bicycle, under-water breath-holding times during swimming lessons, time sitting quietly in church, time standing without assistance, time standing alone, time spent getting ready for meals, etc.

Sometimes information is needed not on the duration of *local* episodes of behavior, but on overall amounts of time that a child exhibits a particular behavior. For a socially-withdrawn child, records might be desired on amounts of time during preschool hours that the child is in physical proximity to other children and adults. On a day-to-day basis this child's social behavior might be measured by cumulating the time the child spends within 5 feet of another person. Caregivers who are working directly with children can usually obtain these records themselves by simply starting a stopwatch when the child exhibits the desired behavior (moves within 5 feet of another person) and stopping the stopwatch when the target behavior is no longer occurring (when the child again moves away from the others).

Some teachers and therapists may find it possible to keep these kinds of records on one or more children during lengthy group training periods. When uninterrupted observations are possible, the daily duration records may be summarized by dividing the accumulated time during which the target behavior has occurred by the overall duration of the training session. For example, a child may have been observed to be within 5 feet of another person for a total of 24 minutes of a 4-hour (240 minutes) preschool session. Thus, the record from this session would show this child to have been in social proximity for 10% of the session.

[2]It should be noted that this measurement procedure combines a duration measure with a "spotcheck" procedure to be described later in this section.

When duration samples of this sort must be interrupted by activities that demand undivided staff attention, percentage data on the duration of target behaviors may be obtained from briefer observation sessions. For example, a nurse who is keeping duration records on a withdrawn child's conversational behavior may find it impossible to keep accurate records during segments of the day when medications must be administered. In this case, the nurse would be advised to record durations of the child's conversational behavior in relatively equal sampling periods *between* times of the day when she is required to distribute medications (for example, from 9:30 to 10:30 a.m. and from 3:00 to 4:00 p.m. each day)[3].

When data are computed in the form of proportions of time that particular behavior occurs and when the length of sampling intervals varies significantly from one observation to the next, the data should be carefully examined to see if any systematic relationships exist between the duration of each sample and the proportion of time the behavior occurred within each sample. Often the only way to determine the optimal duration of a sampling interval is to systematically compare the data obtained from longer and shorter sampling periods. Observers should always remember that behaviors that occur intermittently will usually be shown to occur for higher proportions of time when observation sessions are long than when observation sessions are brief. Hence, it is especially advisable when recording durations of intermittent behaviors to schedule observations at times when the behaviors are most likely to occur. For example, if one were interested in obtaining 3-hour samples of the duration of grooming behavior for a group of children, an observation time from 6 a.m. to 9 a.m. would be preferable to an observation period from 9 a.m. to noon. (This would only be true, of course, in situations where children routinely awaken early.)

To summarize, duration data may be expressed in several ways: (1) as the actual amount of time a target behavior is observed to occur over successive observation sessions that are equal to each other in length, (2) as the proportion of time that a target behavior is observed to occur across sampling periods that vary in length, or (3) as the "local duration," or the amount of time individual units of a behavior last when they occur (the time between the onset and offset of each response). Records of the standing behavior of a crippled child in a physical therapy program will be used to illustrate each of these types of statements about the duration of behavior: (1) A 3-day record of the child's standing behavior during formal 1-*hour treatment sessions* may show that she stood 18 minutes of the period on Day 1, 26 minutes on Day 2, and 29 minutes on Day 3. (2) Records of this child's standing behavior from daily free-play *sessions that vary in length* may show that she stood during

[3]It should be noted that this recording procedure combines duration measures with "spotcheck" and "interval sampling" procedures to be described later in this section.

6% of the free-play period on Day 1, 11% on Day 2, and 14% on Day 3. (3) Records of the local durations of this child's standing over the same 3-day period may show discrete episodes of standing without assistance to have an average duration of 34 seconds (ranging from 4 seconds to 39 seconds) on Day 1, 41 seconds (ranging from 19 seconds to 52 seconds) on Day 2, and 48 seconds (ranging from 23 seconds to 60 seconds) on Day 3. These three types of information would all be very important in this child's physical therapy program, since they describe different aspects of the child's progress. What is surprising is that although these data may be obtained by teachers and other direct-care personnel using only a stopwatch and pencil and paper, they are not routinely obtained in programs designed to remediate children's behavioral deficits.

Checklists and probes

Often, when working with children who have behavioral deficits, data are needed: (1) to show changes in a number of behaviors that the child may not ordinarily emit within an allotted observation time, i.e., behaviors that are under strict stimulus control, or (2) to show changes in several discrete behaviors that comprise a complex skill. Such data may often be obtained most efficiently by using behavior "checklists" or "probes." Probes usually take the form of relatively brief, intermittent tests in which an observer systematically presents the stimuli that are expected to control specific target behaviors. Figs. 18.2, 18.3, and 18.4 illustrate three different types of checklists that could be used to probe deficits in different areas: physical appearance (Fig. 18.2), naming shapes (Fig. 18.3), and matching numbers to number names (Fig. 18.4). The checklist on physical appearance in Fig. 18.2 shows sample data on six categories over several days. The checklist on shape naming in Fig. 18.3 (Part B) might be administered repeatedly to show changes in a

A. PHYSICAL APPEARANCE

	DAYS														
	1	2	3	4	5	6	7	8	9	10	11	12	13	14	15
HAIR COMBED								✓	✓	✓	✓	✓	✓	✓	✓
FACE CLEAN	✓	✓	✓	✓	✓		✓	✓	✓	✓	✓	✓	✓	✓	✓
CLOTHES CLEAN			✓		✓	✓	✓	✓		✓		✓	✓	✓	✓
SHOES TIED					✓	✓	✓	✓	✓	✓	✓	✓	✓	✓	✓
SHIRT IN						✓	✓	✓	✓	✓	✓	✓	✓	✓	✓
HANDS CLEAN			✓	✓	✓	✓		✓	✓	✓	✓		✓	✓	✓
% OK:	17	17	50	33	67	67	67	100	83	100	83	83	100	100	100

Fig. 18.2. Sample checklist for assessing physical appearance. Checks across days indicate aspects of physical appearance judged to be O.K. Daily percentages of items passed are across the bottom of the figure.

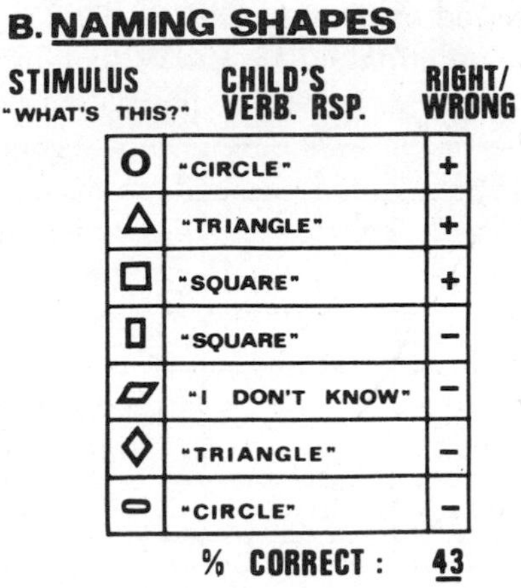

B. NAMING SHAPES

STIMULUS "WHAT'S THIS?"	CHILD'S VERB. RSP.	RIGHT/ WRONG
○ (circle)	"CIRCLE"	+
△ (triangle)	"TRIANGLE"	+
□ (square)	"SQUARE"	+
▯ (rectangle)	"SQUARE"	−
▱ (parallelogram)	"I DON'T KNOW"	−
◇ (diamond)	"TRIANGLE"	−
⬭ (oval)	"CIRCLE"	−

% CORRECT : 43

Fig. 18.3. Sample checklist for shape naming. In assessing shape naming skills, the child would be presented with each of the visual stimuli shown in the left column of the form, together with the question "What's this?" The child's response would then be marked right or wrong, and an overall percent correct score would be computed for this probe.

child's proficiency at giving correct verbal responses to different geometric stimuli. The checklist in Fig. 18.4 (Part C) might also be given repeatedly to provide measures of a child's progress in locating numbers whose names are called out.

Striefel (1974) has provided several additional examples of checklist recording forms that may be used in imitation training programs. Interested readers are also referred to Hedrick & Prather (1972) who have described a checklist that may be used in assessing language development. The Developmental Therapy Objectives Rating Form (Combs, 1975) is yet another example of a general developmental checklist that may be used in remedial programs for children.

Checklists such as these might be administered daily, weekly, or on an aperiodic basis. They may be used advantageously to record changes in behaviors that would be more difficult to record in other ways. Probes can be particularly useful in assessing functional relationships between behaviors; that is, in determining whether training on one behavior on a checklist results in changes in other untrained behaviors.

In using behavioral probes, care must be taken to show that changes in behavior are not occurring as a function of repeated administrations of the probe. In other words, before using a probe to assess training effects, it is important to determine whether probe scores are improving over repeated "baseline" or pretreatment probes, prior to and independent of formal training.

Standardized behavioral probes, tests, scales, and checklists (Nihira *et al.*, 1969; Sanford, 1972; Sailor & Mix, 1975) have recently been developed for

C. MATCHING NUMBERS TO NUMBER NAMES

STIMULUS "FIND":	CHILD'S RESPONSE	RIGHT/ WRONG
"THREE"	7 (3) 9 4	+
"NINE"	1 (8) 7 9	–
"FOUR"	2 6 (4) 3	+
"SIX"	5 6 (1) 8	–
"FIVE"	9 1 (5) 0	+
"TWO"	0 (2) 4 7	+
"SEVEN"	3 (6) 7 8	–

% CORRECT: 57

Fig. 18.4. Sample checklist for matching numbers to number names. In assessing a child's proficiency at matching numbers to number names, the child would be instructed to find each of the numbers listed in the left column of the form. The observer would record whether or not the child pointed to or circled the correct numeral among the four listed in the center column. An overall percent correct score would then be computed for the probe, as shown.

use in diagnosing specific behavioral deficits and evaluating the effects of remedial programs. Unlike traditional psychometric instruments which offer little more than statistical comparisons of scores for handicapped and normal children, these new scales permit identification of specific deficit areas. For example, the TARC Assessment System (Sailor & Mix, 1975) was standardized with a group of 3 through 16-year-old severely-handicapped children. This inventory is to be administered by someone who is familiar enough with a child to provide information about the child's toileting behaviors, washing behaviors, utensil usage, neatness and conduct at mealtime, drinking skills, dressing skills, undressing skills, etc. The child's competence in performing these "Self-Help Skills" may then be compared to his functional level in other performance areas: "Motor Skills," "Communication Skills," and "Social Skills," each of which consists of numerous probe items (194 in all). The authors of this behavioral assessment inventory report statistically significant correlations among scores on its 16 subsections and statistically significant inter-rater correlation coefficients. More research is needed to determine the usefulness of this instrument and others like it (e.g., Sanford, 1972) in formulating training goals and providing frequent data on progress toward training goals. An immediate need is for more information on test/re-test reliability when these probe instruments are repeated (as would be necessary in gathering baseline records for a time series experimental design).

Automatic measures

Sometimes it is possible to design measurement or recording devices that are operated directly by children's movements. In fact, certain subtle behavior changes can only be detected when special instruments are used. An increasing number of devices for automatically measuring behavioral deficits have recently been constructed. Voice-operated relays have been used to measure changes in voice loudness (Jackson & Wallace, 1974) and in the nasality of speech (Roll, 1973). Instruments have also been developed for automatically recording changes in muscle tension (Budzynski & Stoyva, 1969), posture (O'Brien & Azrin, 1970), sphincter pressure (Kohlenberg, 1973), and urine flow (Azrin, Bugle & O'Brien, 1971; VanWagenen *et al.*, 1969).

Other devices, though not operated directly by the target behavior, have been developed to simplify the mechanics of data collection. For example, timing signals may be recorded on audio tapes so that technicians may observe without having to glance repeatedly at a stopwatch; audio and video-tape recorders permit behavioral episodes to be preserved for re-scoring; and manual counters (Mattos, 1968) have been developed so that observers may obtain frequency counts.

Automatic behavior measurement instruments can save time and effort and can yield data on extremely subtle events. However, two important questions should be asked when such instruments are being considered: (1) Do the advantages of the device justify its cost? (2) Is the device relatively unobtrusive, or does the device alone produce significant effects on the target behavior(s)?

Spotchecks

Spotchecks are very similar to probes, except that when performing a spotcheck, no attempt is made to set the occasion for the response to be measured. Spotchecks are like probes in that they are typically brief and they are performed intermittently.

The Planned Activity Check (PLA-Check) evaluation of group care is a type of spotchecking procedure that may be used to gauge the participation of groups or individuals in training activities. The PLA-Check was developed at the University of Kansas and has been used in several investigations (Doke, 1975; Doke & Risley, 1972; LeLaurin & Risley, 1972; McClannahan & Risley, 1973; Quilitch, 1975; Quilitch & Risley, 1973; Twardosz, Cataldo & Risley, 1974). This measure involves counting the number of residents in a program who are involved in planned activities at fixed or variable intervals. For example, in a 30-minute activity designed to improve or develop new manipulative skills, PLA-Checks might involve counting, at 1-minute intervals, the numbers of children appropriately using materials that are available in the manipulation training area. By also counting the total number of children present each minute, check-by-check percentages of children involved in the manipulation training activity may be obtained. These data may be used to trouble-shoot the activity; that is, to reveal times during the activity when group participation levels drop so that these parts of the activity may be improved. The minute-by-minute PLA-Check data may also be summarized for entire activity periods or across activity periods (for example, in the form of an overall mean or median participation index). Such data may be reviewed over a longer period of time to determine, *on the basis of children's participation*, whether staff are proficient in implementing specific training programs.

By altering the basic PLA-Check procedure slightly, information may be also obtained on *individual* children's involvement in training activities. Fig. 18.5 shows a data form that might be used in quantifying individual children's attention to an educational television program being shown to a group of children. Using this form, spotchecks might be made every 3 minutes by glancing quickly from one child to the next and noting (as shown in Fig. 18.5) whether or not each of eight children is attending to the television program at the instant he is observed. Ideally, one would begin these spotchecks at the same point in time from one viewing session to the next (for example, from the time when the title of the television program first flashes on the screen, from a point 5 minutes into the program, etc.). Also, it would be important to standardize the order in which children in the group are checked. Using the form shown in Fig. 18.5, one might glance at each child in the order by which the names are listed across the top of the data form, and note whether or not each child is looking at the television. The observer would wait for 3 more minutes (or gather a different type of data during this time), then glance again at each of the children, placing checks in their respective blocks on the data form if they were attending. PLA-Check data on group participation may be summarized from this record as shown in the far right column in Fig. 18.5. In addition, a percentage of overall time attending to the program may be derived for each child as shown in the bottom row in Fig. 18.5. This measure is particularly applicable in remedial programs, since the numbers of children in such programs are, of necessity, typically small. In fact, for a group of only eight children, as described in the example above, it should be possible to conduct PLA-Checks at 30-second intervals, should a more fine-grained analysis of the children's attention be required. Aside from its uses in therapeutic and educational programs, this measure should also be useful to persons who are interested in evaluating advertisements of children's products or in designing entertaining games, activities, or toys for children.

Another similar type of spotcheck procedure is the MANIFEST Description of Ward Activities (Cataldo & Risley, 1974). This measure was also designed as an evaluation of group living environments, and it, like the PLA-Check,

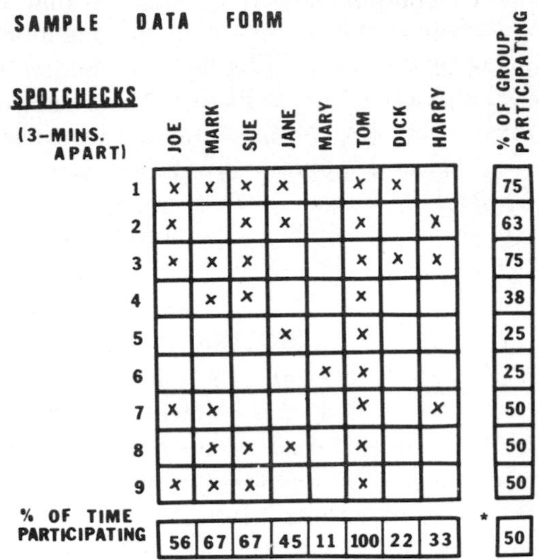

SAMPLE DATA FORM

SPOTCHECKS (3-MINS. APART)	JOE	MARK	SUE	JANE	MARY	TOM	DICK	HARRY	% OF GROUP PARTICIPATING
1	X	X	X	X		X	X		75
2	X		X	X		X		X	63
3	X	X	X			X	X	X	75
4		X	X			X			38
5				X		X			25
6					X	X			25
7	X	X				X		X	50
8		X	X	X		X			50
9	X	X	X			X			50
% OF TIME PARTICIPATING	56	67	67	45	11	100	22	33	* 50

Fig. 18.5. Sample data form for assessing individual children's participation in planned activities from one "spotcheck" to the next. In this example the spotchecks are spaced 3 minutes apart. Percentages of children participating from one spotcheck to the next are shown in the right column. Overall participation percentages for each child are shown across the bottom of was the form. The figure marked by the asterisk, the overall % of child participation time, obtained by dividing the number of scored blocks (36) by the total number of spotchecks across children (72).

may be used to obtain data on individual children. The MANIFEST instrument is unique in that it may be used even in programs that do not feature planned training activities. A major difference between this measure and the PLA-Check is that the MANIFEST instrument provides descriptions of *what* children are doing, and (if they are interacting) *how* they are interacting with the environment. Following is a very brief description of the MANIFEST recording procedures: At fixed intervals (e.g., every 15 minutes) an observer glances sequentially at children, noting on a recording form: (1) whether or not the child is vocalizing, (2) what the child is attending to, (3) what the child is touching with each of his hands, (4) the position or motion of the child, and (5) the child's location. By reviewing data of this sort from repeated spotchecks, it becomes possible to identify children in a group with marked vocal, attentive, manipulative, and motoric deficits. A minor variation of the MANIFEST instrument is appropriate for use in situations where training activities and materials *are* provided. Following procedures that are essentially the same as those just described, observers note *how* children are participating in a planned activity; for example, "playing with the truck," "talking to another child," "throwing a block at the teacher," etc. This measurement variation thus provides information not only as to whether a child is *in contact* with his environment, but also whether and in what way he is *interacting* with the environment. Interested readers are referred to Cataldo and Risley (1974) for further details in using the MANIFEST instrument.

It should be noted in reference to the PLA-Check and MANIFEST instruments that measures of children's participation in planned activities provide no information as to whether or not children who show sustained involvement in these activities benefit from them. Such measures must therefore be used in conjunction with measures of change in specific behaviors in order to assess fully whether a training program is reaching its goals. This is not to say that participation measures are any less important than measures of behavior change. In fact, without participation data, conclusions could often not be drawn regarding the adequacy of a curriculum or treatment procedure. It may be stating the obvious to say that a child must be involved in training before a training program can be expected to affect his behavior. Nevertheless, children's programs continue to be evaluated solely on the basis of whether target behaviors have changed during a program, without regard to whether children were even involved in the program. PLA-Check data might indicate that a child participates during only 30-40% of each reading period. Should this child fail to show progress in reading, one could not conclude that the reading materials were faulty. Instead, one might question the teacher's skill in implementing the reading curriculum: that is, in keeping this child involved in reading instruction. It may be putting the cart before the horse to ask whether activities that are planned for children are beneficial to them. In many programs, the first question to be asked is whether children are involved in *whatever* has been planned for them. Spotcheck procedures are useful in answering this question.

Sometimes, individual spotchecks consist of uninterrupted observations for a specified period of time, in contrast to the instantaneous observations that are made in the PLA-Check and MANIFEST measures. For example, spotchecks might be made by recording the frequency of an event or set of events during 30-second samples every 5 minutes, as opposed to simply noting whether or not an event is occurring when an instantaneous check is made every 5 minutes. This particular recording system shows how different types of measures—spotchecks, frequency counts, and interval records (described below)—can be used in combination.

Interval sampling

It is very difficult to record the frequency or duration of some types of behavior. Consider, for example, the task of recording the frequency or duration of vocal behavior that consists of erratic, unbroken chains of vowel sounds blended together. Such behavior would be difficult to measure due to problems in defining discrete vocal units; that is, problems would be encountered in discriminating the onset and offset of each separate response. Another common obstacle to frequency or duration measurement is the need in many situations for simultaneous data on several behaviors. In these situations, observers typically have trouble reaching agreement on rates and durations. When this is the case, "interval sampling" is usually appropriate. This measurement procedure involves dividing each observation session into intervals of equal length, then recording whether a behavior or set of behaviors occurs or does not occur in each interval. For example, idiosyncratic vocal behavior described above might be recorded, using the sample data form shown in Fig. 18.6. Watching the child throughout successive 10-second intervals, the observer would note whether at any time during each interval the target vocalization occurred. Hence, a vocalization beginning 25 seconds after starting the measure and ending after the 87th second of the measure would be recorded as shown in the first and second rows of the sample data form in Fig. 18.6. This figure shows that the target behavior was observed to occur within 22% of the 90 ten-second intervals sampled. An actual application of this basic interval sampling procedure can be found in a report by Hawkins *et al.* (1966).

When using an interval sampling procedure to obtain simultaneous records on several behavioral categories, it is sometimes very difficult to observe and record concurrently. To avoid having to divert his attention away from the

SAMPLE DATA FORM: INTERVAL SAMPLING

CHILD: ____________ DATE: ____________
OBSERVER: ____________ START TIME: ____________

SUCCESSIVE 10-SEC. INTERVALS

MINUTE						
1			X	X	X	X
2	X	X	X			
3						
4			X	X		X
5	X	X				
6					X	X
7	X	X	X			
8						
9						
10						
11						
12						
13						
14		X				X
15				X		

SUMMARY: % OF INTERVALS IN WHICH BEHAVIOR WAS OBSERVED ...... * 22 %

Fig. 18.6. Example of data form used in interval sampling. Each block corresponds to a 10-second observation interval. Intervals in which a target vocalization occurred are marked with X's. Of the 90 observation intervals, 20 (22%) were thus scored (see the summary figure marked with an asterisk).

target child to record behavioral occurrences on the data sheet, the observer might consider using a *discontinuous* or alternating interval-sampling procedure. Instead of observing and recording in every 10-second interval, the observer could observe the child for 10 seconds, record the child's behavior(s) for the next 10 seconds, observe again for 10 seconds, record for 10 seconds, observe for 10 seconds, and so forth. This alternating interval sampling procedure is obviously much less demanding on observers. In addition, this recording system may result in fewer observer errors when compared to *continuous* interval sampling, particularly if several behavior categories are being recorded at the same time.[4] Additional research is needed to determine whether continuous and discontinuous interval sampling procedures yield significantly different data on the same phenomenon. An actual application of discontinuous interval sampling can be found in a report by O'Leary and Becker (1967).

Interval samples usually cover relatively brief periods of time, for example, 15-30 minutes. However, they may cover much longer periods of time, depending upon the phenomenon of interest. When interval sampling sessions are relatively brief, they may be conducted as spotchecks. For example, instead of glancing at a child once every 2 hours and recording whether at that instant the child was standing, one might observe for 15-minute interval sampling sessions once every 2 hours.[5] This combination of spotchecking and interval sampling may be particularly applicable to the measurement of children's behavioral deficits. Records of a child's standing behavior when obtained via instantaneous spotchecks every 2 hours might show the child to be standing 0% of the time. However, a 15-minute continuous or alternating interval sample every 2 hours may show this same child to be standing 10% of the time. In general, the more continuous the behavioral recording system, the more precise (accurate) will be the behavioral data.

Rating scales

Many discussions of behavioral measurement eschew the use of rating scales because they are often not reliable. Too often, therapists and investigators have used rating scales to quantify behavioral phenomena that may be

[4]Hall *et al.* (1968) has described yet another variation in interval sampling that has the same advantages of alternating interval samples. Rather than observing throughout each interval, the observer may simply glance up in spotcheck fashion at the beginning (or end) of each interval, then look back at the data sheet to record the behavior he saw when he glanced at the child. An advantage of this procedure over alternating interval samples is that it avoids reducing the total number of sampling episodes. However, the procedure has the potential disadvantage of not being as sensitive as alternating interval samples to very brief or low-rate behaviors.

[5]The Behavior Observation Instrument, developed by Liberman *et al.* (1974) is a good example of this combination of measurement procedures.

measured directly. It is also easy to find published records of clinical progress that are based entirely upon progress ratings (by the therapist or by the client), with no accompanying data on the reliability of these ratings. However, observations such as these should not lead us to condemn rating scales, since rating scales may be found to be the most reliable and efficient way to quantify certain behavioral phenomena.

For some time now the rating scale has been the measure of choice for such events as gymnastic and diving performance. Ratings for these phenomena are not very time-consuming, and they usually turn out to be highly reliable. Christophersen *et al.* (1975) used rating scales to assess the condition of urban residential property and found high degrees of inter-rater agreement. Rating scales may be useful in programs for children, when the objective is to assign a value to the quality or form of a behavior or product that would be difficult to measure directly. Fig. 18.7 shows a checklist recording form in which an observer has rated the legibility with which a child has copied letters and numerals, the quality of the child's products in a daily arts and crafts activity, the overall neatness of the child's room at a standard spotchecking time, and the child's style or form when doing various physical exercises. Written criteria and guidelines may be used to improve agreement between rates should initial ratings not prove to be reliable.

SAMPLE DATA FORM: BEHAVIORAL RATINGS

CHILD: ______________ DATE: ______________
OBSERVER: ______________ TIME: ______________

SCALE: 0 1 2 3 4 5 6 7 8 9 10
(VERY POOR) (EXCELLENT)

	DAYS				
	M	T	W	TH	F
COPYING LETTERS & NUMERALS	3	3	6	4	5
ARTS & CRAFTS PRODUCTS	4	4	4	5	4
NEATNESS OF ROOM	6	7	5	7	8
EXERCISES: SIT-UPS	2	2	3	2	3
CHINS	4	3	4	4	5
PUSH-UPS	3	3	4	5	4
HEAD STANDS	2	5	3	2	5

Fig. 18.7. Sample form for daily ratings of various child behaviors on a scale from 0 (very poor) to 10 (excellent).

Combining measurement procedures

As shown for several of the measures just described, no recording system need be used independently. By recording both the frequency and duration of a behavior, an index of a behavior's duration per occurrence may be obtained. Rating and checklist systems may be combined to obtain information on the quality of a behavior as well as its probability of occurrence. Interval sampling records and repeated measures of frequency and duration may take the form of spotchecks conducted aperiodically or at fixed intervals.

The following example will show how duration and frequency measures can be used in combination. The measurement of inter-response times will be illustrated by referring to a hypothetical child whose reading behavior is characterized by erratic pauses. It would be possible for such a child to show normal overall reading rates, providing that his reading speed between pauses was rapid. This child's behavioral deficit would be indicated not by his reading rate, but by the *rhythm* of his reading. Before starting measures of inter-response times in such a case, it would be necessary to decide whether all response-response intervals would be recorded, or whether only the longer intervals would be counted. The task of measuring *all* inter-response times would be very difficult in a natural setting and would probably require expensive voice-operated electromechanical timing devices. In situations where instrumentation would not be practical, other methods of measuring inter-response time are available. Following is a description of one way to record inter-response times for the reading deficit described above:

A set of ten standard paragraphs could be randomly presented for the child to read. (To permit later comparisons across sessions, each paragraph should be presented the same number of times per session.) Using a stopwatch and a data form like that shown in Fig. 18.8, an observer could record distributions of inter-response times for each of the paragraphs that the child reads. Tally marks would be made in columns appropriate to reading pauses of different lengths. The data in Fig. 18.8 show that on his initial reading of paragraph number 5, this child exhibited one pause of 2-4 seconds, one pause of 5-7 seconds, two pauses of 11-13 seconds, and one pause of 14-16 seconds. The totals at the bottom of the form in Fig. 18.8 show frequencies for each pause length. These data could be readily transferred to graphs of the frequency of each pause duration across sessions. Training for the child in this example would presumably be directed at first reducing the frequency of pauses greater than 16 seconds, then pauses from 14-16 seconds, then pauses from 11-13 seconds, and so forth. Data like those in Fig. 8 would be useful in deciding (on the basis of the child's performance) when to make each adjustment in training goals. Training details in this example would require elaboration that would not be pertinent to this chapter. However, measurement procedures have been presented to illustrate another way of combining different recording techniques.

SAMPLE DATA FORM

CHILD: ______________ OBSERVER: ______________ DATE: ______________

INTER-RESPONSE TIMES (IN SECS.)

PARAGRAPH #	2–4	5–7	8–10	11–13	14–16	> 16
5	I	I		II	I	
9	I		I		I	
2	I	I		II		
3	I	I				
6			I			
7				I		
8	I	I	I		I	
10	II					
4	I		I			
1						
6		I			I	
3	I					
10	I		I		I	
5	II		I	I		I
1	I	I				
8		I				
2	I	I	II			
9	I		I	I		
7				I	I	
4		I	I			
TOTALS:	15	9	10	8	6	1

Fig. 18.8. Sample form for recording the frequencies of various durations of pauses (inter-response times) as a child reads test paragraphs coded along the left column. Total frequencies for pauses of each length are shown across the bottom of the form.

Another assessment procedure that combines several types of behavioral measures is the Behavior Observation Instrument (BOI) developed by Liberman *et al.* (1974). The purpose of the BOI is to determine the proportion of time that persons in a group engage in various categories of mutually exclusive and concomitant behaviors. Observations are conducted on a spotcheck basis (e.g., four times per day with at least 1 hour between observation sessions). Each observation session consists of one set of alternating interval samples of target behaviors for each member of the group. One person is observed for 5 seconds and his behavior is coded according to the pre-designated behavior categories (in checklist fashion). Then, after 30 seconds have passed, the second group member is observed for 5 seconds after which his behaviors are coded. This process is repeated until all the group members have been observed once. Recording is then discontinued until time for the next observation session (set of spotchecks). The BOI is innovative in that it combines checklist, interval sampling, and spotcheck measures to obtain simultaneous data on several behaviors of individual members of a group.

Although different measures may be used in combination, observers should be cautioned against creating recording systems that are unnecessarily complicated. The ideal single behavioral measure or combination of measures will be that which yields the greatest amount of reliable and useful information, at the same time minimizing expenditures of time, money, and effort.

Organizing and Using Behavioral Data

In many programs considerable amounts of time are spent collecting data that are never used. In view of this fact, it is not surprising to see observational behaviors extinguish rapidly. This section will present some recommendations for strengthening the reinforcing properties of behavioral data. The rationale for these recommendations is that data assume reinforcing properties by prompting or stimulating new educational/therapeutic techniques that are effective in changing important behaviors. This logic assumes (perhaps incorrectly for some service programs and agencies) that improvements in children's behavior have already been established as long-range reinforcers.

Summary data forms

A first step toward making data useful is to construct summary data sheets. A sample summary sheet is shown in Fig. 18.9. Note that each target behavior for this child is identified across the top of the sheet. The values computed from each observation session are then entered in the appropriate columns, and the dates of each summary computation are recorded in the far left column of the summary sheet. It is also advisable to allow space on the summary sheet for notes and comments about changes in recording or treatment conditions (as shown on the right side of the form in Fig. 18.9). Note also that each column of the form in Fig. 18.9 has been divided so that reliability data may be listed along with prime data, whenever independent observers are available to obtain independent records on one or more of the behaviors (refer to the columns in Fig. 18.9 marked "r"). Data may be summarized by child (as in Fig. 18.9), by group, by behavior, or by setting, depending upon the purpose of the records.

The summary sheet should appear in the front of the child's folder, along with definitions of behaviors that are being recorded and descriptions of observation procedures for each behavior. Entries on the summary sheet should be made as soon as possible after each observation. In order that computations may be entered properly on the summary sheets, it is important to enter on each raw data form the date of the observation, the identity of the child (or group of children) observed, and the name(s) of the person(s)

SAMPLE SUMMARY SHEET

CHILD: SUSIE Q.

OBSERVER(S): Mike A. (prime)
Joe B. (reliab.)
Jan C. (reliab.)

DATE	steps w/out help # per hour	r	% instructions followed	r	time taken to get dressed (mins)	r	% of time using toys appropriately	r	% participation during lessons	r	quality of letters & numerals (ratings)	r	
3/24	14.3		15		22		60		30		5		
3/25	12.1		10		20		55		20		5		
3/27 am	11.7		20		18		60		30		6		
3/27 pm	15.1	15.3	–		–		–		–		–		reliab. chk. - Joe B.
3/29	14.3		15	15	20	23	60	65	40	30	5	5	reliab. chk. - Jan C. snacks used w/ lesson
3/30	13.6		20		18		70		20		5		
3/31	15.0		15		15		55		30		6		
4/3	10.1	10.7	25	25	15	15	60	60	40	40	6	6	reliab. chk. - Jan C.
4/5	10.3		–		13		75		40		7		'instruction" data lost
4/6	14.6		20		15		65		50		6		1st day trng. prog. B (physical therapy)
4/7	15.7		25		12		70		40		6		
4/10	16.1	15.8	15	15	11	13	70	70	50	50	7	6	reliab. chk. - Joe B.

Fig. 18.9. Sample form for summarizing data on several behaviors for one child. Data obtained by independent observers are shown in subdivided columns marked with r's. Sample procedural notes are shown to the right of each day's quantitative data.

collecting the data. It is also important, when starting a new treatment procedure, to clearly indicate which data value was obtained on the first day of treatment (see, for example, the note on 4/6 in Fig. 18.9). An accurate ongoing log of procedural changes can avoid later confusion over which days marked the end of one training phase and the beginning of the next.

Summary data forms are especially useful in preparing or revising graphic records of behavior. Occasionally, during the course of training or as results become ready for publication, it is necessary to reconstruct graphs, plotting data in different ways, changing the scales on the graphs, re-summarizing data values over blocks of days, etc. Information needed to perform these tasks is much easier to obtain from a summary sheet than from individual raw data sheets.

Graphing

Once data have been arranged in a systematic and easily-retrievable form as described above, consideration should be given to preparing visual displays of the data so that changes in each target behavior can be readily seen. Although basic rules have been presented for constructing graphs (Foster, 1974; Hall, 1971; Katzenberg, 1975), technicians are advised to be flexible in choosing a format for displaying results. Graphs should be constructed for the purpose of giving the clearest possible picture of only those aspects of behavior that are of primary interest. Following are examples of graphic formats that are most commonly used in summarizing behavioral data.

Bar Graphs. Sometimes called histograms, bar graphs are most commonly used to summarize data on phenomena that can not be logically grouped together; that is, whose values lie along different continua. For example, the bar graph in Fig. 18.10 shows for each child in a group, the number of products completed during 1 week in an arts and crafts activity. Such a graph allows ready comparisons across children. Fig. 18.11 shows averaged data that might be obtained for a child (Daisy) across checklist-type probe sessions during the first month of a language development program. Note that Daisy's performance is best on the checklist in which pictures of fruits, household objects, and clothing items are presented. Such data might be used to determine the initial target training categories for Daisy. The I-shaped line within bars shows the range of scores over the repeated probe sessions that are summarized in this figure. Interested readers are referred to studies by Bailey *et al.* (1971), Garcia, Baer & Firestone (1971), and Hart & Risley (1968) for other examples of how bar graphs may be used to summarize the effects of development procedures.

Line Graphs. Line graphs are typically used in behavioral research to show changes in behavior over time. Two examples of line graphs are presented in Fig. 18.12. Units of time are routinely indicated across the bottom of line graphs, and response units are calibrated up the side (as shown in both of the graphs in Fig. 18.12). The upper graph in Fig. 18.12 presents data that might be obtained from successive spotchecks every 10 minutes on the percentage of

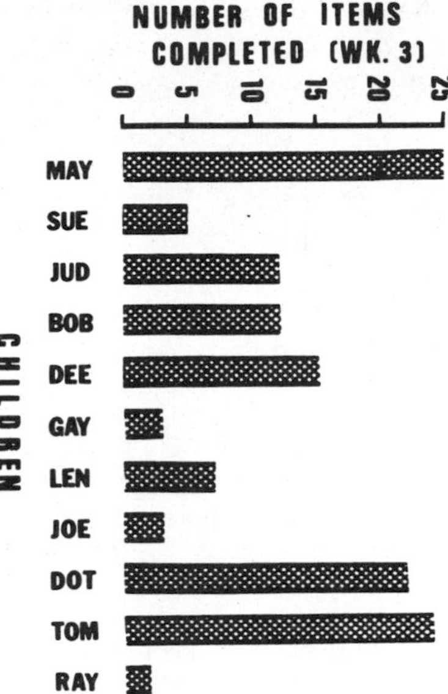

Fig. 18.10. Sample bar graph showing the number of arts and crafts products completed by eleven children during 1 week.

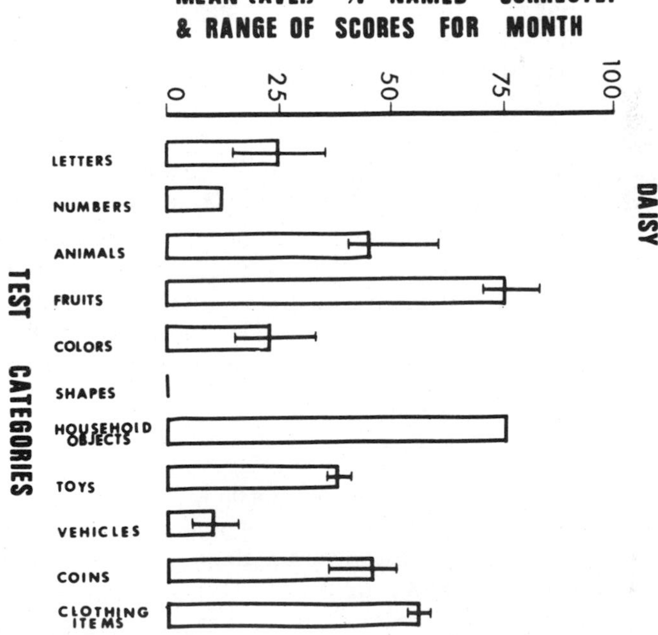

Fig. 18.11. Sample bar graph showing Daisy's proficiency at naming items across visual stimulus categories. The I-shaped lines within some of the bars show the range of percentage scores across tests conducted during the first month.

children in a group-care program who were involved in planned activities. The data summarized in this graph show several reductions in the level of group participation during the morning and a gradual decrement in group participation during the morning and a gradual decrement in group participation in the early afternoon. These data might prompt the supervisor of this program to make some changes in the activities that occur between 9:10 and 10:10 a.m., and from noon to the end of the day.

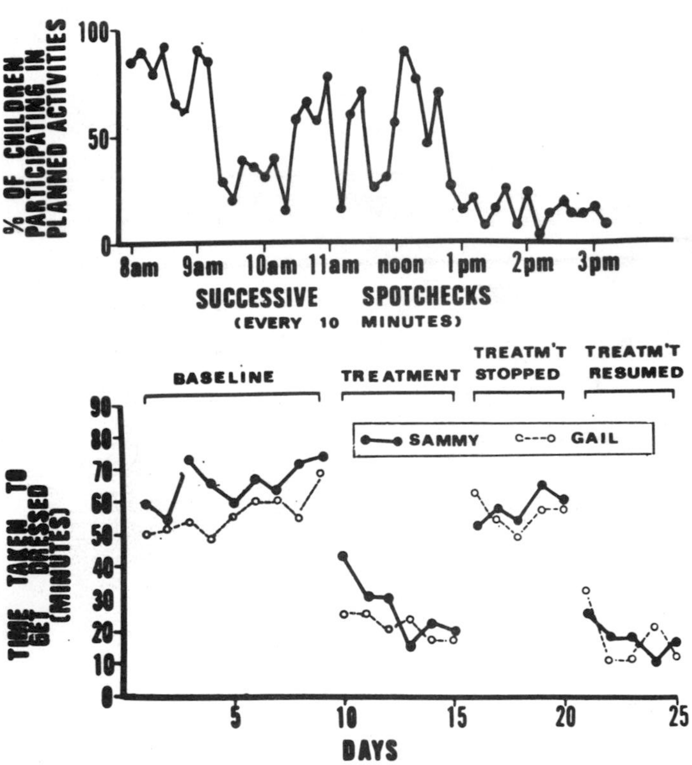

Fig. 18.12. Sample line graphs showing percentages of children participating in planned activities across 10-minute spotchecks (top) and amounts of time taken by Sammy and Gail to get dressed each day (bottom).

The lower graph in Fig. 18.12 presents the daily time that Sammy and Gail take to get dressed each morning. Note that some data points in this figure have not been connected in order to show changes in treatment conditions. Note too that each treatment condition has been labeled above the graph. Results for each child are represented by different symbols in order that both sets of results may be plotted for comparison on one graph.

Figure 18.13 presents two line graphs in the form of "cumulative records". These graphs are like other line graphs, except that each data point is plotted as though the previous point were zero. In other words, each data point represents the growing sum of data values. By plotting results in this way, one can gauge the *rates* in which behaviors are changing by the slopes of the lines. That is, if the line is flat no change is occurring; if the slope is gradual, change is slow; and if the slope is steep, change is rapid. The top half of Fig. 18.13 shows the cumulative record of one child's (Erin's) functional vocabulary from day to day. The lower graph in Fig. 18.13 shows data that might result from records of (Shelly's) eye contact durations over several weeks of speech therapy. Note increases in the slopes when training began for Erin and when treatment started for Shelly. A recovery of a baseline slope upon interrupting

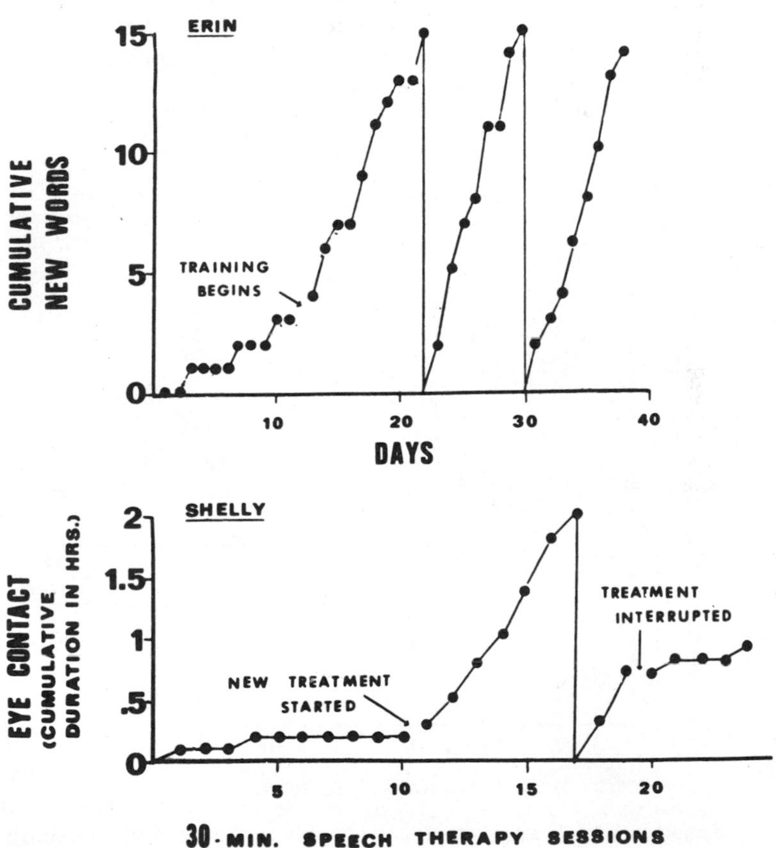

Fig. 18.13. Sample "cumulative records" (line graphs) showing changes in Erin's vocabulary and changes in the duration of Shelly's eye contact across speech therapy sessions (bottom graph). Each new data point in these records has been added to the preceding point.

treatment (as shown for Shelly after Session 19) would support a conclusion that the longer eye contact durations from Sessions 11-19 were produced by the treatment program.

The cumulative record provides a very good format for presenting developmental data. Each new value is added to the last, just as in a training program skills are being "added" to the child's repertoire. Since children's behavioral repertoires do not drop to zero at the beginning of each training session, cumulative records like those shown in Fig. 18.13 may provide more accurate analogues to new skill acquisition.

In a study of imitative speech development with schizophrenic children, Lovaas, Berberich, Perloff & Schaeffer (1966) used an innovative variation of the cumulative record to summarize a child's performance. The basic format used by Lovaas *et al.* (1966) is shown in Fig. 18.14 using hypothetical data. Such data might be obtained from training sessions in which one or more words would be modeled at fixed intervals for a child who would be reinforced for correctly imitating these words. A criterion (e.g., 10 consecutive correct imita-

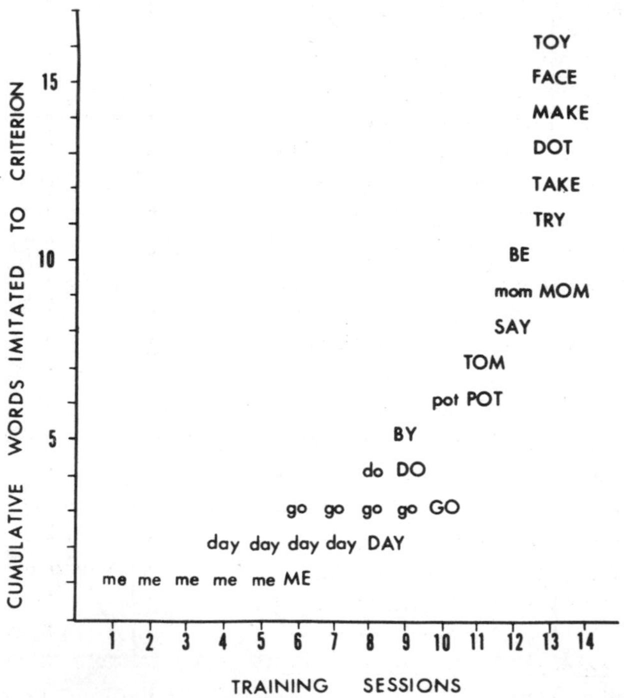

Fig. 18.14. Sample cumulative record of a child's progress in a verbal imitation training program. Words presented during each training session appear in lower-case letters for sessions when the child failed to imitate them to criterion, and in capital letters for sessions when the child did imitate them to criterion. This graphing format is modeled after that used by Lovaas *et al.* (1966).

tions) might be used to determine when the child had learned to imitate each word. In Fig. 18.14 the words presented during each training session appear in the *lower-case letters* if during that session the child failed to imitate to criterion. Training words appear in *capital letters* corresponding to sessions when the child did imitate them to criterion. Data in Fig. 18.14 would indicate steady improvement in this child's imitative performance across training sessions. By presenting actual training words, such a graph also provides topographic information that might not be so obvious in a standard featuring geometric symbols.

There is no sacred way to construct a visual summary of a set of results. Informative graphs are usually the result of several attempts at making results as easy as possible for others to understand, and the best graph is one that requires minimal description (which may be another way of saying that a picture is worth a thousand words).

Procedural Assessment in Developmental and Remedial Programs

The continued growth of a behavior management technology will require the measurement of *procedures* as well as results. An investigation can include precise definitions of target behaviors, reliable data on dependent variables, accurate computations, and clear demonstrations of systematic behavior change. Yet such a study, if it lacks clear procedural descriptions will still be of little use to practitioners. It is crucial when demonstrating the effects of a remedial technique to include as much descriptive and quantitative data as possible on the procedures used to bring about the behavior change. For example, in order to replicate a program for teaching a physically handicapped child to walk, one might need information regarding the frequency and distribution of food reinforcers from session to session, the proportion of food reinforcers that were accompanied by gestures of approval, the durations of training sessions, the amount and nature of physical guidance used, the amount of time when prosthetic devices were used, and detailed descriptions of prosthetic devices, etc. Information of this sort would make the recommended training program much easier for someone else to replicate.

Precise and quantitative procedural descriptions also help in identifying the procedural components that are necessary in affecting a desired behavior change. For example, Herbert *et al.* (1973) instructed mothers to vary systematically the amounts of time they attended to appropriate and to inappropriate behaviors of their children. By measuring actual distributions of maternal attention, these investigators were able to show functional relationships between subtle, but measured changes in the mothers' behavior and consequent changes in the behavior of their children. Kazdin & Klock (1973) were also careful to measure independent variables (procedures) in their study of the effects of non-verbal teacher attention in the classroom. These investigators systematically measured teacher behavior as well as child behavior. They were able to show that teachers, when instructed to alter their amounts of verbal and non-verbal attention to students, did in fact follow instructions. Similarly, Scott & Bushell (1974), in comparing the effects of different durations of teacher contact with individual children, were careful to document the durations of teachers' contacts with students across phases of the study in which teachers were asked to decrease and increase durations of one-to-one contacts. These studies have in common the fact that they include deliberate measures of training or treatment procedures, as well as measures of the child behaviors to be changed.

Procedural assessments of training have their place in ongoing educational and clinical programs. For example, spotchecking procedures that might be used to assess levels of children's participation in a group-care program might also be used to obtain data on percentages of time that *staff* are involved in training activities; for example, how much time staff spend looking at or talking to children; proportions of training time that involve one-to-one contacts with children; actual amounts of time spent in planning activities; etc. Surprisingly, programs are often "evaluated" in the absence of data such as these to show whether the program *is* what it is described to be. By including procedural staff assessments in program evaluation, program developers may be better able to identify and change the undesirable aspects of a program before they produce regrettable and permanent effects upon children enrolled in the program.

Assessing Behavior in Shaping Programs

Much of the work in remediating children's deficits involves increasing the rate, strength, or probability of behaviors that already exist. In other words, a child may "know how" to do something but may need a good reason to do it. Often, however, the process of remediation involves "shaping" new skills or changing (refining) the topography of an existing behavior. Several special considerations must be taken into account when measuring a child's progress toward the changing goals in a shaping program. *First*, the therapist or educator must be familiar enough with the child to set initial expectations that the child is likely to meet. *Second*, the therapist must be familiar enough with the target skill to plan or "map out" the sequence of specific behavioral steps that the child must master in training. *Third*, the therapist must establish clear criteria for determining when each behavioral component of the target skill has been acquired. Each step in a shaping sequence should be defined in advance so that it may be measured reliably. Although it is rarely done, behaviors mastered early in a shaping program should continue to be measured. Some trainers mistakenly assume that steps in a shaping program, once acquired to criterion, will remain permanent. Shaping rarely proceeds that smoothly. Instead, it is usually necessary to back up from time to time and re-establish behaviors that weaken, deteriorate, or drift, after attention has shifted to developing later, more complex components of the target skill.

To gather information that will be useful in deciding when to proceed and when to back up in shaping, observers are advised to continue intermittent measurement of behaviors that have already been taught in the shaping program. For example, if sustained eye contact has been developed as a prerequisite skill in a language shaping program, intermittent records of eye contact should continue to be obtained, even when the child has progressed to using complete sentences. Unless this is done, the speech therapist may waste time working on advanced skills in the training program when further remediation is needed for a behavior that was thought to be established earlier in the shaping program. An occasional probe or spotcheck should be sufficient to detect set-backs in fundamental skills before a shaping program becomes seriously disrupted.

The topographies of each component behavior in a shaping program must be specified before any other measures can be obtained. Yet in most shaping programs, the individual components of the target skill are not defined in advance. Consequently, the therapist shapes haphazardly, deciding as he proceeds which behaviors are closer approximations to the terminal skill. Decisions about when to begin differentially reinforcing each new component behavior are frequently made in the absence of data. Instead, they are based upon whether the therapist "thinks" the prerequisite behaviors have been learned. In short, shaping is too often "intuitive," rather than "programmed." Better descriptions of shaping procedures are needed if the shaping procedures are themselves to be taught. Before starting a shaping program, the therapist should define the component behaviors of the skill to be developed and specify the order in which these component behaviors will be taught. The steps in a shaping program, once they are formalized, may be put into the form of a checklist. As training proceeds, an observer might keep simple records of which steps occur and are reinforced. Procedures for measuring each component behavior should be outlined in advance, and decisions about progressing from one training sub-goal to the next should be based upon data showing whether the prerequisite behaviors have been learned. Data on children's progress can then be used to compare the effectiveness of new training techniques and systematic procedural variations.

Assessing the Quality of Behavioral Data

The technology for remediating children's behavioral deficits will be only as good as the data upon which it is based. Yet most behavioral data in naturalistic settings are obtained not by mechanical instruments, but by humans, who are known to make mistakes and to vary in sensitivity to environmental events. Hence, it is important when measuring behavior to show that mistakes are minimized and that the data indeed represent the phenomenon of interest.

The quality or "goodness" of behavioral data is typically described in terms of "inter-observer agreement," "validity," "accuracy," and "reliability,"[6] each of which involves a comparison of two or more obtained values for the same phenomenon. To be believable and useful, behavioral assessment procedures should be shown to approximate generally-accepted standards along each of these closely-related evaluative dimensions. (For discussion of inter-observer agreement, reliability, and accuracy see Chapter 17 on Assessment of Behavioral Excesses in Children.)

Validity

The validity of a measure refers to whether its values correlate with values obtained via *different* (independent) measures. Validity questions typically pertain to whether the phenomenon of interest is in fact being measured. For example, a child might be referred to a clinic because of poor self-concept. The therapist in this clinic might choose to assess the child's progress by observing him during repeated conversation periods and counting the number of positive and negative statements the child makes about himself. The validity of such data might be assessed by comparing them to repeated independent ratings of the child's self-concept by those with whom he converses. Or, the observational data might be compared to the child's scores on intermittent standardized self-concept scales.

In remediating children's behavioral deficits it is often necessary to define goals like "independence," "cooperative play," "creativity," "persistence," etc. in terms of individual behaviors that are assumed to be components of each generic category. Direct measures of these behaviors can be said to be valid only if they can be shown to correlate with independent measures of the broad dimensions that they are presumed to represent.

Two specific validity questions are relevant to the assessment of techniques for remediating children's deficits. *First*, when new skills are taught, what effects can be seen on behaviors that are not targets of training? In other words, does training on one behavior produce desirable or undesirable

[6]Indeed, "constancy" may be a more descriptive label for this type of data comparison. By substituting this term for "reliability," some of the current confusion over the meaning of reliability might be resolved. Occasionally there are payoffs in discarding terms that have taken on too many different meanings.

changes in other behaviors? *Second,* does a training effect in one situation generalize to new situations? In other words, are the results of training limited to the time and setting in which the training occurs? To be resolved, both of these questions would require independent measures during training. They will, therefore, be discussed in this section on validity.

Several recent studies have documented behavioral side-effects of training or treatment (Epstein *et al.*, 1974; Sajwaj, Twardosz & Burke, 1972; Wahler, 1975; Wahler *et al.*, 1970). In each of these studies, measures were conducted not only on the target behaviors, but on other desirable and undesirable behaviors as well. The authors of each study sought to determine whether non-target behaviors "co-vary" with target behaviors; that is, whether training effects "generalize" across behaviors. For children with behavioral deficits, certain skills may prove to be prime training targets if their development results in the appearance of other desirable but untrained skills. Conversely, one may not wish to teach certain other skills if they are regularly accompanied by *undesirable* behaviors. Measures of desirable and undesirable side-effects should be scheduled from the beginning of a training or treatment program. By obtaining more data on side-effects, therapists and educators will be in a better position to decide which interventions should be adopted and which require more extensive analysis and refinement.

Unfortunately, skills that are learned in hospitals, schools, and clinics do not invariably continue to occur outside these settings. The regularity of this observation has probably discouraged the collection of data on setting generality. Yet, much more needs to be learned about the conditions under which new behaviors do and do not persist away from original training situations. Therapists also need generality data in deciding when to extend training or maintenance contingencies to new settings. Ideally, generality measures would begin in the early phases of training.

The validity of data supporting remedial procedures will depend largely upon demonstrations that training effects last. Even the most dramatic finding will be weakened, unless it can be shown to hold outside the setting in which it was established.

Common Contaminators of Observational Data

Inter-observer agreement, validity, accuracy, and reliability are influenced by several factors that are all within the control of therapists, educators, and program evaluators. Each of these factors will therefore be discussed briefly.

Observer bias. Preliminary information about the expected results of a training or treatment program can influence observational data (Kass &

O'Leary, 1970), particularly if someone important responds favorably to data that show the expected effect (O'Leary, Kent & Kanowitz, 1975). This finding, that observers can be biased toward seeing changes that do not exist, is especially important in programs for remediating children's deficits, since in these programs the direction of desired behavior change is usually obvious. One approach to minimize observer bias would involve informing observers that their records are to be compared to data obtained intermittently and covertly by an independent observer. Or, independent observations might be made from "scrambled" videotapes of various training sessions. It may also be possible to minimize observer bias by discussing it with the observers, cautioning them to avoid letting their expectations affect their data. Finally, whenever possible, therapists should avoid announcing changes in training or experimental conditions and informing observers about expected behavioral effects.

Observer drift or instrument decay. Another process that can affect the quality of behavioral measures is "instrument decay" (Campbell & Stanley, 1966). Instrument decay refers to unintended changes in a measurement device or in measurement operations that may result in spurious findings. When humans are collecting data over relatively long periods of time, as when documenting remedial activities, instrument decay is particularly likely to occur. The process is referred to as "observer drift" when the inadvertent measurement changes are totally attributable to changes in the observer. As time passes, observers may: (1) forget some of the fine points of the initial response definitions or measurement details, (2) make changes on their own in definitions or measurement operations when the child begins exhibiting a slightly different form of the target behavior, (3) miss episodes of behavior due to distractability or "boredom", (4) fabricate data, or (5) adopt "shortcut" methods of data collection (e.g., recording during only half as many intervals). As time goes on, the possibility of observer drift (instrument decay) increases. Random and covert checks on observer agreement and measurement validity, accuracy, and reliability help in detecting instrument decay. In fact, advance notice to observers that these checks will occur may themselves prevent instrument decay, as suggested by the findings of Romanczyk *et al.* (1973) and Taplin & Reid (1973). As noted earlier in this chapter, written response definitions and clear initial descriptions of measurement procedures may also serve to minimize instrument decay, providing that they are reviewed routinely.

Awareness that data are being checked. The studies mentioned in the preceding paragraph indicate that measurement accuracy and observer agreement coefficients are higher when observers "know" their data are being checked.

Hence, data would ideally be checked at unpredictable or unknown times, and observers would be informed in advance that their data would be checked in this way. However, in practice it is difficult to schedule covert data checks, unless the observation setting should be equipped with videotape units that are always running or with one-way observation areas. When these conveniences are not available, it may be possible to check data by routinely assigning two observers to the same setting and giving each observer a different measurement task, except on days when data are to be checked. On these days the second observer would covertly collect data on the phenomena that the first observer had been recording. In this way, the first observer would always know that the second observer is taking data, but he would never know when *his* data were being checked.

Inappropriate or inaccurate data computation. As indicated in the earlier discussion of inter-observer agreement, some problems also arise in regard to procedures for computing agreement, validity, accuracy, and reliability. When comparing two values on any of these dimensions, it is not uncommon to see the relationship between two values expressed as the smaller value divided by the larger value. This quotient tends to be oversensitive to differences in values for low-rate behaviors and undersensitive to differences in values for high-rate behaviors. Hence, it would be preferable to compare values such as these using a correlation statistic. Readers who have more interest in issues related to formal statistical comparisons of observational data are referred to an excellent discussion by Kazdin (in press).

In addition, one should not lose sight of the possibility of error by technicians when *computing* as well as when collecting data. Although it is commonly known that people make mistakes in adding, subtracting, multiplying, and dividing, rarely are assessments of computational accuracy performed. To maximize the believability of behavioral data, occasional checks should be made on the quality of data calculations.

To summarize, the factors above can either directly affect the quality of behavioral measures, or they can limit the conclusions that can be drawn when data quality is examined. Behavioral data are clearly susceptible to a wide variety of contaminating influences. Yet these are the data that form the basis for future extensions and refinements in our teaching and training technologies. Therefore, observers and practitioners are cautioned not to expect their own records (or anyone else's) to be uncontaminated. Instead, we would be better off viewing data contamination as inevitable whenever information is being observed, recorded, or summarized by human technicians. At the same time, we must do everything possible to minimize data contamination and to show that the data represent what they are meant to represent.

References

American Psychological Association, *Ethical principles in the conduct of research with human participants*. Washington, D. C.: American Psychological Association, 1973.

Azrin, N. H., Bugle, C., & O'Brien, F. Behavioral engineering: Two apparatuses for toilet training retarded children. *Journal of Applied Behavior Analysis*, 1971, **4**, 249–253.

Bailey, J. S., Timbers, G. D., Phillips, E. L., & Wolf, M. M. Modification of articulation errors of pre-delinquents by their peers. *Journal of Applied Behavior Analysis*, 1971, **4**, 265–281.

Budzynski, T. H., & Stoyva, J. M. An instrument for producing deep muscle relaxation by means of analog information feedback. *Journal of Applied Behavior Analysis*, 1969, **2**, 231–237.

Campbell, D. T., & Stanley, J. C. *Experimental and quasi-experimental designs for research*. Chicago: Rand McNally, 1966.

Cataldo, M. F., & Risley, T. R. Evaluation of Living Environments: The MANIFEST Description of Ward Activities. In P. O. Davidson, F. W. Clark, & L. A. Hamerlynck (Eds.), *Evaluation of behavioral programs in community, residential and school settings*. Champaign: Research Press, 1974.

Christophersen, E. R., Doke, L. A., Messmer, D. O., & Risley, T. R. Measuring urban problems: A brief report on rating grass coverage. *Journal of Applied Behavior Analysis*, 1975, **8**, 230.

Combs, C. Developmental therapy curriculum objectives. In M. Wood (Ed.), *Developmental therapy*. Baltimore: University Park Press, 1975.

Doke, L. A. The organization of daycare environments: "Formal" versus "Informal" activities. *Child Care Quarterly*, 1975, **4**, in press.

Doke, L. A., & Risley, T. R. The organization of day-care environments: Required vs. optional activities. *Journal of Applied Behavior Analysis*, 1972, **5**, 405–420.

Epstein, L. H., Doke, L. A., Sajwaj, T. E., Sorrell, S., & Rimmer, B. Generality and side-effects of overcorrection. *Journal of Applied Behavior Analysis*, 1974, **7**, 385–390.

Foster, C. *Developing self control*. Kalamazoo: Behaviordelia, 1974.

Garcia, E., Baer, D. M., & Firestone, I. The development of generalized imitation within topographically determined boundaries. *Journal of Applied Behavior Analysis*, 1971, **4**, 101–112.

Hall, R. V. *Managing behavior* (Vol. 1). Lawrence, Kansas: H & H Enterprises, Inc., 1971.

Hall, R. V., Panyan, M., Rabon, D., & Broden, M. Instructing beginning teachers in reinforcement procedures which improve classroom control. *Journal of Applied Behavior Analysis*, 1968, **1**, 315–322.

Hart, B., & Risley, T. R. Establishing the use of descriptive adjectives in the spontaneous speech of disadvantaged preschool children. *Journal of Applied Behavior Analysis*, 1968, **1**, 109–120.

Hart, B., & Risley, T. R. Using preschool materials to modify the language of disadvantaged children. *Journal of Applied Behavior Analysis*, 1974, **7**, 243–256.

Hawkins, R. P., Peterson, R. F., Schweid, E., & Bijou, S. W. Behavior therapy in the home: Amelioration of problem parent-child relations with the parent in the therapeutic role. *Journal of Experimental Child Psychology*, 1966, **4**, 99–107.

Hedrick, D., & Prather, E. A behavioral system for assessing language development. In R. L. Schiefelbusch (Ed.), *Language of the mentally retarded*. Baltimore: University Park Press, 1972.

Herbert, E. W., Pinkston, E. M., Hayden, M. L., Sajwaj, T. E., Pinkston, S., Cordua, G., & Jackson, C. Adverse effects of differential parental attention. *Journal of Applied Behavior Analysis*, 1973, **6**, 15–30.

Jackson, D. A., & Wallace, R. F. The modification and generalization of voice loudness in a fifteen-year-old retarded girl. *Journal of Applied Behavior Analysis*, 1974, **7**, 461–471.

Kass, R. E., & O'Leary, K. D. The effects of observer bias in field-experimental settings. Paper presented at a Symposium on Behavior Analysis in Education, University of Kansas, Lawrence, Kansas, April 1970.

Katzenberg, A. *How to draw graphs*. Kalamazoo: Behaviordelia, 1975.

Kazdin, A. E. Statistical analyses for single-case experimental designs. In M. Hersen, & D. H. Barlow, *Single case experimental designs: Strategies for studying behavior change.* New York: Pergamon, in press.

Kazdin, A. E., & Klock, J. The effect of nonverbal teacher approval on student attentive behavior. *Journal of Applied Behavior Analysis*, 1973, **6**, 643–654.

Kohlenberg, R. J. Operant control of human anal sphincter pressure. *Journal of Applied Behavior Analysis*, 1973, **6**, 201–208.

LeLaurin, K., & Risley, T. R. The organization of day-care environments: "Zone" versus "man-to-man" staff assignments. *Journal of Applied Behavior Analysis*, 1972, **5**, 225–232.

Liberman, R. P., DeRisi, W. J., King, L. W., Eckman, T. A., & Wood, D. Behavioral measurement in a community mental health center. In P. O. Davidson, F. W. Clark, & L. A. Hamerlynck (Eds.), *Evaluation of behavioral programs in community, residential and school settings.* Champaign: Research Press, 1974.

Lovaas, O. I., Berberich, J. P., Perloff, B. F., & Schaeffer, B. Acquisition of imitative speech in schizophrenic children. *Science*, 1966, **151**, 705–707.

Lovaas, O. I., Koegel, R., Simmons, J. Q., & Long, J. S. Some generalization and follow-up measures on autistic children in behavior therapy. *Journal of Applied Behavior Analysis*, 1973, **6**, 131–166.

Mattos, R. L. A manual counter for recording multiple behavior. *Journal of Applied Behavior Analysis*, 1968, **1**, 130.

McClannahan, L. E., & Risley, T. R. A store for nursing home residents. *Nursing Homes*, 10+, 1973, **22**.

O'Brien, F., & Azrin, N. H. Behavioral engineering: Control of posture by informational feedback. *Journal of Applied Behavior Analysis*, 1970, **3**, 235–240.

O'Leary, K. D., & Becker, W. C. Behavior modification of an adjustment class: A token reinforcement program. *Exceptional children*, 1967, **33**, 637–642.

O'Leary, K. D., Kent, R. N., & Kanowitz, J. Shaping data collection congruent with experimental hypotheses. *Journal of Applied Behavior Analysis*, 1975, **8**, 43–51.

Quilitch, H. R. A comparison of three staff-management procedures. *Journal of Applied Behavior Analysis*, 1975, **8**, 59–66.

Quilitch, H. R., & Risley, T. R. The effects of play materials on social play. *Journal of Applied Behavior Analysis*, 1973, **6**, 573–578.

Redd, W. H. Generalization of adults' stimulus control of children's behavior. *Journal of Experimental Child Psychology*, 1970, **9**, 286–296.

Risley, T. R. Behavior modification: An experimental-therapeutic endeavor. In L. A. Hamerlynck, P. O. Davidson, & L. E. Acker (Eds.), *Behavior modification and ideal mental health services.* Calgary, Alberta: University of Calgary, 1969.

Roll, D. L. Modification of nasal resonance in cleft-palate children by informative feedback. *Journal of Applied Behavior Analysis*, 1973, **6**, 397–403.

Romanczyk, R. G., Kent, R. N., Diament, D., & O'Leary, K. D. Measuring the reliability of observational data: A reactive process. *Journal of Applied Behavior Analysis*, 1973, **6**, 175–184.

Sailor, W., & Mix, B. *The TARC Assessment System.* Lawrence, Kansas: H & H Enterprises, Inc., 1975.

Sajwaj, T., Twardosz, S., & Burke, M. Side effects of extinction procedures in a remedial preschool. *Journal of Applied Behavior Analysis*, 1972, **5**, 163–175.

Sanford, A. *Learning Accomplishment Profile.* Chapel Hill. North Carolina: University of North Carolina Printing Department, 1972.

Scott, J. W., & Bushell, D. The length of teacher contacts and students' off-task behavior. *Journal of Applied Behavior Analysis*, 1974, **7**, 39–44.

Stokes, T. F., Baer, D. M., & Jackson, R. L. Programming the generalization of a greeting response in four retarded children. *Journal of Applied Behavior Analysis*, 1974, **7**, 599–610.

Striefel, S. *Managing behavior, Vol. 4, Behavior modification: Teaching a child to imitate.* Lawrence, Kansas: H & H Enterprises, Inc., 1974.

Taplin, P. S., & Reid, J. B. Effects of instructional set and experimenter influence on observer reliability. *Child Development*, 1973, **44**, 547–554.

Twardosz, S., Cataldo, M. F., & Risley, T. R. Open environment design for infant and toddler day care. *Journal of Applied Behavior Analysis*, 1974, **7**, 529–546.

VanWagenen, R. K., Meyerson, L. Kerr, N. J., & Mahoney, K. Field trials of a new procedure for toilet training. *Journal of Experimental Child Psychology*, 1969, **8**, 147–159.

Wahler, R. G. Some structural aspects of deviant child behavior. *Journal of Applied Behavior Analysis*, 1975, **8**, 27–42.

Wahler, R. G., Sperling, K. A., Thomas, M. R., Teeter, N. C., & Luper, H. L. The modification of childhood stuttering: Some response-response relationships. *Journal of Experimental Child Psychology*, 1970, **9**, 411–428.

Author Index

Subject Index